中国周边海洋问题有关文件汇编

A Compilation of the Documents on the Issues Related to China Seas

中华人民共和国外交部
边界与海洋事务司◎编

世界知识出版社

图书在版编目（CIP）数据

中国周边海洋问题有关文件汇编 / 中华人民共和国外交部边界与海洋事务司编著. -- 北京：世界知识出版社，2016.12
ISBN 978-7-5012-5426-2

Ⅰ. ①中… Ⅱ. ①中… Ⅲ. ①国家安全—海洋战略—文件—汇编—中国 Ⅳ. ①D631

中国版本图书馆CIP数据核字（2017）第047140号

责任编辑　何以多　侯新鹏
责任出版　王勇刚
责任校对　陈可望
装帧设计　肖　博

书　　名　**中国周边海洋问题有关文件汇编**
A Compilation of the Documents on the Issues Related to China Seas

编　　著　中华人民共和国外交部边界与海洋事务司

出版发行　世界知识出版社
地址邮编　北京市东城区干面胡同51号（100010）
网　　址　www.ishizhi.cn
经　　销　新华书店
印　　刷　北京朝阳印刷厂有限责任公司
开本印张　710×1000毫米　1/16　35¾印张
字　　数　600千字
版次印次　2017年9月第一版　2017年9月第一次印刷
标准书号　ISBN 978-7-5012-5426-2
定　　价　72.00元

目 录
CONTENTS

第一部分 有关法律和立场文件
Relevant Laws and Position Papers

第二部分 地区和双边文件
Regional and Bilateral Documents

中华人民共和国和菲律宾共和国双边文件
Bilateral Documents between the People's Republic of China and the Republic of the Philippines

中华人民共和国和马来西亚双边文件

Bilateral Documents between the People's Republic of China and Malaysia

中华人民共和国和文莱达鲁萨兰国双边文件

Bilateral Documents between the People's Republic of China and the Brunei Darussalam

中华人民共和国和印度尼西亚共和国双边文件

Bilateral Documents between the People's Republic of China and the Republic of Indonesia

中华人民共和国和日本国双边文件
中華人民共和国と日本国両国間の文書

中华人民共和国和大韩民国双边文件
중화인민공화국 과 대한민국 양자 문건

第一部分
有关法律和立场文件

Relevant Laws and Position Papers

中华人民共和国政府关于领海的声明

（1958年9月4日）

中华人民共和国政府宣布：

（一）中华人民共和国的领海宽度为12海里。这项规定适用于中华人民共和国的一切领土，包括中国大陆及其沿海岛屿，和同大陆及其沿海岛屿隔有公海的台湾及其周围各岛、澎湖列岛、东沙群岛、西沙群岛、中沙群岛、南沙群岛以及其他属于中国的岛屿。

（二）中国大陆及其沿海岛屿的领海以连接大陆岸上和沿海岸外缘岛屿上各基点之间的各直线为基线，从基线向外延伸12海里的水域是中国的领海。在基线以内的水域，包括渤海湾、琼州海峡在内，都是中国的内海。在基线以内的岛屿，包括东引岛、高登岛、马祖列岛、白犬列岛、乌丘岛、大小金门岛、大担岛、二担岛、东碇岛在内，都是中国的内海岛屿。

（三）一切外国飞机和军用船舶，未经中华人民共和国政府的许可，不得进入中国的领海和领海上空。

任何外国船舶在中国领海航行，必须遵守中华人民共和国政府的有关法令。

（四）以上（二）（三）两项规定的原则同样适用于台湾及其周围各岛、澎湖列岛、东沙群岛、西沙群岛、中沙群岛、南沙群岛以及其他属于中国的岛屿。

台湾和澎湖地区现在仍然被美国武力侵占，这是侵犯中华人民共和国领土完整的和主权的非法行为。台湾和澎湖等地尚待收复，中华人民共和国政府有权采取一切适当的方法，在适当的时候，收复这些地区，这是中国的内政，不容外国干涉。

Declaration of the Government of the People's Republic of China on China's Territorial Sea

(4 September 1958)

The Government of the People's Republic of China declares:

1. The breadth of the territorial sea of the People's Republic of China shall be twelve nautical miles. This provision applies to all territories of the People's Republic of China, including the Chinese mainland and its coastal islands, as well as Taiwan and its surrounding islands, the Penghu Islands, the Dongsha Islands, the Xisha Islands, the Zhongsha Islands, the Nansha Islands and all other islands belonging to China which are separated from the mainland and its coastal islands by the high seas.

2. China's territorial sea along the mainland and its coastal islands takes as its baseline the line composed of the straight lines connecting base-points on the mainland coast and on the outermost of the coastal islands; the water area extending twelve nautical miles outward from this baseline is China's territorial sea. The water areas inside the baseline, including Bohai Bay and the Qiongzhou Straits, are Chinese inland waters. The islands inside the baseline, including Dongyin Island, Gaodeng Island, the Mazu Islands, the Baiquan Islands, Wuqiu Island, the Greater and Lesser Jinmen Islands, Dadan Island, Erdan Island and Dongding Island, are islands of the Chinese inland waters.

3. No foreign aircraft and no foreign vessels for military use may enter China's territorial sea and the air space above it without the permission of the Government of the People's Republic of China.

While navigation Chinese territorial sea, every foreign vessel must observe the relevant laws and regulations laid down by the Government of the People's Republic of China .

4. The principles provided in paragraphs 2 and 3 likewise apply to Taiwan and its surrounding islands, the Penghu Islands, the Dongsha Islands, the Xisha Islands, the Zhongsha Islands, the Nansha islands, and all other islands belonging to China.

The Taiwan and Penghu areas are still occupied by the United States by armed force. This is an unlawful encroachment on the territorial integrity and sovereignty of the People's Republic of China. Taiwan, Penghu and such other areas are yet to be recovered, and the Government of the People's Republic of China has the right to recover these areas by all suitable means at a suitable time. This is China's internal affair, in which no foreign interference is tolerated.

中国对西沙群岛和南沙群岛的主权无可争辩

——中华人民共和国外交部文件

（1980年1月30日）

西沙群岛和南沙群岛，是中国南海诸岛中两个较大的岛群，它们和东沙群岛、中沙群岛一样，自古以来就是中国的领土。这不仅有古今中外的大量史料、文件、地图和文物可作证明，而且也为世界上许多国家和广泛国际舆论所承认。在近代历史上，这两个群岛虽曾一度被外国非法侵占，但并不能改变它们属于中国的历史事实和法理基础。

越南当局怀着地区霸权主义扩张野心，在向印度支那和东南亚加紧侵略扩张的同时，一反过去承认西沙群岛、南沙群岛属于中国领土的立场，在一九七五年非法占领了中国南沙群岛中的一些岛屿，并公然对中国西沙、南沙两群岛提出领土要求。一九七九年九月二十八日，越南外交部公布一份题为《越南对于黄沙和长沙两群岛的主权》的白皮书，拼凑和编造了一些自相矛盾的、根本站不住脚的所谓“证明资料”，妄图为其非法占领和扩张野心寻找法理依据，这是徒劳的。

历史事实不能伪造，国际法原则不容践踏。我们在这里引用确凿的史实记载和官方文件，以揭穿和驳斥越南当局所编造的谎言，明白无误地证明中华人民共和国对西沙群岛和南沙群岛享有无可争辩的主权。

一、西沙群岛和南沙群岛自古以来就是中国的领土

早在公元前两世纪的汉武帝时代，中国人民就开始在南海航行。中国人民通过长期的航海实践，先后发现了西沙群岛和南沙群岛。三国时代（公元二二

〇年至二六五年）万震的《南州异物志》和康泰的《扶南传》，就已对西沙群岛和南沙群岛的地形地貌特征作了描述〔注一〕。

中国人民在发现西沙群岛、南沙群岛之后，克服种种困难，陆续来到这两个群岛，辛勤开发经营。我国宋代的《梦粱录》，元代的《岛夷志略》，明代的《东西洋考》、《顺风相送》，清代的《指南正法》、《海国闻见录》以及历代渔民的《更路簿》等著作，记载了中国人民千百年来到西沙群岛、南沙群岛航行、生产的情况和这两个群岛的位置及岛礁分布状况。这些著作不仅相继把西沙群岛和南沙群岛命名为“九乳螺洲”、“石塘”、“千里石塘”、“万里石塘”、“长沙”、“千里长沙”、“万里长沙”等，而且给这两个群岛的各个岛、礁、沙、滩起了许多形象生动的名字。近些年来，在西沙群岛发现了我国唐、宋时代的居住遗址和陶瓷器皿、铁刀、铁锅等生活用具，以及明、清时代的水井、庙宇、坟墓等历史文物。这些事实证明：中国人民至少自唐、宋以来就已经在西沙群岛和南沙群岛生活和从事捕捞等生产活动。

随着中国人民对西沙群岛和南沙群岛的开发经营，中国历代政府对这两个群岛进行了管辖。

早在北宋（公元九六〇年至一一二七年），中国的海军就已巡海至西沙群岛一带。北宋仁宗皇帝（公元一〇二三年至一〇六三年）亲作“御序”的《武经总要》〔注二〕记载：北宋朝廷“命王师出戍，置巡海水师营垒”于广南（即今广东），“治舠鱼入海战舰”，“从屯门山用东风西南行，七日至九乳螺洲”（见附件一）。“九乳螺洲”就是今天的西沙群岛。这表明北宋朝廷已把西沙群岛置于自己的管辖范围内，因而派出海军“战舰”去该处巡逻。

元代初年在全国二十七个地方进行了天文测量。至元十六年（公元一二七九年），元世祖忽必烈亲派著名天文学家、同知太史院事〔注三〕郭守敬到南海进行测量。据元史记载，南海测点“南逾朱崖”，“测得南海北极出地一十五度”。“南海”这个天文点就在今天的西沙群岛上〔注四〕。这说明西沙群岛在元代是在中国的疆域之内。

明、清时代，由中国官方修纂的《广东通志》、《琼州府志》和《万州志》，都在“疆域”或“舆地山川”条目中记载：“万州有千里长沙、万里石塘”。这表明，西沙群岛和南沙群岛当时属广东省琼州府万州（今海南岛万宁、陵水县境）所有。

清康熙四十九年至五十一年（公元一七一〇年至一七一二年）间，广东水师副将吴陞曾率领水师巡海，“自琼崖，历铜鼓，经七洲洋、四更沙，周遭三千里，躬自巡视”〔注五〕。这里所称七洲洋即今西沙群岛一带海域，当时由广东省海军负责巡逻。一八七六年赴任的清朝驻英国公使郭嵩焘在其所著《使西纪程》中记载:(光绪二年十月)"二十四日午正行八百三十一里，在赤道北十七度三十分，计当在琼南二、三百里，船人名之曰齐纳细(按即CHINA SEA)，犹言中国海也。……左近柏拉苏岛(按即PARACEL ISLANDS，即西沙群岛)，出海蔆(参)，亦产珊瑚而不甚佳，中国属岛也。"

光绪九年(公元一八八三年)，德国曾对西沙、南沙群岛进行调查测量，清朝政府提出抗议后，德国不得不停止调查。

西沙群岛、南沙群岛自古以来就是中国的领土，这不仅见诸大量的史籍志书记载，而且有许多官方舆图可资佐证，如清乾隆二十年(公元一七五五年)绘制的《皇清各直省分图》、嘉庆十五年(公元一八一〇年)绘制的《大清万年一统地理全图》和嘉庆二十二年(公元一八一七年)绘制的《大清一统天下全图》等。

宣统元年(公元一九〇九年)四月，两广总督张人骏派遣广东水师提督李准率领海军官兵一百七十余人，分乘伏波、广金、琛航三艘军舰巡海视察西沙群岛，查明岛屿十五座，命名勒石，并在永兴岛上升旗鸣炮，重申主权。

一九一一年，中国广东省政府宣布把西沙群岛划归海南岛崖县管辖。一九二一年，中国政府内务部批准广东省商人何瑞年在西沙群岛开办渔业、垦殖、采矿等实业。后发现何瑞年竟将经营权转让给日本商人，即撤销其经营权。

一九二八年五月，广东省政府派出军、政官员和科技专家组成调查队，乘军舰到西沙群岛作实地调查，并提出详尽的调查报告书。

上述大量历史事实充分证明：西沙群岛和南沙群岛是中国最早发现、最早开发经营、最早管辖的。千百年来，中国历代政府对这两个群岛一直行使着管辖权，中国人民是这两个群岛无可争辩的主人。

二、中国捍卫西沙群岛和南沙群岛主权的斗争

法国于十九世纪末在越南建立殖民主义统治之后的一段时间内，仍然是承认中国对西沙群岛的主权的。一九二一年八月二十二日，法国内阁总理兼外长白里安在西沙群岛问题上承认："由于中国政府自一九〇九年已确立自己的主权(按：指上述李准巡视西沙群岛事)，我们现在对这些岛屿提出要求是不可能的。"一九二九年法国驻印度支那署理总督也承认："根据多方报告，帕拉塞尔群岛(按：即西沙群岛)应认为属中国所有"〔注六〕。

但是，那时觊觎中国领土的法国殖民主义者看到西沙群岛具有的战略重要性，便乘一九三一年日本发动九·一八事件，侵略中国东北的时机，企图侵占这些海岛。同年十二月四日，法国政府向中国驻法国公使馆发出照会，声称安

南帝国对西沙群岛拥有所谓“先有权”，公然对中国的这些岛屿提出了领土要求。当时中国政府曾给予严正批驳，指出西沙群岛早已属中国管辖。一九三二年十一月三十日，中国政府外交部视察专员朱兆莘在给法国驻广州领事的公函中又严正指出：“西沙群岛隶属中国版图实无疑义。”

一九三三年，当时的法国当局进一步侵占了中国南沙群岛的九个岛屿。对此，中国人民群起抗议，当时中国政府也通过外交途径向法国当局提出了严正交涉。

由中国外交部、内政部、海军部等部门组成的“水陆地图审查委员会”，于一九三四年至一九三五年专门审定我国南海诸岛各个岛名，编印《中国南海各岛屿图》，明确标绘东沙、西沙、中沙、南沙群岛属中国版图。

第二次世界大战期间，日本于一九三九年侵占了西沙群岛和南沙群岛。一九四五年日本投降后，当时中国政府于一九四六年十一月、十二月指派高级官员，乘军舰分赴西沙群岛、南沙群岛进行接收，在岛上举行了接收仪式，并立碑纪念（见附件二），派兵驻守。随后又重新命定东沙、西沙、中沙、南沙四个群岛及各个岛、礁、沙、滩的名称。这样，一度被外国非法侵占的西沙群岛和南沙群岛又重新置于中国政府的管辖之下。

中华人民共和国成立后，周恩来外长于一九五一年八月十五日发表《关于美英对日和约草案及旧金山会议声明》，庄严指出：西沙、南沙群岛和东沙、中沙群岛一样，“向为中国领土”，“在日本帝国主义发动侵略战争时虽曾一度沦陷，但日本投降后已为当时中国政府全部接收”，中国对西沙群岛、南沙群岛的主权，“不论美英对日和约草案有无规定和如何规定，均不受任何影响”。

此后，针对外国对中国西沙、南沙群岛主权的侵犯，中华人民共和国政府及外交部曾多次发表严正声明，重申中国对西沙群岛、南沙群岛拥有不可侵犯的主权。

中华人民共和国成立以来，中国政府和人民继续对西沙群岛和南沙群岛进行管辖和经营建设。一九五〇年至一九五六年，广东省琼海县大批渔民不断前往南沙群岛进行渔业生产。广东省海南行政区有关部门不断派遣人员到西沙群岛调查勘测、捕捞水产、开采磷肥、建立气象台，并对西沙群岛的渔民进行管理。一九五九年三月，海南行政区在西沙群岛的永兴岛设立了“西、南、中沙群岛办事处”。一九六九年三月，该办事处改称“广东省西沙、中沙、南沙群岛革命委员会”。

一九七四年一月，中国人民解放军和民兵驱走了入侵西沙群岛的南越西贡当局军队，捍卫了中国的领土主权。

多年来，中国台湾当局一直派军队驻守在南沙群岛的最大岛屿太平岛。

三、中国对西沙群岛和南沙群岛的主权得到国际上的广泛承认

世界上许多国家和国际舆论都承认西沙群岛和南沙群岛是中国的领土。

一九三〇年四月，在香港召开的由中国、法国、菲律宾和香港当局代表参加的远东气象会议，曾经通过决议，要求中国政府在西沙群岛建立气象台。

一九三八年法国殖民当局的安南警察入侵西沙群岛后，日本外务省发言人曾说：安南警察登上的西沙群岛，“我们承认是属于中国领土”〔注七〕。

一九五一年旧金山对日和约会议规定日本应放弃西沙群岛和南沙群岛。当时，苏联代表团团长葛罗米柯在会上曾发言指出：西沙群岛和南沙群岛等岛屿是中国的“不可分割的领土”。虽然美英起草的对日和约没有提及西沙、南沙群岛在日本放弃后归谁所有，但就在签署旧金山对日和约的第二年，即一九五二年，由当时日本外务大臣冈崎胜男亲笔签字推荐的《标准世界地图集》第十五图《东南亚图》，就把和约规定日本必须放弃的西沙、南沙群岛及东沙、中沙群岛全部标绘属于中国（见附件三）。因为这些岛屿本来就是中国领土，理所当然要归还给中国。

一九五五年十月，国际民航组织在马尼拉召开会议，美国、英国、法国、日本、加拿大、澳大利亚、新西兰、泰国、菲律宾、南越和中国台湾当局派了代表出席。会议通过的第二十四号决议要求中国台湾当局在南沙群岛加强气象观测，而会上没有任何一个代表对此提出异议或保留。

二十世纪以来，世界上许多国家权威性的百科全书都承认西沙群岛和南沙群岛是中国领土。例如：一九六三年美国出版的《威尔德麦克各国百科全书》说：中华人民共和国各岛屿“还包括伸展到北纬四度的南中国海的岛屿和珊瑚礁，这些岛屿和珊瑚礁包括东沙（普拉塔斯）、西沙（帕拉塞尔）、中沙和南沙群岛。”一九七三年出版的《苏联大百科全书》和一九七九年日本共同社出版的《世界年鉴》也都明确指出西沙群岛和南沙群岛是中国领土。

世界许多国家出版的地图也都标注西沙群岛和南沙群岛属于中国。例如：一九五四年德意志联邦共和国出版的《世界大地图集》、一九五四年至一九六七年间苏联出版的《世界地图集》、一九五七年罗马尼亚出版的《世界地理图集》、一九六八年法国国家地理研究院出版的《世界普通地图》、一九六八年德意志民主共和国出版的《哈克世界大地图集》、一九七〇年西班牙《阿吉拉尔大地图集》、一九七三年日本平凡社《中国地图集》等等，都把西沙群岛和南沙群岛标注为中国领土。总之，现代世界上许多国家出版的图籍都公认西沙群岛和南沙

群岛是中国领土的一部分。

四、越南当局出尔反尔的恶劣行径

必须指出，中越双方过去在西沙群岛和南沙群岛的归属问题上，本来并不存在争议。在一个相当长的时期内，越南方面无论在其政府的声明、照会中，还是在报刊、地图和教科书中，都正式承认西沙群岛和南沙群岛自古以来就是中国的领土。

一九五六年六月十五日，越南民主共和国外交部副部长雍文谦接见中国驻越南大使馆临时代办李志民，郑重表示："根据越南方面的资料，从历史上看，西沙群岛和南沙群岛应当属于中国领土。"当时在座的越南外交部亚洲司代司长黎禄进一步具体介绍了越南方面的材料，指出："从历史上看，西沙群岛和南沙群岛早在宋朝时就已经属于中国了。"

一九五八年九月四日，中华人民共和国政府发表声明，宣布中华人民共和国的领海宽度为十二海里，并且明确指出："这项规定适用于中华人民共和国的一切领土，包括……东沙群岛、西沙群岛、中沙群岛、南沙群岛以及其他属于中国的岛屿。"九月六日，越南劳动党中央机关报《人民报》就在第一版显著位置报道了中国政府这一声明的详细内容。《人民报》说："一九五八年九月四日，中华人民共和国政府发表了关于领海问题的声明。声明规定：中国领海的宽度为十二海里（约二十二公里多）。这项规定适用于中华人民共和国的一切领土，包括中国大陆及其沿海岛屿和台湾及其周围各岛，澎湖、东沙、西沙、中沙、南沙各群岛，以及其它远离中国大陆和远离中国沿海岛屿的属于中国的岛屿。"同年九月十四日，越南政府总理范文同照会中国国务院总理周恩来，郑重表示："越南民主共和国政府承认和赞同中华人民共和国政府一九五八年九月四日关于领海决定的声明。""越南民主共和国政府尊重这项决定"。范文同的照会清楚地表明越南政府承认西沙群岛和南沙群岛是中国领土（见附件四）。

一九六五年五月九日，越南民主共和国政府就美国政府确定美军在越南的"作战区域"问题发表声明，指出："美国总统约翰逊把整个越南和越南海岸以外宽约一百海里的附近海域，以及中华人民共和国西沙群岛的一部分领海规定为美国武装力量的作战区域"，这是"对越南民主共和国及其邻国安全的直接威胁"。越南政府在这里再次明确承认西沙群岛是中国的领土。

越南方面在报道外国侵犯西沙群岛的行动时，也曾明确承认西沙群岛属于中国。例如，越南《人民报》一九六九年五月十三日报道说："五月十日，美国军用飞机一架侵犯了中国广东省西沙群岛永兴岛和东岛领空。"越南报纸还曾多次作过类似的报道。

越南出版的官方地图和教科书都曾明确承认西沙群岛和南沙群岛是中国的领土。例如，一九六〇年越南人民军总参谋部地图处编绘的《世界地图》，按中国名称标注西沙群岛和南沙群岛，并在这两个群岛名称之后，括注属于中国。一九七二年五月越南总理府测量和绘图局印制的《世界地图集》，也仍用中国名称标注西沙群岛和南沙群岛（见附件五）。又如，一九七四年越南教育出版社出版的普通学校九年级《地理》教科书，在《中华人民共和国》一课中写道："从南沙、西沙各岛到海南岛、台湾岛、澎湖列岛、舟山群岛，……这些岛呈弓形状，构成了保卫中国大陆的一座'长城'。"

越南方面煞有介事地强调，要想证明领土主权，必须拿出"属于国家的正式材料"和"具有法理价值的文件"。我们上面所引证的恰恰都是越南方面"属于国家的正式材料"和"具有法理价值的文件"。这清楚地说明了越南政府在一九七四年以前一直承认西沙群岛和南沙群岛是中国的领土。现在，越南当局竟出尔反尔，自食其言，完全背离了它原来承认西沙群岛和南沙群岛是中国领土的立场，这是国际法所绝对不能允许的。

五、越南《白皮书》的论据是根本站不住脚的

越南外交部《白皮书》中所引用的十九条所谓"证明资料"大体可分为两部分，前一部分（一至五条）搜罗了一些越南的"古籍资料"，后一部分（六至十九条）列举一九三三年以后法国殖民当局和南越西贡当局侵占中国西沙群岛、南沙群岛的一些材料，妄图以此证明中国的西沙群岛和南沙群岛是越南的领土。但只要认真地研究分析一下，就不难看出：这些"证明资料"的前一部分不过是玩弄指鹿为马的手法，而后一部分则是根本站不住脚的，在法律上也是无效的。

越南当局把史籍上记载的黄沙滩和黄沙渚，说成是今天越南所指的黄沙群岛、西方所称的帕拉塞尔群岛，因此也就是中国的西沙群岛。他们提出的最主要的"历史根据"，就是十七世纪一个名叫杜伯的越南人所编制的"越南地图中的广义地区图"和十八世纪的黎贵敦撰写的《抚边杂录》。越南《白皮书》引用这两个材料对黄沙滩和黄沙渚有如下描述：

"海中有一长沙，名娗葛鐄（意即黄沙滩），……自大占门越海至此一日半。自沙淇门至此半日"。

"广义府平山县安永社居近海，海外之东北有岛屿焉。群山零星一百三十余嶺（岭）。山间出海相隔或一日或数更。山上间有甘泉，岛之中有黄沙渚，长约

三十余里，平坦广大，水清彻底”。

越南当局搬出这两段文字作为“最早、最具根本性”的两个材料，但上述记载恰恰说明：越南所说的黄沙群岛根本不是中国的西沙群岛，二者是完全不同的两个地方。

一看地理位置。越南的材料说，从大占门（今越南广南——岘港省的大海门）渡海至黄沙滩只要一天半，从沙淇门（今越南广义省平山县附近海口）渡海至黄沙滩只要半天。而中国的西沙群岛距离越南中部海岸远达二百海里，按当时的航海技术，乘帆船航行半天或一天半是无论如何也到达不了的。

二看长度、面积。越南的材料说，“黄沙渚”“长约三十余里”，且“平坦广大”。而中国的西沙群岛中最大的永兴岛，也仅长不到两公里，面积不过一点八五平方公里。

三看地形地貌特征。越南的材料说，黄沙群岛有“群山零星一百三十余嶺”。而中国的西沙群岛各岛屿海拔只有五六米，最高处也不过十五点九米，且地势低平，根本不存在所谓“群山”。西沙群岛全部岛、礁、沙、滩一共只有三十五个，更谈不上“一百三十余嶺”。

上述种种对比清楚地说明，越南所说的黄沙群岛根本不是中国的西沙群岛，而只能是越南中部沿海的一些岛屿、沙洲。

越南《白皮书》声称《大南实录正编》“记载了嘉隆于一八一六年占有黄沙群岛的事件”，但遍查这一史书，却不见有“占有”的记载。所谓嘉隆皇帝“占有黄沙群岛”之说，源出自法国殖民主义者路易·塔伯尔主教所写的《交趾支那地理札记》。它说：“普拉塞尔，又名帕拉塞尔群岛，是由一些小岛、岩石和沙滩组成的迷宫，位于巴黎算起的东经107°上，似乎一直延伸到北纬11°。”还说一八一六年嘉隆“庄严地在那儿插上它的旗帜，并正式占有这些岩石，大概不会有任何人同他就此发生争议。”巴黎子午线东经107°就是格林威治东经109°10′，离越南中部海岸不远，而我国的西沙群岛在东经110°10′以东。塔伯尔说的帕拉塞尔，一直延伸到北纬11°，而西沙群岛的最南点仅在北纬15°47′。很明显，塔伯尔主教所讲的帕拉塞尔，是指越南中部沿海的一些岛屿、沙洲，而不是我国的西沙群岛。

至于越南方面所说的“长沙群岛”，也决不是中国的南沙群岛。《白皮书》说“长沙群岛”以前称“大长沙”。在中、越许多史籍中都有关于“大长沙”的记载，其位置显然不是在中国的南沙群岛，而是指越南沿海的一些岛屿和沙洲。越南《白皮书》找不出任何有价值的史实材料来证明“长沙”就是中国的南沙群岛，于是搬出了一张来历不明的所谓《大南一统全图》。但是，从这张地图中人们可以清楚地看到，“黄沙”和“万里长沙”是标绘在同越南中部海岸相平行、距离越南海岸不远的地方，而不在中国西沙群岛和南沙群岛的地理位置上。

越南当局妄图用指鹿为马的手法来为其领土野心寻找依据，欺骗世界人民，这是枉费心机的。

至于越南《白皮书》列举一九三三年以后法国殖民当局和南越西贡当局侵占中国西沙群岛和南沙群岛的材料，来证明今天越南当局对中国西沙群岛和南沙群岛提出领土要求的合法性，更是站不住脚的。根据国际法，侵略行为不能产生主权，对侵占得来的别国领土的所谓“继承”，当然也是非法的，因而也是无效的。

西沙群岛和南沙群岛自古以来就是中国的领土，这是具有充分法理根据的。人们通过上面列举的大量事实和材料，可以得出公正的结论。越南当局非法占领中国南沙群岛部分岛屿，对中国西沙、南沙群岛提出领土要求，只能暴露他们地区霸权主义和侵略扩张的野心。中国对西沙群岛和南沙群岛的主权是无可争辩的。

注 释

一、万震《南州异物志》在记述汉代从马来半岛到中国大陆的航行路线时写道：“……东北行，极大崎头，出涨海，中浅而多磁石”。涨海即今南海。这里所说的“磁石”，包括西沙、南沙群岛当时尚未露出水面的暗沙、暗礁，由于船只碰到这些暗礁就搁浅遇难，无法脱身，故称之为“磁石”。康泰在《扶南传》中写道：“涨海中，倒珊瑚洲，洲底有盘石，珊瑚生其上也。”

二、《武经总要》是宋朝记载军事制度和国防大事的权威性很高的重要文献，是由当时朝廷命官尚书工部侍郎参知政事丁度和天章阁待制曾公亮主持编写的。“尚书工部侍郎参知政事”的地位相当于副宰相，“天章阁待制”相当于皇帝的顾问。

三、元代主管天文历法的“同知太史院事”相当于现代的天文总局副总局长。

四、郭守敬在当时元朝疆域范围内主持建立天文测量点。“南海”这个测点“南逾朱崖”，就是在海南岛以南。当时测得“琼州北极出地一十九度太”（即19.75度），“南海北极出地一十五度”，说明南海测点远在海南岛上的琼州测点以南四度多，正好在今西沙群岛一带。由于当时的科学技术条件所限，二十七个测点所测“北极出地”（相当于今天的北纬）数值大都和现代纬度相差一度左右。从一圆周365.25度的元制换算成现代的360度制，南海这个测点“北极出地一十五度”应为北纬14°47′，加上一度左右的误差，其位置也正好在今西沙群岛。

五、见清代乾隆《泉州府志》卷五十六。

六、见《外交评论》杂志一九三四年四月号第七十七页。

七、见路透社一九三八年七月四日电。

附件一
ANNEX 1

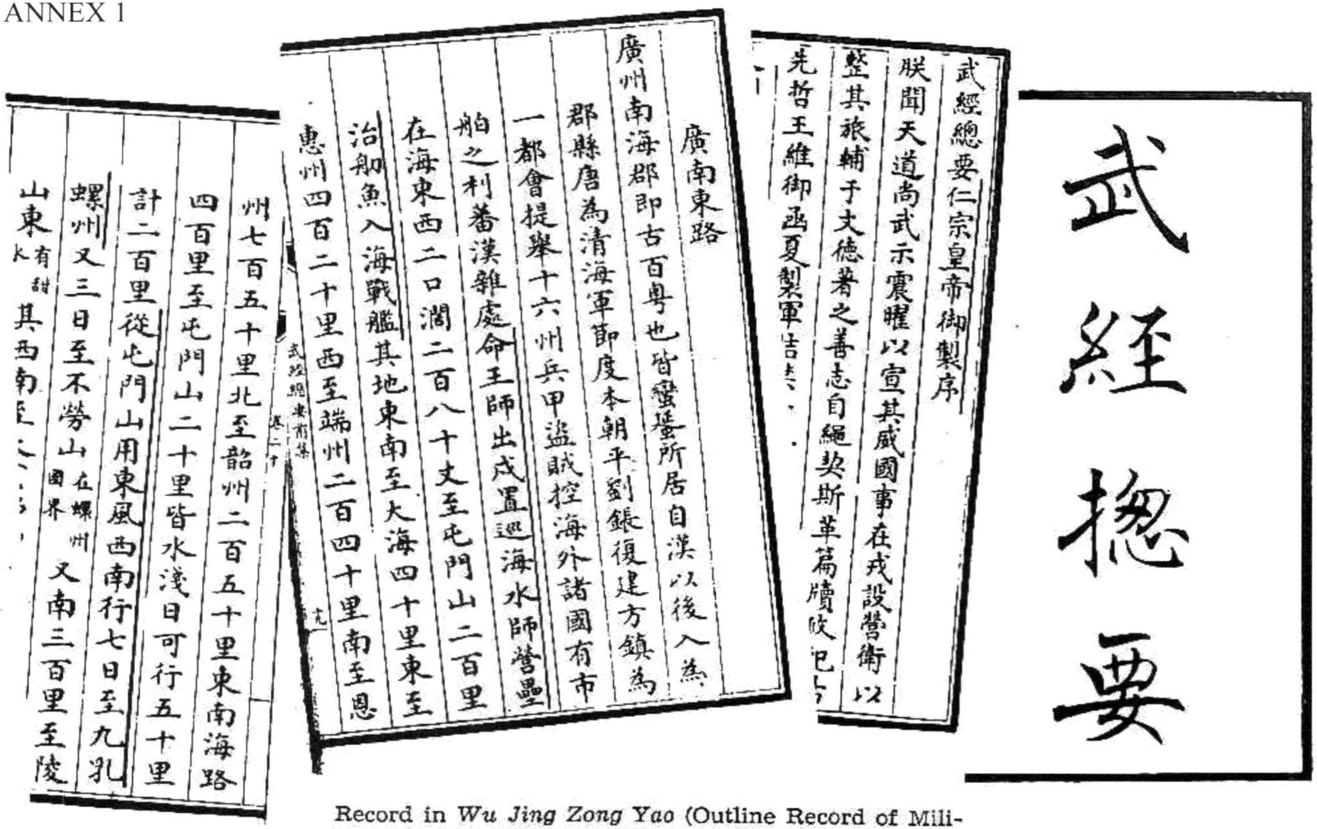
武經總要

武經總要仁宗皇帝御製序
朕聞天道尚武示震曜以宣其威國事在戎設營衛以
整其旅輔于文德著之善志自緝契斯革篇牘攸
先哲王維御函夏製軍

廣南東路
廣州南海郡即古百粵也皆蠻蜑所居自漢以後入爲
郡縣唐爲清海軍節度本朝平劉鋹復建方鎮爲
一都會提舉十六州兵甲盜賊控海外諸國有市
舶之利蕃漢雜處命王師出戍置巡海水師營壘
在海東西二口闊二百八十丈至屯門山二百里
治舠魚入海戰艦其地東南至大海四十里東至
惠州四百二十里西至端州二百四十里南至恩
州七百五十里北至韶州二百五十里東南海路
四百里至屯門山二十里皆水淺日可行五十里
計二百里從屯門山用東風西南行七日至九乳
螺州又三日至不勞山在環州國界又南三百里至陵
山東有甜水其西南

Record in *Wu Jing Zong Yao* (Outline Record of Military Affairs) of the Northern Song dynasty about the patrol of the Guangnan Fleet reaching Jiuruluozhou.

附件二
ANNEX 2

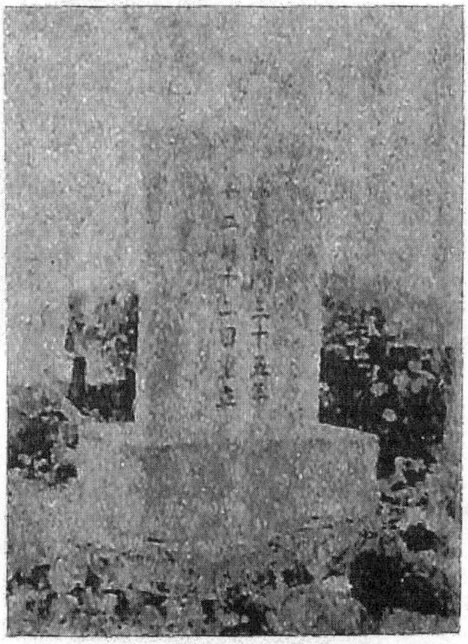

When the Chinese Government officials and naval officers and men took over the Nansha Islands in December 1946, they had a photo taken on Taiping Island as a memento and erected a stone tablet to reassert China's sovereignty over these islands. The photo below left shows the front of the stone tablet and the one below right shows its back.

附件三
ANNEX 3

SOUTH-EAST ASIA

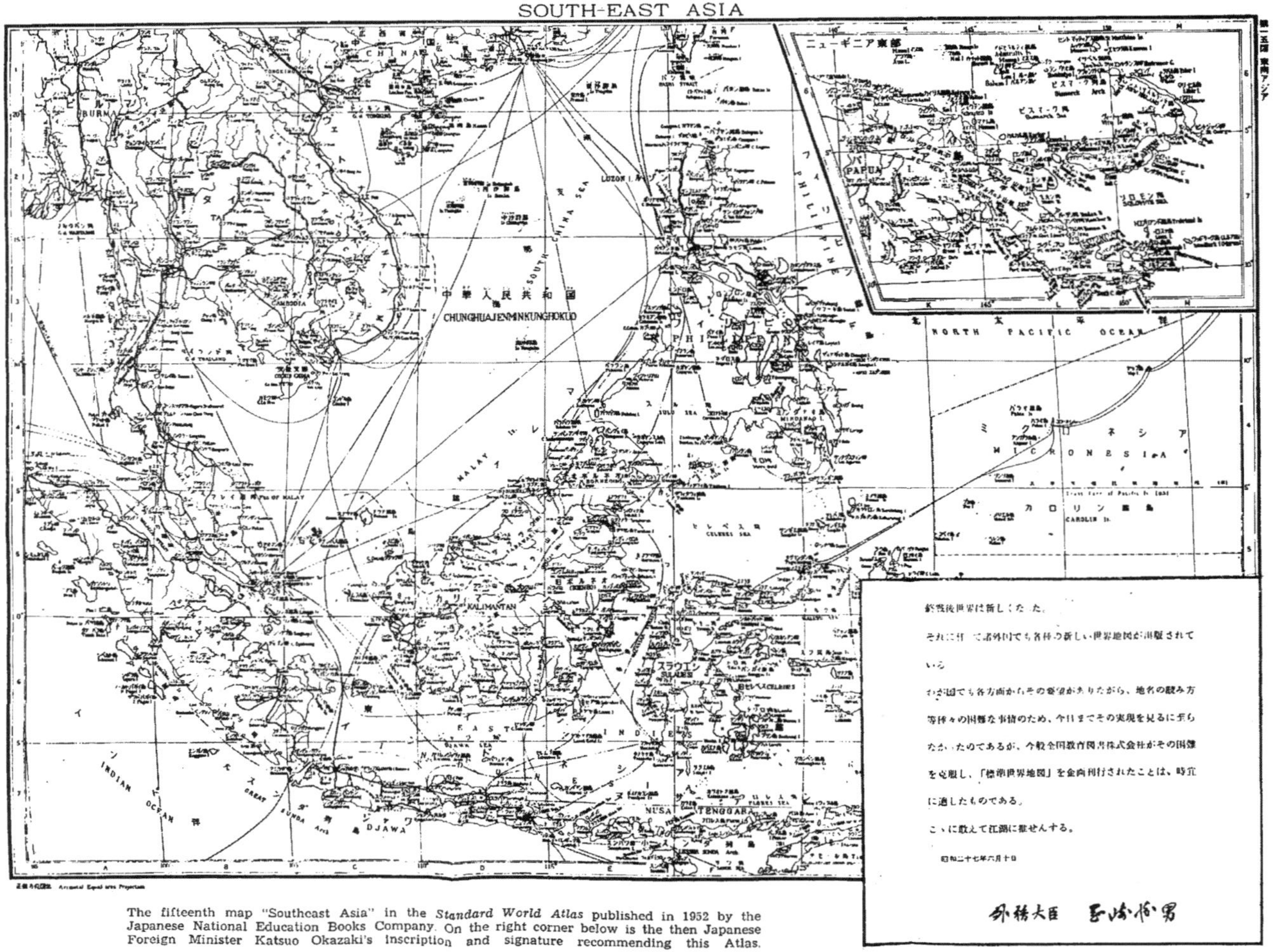

The fifteenth map "Southeast Asia" in the *Standard World Atlas* published in 1952 by the Japanese National Education Books Company. On the right corner below is the then Japanese Foreign Minister Katsuo Okazaki's inscription and signature recommending this Atlas.

附件四

ANNEX 4

THỦ TƯỚNG PHỦ
NƯỚC VIỆT-NAM DÂN-CHỦ CỘNG-HÒA

Thưa Đồng chí Tổng lý,

Chúng tôi xin trân trọng báo tin để Đồng chí Tổng lý rõ :

Chính phủ nước Việt-nam Dân chủ Cộng hoà ghi nhận và tán thành bản tuyên bố, ngày 4 tháng 9 năm 1958, của Chính phủ nước Cộng hoà Nhân dân Trung-hoa, quyết định về hải phận của Trung-quốc.

Chính phủ nước Việt-nam Dân chủ Cộng hoà tôn trọng quyết định ấy và sẽ chỉ thị cho các cơ quan Nhà nước có trách nhiệm triệt để tôn trọng hải phận 12 hải lý của Trung-quốc, trong mọi quan hệ với nước Cộng hoà Nhân dân Trung hoa trên mặt bể.

Chúng tôi xin kính gửi Đồng chí Tổng lý lời chào rất trân trọng./.

Hà-nội, ngày 14 tháng 9 năm 1958

PHẠM VĂN ĐỒNG
Thủ tướng Chính phủ
Nước Việt-nam Dân chủ Cộng hoà

Kính gửi :
Đồng chí CHU AN LAI
Tổng lý Quốc vụ viện
Nước Cộng hoà Nhân dân Trung-hoa
tại
BẮC-KINH.

Vietnamese Premier Pham Van Dong's note to Premier Zhou Enlai, dated September 14, 1958.

附件五
ANNEX 5

PHI LIP PIN, MA LAI XI A, IN ĐÔ NÊ XI A, XIN GA PO

19

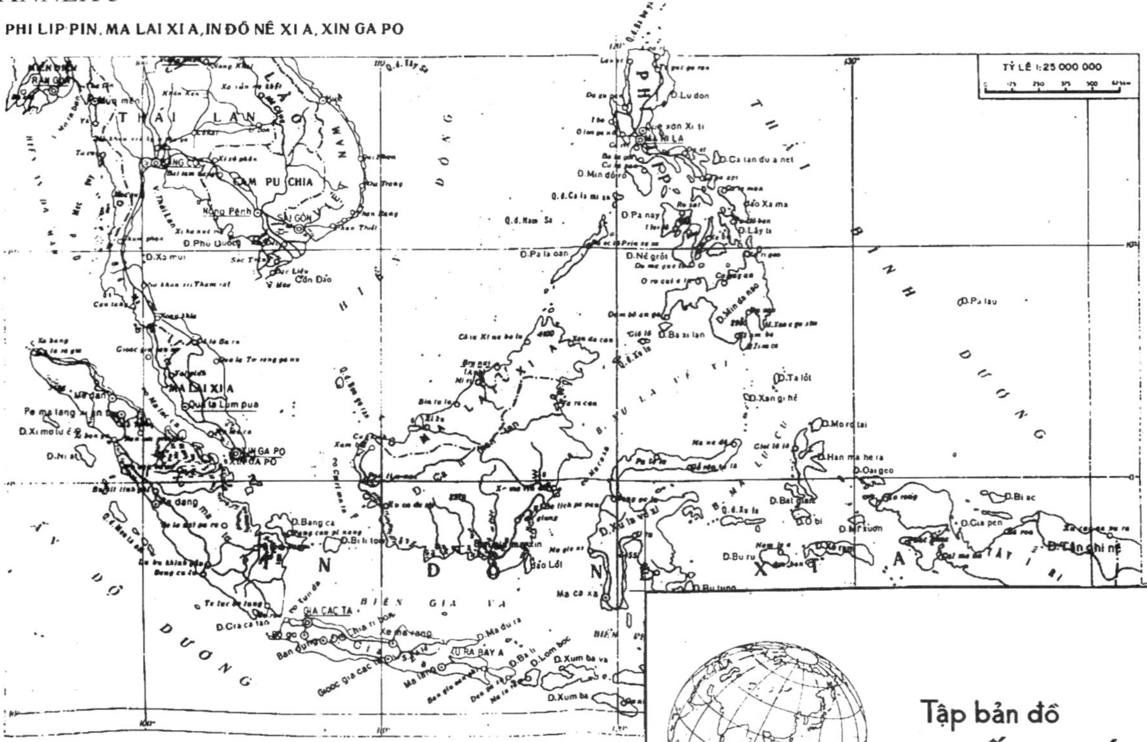

World Atlas printed by Viet Nam in May 1972, page 19. On the right corner below is the cover of the Atlas. The Vietnamese words on the right corner below give the name of the compiler: "The Bureau of Survey and Cartography Under the Office of the Premier of Viet Nam".

China's Indisputable Sovereignty Over the Xisha and Nansha Islands

— Document of the Ministry of Foreign Affairs of the People's Republic of China

(30 January 1980)

The Xisha and Nansha Islands are two large island groups in the South China Sea. Like the Dongsha and Zhongsha Islands, they have been China's territory since ancient times. This is not only proved by numerous Chinese and foreign historical records, documents, maps and cultural relics of ancient or modern times, but also recognized by many countries and extensive world opinion. These island groups were for a time in modern history illegally seized by foreign countries, but this in no way changes the historical fact and legal basis of their belonging to China.

The Vietnamese authorities cherish regional hegemonic and expansionist designs. While stepping up aggression and expansion in Indochina and Southeast Asia, they illegally occupied some islands of China's Nansha island group in 1975 and flagrantly laid a territorial claim to China's Xisha and Nansha Islands, reversing their earlier position of recognizing these islands as Chinese territory. On September 28, 1979 the Vietnamese Foreign Ministry issued a *White Book* entitled "Viet Nam's Sovereignty over the Hoang Sa and Truong Sa Archipelagoes", in which it pieced together or contrived some self-contradictory and utterly untenable "proving materials" in a vain attempt to find legal grounds for their illegal occupation and expansionist designs. This is completely futile.

It is impermissible to falsify historical facts or trample upon principles of international law. Here we cite authentic historical records and official documents to refute and explode the lies of the Vietnamese authorities and clearly prove the indisputable sovereignty of the People's Republic of China over the Xisha and Nansha Islands.

(1) The Xisha and Nansha Islands have been China's territory since ancient times

As early as the 2nd century B.C., at the time of Emperor Wu Di of the Han dynasty, Chinese people began sailing the South China Sea. After long years of navigation, they discovered successively the Xisha and Nansha Islands. The geographical features of these islands are described in *Nanzhou Yi Wu Zhi* (Strange Things of the Southern Provinces) by Wan Zhen and *Fu Nan Zhuan* (An Account of Fu Nan) by Kang Tai, both of which were written in the Three Kingdoms period (220–265).[1]

After the discovery of the Xisha and Nansha Islands, groups of Chinese people, surmounting all kinds of difficulties, came to visit and develop them. Their voyages to the Xisha and Nansha Islands and their productive activities there during more than a thousand years and the location and distribution of these islands are recorded in *Meng Liang Lu* (Record of a Day-Dreamer) of the Song dynasty, *Dao Yi Zhi Lüe* (Brief Account of the Islands) of the Yuan dynasty, *Dong Xi Yang Kao* (Studies on the Oceans East and West) and *Shun Feng Xiang Song* (Fair Winds for Escort) of the Ming dynasty, *Zhi Nan Zheng Fa* (Compass Directions) and *Hai Guo Wen Jian Lu* (Records of Things Seen and Heard About the Coastal Regions) of the Qing dynasty and *Geng Lu Bu* (Manuals of Sea Routes) of fishermen of various generations. In these works, the Xisha and Nansha Islands were variously named Jiuruluozhou (nine isles of cowry), Shitang (rocky reefs), Qianlishitang (thousand-li rocky reefs), Wanlishitang (ten thousand-li rocky reefs), Changsha (long sand cays), Qianlichangsha (thousand-li sand cays) and Wanlichangsha (ten thousand-li sand cays), and the numerous islands, reefs, sand cays and banks of these two archipelagoes were also given many descriptive names. In recent years, there have been discovered in the Xisha

Islands ruins of living quarters, pottery and porcelain utensils, iron knives, iron cooking pots, and other articles of daily use belonging to the Tang and Song dynasties, and wells, shrines, tombs and other relics of the Ming and Qing dynasties. These facts prove that, since at least the Tang and Song dynasties, Chinese people have lived on the Xisha and Nansha Islands and engaged in fishing and other productive activities there.

Along with the exploitation and development of the Xisha and Nansha Islands by Chinese people, the successive Chinese Governments exercised jurisdiction over them.

As early as the Northern Song dynasty (960–1127), Chinese naval patrols reached the Xisha Islands. It is recorded in *Wu Jing Zong Yao* (Outline Record of Military Affairs),[2] to which the Northern Song Emperor Ren Zong (1023–1063) personally wrote a preface, that the Northern Song court "ordered patrols by imperial forces and the building of a barracks for naval patrols" in Guangnan (now Guangdong),"commissioned the building of keeled sea-faring warships" which, "sailing in the southwestern direction from Tunmenshan, with a fair east wind, can reach Jiuruluozhou in seven days" (See annex 1). Jiuruluozhou was the name for today's Xisha Islands. It shows that the Northern Song court already put the Xisha Islands under its jurisdiction and therefore dispatched naval "warships" to patrol them.

Early in the Yuan dynasty, an astronomical observation was carried out at 27 places throughout the country. In the 16th year of the reign of Zhiyuan (1279) Kublai Khan or Emperor Shi Zu, personally assigned Guo Shoujing, famous astronomer and Deputy Director of the Astronomical Bureau,[3] to do the observation in the South China Sea. According to the official *History of the Yuan Dynasty*, Nanhai, Guo's observation point, was "to the south of Zhuya" and "the result of the survey showed that the latitude of Nanhai is15°N". The astronomical observation point Nanhai was on today's Xisha Islands.[4] It shows that Xisha Islands were within the bounds of China at the time of the Yuan dynasty.

During the Ming and Qing dynasties, the officially compiled local chronicles *Guangdong Tong Zhi, Qiongzhoufu Zhi and Wanzhou Zhi* all record, in the section of "territory" or "geography, mountains and waters", that "Wanzhou covers Qianlichangsha (thousand-li sand cays) and Wanlishitang (ten thousand-li rocky reefs)". This shows that at the time, the Xisha and Nansha Islands were under the administration of Wanzhou of Qiongzhou Prefecture (now Wanning and Lingshui Counties, Hainan Island), Guangdong Province.

In the 49th to 5lst years of the reign of Kangxi (1710–1712) of the Qing dynasty, Wu Sheng Vice-Admiral of the Guangdong Fleet led a naval patrol and "went personally on an inspection tour, setting out for Qiongya, rounding Tonggu and passing through Qizhouyang and Sigengsha, covering 3,000 li".[5] The Qizhouyang (sea of seven islands) mentioned here refers to the sea area around the Xisha Islands, whose patrol was the responsibility of the Guangdong Fleet. In the book *Shi Xi Ji Cheng* (Travel Notes of an Envoy to the West) by Guo-Songtao, the Qing dynasty Minister to Britain, the account of his voyage to his post made in 1876 includes this passage: "by noon on the 24th day [of the tenth moon, 2nd year of the reign of Guangxu], the ship had sailed 831 li and reached 17 degrees 30 minutes north of the Equator, 200 to 300 li south of Qiongzhou. The sailors called this place China Sea.... Nearby to the left were the Paracel Islands [the Xisha Islands] which yielded sea slugs, and also coral, which was not of very good quality. These islands belong to China."

In the 9th year of the reign of Guangxu (1883), Germany carried out surveys on the Xisha and Nansha Islands but had to stop them under the protest of the Qing Government.

The fact that the Xisha and Nansha Islands have been China's territory since ancient times is not only recorded in a large number of history books and local chronicles but also corroborated by many official maps, e.g., *Huang Qing Ge Zhi Sheng Fen Tu* (Map of the Provinces Directly Under the Imperial Qing Authority) made in the 20th year of Qianlong (1755), *Da Qing Wan Nian Yi Tong Di Li Quan Tu* (Map of the Eternally Unified Great Qing Empire) made in the 15th year of Jiaqing (1810) and *Da Qing Yi Tong Tian Xia Quan Tu* (Map of the Unified Territory of the Great Qing Empire) made in the 22nd year of Jiaqing (1817).

In the fourth moon of the first year of Emperor Xuantong (1909), Zhang Renjun, Governor of Guangdong and Guangxi, sent Li Zhun, Admiral of the

Guangdong Fleet, with more than 170 naval officers and men on an inspection tour of the Xisha Islands in three warships, the *Fubo*, the *Guangjin* and the *Chenhang*. They inspected 15 islands and set up stone tablets engraved with the names of the islands. They hoisted the flag and fired a salvo on Yongxing Island by way of reasserting Chinese sovereignty.

In 1911 the Chinese Guangdong Provincial Government announced the putting of the Xisha Islands under the administration of Yaxian County, Hainan Island. In 1921 the Ministry of Interior of the Chinese Government approved a license for He Ruinian, a merchant of Guangdong Province, to engage in fishing, plantation and mining on the Xisha Islands. Later he was found to have transferred the license to Japanese merchants, and the license was withdrawn.

In May 1928 the Guangdong Provincial Government sent a study group consisting of military and civil officers, scientists and technicians to go to the Xisha Islands by warship to make investigations on the spot. The group submitted a detailed report on the results of the investigations.

The above historical facts fully prove that China was the first to discover, develop and administer the Xisha and Nansha Islands. Consecutive jurisdiction was exercised over them by successive Chinese Governments for more than a thousand years. The Chinese are indisputable owners of these island groups.

(2) China's struggle in defence of its sovereignty over the Xisha and Nansha Islands

For a period of time after the establishment of its colonial rule in Viet Nam towards the end of the 19th century, France still recognized China's sovereignty over the Xisha Islands. In connection with the Xisha Islands, the French Premier and Foreign Minister Aristide Briand admitted on August 22, 1921 "the impossibility in which we currently find ourselves to claim these Islands as the Chinese Government has since 1909 exercised its rights to their ownership [referring to the above-mentioned inspection tour of the Xisha Islands by Li Zhun]". In 1929 French Acting Governor General in Indochina also conceded that "according to reports from various sources, the Paracels [the Xisha Islands] should be regarded as belonging to China".[6]

But the then French colonialists, covetous of Chinese territory and aware of the great strategic importance of the Xisha Islands, tried to seize these islands by taking the opportunity of Japanese aggression against China's northeastern provinces starting with the September 18th Incident of 1931. In a note addressed to the Chinese Legation in France on December 4 the same year, the French Government asserted that the Empire of Annam had a so-called "prior title" to the Xisha Islands, thus flagrantly laying a territorial claim to these Chinese Islands. The then Chinese Government gave a rebuttal in categorical terms, pointing out that the Xisha Islands had long been under China's jurisdiction. In his note of November 30, 1932 to the French Consul in Guangzhou, Zhu Zhaoxin, Special Inspector of the Ministry of Foreign Affairs of the Chinese Government, again affirmed that "there is no doubt whatsoever that the Xisha Islands are part of China's territory".

However, the then French authorities went a step further and invaded and occupied nine of China's Nansha Islands in 1933. The Chinese people rose in protest, and the then Chinese Government made strong representations to the French authorities through diplomatic channels.

A "Committee for the Examination of Land and Sea Maps" composed of the representatives of the Chinese Foreign, Interior and Naval Ministries and other institutions in1934–35 specially checked and approved the names of the South China Sea islands and compiled and printed the "Map of the South China Sea Islands", on which the Dongsha, Xisha, Zhongsha and Nansha Islands were clearly marked as belonging to China.

During World War II, Japan invaded and occupied the Xisha and Nansha Islands in 1939. Following the Japanese surrender in 1945, the then Chinese Government in November and December 1946 designated senior officials to proceed to the Xisha and Nansha Islands by warships to take over these islands, where take-over ceremonies were held and stone tablets erected (See annex 2) and troops garrisoned. These were followed by the renaming of the Dongsha, Xisha, Zhongsha and Nansha Islands and their various islands, sand cays, reefs and banks. Thus, the Xisha and Nansha Islands, once illegally seized by foreign powers, were restored to the jurisdiction of the Chinese Government.

After the founding of the People's Republic of China, Foreign Minister Zhou Enlai, in his Statement on the U.S.-U.K. Draft of Peace Treaty with Japan and the San Francisco Conference, solemnly declared on August 15,1951 that, like the Dongsha and Zhongsha Islands, the Xisha and Nansha Islands "have always been China's territory", that "although they had been occupied by Japan for some time during the war of aggression waged by Japanese imperialism, they were all taken over by the then Chinese Government, following Japan's surrender", and that "whether or not the U.S.-U.K. draft treaty contains provisions on this subject and no matter how these provisions are worded", China's sovereignty over the Xisha and Nansha Islands "will not be in any way affected".

Thereafter, the Government and Foreign Ministry of the People's Republic of China have issued many solemn statements opposing foreign infringement on China's sovereignty over the Xisha and Nansha Islands and reaffirming China's inviolable sovereignty over them.

Since the founding of the People's Republic of China, the Chinese Government and people have continued to administer and develop the Xisha and Nansha Islands. From 1950 to 1956, large numbers of fishermen from Qionghai County, Guangdong Province, continually went to the Nansha Islands for fishing. The departments concerned of the Hainan Administrative Area of Guangdong Province have continually sent people to the Xisha Islands for surveys, collection of marine products and guano and the setting up of a meteorological station, and exercised administration over the fishermen on the Xisha Islands. In March 1959 the Hainan Administrative Area set up on Yongxing Island of the Xisha Islands an "Office of the Xisha, Nansha and Zhongsha Islands", which in March 1969 was renamed the "Revolutionary Committee of the Xisha, Zhongsha and Nansha Islands of Guangdong Province".

In January 1974 the Chinese People's Liberation Army and militia drove out the troops of the South Vietnamese authorities in Saigon who had invaded the Xisha Islands and thus defended China's sovereignty and territorial integrity.

For years the Taiwan authorities of China have maintained a military garrison on Taiping Island, the biggest among the Nansha Islands.

(3) China's sovereignty over the Xisha and Nansha Islands is widely acknowledged internationally

Many countries and world opinion recognize the fact that the Xisha and Nansha Islands are part of China's territory.

In April 1930 the Far East Conference on Meteorology held in Hong Kong, with the participation of the representatives of China, France, the Philippines and the Hong Kong authorities, adopted a resolution requesting the Chinese Government to establish a meteorological observation station on the Xisha Islands.

After the Annamese police of the French colonial authorities intruded into the Xisha Islands in 1938, a spokesman of the Japanese Foreign Ministry stated that the Xisha Islands on which the Annamese police had landed were "recognized by us as part of China's territory".[7]

The 1951 San Francisco Conference on the peace treaty with Japan decided that Japan should renounce the Xisha and Nansha Islands. The leader of the Soviet Delegation Andrei Gromyko pointed out at the Conference that the Xisha and Nansha Islands... are China's "inalienable territory". Although the U.S.-U.K. drafted peace treaty with Japan did not mention the ownership of these islands after Japan's renunciation, yet in 1952, the year after the San Francisco Peace Treaty with Japan was signed, the fifteenth map, *Southeast Asia, of the Standard World Atlas*, which was recommended by the signature of the then Japanese Foreign Minister Katsuo Okazaki, marks as part of China all the Xisha and Nansha Islands, which Japan had to renounce as stipulated by the Peace Treaty, as well as the Dongsha and Zhongsha Islands (See annex 3). Since these islands were originally China's territory, they should of course be returned to China.

In October 1955 the International Civil Aviation Organization held a conference in Manila, which was attended by representatives of the United States, Britain, France, Japan, Canada, Australia, New Zealand, Thailand, the Philippines and the authorities of South Viet Nam and China's Taiwan. Resolution No. 24 adopted by the conference requested the Taiwan authorities of China to improve meteorological observation on the Nansha Islands, and no opposition or reservation was registered in this regard.

Since the beginning of the twentieth century, most of the authoritative encyclopaedias recognize the Xisha and Nansha Islands as China's territory. For instance, the *Worldmark Encyclopaedia of the Nations* published in the United States in 1963 states that the islands [of the People's Republic of China] "include the reefs and islands of the South China Sea, extending as far as 4°N. These reefs and islands include the Tungsha (Pratas), Sisha (Paracels), Chungsha, and Nansha archipelagoes." The *Bolshaya Sovietskaga Enciclopediya* of 1973 and the Japanese *Kyodo World Manual* of 1979 also explicitly points out that the Xisha and Nansha Islands are China's territory.

Atlases and maps published in many countries mark the Xisha and Nansha Islands as belonging to China. For example, this is done in the *Welt-Atlas* published in the Federal Republic of Germany in 1954, the Soviet *Atlas Mira* from 1954 to 1967, the Romanian *Atlas Geografic Scolar* of 1957, the 1968 *Carte Generale du Monde* published in France by the Institut Geographique National, the 1968 *Haack Grosser Weltatlas* published in the G.D.R., the 1970 *Gran Atlas Aguilar* published in Spain and the 1973 *Atlas of China* published by the Japanese Heibou Sha. In short, the Xisha and Nansha Islands are recognized as part of China's territory in contemporary maps and books published in many countries.

(4) The perfidy of the Vietnamese authorities

It must be pointed out that there used to be no dispute between China and Viet Nam over the ownership of the Xisha and Nansha Islands. During a long period of time the Vietnamese side formally acknowledged these islands as being Chinese territory since ancient times, whether in their government statements and notes, or in their newspapers, periodicals, maps and textbooks.

On June 15, 1956 Vice-Foreign Minister Ung Van Khiem of the Democratic Republic of Viet Nam received Li Zhimin, Charge d'Affaires *ad interim* of the Chinese Embassy in Viet Nam, and stated to him that "according to Vietnamese data, the Xisha and Nansha Islands are historically part of Chinese territory". Le Loc, Acting Director of the Asian Department of the Vietnamese Foreign Ministry, who was present, specifically cited Vietnamese data and pointed out that, "judging from history, these islands were already part of China at the time of the Song dynasty".

In its declaration of September 4, 1958, the Government of the People's Republic of China proclaimed the breadth of the territorial sea of the People's Republic of China to be twelve nautical miles and stated explicitly that "this provision applies to all territories of the People's Republic of China, including… the Dongsha Islands, the Xisha Islands, the Zhongsha Islands, the Nansha Islands and all other islands belonging to China". On September 6, 1958 *Nhan Dan*, central organ of the Vietnamese Workers' Party, prominently featured on its front page details of the Chinese Government's declaration. It wrote, "On September 4, 1958 the Government of the People's Republic of China issued a declaration on China's territorial sea. The declaration provides that the breadth of China's territorial sea is twelve nautical miles (over 22 kilometres). This provision applies to all territories of the People's Republic of China including the Chinese mainland and its coastal islands, as well as Taiwan and its surrounding islands, the Penghu Islands, the Dongsha Islands, the Xisha Islands, the Zhongsha Islands, the Nansha Islands and all other islands belonging to China which are separated from the mainland and its coastal islands by the high seas." On September 14 the same year, Premier Pham Van Dong of the Vietnamese Government solemnly stated in his note to Premier Zhou Enlai of the Chinese State Council that "the Government of the Democratic Republic of Viet Nam recognizes and supports the declaration of the Government of the People's Republic of China on China's territorial sea made on September 4, 1958", and that "the Government of the Democratic Republic of Viet Nam respects this decision". Pham Van Dong's note clearly shows that the Vietnamese Government acknowledged Xisha and Nansha Islands as China's territory (See annex 4).

In its statement of May 9, 1965 on the U.S. Government's designation of a "combat zone" for its forces in Viet Nam, the Government of the Democratic Republic of Viet Nam said that it was "a direct threat to the security of the Democratic Republic of Viet Nam and its neighbouring country" for "U.S. President Lyndon Johnson to designate the whole of Viet Nam and the adjacent waters which extend roughly 100 miles from the coast of Viet Nam and part of the territorial waters of the People's Republic of China in its Xisha Islands as a 'combat zone' of the United States armed forces". Here the Vietnamese Government once again clearly recognized the Xisha Islands as part of Chinese territory.

In reporting foreign intrusions into the Xisha Islands, the Vietnamese press also clearly recognized these islands as belonging to China. For example, on May 13, 1969 *Nhan Dan* reported that "on May 10 a U.S. military aircraft invaded China's air space over Yongxing Island and Dongdao Island of the Xisha Islands of China's Guangdong Province." Many similar reports were carried in Vietnamese papers.

Official maps and textbooks of Viet Nam explicitly acknowledged the Xisha and Nansha Islands as China's territory. For example, the 1960 *World Map* made by the Mapping Section of the General Staff of the Vietnamese People's Army marks the Xisha and Nansha Islands by their Chinese names and notes in brackets that they belong to China. The May 1972 *World Atlas* published by the Bureau of Survey and Cartography Under the Office of the Premier of Viet Nam also marks the Xisha and Nansha Islands by their Chinese names (See annex 5). Another example, the lesson entitled "The People's Republic of China" in the geography textbook for school pupils of grade 9 published by Viet Nam's Educational Press in 1974 reads in part as follows: "The chain of islands from the Nansha and Xisha Islands to Hainan Island, Taiwan Island, the Penghu Islands and the Zhoushan Island… is shaped like a bow and constitutes a Great Wall defending the China mainland."

The Vietnamese in apparent seriousness stressed that in order to establish territorial sovereignty it is necessary to present "formal state materials" and "documents of legal force". What we have cited above are precisely Vietnamese "formal state materials" and "documents of legal force". This clearly shows that up to 1974 the Vietnamese Government had recognized the Xisha and Nansha Islands as Chinese territory. Now, the Vietnamese authorities have gone back on their own word and perfidiously departed from their original position of recognizing the Xisha and Nansha Islands as Chinese territory, and this is something absolutely impermissible under international law.

(5) The arguments of the Vietnamese White Book are totally untenable

The 19 "documents" quoted in the *White Book* of the Vietnamese Foreign Ministry fall roughly into two categories: the first category (documents Nos. 1 to 5) consists of some Vietnamese "historical sources" and the second category (documents Nos. 6 to 19) lists some materials about the occupation of China's Xisha and Nansha Islands by the French colonial authorities and the South Vietnamese authorities in Saigon since 1933. All are intended to prove that China's Xisha and Nansha Islands are Vietnamese territory. But if one makes a serious study and analysis, it will not be difficult to find that the "documents" in the first category are all based on deliberate false attribution, and that those in the second category are totally untenable and legally invalid.

The Vietnamese authorities allege that Bai Cat Vang and Hoang Sa Chu in the historical records is what they now call the Hoang Sa Archipelago or what is known in the West as the Paracels, that is to say, China's Xisha Islands. Their primary "historical sources" are a "Map of the Quang Ngai Region from a Collection of Maps of Viet Nam" compiled in the 17th century by a Vietnamese called Do Ba and *Phu Bien Tap Luc* (Miscellaneous Records on the Pacification of the Frontiers) written by Le Quy Don in the 18th century. Quoted from the map and the record by the Vietnamese *White Book* are the following, descriptions of Bai Cat Vang and Hoang Sa Chu:

"...an elongated sandbank, called Bai Cat Vang (meaning yellow sandbank),...lies in the middle of the sea.... It takes one day and a half from Dai Chiem Port to go there; and only half a day if one embarks at Sa Ky."

"In Binh Son sub-district, Quang Ngai district, there is the An Vinh village on the sea. Off the coast of this village, in the northeast lie islands with over 130 scattered hills. The distance between these hills is covered by a voyage of one day or sometimes of only a few hours. There are fresh water springs on these hills. Among the islands there is a vast and flat yellow sandbank, over 30 li long, where the spring water is crystal clear."

The Vietnamese authorities cite the above two passages as the "earliest and most essential" material. But these records precisely show that what the Vietnamese call the Hoang Sa Archipelago is not China's Xisha Islands. They are two entirely different places.

First, the geographical location. According to the Vietnamese material, it takes one day and a half to get to Bai Cat Vang from Dai Chiem Port (now Cua Dai, Quang Nam-Da Nang Province, Viet Nam) and only half a day from Sa Ky Port (near Binh Son County, Quang Ngai Province, Viet Nam). But China's Xisha Islands are 200 nautical miles from the coast of central Viet Nam, a distance which was absolutely impossible to cover by sailboat in half a day or even one day and a half with navigation techniques as they were.

Secondly, the length and area. It is said in the Vietnamese material that Hoang Sa Chu is "over 30 li long" and "vast and flat". Yet, even Yongxing Island, the biggest among China's Xisha Islands, is less than 2 kilometres (4 li) long and has an area of only 1.85 square kilometres.

Thirdly, the topography. According to the Vietnamese material, there are in the Hoang Sa Archipelago "over 130 scattered hills". But there are no hills at all on China's shallow and flat Xisha Islands, whose elevation is generally only 5 to 6 metres, with the highest point measuring 15.9 metres. And in Xisha there are only a total of 35 islands, reefs, sandbanks and sand cays. There are no "over 130 hills" to speak of.

These comparisons clearly show that the Hoang Sa Archipelago mentioned in the Vietnamese material can only be some islands and shoals off the coast of central Viet Nam and not China's Xisha Islands.

The Vietnamese *White Book* asserts that *Dai Nam Thuc Luc Chinh Bien* (Official Chronicles of Dai Nam) "records the occupation by King Gia Long of the Hoang Sa Islands in 1816". But no record of "occupation" is found anywhere in this history book. The legend that King Gia Long "occupied the Hoang Sa Islands" originated from an article, "Note on the Geography of Cochin-china" by Bishop Louis Taberd, a French colonialist, who wrote:"the Pracel or Parocels, is a labyrinth of small islands, rocks and sandbanks, which appears to extend up to the 11th degree of north latitude, in the 107th parallel of longitude from Paris." He also wrote that in 1816 King Gia Long "went with solemnity to plant his flag and take formal possession of these rocks, which it is not likely anybody will dispute with him". 107°E from Paris meridian is 109°10′ E from Greenwich, which is not far from the coast of central Viet Nam. China's Xisha Islands, however, are to the east of 110°10′ E. Taberd said that the Pracel extended to 11° N, but the southernmost point of the Xisha Islands is at 15°47′ N. Obviously, the Pracel referred to by Bishop Taberd is islands and shoals off the coast of central Viet Nam, but not China's Xisha Islands.

What the Vietnamese call Truong Sa Archipelago cannot be China's Nansha Islands, either. The *White Book* says that Truong Sa Archipelago used to be called Dai Truong Sa. Dai Truong Sa is described in many Chinese and Vietnamese historical records, but it obviously is not situated where China's Nansha Islands are; the reference is to some islands and shoals along the Vietnamese coast. As the Vietnamese authorities fail to find any historical evidence of value to prove that Truong Sa is China's Nansha Islands, they in the *White Book* have recourse to *Dai Nam Nhat Thong Toan Do* (Complete Map of Unified Dai Nam), a map of unknown origin. However, it can clearly be seen from this map that Hoang Sa and Van Ly Truong Sa are close and parallel to the coast of central Viet Nam and not where China's Xisha and Nansha Islands are.

By false attribution the Vietnamese authorities are attempting to find a basis for their ambition for territorial expansion and hoodwink the people of the world. But this is surely futile.

The Vietnamese authorities cite in their *White Book* the occupation of China's Xisha and Nansha Islands by the French colonial authorities and the South Vietnamese authorities in Saigon since 1933 in order to prove the legitimacy of the Vietnamese authorities' territorial claim to China's Xisha and Nansha Islands. This is not at all tenable. According to international law, aggression does not establish sovereignty, and "inheritance" of territory seized from another country through occupation is illegal and therefore invalid.

That the Xisha and Nansha Islands have been China's territory since ancient times is fully proved by legal evidence. And one can draw an impartial conclusion from the ample facts and materials mentioned above. The Vietnamese authorities' illegal occupation of part of China's Nansha Islands and their territorial claim to China's Xisha and Nansha Islands can only serve to reveal their regional hegemonist and aggressor expansionist ambitions. China's sovereignty over the Xisha and Nansha Islands is indisputable.

NOTES

1. Wan Zhen in his *Nanzhou Yi Wu Zhi* (Strange Things of the Southern Provinces) wrote about the navigation route from the Malay Peninsula to the mainland of China in the Han dynasty:"... going northeastward, one reaches Daqitou and then sails through Zhang Hai, which is shallow and has a lot of lodestones underneath. "Zhang Hai was the name for the present South China Sea. The lodestones referred to are the then submerged sand cays and reefs of the Xisha and Nansha Islands. They were called "lodestones" because ships were liable to be stranded on them and unable to extricate themselves. Kang Tai in his *Fu Nan Zhuan* (An Account of Fu Nan) wrote: "In Zhang Hai there are coral islands with flat base rocks, on which coral grows."

2. *Wu Jing Zong Yao* (Outline Record of Military Affairs) was authoritative literature of the Song dynasty, which records the military system and major affairs in national defence. It was edited by Ding Du, Deputy Prime Minister and concurrently Minister of Works, and Zeng Gongliang, Royal Attendant in Tian Zhang Ge, a title equivalent to a privy councillor.

3. The Chinese name of the title was "Tong Zhi Tai Shi Yuan Shi".

4. Guo Shoujing then was responsible for the work of establishing astronomical observation points within the bounds of China in the Yuan dynasty. The Nanhai observation point was "to the south of Zhuya", that is, to the south of Hainan Island. The result of their survey was: "The latitude of Qiongzhou is 19.75°N"; "The latitude of Nanhai is 15°N". This shows that the Nanhai observation point was more than four degrees south of Qiongzhou observation point on Hainan Island, which is exactly the location of the Xisha Islands of today. Owing to technological limitations at that time, the north latitudes obtained of most of the twenty-seven observation points showed an error of about one degree as compared with their present latitudes. Since according to the system of the Yuan dynasty a circumference was divided into 365.25 degrees

instead of 360 degrees as at present, the then 15°N for the Nanhai observation point should actually be 14°47′ N, and discounting the error of about one degree, its location is precisely on the Xisha Islands of today.

5. See Volume 56 of *Quan Zhou Fu Zhi* (History of Quanzhou), written during the reign of Qianlong of the Qing dynasty.

6. See *Review of Foreign Affairs,* April 1934, p.77.

7. A Reuter dispatch, July 4, 1938.

附件一
ANNEX 1

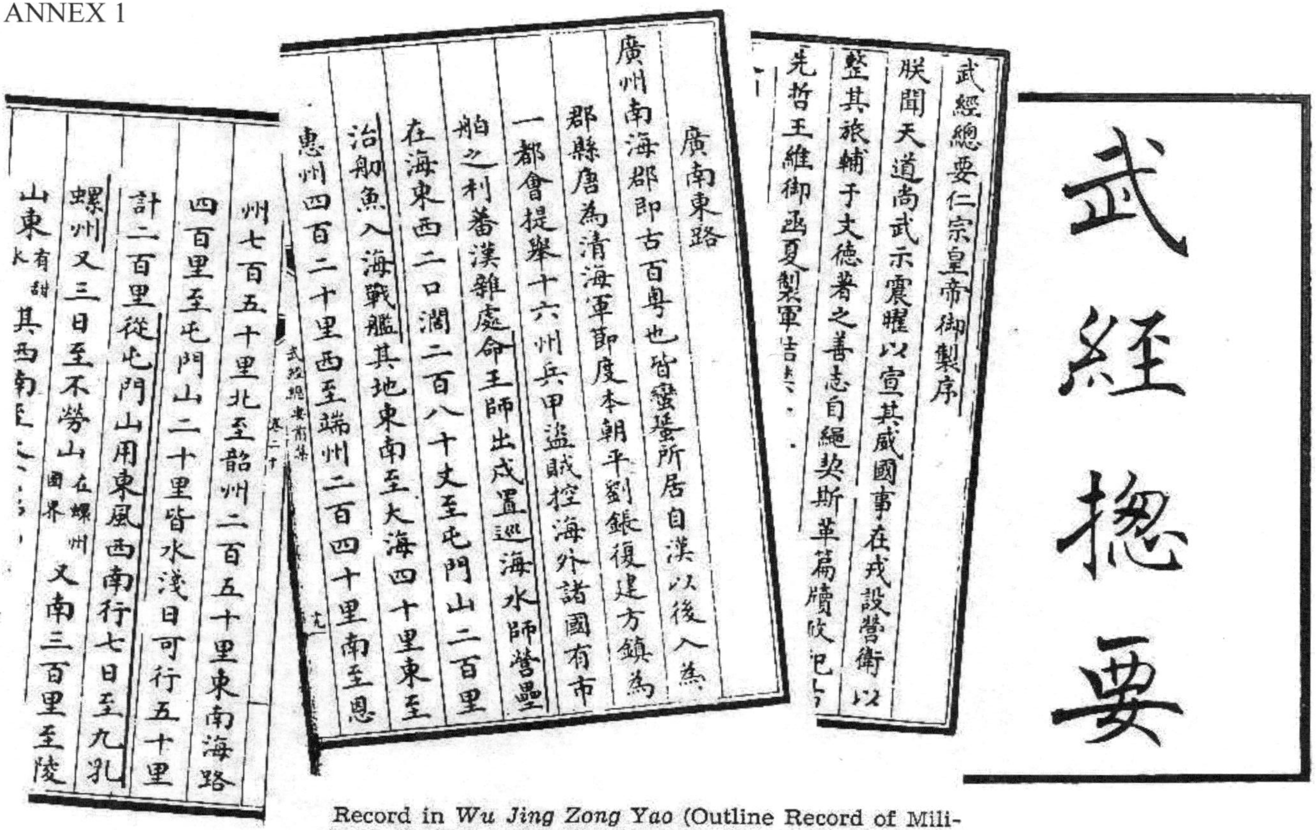

武經總要

武經總要仁宗皇帝御製序

朕聞天道尚武示震曜以宣其威國事在戎設營衛以
整其旅輔于文德著之善志自緄契斯革萹牘攸
先哲王維御函夏製軍

廣南東路

廣州南海郡即古百粵也皆蠻蜑所居自漢以後入為
郡縣唐為清海軍節度本朝平劉鋹復建方鎮為
一都會提舉十六州兵甲盜賊控海外諸國有市
舶之利蕃漢雜處命王師出戍置巡海水師營壘
在海東西二口闊二百八十丈至屯門山二百里
治舠魚入海戰艦其地東南至大海四十里東至
惠州四百二十里西至端州二百四十里南至恩

州七百五十里北至韶州二百五十里東南海路
四百里至屯門山二十里皆水淺日可行五十里
計二百里從屯門山用東風西南行七日至九乳
螺州又三日至不勞山（在螺州國界）又南三百里至陵
山東（有甜水）其西南至

Record in *Wu Jing Zong Yao* (Outline Record of Military Affairs) of the Northern Song dynasty about the patrol of the Guangnan Fleet reaching Jiuruluozhou.

附件二
ANNEX 2

When the Chinese Government officials and naval officers and men took over the Nansha Islands in December 1946, they had a photo taken on Taiping Island as a memento and erected a stone tablet to reassert China's sovereignty over these islands. The photo below left shows the front of the stone tablet and the one below right shows its back.

附件三
ANNEX 3

SOUTH-EAST ASIA

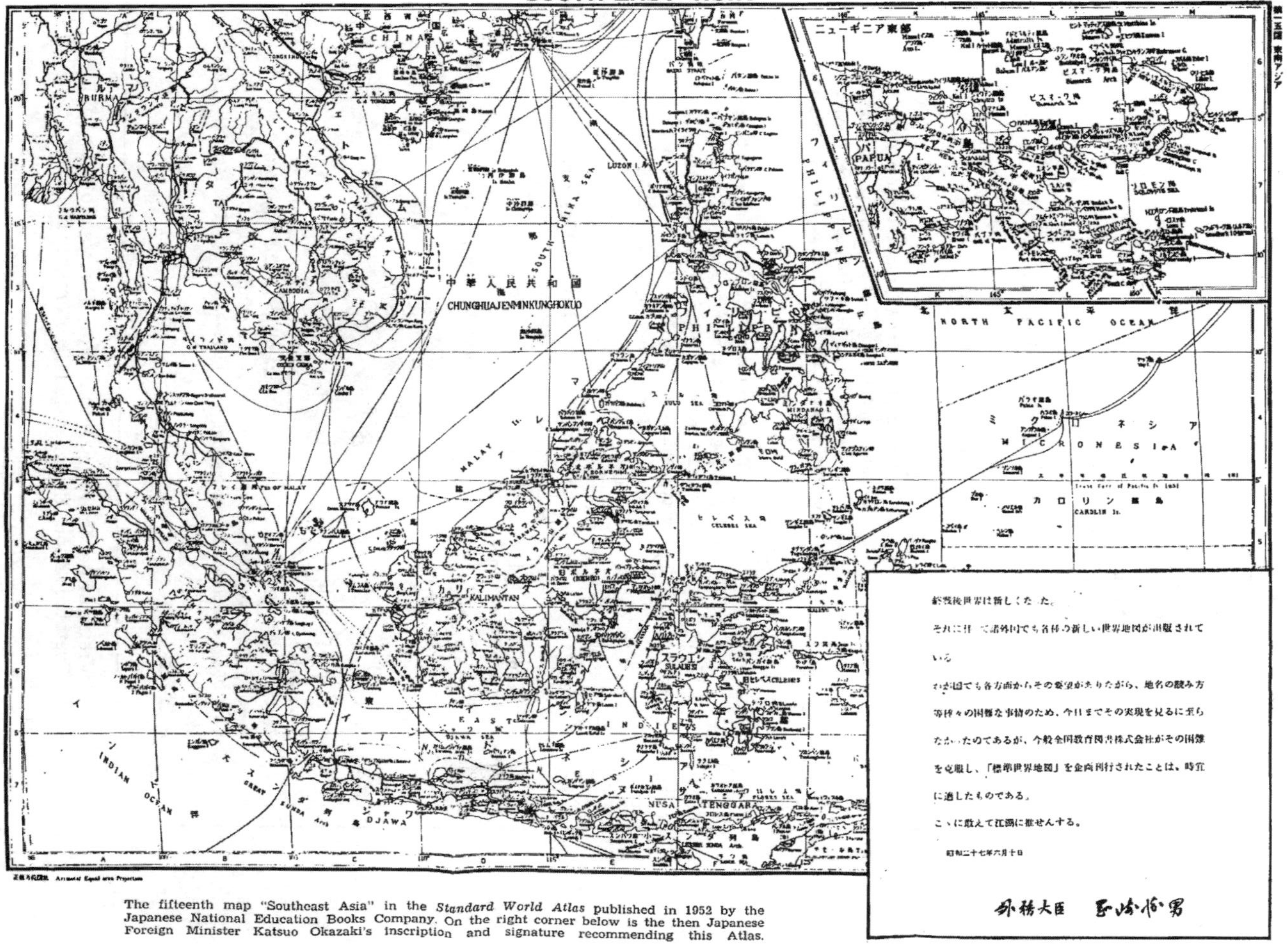

The fifteenth map "Southeast Asia" in the *Standard World Atlas* published in 1952 by the Japanese National Education Books Company. On the right corner below is the then Japanese Foreign Minister Katsuo Okazaki's inscription and signature recommending this Atlas.

附件四
ANNEX 4

THỦ TƯỚNG PHỦ
NƯỚC VIỆT-NAM DÂN-CHỦ CỘNG-HÒA

Thưa Đồng chí Tổng lý,

Chúng tôi xin trân trọng báo tin để Đồng chí Tổng lý rõ :

Chính phủ nước Việt-nam Dân chủ Cộng hoà ghi nhận và tán thành bản tuyên bố, ngày 4 tháng 9 năm 1958, của Chính phủ nước Cộng hoà Nhân dân Trung-hoa, quyết định về hải phận của Trung-quốc.

Chính phủ nước Việt-nam Dân chủ Cộng hoà tôn trọng quyết định ấy và sẽ chỉ thị cho các cơ quan Nhà nước có trách nhiệm triệt để tôn trọng hải phận 12 hải lý của Trung-quốc, trong mọi quan hệ với nước Cộng hoà Nhân dân Trung hoa trên mặt bể.

Chúng tôi xin kính gửi Đồng chí Tổng lý lời chào rất trân trọng./.

Hà-nội, ngày 14 tháng 9 năm 1958

PHẠM VAN ĐỒNG
Thủ tướng Chính phủ
Nước Việt - nam Dân chủ Cộng hoà

Kính gửi :
Đồng chí CHU AN LAI
Tổng lý Quốc vụ viện
Nước Cộng hoà Nhân dân Trung-hoa
tại
BẠC-KINH.

Vietnamese Premier Pham Van Dong's note to Premier Zhou Enlai, dated September 14, 1958.

附件五
ANNEX 5

PHI LIP PIN, MA LAI XI A, IN ĐÔ NÊ XI A, XIN GA PO

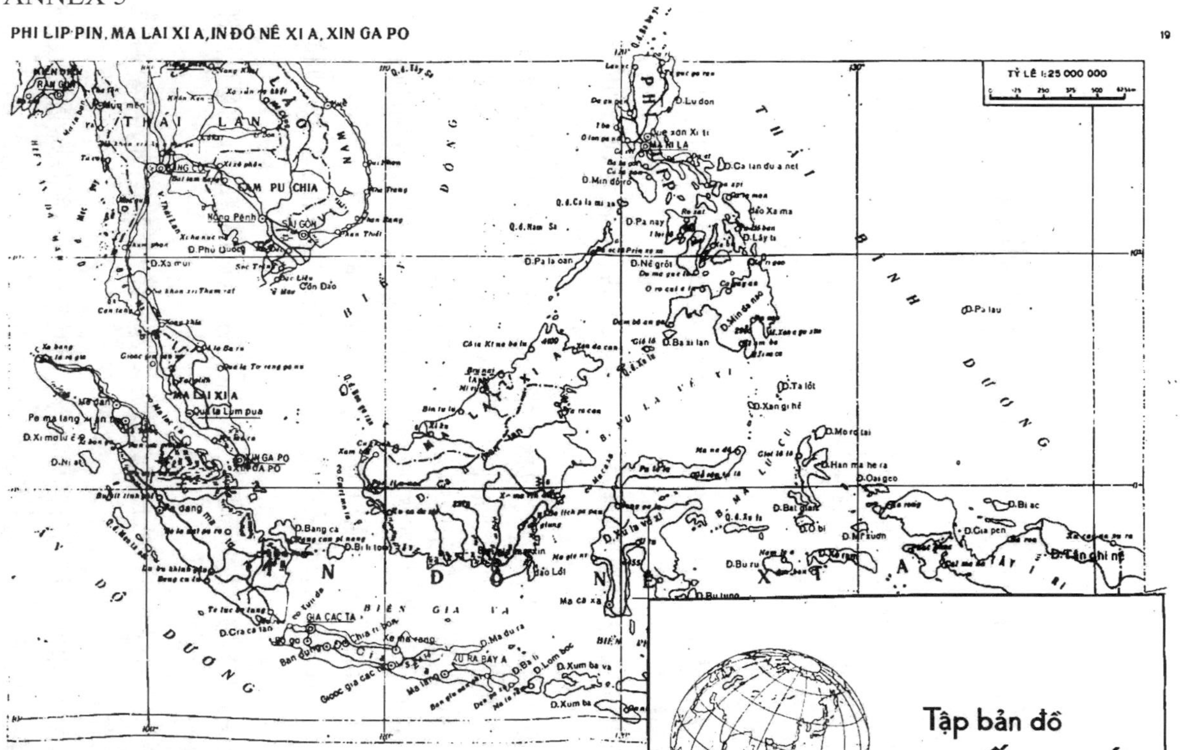

World Atlas printed by Viet Nam in May 1972, page 19. On the right corner below is the cover of the Atlas. The Vietnamese words on the right corner below give the name of the compiler: "The Bureau of Survey and Cartography Under the Office of the Premier of Viet Nam".

中华人民共和国领海及毗连区法

（1992年2月25日第七届全国人民代表大会常务委员会第二十四次会议通过
1992年2月25日中华人民共和国主席令第五十五号发布　自公布之日起施行）

第一条 为行使中华人民共和国对领海的主权和对毗连区的管制权，维护国家安全和海洋权益，制定本法。

第二条 中华人民共和国领海为邻接中华人民共和国陆地领土和内水的一带海域。

中华人民共和国的陆地领土包括中华人民共和国大陆及其沿海岛屿、台湾及其包括钓鱼岛在内的附属各岛、澎湖列岛、东沙群岛、西沙群岛、中沙群岛、南沙群岛以其他一切属于中华人民共和国的岛屿。

中华人民共和国领海基线向陆地一侧的水域为中华人民共和国的内水。

第三条 中华人民共和国领海的宽度从领海基线量起为十二海里。

中华人民共和国领海基线采用直线基线法划定，由各相邻基点之间的直线连线组成。

中华人民共和国领海的外部界限为一条其每一点与领海基线的最近点距离等于十二海里的线。

第四条 中华人民共和国毗连区为领海以外邻接领海的一带海域。毗连区的宽度为十二海里。

中华人民共和国毗连区的外部界限为一条其每一点与领海基线的最近点距离等于二十四海里的线。

第五条 中华人民共和国对领海的主权及于领海上空、领海的海床及底土。

第六条 外国非军用船舶，享有依法无害通过中华人民共和国领海的权利。

外国军用船舶进入中华人民共和国领海，须经中华人民共和国政府批准。

第七条 外国潜水艇和其他潜水器通过中华人民共和国领海，必须在海面航行，并展示其旗帜。

第八条 外国船舶通过中华人民共和国领海，必须遵守中华人民共和国法律、法规，不得损害中华人民共和国的和平、安全和良好秩序。

外国核动力船舶和载运核物质、有毒物质或者其他危险物质的船舶通过中华人民共和国领海，必须持有有关证书，并采取特别预防措施。

中华人民共和国政府有权采取一切必要措施，以防止和制止对领海的非无害通过。

外国船舶违反中华人民共和国法律、法规的，由中华人民共和国有关机关依法处理。

第九条 为维护航行安全和其他特殊需要，中华人民共和国政府可以要求通过中华人民共和国领海的外国船舶使用指定的航道或者依照规定的分道通航制航行，具体办法由中华人民共和国政府或者其有关主管部门公布。

第十条 外国军用船舶或者用于非商业目的的外国政府船舶在通过中华人民共和国领海时，违反中华人民共和国法律、法规的，中华人民共和国有关主管机关有权令其立即离开领海，对所造成的损失或者损害，船旗国应当负国际责任。

第十一条 任何国际组织、外国的组织或者个人，在中华人民共和国领海内进行科学研究、海洋作业等活动，须经中华人民共和国政府或者其有关主管部门批准，遵守中华人民共和国法律、法规。

违反前款规定，非法进入中华人民共和国领海进行科学研究、海洋作业等活动的，由中华人民共和国有关机关依法处理。

第十二条 外国航空器只有根据该国政府与中华人民共和国政府签订的协定、协议，或者经中华人民共和国政府或者其授权的机关批准或者接受，方可进入中华人民共和国领海上空。

第十三条 中华人民共和国有权在毗连区内，为防止和惩处在其陆地领土、内水或者领海内违反有关安全、海关、财政、卫生或者入境出境管理的法律、法规的行为行使管制权。

第十四条 中华人民共和国有关主管机关有充分理由认为外国船舶违反中华人民共和国法律、法规时，可以对该外国船舶行使紧追权。

追逐须在外国船舶或者其小艇之一或者以被追逐的船舶为母船进行活动的其他船艇在中华人民共和国的内水、领海或者毗连区内时开始。

如果外国船舶是在中华人民共和国毗连区内，追逐只有在本法第十三条所列有关法律、法规规定的权利受到侵犯时方可进行。

追逐只要没有中断，可以在中华人民共和国领海或者毗连区外继续进行。在被追逐的船舶进入其本国领海或者第三国领海时，追逐终止。

本条规定的紧追权由中华人民共和国军用船舶、军用航空器或者中华人民共和国政府授权的执行政府公务的船舶、航空器行使。

第十五条 中华人民共和国领海基线由中华人民共和国政府公布。

第十六条 中华人民共和国政府依据本法制定有关规定。

第十七条 本法自公布之日起施行。

Law of the People's Republic of China on the Territorial Sea and the Contiguous Zone

(Adopted at the 24th Meeting of the Standing Committee of the Seventh National People's Congress on February 25,1992)

Article 1 This Law is enacted for the People's Republic of China to exercise its sovereignty over its territorial sea and the control over its contiguous zone, and to safeguard its national security and its maritime rights and interests.

Article 2 The territorial sea of the People's Republic of China is the sea belt adjacent to the land territory and the internal waters of the People's Republic of China.

The land territory of the People's Republic of China includes the mainland of the People's Republic of China and its coastal islands; Taiwan and all islands appertaining thereto including the Diaoyu Islands; the Penghu Islands; the Dongsha Islands; the Xisha Islands; the Zhongsha Islands and the Nansha Islands; as well as all the other islands belonging to the People's Republic of China.

The waters on the landward side of the baselines of the territorial sea of the People's Republic of China constitute the internal waters of the People's Republic of China.

Article 3 The breadth of the territorial sea of the People's Republic of China is twelve nautical miles, measured from the baselines of the territorial sea.

The method of straight baselines composed of all the straight lines joining the adjacent base points shall be employed in drawing the baselines of the territorial sea of the People's Republic of China.

The outer limit of the territorial sea of the People's Republic of China is the line every point of which is at a distance equal to twelve nautical miles from the nearest point of the baseline of the territorial sea.

Article 4 The contiguous zone of the People's Republic of China is the sea belt adjacent to and beyond the territorial sea. The breadth of the contiguous zone is twelve nautical miles.

The outer limit of the contiguous zone of the People's Republic of China is the line every point of which is at a distance equal to twenty-four nautical miles from the nearest point of the baseline of the territorial sea.

Article 5 The sovereignty of the People's Republic of China over its territorial sea extends to the air space over the territorial sea as well as to the bed and subsoil of the territorial sea.

Article 6 Foreign ships for non-military purposes shall enjoy the right of innocent passage through the territorial sea of the People's Republic of China in accordance with the law.

Foreign ships for military purposes shall be subject to approval by the Government of the People's Republic of China for entering the territorial sea of the People's Republic of China.

Article 7 Foreign submarines and other underwater vehicles, when passing through the territorial sea of the People's Republic of China, shall navigate on the surface and show their flag.

Article 8 Foreign ships passing through the territorial sea of the People's Republic of China must comply with the laws and regulations of the People's Republic of China and shall not be prejudicial to the peace, security and good order of the People's Republic of China.

Foreign nuclear-powered ships and ships carrying nuclear, noxious or other dangerous substances, when passing through the territorial sea of the People's Republic of China, must carry relevant documents and take special precautionary measures.

The Government of the People's Republic of China has the right to take all necessary measures to prevent and stop non-innocent passage through its territorial sea.

Cases of foreign ships violating the laws or regulations of the People's

Republic of China shall be handled by the relevant organs of the People's Republic of China in accordance with the law.

Article 9 The Government of the People's Republic of China may, for maintaining the safety of navigation or for other special needs, request foreign ships passing through the territorial sea of the People's Republic of China to use the designated sea lanes or to navigate according to the prescribed traffic separation schemes. The specific regulations to this effect shall be promulgated by the Government of the People's Republic of China or its competent authorities concerned.

Article 10 In the case of violation of the laws or regulations of the People's Republic of China by a foreign ship for military purposes or a foreign government ship for noncommercial purposes when passing through the territorial sea of the People's Republic of China, the competent authorities of the People's Republic of China shall have the right to order it to leave the territorial sea immediately and the flag State shall bear international responsibility for any loss or damage thus caused.

Article 11 All international organizations, foreign organizations or individuals shall obtain approval from the Government of the People's Republic of China for carrying out scientific research, marine operations or other activities in the territorial sea of the People's Republic of China, and shall comply with the laws and regulations of the People's Republic of China.

All illegal entries into the territorial sea of the People's Republic of China for carrying out scientific research, marine operations or other activities in contravention of the provisions of the preceding paragraph of this Article, shall be dealt with by the relevant organs of the People's Republic of China in accordance with the law.

Article 12 No aircraft of a foreign State may enter the air space over the territorial sea of the People's Republic of China unless there is a relevant protocol or agreement between the Government of that State and the Government of the People's Republic of China, or approval or acceptance by the Government of the People's Republic of China or the competent authorities authorized by it.

Article 13 The People's Republic of China has the right to exercise control in the contiguous zone to prevent and impose penalties for activities infringing the laws or regulations concerning security, the customs, finance, sanitation or entry and exit control within its land territory, internal waters or territorial sea.

Article 14 The competent authorities concerned of the People's Republic of China may, when they have good reasons to believe that a foreign ship has violated the laws or regulations of the People's Republic of China, exercise the right of hot pursuit against the foreign ship.

Such pursuit shall be commenced when the foreign ship or one of its boats or other craft engaged in activities by using the ship pursued as a mother ship is within the internal waters, the territorial sea or the contiguous zone of the People's Republic of China.

If the foreign ship is within the contiguous zone of the People's Republic of China, the pursuit may be undertaken only when there has been a violation of the rights as provided for in the relevant laws or regulations listed in Article 13 of this Law.

The pursuit, if not interrupted, may be continued outside the territorial sea or the contiguous zone until the ship pursued enters the territorial sea of its own country or of a third State.

The right of hot pursuit provided for in this Article shall be exercised by ships or aircraft of the People's Republic of China for military purposes, or by ships or aircraft on government service authorized by the Government of the People's Republic of China.

Article 15 The baselines of the territorial sea of the People's Republic of China shall be promulgated by the Government of the People's Republic of China.

Article 16 The Government of the People's Republic of China formulates the relevant regulations in accordance with this Law.

Article 17 This Law shall come into force on the date for promulgation.

中华人民共和国全国人民代表大会常务委员会关于批准《联合国海洋法公约》的决定

（1996年5月15日）

第八届全国人民代表大会常务委员会第十九次会议决定，批准《联合国海洋法公约》，同时声明如下：

一、按照《联合国海洋法公约》的规定，中华人民共和国享有二百海里专属经济区和大陆架的主权权利和管辖权。

二、中华人民共和国将与海岸相向或相邻的国家，通过协商，在国际法基础上，按照公平原则划定各自海洋管辖权界限。

三、中华人民共和国重申对1992年2月25日颁布的《中华人民共和国领海及毗连区法》第二条所列各群岛及岛屿的主权。

四、中华人民共和国重申：《联合国海洋法公约》有关领海内无害通过的规定，不妨碍沿海国按其法律规章要求外国军舰通过领海必须事先得到该国许可或通知该国的权利。

Decision of the Standing Committee of the National People's Congress of the People's Republic of China on the Ratification of the United Nations Convention on the Law of the Sea

(Adopted on 15 May 1996)

The Standing Committee of the Eighth National People's Congress made the decision at its nineteenth session to ratify the United Nations Convention on the Law of the Sea and at the same time made the following statement:

1. In accordance with the provisions of the United Nations Convention on the Law of the Sea, the People's Republic of China shall enjoy sovereign rights and jurisdiction over an exclusive economic zone of 200 nautical miles and the continental shelf.

2. The People's Republic of China will effect, through consultations, the delimitation of the boundary of the maritime jurisdiction with the States with coasts opposite or adjacent to China respectively on the basis of international law and in accordance with the principle of equitability.

3. The People's Republic of China reaffirms its sovereignty over all its archipelagos and islands as listed in article 2 of the Law of the People's Republic of China on the Territorial Sea and the Contiguous Zone, which was promulgated on 25 February 1992.

4. The People's Republic of China reaffirms that the provisions of the United Nations Convention on the Law of the Sea concerning innocent passage through the territorial sea shall not prejudice the right of a coastal State to request, in accordance with its laws and regulations, a foreign State to obtain advance

approval from or give prior notification to the coastal State for the passage of its warships through the territorial sea of the coastal State.

中华人民共和国专属经济区和大陆架法

（中华人民共和国第九届全国人民代表大会常务委员会第三次会议于1998年6月26日通过　1998年6月26日中华人民共和国主席令第六号公布
自公布之日起施行）

第一条 为保障中华人民共和国对专属经济区和大陆架行使主权权利和管辖权，维护国家海洋权益，制定本法。

第二条 中华人民共和国的专属经济区，为中华人民共和国领海以外并邻接领海的区域，从测算领海宽度的基线量起延至二百海里。

中华人民共和国的大陆架，为中华人民共和国领海以外依本国陆地领土的全部自然延伸，扩展到大陆边外缘的海底区域的海床和底土；如果从测算领海宽度的基线量起至大陆边外缘的距离不足二百海里，则扩展至二百海里。

中华人民共和国与海岸相邻或者相向国家关于专属经济区和大陆架的主张重叠的，在国际法的基础上按照公平原则以协议划定界限。

第三条 中华人民共和国在专属经济区为勘查、开发、养护和管理海床上覆水域、海床及其底土的自然资源，以及进行其他经济性开发和勘查，如利用海水、海流和风力生产能等活动，行使主权权利。

中华人民共和国对专属经济区的人工岛屿、设施和结构的建造、使用和海洋科学研究、海洋环境的保护和保全，行使管辖权。

本法所称专属经济区的自然资源，包括生物资源和非生物资源。

第四条 中华人民共和国为勘查大陆架和开发大陆架的自然资源，对大陆架行使主权权利。

中华人民共和国对大陆架的人工岛屿、设施和结构的建造、使用和海洋科学研究、海洋环境的保护和保全，行使管辖权。

中华人民共和国拥有授权和管理为一切目的在大陆架上进行钻探的专属权利。

本法所称大陆架的自然资源，包括海床和底土的矿物和其他非生物资源，以及属于定居种的生物，即在可捕捞阶段在海床上或者海床下不能移动或者其躯体须与海床或者底土保持接触才能移动的生物。

第五条 任何国际组织、外国的组织或者个人进入中华人民共和国的专属经济区从事渔业活动，必须经中华人民共和国主管机关批准，并遵守中华人民共和国的法律、法规及中华人民共和国与有关国家签订的条约、协定。

中华人民共和国主管机关有权采取各种必要的养护和管理措施，确保专属经济区的生物资源不受过度开发的危害。

第六条 中华人民共和国主管机关有权对专属经济区的跨界种群、高度洄游鱼种、海洋哺乳动物、源自中华人民共和国河流的溯河产卵种群、在中华人民共和国水域内度过大部分生命周期的降河产卵鱼种，进行养护和管理。

中华人民共和国对源自本国河流的溯河产卵种群，享有主要利益。

第七条 任何国际组织、外国的组织或者个人对中华人民共和国的专属经济区和大陆架的自然资源进行勘查、开发活动或者在中华人民共和国的大陆架上为任何目的进行钻探，必须经中华人民共和国主管机关批准，并遵守中华人民共和国的法律、法规。

第八条 中华人民共和国在专属经济区和大陆架有专属权利建造并授权和管理建造、操作和使用人工岛屿、设施和结构。

中华人民共和国对专属经济区和大陆架的人工岛屿、设施和结构行使专属管辖权，包括有关海关、财政、卫生、安全和出境入境的法律和法规方面的管辖权。

中华人民共和国主管机关有权在专属经济区和大陆架的人工岛屿、设施和结构周围设置安全地带，并可以在该地带采取适当措施，确保航行安全以及人工岛屿、设施和结构的安全。

第九条 任何国际组织、外国的组织或者个人在中华人民共和国的专属经济区和大陆架进行海洋科学研究，必须经中华人民共和国主管机关批准，并遵守中华人民共和国的法律、法规。

第十条 中华人民共和国主管机关有权采取必要的措施，防止、减少和控制海洋环境的污染，保护和保全专属经济区和大陆架的海洋环境。

第十一条 任何国家在遵守国际法和中华人民共和国的法律、法规的前提下，在中华人民共和国的专属经济区享有航行、飞越的自由，在中华人民共和国的专属经济区和大陆架享有铺设海底电缆和管道的自由，以及与上述自由有关的其他合法使用海洋的便利。铺设海底电缆和管道的路线，必须经中华人民共和国主管机关同意。

第十二条 中华人民共和国在行使勘查、开发、养护和管理专属经济区的生物资源的主权权利时，为确保中华人民共和国的法律、法规得到遵守，可以采取登临、检查、逮捕、扣留和进行司法程序等必要的措施。

中华人民共和国对在专属经济区和大陆架违反中华人民共和国法律、法规的行为，有权采取必要措施，依法追究法律责任，并可以行使紧追权。

第十三条 中华人民共和国在专属经济区和大陆架享有的权利，本法未作规定的，根据国际法和中华人民共和国其他有关法律、法规行使。

第十四条 本法的规定不影响中华人民共和国享有的历史性权利。

第十五条 中华人民共和国政府可以根据本法制定有关规定。

第十六条 本法自公布之日起施行。

Law of the People's Republic of China on the Exclusive Economic Zone and the Continental Shelf

(Adopted at the 3rd Meeting of the Standing Committee of the Ninth National People's Congress on June 26, 1998 and promulgated by Order No.6 of the President of the People's Republic of China on June 26, 1998)

Article 1 This Law is enacted to ensure that the People's Republic of China exercises its sovereign rights and jurisdiction over its exclusive economic zone and its continental shelf and to safeguard its national maritime rights and interests.

Article 2 The exclusive economic zone of the People's Republic of China covers the area beyond and adjacent to the territorial sea of the People's Republic of China, extending to 200 nautical miles from the baselines from which the breadth of the territorial sea is measured.

The continental shelf of the People's Republic of China comprises the sea-bed and subsoil of the submarine areas that extend beyond its territorial sea throughout the natural prolongation of its land territory to the outer edge of the continental margin, or to a distance of 200 nautical miles from the baselines from which the breadth of the territorial sea is measured where the outer edge of the continental margin does not extend up to that distance.

The People's Republic of China shall determine the delimitation of its exclusive economic zone and continental shelf in respect of the overlapping claims by agreement with the states with opposite or adjacent coasts, in accordance with the equitable principle and on the basis of international law.

Article 3 The People's Republic of China exercises its sovereign rights over the exclusive economic zone for the purpose of exploring, exploiting, conserving and managing the natural resources of the waters superjacent to the sea-bed and of the sea-bed and its subsoil, and in its other activities for economic exploitation and exploration of the zone, such as production of energy from water, currents and winds.

The People's Republic of China exercises jurisdiction over the establishment and use of artificial islands, installations and structures, marine scientific research, and the protection and preservation of the marine environment in the exclusive economic zone.

The natural resources in the exclusive economic zone referred to in this Law consist of living and non-living resources.

Article 4 The People's Republic of China exercises its sovereign rights over the continental shelf for the purpose of exploring it and exploiting its natural resources.

The People's Republic of China exercises jurisdiction over the establishment and use of artificial islands, installations and structures, marine scientific research, and the protection and preservation of the marine environment on the continental shelf.

The People's Republic of China has the exclusive right to authorize and regulate drilling on the continental shelf for all purposes.

The natural resources of the continental shelf referred to in this Law consist of the mineral and other non-living resources of the sea-bed and subsoil, and the living organisms that belong to sedentary species--organisms which, at the harvestable stage, either are immobile on or under the sea-bed or are unable to move except in constant physical contact with the sea-bed or the subsoil.

Article 5 All international organizations, foreign organizations or individuals that wish to enter the exclusive economic zone of the People's Republic of China for fishing shall be subject to approval of the competent authorities of the People's Republic of China and shall comply with its laws and regulations as well as the accords and agreements it has signed with the states concerned.

The competent authorities of the People's Republic of China shall have the right to take all necessary conservation and management measures to ensure that the living resources in the exclusive economic zone are protected from the danger of over-exploitation.

Article 6 The competent authorities of the People's Republic of China shall have the right to conserve and manage straddling species, highly migratory species, marine mammals, anadromous stocks that originate in the rivers of the People's Republic of China, and catadromous species that spend the greater part of their life cycle in the waters of the People's Republic of China.

The People's Republic of China enjoys the primary interests in the anadromous stocks that originate in its rivers.

Article 7 All international organizations, foreign organizations or individuals that wish to explore the exclusive economic zone of the People's Republic of China or exploit the natural resources on its continental shelf or for any purpose to drill on the continental shelf shall be subject to approval of the competent authorities of the People's Republic of China and shall comply with the laws and regulations of the People's Republic of China.

Article 8 The People's Republic of China has the exclusive right to construct and to authorize and regulate the construction, operation and use of the artificial islands, installations and structures in its exclusive economic zone and on its continental shelf.

The People's Republic of China exercises exclusive jurisdiction over the artificial islands, installations and structures in its exclusive economic zone and on its continental shelf, including jurisdiction with regard to customs, fiscal, health and safety laws and regulations, and laws and regulations governing entry into and exit from the territory of the People's Republic of China.

The competent authorities of the People's Republic of China shall have the right to establish safety belts around the artificial islands, installations and structures in the exclusive economic zone and on the continental shelf and may take appropriate measures in these belts to ensure safety both of navigation and of the artificial islands, installations and structures.

Article 9 All international organizations, foreign organizations or individuals that wish to conduct marine scientific research in the exclusive economic zone or on the continental shelf of the People's Republic of China shall be subject to approval of the competent authorities of the People's Republic of China and shall comply with the laws and regulations of the People's Republic of China.

Article 10 The competent authorities of the People's Republic of China shall have the right to take all necessary measures to prevent, reduce and control pollution of the marine environment for the protection and preservation of the marine environment in the exclusive economic zone and on the continental shelf.

Article 11 All states shall, on the premise that they comply with international law and the laws and regulations of the People's Republic of China, enjoy the freedom of navigation in and flight over its exclusive economic zone, the freedom to lay submarine cables and pipelines and the convenience of other lawful uses of the sea related to the freedoms mentioned above in the exclusive economic zone and on the continental shelf of the People's Republic of China. The routes for the submarine cables and pipelines shall be subject to consent of the competent authorities of the People's Republic of China.

Article 12 The People's Republic of China may, in the exercise of its sovereign rights to explore its exclusive economic zone and to exploit, conserve and manage the living resources there, take such necessary measures as visit, inspection, arrest, detention and judicial proceedings in order to ensure that the laws and regulations of the People's Republic of China are complied with.

The People's Republic of China has the right to take necessary measures against violations of its laws and regulations in its exclusive economic zone and on its continental shelf and to investigate for legal responsibility according to law, and may exercise the right of hot pursuit.

Article 13 The People's Republic of China exercises, in accordance with international law and other relevant laws and regulations of the People's Republic of China, the rights in its exclusive economic zone and on its continental shelf that are not provided for in this Law.

Article 14 The provisions in this Law shall not affect the historical rights that the People's Republic of China has been enjoying ever since the days of the past.

Article 15 The Government of the People's Republic of China may formulate relevant regulations on the basis of this Law.

Article 16 This Law shall go into effect as of the date of promulgation.

中国根据《联合国海洋法公约》第298条提交排除性声明

（2006年8月25日）

2006年8月25日，中国根据《联合国海洋法公约》第298条的规定向联合国秘书长提交声明。声明如下：

关于《联合国海洋法公约》第298条第1款（a）、（b）和（c）项所述的任何争端（即涉及海域划界、历史性海湾或所有权、军事和执法活动以及安理会执行《联合国宪章》所赋予的职务等争端），中华人民共和国政府不接受《联合国海洋法公约》第十五部分第二节规定的任何程序。

Declaration by the People's Republic of China under Article 298 of the United Nations Convention on the Law of the Sea

(25 August 2006)

The Government of the People's Republic of China does not accept any of the procedures provided for in Section 2 of Part XV of the Convention with respect to all the categories of disputes referred to in paragraph 1 (a) (b) and (c) of Article 298 of the Convention.

中华人民共和国政府关于在南海的领土主权和海洋权益的声明

（2016年7月12日）

为重申中国在南海的领土主权和海洋权益，加强与各国在南海的合作，维护南海和平稳定，中华人民共和国政府声明：

一、中国南海诸岛包括东沙群岛、西沙群岛、中沙群岛和南沙群岛。中国人民在南海的活动已有2000多年历史。中国最早发现、命名和开发利用南海诸岛及相关海域，最早并持续、和平、有效地对南海诸岛及相关海域行使主权和管辖，确立了在南海的领土主权和相关权益。

第二次世界大战结束后，中国收复日本在侵华战争期间曾非法侵占的中国南海诸岛，并恢复行使主权。中国政府为加强对南海诸岛的管理，于1947年审核修订了南海诸岛地理名称，编写了《南海诸岛地理志略》和绘制了标绘有南海断续线的《南海诸岛位置图》，并于1948年2月正式公布，昭告世界。

二、中华人民共和国1949年10月1日成立以来，坚定维护中国在南海的领土主权和海洋权益。1958年《中华人民共和国政府关于领海的声明》、1992年《中华人民共和国领海及毗连区法》、1998年《中华人民共和国专属经济区和大陆架法》以及1996年《中华人民共和国全国人民代表大会常务委员会关于批准〈联合国海洋法公约〉的决定》等系列法律文件，进一步确认了中国在南海的领土主权和海洋权益。

三、基于中国人民和中国政府的长期历史实践及历届中国政府的一贯立场，根据中国国内法以及包括《联合国海洋法公约》在内的国际法，中国在南海的领土主权和海洋权益包括：

（一）中国对南海诸岛，包括东沙群岛、西沙群岛、中沙群岛和南沙群岛拥有主权；

（二）中国南海诸岛拥有内水、领海和毗连区；

（三）中国南海诸岛拥有专属经济区和大陆架；

（四）中国在南海拥有历史性权利。

中国上述立场符合有关国际法和国际实践。

四、中国一向坚决反对一些国家对中国南沙群岛部分岛礁的非法侵占及在中国相关管辖海域的侵权行为。中国愿继续与直接有关当事国在尊重历史事实的基础上，根据国际法，通过谈判协商和平解决南海有关争议。中国愿同有关直接当事国尽一切努力作出实际性的临时安排，包括在相关海域进行共同开发，实现互利共赢，共同维护南海和平稳定。

五、中国尊重和支持各国依据国际法在南海享有的航行和飞越自由，愿与其他沿岸国和国际社会合作，维护南海国际航运通道的安全和畅通。

Statement of the Government of the People's Republic of China on China's Territorial Sovereignty and Maritime Rights and Interests in the South China Sea

(7 July 2016)

To reaffirm China's territorial sovereignty and maritime rights and interests in the South China Sea, enhance cooperation in the South China Sea with other countries, and uphold peace and stability in the South China Sea, the Government of the People's Republic of China hereby states as follows:

I. China's Nanhai Zhudao (the South China Sea Islands) consist of Dongsha Qundao (the Dongsha Islands), Xisha Qundao (the Xisha Islands), Zhongsha Qundao (the Zhongsha Islands) and Nansha Qundao (the Nansha Islands). The activities of the Chinese people in the South China Sea date back to over 2,000 years ago. China is the first to have discovered, named, and explored and exploited Nanhai Zhudao and relevant waters, and the first to have exercised sovereignty and jurisdiction over them continuously, peacefully and effectively, thus establishing territorial sovereignty and relevant rights and interests in the South China Sea.

Following the end of the Second World War, China recovered and resumed the exercise of sovereignty over Nanhai Zhudao which had been illegally occupied by Japan during its war of aggression against China. To strengthen the administration over Nanhai Zhudao, the Chinese government in 1947 reviewed and updated the geographical names of Nanhai Zhudao, compiled *Nan Hai Zhu Dao Di Li Zhi Lüe* (A Brief Account of the Geography of the South China Sea

Islands), and drew *Nan Hai Zhu Dao Wei Zhi Tu* (Location Map of the South China Sea Islands) on which the dotted line is marked. This map was officially published and made known to the world by the Chinese government in February 1948.

II. Since its founding on 1 October 1949, the People's Republic of China has been firm in upholding China's territorial sovereignty and maritime rights and interests in the South China Sea. A series of legal instruments, such as the 1958 *Declaration of the Government of the People's Republic of China on China's Territorial Sea*, the 1992 *Law of the People's Republic of China on the Territorial Sea and the Contiguous Zone*, the 1998 *Law of the People's Republic of China on the Exclusive Economic Zone and the Continental Shelf* and the 1996 *Decision of the Standing Committee of the National People's Congress of the People's Republic of China on the Ratification of the United Nations Convention on the Law of the Sea*, have further reaffirmed China's territorial sovereignty and maritime rights and interests in the South China Sea.

III. Based on the practice of the Chinese people and the Chinese government in the long course of history and the position consistently upheld by successive Chinese governments, and in accordance with national law and international law, including the *United Nations Convention on the Law of the Sea*, China has territorial sovereignty and maritime rights and interests in the South China Sea, including, inter alia:

i. China has sovereignty over Nanhai Zhudao, consisting of Dongsha Qundao, Xisha Qundao, Zhongsha Qundao and Nansha Qundao;

ii. China has internal waters, territorial sea and contiguous zone, based on Nanhai Zhudao;

iii. China has exclusive economic zone and continental shelf, based on Nanhai Zhudao;

iv. China has historic rights in the South China Sea.

The above positions are consistent with relevant international law and practice.

IV. China is always firmly opposed to the invasion and illegal occupation by certain states of some islands and reefs of China's Nansha Qundao, and activities infringing upon China's rights and interests in relevant maritime areas under China's jurisdiction. China stands ready to continue to resolve the relevant disputes peacefully through negotiation and consultation with the states directly concerned on the basis of respecting historical facts and in accordance with international law. Pending final settlement, China is also ready to make every effort with the states directly concerned to enter into provisional arrangements of a practical nature, including joint development in relevant maritime areas, in order to achieve win-win results and jointly maintain peace and stability in the South China Sea.

V. China respects and upholds the freedom of navigation and overflight enjoyed by all states under international law in the South China Sea, and stays ready to work with other coastal states and the international community to ensure the safety of and the unimpeded access to the international shipping lanes in the South China Sea.

第二部分
地区和双边文件

Regional and Bilateral Documents

南海各方行为宣言

（2002年11月4日）

中华人民共和国和东盟各成员国政府，重申各方决心巩固和发展各国人民和政府之间业已存在的友谊与合作，以促进面向21世纪睦邻互信伙伴关系；

认识到为增进本地区的和平、稳定、经济发展与繁荣，中国和东盟有必要促进南海地区和平、友好与和谐的环境；

承诺促进1997年中华人民共和国与东盟成员国国家元首或政府首脑会晤《联合声明》所确立的原则和目标；

希望为和平与永久解决有关国家间的分歧和争议创造有利条件；

谨发表如下宣言：

一、各方重申以《联合国宪章》宗旨和原则、1982年《联合国海洋法公约》、《东南亚友好合作条约》、和平共处五项原则以及其它公认的国际法原则作为处理国家间关系的基本准则。

二、各方承诺根据上述原则，在平等和相互尊重的基础上，探讨建立信任的途径。

三、各方重申尊重并承诺，包括1982年《联合国海洋法公约》在内的公认的国际法原则所规定的在南海的航行及飞越自由。

四、有关各方承诺根据公认的国际法原则，包括1982年《联合国海洋法公约》，由直接有关的主权国家通过友好磋商和谈判，以和平方式解决它们的领土和管辖权争议，而不诉诸武力或以武力相威胁。

五、各方承诺保持自我克制，不采取使争议复杂化、扩大化和影响和平与稳定的行动，包括不在现无人居住的岛、礁、滩、沙或其它自然构造上采取居住的行动，并以建设性的方式处理它们的分歧。

在和平解决它们的领土和管辖权争议之前，有关各方承诺本着合作与谅解的精神，努力寻求各种途径建立相互信任，包括：

（一）在各方国防及军队官员之间开展适当的对话和交换意见；

（二）保证对处于危险境地的所有公民予以公正和人道的待遇；

（三）在自愿基础上向其它有关各方通报即将举行的联合军事演习；

（四）在自愿基础上相互通报有关情况。

六、在全面和永久解决争议之前，有关各方可探讨或开展合作，可包括以下领域：

（一）海洋环保；

（二）海洋科学研究；

（三）海上航行和交通安全；

（四）搜寻与救助；

（五）打击跨国犯罪，包括但不限于打击毒品走私、海盗和海上武装抢劫以及军火走私。

在具体实施之前，有关各方应就双边及多边合作的模式、范围和地点取得一致意见。

七、有关各方愿通过各方同意的模式，就有关问题继续进行磋商和对话，包括对遵守本宣言问题举行定期磋商，以增进睦邻友好关系和提高透明度，创造和谐、相互理解与合作，推动以和平方式解决彼此间争议。

八、各方承诺尊重本宣言的条款并采取与宣言相一致的行动。

九、各方鼓励其他国家尊重本宣言所包含的原则。

十、有关各方重申制定南海行为准则将进一步促进本地区和平与稳定，并同意在各方协商一致的基础上，朝最终达成该目标而努力。

本宣言于2002年11月4日在柬埔寨王国金边签署。

Declaration on the Conduct of Parties in the South China Sea

(Adopted by the Foreign Ministers of ASEAN and the People's Republic of China at the 8th ASEAN Summit in Phnom Penh, Cambodia on 4 November 2002)

The Governments of the Member States of ASEAN and the Government of the People's Republic of China,

REAFFIRMING their determination to consolidate and develop the friendship and cooperation existing between their people and governments with the view to promoting a 21st century-oriented partnership of good neighborliness and mutual trust;

COGNIZANT of the need to promote a peaceful, friendly and harmonious environment in the South China Sea between ASEAN and China for the enhancement of peace, stability, economic growth and prosperity in the region;

COMMITTED to enhancing the principles and objectives of the 1997 Joint Statement of the Meeting of the Heads of State/Government of the Member States of ASEAN and President of the People's Republic of China;

DESIRING to enhance favourable conditions for a peaceful and durable solution of differences and disputes among countries concerned;

HEREBY DECLARE the following:

1. The Parties reaffirm their commitment to the purposes and principles of the Charter of the United Nations, the 1982 UN Convention on the Law of the Sea, the Treaty of Amity and Cooperation in Southeast Asia, the Five Principles of Peaceful Coexistence, and other universally recognized principles of international law which shall serve as the basic norms governing state-to-state relations;

2. The Parties are committed to exploring ways for building trust and confidence in accordance with the above-mentioned principles and on the basis of equality and mutual respect;

3. The Parties reaffirm their respect for and commitment to the freedom of navigation in and overflight above the South China Sea as provided for by the universally recognized principles of international law, including the 1982 UN Convention on the Law of the Sea;

4. The Parties concerned undertake to resolve their territorial and jurisdictional disputes by peaceful means, without resorting to the threat or use of force, through friendly consultations and negotiations by sovereign states directly concerned, in accordance with universally recognized principles of international law, including the 1982 UN Convention on the Law of the Sea;

5. The Parties undertake to exercise self-restraint in the conduct of activities that would complicate or escalate disputes and affect peace and stability including, among others, refraining from action of inhabiting on the presently uninhabited islands, reefs, shoals, cays, and other features and to handle their differences in a constructive manner.

Pending the peaceful settlement of territorial and jurisdictional disputes, the Parties concerned undertake to intensify efforts to seek ways, in the spirit of cooperation and understanding, to build trust and confidence between and among them, including:

a. holding dialogues and exchange of views as appropriate between their defense and military officials;

b. ensuring just and humane treatment of all persons who are either in danger or in distress;

c. notifying, on a voluntary basis, other Parties concerned of any impending joint/combined military exercise; and

d. exchanging, on a voluntary basis, relevant information.

6. Pending a comprehensive and durable settlement of the disputes, the Parties concerned may explore or undertake cooperative activities. These may include the following:

a. marine environmental protection;

b. marine scientific research;

c. safety of navigation and communication at sea;

d. search and rescue operation; and

e. combating transnational crime, including but not limited to trafficking in illicit drugs, piracy and armed robbery at sea, and illegal traffic in arms.

The modalities, scope and locations, in respect of bilateral and multilateral cooperation should be agreed upon by the Parties concerned prior to their actual implementation.

7. The Parties concerned stand ready to continue their consultations and dialogues concerning relevant issues, through modalities to be agreed by them, including regular consultations on the observance of this Declaration, for the purpose of promoting good neighborliness and transparency, establishing harmony, mutual understanding and cooperation, and facilitating peaceful resolution of disputes among them;

8. The Parties undertake to respect the provisions of this Declaration and take actions consistent therewith;

9. The Parties encourage other countries to respect the principles contained in this Declaration;

10. The Parties concerned reaffirm that the adoption of a code of conduct in the South China Sea would further promote peace and stability in the region and agree to work, on the basis of consensus, towards the eventual attainment of this objective.

Done on the Fourth Day of November in the Year Two Thousand and Two in Phnom Penh, the Kingdom of Cambodia.

A Tripartite Agreement for Joint Marine Seismic Undertaking in the Agreement Area in the South China Sea

By and Among
China National Offshore Oil Corporation
And
Vietnam Oil and Gas Corporation
And
Philippine National Oil Company

(March 14, 2005 Manila, Philippines)

This Tripartite Agreement for Joint Marine Seismic Undertaking in the Agreement Area in the South China Sea (hereinafter referred to as the "Agreement") is entered into on this 14th day of March 2005 by and among China National Offshore Oil Corporation (hereinafter referred to as "CNOOC"), a company organized and existing under the laws of the People's Republic of China, having its headquarters domiciled in Beijing and Vietnam Oil and Gas Corporation (hereinafter referred to as "PETROVIETNAM"), a company organized and existing under the laws of the Socialist Republic of Vietnam, having its headquarters domiciled in Hanoi and Philippine National Oil Company (hereinafter referred to as "PNOC"), a company organized and existing under the laws of the Republic of the Philippines, having its headquarters domiciled at Fort Bonifacio, Taguig, Metro Manila.

CNOOC, PETROVIETNAM and **PNOC** are collectively referred to as "Parties" and individually as "Party".

WITNESSETH: That

WHEREAS, CNOOC is a state-owned oil company of the People's Republic of China;

WHEREAS, PETROVIETNAM is the state-owned oil company of the Socialist Republic of Vietnam;

WHEREAS, PNOC is the national oil company of the Republic of the Philippines;

WHEREAS, the Parties' respective governments have expressed the commitment to pursue efforts to transform the South China Sea into an area of peace, stability, cooperation and development;

WHEREAS, the Parties expressed desire to engage in a joint research of petroleum resource potential of a certain area of the South China Sea as a pre-exploration activity;

WHEREAS under the authorization of the Chinese Government, CNOOC has the exclusive right to sign this Agreement with PETROVIETNAM and PNOC for a joint marine seismic undertaking within the Agreement Area;

WHEREAS, under the authorization of the Government of the Socialist Republic of Vietnam, PETROVIETNAM has the exclusive right to sign this Agreement with CNOOC and PNOC for a joint marine seismic undertaking within the Agreement Area;

WHEREAS, under the authorization of the Philippine Government, PNOC has the exclusive right to sign this Agreement with CNOOC and PETROVIETNAM for a joint marine seismic undertaking within the Agreement Area;

WHEREAS, the Parties recognize that the signing of this Agreement shall not undermine the basic position held by the Government of each Party on the South China Sea issue;

NOW, THEREFORE, the Parties hereby agree, as follows:

Article 1 The Agreement Term

Unless otherwise agreed upon by the Parties, the term of this Agreement shall be three (3) years starting from the date of commencement of implementation of the Agreement. The said three-year period is hereinafter referred to as the "Agreement Term".

Article 2 The Agreement Area

The Agreement Area as of the date of signing of this Agreement covers a total area of one hundred forty-two thousand eight hundred eighty-six (1420,886) square kilometers, as defined and marked out by the geographic location and the coordinates of the connecting points of the boundary lines in the Annex "A" attached hereto.

Article 3 Financing

Each Party shall be responsible for the costs of its own personnel designated for the implementation of this Agreement. Such costs shall include but not be limited to salaries or wages, allowance, expenses for travel and accommodation. However, the expenses incurred for carrying out the activities referred to in Article 4.1 hereof and any other necessary activities determined by the Joint Operating Committee referred to in Article 5 hereof to be necessary for the implementation of this Agreement shall be shared by the Parties in equal shares.

Article 4 Seismic Work

4.1 It is agreed that certain amount of 2D and/or 3D seismic lines shall be collected and processed and certain amount of existing 2D seismic lines shall be reprocessed within the Agreement Term. The seismic work shall be conducted in accordance with the seismic program unanimously approved by the Parties taking into account the safety and protection of the environment in the Agreement Area.

4.2 The actual annual work program and budget within the Agreement Term shall be formulated by the Joint Operating Committee referred to in Article 5 hereof pursuant to the Parties' authorization. The interpretation of and evaluation on data should be done by a joint team created by the Parties either in Beijing or Hanoi or Manila.

Article 5 The Joint Operating Committee

5.1 For the proper performance of the joint activity, the Parties shall establish a Joint Operating Committee ("JOC") as soon as possible after the Agreement is signed by the Parties.

5.2 CNOOC, PETROVIETNAM and PNOC shall each appoint three (3) representatives to form the JOC, and each Party shall designate one of its representatives as its chief representative. When a decision is to be made on any proposal, the chief representative from each Party shall be the spokesman on behalf of the Party.

5.3 Decisions of the JOC shall be made unanimously through consultation.

5.4 The Parties shall empower the JOC to:

5.4.1 Formulate the annual work program and budget;

5.4.2 Discuss and determine the manner of data exchange;

5.4.3 Arrange further joint studies;

5.4.4 Formulate the actual plan for seismic line acquisition;

5.4.5 Sign service contracts for seismic acquisition and processing; and

5.4.6 Ensure interpretation of and evaluation on the relevant data and submit final evaluation report to the Parties.

5.5 The JOC will formulate a Joint Operating Procedure ("JOP") covering but not limited to relevant job descriptions, work procedures, the establishment of subordinate bodies, methods of cash calls, accounting methods and other necessary rules and regulations within the JOC as the joint activity may require.

5.6 The JOC shall report to the Parties on a timely basis the progress of the joint activity and be subject to the directions given by the Parties.

Article 6 Service Contracts

6.1 As a general rule, the Parties agree to have effective and equal participation in all activities relevant to the implementation of this Agreement.

6.2 The Parties agree to use vessels of CNOOC's or PETROVIETNAM's or

PNOC's affiliates or other party's vessels to conduct the seismic acquisition in accordance with international bidding procedures. However, preference shall be given to one of the Parties or one of their affiliates whose bid the Parties deem as competitive and reasonable compared with other bids in terms of quality and price for the service required. The Parties shall exert best efforts to allow such vessels of CNOOC's , PETROVIETNAM 's or PNOC's affiliates or those of such other parties to use the ports of the Philippines, Vietnam or China, as the case may be, to get necessary supplies.

6.3 The Parties agree to use CNOOC's or PETROVIETNAM 's or PNOC's affiliates or other parties to process the relevant seismic data in accordance with international bidding procedures. However, preference shall be given to one of the Parties or one of their affiliates whose bid the Parties deem as competitive and reasonable compared with other bids in terms of quality and price for the service required.

Article 7 Mutual Assistance

7.1 The Parties shall use reasonable efforts to obtain all the necessary approvals from their respective governments for the implementation of this Agreement.

7.2 A Party shall facilitate the entrance of the relevant personnel and vessels from the rest of the Parties to enter into relevant areas to conduct joint marine seismic undertaking, to get necessary supply and to obtain all the necessary permits on a timely basis.

7.3 With regard to the joint activity, a Party shall, upon the request of the rest of the Parties, use reasonable efforts to contact and coordinate with its relevant governmental departments.

Article 8 Negotiation Term

In the event the Parties elect to enter into negotiations for signing a more definitive agreement for further cooperation covering all or part of the Agreement Area prior to or at the expiration of the Agreement Term, then such negotiations shall take place during the Agreement Term or during the period of ninety (90) days following the date of expiration of the Agreement Term (all of which periods are hereinafter referred to as the "Negotiation Term"). The Negotiation Term shall be reserved for the sole purpose of negotiations among CNOOC, PETROVIETNAM and PNOC. During such Negotiation Term, unless otherwise agreed by the Parties, no Party shall have the right to negotiate an agreement for a marine seismic undertaking or any other agreement(s) with any other party with respect to all or part of the Agreement Area.

After the Parties have decided to pursue a definitive agreement, the Parties will consult with their appropriate authorities with regard to further cooperative activities.

Article 9 Assignment

9.1 Except for the retention of CNOOC's management functions, CNOOC shall assign all its rights and obligations under the Agreement to one of its affiliates (it is understood by the Parties that such affiliate shall be CNOOC China Limited). Except for the retention of PETROVIETNAM's management functions, PETROVIETNAM shall assign all its rights and obligations under the Agreement to one of its affiliates (it is understood by the Parties that such affiliate shall be PetroVietnam Investment and Development Company-PIDC). PNOC shall assign all its rights and obligations under the Agreement to one of its affiliates (it is understood by the Parties that such affiliate shall be PNOC Exploration Corporation). Each of CNOOC, PETROVIETNAM and PNOC shall provide one another with copies of the written agreement for such assignment of all of its rights and obligations.

9.2 Except for the assignments described in Article 9.1, no Party shall assign all or part of its rights and obligations under the Agreement to any other parties without the prior written consent of the rest of the Parties.

Article 10 Confidentiality of Information

This Agreement and all relevant documents, information, data and reports with respect to the joint marine seismic undertaking shall be kept confidential during the Agreement Term and within five (5) years after its expiration and shall not be disclosed by a Party to any other party without the written consent of the rest of the Parties. However, no consent shall be required when said documents, information, data and reports are disclosed, for the purpose of implementation of this Agreement, to the Parties' respective governments, affiliates or stock exchanges on which a Party's shares are registered. Provided, however, that after the signing of the Agreement, the Parties agree to issue a joint statement on the purpose, scope and area of the Agreement.

Article 11 Miscellaneous Provisions

11.1 The Parties shall exert their best efforts to settle amicably through consultation any dispute arising in connection with the performance or interpretation of any provision hereof.

11.2 All the data and information acquired for the fulfillment of the Seismic Work referred to in Article 4 hereof and their interpretation shall be jointly owned by the Parties. In the event any Party wishes to sell or disclose the above-mentioned data and information after the expiration of the confidentiality term, prior written consent therefor shall be obtained from the rest of the Parties.

11.3 All notices and documents by one Party to the rest of the Parties shall be delivered by hand or sent by mail, registered airmail or facsimile transmission to the addresses hereunder specified:

For CNOOC:
Cao Yunshi
General Counsel
CNOOC
PO Box 4705, No. 6 Dongzhimenwai Xiaojie
Dongcheng District, Beijing
People's Republic of China
Postcode: 100027

For PETROVIETNAM:
Dr. Tran Ngoc Canh

President and CEO
Vietnam Oil and Gas Corporation
22 Ngo Quyen Street,
Hoan Kiem Dist., Hanoi
Socialist Republic of Vietnam
Postcode: 10000

For PNOC:
Eduardo V. Mañalac
President and CEO
PNOC Building 6, Energy Center,
Merritt Road, Fort Bonifacio, Taguig,
1634, Metro Manila, Philippines

Each Party may change its address or representative by a written notice to the rest of the Parties.

11.4 The Parties' rights, interest and obligations under the Agreement shall be on equal basis.

11.5 The Parties commit to observe and follow all laws and regulations, as well as any international obligation, of their respective countries that may have a bearing on this Agreement, such as the 1982 United Nations Convention on the Law of the Sea (UNCLOS) and the ASEAN-China Declaration on the Conduct of Parties in the South China Sea (DOC), or any further or subsequent agreements that may be signed by the Parties.

11.6 After the Agreement is signed, it shall be approved by the Parties' respective governments. The latest date of such approvals shall be the effective date of the Agreement. The Parties agree that the first day of the month following the effective date of the Agreement shall be the date of commencement of the implementation of the Agreement. The Agreement shall not be binding on the Parties should any Party fail to obtain its government's approval within three (3) months after the date on which the Agreement is signed.

11.7 Within the same period of three (3) months after the Agreement is signed, the Parties shall be obliged to:

— immediately convene the JOC, which shall formulate the Joint Operating Procedure;

— discuss and approve a Work Program and Budget for 2005 prepared by JOC.

11.8 Upon the effectiveness of the Tripartite Agreement and with the implementation thereof, the "Agreement for Joint Marine Seismic Undertaking in Certain Areas in the South China Sea" signed by and between CNOOC and PNOC on the 1st September 2004 in Beijing, China, is not implemented.

11.9 The Agreement shall be signed in six (6) original copies written in the English language, each of which shall have equal force and effect. Each Party shall be entitled to keep two (2) original copies of the Agreement.

The Agreement is signed on this 14th day of March 2005 in Manila, Philippines by the authorized representatives of the Parties hereunder.

China National Offshore Oil Corporation

Signature:________________________

Name: Zhou Shouwei

Title: Vice President

Vietnam Oil and Gas Corporation

Signature:________________________

Name: Tran Ngoc Canh

Title: President and CEO

Philippine National Oil Company

Signature:________________________

Name: Eduardo V. Mañalac

Title: President and CEO

落实《南海各方行为宣言》指导方针

（2011年7月）

重申《南海各方行为宣言》是中国同东盟成员国签署的具有里程碑意义的文件，显示了他们共同促进和平稳定和互信以及确保和平解决南海争议的承诺；

认识到全面、有效落实《宣言》将有助于深化中国—东盟面向和平与繁荣的战略伙伴关系；

本指针旨在指导落实《宣言》框架下可能开展的共同合作活动、措施和项目。

一、落实《宣言》应根据《宣言》条款，以循序渐进的方式进行。

二、《宣言》各方将根据《宣言》的精神，继续推动对话和磋商。

三、落实《宣言》框架下的活动或项目应明确确定。

四、参与活动或项目应建立在自愿的基础上。

五、《宣言》范围内最初开展的活动应是建立信任措施。

六、应在有关各方共识的基础上决定实施《宣言》的具体措施或活动，并迈向最终制订“南海行为准则”。

七、在落实《宣言》框架下达成共识的合作项目时，如有需要，将请专家和名人为有关项目提供协助。

八、每年向中国—东盟外长会报告《宣言》范围内达成共识的合作活动或项目的实施进展情况。

Guidelines for the Implementation of the Declaration on the Conduct of Parties in the South China Sea

(July 2011)

Reaffirming that the DOC is a milestone document signed between the ASEAN Member States and China, embodying their collective commitment to promoting peace, stability and mutual trust and to ensuring the peaceful resolution of disputes in the South China Sea;

Recognizing also that the full and effective implementation of the DOC will contribute to the deepening of the ASEAN-China Strategic Partnership for Peace and Prosperity;

These Guidelines are to guide the implementation of possible joint cooperative activities, measures and projects as provided for in the DOC.

1. The implementation of the DOC should be carried out in a step-by-step approach in line with the provisions of the DOC.

2. The Parties to the DOC will continue to promote dialogue and consultations in accordance with the spirit of the DOC.

3. The implementation of activities or projects as provided for in the DOC should be clearly identified.

4. The participation in the activities or projects should be carried out on a voluntary basis.

5. Initial activities to be undertaken under the ambit of the DOC should be confidence-building measures.

6. The decision to implement concrete measures or activities of the DOC should be based on consensus among parties concerned, and lead to the eventual

realization of a Code of Conduct.

7. In the implementation of the agreed projects under the DOC, the services of the Experts and Eminent Persons, if deemed necessary, will be sought to provide specific inputs on the projects concerned.

8. Progress of the implementation of the agreed activities and projects under the DOC shall be reported annually to the ASEAN-China Ministerial Meeting.

纪念《南海各方行为宣言》签署十周年联合声明

（2012年11月19日， 柬埔寨金边）

一、我们，中华人民共和国和东南亚国家联盟成员国的国家元首或政府首脑，于2012年11月19日相聚柬埔寨金边，纪念《南海各方行为宣言》签署十周年。我们重申2003年10月8日中国和东盟成员国国家元首或政府首脑关于面向和平与繁荣的战略伙伴关系的联合宣言。

促进相互信任的十年

二、我们重申，2002年在柬埔寨金边签署的《南海各方行为宣言》是具有里程碑意义的文件，体现了中国和东盟成员国共同促进南海和平稳定和增进互信的承诺。

三、我们注意到2011年7月各方就落实《南海各方行为宣言》指导方针达成一致后，《南海各方行为宣言》框架下商定的合作项目的落实取得进展，促进了各方在南海的互信与合作。

四、我们还认识到，全面有效落实《南海各方行为宣言》将促进中国与东盟的战略伙伴关系以及更广范围的东亚地区的和平、稳定与繁荣。为此，我们重申希望为和平与永久解决有关国家间的分歧和争议创造有利条件。

和平、友谊与合作的未来

五、我们重申以《联合国宪章》宗旨和原则、1982年《联合国海洋法公约》、《东南亚友好合作条约》、和平共处五项原则以及其他公认的国际法原则作为处理国家间关系的基本准则。

六、我们重申根据国际法及不干涉别国内政的原则，相互尊重彼此独立、主权和领土完整。

七、我们同意继续坚持《南海各方行为宣言》的精神和原则，促进中国与东盟国家间的和平、友谊、互信与合作。

八、值此《南海各方行为宣言》签署十周年之际，我们重申遵守《南海各方行为宣言》的原则并承诺：

——继续全面有效落实《南海各方行为宣言》；

——根据落实《南海各方行为宣言》指导方针，实施已经达成一致的合作项目和活动；

——根据国际法，包括1982年《联合国海洋法公约》，继续开展合作，加强海上安全，包括确保商贸自由、航行及海上交通安全；

——继续鼓励有关各方根据公认的国际法原则，包括1982年《联合国海洋法公约》，由直接有关的主权国家通过友好磋商和谈判，以和平方式解决领土和管辖权争议，而不诉诸武力或以武力相威胁；

——继续保持自我克制，不采取使争议复杂化、扩大化和影响和平与稳定的行动，包括不在现无人居住的岛、礁、滩、沙或其他自然构造上采取居住的行动，并以建设性的方式处理他们的分歧；

——保持对话和磋商势头，增进互信，促进合作，在协商一致的基础上朝达成"南海行为准则"而努力。

九、我们交由各国部长和高官落实此声明确定的目标、倡议和活动。

二〇一二年十一月十九日于柬埔寨金边通过。一式两份，均为英文文本。

Joint Statement of the 15th ASEAN-China Summit on the 10th Anniversary of the Declaration on the Conduct of Parties in the South China Sea

(Phnom Penh, Cambodia, 19 November 2012)

1. We, the Heads of State/Government of the Member States of the Association of Southeast Asian Nations (ASEAN) and the People's Republic of China gathered on 19 November 2012 in Phnom Penh, Cambodia, to commemorate the 10th Anniversary of the Declaration on the Conduct of Parties in the South China Sea (DOC). We reaffirm the Joint Declaration of the Heads of State/Government of the Association of the Southeast Asian Nations and the People's Republic of China on Strategic Partnership for Peace and Prosperity of 8 October 2003.

A Decade of Enhancing Mutual Confidence and Trust

2. We reaffirm that the DOC signed in 2002 in Phnom Penh, Cambodia, is a milestone document which embodies the collective commitment of ASEAN Member States and China to promote peace, stability and mutual trust in the South China Sea.

3. Following the successful conclusion of the Guidelines for the Implementation of the DOC in July 2011, we note the progress in the implementation of agreed joint cooperative projects under the DOC, which has contributed to the promotion of mutual confidence, trust and cooperation in the South China Sea.

4. We also recognise that the full and effective implementation of the DOC

would strengthen the strategic relations and partnership between ASEAN and China, and promote peace, stability and prosperity in the wider East Asian region. In this regard, we reiterate our desire to enhance favorable conditions for a peaceful and durable solution of differences and disputes among the countries concerned.

A Future of Peace, Friendship and Cooperation

5. We reaffirm our commitment to the purposes and principles of the Charter of the United Nations (UN), the 1982 UN Convention on the Law of the Sea (UNCLOS), the Treaty of Amity and Cooperation in Southeast Asia (TAC), the Five Principles of Peaceful Coexistence, and other universally recognised principles of international law which shall serve as the basic norms governing state-to-state relations.

6. We reaffirm our mutual respect for each other's independence, sovereignty and territorial integrity in accordance with international law, and the principle of non-interference in the internal affairs of other states.

7. We agree to continue to uphold the spirit and principles of the DOC to contribute to the promotion of peace, friendship, mutual trust, confidence and cooperation between and among ASEAN Member States and China.

8. On the occasion of this 10th Anniversary of the DOC, we reaffirm our commitment to the principles of the DOC by undertaking to:

- Continue to fully and effectively implement the DOC;

- Carry out agreed joint cooperative projects and activities in accordance with the Guidelines for the Implementation of the DOC;

- Continue to cooperate to enhance maritime security, including to ensure freedom of commerce, safety of navigation and maritime traffic, in accordance with international law, including the 1982 UNCLOS;

- Continue to encourage the parties concerned to resolve territorial and jurisdictional disputes by peaceful means, without resorting to the threat or use of force, through friendly consultations and negotiations by sovereign states directly concerned, in accordance with universally recognised principles of international law, including the 1982 UNCLOS;

- Continue exercising self-restraint by all parties concerned in the conduct of activities that would complicate or escalate disputes and affect peace and stability including, among others, refraining from action of inhabiting on the presently uninhabited islands, reefs, shoals, cays, and other features and to handle their differences in a constructive manner;

- Keep the momentum of dialogue and consultation to enhance trust, confidence and cooperation, and work together for the adoption of a code of conduct in the South China Sea on the basis of consensus.

9. We task our Ministers and Senior Officials to realise the goals, initiatives and activities outlined in this Statement.

ADOPTED in Phnom Penh, Cambodia, on the Nineteenth Day of November in the Year Two Thousand and Twelve, in two original copies in the English Language.

中国和东盟国家外交部长关于全面有效落实《南海各方行为宣言》的联合声明

（2016年7月25日）

我们，中国和东盟国家外长，于2016年7月25日在老挝万象举行会晤，

认识到维护南海的和平与稳定符合中国与东盟国家以及国际社会的基本利益；

重申2002年《南海各方行为宣言》是具有里程碑意义，展现了各方依据《联合国宪章》以及包括1982年《联合国海洋法公约》在内的公认国际法原则，共同维护地区和平稳定、增进互信和信心的共同承诺；

重申《宣言》在维护地区和平稳定中发挥的重要作用；

承诺全面有效完整落实《宣言》，并在协商一致的基础上实质性推动早日达成“南海行为准则”；

忆及2012年第15届中国东盟峰会关于《宣言》十周年纪念的联合声明；

鉴此，谨作出如下声明：

一、各方重申尊重并承诺，包括1982年《联合国海洋法公约》在内的公认的国际法原则所规定的在南海的航行及飞越自由。

二、有关各方承诺根据公认的国际法原则，包括1982年《联合国海洋法公约》，由直接有关的主权国家通过友好磋商和谈判，以和平方式解决它们的领土和管辖权争议，而不诉诸武力或以武力相威胁。

三、各方承诺保持自我克制，不采取使争议复杂化、扩大化和影响和平与稳定的行动，包括不在现无人居住的岛、礁、滩、沙或其它自然构造上采取居住的行动，并以建设性的方式处理它们的分歧。

四、各方可在包括航行安全、搜救、海洋科研、环境保护以及打击海上跨国

犯罪等各领域探讨或开展合作。

五、各方鼓励其他国家尊重《宣言》所包含的原则。

六、有关各方重申制定“南海行为准则”将进一步促进本地区和平与稳定，并同意在各方协商一致的基础上，朝最终达成该目标而努力。

Joint Statement of the Foreign Ministers of ASEAN Member States and China on the Full and Effective Implementation of the Declaration on the Conduct of Parties in the South China Sea

(25 July 2016)

We, the Foreign Ministers of ASEAN Member States and the People's Republic of China met in Vientiane, Lao People's Democratic Republic, on 25 July 2016.

RECOGNISING that maintaining peace and stability in the South China Sea region serves the fundamental interests of ASEAN Member States and China ("the Parties") as well as the international community;

REAFFIRMING that the Declaration on the Conduct of Parties in the South China Sea (DOC) is a milestone document that embodies the collective commitment of the Parties to promote peace, stability, mutual trust and confidence in the region, in accordance with the UN Charter and universally recognized principles of international law, including the 1982 United Nations Convention on the Law of the Sea (UNCLOS);

REAFFIRMING the importance and role of the DOC in maintaining peace and stability in the region;

COMMITTED to the full and effective implementation of the DOC in its entirety and working substantively towards the early adoption of a Code of Conduct in the South China Sea (COC) based on consensus;

RECALLING the Joint Statement of the 15th ASEAN-China Summit on the 10th Anniversary of the DOC adopted in 2012;

HEREBY state the following:

1. The Parties reaffirm their respect for and commitment to the freedom of navigation in and overflight above the South China Sea as provided for by the universally recognised principles of international law, including the 1982 UNCLOS.

2. The Parties concerned undertake to resolve their territorial and jurisdictional disputes by peaceful means, without resorting to the threat or use of force, through friendly consultations and negotiations by sovereign states directly concerned, in accordance with universally recognised principles of international law, including the 1982 UNCLOS.

3. The Parties undertake to exercise self-restraint in the conduct of activities that would complicate or escalate disputes and affect peace and stability including, among others, refraining from action of inhabiting on the presently uninhabited islands, reefs, shoals, cays, and other features and to handle their differences in a constructive manner.

4. The Parties may explore or undertake cooperative activities, in fields such as navigation safety, search and rescue, marine scientific research, environmental protection, and combating transnational crimes at sea.

5. The Parties encourage other countries to respect the principles contained in the DOC.

6. The Parties concerned reaffirm that the adoption of a code of conduct in the South China Sea would further promote peace and stability in the region and agree to work, on the basis of consensus, towards the eventual attainment of this objective.

中华人民共和国和菲律宾共和国
双边文件

Bilateral Documents between the People's Republic of China and the Republic of the Philippines

中华人民共和国和菲律宾共和国关于南海问题和其他领域合作的磋商联合声明

（1995年8月10日）

1995年8月9日至10日，中国和菲律宾代表团在马尼拉就南海问题和其他领域合作进行了磋商。

磋商是以坦诚和建设性态度在友好的气氛中进行的。

双方重申对双边关系的重视，一致认为两国经济的持续发展有赖于地区的和平和稳定，重申致力于促进本地区的和平稳定与合作。

双方就美济礁问题坦率地交换了意见，各自阐述了在此问题上的立场。双方同意为解决分歧继续磋商。双方并就整个南海问题上各自立场的法理和历史依据交换了意见。

在争议解决前，双方同意为在该地区确立行为准则而遵守下列原则：

1. 双方的领土争议不应影响两国关系的正常发展。有关争议应通过平等和相互尊重基础上的磋商和平友好地加以解决。

2. 双方将努力建立相互信任，加强本地区和平与稳定的气氛，不诉诸武力或以武力相威胁解决争端。

3. 本着扩大共同点缩小分歧的精神，双方承诺循序渐进地进行合作，最终谈判解决双方争议。

4. 双方同意根据公认的国际法包括《联合国海洋法公约》的原则解决双方间的争议。

5. 对本地区国家为寻求适当时候在南海开展多边合作所提出的建设性主张和建议，双方将持开放态度。

6. 双方同意推动在海洋环境、航行安全、打击海盗、海洋科研、减灾防灾、搜救、气象和海洋的污染控制方面的合作，他们还同意在上述某些领域，可以最终进行多边合作。

7. 有关各方将就南海海洋资源的养护进行合作。

8. 争议由直接有关国家解决，不影响南海的航行自由。

为推动解决进程，双方同意由专家就法律问题和南沙长期经济合作，包括争议地区的渔业合作交换意见。

双方同意双边合作活动本身及对建立信任措施都是重要的，有益的。双方同意对合作采取务实的态度。

除南海问题外，双方讨论了其他领域的双边合作，强调各层次的交往对加强合作是有益的。他们注意到中菲贸易联委会成功地举行了第十八次会议，期待着完成避免双重征税和偷漏税协定的谈判。双方注意到菲律宾方面已批准中菲促进和保护投资协定。

双方对磋商取得的进展表示满意，磋商极大地改善了两国关系的气氛。通过对争议问题进行直接和坦率的讨论，扩大了一致的领域。双方承诺将本着同样的建设性精神继续进行磋商。

Joint Statement between the People's Republic of China and the Republic of the Philippines concerning Consultations on the South China Sea and on Other Areas of Cooperation

(9-10 August 1995)

Delegation from China and the Philippines met in Manila on 9-10 August 1995 for consultations on the South China Sea and on other areas of cooperation.

The consultations were held in an atmosphere of cordiality and in a frank and constructive manner.

The two sides reiterated the importance they attach to the bilateral relations. They recognized that the continued prosperity of their economies depends upon the peace and stability of the region. They reaffirmed their commitment to regional peace, stability and cooperation.

Frank discussions on Meiji Reef ("Mischief Reef") were held. The two sides expressed their respective positions on the matter. They agreed to hold further consultations in order to resolve their differences. On the South China Sea issue as a whole, they exchanged views on the legal and historical bases of their respective positions.

Pending the resolution of the dispute, the two sides agreed to abide by the following principles for a code of conduct on the area:

1. Territorial disputes between the two sides should not affect the normal development of their relations. Disputes shall be settled in a peaceful and friendly manner through consultations on the basis of equality and mutual respect.

2. Efforts must be undertaken to build confidence and trust between the two

parties, to enhance an atmosphere of peace and stability in the region, and to refrain from using force or threat of force to resolve disputes.

3. In the spirit of expanding common ground and narrowing differences, a gradual and progressive process of cooperation shall be adopted with a view to eventually negotiating a settlement of the bilateral disputes.

4. The two sides agree to settle their bilateral disputes in accordance with the recognized principles of international law, including the UN Convention on the Law of the Sea.

5. Both sides shall keep an open-minded attitude on the constructive initiatives and proposals of regional states to pursue multilateral cooperation in the South China Sea at the appropriate time.

6. The two sides agree to promote cooperation in fields such as protection of the marine environment, safety of navigation, prevention of piracy, marine scientific research, disaster mitigation and control, search and rescue operations, meteorology, and maritime pollution control. They also agree that on some of the above mentioned issues, multilateral cooperation could eventually be conducted.

7. All parties concerned shall cooperate in the protection and conservation of the marine resources of the South China Sea.

8. Disputes shall be settled by the countries directly concerned without prejudice to the freedom of navigation in the South China Sea.

In order to push the process forward, the two sides agreed to hold discussions among experts on legal issues and sustainable economic cooperation in the South China Sea. They agreed further that experts from the two countries shall hold consultations at a mutually acceptable date in order to explore the possibilities of fisheries cooperation in the disputed area.

The two sides agreed on the importance of bilateral cooperative activities as useful in and of themselves, and as confidence-building measures. They are dedicated to a pragmatic approach to cooperation.

In addition to the South China Sea issue, the two sides reviewed other fields of bilateral cooperation. They emphasized the usefulness of exchanging contacts at various levels in strengthening cooperation. They noted the successful conclusion of the 18th Philippines-China Joint Trade Committee Meeting. They looked forward to concluding negotiations on the avoidance of double taxation and fiscal evasion. They noted the ratification by the Philippines side of the Bilateral Agreement on the Promotion and Mutual Protection of Investments.

The talks ended with both sides satisfied that some progress had been made in terms of substantially improving the atmosphere of relations and identifying and expanding areas of agreement by holding frank exchanges directly addressing contentious issues. They pledged to continue consultations in the same constructive spirit.

中菲建立信任措施工作小组会议
联合公报

（1999年3月23日）

根据1996年3月中菲磋商达成的共识，双方建立信任措施工作小组会议于1999年3月22—23日在马尼拉召开。

双方团长分别为王毅部长助理和副外长巴哈。

中菲双方一致同意，通过大量的官方往来和致力于促进各领域关系的共同努力，双方建立了传统友谊。双方就建立信任措施进行了广泛的探讨。双方还就有关美济礁的最近事态坦诚地交换了意见。

关于信任措施，双方重申以下承诺：

1. 遵守继续通过友好磋商寻求解决分歧方法的谅解。

2. 根据广泛接受的国际法原则包括联合国海洋法公约解决分歧。

3. 维护地区稳定与和平，不使用武力或以武力相威胁。

4. 在渔业、海洋环境、气象、海洋科研、海上生命安全、减灾防灾和航行安全领域，改善现有的接触和对话机制。

5. 扩大双边军事对话与合作，包括增加高级防务和军事官员的互访，加强信息交流，建立避免海上冲突的措施。

关于美济礁问题，双方各自阐述了自己的立场。菲方对近期有关事态表示十分关切。中方表示，美济礁上的设施将是民政用途的。双方还就缓和紧张，增进信任，包括菲律宾方面提出的利用这些民用设施的设想和中方提出的停止抓扣渔民的要求交换了意见。针对本地区形势可能出现进一步发展的关切，双方同意保持克制，不采取可能导致事态扩大化的行动。

双方认为召开建立信任措施会议本身即是一项信任措施，增进了相互了解。

双方认为，中菲之间的磋商渠道是畅通的。他们同意通过协商和平解决争议，双方之间的分歧不应影响两国关系的正常发展。双方重申将本着建设性、友好和互让的精神努力解决悬而未决的问题。双方同意尽早召开建立信任措施第二次会议，中方愿意在双方同意的时间和地点主办会议。

中华人民共和国政府和菲律宾共和国政府关于21世纪双边合作框架的联合声明

（2000年5月16日）

中华人民共和国和菲律宾共和国自1975年6月9日建立外交关系以来，在平等互利的基础上，在政治、经济、文化、教育、科技等各个领域的合作均得到长足发展，为两国人民带来了切实利益。

中华人民共和国政府和菲律宾共和国政府（以下简称“双方”）认为目前是为未来双边合作制订一个框架的合适时机。这一新的框架将利用双方具有历史悠久的传统友谊和地理上邻近的优势，促进两国人民的根本利益，并为亚洲和世界的和平、安全、稳定、持续增长和发展作出贡献。双方将在睦邻合作、互信互利的基础上建立长期、稳定的关系，努力使中菲关系在21世纪更上一层楼。为此，特声明如下：

一、双方确认，《联合国宪章》的宗旨和原则、和平共处五项原则、《东南亚友好合作条约》所确定的原则以及公认的国际法原则是处理两国关系的基本准则。

二、双方同意经常保持密切的高层接触和各个层次的互访，包括政府官员、私营部门、民间组织、学术界、新闻界以及两国人民之间的交往，促进双边关系全面、稳定、持续地发展。

三、双方同意保持和加强两国高官及外交部之间的年度会晤制度，就共同关心的双边、地区和国际问题进行磋商。

四、双方同意进一步开展在防务和军事领域的交流与合作，加强两国军事、防务人员及外交官之间有关安全问题的磋商，两国军事机构间就人道主义救助、救灾减灾问题进行交流，加强双方战略安全研究机构间的合作。

五、双方认为两国的发展目标相似，同意充分发挥双方在贸易、投资、科技、农业、教育、文化、旅游、民航、税收等领域现有的合作框架的作用。双方将：

（一）通过以下方式，进一步促进贸易、投资往来及工业合作：

1. 探讨一切可能的措施，增加贸易额、扩大产品的选择范围；

2. 同意通过确认并消除贸易投资障碍创造良好的市场环境；

3. 提高贸易规则的透明度；

4. 促进相互投资及合作到第三国投资；

5. 鼓励双方工商界发挥积极的作用。

（二）在互惠基础上加强金融领域的交流与合作，共同致力于改革国际金融体制。

（三）根据两国1978年3月14日签订的科技合作协定，扩大两国科技合作，通过合作研究以及技术转让等形式开拓新的合作领域。

（四）落实两国1999年9月13日签订的农业合作协定，促进农业领域的经济技术合作，加强信息交流，开展合作研究，鼓励两国有关企业、科研院所和商业团体积极参与农业领域的合作，以促进两国经济的共同发展。

（五）根据1979年7月8日签订的文化合作协定，继续实施两年执行计划。双方将通过互派代表团和文艺团组、专家互访、互办展览等活动，进一步加强两国在文化、艺术、教育、电影、体育、卫生、宗教、社会科学、图书出版等领域的交流与合作。

（六）进一步发展双边旅游合作，拓展旅游市场，促进两国旅游业的共同发展。

六、双方将依据国际准则提供必要便利，使在各自领土上居住、工作和旅游的对方国民在陷入困境或卷入法律、劳务等纠纷时可获得其本国适当官员所提供的领事保护。

七、双方将继续探讨执法、司法、安全及防务机构间新的合作领域，应对跨国有组织犯罪行为所构成的严重威胁。

八、两国政府将继续为各自的国家机构提供政策指导，以进一步发挥各联委会在所确定的合作领域里的作用。

九、双方致力于维护南海的和平与稳定，同意根据公认的国际法原则，包括1982年《联合国海洋法公约》，通过双边友好协商和谈判促进争议的和平解决。双方重申遵守1995年中菲两国关于南海问题的联合声明，同意不采取可能使事态复杂化和扩大化的行动，决心完成建立中菲信任措施工作小组的工作，促进本地区的和平与稳定。双方重申将为制订和达成南海地区行为准则作出积极贡献。

十、结合各自独特的文化、传统和习俗，双方承认并尊重人权的普遍性原则。双方应在平等和相互尊重的基础上，鼓励人权领域的交流与合作，增进相互了解。双方将共同致力于促进和保护人权事业。

十一、双方表示将尊重对方的独立、主权和领土完整。菲律宾政府重申其一个中国的政策，承认台湾是中国领土不可分割的一部分。

十二、双方同意深化中华人民共和国与东盟之间的合作，认识到密切的中菲关系有助于中国与东盟以及东盟+3（中、日、韩）关系的发展。双方将根据1999年11月28日在马尼拉发表的《东亚合作联合声明》，共同促进东亚对话与合作，为促进地区及世界的和平、稳定与繁荣作出重要贡献。

十三、双方同意继续加强在东盟、东盟地区论坛、亚太经济合作组织、亚欧会议、世贸组织和联合国等多边场合的协调与合作。双方将在地区和国际场合积极促进和维护发展中国家的共同利益，特别是在贸易、金融、人力资源开发以及促进劳工、农民和妇女儿童权益领域。

十四、双方同意推动建立公正合理的世界秩序。

如一方要求，双方外交部长将共同对本声明进行复审。

本声明于2000年5月16日在北京签署。

Joint Statement between the Government of the People's Republic of China and the Government of the Republic of the Philippines on the Framework of Bilateral Cooperation in the Twenty-First Century

(16 May 2000)

The People's Republic of China and the Republic of the Philippines have made great progress in their cooperation in the political, economic, cultural, educational, scientific and technological and other fields on the basis of equality and mutual benefit since the establishment of diplomatic relations on 9 June 1975, brining concrete benefits to the two peoples.

The Government of the People's Republic of China and the Government of the Republic of the Philippines (hereinafter referred to as "the two sides") believe that it is now opportune to establish a framework for further bilateral cooperation.

This new framework will draw on the strength of their long, historical friendship and geographical proximity in order to advance the fundamental interests of their two peoples and thereby contribute to peace, security, stability, sustained growth, and development in Asia and the rest of the world.

The two sides will establish a long-term and stable relationship on the basis of good neighborliness, cooperation, an mutual trust and benefit.

They will undertake to elevate China-Philippines relations to greater heights in the 21st century and to this end, state the following:

1. The two sides reaffirm that the purposes and principles of the United

Nations Charter, the Five Principles of Peaceful Coexistence, the principles established in the Treaty of Amity and Cooperation in Southeast Asia and other universally recognized principles of international law are the basic norms governing the relations between the two countries.

2. The two sides agree to maintain close and frequent high-level contacts and exchange of visits at all levels, including government officials, the private sector, non-government organizations, the academic community, press and media, and their peoples to contribute to a comprehensive, stable and sustained development of bilateral relations.

3. The two sides agree to maintain and strengthen the mechanism of annual meetings between senior officials and their respective foreign ministries for consultations on bilateral, regional, and international issues of mutual concern.

4. The two sides agree to make further exchanges and cooperation in the defense and military fields, strengthen consultations between their military and defense personnel and diplomatic officials on security issues, to include exchanges between their military establishments on matters relating to humanitarian rescue and assistance, disaster relief and mitigation, and enhance cooperation between their respective strategic and security research institutes.

5. The two sides acknowledge the similarities in their respective national development goals, and agree to optimize the use of existing frameworks for cooperation in the fields of trade, investment, science and technology, agriculture, education and culture, tourism, civil aviation, and taxation. They will undertake the following:

a) Promote better bilateral trade and investment flows, and improve industrial cooperation by:

i. Exploring all possible measures to effect increases in trade volumes and product choices;

ii. Agreeing to provide a conducive market environment through identification and removal of trade and investment impediments;

iii. Improving transparency of trade-related regulations;

iv. Undertaking investment promotion, and joint investment in third countries; and

v. Encouraging a proactive role for the business sectors of both sides.

b) Intensify exchanges and cooperation in the financial field on the basis of reciprocity. They will work together for the reform of the international financial system.

c) Expand scientific and technological cooperation in accordance with the Agreement on Science and Technology Cooperation signed on 14 March 1978, and enter into new areas of cooperation through joint research, technology transfer and other means.

d) Implement the Agreement on the Cooperation in the Field of Agriculture signed on 13 September 1999, by promoting economic and technological cooperation in the agricultural field, increasing data exchange, conducting joint research, and encouraging their enterprises, scientific research institutes, and business groups concerned to take an active part in agricultural cooperation, so as to bring about common growth of the two economies.

e) Continue to implement the biennial executive programs in accordance with the Cultural Agreement signed on 8 July 1979. They will further enhance their exchanges and cooperation in the fields of culture, arts, education, film, sports, health care, religion, social science and book publication through, among others, the exchange of delegations and art troupes, visits by experts, and exhibitions held in each other's country.

f) Further develop bilateral tourism cooperation and expand the tourism market in an effort to achieve common development of their tourism industries.

6. Either side shall accord to the other due facilitation in accordance with international norms so that the nationals of either country who reside, work or travel in the territory of the other country may receive consular protection by the appropriate officials of their own country when they are in distress or involved in legal, labor or other disputes.

7. The two sides will continue to explore new areas for cooperation among their law enforcement, judicial, security, and defense agencies in order to address the serious threats posed by organized transnational crimes.

8. The two sides will continue to provide policy guidance to their respective national agencies in order to strengthen the role of the various joint committees

in identified areas of cooperation.

9. The two sides commit themselves to the maintenance of peace and stability in the South China Sea. They agree to promote a peaceful settlement of disputes through bilateral friendly consultations and negotiations in accordance with universally-recognized principles of international law, including the 1982 United Nations Convention on the Law of the Sea. They reaffirm their adherence to the 1995 joint statement between the two countries on the South China Sea and agree not to take actions that might complicate or escalate the situation. The two sides expressed their determination to follow through the work of the China-Philippines Working Group on Confidence Building Measures to enhance peace and stability in the region. They reiterate that they will contribute positively toward the formulation and adoption of the regional Code of Conduct in the South China Sea.

10. The two sides recognize and respect the universality of human rights taking into account their distinct culture, tradition, and practices. They shall encourage exchanges and cooperation on human rights on the basis of equality, mutual respect, with a view to enhancing mutual understanding. They will work together for the progress and protection of the cause of human rights.

11. The two sides affirm their commitment to respect the independence, sovereignty, and territorial integrity of each other. The Philippine Government reaffirms its one China policy and recognizes that Taiwan is an integral part of Chinese territory.

12. The two sides agree to deepen cooperation between the People's Republic of China (PRC) and the Association of Southeast Asian Nations (ASEAN), recognizing that close China-Philippines relations contribute to the promotion of PRC-ASEAN and ASEAN+3 (PRC, Republic of Korea, and Japan) relations. They will jointly promote dialogue and cooperation in East Asia in accordance with the Joint Statement on East Asia Cooperation issued in Manila on 28 November 1999 to make a significant contribution to the peace, stability and prosperity of the region and the world.

13. The two sides agree to continue their coordination and cooperation at the Association of Southeast Asian Nations, ASEAN Regional Forum, Asia-Pacific

Economic Cooperation, ASEM, World Trade Organization, United Nations, and other multilateral fora. They will actively promote and protect the common interests of developing countries in regional and international fora, particularly in the areas of trade and finance, human resources development, and the promotion of the interests of labor, farmers, and women and children, among others.

14. The two sides agree to promote the establishment of an equitable and rational world order.

The above statement will be jointly reviewed by the ministers of foreign affairs of the two sides, if requested by either side.

Done in Beijing, China, on this 16th day of May 2000.

中华人民共和国和菲律宾共和国第三次建立信任措施专家组会议联合新闻声明

（2001年4月3日至4日）

中国—菲律宾第三次建立信任措施专家组（CBMs）会议于2001年4月3日至4日在马尼拉召开。中国外交部亚洲司司长傅莹与菲律宾外交部部长助理兼亚太司司长戈阿共同主持了会议。会议期间，菲律宾总统阿罗约和副总统兼外交部长金戈纳分别会见了傅莹等一行。

一、双方回顾了1995年8月《中菲关于南海及其他领域合作磋商的联合声明》、1999年3月《中菲第一次CBMs专家组会议联合声明》和1999年10月中菲第二次CBMs专家组会议成果等文件中所达成的共识与谅解。

二、双方对会议所体现出的维护和推进两国良好关系的意愿表示满意。双方认为，中菲发展友好合作符合两国人民的根本利益。双方应根据《中菲关于21世纪双边合作框架的联合声明》，在睦邻合作、互信互利的基础上建立长期、稳定的关系。

三、双方回顾了南海形势，同意将继续致力于不让有关分歧影响两国关系发展的大局。双方认为中菲关系发展潜力巨大。

四、双方认识到两国就探讨南海合作方式所建立的双边磋商机制是富有成效的，双方所达成的一系列谅解与共识对维护中菲关系的健康发展和南海地区的和平与稳定发挥了建设性作用。

五、双方就黄岩岛有关事态交换了意见，并同意不应在这一地区采取任何可能使事态扩大化和复杂化的行动。

六、关于建立信任措施，双方确认以下谅解与共识：

（一）双方强调了保护海洋物种及其栖息地的重要性，并就包括休渔等措施交换了意见。

（二）双方同意讨论并筹备联合搜救沙盘演习。

（三）中方将积极考虑菲方提出的举行菲中研讨会的建议。

（四）双方原则同意在两国渔业部门之间建立直线联系，具体方式将交由渔业合作专家组讨论。

（五）双方同意研究在建立信任措施专家组框架内建立解决渔业纠纷的机制。

（六）双方同意研究尽快召开中菲渔业合作专家组和海洋环保专家组会议的可能性。菲方对中方提议尽快主办上述两个会议表示赞赏，有关会期将通过外交渠道商定。

（七）双方同意在海洋环境保护专家组框架下讨论中国提议的三个合作项目，即“赤潮的对比研究”、“海洋环境保护容量”和“南海风暴潮的分析、预报”。

（八）双方将扩大双边军事对话与合作，包括增加双边高级国防和军事官员的互访，积极探讨在语言培训方面进行互惠合作。

（九）中方欢迎菲律宾军舰在对双方都方便的时候访问中国港口，作为此前中国军舰访菲的回访。

（十）双方同意避免采取任何可能使事态扩大化和复杂化的行动，或发表任何挑衅性言论，以利于维护地区和平与稳定。

七、双方同意研究落实本专家组前两次会议所提出的下列信任措施：

（一）双方军队就抢险救灾和工程技术交流经验。

（二）双方就相互提供航海公告、发布航行通告和航海警报问题进行磋商，并就海上航行安全的相关问题进行深入细致的讨论。

八、双方将加强合作，为制定和达成中国—东盟南海地区行为准则作出积极贡献。

九、中方感谢菲方所给予的热情款待。

Joint Press Statement of the 3rd China–Philippines Experts' Group Meeting on Confidence-Building Measures

(3–4 April 2001)

The 3rd China–Philippines Experts' Group Meeting on Confidence-Building Measures convened in Manila on 3–4 April 2001. The meeting was co-chaired by Director-General of the Asian Department Madame Fu Ying and Assistant Secretary of the Office of Asian and Pacific Affairs Willy C. Gaa. During the Meeting, Madame Fu Ying paid a courtesy call on His Excellency Vice President and Foreign Secretary Teofisto G. Guingona, Jr. and His Excellency Foreign Affairs Undersecretary Lauro L. Baja, Jr..

I. The two sides reviewed previous agreements and understandings on principles provided under the Joint Statement on China–Philippine Consultations on the South China Sea and on Other Areas of Cooperation of August 1995, the Joint Statement of the 1st China–Philippines Experts' Group Meeting on Confidence Building Measures of March 1999, and the results of the 2nd China–Philippines Experts' Working Group on Confidence Building Measures of October 1999.

II. The two sides expressed satisfaction that the meeting manifested the determination of both countries to preserve and advance the excellent relations that prevail between them. They agreed that developing friendship and cooperation between China and the Philippines conforms with the basic interest of the two peoples, and that the two sides should establish a long-term and stable relationship on the basis of good neighborliness, cooperation, and mutual trust and benefit in accordance with the China–Philippines Joint Statement on the

Framework of Bilateral Cooperation in the 21st Century.

III. The two sides reviewed the situation in the South China Sea. They agreed to continue with the commitment not to allow bilateral differences to affect the overall development of China–Philippines relations, the enormous potentials of which remain unexplored.

IV. The two sides noted that the bilateral consultation mechanism to explore ways of cooperation in the South China Sea has been effective. The series of understanding and consensus reached by the two sides have played a constructive role in the maintenance of the sound development of China–Philippines relations and peace and stability of the South China Sea area.

V. The two sides exchanged views on the incidents around Huangyan Island/Scarborough Shoal, and agreed that neither side shall take any action that might complicate and escalate the situation in this area.

VI. In regard to confidence-building measures, the two sides confirmed the following understanding and consensus:

1. The two sides stated the importance of the preservation of the marine species and habitats and exchanged views on such measures including moratorium on fishing.

2. The two sides agreed to discuss and prepare for joint search and rescue table-top exercises.

3. China will consider positively the Philippine proposal of holding a Philippines–China symposium/workshop.

4. The two sides agreed, in principle, to set-up a direct line of communication between the fisheries departments of both countries, the modalities of which shall be discussed at the Working Group on Fisheries Cooperation.

5. The two sides agreed to study a mechanism for settling fishery disputes under the framework of the Experts' Group Meeting on Confidence-Building Measures.

6. The two sides agreed to look into the possibility of convening soon the China-Philippines Working Group on Fisheries Cooperation and on Marine Environmental Protection. The Philippine side expressed appreciation for China's offer to host both meeting in the near future, the dates of which shall be

mutually agreed upon through diplomatic channels.

7. The two sides agreed to discuss the three Chinese proposed cooperation projects: " Comparative Studies on Red Tide", "Marine Environment Protection Capacity", and "Analysis and Prediction of Surge Affection the South China Sea" under the framework of the Working Group on Marine Environmental Protection.

8. The two sides will expand bilateral military dialogue and cooperation, including more exchanges of visits by senior defense and military officials and active exploration of reciprocal cooperation in language training.

9. China welcomes the proposed port call on China of a Philippine naval vessel to reciprocate previous visits of Chinese naval vessels to the Philippines at a time convenient to both sides.

10. The two sides agreed to refrain from making any actions or provocative statements that might complicate or escalate the situation in the interest of maintaining regional peace and stability.

VII. The two sides agreed to look into ways of implementing the following confidence-building measures agreed upon in the previous two meetings of this group:

1. The Armed Forces of the two sides to exchange and share experience in rescue operation, disaster relief and engineering technology.

2. The two sides to hold consultations on issues concerning the exchange of navigational bulletins, release of notices to mariners and navigational warnings, and have indepth and detailed discussions on the issues concerning marine navigation safety.

VIII. The two sides will strengthen their cooperation to contribute positively toward the formulation and adoption of an ASEAN-China regional code of conduct in the South China Sea.

IX. The Chinese side appreciated the warm reception and hospitality by the Philippine side.

中华人民共和国政府与菲律宾共和国政府联合新闻公报

（2004年9月3日）

应中华人民共和国主席胡锦涛的邀请，菲律宾共和国总统格洛丽亚·马卡帕加尔·阿罗约于2004年9月1日至3日对中国进行了国事访问。

此访旨在促进中菲两国之间紧密的传统友谊和睦邻友好关系，增进相互了解和信任，促进经济合作与共同发展。

访问期间，中国国家主席胡锦涛与阿罗约总统举行了会谈，中央军委主席江泽民、国务院总理温家宝分别会见了阿罗约总统。

两国领导人在坦诚友好的气氛中就双边关系及共同关心的国际和地区问题交换了意见。双方对中菲关系取得的积极进展和各领域合作的不断扩大和深化表示满意。双方重申将继续促进两国关系全面发展，一致同意在两国政府2000年签署的关于21世纪双边合作框架《联合声明》有关原则的指导下，进一步推动中菲关系健康稳定地向前发展。

双方同意于2005年共同举办庆祝活动，纪念中菲建交30周年。

双方同意保持和促进高层接触与各层次的交流，同意加强两国政府各部门、工商界、学术界、新闻界、非政府组织之间的交往。

双方同意进一步加强各种磋商与合作机制，包括两国外交磋商、领事磋商、贸易联委会、农业联委会和科技联委会等磋商与合作机制。

双方一致认为中菲两国经济互补性很强，注意到两国贸易近年来取得显著发展，同意进一步扩大双边贸易、改善贸易结构并拓展服务贸易合作。

双方期待着菲律宾于2005年1月1日加入东盟—中国自由贸易区“早期收

获”计划。菲方对中国的灵活性表示感谢。

菲律宾承认中国的市场经济地位。

为继续扩大相互投资，双方同意鼓励各自企业赴对方国家投资兴业，特别是在基础设施建设、农业、资源、信息和通信技术等领域开展合作。菲方感谢中方对菲农业发展和北部铁路建设提供的支持。

双方表示将进一步促进两国旅游合作，鼓励各自公民赴对方国家旅游。

双方同意促进两国人员交流，加强在教育、文化等领域的交流与合作。

双方一致认为扩大中菲军事和安全领域的交流与合作对增进两国政治互信具有重要意义，同意探讨建立中菲国防部门防务安全磋商机制。双方同意积极落实两国在司法协助、打击贩毒等跨国犯罪领域的合作协议。

菲方重申坚持一个中国政策，表示理解中国政府为维护国家统一所作的努力。

双方重申将继续致力于维护南海地区的和平与稳定。在尚未全面并最终解决南海地区的领土和海洋权益争端前，双方将继续探讨共同开发等合作。双方同意根据包括1982年《联合国海洋法公约》在内的公认的国际法准则，推动和平解决有关争议。双方一致认为尽快积极落实中国与东盟于2002年签署的《南海各方行为宣言》有助于将南海变为合作之海。

双方同意继续推动中国与东盟的合作，积极建设中国与东盟自贸区，并进一步促进东盟与中日韩合作。

双方认为中菲两国应继续与发展中国家合作，寻求建立公正平衡的全球自由贸易体系。

双方一致认为维护本地区的和平与稳定至关重要。菲方赞赏中方为实现朝鲜半岛无核化所作的积极努力。

阿罗约总统对访华期间中方给予其本人及菲方代表团的热情友好接待表示感谢。

阿罗约总统邀请胡锦涛主席在方便的时候访问菲律宾，胡锦涛主席对此表示感谢。双方将做好胡锦涛主席对菲律宾进行国事访问的准备工作。

Joint Press Statement of the Government of the People's Republic of China and the Government of the Republic of the Philippines

(3 September 2004)

Upon the invitation of His Excellency Hu Jintao, President of the People's Republic of China, Her Excellency Gloria Macapagal-Arroyo, President of the Republic of the Philippines paid a state visit to China from 1 to 3 September 2004.

The visit was aimed at promoting the existing close traditional friendship and good neighborly relationship between the two countries, enhancing mutual understanding and trust and facilitating economic cooperation and development.

During the visit, President Hu Jintao held talks with President Arroyo. His Excellency Jiang Zemin, Chairman of the Central Military Commission, and His Excellency Wen Jiabao, Premier of the State Council, also met President Arroyo.

Leaders of the two countries exchanged views on bilateral ties as well as international and regional issues of common interest in a sincere and friendly atmosphere. They noted with satisfaction the significant progress in the bilateral relationship and the steady expansion and deepening of cooperation in all fields. They reaffirmed their commitment to work on the comprehensive development of their ties. They agreed to further promote the healthy and steady development of the relationship, guided by the principles enshrined in the Joint Statement on the Framework of Bilateral Cooperation in the 21st Century signed by the two Governments in 2000.

The two sides agreed to prepare for the celebrations of the 30th anniversary of the establishment of China–Philippines diplomatic relations in 2005.

The two sides agreed to strengthen ties and to sustain high-level contacts exchanges at all levels in all fields of government, business, academic communities, media and non-government organizations of the two countries.

They also agreed to further strengthen various consultation and cooperation mechanisms, including the foreign ministry consultations, consular consultations, the Joint Trade Committee, the Joint Committee on Agriculture and the Joint Committee on Science and Technology.

Both sides acknowledged the strong complementarity between the two economies. Noting the remarkable progress achieved in bilateral trade in the recent years, they agreed to promote the further expansion of bilateral trade, the improvement of the trade structure and the development of potentials in trade and services.

Both sides expect the Philippines' participation in the Early Harvest Program of the ASEAN–China Free Trade Area on 1 January 2005. The Philippines expressed appreciation for China's flexibility.

The Philippines recognized China's market economy status.

In the interest of expanding mutual investment, they agreed to encourage entrepreneurs to invest in each other's countries, particularly in the fields of infrastructure, agriculture, resources, information and communications technology among others. The Philippine side expressed appreciation for China's support for the agricultural development program and the Northrail project of the Philippine government.

The two sides agreed to promote cooperation in tourism and encourage their nationals to visit each other's countries.

The two sides indicated their readiness to enhance people-to-people exchanges with further cooperation in educational, cultural and other fields.

Both sides believed that expanded exchanges and dialogue in the military and security fields will strengthen the level of mutual political trust between the two countries. They agreed to study the possible establishment of the annual defense security consultation mechanism between their defense departments. They also agreed to strengthen ways and means to implement cooperation agreements concerning judicial assistance, drug control and transnational crimes.

The Philippine side reaffirmed its adherence to the One-China policy and understands efforts by the Chinese government to maintain national unity.

The two sides reaffirmed their commitment to the peace and stability in the South China Sea and their readiness to continue discussions to study cooperative activities like joint development pending the comprehensive and final settlement of territorial disputes and overlapping maritime claims in the area. They agreed to promote the peaceful settlement of disputes in accordance with universally-recognized principles of international law, including the 1982 United Nations Convention on the Law of the Sea. They agreed that the early and vigorous implementation of the 2002 ASEAN-China Declaration on the Conduct of Parties in the South China Sea will pave the way for the transformation of the South China Sea into an area of cooperation.

The two sides agreed to continue to promote cooperation between China and ASEAN, pursue the realization of the China-ASEAN free trade area and strengthen the ASEAN plus 3 process.

They recognized that the China and Philippines should continue to work with other developing countries for fairness and balance in the global free trade regime.

They shared the view that maintaining peace and stability in the region was of critical importance. The Philippines acknowledged China's efforts to bring about denuclearization and development in the Korean Peninsula.

President Arroyo expressed appreciation for the warm hospitality and friendship extended to her delegation during her visit to China.

President Arroyo invited President Hu Jintao to visit the Philippines at a mutually convenient date. President Hu expressed appreciation for the invitation. Both sides will prepare for the State Visit of President Hu to the Philippines.

中华人民共和国与菲律宾共和国联合声明

（2005年4月28日）

值此中华人民共和国与菲律宾共和国建交30周年之际，应菲律宾共和国总统格洛丽亚·马加帕加尔·阿罗约阁下邀请，中华人民共和国主席胡锦涛于2005年4月26日至28日对菲律宾共和国进行了国事访问。

胡锦涛主席与阿罗约总统在诚挚友好的气氛中进行了会谈，就双边关系及共同关心的国际和地区问题深入交换了意见。

两国领导人对中菲建交30年来在政治、经贸、农业、文化、科技、教育、防务、打击跨国犯罪等各领域合作取得的显著进展表示满意，认为两国各界人士长期以来为促进中菲关系发展作出了重要贡献。

双方确认《联合国宪章》的宗旨和原则、和平共处五项原则、《东南亚友好合作条约》的宗旨和原则及公认的国际法准则是处理两国关系的基本准则。

双方强调中菲关系已经进入伙伴关系的黄金时期，持续拓展和全面发展两国友好关系符合双方的根本利益，也有利于本地区的和平、稳定与繁荣。

两国领导人回顾了1975年中菲《建交公报》有关原则，重申将继续坚持两国于2000年5月14日签署的关于21世纪双边合作框架《联合声明》的精神，愿在中国与东盟面向和平与繁荣的战略伙伴关系的框架下，积极推动中菲建立致力于和平与发展的战略性合作关系，并达成如下共识：

——保持高层经常交往与接触。两国领导人将通过互访、互致信函和多边场合会晤等方式，及时就双边关系和共同关心的重大国际地区问题交换意见，协调立场。

——大力推进经贸合作。进一步发挥双方现有经贸合作机制的作用，充分利用两国经济的互补优势，挖掘合作潜力，在广度和多样性方面改善贸易结构，不断扩大贸易和投资规模，并争取在未来5年内实现中菲年贸易额突破300亿美元。

——继续深化农业合作。双方愿共同努力，进一步发挥中国援建的中菲农技中心的作用，推动双方在优质杂交种子、农业基础设施、农业机械等方面的合作。双方将继续根据两国《渔业合作谅解备忘录》的精神探讨渔业合作，以友好、合作的方式处理非法捕捞问题，减少渔业纠纷。

——加强基础设施建设合作。双方强调基础设施建设是中菲经贸合作的重点领域，认为两国就菲律宾北部铁路工程开展的有效合作已成为中菲友好合作新的象征。中方表示将继续支持菲北部铁路和南部铁路等基础设施的建设。两国已建立基础设施建设合作机制，专门探讨、协调双方公司在这一领域的合作，并提供相关便利。

——拓展矿产资源开发合作。双方将在互利双赢的基础上大力拓展矿产资源开发合作，并将这一领域作为中菲合作新的支柱。两国有关部门将启动中菲矿业合作磋商和协调机制。

——密切人员交往。双方同意共同推动两国政府、议会、政党和民间团体加强友好交流与合作，鼓励两国青年交流，深化旅游合作。

——加强中国南部省份与菲律宾北吕宋的联系。双方确认，在具有互补性的经济结构、地缘优势和市场需求的基础上，逐步发展中国与菲律宾北吕宋的经贸关系，支持双方商务和人员往来。菲律宾欢迎中国在菲增设驻拉瓦格市领事馆，认为这是为推动上述合作迈出的积极一步。

——促进防务与安全合作。双方欢迎两国防务部门签署防务合作谅解备忘录并建立防务安全磋商机制，宣布将于今年5月举行首次防务安全磋商。双方还表示愿加强在禁毒、打击跨国犯罪等非传统安全领域的合作。

——双方承诺在涉及国家主权和领土完整的重大问题上相互理解、相互支持。菲律宾重申坚持一个中国政策，理解中国政府为实现国家统一所作的努力，支持并赞赏中国为和平解决台湾问题所作的努力。

——双方同意继续致力于维护南海地区的和平与稳定，愿与其他东盟国家一道，积极落实《南海各方行为宣言》。双方一致认为，中菲率先启动南海共同开发促进了中菲关系发展，为推动有关国家在南海开展务实合作、促进本地区的和平、稳定与繁荣作出了历史性贡献。双方对中国海洋石油总公司、越南油气总公司和菲律宾国家石油公司签订《南中国海协议区三方联合海洋地震工作协议》表示欢迎，认为这是具有历史意义的一步，将使南海成为友谊之海、合作之海。

——双方高度评价中国与东盟关系近年来取得的长足进展，一致认为这一良好的关系已成为促进本地区和平、稳定与繁荣的重要支柱。双方表示将继续致力于推进中国与东盟面向和平与繁荣的战略伙伴关系和中国—东盟自贸区建设，积极推动东亚合作进程。中方重申将一如既往地支持东盟一体化进程，支持东盟在区域合作中发挥主导作用，并将积极参加东盟东部增长区建设。菲律宾感谢中国承诺支持东盟东部增长区的发展，支持中国成为增长区的观察员。双方欢迎菲律宾加入中国—东盟早期收获计划。

——双方同意进一步加强在联合国、东盟地区论坛、亚太经合组织、亚欧会议、世界贸易组织及其他多边组织中的协调与配合。

——双方认为，和平与发展是当今世界的主题。国际社会应尊重世界多样性，提倡国际关系公正、平衡，充分发挥联合国在重大国际事务中的主导作用。双方表示支持通过必要和合理的改革加强联合国的作用，并主张推动落实发展问题、维护发展中国家合法权益、加强发展中国家在国际事务中的发言权和代表性，应成为联合国改革的重点。

——双方表示将加强在国际组织中的合作，推动经济全球化在公平的基础上平衡发展，以确保发展中国家在全球化进程中能充分受益。

——双方表示反对一切形式恐怖主义，认为国际社会有必要共同防范恐怖主义威胁。

胡锦涛主席还会见了菲律宾参议长弗兰克林·德里隆和众议长何塞·德贝内西亚等菲律宾领导人，并在菲律宾参、众两院联席会议上发表演讲。

中方对胡锦涛主席访菲期间受到的热情友好接待表示感谢。胡锦涛主席邀请菲方领导人在方便的时候访问中国，菲方领导人愉快地接受了邀请。

二〇〇五年四月二十八日于马尼拉

Joint Statement of the People's Republic of China and the Republic of the Philippines

(28 April 2005)

At the invitation of Her Excellency President Gloria Macapagal-Arroyo of the Republic of the Philippines and on the occasion of the 30th anniversary of diplomatic relations between the People's Republic of China and the Republic of the Philippines, President Hu Jintao of the People's Republic of China paid a state visit to the Philippines between 26–28 April 2005.

During their meeting, President Hu Jintao and President Arroyo had an indepth exchange of views on bilateral relations and international and regional issues of shared interest in a cordial and friendly atmosphere.

The two leaders expressed their satisfaction with the remarkable progress made in the cooperation in the political, economic, trade, cultural, scientific, educational, defense, transnational crimes, agriculture, and other fields over the past 30 years since China and the Philippines established diplomatic relations. They acknowledged the important contributions of individuals from all circles in the two countries who have made long-term commitments to the promotion of China–Philippines relations.

The two sides affirmed the purposes and principles of the United Nations Charter, the Five Principles of Peaceful Coexistence, the purposes and principles of the Treaty of Amity and Cooperation in Southeast Asia and other universally recognized norms of international law as the principles guiding their relations.

The two sides stressed that China–Philippines relations have reached the golden age of partnership and that continuous expansion and comprehensive development of friendly relations between the two countries not only serves the fundamental interests of the two sides but also contributes to peace, stability and prosperity in the region.

The two leaders recalled the principles enshrined in the Joint Communiqué of the Government of the People's Republic of China and the Government of the Republic of the Philippines on the Establishment of Diplomatic Relations signed in 1975 and reiterated that while continuing to act in the spirit of the Joint Statement on the Framework of Bilateral Cooperation in the 21st Century signed between the two sides on 14 May 2000, under the framework of China-ASEAN strategic partnership geared to peace and prosperity, the two sides stand ready to work vigorously for the establishment of a strategic and cooperative relationship for peace and development between China and the Philippines. They agreed as follows:

— Maintain frequent high-level contacts and exchanges. Leaders of the two countries will promptly exchange views and coordinate positions on bilateral relations as well as major international and regional issues of shared interest through exchange of visits, correspondence, meetings on multilateral occasions and other means.

— Vigorously promote economic cooperation and trade. The two sides should give full play to the existing economic cooperation and trade mechanisms, tap into their economic complementarity and potential for cooperation, broaden and diversify trade structure, further expand trade and investment and make efforts to raise bilateral trade to over USD 30 billion within the next 5 years.

— Further deepen cooperation in agriculture. China and the Philippines will intensify cooperation in agriculture. The two sides are ready to work together to optimize role of the China-Philippines Agricultural Technology Center and push forward bilateral cooperation in such areas as quality hybrid seeds, agricultural infrastructure development and agricultural machinery. They will continue discussions on fishery cooperation in the spirit of the Memorandum of Understanding on Fisheries Cooperation, and to address illegal fishing in a friendly and cooperative manner.

— Enhance infrastructure cooperation. Stressing that infrastructure development is a priority in economic cooperation and trade between China and the Philippines, the two sides maintained that their effective cooperation on the North Rail project has become a new symbol of China-Philippine friendship and cooperation. The Chinese side stated that it will continue to support infrastructure projects in the Philippines such as the North Rail and the South Rail projects. The two sides established a mechanism to discuss, coordinate and facilitate partnerships between their companies in the infrastructure sector.

— Expand cooperation in mineral resource development. The two sides will vigorously expand cooperation in mineral resource development on a mutually-beneficial and win-win basis and to transform this sector as a new pillar of China-Philippines cooperation. Their relevant departments will activate consultation and coordinative mechanisms for bilateral cooperation in mining.

— Increase personnel exchanges. The two sides agreed to jointly push forward friendly exchanges and cooperation between governments, parliaments, political parties and non-governmental organizations of the two countries, promote youth exchanges and deepen tourism cooperation.

— Strengthen linkages between southern China and northern Luzon. Both sides acknowledged the gradual development of economic and trade ties, including people to people exchanges and air services, between China and the northern part of Luzon, the Philippines on the basis of complementing economic structure, geographic advantages and market forces. They agreed to promote port and air linkages and support exchanges between business and people. The Philippines welcomed the opening of a new Chinese Consulate in Laoag as a positive step towards this direction.

— Promote defense and security cooperation. The two sides welcomed the signing of the Memorandum of Understanding on Defense Cooperation and the launching of the defense and security consultation mechanism between the two Defense Departments and announced that the first defense and security consultations will be held in May this year. The two sides also expressed their willingness to strengthen cooperation in non-traditional security areas such as combating drugs and transnational crimes.

— The two sides committed themselves to mutual understanding and mutual support with respect to major issues bearing on state sovereignty and territorial integrity. The Philippines reaffirmed its adherence to the one China policy and understanding of the Chinese Government's efforts for national reunification. The Philippines supports and appreciates China's efforts to resolve the Taiwan issue peacefully.

— The two sides agreed to continue efforts to maintain peace and stability in the South China Sea and work with other ASEAN countries to actively implement the Declaration on the Conduct of Parties in the South China Sea. The two sides agreed that the collaboration between China and the Philippines in pioneering the joint development in the South China Sea had given a boost to China-Philippines relations and made historic contributions to pragmatic cooperation among relevant countries in the South China Sea and to peace, stability and prosperity in the region. The two sides welcomed the signing of the Tripartite Agreement for Joint Marine Seismic Undertaking in the Agreement Area in the South China Sea by China National Offshore Oil Corporation, Vietnam Oil and Gas Company and Philippines National Oil Corporation as a historic step towards the transformation of the South China Sea into a sea of friendship and cooperation.

— The two sides highly commended the remarkable progress achieved in China-ASEAN relations in recent years. They agreed that the sound relationship had become an important pillar for the promotion of peace, stability and prosperity in the region. The two sides reaffirmed their commitments to the China-ASEAN strategic partnership for peace and prosperity, the China-ASEAN Free Trade Area and the process of East Asian cooperation. The Chinese side reaffirmed its support to the ASEAN integration process and ASEAN's leading role in regional cooperation and its active participation in the development of East ASEAN Growth Area. The Philippine side expressed appreciation for China's commitment to support the development of the BIMP-EAGA and support for China's request for observer status in the BIMP-EAGA process. Both sides welcomed the participation of the Philippines in the China-ASEAN Early Harvest Program.

— The two sides agreed to further strengthen their coordination and cooperation in the UN, ARF, APEC, ASEM, WTO and other multilateral organizations.

— The two sides agreed that peace and development were the themes of the present-day world. The international community should respect the diversity of the world, promote fairness and balance in international relations and bring into full play the leading role of the UN in major international affairs. The two sides expressed their support for necessary and rational reform aimed at enhancing the role of the UN. They agreed that UN reform should focus on addressing the development issue and uphold the legitimate rights and interests of developing countries and enhance the voice and representation of developing countries in international affairs.

— The two sides expressed their willingness to strengthen cooperation in international organizations and promote the balanced development of economic globalization on the basis of equality so as to ensure that developing countries will fully benefit from the globalization process.

— The two sides reaffirmed their opposition to terrorism of all forms and affirmed the need for international collaboration in response to the threat of terrorism.

President Hu Jintao also met with senior Philippine officials including Senate President Franklin M. Drilon and Speaker Jose C. De Venecia, Jr. of the House of Representatives and addressed a joint session of the Philippine Congress.

The Chinese side expressed its thanks for the hospitality accorded to President Hu Jintao during his visit to the Philippines. President Hu Jintao invited Philippine leaders to visit China at their convenience, and the Philippine leaders accepted with pleasure.

Manila, 28 April 2005

中华人民共和国和菲律宾共和国联合声明

（2007年1月16日）

应菲律宾总统格洛丽亚·马卡帕加尔·阿罗约阁下邀请，中华人民共和国国务院总理温家宝阁下于2007年1月15日至16日对菲律宾进行正式访问。

访问期间，温家宝总理与阿罗约总统就中菲关系和共同关心的国际和地区问题进行了成果丰富、意义深远的讨论。温家宝总理也会见了参议长曼努埃尔·维拉和众议长何塞·德贝内西亚。上述会见是在诚挚友好的气氛中进行的。

两国领导人重申了1975年中菲《建交公报》有关原则，并重申了对两国于2000年5月14日签署的关于21世纪双边合作框架《联合声明》和2005年4月28日胡锦涛主席访菲期间发表的《联合声明》所作的承诺。

两国领导人对双方在政治、安全、防务、经济、贸易、旅游、农业渔业、能源、矿业、社会文化、卫生、教育及其他领域开展合作与对话所取得的进展表示满意，并重申中菲关系正处于伙伴关系的黄金时期。双方也认为中菲关系的发展给两国和两国人民带来了实实在在的利益，为促进本地区的和平、稳定与繁荣作出了积极贡献。

两国领导人同意进一步深化中菲致力于和平与发展的战略性合作关系。为此，他们指示两国外交部制定共同行动计划，对两国各领域战略性合作进行规划。双方同意该共同行动计划应与两国各自的发展战略和区域合作进程保持一致。

温家宝总理和阿罗约总统高兴地看到，两国高层互访和民间交往持续增多，使得两国和两国人民相互了解加深，关系更加密切。双方同意鼓励开展更多交流，特别是加强两国议员、地方政府官员、青年、企业家、教育工作者、新闻从业人员和艺术家之间的交流。

双方认为，根据目前双边贸易的增长速度，对在2010年前实现300亿美元的贸易额目标表示乐观。双方同意进一步扩大双边贸易额、优化贸易结构、促进相互投资、并积极开拓经济合作的新领域。

双方宣布，《中华人民共和国政府和菲律宾共和国政府关于扩大和深化双边经济贸易合作的框架协定》正式签署，中菲双边经贸合作将在未来10年不断加强。双方将进一步推动在农业、渔业、公共工程与基础设施、住房、矿业、能源、制造业、纺织与服装、工业园与经济开发区、旅游、远程教育、集装箱检查设备和贸易促进等方面的合作。

两国领导人共同见证了各领域合作多项协议的签署。

双方承诺在涉及国家主权和领土完整的重大问题上相互理解、相互支持。菲律宾重申坚持一个中国政策，支持中国政府为实现国家统一所作的努力，支持并赞赏中国为和平解决台湾问题所作的努力。

两国领导人对中国与东盟关系16年来的发展表示满意。双方同意按照《中国—东盟纪念峰会联合声明》的有关精神，把中国—东盟关系推向更高的水平。

双方相信，东盟与中国不久将同意通过具体行动和项目来落实2002年签署的《南海各方行为宣言》，并致力于制定《南海地区行为准则》。双方认为，南海三方联合海洋地震工作可以成为本地区合作的一个示范。双方同意，可以探讨将下一阶段的三方合作提升到更高水平，以加强本地区建立互信的良好势头。

阿罗约总统对在宿务举行的第七次中、日、韩领导人会议表示欢迎，相信这将促进东北亚国家间的相互信任与互利合作。

两国领导人欢迎重启六方会谈，呼吁有关各方继续致力于和平解决朝鲜半岛核问题。

双方同意进一步加强在东盟—中日韩、东盟地区论坛、东亚峰会、亚太经合组织、亚欧会议、联合国、世界贸易组织及其他地区和多边场合中的协调与配合。

温家宝总理对于他和代表团在访菲期间受到热情欢迎与接待表示感谢。阿罗约总统感谢中方支持菲律宾在东盟与中国、东盟与中、日、韩领导人会议以及东亚峰会上履行主席国工作。

二〇〇七年一月十六日于马尼拉

Joint Statement of the People's Republic of China and the Republic of the Philippines

(16 January 2007)

At the invitation of Her Excellency President Gloria Macapagal Arroyo, His Excellency Premier Wen Jiabao of the State Council of the People's Republic of China paid an official visit to the Philippines on 15–16 January 2007.

During the visit, Premier Wen Jiabao and President Arroyo held fruitful and meaningful discussions on China–Philippine relations as well as regional and international issues of mutual interest. Premier Wen Jiabao also met with Senate President Manuel Villar and House Speaker Jose de Venecia. The meetings were conducted in a friendly atmosphere.

The two leaders reaffirmed the principles enshrined in the 1975 Joint Communiqué of the Government of the People's Republic of China and the Government of the Republic of the Philippines, which established diplomatic relations between them. They also reiterated their commitment to the Joint Statement on the Framework of Bilateral Cooperation in the 21st Century signed between the two sides on 14 May 2000 and the Joint Statement issued during President Hu Jintao's visit to the Philippines on 28 April 2005.

Noting with satisfaction the progress of their cooperation and dialogue in the political, security, defense, economic, trade, tourism, agriculture and fisheries, energy, mining, socio-cultural, health, education, and other fields, the two leaders reaffirmed that China–Philippine relations are at a golden age of partnership. They also acknowledged that the development of China–Philippine relations had brought real benefits to the two countries and peoples and contributed to peace, stability and prosperity in the region.

The two leaders agreed to take further steps to deepen the strategic and cooperative relationship for peace and development between China and the Philippines. Towards this end, they directed their respective foreign ministries to formulate a Joint Action Plan that will guide strategic cooperation in all fields. They agreed that the Joint Action Plan should be consistent with the respective development strategies of the two countries and the regional cooperation process.

Premier Wen and President Arroyo expressed pleasure that the growing number of high-level visits and people-to-people exchanges has led to better understanding and closer relations between the two countries and peoples. They agreed to encourage more exchanges, especially among parliamentarians, local government officials, youth, entrepreneurs, educators, media practitioners, and artists.

Both sides expressed optimism that given the current growth rate of bilateral trade, the US$30 billion trade volume targeted for 2010 will be attained earlier. Both sides agreed to further expand trade volume, improve trade structure, promote mutual investments and actively explore new areas of economic cooperation.

They declared that with the signing of the Framework Agreement on Expanding and Deepening Bilateral Economic and Trade Cooperation Between the Government of the People's Republic of China and the Government of the Republic of the Philippines, bilateral economic and trade cooperation would intensify within the next ten years. The two sides will further enhance cooperation in the sectors of agriculture, fisheries, public works and infrastructure, housing, mining, energy, manufacturing, textiles and garments, industrial parks and economic development zones, tourism, ICT-based education, container inspection machines, and trade promotion.

The two leaders witnessed the signing of agreements in various areas of cooperation.

The two sides committed themselves to mutual understanding and mutual support with respect to major issues bearing on state sovereignty and territorial integrity. The Philippines reaffirmed its adherence to the One-China policy and support for the Chinese Government's efforts for national reunification. The Philippines supports and appreciates China's efforts to resolve the Taiwan issue peacefully.

The two leaders expressed satisfaction with China-ASEAN relations in the past 16 years. They agreed to advance China-ASEAN relations to a higher level in the spirit of the Joint Statement of China-ASEAN Commemorative Summit.

They expressed confidence that ASEAN and China would soon agree on activities and projects to implement the 2002 Declaration on the Conduct of Parties in the South China Sea and work towards the conclusion of a Regional Code of Conduct in the South China Sea. They acknowledged that the tripartite Joint Marine Seismic Undertaking in the South China Sea serves as a model for cooperation in the region. They agreed that possible next steps for cooperation among the three parties should be explored to bring collaboration to a higher level and increase the momentum of trust and confidence in the region.

President Arroyo welcomed the seventh "Plus Three Summit" among China, Japan and the Republic of Korea in Cebu and expressed confidence that it would foster greater mutual trust, mutual benefit and cooperation among the countries in Northeast Asia.

The two leaders welcomed the resumption of the Six-Party Talks and urged the concerned parties to continue working towards a peaceful resolution of the nuclear issue in the Korean Peninsula.

They agreed to further strengthen their coordination and cooperation in the ASEAN+3, ARF, EAS, APEC, ASEM, UN, WTO and other regional and multilateral fora.

Premier Wen Jiabao expressed appreciation for the warm welcome and hospitality accorded to him and his delegation throughout their official visit to the Philippines. President Arroyo thanked Premier Wen for China's support during the Philippine Chairmanship of the ASEAN-China, ASEAN+3 and the East Asia Summits.

中华人民共和国与菲律宾共和国联合声明

（2011年9月1日）

应中华人民共和国主席胡锦涛邀请，菲律宾总统贝尼尼奥·阿基诺于8月30日至9月3日对中国进行国事访问。除北京外，阿基诺总统将前往上海和福建访问。双方认为此访对中菲两国关系发展具有里程碑意义。

在京期间，胡锦涛主席和阿基诺总统举行了富有成果的会谈。全国人大常委会委员长吴邦国和国务院总理温家宝分别会见了阿基诺总统。两国领导人积极评价了中菲建交36年来双边关系取得的发展。双方重申将在相互尊重、平等互利的基础上，共同致力于推动中菲战略性合作关系长期稳定发展。双方也同意2009年10月29日签署的《战略性合作共同行动计划》将继续指导双方各领域合作。菲律宾重申坚持一个中国政策。

两国领导人对访问期间签署的各项协议表示欢迎，相信这些协议将进一步加强双方在贸易、经济技术、旅游、海上互联互通、媒体、体育、文化和信息等领域的合作。

双方认为，中菲两国是友好近邻，两国传统友谊绵延数百年，贸易合作富有活力，民间往来持续不断。两国领导人承诺将继续巩固中菲致力于和平与发展的战略性合作关系。

两国领导人认为现有的中菲双边对话机制对增进了解、拓展合作、加强两国关系具有重要意义。

双方同意继续扩大两国领导人、政府部门负责人、议员以及司法、防务和地方政府官员间的定期交流和互访。双方还同意加强两国青年、企业家、教育工作者、媒体工作者和艺术家间的交流，以增进两国和两国人民间的相互了解和信任。

双方认为，在当前世界经济不稳定、新兴发展中国家对促进可持续发展的作用不断扩大的形势下，拓展和加强中菲经贸合作具有重要现实意义。两国领导人认为《中菲经贸合作五年发展规划(2012—2016)》为两国在以下领域开展合作勾画了蓝图：农业和渔业、基础设施与公共工程、矿业、能源、信息通信技术、加工制造业、旅游业、工程服务和林业。

双方同意进一步扩大双边贸易额，并提出到2016年将双边贸易额提高到600亿美元的目标。双方还同意优化贸易结构，扩大相互投资，探索新能源、可再生能源、航运和港口等新的经济合作领域。

中方支持菲律宾政府提出的公私伙伴计划，愿鼓励合格的中国公司参与该计划框架下的项目竞标。

菲律宾感谢中方在菲发展经济、加强农业和基础设施建设方面给予的帮助。

双方将探讨建立联结中菲的海上高速路，为双边经贸关系注入新的活力，这将成为落实中国—东盟互联互通倡议的补充和支持。

两国领导人欢迎两国地方省市缔结友好关系，认为这可以成为两国和两国人民增进相互了解与友谊的桥梁。

两国领导人同意将2012—2013年定为“中菲友好交流年”。双方对两国人员往来已突破100万人次表示满意，提出到2016年将人员往来翻一番达到200万人次的目标。双方愿努力增加航空运力推动实现这一目标。

双方积极评价两国根据现有协议在司法和执法领域开展的良好交流与合作。双方将积极履行法律程序，推动《中菲刑事司法协助条约》尽快生效，愿探讨早日启动两国《移管被判刑人协定》的谈判，重申愿在打击包括贩毒和人口贩卖在内的跨国犯罪活动方面加强合作。

两国领导人就海上争议交换了意见，认为不应让海上争议影响到两国友好合作大局。两国领导人重申将通过和平对话处理争议，继续维护地区和平、安全与稳定以及营造良好的经济增长环境。双方重申尊重和遵守中国与东盟国家于2002年签署的《南海各方行为宣言》。

两国领导人对20年来中国—东盟关系取得的进展表示满意，重申在讨论亚洲未来地区架构的性质和形式时应坚持以东盟为主导的原则。

双方同意进一步加强在联合国、亚太经合组织、亚欧会议、世界贸易组织、联合国气候变化会议及其他地区和多边组织的协调与配合。

二〇一一年九月一日于北京

Joint Statement of the People's Republic of China and the Republic of the Philippines

(1 September 2011)

1. At the invitation of President Hu Jintao of the People's Republic of China, Philippine President Benigno S. Aquino III is undertaking a State Visit to China from 30 August to 3 September 2011. From Beijing, President Aquino is proceeding to Shanghai and Fujian. Both sides agreed that this is a milestone visit in the development of China-Philippines bilateral relations.

2. President Hu and President Aquino had a fruitful meeting. H.E. Wu Bangguo, Chairman of the Standing Committee of the National People's Congress and H.E. Wen Jiabao, Premier of the State Council, met with President Aquino respectively. The two leaders shared a positive assessment of the development of China-Philippines relations in the last 36 years since the establishment of diplomatic relations on 9 June 1975. They reiterated their commitment to jointly pursue a long-term and stable relationship of strategic cooperation on the basis of mutual respect, equality and mutual benefit. They also agreed that the Joint Action Plan for Strategic Cooperation signed by the two sides on 29 October 2009 will continue to guide cooperation in all fields. The Philippines reaffirmed its adherence to the one China policy.

3. The two leaders welcomed the various agreements signed by the two sides in the course of the visit, expressing confidence that these will further strengthen bilateral cooperation in the fields of, among others, trade, economic and technical cooperation, tourism, nautical connectivity, media, sports, culture and information.

4. Acknowledging that the two countries are close neighbors bound by time-honored friendship, vibrant trade and sustained people-to-people contacts over the centuries, the two leaders committed themselves to continue strengthening the strategic and cooperative relationship for peace and development between China and the Philippines.

5. The two leaders affirmed the importance of the existing China–Philippines bilateral dialogue mechanisms in enhancing understanding, broadening cooperation and striving for a stronger relationship.

6. The two sides agreed to increase regular high-level exchanges, visits and meetings between leaders, cabinet members, legislators, judicial offcials, defense and military officials and local government officials. They also agreed to encourage more exchanges among youth, entrepreneurs, educators, media practitioners and artists, among others, to strengthen better understanding and mutual trust between the two countries and peoples.

7. The two leaders agreed that with the current instability of the global economy and the growing role of emerging and developing economies in sustaining growth, it is highly practical and important for China and the Philippines to broaden and strengthen their economic and trade cooperation. The two leaders affirmed that the China–Philippines Five-Year Development Program for Trade and Economic Cooperation (2012–2016) serves as the blueprint for future efforts in the following sectors: agriculture and fishery, infrastructure and public works, mining, energy, information and communications technology (ICT), processing and manufacturing, tourism, engineering services and forestry.

8. Both sides agreed to further expand the volume of bilateral trade and accordingly set a target of US$ 60 billion in total two-way trade by 2016. They also agreed to improve the trade structure, promote a more vigorous exchange of investments and explore new areas of economic cooperation in the fields of, among others, new and renewable energy, shipping and ports.

9. China affirmed its support for the Public Private Partnership (PPP) program of the Philippine government and committed to encourage its qualified companies to participate in the competitive bidding processes of the program.

10. The Philippines expressed appreciation to China for its development

assistance to various economic, agricultural and infrastructure projects in the Philippines.

11. The two sides will discuss the establishment of a nautical highway that will infuse new energy to bilateral trade and economic activities between the two countries which complement and support the connectivity between China and ASEAN.

12. The two leaders welcomed the increasing number of twining arrangements between their cities and provinces and stressed the role of such arrangements as bridges of promoting mutual understanding and friendship between the two countries and peoples.

13. The two leaders agreed that 2012–2013 will be the "China–Philippines Years of Friendly Exchanges" . The two leaders expressed satisfaction that two-way tourist arrivals have breached the one-million mark. They agreed to adopt the goal of doubling two-way tourist arrivals to two million by 2016. They expressed optimism that an expansion of capacity entitlements in air services will contribute to the attainment of this goal.

14. Noting that the two countries have active judicial and law-enforcement exchanges and cooperation through existing bilateral agreements, the two leaders agreed to fulfill the legal procedures to expedite the entry into force of the Treaty between the People's Republic of China and the Republic of the Philippines Concerning Mutual Legal Assistance in Criminal Matters, and begin negotiations at an early date for a bilateral agreement on Transfer of Sentenced Persons. They reaffirmed their commitment to strengthening cooperation in combating transnational crimes, including drug trafficking and trafficking in persons.

15. Both leaders exchanged views on the maritime disputes and agreed not to let the maritime disputes affect the broader picture of friendship and cooperation between the two countries. The two leaders reiterated their commitment to addressing the disputes through peaceful dialogue, to maintain continued regional peace, security, stability and an environment and conducive to economic progress. Both leaders reaffirmed their commitments to respect and abide by the Declaration on the Conduct of Parties in the South China Sea signed by China and the ASEAN member countries in 2002.

16. The two leader expressed satisfaction with the progress of China-ASEAN relations in the past 20 years and affirmed the principle of ASEAN centrality in the discussion on the nature and shape of a future regional architecture in Asia.

17. The two leaders expressed their willingness to further strengthen cooperation in the United Nations, Asia-Pacific Economic Cooperation, Asia-Europe Meeting, World Trade Organization, United Nations Climate Change Conference and other regional and multilateral organizations.

中华人民共和国与菲律宾共和国联合声明

（2016年10月21日）

一、应中华人民共和国主席习近平邀请，菲律宾共和国总统罗德里戈·罗亚·杜特尔特于2016年10月18日至21日对中华人民共和国进行了国事访问。

二、访问期间，习近平主席同杜特尔特总统在亲切友好气氛中进行了富有成果的会谈，就双边关系及共同关心的国际和地区问题深入交换了意见。国务院总理李克强、全国人大常委会委员长张德江分别与杜特尔特总统举行了会见。国务院副总理张高丽与杜特尔特总统共同出席了中菲经贸合作论坛开幕式并致辞。

三、双方认为，中菲人民之间传统友谊历史悠久。双方同意两国人民之间的相互理解和友谊至关重要，将共同致力于巩固两国人民之间的传统友谊。

四、双方同意自建交以来中菲关系发展顺利，在诸多合作领域取得显著进展，造福了两国和两国人民。

五、双方同意进一步丰富建立于相互尊重、真诚、平等和互惠互利原则基础上的双边关系，这也有利于本地区的和平、稳定与繁荣。

六、双方重申了1975年中菲建交公报及其他文件所包含的原则，其中包括通过和平方式解决争端的原则和菲方恪守一个中国政策。

七、双方重申了两国伙伴关系和对争取有益于两国人民的可持续发展、包容性增长的共同愿望，一致认为此访具有里程碑式意义，将为两国关系注入新动力，给两国人民带来实实在在的好处。双方将携手努力，推动两国致力于和平与发展的战略性合作关系健康稳定发展。

八、双方认为保持高层交往对促进双边关系全面发展具有重要意义。

九、双方欢迎访问期间签署的诸多合作协议和谅解备忘录（见附件）。

十、双方表达了在诸如教育、金融、海关、体育等其他领域签署合作协定和谅解备忘录的意愿。

十一、双方重申现有中菲双边对话机制对增进理解、拓展合作、增强双边关系的重要性，同意恢复两国外交磋商、领事磋商、经贸联委会、防务安全磋商、农业联委会、科技联委会及其他双边对话机制。

十二、双方愿鼓励两国高级别政府团组、地方政府、立法机构、政党、民间组织互访，增进沟通交流。

十三、菲方欢迎中方提议中国驻达沃总领馆将尽快开馆。双方将基于国际实践和互惠原则，并遵循1975年建交公报的原则对双边外交馆舍的最急迫问题优先作出妥善安排。

十四、双方认识到共同行动打击跨国犯罪的必要性，两国相关部门将根据共同认可的安排，加强在打击电信诈骗、网络诈骗、计算机犯罪、毒品贩卖、人口贩卖、濒危野生动植物及其制品走私等跨国犯罪方面的交流合作。

十五、双方反对任何形式的恐怖主义和暴力极端主义，将在包括信息交流、能力建设等方面进行合作，以共同防范和应对恐怖主义和暴力极端主义威胁。

十六、中方理解并支持菲政府致力于打击毒品犯罪的努力。双方认识到毒品问题给两国人民健康、安全和福祉构成严重威胁，同意加强信息共享，在打击毒品犯罪、预防教育、戒毒康复等方面分享知识技术。

十七、为加大禁毒行动力度，双方同意建立专案侦办和情报搜集领域的联合行动机制。菲方感谢中方在人员培训和捐赠毒品查缉检验设备等方面向菲禁毒工作提供援助。

十八、双方承诺根据公认的国际法原则，包括1982年《联合国海洋法公约》，加强两国海警部门间合作，应对南海人道主义、环境问题和海上紧急事件，如海上人员、财产安全问题和维护保护海洋环境等。

十九、双方同意继续探讨商签移管被判刑人条约。

二十、双方同意两军关系是两国关系重要组成部分。为增进互信，双方同意执行好《中菲防务合作谅解备忘录》，加强在人道主义援助、减灾、维和领域的交流合作。

二十一、双方一致认为双边经济合作发展强劲并仍存在增长空间。双方承诺将通过开展《关于加强双边贸易、投资和经济合作的谅解备忘录》框架下的活动发挥互补优势，不断促进贸易、投资和经济合作，加强两国在优先领域的经济关系。

二十二、双方认识到《中菲经贸合作五年发展规划（2011—2016年）》所取得的经济和社会成就，并通过签署《关于编制中菲经济合作发展规划的谅解备忘录》表达续签《发展规划》的承诺。

二十三、双方在减贫领域具有共同意愿，鉴此同意加强减贫实践交流和项目合作。

二十四、双方表达了在包括基础设施投资、基础设施项目建设、工业产能等领域共同开展务实合作的意愿。双方同意共同实施的基础设施合作需服从适当招标程序、透明度，符合两国相关国内法律法规和通行的国际实践。

二十五、双方将在优惠贷款、优惠出口买方信贷、债券、贷款、投资、证券及其他双方同意的如开发性专项贷款等领域加强金融合作。双方愿在亚投行和其他国际和地区银行框架下加强合作。

二十六、双方愿扩大双边贸易和投资本币结算，协调积极推进清迈倡议多边化等区域金融合作和双边本币互换安排。中方欢迎菲央行有意参与中国银行间债券市场。

二十七、双方承诺扩大在包括农业科技和基础设施、农业贸易、灌溉、适应和减缓气候变化、遵循动植物卫生标准等领域的合作。

二十八、双方同意加强在动植物检验检疫方面的合作，菲方欢迎中方宣布恢复相关菲企业对华出口香蕉、菠萝许可，将继续进口符合中方标准的设施包装的热蒸处理芒果。

二十九、双方愿共同努力，推动双方在优质杂交水稻种子、农业基础设施、农业机械、进一步发挥中菲农技中心作用及其他同意的领域的合作。中方承诺支持菲方遵照国内法律提升粮食生产能力、培训农业技术人员、发展农渔业和能力建设的努力。

三十、中方愿积极支持于紧急状态下在东盟与中日韩大米储备机制下向菲提供紧急粮食援助。

三十一、中方愿协助菲建立科研产业体系，帮助菲开展科技培训。双方愿探讨共建技术转移中心、联合实验室和科技资源共享平台的可能性。

三十二、双方认识到过去几年双向游客增长状况，注意到2017年“东盟—中国旅游合作年”的推动势头，同意设立旅游合作增长目标。双方愿鼓励本国公民赴对方国家旅游，探讨航空服务领域可能的增长点，鼓励双方航空公司在中国城市和菲律宾达沃及维萨亚、棉兰老地区城市间开设新航线，助力实现上述旅游合作增长目标。

三十三、双方鼓励两国大学间在研究、创新领域开展实质性交流，加强学术和产学研模式交流合作。中方愿在科学、技术、工程和数学领域对菲增加政府奖学金名额。

三十四、双方同意鼓励中国媒体同菲媒体包括“人民广播公司”开展人员互访、新闻产品互换、设备技术和培训等业务合作。中国新闻主管部门愿同菲总统府新闻部加强交流与合作。

三十五、双方表达了在两国省市间缔结更多友好省市关系的意愿，注意到这种安排将鼓励两国人民间增进了解，释放地方合作潜力。

三十六、双方同意在紧急援助和救灾领域开展合作。

三十七、双方重申推进落实《中菲文化合作协定2015年至2018年执行计划》的重要性，鼓励两国文化机构和团体加强互访。双方愿积极考虑在对方国家设立文化中心。

三十八、双方重视两国人员往来，注意到2017年是菲律宾苏禄苏丹访华600周年，愿举办相关纪念活动。

三十九、双方将探讨在包括信息科技、卫生、海关、研发、教育和其他领域的合作，使两国共同受益。

四十、双方就涉及南海的问题交换了看法。双方重申争议问题不是中菲双边关系的全部。双方就以适当方式处理南海争议的重要性交换了意见。双方重申维护及促进和平稳定、在南海的航行和飞越自由的重要性，根据包括《联合国宪章》和1982年《联合国海洋法公约》在内公认的国际法原则，不诉诸武力或以武力相威胁，由直接有关的主权国家通过友好磋商和谈判，以和平方式解决领土和管辖权争议。

四十一、双方回顾了2002年《南海各方行为宣言》和2016年7月25日于老挝万象通过的中国—东盟外长关于全面有效落实《宣言》的声明。双方承诺全面、有效落实《宣言》，愿共同努力在协商一致基础上早日达成“南海行为准则”。

四十二、双方同意继续商谈建立信任措施，提升互信和信心，并承诺在南海采取行动方面保持自我克制，以免使争议复杂化、扩大化和影响和平与稳定。鉴此，在作为其它机制的补充、不损及其他机制基础上，建立一个双边磋商机制是有益的，双方可就涉及南海的各自当前及其他关切进行定期磋商。双方同意探讨在其他领域开展合作。

四十三、中方支持菲担任2017年东盟轮值主席国。双方对过去25年来中国—东盟对话关系的发展感到满意，重申对地区架构中坚持东盟中心原则的承诺。中方重申支持东盟一体化、东盟共同体建设和东盟为实现“东盟2025：携手前行”愿景文件目标所作的努力。

四十四、双方同意进一步加强在联合国、东盟地区论坛、亚太经合组织、亚欧会议、世界贸易组织、联合国气候变化大会及其他地区和国际组织中的合作。

四十五、双方重申恪守《联合国宪章》宗旨中的主权平等、不干涉、不干预原则，强调共同致力于通过在双方均参与的主要人权机制中开展对话合作来保护和增进人权。

四十六、双方支持通过必要和合理的改革加强联合国的作用，并主张推动落实发展问题、维护发展中国家合法权益、加强发展中国家在国际事务中的发言权和代表性，应成为联合国包括安理会改革的重点，不断增强发展中国家在联合国决策过程中的作用。

四十七、杜特尔特总统对中方给予的热情接待表示感谢。杜特尔特总统邀请习近平主席在方便时访问菲律宾，习近平主席愉快地接受了邀请。杜特尔特总统也表示欢迎中方领导人出席2017年东亚合作领导人系列会议。

附件：

签署合作文件清单

一、《中国政府和菲律宾政府经济技术合作协定》

二、《中国国家发展改革委和菲律宾国家经济发展署关于开展产能与投资合作的谅解备忘录》

三、《中国国家发展改革委与菲律宾交通部、公共工程与公路部关于交通基础设施合作项目清单的谅解备忘录》

四、《中国商务部和菲律宾贸工部签署关于加强贸易、投资和经济合作的谅解备忘录》

五、《中国商务部和菲律宾国家经济发展署关于编制中菲经济合作发展规划的谅解备忘录》

六、《中国商务部和菲律宾财政部关于支持开展重大项目可行性研究的谅解备忘录》

七、《中国农业部与菲律宾农业部农业合作行动计划（2017—2019）》

八、《中国国新办和菲律宾总统府新闻部关于新闻、信息交流、培训和其他事宜的备忘录》

九、《中国质检总局和菲律宾农业部关于动植物检验检疫合作谅解备忘录》

十、《中国海警局和菲律宾海岸警卫队关于建立海警海上合作联合委员会的谅解备忘录》

十一、《中国国家旅游局和菲律宾旅游部旅游合作谅解备忘录执行计划（2017—2022）》

十二、《中国公安部禁毒局和菲律宾肃毒局合作议定书》

十三、《中国进出口银行和菲律宾财政部融资合作备忘录》

Joint Statement of the People's Republic of China and the Republic of the Philippines

(21 October 2016)

1. At the invitation of H.E. President Xi Jinping of the People's Republic of China, H.E. President Rodrigo Roa Duterte of the Republic of the Philippines undertook a state visit to China from 18 to 21 October 2016.

2. During the visit, President Xi Jinping and President Rodrigo Roa Duterte had a fruitful meeting in an amicable and friendly atmosphere and conducted in-depth exchanges on bilateral relations as well as international and regional issues of shared interest. H.E. Li Keqiang, Premier of the State Council, and H.E. Zhang Dejiang, Chairman of the Standing Committee of the National People's Congress, met with President Rodrigo Roa Duterte. H.E. Zhang Gaoli, Vice Premier of the State Council, and President Rodrigo Roa Duterte also attended the opening ceremony of China-Philippines Economic and Investment Forum and delivered remarks.

3. Both sides acknowledge the centuries-old bonds of friendship of the two peoples. Both sides agree that the mutual understanding and friendship of the two peoples are important. Both sides will make concerted efforts to cement the traditional friendship of the two peoples.

4. Both sides agree that since the establishment of diplomatic relations, China-Philippines relations have enjoyed smooth development and remarkable progress in many areas of cooperation which have benefited both countries and peoples.

5. Both sides commit to further enrich China-Philippines bilateral relations,

founded on mutual respect, sincerity, equality and mutual benefit, which is conducive to regional peace, stability and prosperity.

6. Both sides reaffirm the principles contained in the China-Philippines Joint Communique of 1975 and other documents, whose principles include, among others, the principle of the peaceful settlement of all disputes and the Philippines' adherence to the One-China Policy.

7. Both sides affirm their partnership and their common aspiration to achieve sustainable development and inclusive growth that will benefit the peoples of both countries. Both sides agree that this is a milestone visit which will infuse new energy to bring tangible benefits to the peoples of the two countries. Both sides will work together to pursue the sound and stable development of the strategic and cooperative relationship for peace and development.

8. Both sides acknowledge the great importance of maintaining high-level exchanges in promoting the all-around development of bilateral relations.

9. Both sides welcome the signing during the visit of various agreements and Memoranda of Understanding (MOU), as listed in the Annex.

10. Both sides express interest in finalizing agreements and MOUs in such areas as education, finance, customs and sports.

11. Both sides affirm the importance of existing China-Philippines bilateral dialogue mechanisms in enhancing understanding, broadening cooperation and striving for a stronger relationship. Both sides agree to resume the Foreign Ministry Consultations, Consular Consultations, Joint Commission on Economic and Trade Cooperation, Annual Defense Security Talks, Joint Committee on Agriculture, Joint Committee on Science and Technology, and other bilateral dialogue mechanisms.

12. Both sides will encourage exchange of visits of high-ranking governmental delegations and leaders at the local level, legislative organs, political parties, and civil organizations, and increase interactions and communications.

13. The Philippines welcomes China's proposal to open a Consulate-General of the People's Republic of China in Davao in due course. Proper arrangements for the diplomatic premises in both countries will be made in the spirit of the

1975 Joint Communique, on the basis of international practice and reciprocity, with priority for the most immediate concerns.

14. Realizing that coordinated action is necessary to combat transnational crimes, the two countries' relevant agencies, subject to mutually agreed arrangements, will enhance cooperation and communication to combat transnational crimes, including telecommunications fraud, on-line fraud, cybercrimes, drug trafficking, trafficking in persons and wildlife trafficking.

15. Both sides oppose violent extremism and terrorism in all forms and will cooperate in the fields of information exchange, capacity building, among others, in order to jointly prevent and address the threat of violent extremism and terrorism.

16. China understands and supports Philippine Government's efforts in fighting against illicit drugs. Realizing that the problem of illicit drugs poses severe threats to the health, safety and welfare of the peoples of both countries, both sides agree to enhance exchange of intelligence, know-how and technology sharing on fighting against drug crimes, preventive education and rehabilitation facilities.

17. To further strengthen the efforts to fight against illicit drugs, both sides agree to establish operation mechanism for joint investigation on special cases and intelligence collection purposes. The Philippines thanks China for its offer of assistance in personnel training and donation of drug detection, seizure, and testing equipment to aid in the fight against illicit drugs.

18. Both sides commit to enhance cooperation between their respective Coast Guards, to address maritime emergency incidents, as well as humanitarian and environmental concerns in the South China Sea, such as safety of lives and property at sea and the protection and preservation of the marine environment, in accordance with universally recognized principles of international law including the 1982 UNCLOS.

19. Both sides agree to continue discussions with a view to signing a bilateral agreement on Transfer of Sentenced Persons.

20. Both sides agree that bilateral defense and military cooperation are important components of bilateral relations. To enhance mutual trust, both

sides agree to implement the China-Philippines MOU on Defense Cooperation, through exchanges and cooperation in areas of humanitarian assistance and disaster alleviation and peacekeeping operations.

21. Both sides agree that bilateral economic cooperation remains strong, but has room for growth. Both sides commit to enhance economic relations in the priority sectors of the two countries by leveraging their complementarity and continuously promoting trade, investment and economic cooperation, through the activities identified under the MOU on Strengthening Bilateral Trade, Investment and Economic Cooperation.

22. Both sides acknowledge the mutual economic and social benefits gained from the Five Year Development Program for Trade and Economic Cooperation (2011-2016), and announced their commitment to its renewal through the Memorandum of Understanding on the Formulation of the Development Program for Economic Cooperation.

23. Both sides identify poverty alleviation as their shared aspiration, and agree to exchange best practices and cooperate in projects in this regard.

24. Both sides express willingness to jointly undertake practical cooperation including infrastructure investment, infrastructure project construction and industrial production capacity. Both sides agree that infrastructure cooperation which are jointly undertaken will be subject to proper procurement process, transparency and in compliance with relevant domestic laws and regulations and international practices.

25. Both sides will develop financial cooperation including in areas such as concessional loans, preferential buyer's credit, bonds issuance, loans, investments, securities, and others as mutually agreed upon including special loans for development. Both sides will strengthen cooperation in the Asian Infrastructure Investment Bank (AIIB) and other multilateral and regional development banks.

26. Both sides express willingness to expand the local currency settlement of bilateral trade and investment, and to coordinate to actively promote the regional financial cooperation which includes the multilateralization of Chiang Mai Initiative (CMIM) and bilateral swap arrangements (BSA). China welcomes

the interest of Bangko Sentral ng Pilipinas (BSP) in participating in the Chinese Interbank Bond Market.

27. Both sides commit to expand cooperation in agriculture, particularly in such areas as (i) agricultural technology and infrastructure;(ii) agricultural trade;(iii) irrigation;(iv) climate change adaption and mitigation and (v) compliance with animal and plant sanitary standards.

28. Both sides agree to strengthen cooperation on animal and plant inspection and quarantine. The Philippines welcomes China's announcement to restore permits of relevant Philippine enterprises that export bananas and pineapples to China, and continue to import vapor heat treated mangoes which were packed in facilities that comply with standards set by China.

29. Both sides will undertake joint efforts to promote cooperation in the fields of high quality hybrid rice seeds, agriculture infrastructure, agricultural machinery, further develop the role of the Sino-Phil Center for Agricultural Technology, and other mutually agreed upon areas. China commits support for the Philippines' effort to improve its food production capacity, training of agricultural technical professionals, and agricultural and fisheries industry development and capacity building, subject to domestic laws.

30. China expresses readiness to support Philippine requests for assistance under the framework of the ASEAN Plus Three Emergency Rice Reserve (APTERR) in times of emergency.

31. China expresses readiness to provide assistance to the Philippines in building scientific research industrial system and in science and technology training. Both sides are willing to explore the possibility of jointly building technology transfer centers, joint laboratories, and science and technology resources sharing platforms.

32. Recognizing the growing two-way tourist arrivals in the past few years and noting momentum that will be driven by the "ASEAN-China Year of Tourism" in 2017, both sides agree to set the goal of intensifying tourism cooperation. Both sides will encourage their citizens to travel to each other's country, explore the possible increase in capacity entitlements in air services, and encourage airlines to open new flights between Philippine cities, including

Davao City and other cities in Visayas and Mindanao, and Chinese cities, which will contribute to the realization of this objective.

33. Both sides encourage the universities of the two countries to promote meaningful exchanges in the field of research and innovation and to strengthen academic exchanges and the model of university-research-industry communications and cooperation. China expresses readiness to increase allocation of Chinese Government Scholarship for the Philippines in the areas of science, technology, engineering and mathematics.

34. Both sides agree to encourage mutual visits of media personnel, exchange of media products, cooperation in facilities, technologies and training between Chinese media and Philippine media including the People's Broadcasting Corporation. The competent media authority of China is willing to enhance exchanges and cooperation with the Presidential Communication Office of the Philippines.

35. Both sides express interest in increasing twinning agreements between their cities and provinces, noting that these arrangements will encourage mutual understanding between their peoples and tap cooperation potentials at the local level.

36. Both sides agree to cooperate in emergency assistance and disaster relief.

37. Both sides reaffirm the importance of further implementing the "Executive Program of Cultural Agreement between the Philippines and China, 2015-2018" and encouraged their cultural institutions and groups to increase exchange of visits. Both sides will positively consider setting up their respective culture centers in each other's country.

38. Both sides attach importance to people-to-people exchanges between the two countries, noting that 2017 marks 600 years of friendly contacts between the Sultanate of Sulu and China, and the Philippines and China expressed interest in holding relevant commemorative activities.

39. Both sides will explore other areas of bilateral cooperation including in information technology, health, customs cooperation, research and development, education, and other fields that will be mutually beneficial to both countries.

40.Both sides exchange views on issues regarding the South China Sea. Both sides affirm that contentious issues are not the sum total of the China–Philippines bilateral relationship. Both sides exchange views on the importance of handling the disputes in the South China Sea in an appropriate manner. Both sides also reaffirm the importance of maintaining and promoting peace and stability, freedom of navigation in and over-flight above the South China Sea, addressing their territorial and jurisdictional disputes by peaceful means, without resorting to the threat or use of force, through friendly consultations and negotiations by sovereign states directly concerned, in accordance with universally recognized principles of international law, including the Charter of the United Nations and the 1982 UNCLOS.

41. Both sides recall the 2002 Declaration on the Conduct of Parties in the South China Sea (DOC) and the Joint Statement of the Foreign Ministers of ASEAN Member States and China on the Full and Effective Implementation of the DOC adopted in Vientiane on 25 July 2016. Both sides commit to the full and effective implementation of DOC in its entirety, and work substantively toward the early conclusion of a Code of Conduct in the South China Sea (COC) based on consensus.

42. Both sides agree to continue discussions on confidence-building measures to increase mutual trust and confidence and to exercise self-restraint in the conduct of activities in the South China Sea that would complicate or escalate disputes and affect peace and stability. In this regard, in addition to and without prejudice to other mechanisms, a bilateral consultation mechanism can be useful, which will meet regularly on current and other issues of concern to either side on the South China Sea. Both sides also agree to explore other areas of cooperation.

43. China expresses support for the Philippines' chairmanship of ASEAN in 2017. Both sides express satisfaction with the growth of ASEAN–China Dialogue Relations over the past 25 years and affirmed their commitment to the principle of ASEAN centrality in the evolving regional architecture. China affirms support for ASEAN integration, ASEAN Community Building, as well as ASEAN's efforts in realizing ASEAN 2025: Forging Ahead Together.

44. Both sides affirm their continued cooperation in UN, ASEAN Regional

Forum, Asia-Pacific Economic Cooperation, Asia-Europe Meeting, World Trade Organization, UN Climate Change Conference and other regional and multilateral organizations.

45. Both sides reaffirm adherence to sovereign equality, non-intervention, and non-interference enshrined in the UN Charter and reiterate their common commitment for the protection and promotion of human rights through dialogue and cooperation in light of the core human rights instruments to which both countries are parties to.

46. Both sides support the enhancement of the UN's role through necessary and reasonable reforms. Both sides held that pushing for the implementation of development issues, upholding the legitimate rights and interests of developing countries, enhancing the voice and representation of developing countries in international affairs should be the priorities in the reform of the UN, including the Security Council, and increasing the role of developing countries in UN decision-making.

47. President Rodrigo Roa Duterte expressed appreciation for the warm welcome extended by the Chinese side. President Rodrigo Roa Duterte invited President Xi Jinping to visit the Philippines at a convenient time. President Xi Jinping accepted the invitation with pleasure. President Rodrigo Roa Duterte also said that he looked forward to welcoming Chinese leaders to the ASEAN and Related Summits in 2017.

ANNEX

List of Signed Cooperation Documents

1. Agreement on Economic and Technical Cooperation between the Government of the People's Republic of China and the Government of the Republic of the Philippines

2. Memorandum of Understanding between the National Development and Reform Commission of the People's Republic of China and the National Economic and Development Authority of the Republic of the Philippines for Developing Cooperation on Production Capacity and Investment

3. Memorandum of Understanding between the National Development and

Reform Commission of the People's Republic of China and the Department of Transportation and the Department of Public Works and Highways of the Republic of the Philippines on Transportation Infrastructure Cooperation Project List

4. Memorandum of Understanding between the Ministry of Commerce of the Government of the People's Republic of China and the Department of Trade and Industry of the Republic of the Philippines on Strengthening Bilateral Trade, Investment and Economic Cooperation

5. Memorandum of Understanding between the Ministry of Commerce of the People's Republic of China and the National Economic and Development Authority of the Republic of the Philippines on Formulation of the Development Program for Economic Cooperation

6. Memorandum of Understanding between the Ministry of Commerce of the People's Republic of China and the Department of Finance of the Republic of the Philippines on Supporting the Conduct of Feasibility Studies for Major Projects

7. Action Plan on Agricultural Cooperation between the Ministry of Agriculture of the People's Republic of China and the Department of Agriculture of the Republic of the Philippines 2017–2019

8. Memorandum of Agreement between the State Council Information Office of the People's Republic of China and the Presidential Communications Operations Office of the Government of the Republic of the Philippines on News, Information Exchange, Training and for other Purposes

9. Memorandum of Understanding between the General Administration of Quality Supervision Inspection and Quarantine of the People's Republic of China and the Department of Agriculture of the Republic of the Philippines on Cooperation of Animal and Plant Inspection and Quarantine

10. Memorandum of Understanding between the China Coast Guard and the Philippine Coast Guard on the Establishment of a Joint Coast Guard Committee on Maritime Cooperation

11. Implementation Program of the Memorandum of Understanding on Tourism Cooperation between the National Tourism Administration of the

People's Republic of China and the Department of Tourism of the Republic of the Philippines 2017–2022

12. Protocol on Cooperation between the Narcotics Control Bureau of the Ministry of Public Security of the People's Republic of China and the Philippines Drug Enforcement Agency

13. Memorandum of Understanding on Financing Cooperation between the Export-Import Bank of China and the Government of the Republic of the Philippines, represented by the Department of Finance

中华人民共和国和越南
社会主义共和国双边文件

Bilateral Documents between the People's Republic of China and the Socialist Republic of Viet Nam

关于解决中华人民共和国和越南社会主义共和国边界领土问题的基本原则协议

（1993年10月19日）

中华人民共和国政府代表团和越南社会主义共和国政府代表团，根据中越两国高级领导人在一九九一年十一月十日和一九九二年十二月四日联合公报中达成的协议，同意双方在解决边界领土问题时将遵循以下原则：

一、基本原则

1. 通过协商和平解决两国间存在的边界领土问题，把中越边界建设成和平、友好的边界，为在互相尊重主权和领土完整、互不侵犯、互不干涉内政、平等互利与和平共处五项原则基础上发展两国睦邻友好关系作出贡献。

2. 双方同意，加快谈判进程，早日解决两国包括海上和陆地上的边界领土问题。在逐步解决这些问题的过程中，从实际出发，双方商定，目前集中解决陆地边界和北部湾问题。与此同时，继续就海上的问题进行谈判，以便取得一项基本和长久的解决办法。在问题解决前，双方均不采取使争端复杂化的行动，不诉诸武力或以武力相威胁。

3. 双方根据公认的国际法准则并参照国际实践解决边界领土问题。

二、关于陆地边界问题

1. 双方同意以中法签订的一八八七年六月二十六日《续议界务专条》和一八九五年六月二十日《续议界务专条附章》及其所确认或根据其规定制定的各项划界和立碑文件、附图以及按规定所立的界碑为依据，核定中越两国边界线的全部走向。

为进行边界线走向和界碑位置核对工作，中方将向越方提供一比五万比例尺的边界地区素图，双方将据此标明各自主张线并尽快交换。

2. 在核定边界线走向和界碑位置过程中，对经过反复核对后仍然不能就界线走向和界碑位置认识取得一致的地段，双方将共同进行实地勘察，考虑该地区存在的各种情况，本着互谅互让的精神，友好协商，寻求公平合理的解决办法。

3. 经核定边界线后，凡属任何一方超越边界线行使管辖的地区，原则上应无条件归还另一方。对一些个别地区，从便于边界管理出发，双方可通过友好协商，本着互谅互让、公平合理的精神作适当调整。

4. 双方同意，对以河为界的地段，将考虑各种情况并参照国际惯例，通过友好协商解决。

5. 在解决中越陆地边界问题过程中，双方保证严格遵守两国在一九九一年十一月七日签订的《中华人民共和国政府和越南社会主义共和国政府关于处理两国边境事务的临时协定》。

6. 双方同意在两国政府代表团下设立陆地边界联合工作组，核定边界线走向。在解决边界争议地区后，双方共同起草中越边界条约，在该条约经两国全权代表正式签署并生效后，成立双方代表人数相等的联合勘界委员会，根据中越边界条约的规定，会勘边界并树立新的界桩，起草边界议定书，绘制边界条约详细附图，呈交两国政府代表签署。

三、关于划分北部湾

1. 双方同意根据国际海洋法并参照国际实践，通过谈判划分北部湾。

2. 为了达成划分北部湾的协议，双方应按照公平原则并考虑北部湾所有有关情况，以取得一项公平的解决办法。

3. 双方同意，在确立北部湾划界原则后，双方应尽快在两国政府代表团下设立划分北部湾联合工作组，就有关划界的范围、内容、法律基础、有关情况及手段协商一致，确定两国在北部湾的界线，起草划界协定，呈交两国全权代表签署。

本协议于一九九三年十月十九日在河内签订，一式两份，用中文和越文写成，两种文本具有同等效力。

Thỏa thuận về những Nguyên tắc cơ bản giải quyết vấn đề biên giới lãnh thổ giữa Cộng hòa Xã hội chủ nghĩa Việt Nam và Cộng hòa nhân dân Trung Hoa

(1993/10/19)

Theo thỏa thuận của lãnh đạo cấp cao giữa hai nước đã được ghi nhận trong các "Thông cáo chung" ngày 10 tháng 11 năm 1991 và ngày 04 tháng 12 năm 1992 giữa hai nước Việt Nam-Trung Quốc, Đoàn Đại biểu Chính phủ nước Cộng hòa Xã hội chủ nghĩa Việt Nam và đoàn đại biểu Chính phủ nước Cộng hòa Nhân dân Trung Hoa đã thỏa thuận trong khi giải quyết các vấn đề biên giới lãnh thổ, hai bên sẽ tuân thủ những nguyên tắc dưới đây:

I. NGUYÊN TẮC CỞ BẢN

1. Thông qua thương lượng giải quyết hòa bình các vấn đề biên giới lãnh thổ giữa hai nước, nhằm xây dựng đường biên giới Việt Nam-Trung Quốc thành biên giới hòa bình, hữu nghị, góp phần phát triển quan hệ hữu nghị và láng giềng thân thiện giữa hai nước trên cơ sở 5 nguyên tắc: tôn trọng chủ quyền và toàn vẹn lãnh thổ của nhau, không xâm phạm lẫn nhau, không can thiệp vào công việc nội bộ của nhau, bình đẳng cùng có lợi và cùng tồn tại hòa bình.

2. Hai bên đồng ý sẽ đẩy nhanh tiến trình đàm phán, sớm giải quyết các vấn đề biên giới, lãnh thổ bao gồm trên biển và trên bộ. Trong quá trình từng bước giải quyết vấn đề này, xuất phát từ tình hình thực tế hai bên thỏa thuận trước mắt tập trung giải quyết vấn đề biên giới trên bộ và vịnh Bắc Bộ, đồng thời tiếp tục đàm phán về các vấn đề liên quan trên biển để đi đến một giải pháp cơ bản, lâu dài. Trong khi đàm phán giải quyết vấn đề, hai bên đều không tiến hành các hoạt

động làm phức tạp thêm tranh chấp, không dùng vũ lực hoặc đe dọa dùng vũ lực.

3. Hai bên căn cứ vào tiêu chuẩn và nguyên tắc luật pháp quốc tế được công nhận và tham khảo thực tiễn quốc tế để giải quyết các vấn đề biên giới lãnh thổ.

II. VỀ VẤN ĐỀ BIÊN GIỚI TRÊN BỘ

1. Hai bên đồng ý, căn cứ vào Công ước hoạch định biên giới ký giữa Trung Quốc và Pháp ngày 26 tháng 6 năm 1887 và Công ước bổ sung Công ước hoạch định biên giới ngày 20 tháng 6 năm 1895 cùng các văn kiện và bản đồ hoạch định và cắm mốc biên giới kèm theo đã được Công ước và Công ước bổ sung nói trên xác nhận hoặc qui định, cũng như các mốc quốc giới cắm theo qui định, đối chiếu xác định lại toàn bộ đường biên giới trên bộ giữa hai nước Việt Nam-Trung Quốc.

Để tiện cho việc tiến hành công tác đối chiếu đường biên giới, vị trí mốc quốc giới, phía Trung Quốc sẽ cung cấp cho phía Việt Nam bản đồ địa hình khu vực biên giới với tỉ lệ 1/50.000. Hai bên sẽ căn cứ vào đó để vẽ đường biên giới theo chủ trương của mình và sớm trao đổi cho nhau.

2. Trong quá trình đối chiếu xác định hướng đi của đường biên giới, và vị trí mốc quốc giới đối với những đoạn biên giới và vị trí mốc quốc giới, sau khi đã đối chiếu xác định nhiều lần mà vẫn không đi đến nhất trí về đường biên giới thì hai bên sẽ cùng nhau khảo sát thực địa, suy tính đến mọi tình hình tồn tại trong khu vực, với tinh thần thông cảm và nhân nhượng lẫn nhau,thương lượng hữu nghị để tìm giải pháp công bằng hợp lý.

3. Sau khi hai bên dối chiếu xác định lại đường biên giới, phàm những vùng do bất cứ bên nào quản lý vượt quá đường biên giới, về nguyên tắc cần trả lại cho bên kia không điều kiện. Đối với một số vùng cá biệt, để tiện cho việc quản lý biên giới, hai bên có thể thông qua thương lượng hữu nghị điều chỉnh thích hợp theo tinh thần thông cảm và nhân nhượng lẫn nhau, công bằng hợp lý.

4. Đối với những đoạn biên giới đi theo sông suối hai bên đồng ý sẽ tính đến mọi tình hình và tham khảo tập quán quốc tế, thông qua thương lượng hữu nghị để giải quyết.

5. Trong quá trình giải quyết vấn đề biên giới trên bộ giữa Việt Nam và Trung Quốc, hai bên cam kết nghiêm trỉnh tôn trọng " Hiệp định tạm thời giải

quyết công việc trên vùng biên giới hai nước giữa Chính phủ Cộng hòa Xã hội chủ nghĩa Việt Nam và Chính phủ Cộng hòa Nhân dân Trung Hoa “ ký ngày 7 tháng 11 năm 1991.

6. Hai bên nhất trí lập nhóm công tác liên hợp về biên giới trên bộ trực thuộc đoàn đại biểu Chính phủ hai nước để đối chiếu và xác định đường biên giới. Sau khi giải quyết xong các vấn đề vùng đất tranh chấp, hai bên cùng nhau dự thảo Hiệp ước biên giới Việt Nam-Trung Quốc. Sau khi Hiệp ước biên giới này được Đại diện toàn quyền hai nước ký chính thức và bắt đầu có hiệu lực, hai Bên sẽ thánh lập Ủy bân liên hợp khảo sát biên giới với số đại biểu bằng nhau, và căn cứ vào qui định của Hiệp ước biên giới Việt Nam-Trung Quốc, hai bên cùng nhau khảo sát biên giới và cắm các mốc quốc giới mới, dư thảo Nghị định thư biên giới, vẽ bản đồ tường tận theo Hiệp ước biên giới, rồi trình Đại diện Chính phủ hai nước ký kết.

III. VỀ VẤN ĐỀ PHÂN ĐỊNH (DELIMITATION) VỊNH BẮC BỘ

1. Hai bên đồng ý sẽ áp dụng Luật biển quốc tế và tham khảo thực tiễn quốc tế, để tiến hành đàm phán phân định (delimitation) vịnh Bắc Bộ.

2. Nhằm đạt thỏa thuận về phân định vịnh Bắc Bộ, hai bên cần theo nguyên tắc công bằng và tính đến mọi hoàn cảnh hữu quan trong vịnh Bắc Bộ để đi đến một giải pháp công bằng.

3. Hai bên đồng ý, sau khi xác định nguyên tắc phân định vịnh Bắc Bộ, hai bên sẽ sớm thành lập nhóm công tác liên hợp phân định (delimitation) vịnh Bắc Bộ trực thuộc đoàn đại biểu Chính phủ hai nước để bàn về phạm vi, nội dung, cơ sở luật pháp, các hoàn cảnh hữu quan và phương pháp phân định nhằm xác định đường biên giới của hai nước trong vịnh Bắc Bộ, dự thảo Hiệp định phân định (delimitation) vịnh Bắc Bộ, trình Đại diện toàn quyền hai nước ký kết.

Thỏa thuận này ký tại Hà Nội, ngày 19 tháng 10 năm 1993, thành hai bản, mỗi bản bằng tiếng Việt và tiếng Trung Quốc, cả hai văn bản đều có giá trị như nhau.

中华人民共和国和越南社会主义共和国关于新世纪全面合作的联合声明

（2000年12月25日）

中华人民共和国和越南社会主义共和国（以下简称“双方”）是有着悠久传统友好关系的社会主义邻邦。建交50年来，中越关系不断得到巩固和发展。

自1991年两国关系正常化以来，在1991年、1992年、1994年、1995年和1999年两国高层领导会晤期间发表的《联合公报》和《联合声明》所确认的各项原则基础上，两国传统友好、互信、平等、互利关系在各个领域得到迅速发展，各部门、各个级别之间的交往频繁。

1999年2月，两党总书记确定了二十一世纪发展两国关系的16字方针，即“长期稳定、面向未来、睦邻友好、全面合作”。这符合两国人民的根本利益，有利于地区和世界的和平、稳定与发展。

双方重申，继续根据《联合国宪章》的宗旨和原则、和平共处五项原则以及公认的国际关系准则，促进国家关系的全面发展。中国共产党和越南共产党继续在独立自主、完全平等、互相尊重、互不干涉内部事务的原则基础上发展友好合作关系。

为有效落实16字指导方针，在二十一世纪把两国关系不断推向新的发展阶段，双方同意在以下领域加强和扩大合作：

一、保持经常性的高层会晤，为推动两国关系发展增添新的动力；进一步加强两国各部门、群众组织和地方的友好往来和多种形式的交流与合作。

二、加强对两国青年一代进行友好传统的宣传教育；开展两国青少年之间的友好交流与往来，为增进两国人民之间的友谊和互信作出贡献，使两国人民的友谊、互信和合作后继有人，深入发展。

三、根据平等互利、注重实效、优势互补、形式多样、共同发展的原则，继续加强和扩大两国经贸、科技等领域的合作。为此，双方同意在以下领域共同努力：

（一）充分发挥两国政府经济贸易合作委员会在加强两国经贸关系和投资合作方面的作用。通过进一步发挥大公司的主渠道作用、扩大大宗商品贸易、鼓励和支持双方企业开展大型项目合作等多种形式，扩大双方经济、贸易和投资合作。培育良好的市场环境，不断挖掘潜力，确保双边贸易的持续稳定增长；保持稳定的投资政策，为双方企业相互投资创造有利条件；积极贯彻实施《边境贸易协定》，加强协调管理，规范两国边境贸易。

（二）发挥两国政府间科技合作联合委员会的宏观指导和协调作用，促进科技交流与合作，引导和鼓励两国有关政府部门、科研院所、大学和科技型企业在信息、生物和农业、气象、海洋、环境保护、和平利用核能以及双方共同感兴趣的领域开展广泛的科技合作。

（三）积极推动两国农、林、渔业的互利合作，鼓励和支持两国有关企业和部门在农作物、家畜家禽良种培育、农林产品加工、农业机械制造、海洋捕捞、水产养殖等方面加强交流和合作。

（四）加强双方在财政和金融领域以及宏观经济调控方面的交流与合作。

（五）加强交通运输领域的合作，共同发展两国之间的国际铁路客货联运，扩大通往第三国的国际铁路联运，促进人员和商品交流。

（六）鼓励两国邮电部门在通讯网络现代化、应用新技术、开拓新业务等方面加强交流与合作。

（七）扩大旅游合作，鼓励两国旅游部门在管理、宣传、营销、人员培训等方面交流经验，加强合作，并为两国公民和第三国公民赴两国旅游提供便利。

（八）加强双方在环境保护、防灾救灾和气象水文等领域的信息交流合作；共同致力于湄公河流域的开发与合作。

（九）在城市规划、建设、管理、发展，以及人员培训等方面扩大合作，交流经验。

四、继续加强双方在联合国、东盟地区论坛、东亚合作、亚太经合组织、亚欧会议等国际和区域多边领域的合作与配合，推进发展中国家的团结与合作，继续致力于建立公正合理的国际政治经济新秩序，为维护地区和世界和平、稳定与发展作出新贡献。

双方赞赏东盟组织在地区稳定与发展中的积极作用，重申将继续致力于加强东盟国家与中国的睦邻互信伙伴关系，为亚洲特别是东亚的持久稳定和繁荣作出积极的努力。

继续强化两国外交部高级官员年度磋商机制，就双边关系以及双方共同关心的地区和国际问题交换意见。

五、通过开展多层次、多领域的军事交往，增进相互了解和信任，进一步密切两国防务机构和两军之间的关系，扩大安全领域的交流与合作。

六、加强两国文化、体育和新闻媒体的交流与合作，包括增加互访、交流经验、开展人员培训等。

七、扩大在教育领域的合作，包括交换留学生、教师，鼓励和支持双方高等院校、教育部门和研究机构加强直接合作。

八、加强双方在预防和打击各种跨国犯罪方面的合作，以及双方法院、检察院、公安、司法行政等机关的交流与合作，增进双方纪检监察部门在反腐倡廉方面的经验交流。

九、双方一致认为，两国签署《中华人民共和国和越南社会主义共和国陆地边界条约》、《中华人民共和国和越南社会主义共和国关于在北部湾领海、专属经济区和大陆架的划界协定》和《中华人民共和国政府和越南社会主义共和国政府北部湾渔业合作协定》，具有深远的历史意义，将进一步推动两国睦邻友好、全面合作关系在二十一世纪取得更大发展。双方承诺认真履行两国签署的有关协议，积极合作，努力把两国边界建设成为和平、友好、长期稳定的边界。

双方同意，继续维持现有海上问题谈判机制，坚持通过和平谈判，寻求一项双方都能接受的基本和长久的解决办法。在问题解决前，双方本着先易后难的精神，积极探讨在海上，诸如海洋环保、气象水文、减灾防灾等领域开展合作的可能性和措施。与此同时，双方均不采取使争端复杂化或扩大化的行动，不诉诸武力或以武力相威胁。双方对产生的分歧应及时进行磋商，采取冷静和建设性的态度，予以妥善处理；不因分歧而影响两国关系的正常发展。

十、双方再次确认，1991年11月10日、1994年11月22日、1995年12月2日《中越联合公报》和1999年2月27日《中越联合声明》达成的共识：越南方面重申一个中国的政策，越南承认中华人民共和国政府是代表全中国的唯一合法政府，台湾是中国领土不可分割的一部分。越南同台湾只进行非官方经贸往来，绝不同台湾发展官方关系。中国方面对越南方面的上述立场表示理解和赞赏。中国方面重申，台湾问题纯属中国内政，坚决反对与中国建立外交关系的国家同台湾建立任何形式的官方关系，或进行任何具有官方性质的往来。

本《联合声明》于2000年12月25日在北京签署，一式二份，每份均用中文和越文写成，两种文本同等作准。

Tuyên bố chung về hợp tác toàn diện trong thế kỷ mới giữa nước Cộng hòa Xã hội chủ nghĩa Việt Nam và nước Cộng hòa nhân dân Trung Hoa

(2000/12/25)

Nước Cộng hòa Xã hội chủ nghĩa Việt Nam và nước Cộng hòa Nhân dân Trung Hoa (dưới đây gọi tắt là "hai bên") là hai nước láng giềng Xã hội Chủ nghĩa có quan hệ hữu nghị truyền thống lâu đời. Trong 50 năm qua kể từ ngày thiết lập quan hệ ngoại giao, quan hệ Việt-Trung đã không ngừng củng cố và phát triển.

Từ khi bình thường hóa quan hệ hai nước năm 1991, trên cơ sở những nguyên tắc được ghi nhận trong các " Thông cáo chung" năm 1991, năm 1992, năm 1994, năm 1995 và " Tuyên bố chung" năm 1999 nhân các cuộc gặp giữa lãnh đạo cấp cao hai nước, quan hệ hữu nghị truyền thống, tin cậy lẫn nhau, bình đẳng, cùng có lợi giữa hai nước đã phát triển nhanh chóng trên tất cả các lĩnh vực, giao lưu giữa các ngành, các cấp diễn ra thường xuyên.

Tháng 2 năm 1999, Tổng Bí thư hai Đảng đã xác định phương châm 16 chữ phát triển quan hệ hai nước trong thế kỷ 21 là "láng giềng hữu nghị, hợp tác toàn diện, ổn định lâu dài, hướng tới tương lai". Điều này phù hợp với lợi ích căn bản của nhân dân hai nước, có lợi cho hòa bình, ổn định và phát triển ở khu vực và trên thế giới.

Hai bên khẳng định lại, tiếp tục căn cứ theo tôn chỉ và nguyên tắc của Hiến chương Liên Hợp quốc, 5 nguyên tắc cùng tồn tại hòa bình và các nguyên tắc quan hệ quốc tế đã được thừa nhận, thúc đẩy quan hệ hai nước phát triển toàn diện. Đảng Cộng sản Việt Nam và Đảng Cộng sản Trung Quốc tiếp tục phát triển quan hệ hợp tác hữu nghị trên cơ sở các nguyên tắc: độc lập tự chủ, hoàn toàn bình đẳng, tôn trọng lẫn nhau, không can thiệp vào công việc nội bộ của nhau.

Để thực hiện có hiệu quả phương châm chỉ đạo 16 chữ, không ngừng thúc đẩy quan hệ hai nước bước sang một giai đoạn phát triển mới trong thế kỷ 21, hai bên đồng ý tăng cường và mở rộng hợp tác trong các lĩnh vực sau:

I. Duy trì gặp gỡ cấp cao thường xuyên, tạo thêm động lực mới thúc đẩy quan hệ hai nước phát triển; tăng cường hơn nữa tiếp xúc hữu nghị và giao lưu hợp tác dưới nhiều hình thức giữa các ban ngành, các tổ chức quần chúng và các địa phương của hai nước.

II. Tăng cường công tác tuyên truyền, giáo dục đối với thế hệ trẻ hai nước về truyền thống hữu nghị; triển khai trao đổi, giao lưu hữu nghị giữa thanh thiếu niên hai nước, góp phần tăng cường sự tin cậy và tình hữu nghị giữa nhân dân hai nước, làm cho tình hữu nghị, sự tin cậy và hợp tác giữa nhân dân hai nước được kế tục và không ngừng phát triển.

III. Trên cơ sở nguyên tắc bình đẳng, cùng có lợi, coi trọng hiệu quả thực tế, bổ sung ưu thế cho nhau, hình thức đa dạng, cùng nhau phát triển, tiếp tục tăng cường và mở rộng hợp tác trong các lĩnh vực kinh tế thương mại và khoa học kỹ thuật giữa hai nước. Vì vậy, hai bên đồng ý cùng nỗ lực trong các lĩnh vực sau:

1. Phát huy đầy đủ vai trò của ủy ban liên Chính phủ về hợp tác kinh tế thương mại trong việc tăng cường quan hệ kinh tế thương mại và hợp tác đầu tư giữa hai nước. Thông qua nhiều hình thức đa dạng như phát huy hơn nữa vai trò chủ đạo của các công ty lớn, mở rộng buôn bán hàng hóa khối lượng lớn, khuyến khích và ủng hộ các doanh nghiệp hai bên triển khai các dự án hợp tác lớn, mở rộng hợp tác kinh tế, thương mại và đầu tư giữa hai bên. Tạo dựng môi trường kinh doanh tốt đẹp, không ngừng khai thác tiềm năng, đảm bảo mậu dịch giữa hai bên tăng trưởng ổn định, liên tục: duy trì chính sách đầu tư ổn định, tạo điều kiện thuận lợi cho việc đầu tư giữa các doanh nghiệp của hai bên; tích cực quán triệt thực hiện “ Hiệp định về mua bán hàng hóa ở vùng biên giới”, tăng cường phối hợp trong công tác quản lý quy phạm hóa buôn bán biên giới giữa hai nước.

2. Phát huy vai trò điều tiết và chỉ đạo vĩ mô của ủy ban liên Chính phủ về hợp tác khoa học kỹ thuật, thúc đẩy hợp tác và trao đổi về khoa học kỹ thuật, hướng dẫn và khuyến khích các cơ quan hữu quan của Chính phủ, các cơ sở và

viện nghiên cứu khoa học, các trường đại học, các xí nghiệp phục vụ khoa học kỹ thuật của hai nước triển khai rộng rãi hợp tác khoa học kỹ thuật trong các lĩnh vực như thông tin, sinh học, nông nghiệp, khí tượng, hải dương, bảo vệ môi trường, sử dụng năng lượng nguyên tử vào mục đích hòa bình và các lĩnh vực mà hai bên cùng quan tâm.

3. Tích cực thúc đẩy hợp tác cùng có lợi giữa hai nước về nông, lâm, ngư nghiệp, khuyến khích và ủng hộ các xí nghiệp và cơ quan hữu quan của hai nước tăng cường trao đổi và hợp tác trên các mặt như tạo ra các giống cây trồng nông nghiệp, giống gia súc gia cầm tốt, chế biến sản phẩm nông, lâm nghiệp, chế tạo máy móc nông nghiệp, đánh bắt trên biển, nuôi trồng thủy sản.

4. Tăng cường trao đổi và hợp tác trong lĩnh vực tài chính, tiền tệ và điều tiết kinh tế vĩ mô.

5. Tăng cường hợp tác trên lĩnh vực giao thông vận tải, cùng nhau phát triển vận chuyển hành khách, hàng hóa qua tuyến đường sắt quốc tế giữa hai nước, mở rộng đường sắt liên vận quốc tế đến nước thứ ba, thúc đẩy trao đổi nhân viên và hàng hóa.

6. Khuyến khích ngành bưu điện hai nước tăng cường trao đổi và hợp tác trên các mặt hiện đại hóa mạng lưới bưu chính, viễn thông, ứng dụng kỹ thuật mới, khai thác nghiệp vụ mới.

7. Mở rộng hợp tác du lịch, khuyến khích ngành du lịch giữa hai nước tăng cường hợp tác, trao đổi kinh nghiệm trên các mặt như quản lý, quảng cáo tiếp thị, đào tạo nguồn nhân lực và tạo thuận lợi cho công dân hai nước và công dân nước thứ 3 đi du lịch hai nước.

8. Tăng cường hợp tác trao đổi thông tin trên các lĩnh vực như bảo vệ môi trường, phòng chống thiên tai và khí tượng thủy văn; cùng nỗ lực hợp tác và khai thác lưuu vực sông Mê Kông.

9. Mở rộng hợp tác, trao đổi kinh nghiệm trên các mặt như qui hoạch, xây dựng, quản lý, phát triển đô thị và đào tạo nguồn nhân lực.

IV. Hai bên tiếp tục tăng cường hợp tác, phối hợp giữa hai bên tại các diễn đàn đa phương quốc tế và khu vực như Liên hợp quốc, Arf, Hợp tác Đông á, Apec, Asem, thúc đẩy sự đoàn kết và hợp tác giữa các nước đang phát triển, tiếp tục ra sức xây dựng trật tự chính trị, kinh tế quốc tế mới công bằng, hợp lý, có đóng góp mới cho việc bảo vệ hòa bình, ổn định và phát triển ở khu vực và trên thế giới.

Hai bên đánh giá cao vai trò tích cực của tổ chức Asean đối với sự ổn định và phát triển của khu vực, khẳng định lại sẽ tiếp tục dốc sức tăng cường quan hệ láng giềng, đối tác tin cậy giữa các nước Asean với Trung Quốc, nỗ lực tích cực vì ổn định và phồn vinh lâu dài của Châu á, đặc biệt là khu vực Đông á.

Tiếp tục tăng cường cơ chế trao đổi ý kiến hàng năm giữa quan chức cấp cao Bộ Ngoại giao hai nước, trao đổi ý kiến về những vấn đề song phương, khu vực và quốc tế mà hai bên cùng quan tâm.

V. Thông qua việc triển khai qua lại quân sự ở các cấp và các lĩnh vực khác nhau, tăng cường sự hiểu biết và tin cậy lẫn nhau, thắt chặt hơn nữa mối quan hệ giữa các cơ quan quốc phòng và quân đội hai nước, mở rộng trao đổi và hợp tác trong lĩnh vực an ninh.

VI. Tăng cường trao đổi và hợp tác về văn hóa, thể dục thể thao, và các phương tiện thông tin đại chúng, bao gồm tăng cường thăm lẫn nhau, trao đổi kinh nghiệm, triển khai đào tạo nhân lực...

VII. Mở rộng hợp tác trong lĩnh vực giáo dục đào tạo, bao gồm trao đổi lưu học sinh, cán bộ giảng dạy, khuyến khích và ủng hộ các trường đại học, các ngành giáo dục và các cơ sở nghiên cứu của hai bên tăng cường hợp tác trực tiếp.

VIII. Tăng cường hợp tác trong các mặt phòng chống các loại tội phạm xuyên quốc gia cũng như trao đổi và hợp tác giữa các cơ quan tư pháp, công an, tòa án, viện kiểm sát của hai bên, tăng cường trao đổi kinh nghiệm giữa các cơ quan kỷ luật, kiểm sát, giám sát của hai bên về chống tham nhũng, đề cao liêm khiết.

IX. Hai bên nhất trí cho rằng, việc hai nước ký kết " Hiệp ước biên giới trên đất liền giữa nước Cộng hòa Xã hội Chủ nghĩa Việt Nam và nước Cộng hòa Nhân dân Trung Hoa", "hiệp định phân định lãnh hải, vùng đặc quyền kinh tế và thềm lục địa trong Vịnh Bắc Bộ giữa nước Cộng hòa Xã hội Chủ nghĩa Việt Nam và nước Cộng hòa Nhân dân Trung Hoa", "hiệp định hợp tác nghề cá ở Vịnh Bắc Bộ giữa Chính phủ nước Cộng hòa Xã hội Chủ nghĩa Việt Nam và Chính phủ nước Cộng hòa Nhân dân Trung Hoa" có ý nghĩa lịch sử sâu rộng, sẽ thúc đẩy hơn nữa quan hệ láng giềng hữu nghị, hợp tác toàn diện giữa hai nước phát triển mạnh hơn nữa trong thế kỷ 21. Hai bên cam kết sẽ nghiêm chỉnh thực hiện các thỏa thuận liên quan đã ký kết giữa hai nước, tích cực hợp tác, nỗ lực xây dựng biên giới hai nước thành biên giới hòa bình, hữu nghị, ổn định lâu dài.

Hai bên khẳng định, tiếp tục duy trì cơ chế đàm phán hiện có về vấn đề trên biển, kiên trì thông qua đàm phán hòa bình để tìm ra một giải pháp cơ bản, lâu dài mà hai bên đều có thể chấp nhận được. Trước khi vấn đề được giải quyết, với tinh thần dễ trước khó sau, hai bên tích cực bàn bạc, tìm kiếm khả năng và giải pháp triển khai hợp tác trên biển trong các lĩnh vực như: bảo vệ môi trường biển, khí tượng thủy văn, phòng chống thiên tai. Đồng thời, hai bên đều không tiến hành các hành động làm phức tạp thêm hoặc mở rộng tranh chấp, không sử dụng vũ lực hoặc đe dọa sử dụng vũ lực. Hai bên cần bàn bạc kịp thời và giải quyết thỏa đáng những bất đồng nảy sinh với thái độ bình tĩnh xây dựng, không để bất đồng ảnh hưởng đến sự phát triển bình thường của quan hệ hai nước.

X. Hai bên khẳng định lại những nhận thức chung đã đạt được trong các Thông cáo chung Việt Nam-Trung Quốc 10/11/1991, 22/11/1994, 2/12/1995 và Tuyên bố chung Việt Nam-Trung Quốc 27/2/1999; phía Việt Nam khẳng định chính sách một nước Trung Quốc, Việt Nam công nhận Chính phủ nước Cộng hòa Nhân dân Trung Hoa là Chính phủ hợp pháp duy nhất đại diện cho toàn Trung Quốc; Đài Loan là một bộ phận lãnh thổ không thể chia cắt của Trung Quốc. Việt Nam chỉ giao lưu về kinh tế, thương mại phi chính phủ với Đài Loan, không phát triển quan hệ chính phủ với Đài Loan. Phía Trung Quốc tỏ sự hiểu biết và hoan nghênh lập trường trên đây của phía Việt Nam. Phía Trung Quốc khẳng định vấn đề Đài Loan hoàn toàn là vấn đề thuộc công việc nội bộ của Trung Quốc và kiên quyết phản đối các nước đã lập quan hệ ngoại giao với Trung Quốc có quan hệ chính phủ dưới bất cứ hình thức nào, hoặc có bất cứ sự đi lại nào mang tính chính phủ với Đài Loan.

Tuyên bố chung được ký tại Bắc Kinh ngày 25 tháng 12 năm 2000 thành hai bản, mỗi bản bằng tiếng Việt và tiếng Trung, cả hai văn bản đều có giá trị như nhau.

中华人民共和国和越南社会主义共和国关于两国在北部湾领海、专属经济区和大陆架的划界协定

（2000年12月25日）

中华人民共和国和越南社会主义共和国(以下简称“缔约双方”)，为巩固和发展中越两国和两国人民之间的传统睦邻友好关系，维护和促进北部湾的稳定和发展，在相互尊重独立、主权和领土完整，互不侵犯，互不干涉内政，平等互利和和平共处的原则基础上，本着互谅互让、友好协商和公平合理地解决划分北部湾问题的精神，达成协议如下：

第一条

一、缔约双方根据一九八二年《联合国海洋法公约》，公认的国际法各项原则和国际实践，在充分考虑北部湾所有有关情况的基础上，按照公平原则，通过友好协商，确定了两国在北部湾的领海、专属经济区和大陆架的分界线。

二、在本协定中，“北部湾”系指北面为中国和越南两国陆地领土海岸、东面为中国雷州半岛和海南岛海岸、西面为越南大陆海岸所环抱的半封闭海湾，其南部界限是自地理坐标为北纬18度30分19秒、东经108度41分17秒的中国海南岛莺歌嘴最外缘突出点经越南昏果岛至越南海岸上地理坐标为北纬16度57分40秒、东经107度08分42秒的一点之间的直线连线。

缔约双方确定，上述区域构成本协定的划界范围。

第二条

缔约双方同意，两国在北部湾的领海、专属经济区和大陆架分界线由以下

21个界点以直线顺次连接确定，其地理坐标如下：

第1界点　北纬21度28分12.5秒，东经108度06分04.3秒；

第2界点　北纬21度28分01.7秒，东经108度06分01.6秒；

第3界点　北纬21度27分50.1秒，东经108度05分57.7秒；

第4界点　北纬21度27分39.5秒，东经108度05分51.5秒；

第5界点　北纬21度27分28.2秒，东经108度05分39.9秒；

第6界点　北纬21度27分23.1秒，东经108度05分38.8秒；

第7界点　北纬21度27分08.2秒，东经108度05分43.7秒；

第8界点　北纬21度16分32秒，东经108度08分05秒；

第9界点　北纬21度12分35秒，东经108度12分31秒；

第10界点 北纬20度24分05秒，东经108度22分45秒；

第11界点 北纬19度57分33秒，东经107度55分47秒；

第12界点 北纬19度39分33秒，东经107度31分40秒；

第13界点 北纬19度25分26秒，东经107度21分00秒；

第14界点 北纬19度25分26秒，东经107度12分43秒；

第15界点 北纬19度16分04秒，东经107度11分23秒；

第16界点 北纬19度12分55秒，东经107度09分34秒；

第17界点 北纬18度42分52秒，东经107度09分34秒；

第18界点 北纬18度13分49秒，东经107度34分00秒；

第19界点 北纬18度07分08秒，东经107度37分34秒；

第20界点 北纬18度04分13秒，东经107度39分09秒；

第21界点 北纬17度47分00秒，东经107度58分00秒。

第三条

一、本协定第二条所规定的第1界点至第9界点的分界线是两国在北部湾的领海分界线。

二、本条第一款所规定的两国领海分界线沿垂直方向划分两国领海的上空、海床和底土。

三、除非缔约双方另有协议，任何地形变化不改变本条第一款所规定的第1界点至第7界点的两国领海分界线。

第四条

本协定第二条所规定的第9界点至第21界点的分界线是两国在北部湾的专属经济区和大陆架的分界线。

第五条

本协定第二条所规定的第1界点至第7界点的两国领海分界线用黑线标绘在缔约双方于二〇〇〇年共同测制的比例尺为一万分之一的北仑河口专题地图上，第7界点至第21界点的两国领海、专属经济区和大陆架分界线用黑线标绘在由缔约双方于二〇〇〇年共同测制的比例尺为五十万分之一的北部湾全图上。上述分界线均为大地线。

上述北仑河口专题地图和北部湾全图为本协定的附图。上述地图采用ITRF-96坐标系。本协定第二条所规定各界点的地理坐标均系从上述地图上量取。本协定所规定的分界线标绘在本协定附图上，仅用于说明的目的。

第六条

缔约双方应相互尊重按照本协定所确定的两国各自在北部湾的领海、专属经济区和大陆架的主权、主权权利和管辖权。

第七条

如果任何石油、天然气单一地质构造或其他矿藏跨越本协定第二条所规定的分界线，缔约双方应通过友好协商就该构造或矿藏的最有效开发以及公平分享开发收益达成协议。

第八条

缔约双方同意就北部湾生物资源的合理利用和可持续发展以及两国在北部湾专属经济区的生物资源养护、管理和利用的有关合作事项进行协商。

第九条

两国根据本协定对北部湾领海、专属经济区和大陆架分界线的划定对缔约各方有关海洋法方面国际法规则的立场不造成任何影响或妨害。

第十条

缔约双方对本协定的解释或适用所产生的任何争议，应通过友好协商和谈判予以解决。

第十一条

本协定须经缔约双方批准，并自互换批准书之日起生效。批准书在河内互换。

本协定于二〇〇〇年十二月二十五日在北京签订，一式两份，每份都用中文和越文写成，两种文本同等作准。

Hiệp định giữa Cộng hòa xã hội chủ nghĩa Việt Nam và nước Cộng hòa nhân dân Trung Hoa về phân định lãnh hải, vùng đặc quyền kinh tế và thềm lục địa của hai nước trong Vịnh Bắc Bộ

(2000/12/25)

Nước Cộng hòa xã hội chủ nghĩa Việt Nam và nước Cộng hòa Nhân dân Trung Hoa (dưới đây gọi là "hai Bên ký kết").

Nhằm củng cố và phát triển mối quan hệ láng giềng hữu nghị truyền thống giữa hai nước và nhân dân hai nước Việt Nam và Trung Quốc, giữ gìn và thúc đẩy sự ổn định và phát triển của Vịnh Bắc Bộ;

Trên cơ sở các nguyên tắc tôn trọng độc lập, chủ quyền và toàn vẹn lãnh thổ của nhau, không xâm phạm lẫn nhau, không can thiệp vào công việc nội bộ của nhau, bình đẳng cùng có lợi, cùng tồn tại hòa bình;

Trên tinh thần thông cảm, nhân nhượng lẫn nhau, hiệp thương hữu nghị và giải quyết một cách công bằng, hợp lý vấn đề phân định Vịnh Bắc Bộ;

Đã thỏa thuận như sau :

Điều 1:

1. Hai Bên ký kết căn cứ vào Công ước của Liên hợp quốc tế Luật Biển năm 1982, các nguyên tắc luật pháp và thực tiễn quốc tế được công nhận, trên cơ sở suy xét đầy đủ mọi hoàn cảnh hữu quan trong Vịnh Bắc Bộ, theo nguyên tắc công bằng, qua thương lượng hữu nghị đã phân định lãnh hải, vùng đặc quyền kinh tế và thềm lục địa của hai nước trong Vịnh Bắc Bộ.

2. Trong Hiệp định này, Vịnh Bắc Bộ là vịnh nửa kín được bao bọc ở phía Bắc bởi bờ biển lãnh thổ đất liền của hai nước Việt Nam và Trung Quốc, phía Đông bởi bờ biển bán đảo Lôi Châu và đảo Hải Nam của Trung Quốc, phía Tây

bởi bờ biển đất liền Việt Nam và giới hạn phía Nam bởi đoạn thẳng nối liền từ điểm nhô ra nhất của mép ngoài cùng của mũi Oanh Ca-đảo Hải Nam của Trung Quốc có tọa độ địa lý là vĩ tuyến 18°31′19″ Bắc, kinh tuyến 18°41′17″ Đông, qua đảo Cồn Cỏ của Việt Nam đến một điểm trên bờ biển của Việt Nam có tọa độ địa lý là vĩ tuyến16°57′40″ Bắc và kinh tuyến 107°08′42″ Đông.

Hai Bên ký kết xác định khu vực nói trên là phạm vi phân định của Hiệp định này.

Điều 2:

Hai Bên ký kết đồng ý đường phân định lãnh hải, vùng đặc quyền kinh tế và thềm lục địa giữa hai nước trong Vịnh Bắc Bộ được xác định bằng 21 điểm nối tuần tự với nhau bằng các đoạn thẳng, tọa độ địa lý của 21 điểm này như sau :

Điểm số 1:	Vĩ độ Bắc	21°28′12.5″
	Kinh độ Đông	108°06′04.3″
Điểm số 2:	Vĩ độ Bắc	21°28′01.7″
	Kinh độ Đông	108°06′01.6″
Điểm số 3	Vĩ độ Bắc	21°27′50.5″
	Kinh độ Đông	108°05′57.7″
Điểm số 4:	Vĩ độ Bắc	21°27′39.5″
	Kinh độ Đông	108°05′51.5″
Điểm số 5:	Vĩ độ Bắc	21°27′28.2″
	Kinh độ Đông	108°05′39.9″
Điểm số 6:	Vĩ độ Bắc	21°27′23.1″
	Kinh độ Đông	108°05′38.8″
Điểm số 7:	Vĩ độ Bắc	21°27′08.2″
	Kinh độ Đông	108°05′43.7″
Điểm số 8:	Vĩ độ Bắc	21°16′32″
	Kinh độ Đông	108°08′05″
Điểm số 9:	Vĩ độ Bắc	21°12′35″
	Kinh độ Đông	108°12′31″
Điểm số 10:	Vĩ độ Bắc	20°24′05″
	Kinh độ Đông	108°22′45″
Điểm số 11:	Vĩ độ Bắc	19°57′33″

	Kinh độ Đông	107°55′47″
Điểm số 12:	Vĩ độ Bắc	19°39′33″
	Kinh độ Đông	107°31′40″
Điểm số 13:	Vĩ độ Bắc	19°25′26″
	Kinh độ Đông	107°21′00″
Điểm số 14:	Vĩ độ Bắc	19°25′26″
	Kinh độ Đông	107°12′43″
Điểm số 15:	Vĩ độ Bắc	19°16′04″
	Kinh độ Đông	107°11′23″
Điểm số 16:	Vĩ độ Bắc	19°12′55″
	Kinh độ Đông	107°09′34″
Điểm số 17:	Vĩ độ Bắc	18°42′52″
	Kinh độ Đông	107°09′34″
Điểm số 18:	Vĩ độ Bắc	18°13′49″
	Kinh độ Đông	107°34′00″
Điểm số 19:	Vĩ độ Bắc	18°07′08″
	Kinh độ Đông	107°37′34″
Điểm số 20:	Vĩ độ Bắc	18°04′13″
	Kinh độ Đông	107°39′09″
Điểm số 21:	Vĩ độ Bắc	17°47′00″
	Kinh độ Đông	107°58′00″

Điều 3:

1. Đường phân định từ điểm số 1 đến điểm số 9 quy định tại Điều II của Hiệp định này là biên giới lãnh hải của hai nước trong vịnh Bắc Bộ.

2. Mặt thẳng đứng đi theo đường biên giới lãnh hãi của hai nước quy định tại khoản 1 Điều này phân định vùng trời, đáy biển và lòng đất dưới đáy biển của lãnh hải hai nước.

3. Mọi sự thay đổi địa hình đều không làm thay đổi đường biên giới lãnh hải hai nước từ điểm số 1 đến điểm số 7 quy định tại khoản 1 Điều này, trừ khi hai Bên ký kết có thỏa thuận khác.

Điều 4:

Đường phân định từ điểm số 9 đến điểm số 21 quy định tại Điều II của Hiệp định này là ranh giới giữa vùng đặc quyền kinh tế và thềm lục địa của hai nước trong Vịnh Bắc Bộ.

Điều 5:

Đường phân định lãnh hải của hai nước quy định tại Điều II từ điểm số 1 đến điểm số 7 được thể hiện bằng đường mầu đen trên bản đồ chuyên đề cửa sông Bắc Luân tỷ lệ : 10.000 do hai Bên ký kết cùng nhau thành lập năm 2000. Đường phân định lãnh hải, vùng đặc quyền kinh tế và thềm lục địa của hai nước từ điểm số 7 đến điểm số 21 được thể hiện bằng đường mầu đen trên Tổng đồ toàn diện Vịnh Bắc Bộ tỷ lệ 1: 500.0000 do hai Bên ký kết cùng nhau thành lập năm 2000. Các đường phân định này đều là đường trắc địa.

Bản đồ chuyên đề cửa sông Bắc Luân và Tổng đồ toàn diện Vịnh Bắc Bộ nói trên là bản đồ đính kèm Hiệp định. Các bản đồ trên sử dụng hệ tọa độ ITRF-96. Các tọa độ địa lý của các điểm quy định tại Điều II Hiệp định này đều được xác định trên các bản đồ nói trên. Đường phân định quy định trong Hiệp định này được thể hiện trên các bản đồ kèm theo Hiệp định chỉ nhằm mục đích minh họa.

Điều 6:

Hai Bên ký kết phải tôn trọng chủ quyền, quyền chủ quyền và quyền tài phán của mỗi Bên đối với lãnh hải, vùng đặc quyền kinh tế và thềm lục địa trong Vịnh Bắc Bộ được xác định theo Hiệp định này.

Điều 7:

Trong trường hợp có các cấu tạo mỏ dầu, khí tự nhiên đơn nhất hoặc mỏ khoáng sản khác nằm vắt ngang đường phân định quy định tại Điều II của Hiệp định này, hai Bên ký kết phải thông qua hiệp thương hữu nghị để đạt được thỏa thuận về việc khai thác hữu hiệu nhất các cấu tạo hoặc mỏ khoáng sản nói trên cũng như việc phân chia công bằng lợi ích thu được từ việc khai thác.

Điều 8:

Hai Bên ký kết đồng ý tiến hành hiệp thương về việc sử dụng hợp lý và phát triển bền vững tài nguyên sinh vật ở Vịnh Bắc Bộ cũng như các công việc hợp tác có liên quan đến bảo tồn, quản lý và sử dụng tài nguyên sinh vật ở vùng đặcquyền kinh tế hai nước trong Vịnh Bắc Bộ.

Điều 9:

Việc phân định lãnh hải, vùng đặc quyền kinh tế và thềm lục địa hai nước trong Vịnh Bắc Bộ theo Hiệp định này không gây bất kỳ ảnh hưởng hoặc phương hại nào đến lập trường của mỗi Bên ký kết đối với các quy phạm luật pháp quốc tế về luật Biển.

Điều 10:

Mọi tranh chấp giữa hai Bên ký kết liên quan đến việc giải thích hoặc thực hiện Hiệp định này phải được giải quyết thông qua hiệp thương và đàm phán hữu nghị.

Điều 11:

Hiệp định này phải được hai Bên ký kết phê chuẩn và có hiệu lực kể từ ngày trao đổi các văn kiện phê chuẩn. Các văn kiện phê chuẩn được trao đổi tại Hà Nội.

Hiệp định này được ký tại Bắc Kinh, ngày 25 tháng 12 năm 2000 thành hai bản, mỗi bản bằng tiếng Việt và tiếng Trung, cả hai văn bản đều có giá trị như nhau.

中华人民共和国政府和越南社会主义共和国政府北部湾渔业合作协定

（2000年12月25日）

中华人民共和国政府和越南社会主义共和国政府（以下简称“缔约双方”），为了维护和发展中越两国和两国人民之间的传统睦邻友好关系，养护和持续利用北部湾协定水域的海洋生物资源，加强两国在北部湾的渔业合作，根据国际法，特别是一九八二年十二月十日《联合国海洋法公约》的有关规定以及二〇〇〇年十二月二十五日签订的《中华人民共和国和越南社会主义共和国关于两国在北部湾领海、专属经济区和大陆架的划界协定》（以下简称“北部湾划界协定”），经友好协商，在相互尊重各自在北部湾的主权、主权权利和管辖权、平等互利的基础上，达成协议如下：

第一部分 总则

第一条

本协定适用于北部湾两国专属经济区的一部分和两国领海相邻水域的一部分（以下简称“协定水域”）。

第二条

缔约双方在相互尊重主权、主权权利和管辖权的基础上，在协定水域进行渔业合作。这种渔业合作不影响两国各自的领海主权和两国各自在专属经济区享有的其他权益。

第二部分 共同渔区

第三条

一、缔约双方同意在北部湾封口线以北、北纬20度以南、距北部湾划界协定所确定的分界线（以下简称“分界线”）各自30.5海里的两国各自专属经济区设立共同渔区。

二、共同渔区的具体范围为下列各点顺次用直线连接而围成的水域：

1. 北纬17度23分38秒，东经107度34分43秒之点
2. 北纬18度09分20秒，东经108度20分18秒之点
3. 北纬18度44分25秒，东经107度41分51秒之点
4. 北纬19度08分09秒，东经107度41分51秒之点
5. 北纬19度43分00秒，东经108度20分30秒之点
6. 北纬20度00分00秒，东经108度42分32秒之点
7. 北纬20度00分00秒，东经107度57分42秒之点
8. 北纬19度52分34秒，东经107度57分42秒之点
9. 北纬19度52分34秒，东经107度29分00秒之点
10. 北纬20度00分00秒，东经107度29分00秒之点
11. 北纬20度00分00秒，东经107度07分41秒之点
12. 北纬19度33分07秒，东经106度37分17秒之点
13. 北纬18度40分00秒，东经106度37分17秒之点
14. 北纬18度18分58秒，东经106度53分08秒之点
15. 北纬18度00分00秒，东经107度01分55秒之点
16. 北纬17度23分38秒，东经107度34分43秒之点

第四条

缔约双方本着互利的精神，在共同渔区内进行长期渔业合作。

第五条

缔约双方根据共同渔区的自然环境条件、生物资源特点、可持续发展的需要和环境保护以及对缔约各方渔业活动的影响，共同制订共同渔区生物资源的养护、管理和可持续利用措施。

第六条

缔约双方尊重平等互利的原则，根据在定期联合渔业资源调查结果的基础上所确定的可捕量和对缔约各方渔业活动的影响，以及可持续发展的需要，通过根据本协定第十三条设立的中越北部湾渔业联合委员会每年确定缔约各方在共同渔区内的作业渔船数量。

第七条

一、缔约各方对在共同渔区从事渔业活动的己方渔船实行捕捞许可制度。捕捞许可证须按照中越北部湾渔业联合委员会确定的当年作业渔船数量发放，并将获得许可证的渔船船名号通报缔约另一方。缔约双方有义务对进入共同渔区从事渔业活动的渔民进行教育和培训。

二、凡进入共同渔区从事渔业活动的渔船均须向本国政府授权机关提出申请，并在领取捕捞许可证后，方可进入共同渔区从事渔业活动。缔约双方进入共同渔区从事渔业活动的渔船应按照中越北部湾渔业联合委员会的规定进行标识。

第八条

缔约各方进入共同渔区从事渔业活动的国民和渔船在进行渔业活动时须遵守中越北部湾渔业联合委员会关于渔业资源养护和管理的规定，依照中越北部湾渔业联合委员会的要求正确填写捕捞日志并在规定时间内上交本国政府授权机关。

第九条

一、根据中越北部湾渔业联合委员会在符合共同渔区特点以及符合两国各自关于渔业资源养护和管理的国内法的基础上制订的规定，缔约各方授权机关对进入共同渔区内己方一侧水域的缔约双方国民和渔船进行监督检查。

二、缔约一方授权机关发现缔约另一方国民和渔船在共同渔区内己方一侧水域违反中越北部湾渔业联合委员会的规定时，有权按中越北部湾渔业联合委员会的规定对该违规行为进行处理，并应通过中越北部湾渔业联合委员会商定的途径，将有关情况和处理结果迅速通知缔约另一方。被扣留的渔船和船员，在提出适当的保证书或其他担保后，应迅速获得释放。

三、必要时，缔约双方授权机关可相互配合进行联合监督检查，对在共同渔区内违反中越北部湾渔业联合委员会关于渔业资源养护和管理规定的行为进行处理。

四、缔约各方有权根据各自国内法对未获许可证进入共同渔区内己方一侧水域从事渔业活动或虽获许可证进入共同渔区但从事渔业活动以外不合法活动的渔船进行处罚。

五、缔约各方应为获得许可证进入共同渔区的缔约另一方渔船提供便利。缔约各方授权机关不得滥用职权，妨碍缔约另一方获得许可证的国民和渔船在共同渔区内从事正常渔业活动。缔约一方如发现缔约另一方授权机关未按照中越北部湾渔业联合委员会制订的共同管理措施进行执法，有权要求该授权机关做出解释，必要时，可提交中越北部湾渔业联合委员会予以讨论和解决。

第十条

缔约各方在共同渔区己方作业规模框架内，可采取任何一种国际合作或联营方式。所有获许可证在共同渔区内以上述合作或联营方式从事渔业活动的渔船均须遵守中越北部湾渔业联合委员会制订的渔业资源养护和管理的规定，悬挂向其颁发许可证的缔约一方的国旗，按中越北部湾渔业联合委员会的规定进行标识，在共同渔区向其颁发许可证的缔约一方一侧水域从事渔业活动。

第三部分 过渡性安排

第十一条

一、缔约各方应对共同渔区以北（自北纬20度起算）本国专属经济区内缔约另一方的现有渔业活动做出过渡性安排。自本协定生效之日起，过渡性安排开始实施。缔约另一方应采取措施，逐年削减上述渔业活动。过渡性安排自本协定生效之日起四年内结束。

二、关于过渡性安排水域的范围和过渡性安排的管理办法，由缔约双方以补充议定书形式加以规定，该补充议定书为本协定不可分割的组成部分。

三、过渡性安排结束后，缔约各方应在相同条件下优先准许缔约另一方在本国专属经济区入渔。

第四部分 小型渔船缓冲区

第十二条

一、为避免缔约双方小型渔船误入缔约另一方领海引起纠纷，缔约双方在两国领海相邻部分自分界线第一界点起沿分界线向南延伸10海里、距分界线各自3海里的范围内设立小型渔船缓冲区，具体范围为下列各点顺次用直线连接而围成的水域：

1. 北纬21度28分12.5秒，东经108度06分04.3秒之点
2. 北纬21度25分40.7秒，东经108度02分46.1秒之点
3. 北纬21度17分52.1秒，东经108度04分30.3秒之点
4. 北纬21度18分29.0秒，东经108度07分39.0秒之点
5. 北纬21度19分05.7秒，东经108度10分47.8秒之点
6. 北纬21度25分41.7秒，东经108度09分20.0秒之点
7. 北纬21度28分12.5秒，东经108度06分04.3秒之点

二、缔约一方如发现缔约另一方小型渔船进入小型渔船缓冲区己方一侧水域从事渔业活动，可予以警告，并采取必要措施令其离开该水域，但应克制：不扣

留，不逮捕，不处罚或使用武力。如发生有关渔业活动的争议，应报告中越北部湾渔业联合委员会予以解决；如发生有关渔业活动以外的争议，由两国各自相关授权机关依照国内法予以解决。

第五部分 中越北部湾渔业联合委员会

第十三条

一、为实施本协定，缔约双方决定设立中越北部湾渔业联合委员会（以下简称“渔委会”）。渔委会由两国政府各自任命的一名代表和若干名委员组成。

二、渔委会将对其活动机制做出具体规定。

三、渔委会的职责如下：

（一）协商协定水域渔业资源养护和可持续利用的有关问题，并向两国政府提出建议；

（二）协商两国在协定水域渔业合作的有关事项，并向两国政府提出建议；

（三）根据本协定第五条，制订共同渔区的渔业资源养护和管理规定及其实施办法；

（四）根据本协定第六条，每年确定缔约各方进入共同渔区的作业渔船数量；

（五）协商和决定与共同渔区有关的其他事项；

（六）根据过渡性安排补充议定书的规定履行其职能；

（七）解决发生在小型渔船缓冲区内的有关渔业活动的争议；

（八）在其职能范围内对渔业纠纷和海损事故的处理进行指导；

（九）对本协定执行情况进行评估并向两国政府报告；

（十）可就本协定、本协定附件和本协定补充议定书的补充和修改向两国政府提出建议；

（十一）对缔约双方共同关注的其他事项进行协商。

四、渔委会的一切建议和决定均须经缔约双方代表一致同意。

五、渔委会每年举行一至二次会议，在两国轮流举行。必要时，经缔约双方同意可举行临时会议。

第六部分 其他条款

第十四条

为确保航行安全，维护海上捕捞作业秩序和安全，并顺利及时处理协定水域海上事故，缔约各方应对本国国民和渔船进行指导、法律教育并采取其他必要措施。

第十五条

一、缔约一方国民和渔船在缔约另一方一侧海域遭遇海难或发生其他紧急事态需要救助时，缔约另一方有义务予以救助和保护，同时迅速将有关情况通报缔约一方的有关部门。

二、缔约一方的国民和渔船因天气恶劣或其他紧急事态需要避难时，可按本协定附件和渔委会的规定，经与缔约另一方有关部门联系，到缔约另一方避难。该国民和渔船在避难期间须遵守缔约另一方的有关法律和法规，并服从缔约另一方有关部门的管理。

第十六条

缔约各方按照一九八二年十二月十日《联合国海洋法公约》的规定确保缔约另一方渔船的无害通过权和航行便利。

第十七条

一、缔约双方应在协定水域就渔业科学研究和海洋生物资源养护进行合作。

二、缔约各方可在协定水域己方一侧进行国际渔业科研合作。

第七部分 最后条款

第十八条

缔约双方之间对本协定的解释或适用而产生的任何争端，应通过友好协商予以解决。

第十九条

本协定附件和本协定补充议定书为本协定不可分割的组成部分。

第二十条

经协商，缔约双方可对本协定、本协定附件和本协定补充议定书进行补充和修改。

第二十一条

本协定第三条第二款规定的共同渔区的地理坐标和本协定第十二条第一款规定的小型渔船缓冲区的地理坐标均从作为北部湾划界协定附图的北部湾全图和北仑河口专题地图上量取。

第二十二条

一、本协定经缔约双方履行各自国内法律程序后，自两国政府换文商定之日起生效。

二、本协定有效期为十二年，其后自动顺延三年。顺延期满后，继续合作事宜由缔约双方通过协商商定。

本协定于二〇〇〇年十二月二十五日在北京签订，一式两份，每份均用中文和越文写成，两种文本同等作准。

附件：

关于紧急避难的规定

为实施本协定第十五条第二款的规定：

一、中华人民共和国政府指定的联络部门为农业部南海区渔政渔港监督管理局。越南社会主义共和国政府指定的联络部门为水产部水产资源保护局。

二、紧急避难的联络办法由缔约双方在渔委会上相互通报。

三、紧急避难的联系内容应包括：船名、呼号、当时船位（纬度、经度）、船籍港、总吨位、全长、船长姓名、船员数、避难理由、请求避难的目的地、预计到达时间和联络方法。

Hiệp định hợp tác nghề cá ở Vịnh Bắc Bộ giữa Chính phủ nước CHXHCN Việt Nam và Chính phủ nước CHND Trung Hoa

(2000/12/25)

Chính phủ nước Cộng hoà xã hội chủ nghĩa Việt Nam và Chính phủ nước Cộng hoà nhân dân Trung Hoa (dưới đây gọi tắt là "hai Bên ký kết"); Nhằm giữ gìn và phát triển mối quan hệ láng giềng hữu nghị truyền thống giữa hai nước và nhân dân hai nước Việt Nam và Trung Quốc; Nhằm bảo tồn và khai thác bền vững tài nguyên sinh vật biển trong Vùng nước Hiệp định ở vịnh Bắc Bộ; Nhằm mục đích tăng cường hợp tác nghề cá giữa hai nước trong vịnh Bắc Bộ;Chính phủ nước Cộng hoà xã hội chủ nghĩa Việt Nam và Chính phủ nước Cộng hoà nhân dân Trung Hoa (dưới đây gọi tắt là "hai Bên ký kết"); Nhằm giữ gìn và phát triển mối quan hệ láng giềng hữu nghị truyền thống giữa hai nước và nhân dân hai nước Việt Nam và Trung Quốc; Nhằm bảo tồn và khai thác bền vững tài nguyên sinh vật biển trong Vùng nước Hiệp định ở vịnh Bắc Bộ; Nhằm mục đích tăng cường hợp tác nghề cá giữa hai nước trong vịnh Bắc Bộ;Căn cứ theo luật pháp quốc tế, đặc biệt là các quy định liên quan trong "Công ước của Liên hợp quốc về luật biển" ký ngày 10 tháng 12 năm 1982 cũng như Hiệp định giữa nước Cộng hoà xã hội chủ nghĩa Việt Nam và nước Cộng hoà nhân dân Trung Hoa về phân định lãnh hải, vùng đặc quyền kinh tế và thềm lục địa của hai nước ký ngày 25 tháng 12 năm 2000 (dưới đây gọi tắt là "Hiệp định phân định vịnh bắc Bộ"); Qua hiệp thương hữu nghị, trên cơ sở tôn trọng chủ quyền, quyền chủ quyền và quyền tài phán của nhau trong vịnh Bắc Bộ, bình đẳng cùng có lợi; Đã thoả thuận như sau:

PHẦN I: CÁC QUY ĐỊNH CHUNG

ĐIỀU 1

Hiệp định này áp dụng cho một phần vùng đặc quyền kinh tế và một phần vùng giáp giới lãnh hải của hai nước trong vịnh Bắc Bộ (dưới đây gọi tắt là "Vùng nước Hiệp định").

ĐIỀU 2

Hai bên ký kết tiến hành hợp tác nghề cá trong Vùng nước Hiệp định trên cơ sở tôn trọng chủ quyền, quyền chủ quyền và quyền tài phán của nhau. Việc hợp tác nghề cá này không ảnh hưởng đến chủ quyền lãnh hải của mỗi nước và các quyền lợi khác mà mỗi Bên ký kết được hưởng trong vùng đặc quyền kinh tế của mình.

PHẦN II: VÙNG ĐÁNH CÁ CHUNG

ĐIỀU 3

1. Hai bên ký kết nhất trí thiết lập Vùng đánh cá chung trong vùng đặc quyền kinh tế của mỗi nước, nằm về phía Bắc của đường đóng cửa vịnh Bắc Bộ, về phía Nam của vĩ tuyến 200 Bắc và cách đường phân định được xác định trong Hiệp định phân định vịnh Bắc Bộ (dưới đây gọi tắt là "Đường phân định") 30,5 hải lý về mỗi phía.

2. Phạm vi cụ thể của Vùng đánh cá chung là vùng nước nằm trong các đoạn thẳng tuần tự nối liền các điểm sau đây:

Điểm 1: Vĩ độ Bắc 17°23′38″	Kinh độ Đông 107°34′43″
Điểm 2: Vĩ độ Bắc18°09′20″	Kinh độ Đông 108°20′18″
Điểm 3: Vĩ độ Bắc 18°44′25″	Kinh độ Đông 107°41′51″
Điểm 4: Vĩ độ Bắc 19°08′09″	Kinh độ Đông 107°41′51″
Điểm 5: Vĩ độ Bắc 19°43′00″	Kinh độ Đông 108°20′30″
Điểm 6: Vĩ độ Bắc20°00′00″	Kinh độ Đông 108°42′32″
Điểm 7: Vĩ độ Bắc 20°00′00″	Kinh độ Đông107°57′42″
Điểm 8: Vĩ độ Bắc 19°52′34″	Kinh độ Đông 107°57′42″
Điểm 9: Vĩ độ Bắc 19°52′34″	Kinh độ Đông 107°29′00″
Điểm 10: Vĩ độ Bắc 20°00′00″	Kinh độ Đông 107°29′00″
Điểm 11: Vĩ độ Bắc20°00′00″	Kinh độ Đông 107°07′41″

Điểm 12: Vĩ độ Bắc 19°33′07″ Kinh độ Đông 106°37′17″
Điểm 13: Vĩ độ Bắc 18°40′00″ Kinh độ Đông 106°37′17″
Điểm 14: Vĩ độ Bắc 18°18′58″ Kinh độ Đông 106°53′08″
Điểm 15: Vĩ độ Bắc18°00′00″ Kinh độ Đông 107°01′55″
Điểm 16: Vĩ độ Bắc17°23′38″ Kinh độ Đông 107°34′43″

ĐIỀU 4

Hai Bên ký kết tiến hành hợp tác nghề cá lâu dài trong Vùng đánh cá chung trên tinh thần cùng có lợi.

ĐIỀU 5

Hai Bên ký kết căn cứ theo điều kiện môi trường tự nhiên, đặc điểm của tài nguyên sinh vật, nhu cầu phát triển bền vững và bảo vệ môi trường, cũng như những ảnh hưởng đối với hoạt đọng nghề cá của mỗi Bên ký kết trong Vùng đánh cá chung, cùng đặt ra những biện pháp về việc bảo tồn, quản lý và khai thác bền vững tài nguyên sinh vật trong Vùng đánh cá chung.

ĐIỀU 6

Hai Bên ký kết tôn trọng nguyên tắc bình đẳng cùng có lợi, căn cứ vào sản lượng được phép đánh bắt được xác định trên cơ sở kết quả điều tra liên hợp định kỳ về nguồn lợi thuỷ sản và những ảnh hưởng đối với hoạt động nghề cá của mỗi Bên ký kết cũng như nhu cầu của sự phát triển bền vững, thông qua Uỷ ban Liên hợp nghề cá vịnh Bắc Bộ Việt-Trung được thành lập theo điều 13 của Hiệp định này, hàng năm xác định số lượng tàu cá của mỗi Bên ký kết vào hoạt động đánh bắt trong Vùng đánh cá chung.

ĐIỀU 7

1. Mỗi Bên ký kết thực hiện chế độ cấp phép đánh bắt đối với tàu cá Bên mình tiến hành hoạt động nghề cá trong Vùng đánh cá chung. Việc cấp phép đánh bắt phải căn cứ theo số lượng tàu cá hoạt động đánh bắt mà Uỷ ban Liên hợp nghề cá vịnh Bắc Bộ Việt-Trung định ra cho năm đó, đồng thời thông báo cho Bên ký kết kia tên, số hiệu tàu cá được cấp phép. Hai Bên ký kết có nghĩa vụ giáo dục và đào tạo những ngư dân vào tiến hành hoạt động nghề cá trong Vùng đánh cá chung.

2. Tất cả những tàu cá vào tiến hành hoạt động nghề cá trong Vùng đánh cá chung đều phải xin phép cơ quan được trao thẩm quyền của Chính phủ nước

mình và sau khi nhận được giấy phép đánh bắt mới có thể vào tiến hành hoạt động nghề cá trong Vùng đánh cá chung. Tàu cá của hai Bên ký kết vào hoạt động nghề cá trong Vùng đánh cá chung cần phải được đánh dấu theo qui định của Uỷ ban Liên hợp nghề cá vịnh Bắc Bộ Việt-Trung.

ĐIỀU 8

Khi tiến hành hoạt động nghề cá trong Vùng đánh cá chung, công dân và tàu cá của mỗi Bên ký kết phải tuân thủ những quy định về bảo tồn và quản lý nguồn lợi thuỷ sản của Uỷ ban Liên hợp nghề cá vịnh Bắc Bộ Việt-Trung; phải viết chính xác nhật ký đánh bắt theo yêu cầu của Uỷ ban Liên hợp nghề cá vịnh Bắc Bộ Việt-Trung, đồng thời phải nộp cho cơ quan được trao thẩm quyền của Chính phủ nước mình trong thời gian quy định.

ĐIỀU 9

1. Căn cứ vào các quy định do Uỷ ban Liên hợp nghề cá vịnh Bắc Bộ Việt-Trung đặt ra trên cơ sở phù hợp với đặc điểm của Vùng đánh cá chung cũng như phù hợp với luật pháp của mỗi nước về bảo tồn và quản lý nguồn lợi thuỷ sản, cơ quan có thẩm quyền của mỗi Bên ký kết thực hiện việc kiểm tra, kiểm soát đối với công dân và tàu cá của hai Bên ký kết ở Vùng đánh cá chung thuộc vùng nước của mình.

2. Khi cơ quan có thẩm quyền của một Bên ký kết phát hiện công dân và tàu cá bên ký kết kia vi phạm các quy định của Uỷ ban Liên hợp nghề cá vịnh Bắc Bộ Việt-Trung ở Vùng đánh cá chung thuộc vùng nước của mình thì có quyền xử lý các hành vi vi phạm đó theo các quy định của Uỷ ban Liên hợp nghề cá vịnh Bắc Bộ Việt-Trung, và nên thông báo nhanh chóng cho bên ký kết kia tình hình liên quan và kết quả xử lý theo đường do Uỷ ban Liên hợp nghề cá vịnh Bắc Bộ Việt-Trung thoả thuận. Các tàu cá và thuyền viên bị bắt giữ cần phải được phóng thích nhanh chóng sau khi có sự bảo lãnh thích đáng hoặc những bảo đảm khác.

3. Khi cần thiết, cơ quan có thẩm quyền của hai Bên ký kết có thể phối hợp với nhau cùng kiểm tra, kiểm soát và xử lý các hành vi vi phạm các quy định về bảo tồn và quản lý nguồn lợi thuỷ sản của Uỷ ban Liên hợp nghề cá vịnh Bắc Bộ Việt-Trung trong Vùng đánh cá chung.

4. Mỗi Bên ký kết có quyền căn cứ vào luật pháp của nước mình xử phạt những tàu cá chưa được cấp phép mà vào Vùng đánh cá chung thuộc vùng nước

của mình tiến hành hoạt động nghề cá, hoặc tuy được cấp phép vào Vùng đánh cá chung nhưng có các hoạt động bất hợp pháp ngoài hoạt động nghề cá.

5. Mỗi Bên ký kết nên tạo thuận lợi cho những tàu cá đã được cấp phép của Bên ký kết kia được vào Vùng đánh cá chung. Cơ quan có thẩm quyền của mỗi Bên ký kết không được lạm dụng chức quyền, cản trở những công dân và tàu cá đã được cấp phép của Bên ký kết kia tiến hành hoạt động nghề cá bình thường trong Vùng đánh cá chung. Nếu một Bên ký kết phát hiện cơ quan có thẩm quyền của Bên ký kết kia tiến hành thực thi pháp luật không theo biện pháp quản lý chung do Uỷ ban Liên hợp nghề cá vịnh Bắc Bộ Việt−Trung đặt ra thì có quyền yêu cầu cơ quan có thẩm quyền đó giải thích, khi cần thiết, có thể đưa ra thảo luận và giải quyết tại Uỷ ban Liên hợp nghề cá vịnh Bắc Bộ Việt-Trung.

ĐIỀU 10

Mỗi Bên ký kết có thể áp dụng bất kỳ một phương thức hợp tác hoặc liên doanh quốc tế nào trong khuôn khổ quy mô đánh bắt của Bên mình trong Vùng đánh cá chung. Tất cả tàu cá được cấp phép hoạt động nghề cá theo các phương thức hợp tác hoặc liên doanh nói trên trong Vùng đánh cá chung đều phải tuân theo những quy định về bảo tồn và quản lý nguồn lợi thuỷ sản do Uỷ ban Liên hợp nghề cá vịnh Bắc Bộ Việt-Trung đặt ra, treo quốc kỳ của Bên ký kết cấp phép đó và tiến hành đánh dấu theo quy định của Uỷ ban Liên hợp nghề cá vịnh Bắc Bộ Việt-Trung, hoạt động nghề cá trong Vùng đánh cá chung tại Vùng nước của Bên ký kết cấp phép đó.

PHẦN III: DÀN XẾP QUÁ ĐỘ

ĐIỀU 11

1. Mỗi Bên ký kết nên đưa ra dàn xếp quá độ đối với hoạt động nghề cá hiện có của Bên ký kết kia trong vùng đặc quyền kinh tế nước mình nằm về phía Bắc Vùng đánh cá chung (tính từ vĩ tuyến 200 Bắc). Việc dàn xếp quá độ bắt đầu được thực thi kể từ ngày Hiệp định này có hiệu lực. Bên ký kết kia nên áp dụng biện pháp giảm dần hàng năm hoạt động nghề cá nói trên. Việc dàn xếp quá độ sẽ kết thúc trong vòng bốn năm kể từ ngày Hiệp định này có hiệu lực.

2. Phạm vi vùng nước dàn xếp quá độ và biện pháp quản lý đối với việc dàn xếp quá độ sẽ do hai Bên ký kết quy định bằng hình thức Nghị định thư bổ sung.

Nghị định thư bổ sung đó là bộ phận không thể tách rời của Hiệp định này.

3. Sau khi dàn xếp quá độ kết thúc, trong điều kiện giống nhau, mỗi Bên ký kết nên ưu tiên cho phép Bên ký kết kia vào đánh bắt theo chế độ vùng đặc quyền kinh tế trong vùng đặc quyền kinh tế nước mình.

PHẦN IV: VÙNG ĐỆM CHO TÀU CÁ NHỎ

ĐIỀU 12

1. Để tránh xảy ra tranh chấp do việc tàu cá loại nhỏ của hai Bên ký kết đi nhầm vào lãnh hải của Bên ký kết kia, hai Bên ký kết thiết lập vùng đệm cho tàu cá loại nhỏ ở vùng giáp giới lãnh hải của hai nước, chiều dài tính từ điểm đầu tiên của đường phân định kéo về phía Nam theo đường phân định 10 hải lý, chiều rộng lùi về mỗi phía 3 hải lý tính từ đường phân định, phạm vi cụ thể được tạo thành bởi các đoạn thẳng tuần tự nối các điểm sau đây:

Điểm 1: Vĩ độ Bắc 21°28′12.5″ Kinh độ Đông 108°06′04.3″
Điểm 2: Vĩ độ Bắc 21°25′40.7″ Kinh độ Đông 108°02′46.1″
Điểm 3: Vĩ độ Bắc 21°17′52.1″ Kinh độ Đông 108°04′30.3″
Điểm 4: Vĩ độ Bắc 21°18′29.0″ Kinh độ Đông 108°07′39.0″
Điểm 5: Vĩ độ Bắc 21°19′05.7″ Kinh độ Đông 108°10′47.8″
Điểm 6: Vĩ độ Bắc 21°25′41.7″ Kinh độ Đông 108°09′20.0″
Điểm 7: Vĩ độ Bắc 21°28′12.5″ Kinh độ Đông 108°06′04.3″

2. Nếu một Bên ký kết phát hiện tàu cá loại nhỏ của Bên ký kết kia vào hoạt động nghề cá trong vùng đệm cho tàu cá loại nhỏ thuộc vùng nước của mình có thể cảnh cáo và áp dụng các biện pháp cần thiết để buộc tàu đó rời khỏi vùng nước đó, nhưng nên kiềm chế: không bắt bớ, giam giữ, xử phạt hoặc dùng vũ lực; nếu xảy ra tranh chấp liên quan đến hoạt động nghề cá thì nên báo cáo Uỷ ban Liên hợp nghề cá vịnh Bắc Bộ Việt-Trung để giải quyết; nếu xảy ra những tranh chấp ngoài hoạt động nghề cá thì do các cơ quan có thẩm quyền liên quan của mỗi nước giải quyết theo luật pháp của nước mình.

PHẦN V: UỶ BAN LIÊN HỢP NGHỀ CÁ VỊNH BẮC BỘ VIỆT-TRUNG

ĐIỀU 13

1. Để thực thi Hiệp định này, hai Bên ký kết quyết định thành lập Uỷ ban

Liên hợp nghề cá vịnh Bắc Bộ Việt-Trung (sau đây gọi tắt là "Uỷ ban Liên hợp nghề cá"). Uỷ ban Liên hợp nghề cá gồm mỗi Bên ký kết một đại diện do Chính phủ Bên ký kết đó bổ nhiệm và một số uỷ viên.

2. Uỷ ban Liên hợp nghề cá sẽ đặt ra những quy định cụ thể về cơ chế hoạt động của mình.

3. Uỷ ban Liên hợp nghề cá có chức trách như sau:

3.1 Hiệp thương những vấn đề liên quan đến bảo tồn và khai thác bền vững nguồn lợi thuỷ sản trong Vùng nước Hiệp định, đồng thời đề xuất kiến nghị với Chính phủ hai nước.

3.2 Hiệp thương về những việc liên quan tới hợp tác nghề cá của hai nước ở Vùng nước Hiệp định, đồng thời đề xuất kiến nghị với Chính phủ hai nước.

3.3 Căn cứ theo Điều 5 của Hiệp định này đặt ra những quy định về bảo tồn và quản lý nguồn lợi thuỷ sản trong Vùng đánh cá chung cũng như các biện pháp thực thi các quy định đó.

3.4 Căn cứ theo Điều 6 của Hiệp định này hàng năm xác định số lượng tàu cá của mỗi Bên ký kết vào hoạt động đánh bắt trong Vùng đánh cá chung.

3.5 Hiệp thương và quyết định những việc khác liên quan tới Vùng đánh cá chung.

3.6 Thực hiện chức năng của mình theo các quy định của Nghị định thư bổ sung về dàn xếp quá độ.

3.7 Giải quyết tranh chấp liên quan đến hoạt động nghề cá xảy ra trong Vùng đệm cho tàu cá loại nhỏ.

3.8 Tiến hành chỉ đạo việc xử lý đối với những tranh chấp nghề cá và sự cố gây thiệt hại trên biển trong phạm vi chức năng của mình.

3.9 Tiến hành đánh giá tình hình chấp hành Hiệp định này và báo cáo Chính phủ hai nước.

3.10 Có thể kiến nghị với Chính phủ hai nước về việc bổ sung, sửa đổi Hiệp định này, Phụ lục của Hiệp định này và Nghị định thư bổ sung của Hiệp định này.

3.11 Tiến hành hiệp thương những công việc khác mà hai Bên ký kết cùng quan tâm.

4. Tất cả mọi kiến nghị và quyết định của Uỷ ban Liên hợp Nghề cá đều

phải được sự nhất trí của đại diện hai Bên ký kết.

5. Uỷ ban Liên hợp nghề cá mỗi năm họp một đến hai lần và luân phiên tổ chức tại hai nước. Khi cần thiết, có thể triệu tập hội nghị bất thường sau khi có sự nhất trí của đại diện hai Bên ký kết.

PHẦN VI: NHỮNG ĐIỀU KHOẢN KHÁC

ĐIỀU 14

Để đảm bảo an toàn hàng hải, giữ gìn an ninh và trật tự hoạt động đánh bắt trên biển, xử lý kịp thời, thuận lợi các tai nạn trên biển trong Vùng nước Hiệp định, mỗi Bên ký kết nên có sự chỉ đạo, giáo dục pháp luật và áp dụng các biện pháp cần thiết khác đối với công dân và tàu cá của nước mình.

ĐIỀU 15

1. Khi công dân và tàu các của một Bên ký kết gặp nạn hoặc tình hình khẩn cấp khác tại vùng biển của Bên ký kết kia cần cứu giúp thì Bên ký kết kia có nghĩa vụ tiến hành việc cứu trợ và bảo hộ, đồng thời nhanh chóng thông báo tình hình liên quan cho cơ quan hữu quan của Bên ký kết đó.

2. Khi công dân và tàu cá của một Bên ký kết do thời tiết xấu hoặc gặp tình hình khẩn cấp khác phải lánh nạn, thì có thể thông qua liên hệ với cơ quan hữu quan của Bên ký kết kia căn cứ vào Phụ lục của Hiệp định này và các quy định của Uỷ ban Liên hợp nghề cá để tới Bên ký kết kia lánh nạn. Công dân và tàu cá trong thời gian lánh nạn cần phải tuân thủ pháp luật và quy định liên quan của Bên ký kết kia, đồng thời phải phục tùng sự quản lý của cơ quan hữu quan của Bên ký kết kia.

ĐIỀU 16

Mỗi Bên ký kết căn cứ theo các quy định của "Công ước của Liên hợp quốc về luật biển" ngày 10 tháng 12 năm 1982 bảo đảm quyền đi qua vô hại và đi lại thuận lợi cho tàu cá của Bên ký kết kia.

ĐIỀU 17

1. Hai Bên ký kết nên tiến hành hợp tác nghiên cứu khoa học về nghề cá và bảo tồn tài nguyên sinh vật biển trong Vùng nước Hiệp định.

2. Mỗi Bên ký kết có thể tiến hành hợp tác quốc tế về nghiên cứu khoa học nghề cá trong Vùng nước Hiệp định thuộc Bên mình.

PHẦN VII: CÁC ĐIỀU KHOẢN CUỐI CÙNG

ĐIỀU 18

Bất cứ tranh chấp nào nảy sinh giữa hai Bên ký kết trong việc giải thích hoặc áp dụng Hiệp định này nên được giải quyết thông qua thương lượng hữu nghị.

ĐIỀU 19

Những Phụ lục của Hiệp định này và Nghị định thư bổ sung của Hiệp định này là bộ phận không thể tách rời của Hiệp định này.

ĐIỀU 20

Hiệp định này, những Phụ lục của Hiệp định này và Nghị định thư bổ sung của Hiệp định này có thể được bổ sung, sửa đổi thông qua thương lượng giữa hai Bên ký kết.

ĐIỀU 21

Các toạ độ địa lý của Vùng đánh cá chung được quy định trong khoản 2 điều 3 của Hiệp định này và các toạ độ địa lý của Vùng đệm cho tàu cá nhỏ được quy định trong khoản 1 Điều 12 của Hiệp định này được xác định trên Tổng đồ toàn diện vịnh Bắc Bộ và Bản đồ chuyên đề cửa sông Bắc Luân, là các bản đồ được đính kèm theo Hiệp định phân định vịnh Bắc Bộ.

ĐIỀU 22

1. Hiệp định này, sau khi được hai Bên ký kết hoàn thành trình tự pháp luật của mỗi nước, sẽ có hiệu lực vào ngày được thoả thuận trong văn kiện trao đổi giữa Chính phủ hai nước.

2. Hiệp định này có hiệu lực trong vòng 12 năm và mặc nhiên gia hạn thêm ba năm. Sau khi thời gian gia hạn kết thúc, việc hợp tác tiếp theo do hai Bên ký kết hiệp thương thoả thuận.

Hiệp định này được ký tại Bắc Kinh ngày 25 tháng 12 năm 2000, thành hai bản, mỗi bản bằng tiếng Việt và tiếng Trung, cả hai văn bản đều có giá trị như nhau.

中越联合声明

（2001年12月3日）

一、应中国共产党中央委员会总书记、中华人民共和国主席江泽民的邀请，越南共产党中央委员会总书记农德孟于2001年11月30日至12月4日对中华人民共和国进行了正式友好访问。

中共中央总书记、中华人民共和国主席江泽民同越共中央总书记农德孟举行了会谈。中共中央政治局常委、中华人民共和国全国人民代表大会常务委员会委员长李鹏，中共中央政治局常委、中华人民共和国国务院总理朱镕基，中共中央政治局常委、中国人民政治协商会议全国委员会主席李瑞环和中共中央政治局常委、中华人民共和国副主席胡锦涛分别会见了农德孟总书记。双方互相通报了各自党和国家的情况，并就共同关心的地区和国际问题广泛交换了意见。会谈与会见是在亲切、友好的气氛中进行的。

双方认为，越共中央总书记农德孟对中国的访问取得了圆满成功，这次访问是新世纪初两党、两国关系中的重大事件，对加强和深化21世纪中越两党、两国全面友好合作关系作出了重要贡献，并将对本地区和世界的和平、稳定、合作与发展产生积极而深远的影响。

二、越南方面高度评价中国共产党和中国人民在过去的80年中所取得的历史性成就，并坚信中国共产党和中国人民一定会在建设有中国特色社会主义事业中取得新的更大的成就。中国方面高度评价越南共产党和越南人民在过去70多年中所取得的历史性成就，并坚信越南共产党和越南人民一定会在建设民富国强、社会公平、民主、文明的社会主义祖国的事业中取得新的更大的成就。双方决心从各自国家的实际出发，继续探索和解决党和国家建设面临的重大理论和实践问题，推动经济发展和社会进步。

三、双方满意地指出，两国关系正常化以来，双方在各个领域的交往与合作日益扩大和深化。两国发表了1991年、1992年、1994年、1995年《联合公报》和1999年、2000年《联合声明》，陆续签署了陆地边界条约、北部湾划界协定和北部湾渔业合作协定；两党、两国开展了广泛深入的改革开放、革新、治党治国和社会主义建设理论与实践经验的交流；两国的经贸合作迈上了新的台阶。两党、两国政府和两国人民对中越全面友好合作关系的良好而重大的发展感到高兴。

四、双方认为，中越友好是两党、两国、两国人民共同的宝贵财富。在新的世纪里，不断加强中越两党、两国全面友好合作关系，不仅符合两党、两国和两国人民的根本利益，而且有利于本地区和世界的和平、稳定、合作与发展。双方决心坚持“长期稳定、面向未来、睦邻友好、全面合作”的16字指导方针，全面贯彻落实两国《关于新世纪全面合作的联合声明》提出的明确目标和任务，不断提高中越传统友好合作关系的质量和水平，使中越两国和两国人民世代友好下去。

五、双方同意，为进一步加强和发展新世纪中越两党、两国全面友好合作关系，将继续保持两党、两国高层交往的良好传统；推动两国党政部门、议会、群众团体及地方之间在政治、经济、文化、教育等各个领域的交往与合作，提高合作效果；加强双方治党治国经验的交流，相互借鉴改革开放、革新和党的建设等各方面的经验；加强两国青少年之间形式多样、内容丰富的友好交往，使两国老一辈革命家精心培育的传统友谊和两国全面友好合作事业后继有人。

六、双方确认，新世纪要按照平等互利、注重实效、优势互补、形式多样、共同发展的方针，继续加强和扩大两国经贸、科技等领域的合作。积极鼓励和支持双方企业进一步开拓两国商品市场，加强投资合作，扩大经济技术合作规模，落实能带来切实经济效益和社会效益的合作项目。

双方签署了《中华人民共和国政府和越南社会主义共和国政府关于中国向越南提供优惠贷款的框架协议》和《中华人民共和国政府和越南社会主义共和国政府经济技术合作协定》，并同意将积极推动企业在多农铝矿项目上长期合作。

越南热烈祝贺中国成为世界贸易组织成员，中国积极支持越南早日加入世界贸易组织。

七、双方一致认为，两国签署陆地边界条约、北部湾划界协定和北部湾渔业合作协定，是具有重大意义的事件，为推动两国睦邻友好与全面合作关系的进一步发展和地区的稳定作出了积极贡献。双方同意，按照两国领导人的共识，加快完成北部湾渔业合作协定的有关后续谈判工作，使北部湾划界协定与渔业合作协定尽早一并生效。积极推动并加快陆地边界勘界立碑工作进程，把两国边界建设成为和平、友好、长期稳定的边界。

双方同意，继续维持现有海上问题谈判机制，坚持通过和平谈判，寻求一项双方都能接受的基本和长久的解决办法。在问题解决前，双方本着先易后难的精神，积极探讨在海上，诸如海洋环保、气象水文、减灾防灾等领域开展合作的可能性和措施。与此同时，双方均不采取使争端复杂化或扩大化的行动，不诉诸武力或以武力相威胁。对产生的分歧应及时进行磋商，采取冷静和建设性的态度，予以妥善处理；不因分歧而影响两国关系的正常发展。

八、越南方面重申，越南承认中华人民共和国政府是代表全中国的唯一合法政府，台湾是中国领土不可分割的一部分。越南同台湾只进行非官方经贸往来，绝不同台湾发展官方关系。中国方面对越南方面的上述立场表示理解和赞赏。中国方面重申，台湾问题纯属中国内政，坚决反对与中国建立外交关系的国家同台湾建立任何形式的官方关系，或进行任何具有官方性质的往来。

九、双方对就共同关心的地区和国际问题达成的广泛共识表示满意。双方认为，谋求和平、合作、发展和社会进步，已成为当今时代的潮流。中越两国和两国人民渴望世界持久和平，渴望过上长期稳定安宁的生活，渴望建立公正合理的国际新秩序，渴望促进各国共同繁荣和发展。

双方反对在国际事务中的霸权主义和强权政治，反对一切形式的恐怖主义。双方主张尊重各国的历史文化、社会制度、发展模式以及世界各种文明。双方赞赏东盟组织在维护和促进地区稳定与发展中发挥的积极作用，重申将继续致力于加强中国与东盟国家的睦邻互信伙伴关系，为亚洲特别是东亚的持久稳定和繁荣作出积极的努力和贡献。

十、越共中央总书记农德孟对中国共产党、中国政府和中国人民所给予的隆重、热情和友好的接待表示衷心感谢。农德孟总书记邀请中共中央总书记、国家主席江泽民在明年方便的时候对越南进行正式友好访问。江泽民总书记、国家主席对此表示感谢并愉快地接受了邀请。

Tuyên bố chung Trung Quốc-Việt Nam

(2001/12/3)

1. Nhận lời mời của Tổng Bí thư Ban Chấp hành Trung ương Đảng Cộng sản Trung Quốc, Chủ tịch nước Cộng hòa Nhân dân Trung Hoa Giang Trạch Dân, Tổng Bí thư Ban Chấp hành Trung ương Đảng Cộng sản Việt Nam Nông Đức Mạnh đã thăm hữu nghị chính thức nước Cộng hòa Nhân dân Trung Hoa từ ngày 30 tháng 11 đến ngày 4 tháng 12 năm 2001.

Tổng Bí thư Nông Đức Mạnh đã hội đàm với Tổng Bí thư, Chủ tích nước Giang Trạch Dân; lần lượt hội kiến với ủy viên.

Thường vụ Bộ Chính trị Ban Chấp hành Trung ương Đảng Cộng sản Trung Quốc, ủy viên Trưởng ủy ban Thường vụ Đại hội Đại biểu Nhân dân toàn quốc nước Cộng hòa Nhân dân Trung Hoa Lý Bằng; ủy viên Thường vụ Bộ Chính trị Ban Chấp hành Trung ương Đảng Cộng sản Trung Quốc, Thủ tường Quốc vụ viện nước Cộng hòa Nhân dân Trung Hoa Chu Dung Cơ; ủy viên Thường vụ Bộ Chính trị Ban Chấp hành Trung ương Đảng Cộng sản Trung Quốc, Chủ tịch ủy ban toàn quốc Hội nghị Hiệp thương chính trị nhân dân Trung Quốc Lý Thụy Hoàn; ủy viên Thường vụ Bộ Chính trị Ban Chấp hành Trung ương Đảng Cộng sản Trung Quốc, Phó Chủ tịch nước Cộng hòa Nhân dân Trung Hoa Hồ Cẩm Đào. Hai bên đã thông báo cho nhau tình hình mỗi Đảng, mỗi nước; trao đổi ý kiến sâu rộng về các vấn đề khu vực và quốc tế cùng quan tâm. Các cuộc hội đàm, hội kiến đã diễn ra trong bầu không khí thân thiết và hữu nghị.

Hai bên cho rằng, chuyến thăm Trung Quốc của Tổng Bí thư Ban Chấp hành Trung ương Đảng Cộng sản Việt Nam Nông Đức Mạnh đã thành công tốt đẹp, chuyến thăm này là một sự kiện trọng đại trong quan hệ hai Đảng, hai nước vào đầu thế kỷ mới, góp phần quan trọng vào việc tăng cường và làm sâu sắc thêm quan hệ hữu nghị và hợp tác toàn diện giữa hai Đảng, hai nước Việt Nam-Trung Quốc trong thế kỷ Xxi, và sẽ có ảnh hưởng tích cực và sâu sắc đối với hòa bình, ổn định, hợp tác và phát triển của khu vực và thế giới.

2. Phía Việt Nam đánh giá cao những thành tựu lịch sử mà Đảng Cộng sản và nhân dân Trung Quốc đã đạt được trong 80 năm qua, và tin chắc rằng Đảng Cộng sản và nhân dân Trung Quốc nhất định giành được nhiều thành tưu mới to lớn hơn nữa trong công cuộc xây dựng chủ nghĩa xã hội mang đặc sắc Trung Quốc. Phía Trung Quốc đánh giá cao những thành tưu lịch sử mà Đảng Cộng sản và nhân dân Việt Nam đã đạt được trong hơn 70 năm qua, và tin chắc rằng Đảng Cộng sản và nhân dân Việt Nam nhất định giành được những thành tựu mới to lớn hơn nữa trong công cuộc xây dựng Tổ quốc xã hội chủ nghĩa, dân giàu, nước mạnh, xã hội công bằng, dân chủ, văn minh. Hai bên quyết tâm, xuất phát từ thực tế của mỗi nước, tiếp tục tìm tòi và giải quyết những vấn đề lý luận và thực tiễn trọng đại trong việc xây dựng Đảng và Nhà nước, thúc đẩy kinh tế phát triển và xã hội tiến bộ.

3. Hai bên hài lòng chỉ rõ, kể từ khi bình thường hóa quan hệ hai nước, sự giao lưu và hợp tác trên các lĩnh vực giữa Việt Nam và Trung Quốc ngày càng mở rộng và đi vào chiều sâu. Hai bên đã ra các Thông cáo chung năm 1991, 1992, 1994, 1995 và các Tuyên bố chung năm 1999 và 2000, lần lượt ký Hiệp ước biên giới trên đất liền, Hiệp định phân định Vịnh Bắc Bộ và Hiệp định hợp tác nghề cá ở Vịnh Bắc Bộ. Hai Đảng, hai nước đã trao đổi rộng rãi và sâu sắc về những kinh nghiệm đổi mới, cải cách mở cửa, xây dựng Đảng và quản lý Nhà nước, lý luận và thực tiễn xây dựng chủ nghĩa xã hội. Sự hợp tác kinh tế và thương mại giữa hai nước đã nâng lên một tầm cao mới. Hai Đảng, Chính phủ và nhân dân hai nước vui mừng trước sự phát triển tốt đẹp và quan trọng của quan hệ hữu nghị và hợp tác toàn diện Việt Nam-Trung Quốc.

4. Hai bên cho rằng, tình hữu nghị Việt-Trung là tài sản chung quý báu của hai Đảng, hai nước và nhân dân hai nước; không ngừng tăng cường quan hệ hữu nghị và hợp tác toàn diện giữa hai Đảng, hai nước Việt Nam-Trung Quốc trong thế kỷ mới không những phù hợp với lợi ích căn bản của hai Đảng, hai nước và nhân dân hai nước, mà còn có lợi cho hòa bình, ổn định, hợp tác và phát triển

trong khu vực và trên thế giới. Hai bên quyết tâm kiên trì phương châm chỉ đạo 16 chữ "láng giềng hữu nghị, hợp tác toàn diện, ổn định lâu dài, hướng tới tương lai", quán triệt và thực hiện một cách toàn diện mục tiêu và nhiệm vụ đã được nêu rõ trong bản Tuyên bố chung về hợp tác toàn diện trong thế kỷ mới giữa hai nước, không ngừng nâng tầm cao và chất lượng của quan hệ hữu nghị và hợp tác truyền thống Việt-Trung, làm cho hai nước và nhân dan hai nước Việt Nam-Trung Quốc đời đời hữu nghị.

5. Nhằm tăng cường và phát triển hơn nữa quan hệ hữu nghị và hợp tác toàn diện giữa hai Đảng, hai nước Việt Nam-Trung Quốc trong thế kỷ mới, hai bên nhất trí tiếp tục duy trì truyền thống tốt đẹp giao lưu cấp cao giữa hai Đảng, hai nước; thúc đẩy sự giao lưu và hợp tác, nâng cao hiệu quả hợp tác giữa các ban ngành Đảng, Chính quyền, Quốc hội, các đoàn thể nhân dân và các địa phương, trên các lĩnh vực chính trị, kinh tế, văn hóa, giáo dục... giữa hai nước; tăng cường việc trao đổi kinh nghiệm về xây dựng Đảng, quản lý Nhà nước giữa hai bên; tham khảo lẫn nhau về kinh nghiệm đổi mới, cải cách mở cửa và xây dựng Đảng; tăng cường sự giao lưu hữu nghị với hình thức đa dạng và nội dung phong phú giữa thanh, thiếu niên hai nước, làm cho mối tình hữu nghị truyền thống đã được các bậc tiền bối cách mạng hai nước dày công vun đắp cũng như sự nghiệp hữu nghị và hợp tác toàn diện giữa hai nước truyền tiếp cho các thế hệ mai sau.

6. Hai bên xác định trong thế kỷ mới cần tiếp tục tăng cường và mở rộng hợp tác kinh tế, thương mại, khoa học-kỹ thuật và các lĩnh vực khác giữa hai nước theo phương châm bình đẳng, cùng có lợi, chú trọng hiệu quả, bổ sung ưu thế cho nhau, hình thức đa dạng, cùng nhau phát triển; tích cực khuyến khích và ủng hộ các doanh nghiệp hai bên khai thác thêm thị trường hàng hóa của hai nước, tăng cường đầu tư và hợp tác, mở rộng quy mô hợp tác kinh tế và kỹ thuật, thực hiện các dự án hợp tác đem lại hiệu quả kinh tế và xã hội thiết thực.

Nhân dịp này, hai bên đã ký Hiệp định khung giữa Chính phủ nước Cộng hòa Xã hội chủ nghĩa Việt Nam và Chính phủ nước Cộng hòa Nhân dân Trung Hoa về việc Trung Quốc cung cấp cho Việt Nam khoản tín dụng ưu đãi và Hiệp định hợp tác kinh tế kỹ thuật giữa Chính phủ nước Cộng hòa Xã hội Chủ nghĩa Việt Nam và Chính phủ nước Cộng hòa Nhân dân Trung Hoa; và nhất trí sẽ tích cực thúc đẩy các doanh nghiệp hợp tác lâu dài trên dự án bô-xít nhôm Đắc Nông.

Việt Nam nhiệt liệt chúc mừng Trung Quốc trở thành thành viên Tổ chức thương mại thế giới. Trung Quốc tích cực ủng hộ Việt Nam sớm gia nhập Tổ chức thương mại thế giới.

7. Hai bên nhất trí cho rằng, việc hai nước ký Hiệp định biên giới trên đất liền, Hiệp định phân định Vịnh Bắc Bộ và Hiệp định hợp tác nghề cá ở Vịnh Bắc Bộ là sự kiện có ý nghĩa trọng đại, góp phần tích cực vào việc thúc đẩy phát triển hơn nữa quan hệ láng giềng hữu nghị và hợp tác toàn diện giữa hai nước và sự ổn định của khu vực. Hai bên đồng ý tuân theo nhận thức chung của các nhà lãnh đạo hai nước, nhanh chóng hoàn thành các công việc đàm phán tiếp theo có liên quan đến Hiệp định hợp tác nghề cá ở Vịnh Bắc Bộ, để Hiệp định phân định Vịnh Bắc Bộ cùng với Hiệp định hợp tác nghề cá ở Vịnh Bắc Bộ sớm có hiệu lực, tích cực thúc đẩy và tăng nhanh tiến trình công tác phân giới cắm mốc biên giới trên đất liền, xây dựng biên giới hai nước thành biên giới hòa bình, hữu nghị, ổn định lâu dài.

Hai bên đồng ý tiếp tục duy trì cơ chế đàm phán hiện có về vấn đề trên biển, kiên trì thông qua đàm phán hòa bình để tìm ra một giải pháp cơ bản, lâu dài mà hai bên đều có thể chấp nhận được. Trước khi vấn đề được giải quyết, với tinh thần dễ trước khó sau, hai bên tích cực tìm kiếm khả năng và biện pháp triển khai hợp tác trên biển trong các lĩnh vực như: bảo vệ môi trường biển, khí tượng thủy văn, phòng chống thiên tai. Đồng thời, hai bên đều không tiến hành các hành động làm phức tạp thêm hoặc mở rộng tranh chấp, không sử dụng vũ lực hoặc de dọa sử dụng vũ lực đối với những bất đồng nảy sinh, cần bàn bạc kịp thời và giải quyết thỏa đáng với thái độ bình tĩnh, xây dựng không để bất đồng ảnh hưởng đến sự phát triển bình thường của quan hệ hai nước.

8. Phía Việt Nam khẳng định Việt Nam công nhận Chính phủ nước Cộng hòa Nhân dân Trung Hoa là Chính phủ hợp pháp duy nhất đại diện cho toàn Trung Quốc. Đài Loan là một bộ phận lãnh thổ không thể chia cắt của Trung Quốc. Việt Nam chỉ giao lưu về kinh tế, thương mại phi chính phủ với Đài Loan, không phát triển quan hệ chính phủ với Đài Loan. Phía Trung Quốc tỏ sự hiểu biết và hoan nghênh lập trường trên đây của phía Việt Nam. Phía Trung Quốc khẳng định vấn đề Đài Loan hoàn toàn là vấn đề thuộc công việc nội bộ của Trung Quốc và kiên quyết phản đối các nước đã lập quan hệ ngoại giao với

Trung Quốc có quan hệ chính phủ dưới bất cứ hình thức nào, hoặc có bất cứ sự đi lại nào mang tính chính phủ với Đài Loan.

9. Hai bên hài lòng với những nhận thức chung rộng rãi về các vấn đề khu vực và quốc tế mà hai bên cùng quan tâm. Hai bên cho rằng hòa bình, hợp tác, phát triển và tiến bộ xã hội đã trở thành trào lưu của thời đại hiện nay. Hai nước và nhân dân hai nước Việt Nam-Trung Quốc tha thiết mong muốn thế giới hòa bình bền vững, cuộc sống yên ổn lâu dài; tha thiết mong muốn xây dựng một trật tự quốc tế mới công bằng và hợp lý, thúc đẩy các nước cùng phồn vinh và phát triển. Hai bên phản đối chủ nghĩa bá quyền và chính trị cường quyền trong công việc quốc tế; phản đối chủ nghĩa khủng bố dưới mọi hình thức. Hai bên chủ trương tôn trọng lịch sử văn hóa, chế độ xã hội, mô hình phát triển của các nước và các nền văn minh trên thế giới.

Hai bên đánh giá cao vai trò tích cực của tổ chức Asean trong việc giữ gìn và thúc đẩy sự ổn định và phát triển của khu vực, khẳng định lại sẽ tiếp tục góp sức tăng cường quan hệ đối tác láng giềng tin cậy giữa Trung Quốc và các nước Asean, nỗ lực và đóng góp tích cực vào sự ổn định và phồn vinh lâu dài của Châu á, đặc biệt là khu vực Đông á.

10.Tổng Bí thư Ban Chấp hành Trung ương Đảng Cộng sản Việt Nam Nông Đức Mạnh chân thành cảm ơn sự đón tiếp trọng thể, nồng nhiệt và hữu nghị của Đảng Cộng sản, Chính phủ và nhân dân Trung Quốc. Tổng Bí thư Nông Đức Mạnh mời Tổng Bí thư, Chủ tịch nước Giang Trạch Dân thăm hữu nghị chính thức Việt Nam vào thời gian thuận tiện trong năm tới. Tổng Bí thư, Chủ tịch nước Giang Trạch Dân đã cảm ơn và vui vẻ nhận lời.

中华人民共和国政府和越南社会主义共和国政府联合公报

（2004年10月8日）

一、应越南社会主义共和国政府总理潘文凯的邀请，中华人民共和国国务院总理温家宝于2004年10月6日至7日对越南进行了正式访问。访问期间，温家宝总理和潘文凯总理举行了会谈，并会见了越南共产党中央委员会总书记农德孟、国家主席陈德良和国会主席阮文安。两国领导人在诚挚、友好和务实的气氛中就加强双边关系及共同关心的国际和地区问题深入交换了意见，达成广泛共识。访问取得了圆满成功。

二、双方高兴地看到，在两国领导人确定的“长期稳定、面向未来、睦邻友好、全面合作”16字方针指引下，中越关系正在迅速、全面和深入发展。两国领导人往来频繁，双方政治互信增强，经贸合作成果显著，边界领土等历史遗留问题的解决取得积极进展，其他领域的交流与合作日益扩大，在国际和地区事务中相互支持，协调配合。

三、双方认为，中越两国在许多重大问题上具有共同的战略利益。在国际形势深刻演变的背景下，保持双边关系始终稳定、健康和顺利发展，符合两国和两国人民的根本利益，同时也有利于地区和世界的和平与发展。两国政府决心从全局和战略高度出发，继续秉承16字方针，弘扬传统友谊，拓展互利合作，及时妥善处理敏感问题，把中越关系不断推向新的更高水平。

双方一致同意，继续保持高层接触，加强两国各部门、地方和群众团体的友好往来和交流，认真落实双方外交、国防、公安等部门签署的合作文件，切实增进相互理解和信任；深化全面合作，鼓励和支持双方在经贸、科技、教育、文化等领域开展务实合作，努力寻求和扩大共同利益；加强双方治党治国和社会主义理论与实践的经验交流，深入开展“中越青年友好会见”活动和促进两国青年一代的交往，加强中越友好的宣传教育。

四、双方对两国经贸关系取得的长足进展表示满意。双方愿继续深化经贸领域的互利合作，扩大大宗商品交易，确保双边贸易持续快速增长和实现2010年贸易额100亿美元目标，逐渐缩小双边贸易的失衡；抓紧实施双方业已确定的合作项目，积极鼓励和支持双方企业就重大基础设施和工业项目开展长期合作，努力提高两国经贸合作的水平和质量。双方同意在两国政府经贸合作委员会框架下成立专家组，积极探讨“昆明—老街—河内—海防—广宁”、“南宁—谅山—河内—海防—广宁”经济走廊和环北部湾经济圈的可行性。

双方同意共同推动中国—东盟自由贸易区建设进程。越南承认中国完全市场经济地位，并承诺不对中国使用《中国加入世界贸易组织议定书》第15、16条和《中国加入世界贸易组织工作组报告书》第242段。中国承认越南经济为市场经济，支持越南早日加入世界贸易组织，并愿同越方共同努力。双方本着务实和灵活的精神，尽快完成双边市场准入谈判。

五、双方一致认为，2004年8月两国边界谈判政府代表团团长举行特别会晤，就具体落实两国领导人重要共识达成一致并签署会谈纪要，有利于进一步增进双方互信，切实预防和及时妥善处理边界领土发生问题。双方同意采取有效措施，尽快将纪要内容落到实处。

双方同意进一步加快中越陆地边界勘界立碑进程，指导双方有关部门和地方加倍努力，增进互信，真诚合作，力争如期完成勘界立碑工作，早日把陆地边界建成中越两国之间和平、友好与合作的边界。在勘界立碑期间，双方将切实维护边界现状，并严格按照1991年《中华人民共和国政府和越南社会主义共和国政府关于处理两国边境事务的临时协定》管理边界。

双方对北部湾划界协定和渔业合作协定于2004年6月30日同时生效予以高度评价，认为这是中越关系中的一件大事，有利于北部湾地区的长治久安，对中越关系长期稳定发展具有重要意义。双方对两个协定生效后的实施情况感到满意，并强调将继续密切配合，严格落实两协定的规定，同时本着互谅互让的精神，不采取过激和武力行动，共同维护北部湾的和平与稳定，致力于长远合作，造福两国人民。

双方同意严格遵循两国高层共识和中国与东盟各成员国签署的《南海各方行为宣言》（DOC）的宗旨和原则，切实保持克制，双方均不采取任何使争端复杂化或扩大化的单方面行动，不诉诸武力或以武力相威胁，包括不对渔船采取武力行动，以实际行动维护南海局势的稳定。

双方强调，继续维持海上问题谈判机制并增加谈判次数，坚持通过和平谈判，寻求双方均能接受的基本和长久的解决办法。在问题解决前，本着先易后难的精神，继续加强共同关心的低敏感领域的合作，逐步探讨在双方商定的其他领域扩大合作。

六、越南政府重申坚定奉行一个中国政策，支持中国统一大业，坚决反对任何形式的“台独”分裂活动。越南同台湾只进行非官方经贸往来，绝不同台湾发展官方关系。

七、双方同意继续加强在联合国、东盟、东盟地区论坛、亚太经合组织、亚欧会议、大湄公河次区域开发等多边领域的合作与配合，继续致力于建立公正合理的国际政治和经济新秩序，为维护地区和世界和平、稳定与发展作出贡献。

Thông cáo báo chí chung Trung Quốc-Việt Nam

(2004/10/8)

Nhận lời mời của Thủ tướng Chính phủ nước Cộng hòa xã hội chủ nghĩa Việt Nam Phan Văn Khải, Thủ tướng Quốc vụ viện nước Cộng hòa Nhân dân Trung Hoa Ôn Gia Bảo đã thăm chính thức nước Việt Nam từ ngày 6 đến ngày 7 tháng 10 năm 2004.

Trong thời gian chuyến thăm, Thủ tướng Ôn Gia Bảo đã tiến hành hội đàm với Thủ tướng Phan Văn Khải, hội kiến với Tổng Bí thư Ban Chấp hành Trung ương Đảng Cộng sản Việt Nam Nông Đức Mạnh, Chủ tịch nước Trần Đức Lương, Chủ tịch Quốc hội Nguyễn Văn An. Trong không khí chân thành, hữu nghị và cầu thị, lãnh đạo hai nước đã trao đổi ý kiến và đạt được nhận thức chung sâu rộng về việc tăng cường quan hệ song phương và các vấn đề quốc tế, khu vực cùng quan tâm. Chuyến thăm đã thành công tốt đẹp.

Hai bên vui mừng nhận thấy, quan hệ Việt-Trung đang phát triển nhanh chóng, toàn diện và sâu sắc theo phương châm 16 chữ “láng giềng hữu nghị, hợp tác toàn diện, ổn định lâu dài, hướng tới tương lai” do lãnh đạo hai nước xác định. Lãnh đạo hai nước thường xuyên thăm viếng lẫn nhau, sự tin cậy về chính trị giữa hai bên được tăng cường, hợp tác kinh tế thương mại thu được thành quả rõ rệt, việc giải quyết các vấn đề do lịch sử để lại như biên giới lãnh thổ đạt được tiến triển tích cực, giao lưu và hợp tác trong các lĩnh vực khác ngày càng được mở rộng, hai bên ủng hộ lẫn nhau và phối hợp nhịp nhàng trong các vấn đề quốc tế và khu vực.

Hai bên cho rằng, Việt Nam và Trung Quốc có lợi ích chiến lược chung trên nhiều vấn đề quan trọng. Trong bối cảnh tình hình quốc tế diễn biến sâu sắc, việc duy trì quan hệ hai bên luôn luôn phát triển ổn định, lành mạnh và thuận lợi phù hợp với lợi ích căn bản của hai nước và nhân dân hai nước, đồng thời cũng có lợi cho hòa bình, phát triển ở khu vực và trên thế giới. Chính phủ hai nước quyết tâm xuất phát từ toàn cục và tầm cao chiến lược, tiếp tục tuân theo phương châm 16 chữ, phát huy tình hữu nghị truyền thống, mở rộng hợp tác cùng có lợi, kịp thời xử lý thỏa đáng các vấn đề nhạy cảm, không ngừng đưa quan hệ Việt-Trung lên tầm cao mới.

Hai bên nhất trí tiếp tục duy trì tiếp xúc cấp cao, tăng cường trao đổi và giao lưu hữu nghị giữa các ngành, địa phương và đoàn thể quần chúng hai nước, nghiêm túc thực hiện các văn kiện hợp tác được ký kết giữa các ngành của hai bên như ngoại giao, quốc phòng, công an, v.v..., thực sự tăng cường hiểu biết và tin cậy lẫn nhau; đi sâu hợp tác toàn diện, khuyến khích và hỗ trợ việc triển khai hợp tác thiết thực giữa hai bên trên các lĩnh vực kinh tế thương mại, khoa học kỹ thuật, giáo dục, văn hóa, v.v..., nỗ lực tìm tòi và mở rộng lợi ích chung; tăng cường trao đổi kinh nghiệm về lý luận và thực tiễn lãnh đạo Đảng, quản lý đất nước và xây dựng chủ nghĩa xã hội, triển khai sâu rộng hoạt động "Gặp gỡ hữu nghị thanh niên Việt-Trung" và thúc đẩy giao lưu giữa thế hệ thanh niên hai nước, tăng cường tuyên truyền giáo dục tình hữu nghị Việt-Trung.

Hai bên hài lòng về những tiến triển đáng kể trong quan hệ kinh tế-thương mại hai nước. Hai bên mong muốn tiếp tục đi sâu hợp tác cùng có lợi trong lĩnh vực kinh tế-thương mại, mở rộng buôn bán hàng hóa khối lượng lớn, bảo đảm buôn bán song phương tiếp tục tăng trưởng nhanh, liên tục và hoàn thành mục tiêu nâng kim ngạch thương mại song phương lên 10 tỷ USD vào năm 2010, thu hẹp dần sự mất cân đối trong cán cân thương mại hai chiều; khẩn trương thực hiện các dự án hợp tác hai bên đã xác định, tích cực khuyến khích và hỗ trợ doanh nghiệp hai bên triển khai hợp tác lâu dài đối với các dự án cơ sở hạ tầng và công nghiệp quan trọng, nỗ lực nâng cao trình độ và chất lượng hợp tác kinh tế thương mại giữa hai nước. Hai bên đồng ý thành lập Nhóm chuyên gia trong khuôn khổ Ủy ban hợp tác kinh tế, thương mại liên Chính phủ hai nước, tích cực trao đổi về tính khả thi của hành lang kinh tế "Côn Minh-Lào Cai-Hà Nội-Hải Phòng-Quảng Ninh", "Nam Ninh-Lạng Sơn-Hà Nội-Hải Phòng-Quảng Ninh" và vành đai kinh tế xung quanh Vịnh Bắc Bộ.

Hai bên đồng ý cùng nhau thúc đẩy tiến trình xây dựng khu vực mậu dịch tự do Trung Quốc-ASEAN. Việt Nam công nhận địa vị kinh tế thị trường hoàn toàn của Trung Quốc và cam kết không sử dụng điều 15, điều 16 của "*Nghị định thư Trung Quốc gia nhập WTO*" và đoạn 242 "*Báo cáo của tổ công tác Trung Quốc gia nhập WTO*" đối với Trung Quốc. Trung Quốc công nhận nền kinh tế Việt Nam là nền kinh tế thị trường, ủng hộ Việt Nam sớm gia nhập WTO và nguyện cùng phía Việt Nam nỗ lực. Hai bên với tinh thần thực tế và linh hoạt kết thúc đàm phán song phương về mở cửa thị trường trong thời gian sớm nhất.

Hai bên nhất trí cho rằng, tháng 8 năm 2004, hai Trưởng đoàn đại biểu Chính phủ đàm phán về biên giới lãnh thổ hai nước tiến hành cuộc gặp đặc biệt, đạt được nhất trí và ký Biên bản hội đàm về việc triển khai cụ thể nhận thức chung quan trọng của Lãnh đạo cấp cao hai nước là có lợi cho việc tăng cường hơn nữa sự tin cậy lẫn nhau giữa hai bên, thiết thực phòng ngừa và xử lý thỏa đáng, kịp thời những vấn đề nảy sinh liên quan đến biên giới lãnh thổ. Hai bên đồng ý áp dụng các biện pháp hữu hiệu, nhanh chóng thực hiện các nội dung của Biên bản.

Hai bên đồng ý đẩy nhanh hơn nữa tiến trình phân giới cắm mốc biên giới trên đất liền Việt-Trung, chỉ đạo các cơ quan và địa phương hữu quan hai bên ra sức nỗ lực, tăng cường tin cậy, hợp tác chân thành, cố gắng hoàn thành đúng kế hoạch công tác phân giới cắm mốc, sớm xây dựng đường biên giới trên đất liền trở thành đường biên giới hòa bình, hữu nghị và hợp tác giữa hai nước Việt Nam và Trung Quốc. Trong thời gian phân giới cắm mốc, hai bên thực sự duy trì hiện trạng biên giới và nghiêm chỉnh quản lý biên giới theo "Hiệp định tạm thời về việc giải quyết công việc trên vùng biên giới hai nước giữa Chính phủ Cộng hòa xã hội chủ nghĩa Việt Nam và Chính phủ Cộng hòa Nhân dân Trung Hoa" năm 1991.

Hai bên đánh giá cao việc Hiệp định phân định và Hiệp định hợp tác nghề cá ở Vịnh Bắc Bộ đồng thời có hiệu lực từ ngày 30 tháng 6 năm 2004, cho rằng đây là một sự kiện lớn trong quan hệ Việt-Trung, có lợi cho ổn định lâu dài ở khu vực Vịnh Bắc Bộ, có ý nghĩa quan trọng đối với sự phát triển ổn định lâu dài của quan hệ Việt-Trung. Hai bên hài lòng về tình hình thực hiện sau khi hai Hiệp định có hiệu lực, nhấn mạnh sẽ tiếp tục phối hợp chặt chẽ, thực hiện nghiêm chỉnh các quy định của hai Hiệp định, đồng thời theo tinh thần thông cảm nhân nhượng lẫn nhau không có các hành động quá khích và sử dụng vũ lực, cùng nhau duy trì hòa bình và ổn định ở Vịnh Bắc Bộ, nỗ lực vì sự hợp tác lâu dài, tạo dựng hạnh phúc cho nhân dân hai nước.

Hai bên đồng ý nghiêm chỉnh tuân theo nhận thức chung của lãnh đạo cấp cao hai nước, tôn chỉ, nguyên tắc của "Tuyên bố về cách ứng xử của các bên ở Biển Đông" (DOC) giữa các nước thành viên ASEAN và Trung Quốc, thực sự kiềm chế, hai bên đều không có bất cứ hành động đơn phương nào làm phức tạp hoặc mở rộng tranh chấp, không sử dụng vũ lực hoặc đe dọa sử dụng vũ lực, kể cả không có hành động vũ lực đối với tàu thuyền đánh cá, duy trì ổn định tình hình biển Đông bằng hành động thực tế.

Hai bên nhấn mạnh, tiếp tục duy trì cơ chế đàm phán về vấn đề trên biển, tăng số lần đàm phán, kiên trì thông qua đàm phán hòa bình, tìm kiếm giải pháp cơ bản và lâu dài hai bên đều chấp nhận được. Trước khi vấn đề được giải quyết, với tinh thần dễ trước khó sau, hai bên tiếp tục tăng cường hợp tác trong các lĩnh vực ít nhạy cảm mà hai bên cùng quan tâm, từng bước tiến hành trao đổi mở rộng hợp tác trong các lĩnh vực khác do hai bên thỏa thuận.

Chính phủ Việt Nam khẳng định lại kiên định thi hành chính sách một nước Trung Quốc, ủng hộ sự nghiệp lớn thống nhất Trung Quốc, kiên quyết phản đối các hoạt động "Đài Loan độc lập" dưới bất cứ hình thức nào. Việt Nam chỉ tiến hành trao đổi kinh tế mậu dịch phi chính phủ với Đài Loan, không phát triển quan hệ chính phủ với Đài Loan.

Hai bên đồng ý tiếp tục tăng cường hợp tác và phối hợp trong các lĩnh vực đa phương như Liên hợp quốc, ASEAN, ARF, APEC, ASEM, phát triển tiểu vùng sông Mê Công mở rộng, tiếp tục nỗ lực xây dựng trật tự chính trị, kinh tế quốc tế mới công bằng hợp lý, góp phần duy trì hòa bình, ổn định và phát triển trong khu vực và trên thế giới.

中越联合声明

（2005年11月2日）

一、应越南共产党中央委员会总书记农德孟和越南社会主义共和国主席陈德良的邀请，中国共产党中央委员会总书记、中华人民共和国主席胡锦涛于2005年10月31日至11月2日对越南进行了正式友好访问。访问期间，胡锦涛总书记、国家主席与农德孟总书记、陈德良国家主席举行了会谈，分别会见了越南政府总理潘文凯、国会主席阮文安，并应邀在越南国会发表了演讲。双方领导人在亲切、友好的气氛中，就进一步加强和发展两党两国关系以及共同关心的地区和国际问题深入交换了意见，取得了广泛共识。

双方认为这次成功访问将中越两党两国睦邻友好与全面合作关系提高到了一个新的发展水平，同时也将对本地区和世界的和平、稳定、发展与合作产生积极影响。

二、双方对两党两国在探索符合各自国情的社会主义发展道路中取得的历史性成就感到高兴。中国方面衷心祝愿并相信越南共产党和越南人民在建设民富国强、社会公平、民主、文明的社会主义祖国的宏伟事业中取得新的更大的成就。越南方面坚信中国共产党和中国人民在建设中国特色社会主义的宏伟事业中一定会不断取得新的成就。

三、双方回顾和总结了中越两国建交55年来，特别是关系正常化以来，两党两国睦邻友好与全面合作关系取得的丰硕成果，一致认为，相互尊重、相互理解、相互支持、相互信任、相互合作是两党两国关系稳定、健康和顺利发展的重要经验，中越友好是两党两国和两国人民的宝贵财富，长期稳定、面向未来、睦邻友好、全面合作是新时期发展两党两国关系的指导方针，永做好邻居、好朋友、好同志、好伙伴是两党两国和两国人民的共同目标。

双方认为，增进友好互信，推动互利合作，促进共同发展，符合中越两国的根本利益。为此，双方决心从大局和战略高度出发，采取行之有效的措施，全面深化和拓展两党两国关系，继续保持高层互访的良好传统，加强党政部门、议会、群众团体和地方在政治、经济、外交、国防、公安、安全、文化、教育等各个领域的交流与合作，深化治党治国和社会主义理论与实践的经验交流，进一步巩固和加深两国人民的相互了解和友谊，特别是加强对中越两国青年进行中越友好传统的宣传和教育，使中越世代友好深深植根于两国人民心中，推动两党两国关系不断开创新局面。

四、双方对近年来两国经贸关系发展表示满意。双方一致同意，力争提前实现2010年双边贸易额达到100亿美元的目标。

双方表示愿意进一步推动两国经贸关系的发展，实现优势互补、互利双赢。双方同意本着积极务实的精神，进一步扩大贸易规模，并共同采取措施促进双边贸易平衡发展；双方密切配合，积极推动两国大型经济合作项目；共同鼓励和推动两国企业开展长期合作，积极开展双向投资和多种形式的互利经济合作；加强配合，共同为双方企业合作创造便利条件。双方对中越"两廊一圈"经济合作研究取得的进展表示满意，并对其合作前景充满信心。

双方对两国顺利完成关于越南加入世贸组织的双边市场准入谈判给予高度评价。中方表示，坚决支持越南早日加入世贸组织。双方同意加强在地区和国际经贸事务上的合作，共同推进中国—东盟自由贸易区的建设进程。

双方签署了经济技术合作协定等文件。越方对中方的援助及一贯支持越南经济发展表示感谢。

五、双方认为，两国陆地边界勘界立碑工作取得了显著进展。双方同意密切配合，进一步加快工作进程，确保如期实现最迟于2008年完成陆地边界全线勘界立碑工作并签署新的边界管理制度文件的目标，把两国边界建成和平友好和长期稳定的边界。

双方积极评价北部湾划界协定和渔业合作协定的落实情况，同意继续认真落实这两个协定，共同维护海上治安和渔业生产秩序，积极开展北部湾共同渔区渔业资源联合调查，启动跨界油气构造勘采合作，早日实施两国海军北部湾联合巡逻。双方同意尽早开始湾口外海域的划界谈判并商谈该海域的共同开发问题。

双方高度评价中国、越南和菲律宾三国石油公司今年3月签署的《南中国海协议区三方联合海洋地震工作协议》，认为协议的签署是落实《南海各方行为宣言》（DOC）的重要贡献，对促进海上共同开发和局势稳定，加强有关国家睦邻互信具有积极影响。双方同意对有关公司予以积极支持，确保协议得到认真实施，使合作早日取得具体成果。双方同意维持海上问题谈判机制，坚持通过和平谈判，寻求双方均能接受的基本和长久的解决办法；在此过程中，双方将认真研究共同开发问题，以便找到双方都能接受的符合国际法、国际实践特别是1982年《联合国海洋法公约》和《南海各方行为宣言》精神的共同开发模式和区域。同时双方同意恪守两国高层共识，遵循《南海各方行为宣言》的宗旨和原则，共同维护南海局势的稳定。

六、越南方面重申坚定奉行一个中国政策，支持中国统一大业，坚决反对任何形式的“台独”分裂活动，充分理解和支持中国全国人大通过《反分裂国家法》，欢迎近年来两岸关系的缓和趋势。越南绝不同台湾发展任何官方关系。中国方面对越南方面的上述立场表示赞赏。

七、双方一致认为中越两国在许多重大问题上具有共同的战略利益。要和平、促发展、谋合作是当今时代的主旋律。双方强调，要坚持国际事务中的多边主义，实现共同繁荣，在平等和相互尊重的基础上开展多边合作，反对一切形式的恐怖主义。双方主张尊重各国的历史文化、社会制度、发展模式以及世界文明的多样性，促进国际关系民主化，共建持久和平、共同繁荣的和谐的亚洲和世界。

八、双方欢迎2005年9月联合国成立60周年首脑会议通过的《成果文件》，认为当务之急是要落实千年发展目标，切实帮助发展中国家解决发展问题。双方一致认为，联合国改革应有助于提高联合国的作用、权威和效率，维护世界和平与安全以及应对新挑战和新威胁的能力，推动各成员国的共同发展，为落实千年发展目标服务。双方认为，安理会改革应从联合国长远利益出发，根据国际关系民主化原则，在广泛协商的基础上增加发展中国家的代表性，寻求兼顾各方利益的解决办法。本着上述精神，双方将就此问题继续加强磋商与合作。

双方同意继续加强在联合国、中国与东盟、东盟—中日韩、亚洲合作对话、东盟地区论坛、亚太经合组织、亚欧会议、大湄公河次区域开发等多边框架下的合作与配合。中方重申支持越南主办2006年第十四次亚太经合组织领导人非正式会议。

九、中共中央总书记、国家主席胡锦涛对越南共产党、越南政府和越南人民所给予的隆重、热情和友好的接待表示衷心感谢，并邀请农德孟总书记和陈德良国家主席在方便的时候对中国进行访问。农德孟总书记和陈德良国家主席对此表示感谢并愉快地接受了邀请。

越方再次邀请胡锦涛总书记、国家主席出席2006年底在河内举行的第十四次亚太经合组织领导人非正式会议。胡锦涛总书记、国家主席愉快地接受了邀请。

二〇〇五年十一月二日于河内

Tuyên bố chung Trung Quốc-Việt Nam

(2005/11/2)

1. Nhận lời mời của Tổng Bí thư Ban chấp hành Trung ương Đảng Cộng sản Việt Nam Nông Đức Mạnh và Chủ tịch nước Cộng hoà xã hội chủ nghĩa Việt Nam Trần Đức Lương, Tổng Bí thư Ban chấp hành Trung ương Đảng Cộng sản Trung Quốc, Chủ tịch nước Cộng hoà nhân dân Trung Hoa Hồ Cẩm Đào đã thăm hữu nghị chính thức Việt Nam từ ngày 31 tháng 10 đến ngày 2 tháng 11 năm 2005.

Trong thời gian thăm, Tổng Bí thư, Chủ tịch nước Hồ Cẩm Đào đã tiến hành hội đàm với Tổng Bí thư Nông Đức Mạnh, Chủ tịch nước Trần Đức Lương, lần lượt gặp Thủ tướng Phan Văn Khải, Chủ tịch Quốc hội Nguyễn Văn An và đã nhận lời mời đến phát biểu tại Quốc hội Việt Nam. Trong không khí thân mật, hữu nghị, lãnh đạo hai bên đã đi sâu trao đổi và đạt được nhận thức chung rộng rãi về việc tăng cường và phát triển hơn nữa quan hệ giữa hai Đảng, hai nước và các vấn đề khu vực, quốc tế cùng quan tâm.

Hai bên cho rằng, chuyến thăm thành công lần này sẽ đưa quan hệ láng giềng hữu nghị và hợp tác toàn diện giữa hai Đảng, hai nước Việt-Trung phát triển lên một tầm cao mới, đồng thời sẽ có ảnh hưởng tích cực đối với hoà bình, ổn định, phát triển và hợp tác ở khu vực và thế giới.

2. Hai bên vui mừng trước những thành tựu mang tính lịch sử mà hai Đảng, hai nước giành được trong việc tìm tòi con đường phát triển xã hội chủ nghĩa phù hợp với tình hình của mỗi nước. Phía Trung Quốc chân thành chúc và tin tưởng Đảng Cộng sản Việt Nam và nhân dân Việt Nam sẽ giành được những thành tựu mới, to lớn hơn nữa trong sự nghiệp vĩ đại xây dựng Tổ quốc xã hội chủ nghĩa,

dân giàu nước mạnh, xã hội công bằng, dân chủ, văn minh. Phía Việt Nam tin tưởng vững chắc rằng Đảng Cộng sản Trung Quốc và nhân dân Trung Quốc nhất định sẽ không ngừng giành được những thành tựu mới trong sự nghiệp vĩ đại xây dựng xã hội chủ nghĩa đặc sắc Trung Quốc.

3. Hai bên đã điểm lại và tổng kết những thành quả to lớn mà quan hệ láng giềng hữu nghị và hợp tác toàn diện giữa hai Đảng, hai nước đã giành được trong 55 năm qua kể từ khi hai nước Việt Nam và Trung Quốc thiết lập quan hệ ngoại giao, đặc biệt là từ khi bình thường hóa quan hệ đến nay, nhất trí cho rằng, tôn trọng lẫn nhau, hiểu biết lẫn nhau, ủng hộ lẫn nhau, tin cậy lẫn nhau và hợp tác cùng nhau là kinh nghiệm quan trọng để quan hệ hai Đảng, hai nước phát triển ổn định, lành mạnh và thuận lợi. Tình hữu nghị Việt–Trung là tài sản quý báu của hai Đảng, hai nước và nhân dân hai nước. Láng giềng hữu nghị, hợp tác toàn diện, ổn định lâu dài, hướng tới tương lai là phương châm chỉ đạo phát triển quan hệ hai Đảng, hai nước trong thời kỳ mới. Mãi mãi là láng giềng tốt, bạn bè tốt, đồng chí tốt, đối tác tốt là mục tiêu chung của hai Đảng, hai nước và nhân dân hai nước.

Hai bên cho rằng, tăng thêm hữu nghị và tin cậy lẫn nhau, đẩy mạnh hợp tác cùng có lợi, thúc đẩy cùng phát triển là phù hợp với lợi ích căn bản của hai nước Việt-Trung. Vì vậy, hai bên quyết tâm xuất phát từ đại cục và tầm cao chiến lược, áp dụng các biện pháp có hiệu quả, làm sâu sắc và triển khai toàn diện quan hệ hai Đảng, hai nước, tiếp tục duy trì truyền thống tốt đẹp thăm viếng lẫn nhau ở cấp cao, tăng cường trao đổi và hợp tác giữa các ngành của Đảng và chính phủ, quốc hội, đoàn thể quần chúng và địa phương trong các lĩnh vực chính trị, kinh tế, ngoại giao, quốc phòng, công an, an ninh, văn hóa, giáo dục, đi sâu trao đổi kinh nghiệm về xây dựng Đảng, quản lý đất nước cũng như lý luận và thực tiễn về chủ nghĩa xã hội, củng cố và làm sâu sắc hơn nữa sự hiểu biết lẫn nhau và tình hữu nghị giữa nhân dân hai nước, đặt biệt là tăng cường tuyên truyền và giáo dục thanh niên hai nước về truyền thống hữu nghị Việt-Trung, để tình hữu nghị muôn đời Việt-Trung thấm sâu vào lòng nhân dân hai nước, thúc đẩy quan hệ giữa hai Đảng, hai nước không ngừng mở ra cục diện mới.

4. Hai bên hài lòng về sự phát triển quan hệ kinh tế thương mại giữa hai nước trong những năm gần đây. Hai bên nhất trí phấn đấu thực hiện trước thời

hạn mục tiêu đưa kim ngạch thương mại hai nước đạt 10 tỷ USD vào năm 2010.

Hai bên bày tỏ mong muốn thúc đẩy quan hệ kinh tế thương mại giữa hai nước phát triển hơn nữa, thực hiện bổ sung ưu thế cho nhau, hai bên cùng có lợi cùng thắng. Trên tinh thần tích cực, thực tế, hai bên nhất trí mở rộng hơn nữa quy mô thương mại, đồng thời cùng có biện pháp thúc đẩy thương mại song phương phát triển cân đối; hai bên phối hợp chặt chẽ, tích cực thúc đẩy những dự án hợp tác kinh tế lớn giữa hai nước; cùng khuyến khích và thúc đẩy doanh nghiệp hai nước tiến hành hợp tác lâu dài, tích cực triển khai đầu tư hai chiều và hợp tác kinh tế cùng có lợi với nhiều hình thức; tăng cường phối hợp cùng tạo điều kiện thuận lợi cho sự hợp tác giữa doanh nghiệp hai nước. Hai bên bày tỏ hài lòng trước những tiến triển đạt được trong việc nghiên cứu về hợp tác kinh tế "hai hành lang, một vành đai" và hết sức tin tưởng vào triển vọng hợp tác của dự án này.

Hai bên đánh giá cao việc hai nước hoàn thành thuận lợi đàm phán về mở cửa thị trường liên quan đến việc Việt Nam gia nhập WTO. Phía Trung Quốc bày tỏ kiên quyết ủng hộ Việt Nam sớm gia nhập WTO. Hai bên đồng ý tăng cường hợp tác trong các vấn đề kinh tế thương mại khu vực và quốc tế; cùng nhau thúc đẩy tiến trình xây dựng Khu mậu dịch tự do ASEAN-Trung Quốc.

Hai bên đã ký kết nhiều Thỏa thuận hợp tác kinh tế kỹ thuật. Phía Việt Nam cảm ơn sự giúp đỡ và ủng hộ nhất quán của Trung Quốc đối với công cuộc phát triển kinh tế của Việt Nam.

5. Hai bên cho rằng, công tác phân giới cắm mốc biên giới trên đất liền giữa hai nước đã đạt được tiến triển rõ rệt. Hai bên đồng ý phối hợp chặt chẽ, đẩy nhanh hơn nữa tiến trình công tác, bảo đảm thực hiện đúng thời hạn mục tiêu hoàn thành công tác phân giới cắm mốc trên toàn tuyến biên giới và ký văn kiện mới về qui chế quản lý biên giới chậm nhất vào năm 2008, xây dựng biên giới hai nước trở thành biên giới hoà bình, hữu nghị và ổn định lâu dài.

Hai bên đánh giá tích cực tình hình thực hiện Hiệp định phân định và Hiệp định Hợp tác nghề cá Vịnh Bắc bộ, đồng ý tiếp tục thực hiện nghiêm túc hai Hiệp định này; cùng giữ gìn an ninh trên biển và trật tự sản xuất nghề cá; tích cực triển khai điều tra liên hợp nguồn lợi thuỷ sản trong vùng đánh cá chung ở Vịnh Bắc Bộ; khởi động hợp tác thăm dò khai thác các cấu tạo dầu khí vắt ngang đường phân định; sớm thực hiện việc tuần tra chung giữa Hải quân hai nước ở

Vịnh Bắc Bộ. Hai bên đồng ý sớm bắt đầu đàm phán về phân định vùng biển ngoài cửa vịnh và trao đổi về vấn đề hợp tác cùng phát triển ở khu vực này.

Hai bên đánh giá cao "Thỏa thuận công tác địa chấn biển liên hợp 3 bên tại khu vực thỏa thuận ở biển Đông" do Công ty dầu khí 3 nước Việt Nam, Trung Quốc, Philipin ký tháng 3 năm nay, cho rằng việc ký kết Thỏa thuận này là đóng góp quan trọng thực hiện "Tuyên bố về cách ứng xử của các bên ở Biển Đông" (DOC), có ảnh hưởng tích cực đối với việc thúc đẩy hợp tác cùng phát triển và ổn định tình hình trên biển, tăng cường tình hữu nghị láng giềng và sự tin cậy lẫn nhau giữa các nước liên quan. Hai bên đồng ý tích cực ủng hộ các công ty liên quan, bảo đảm thực hiện Thỏa thuận một cách nghiêm chỉnh, làm cho việc hợp tác sớm đạt được thành quả cụ thể. Hai bên đồng ý tiếp tục duy trì cơ chế đàm phán về vấn đề trên biển, kiên trì thông qua đàm phán hoà bình, tìm kiếm giải pháp cơ bản và lâu dài mà hai bên đều chấp nhận được; trong quá trình đó, hai bên sẽ nghiên cứu kỹ vấn đề hợp tác cùng phát triển để tìm được mô hình và khu vực hợp tác cùng phát triển phù hợp với Luật pháp quốc tế và thực tiễn quốc tế, đặc biệt là "Công ước Luật biển" năm 1982 của Liên Hợp Quốc và "Tuyên bố về cách ứng xử của các bên ở Biển Đông" mà hai bên có thể chấp nhận được. Đồng thời, hai bên đồng ý nghiêm túc tuân thủ nhận thức chung cấp cao, tuân thủ tôn chỉ và nguyên tắc của "Tuyên bố về cách ứng xử của các bên ở Biển Đông", cùng giữ gìn ổn định tình hình biển Đông.

6. Phía Việt Nam khẳng định kiên trì thực hiện chính sách một nước Trung Quốc, ủng hộ sự nghiệp lớn thống nhất Trung Quốc, kiên quyết phản đối hành động chia rẽ "Đài Loan độc lập" dưới mọi hình thức, hoàn toàn hiểu và ủng hộ Đại hội đại biểu Nhân dân toàn quốc Trung Quốc thông qua "Luật chống chia cắt đất nước", hoan nghênh xu thế hoà dịu của quan hệ hai bờ trong những năm gần đây. Việt Nam không phát triển bất kỳ quan hệ chính thức nào với Đài Loan. Phía Trung Quốc bày tỏ hoan nghênh lập trường trên của phía Việt Nam.

7. Hai bên nhất trí cho rằng Việt Nam và Trung Quốc có lợi ích chiến lược chung trên nhiều vấn đề quan trọng. Mong muốn hoà bình, thúc đẩy phát triển và tìm kiếm hợp tác là nhịp điệu chính của thời đại hiện nay. Hai bên nhấn mạnh cần phải kiên trì chủ nghĩa đa phương trong các vấn đề quốc tế, thực hiện cùng phồn vinh, phát triển hợp tác nhiều bên trên cơ sở bình đẳng và tôn trọng lẫn

nhau, phản đối chủ nghĩa khủng bố dưới mọi hình thức.

Hai bên chủ trương tôn trọng văn hoá lịch sử, chế độ xã hội, mô hình phát triển của các nước cũng như tính đa dạng của nền văn minh thế giới, thúc đẩy dân chủ hoá quan hệ quốc tế, cùng nhau xây dựng một khu vực châu Á cũng như thế giới hoà hợp, hoà bình lâu dài, cùng thịnh vượng.

8. Hai bên hoan nghênh Văn kiện cuối cùng được thông qua tại Hội nghị cấp cao Đại hội đồng Liên hợp quốc tháng 9 năm 2005 nhân 60 năm thành lập Liên hợp quốc và cho rằng việc cấp bách hiện nay là thực hiện Mục tiêu phát triển Thiên niên kỷ, thiết thực giúp đỡ các nước đang phát triển giải quyết vấn đề phát triển. Hai bên nhất trí cho rằng cải tổ Liên Hợp quốc cần góp phần nâng cao vai trò, uy tín, hiệu quả và năng lực của Liên Hợp quốc trong việc duy trì hòa bình và an ninh quốc tế, đối phó với những thách thức và đe doạ mới, thúc đẩy sự phát triển chung của các nước thành viên, phục vụ cho việc thực hiện các Mục tiêu phát triển thiên niên kỷ. Hai bên cho rằng việc cải tổ Hội đồng bảo an Liên Hợp quốc cần xuất phát từ lợi ích lâu dài của Liên Hợp quốc, tuân theo nguyên tắc dân chủ hóa quan hệ quốc tế và cần tăng thêm tính đại diện của các nước đang phát triển trên cơ sở hiệp thương rộng rãi, tìm kiếm giải pháp có tính đến lợi ích các bên. Trên tinh thần đó, hai bên sẽ tiếp tục tăng cường trao đổi ý kiến và hợp tác về vấn đề này.

Hai bên đồng ý tiếp tục tăng cường hợp tác và phối hợp trong khuôn khổ đa phương tại các diễn đàn Liên Hợp quốc, Trung Quốc-ASEAN, ASEAN+3, ACD, ARF, APEC, ASEM, GMS . Phía Trung Quốc khẳng định ủng hộ Việt Nam đăng cai Hội nghị không chính thức các nhà lãnh đạo APEC lần thứ 14 năm 2006.

9. Tổng Bí thư Ban chấp hành Trung ương Đảng Cộng sản Trung Quốc, Chủ tịch nước Hồ Cẩm Đào bày tỏ sự cảm ơn chân thành đối với sự đón tiếp trọng thị, nhiệt tình và thắm tình hữu nghị của Đảng Cộng sản, Chính phủ và nhân dân Việt Nam, đồng thời mời Tổng Bí thư Nông Đức Mạnh và Chủ tịch nước Trần Đức Lương sang thăm Trung Quốc vào thời gian thuận tiện. Tổng Bí thư Nông Đức Mạnh và Chủ tịch nước Trần Đức Lương bày tỏ cảm ơn và vui vẻ nhận lời.

Phía Việt Nam nhắc lại lời mời Tổng Bí thư, Chủ tịch nước Hồ Cẩm Đào dự Hội nghị không chính thức các nhà lãnh đạo APEC lần thứ 14 tại Hà Nội vào cuối năm 2006. Tổng Bí thư, Chủ tịch nước Hồ Cẩm Đào đã vui vẻ nhận lời.

中越联合声明

（2006年11月17日）

一、应越南共产党中央委员会总书记农德孟、越南社会主义共和国主席阮明哲的邀请，中国共产党中央委员会总书记、中华人民共和国主席胡锦涛于2006年11月15日至17日对越南进行国事访问。访问期间，胡锦涛总书记、国家主席与农德孟总书记、阮明哲国家主席举行会谈，并分别会见了越南政府总理阮晋勇、国会主席阮富仲。双方相互通报了各自党和国家的情况，并就两党、两国关系及共同关心的国际和地区问题深入交换意见，达成广泛共识。双方一致认为，访问取得了圆满成功，必将有力地推动中越睦邻友好与全面合作关系继续向前发展。

二、双方对两党、两国在探索符合各自国情的社会主义发展道路上取得的历史性成就感到高兴。越方高度评价中国在改革开放和中国特色社会主义建设事业中取得的伟大成就，相信中国人民在中国共产党领导下，一定能实现全面建设小康社会、加快推进社会主义现代化的宏伟目标。中方高度评价越南推行革新事业20年来取得的具有历史意义的重大成就，支持越共十大确定的方针政策，相信越南人民在越南共产党的领导下，一定能胜利实现越共十大确定的各项目标和任务，把越南建设成为民富国强、社会公平、民主、文明的社会主义现代化国家。

三、双方对两党、两国关系不断巩固和发展表示满意，一致认为，中越两国在许多重大问题上具有共同的战略利益。在国际形势发生深刻变化的情况下，加强中越睦邻友好和全面合作，符合两党、两国和两国人民的根本利益，有利于地区和世界的和平与发展。

双方同意，加强高层往来，深化治党理政和社会主义理论与实践的交流，充分发挥外交、国防、公安、安全等各部门合作机制的作用，扩大经贸、科技、教育、文化等领域的务实合作，大力开展青少年友好交往，使中越友好世代相传。共同致力于发展“长期稳定、面向未来、睦邻友好、全面合作”的中越关系，永远做“好邻居、好朋友、好同志、好伙伴”。

四、双方积极评价中越双边合作指导委员会正式成立和首次会议的召开。双方一致认为，这有利于加强对中越各领域合作的宏观指导、统筹规划和全面推进，协调解决合作中出现的问题，将为两国睦邻友好与全面合作关系长期、稳定、健康、持续发展发挥重要作用。

五、双方对两国经贸合作取得的进展表示满意。同意本着“优势互补、互利共赢”的精神，进一步扩大经贸合作规模，提高合作质量和水平。积极开拓新的贸易增长点，保持双边贸易额快速增长，实现到2010年双边贸易额150亿美元的新目标。逐步改善贸易结构，努力实现双边贸易的平衡发展和可持续增长。积极支持和推进双方企业在基础设施、制造业、人力资源开发、能源、矿产加工及其他重要领域的长期互利合作。抓紧商谈和落实多农铝矿等大型项目。加快“两廊一圈”建设进程，切实稳步推进具体项目合作。加强在地区、跨地区和国际经济机制中的合作，推动东盟与中国的全面经济合作关系。

中国祝贺越南加入世界贸易组织，并相信越南成为正式成员之后，将会为世界贸易组织的运作作出积极贡献。

双方签署了《关于扩大和深化双边经济贸易合作的协定》，并一致同意尽快付诸实施，全面规划两国未来5至10年的经贸合作方向，确定重点合作领域，为促进两国经贸合作发挥积极作用。

双方还签署了《关于开展“两廊一圈”合作的谅解备忘录》和其他经济合作文件。

六、双方积极评价两国在解决边界领土问题方面取得的进展。同意进一步密切配合，采取更加切实有效的措施，加快陆地边界勘界立碑工作进度，确保最迟于2008年完成陆地边界全线勘界立碑工作并签署新的边界管理制度文件。继续落实好《北部湾划界协定》和《北部湾渔业合作协定》，做好两国海军联合巡逻及共同渔区资源联合调查和联合检查工作，加快落实《北部湾协议区油气合作框架协议》，开展跨界油气构造的共同勘探工作，维护正常的渔业生产秩序，积极开展北部湾渔业、环保、海上搜救等其他方面的合作。稳步推进北部湾湾口外海域的划界谈判并积极商谈该海域的共同开发问题。双方同意恪守两国高层有关共识，继续维持海上问题谈判机制，坚持通过和平谈判寻求双方均能接受的基本和长久的解决办法。双方共同努力保持南海局势稳定，同时积极研究和商谈共同开发问题，以便找到适合的模式和区域。

七、越方重申坚定奉行一个中国政策，支持中国统一大业，支持《反分裂国家法》，坚决反对任何形式的“台独”分裂活动。希望中国早日实现国家统一。越南绝不同台湾发展官方关系。中方对越方的上述立场表示赞赏。

八、双方对两国在国际和地区事务中的合作表示满意。重申将继续加强在联合国、亚太经合组织、亚欧会议、中国—东盟、东盟—中日韩、东亚峰会、东盟地区论坛、大湄公河次区域等多边框架下的协调与配合，共同致力于维护和促进本地区和世界的和平、稳定与发展。

双方一致认为，联合国应加强在应对新挑战和威胁，维护国际和平及安全，推动各成员国共同发展，实现千年发展目标等方面的作用及效果。

中方表示支持越南成为2008—2009年任期联合国安理会非常任理事国。

九、胡锦涛总书记、国家主席对农德孟总书记、阮明哲国家主席以及越南共产党、越南政府和越南人民所给予的隆重、热情和友好的接待表示感谢，邀请农德孟总书记、阮明哲国家主席方便时访华，农德孟总书记、阮明哲国家主席对此表示感谢并愉快地接受了邀请。

二○○六年十一月十七日于河内

Tuyên bố chung Trung Quốc-Việt Nam

(2006/11/17)

1. Nhận lời mời của Tổng Bí thư Ban Chấp hành Trung ương Đảng Cộng sản Việt Nam Nông Đức Mạnh và Chủ tịch nước Cộng hòa Xã hội chủ nghĩa Việt Nam Nguyễn Minh Triết, Tổng Bí thư Ban Chấp hành Trung ương Đảng Cộng sản Trung Quốc, Chủ tịch nước Cộng hòa Nhân dân Trung Hoa Hồ Cẩm Đào đã sang thăm hữu nghị chính thức Việt Nam từ ngày 15 đến 17-11-2006. Trong thời gian thăm, Tổng Bí thư, Chủ tịch nước Hồ Cẩm Đào đã hội đàm với Tổng Bí thư Nông Đức Mạnh, Chủ tịch nước Nguyễn Minh Triết, hội kiến với Thủ tướng Nguyễn Tấn Dũng, Chủ tịch Quốc hội Nguyễn Phú Trọng. Hai bên thông báo cho nhau tình hình mỗi Đảng, mỗi nước; trao đổi ý kiến sâu rộng về quan hệ giữa hai Đảng, hai nước cũng như các vấn đề quốc tế và khu vực mà hai bên cùng quan tâm và đã đạt được nhận thức chung rộng rãi. Hai bên nhất trí cho rằng, chuyến thăm lần này đã thành công tốt đẹp, chắc chắn sẽ thúc đẩy mạnh mẽ quan hệ láng giềng hữu nghị và hợp tác toàn diện giữa Việt Nam và Trung Quốc tiếp tục phát triển.

2. Hai bên bày tỏ vui mừng trước những thành tựu có tính chất lịch sử mà hai Đảng, hai nước đã giành được trong quá trình tìm tòi con đường phát triển xã hội chủ nghĩa phù hợp với tình hình của mỗi nước. Việt Nam đánh giá cao những thành tựu vĩ đại mà Trung Quốc đã giành được trong sự nghiệp cải cách, mở cửa và xây dựng chủ nghĩa xã hội đặc sắc Trung Quốc, tin tưởng rằng dưới sự lãnh đạo của Đảng Cộng sản Trung Quốc, nhân dân Trung Quốc nhất định sẽ thực hiện được mục tiêu hùng vĩ xây dựng toàn diện xã hội khá giả và đẩy nhanh hiện đại hóa xã hội chủ nghĩa. Trung Quốc đánh giá cao những thành tựu to lớn có ý

nghĩa lịch sử mà Việt Nam đã giành được trong công cuộc đổi mới 20 năm qua, ủng hộ các phương châm và chính sách do Đại hội X của Đảng Cộng sản Việt Nam đề ra và tin tưởng rằng, dưới sự lãnh đạo của Đảng Cộng sản Việt Nam, nhân dân Việt Nam nhất định sẽ thực hiện thắng lợi các mục tiêu và nhiệm vụ do Đại hội X của Đảng xác định, xây dựng Việt Nam thành một nước xã hội chủ nghĩa hiện đại, dân giàu, nước mạnh, xã hội công bằng, dân chủ, văn minh.

3. Hai bên hài lòng nhận thấy quan hệ giữa hai Đảng, hai nước không ngừng được củng cố và phát triển, nhất trí cho rằng Trung Quốc và Việt Nam có lợi ích chiến lược chung trên nhiều vấn đề quan trọng. Trong bối cảnh tình hình quốc tế đang có những diễn biến sâu sắc, việc tiếp tục tăng cường quan hệ láng giềng hữu nghị và hợp tác toàn diện Việt Nam-Trung Quốc phù hợp với lợi ích căn bản của hai Đảng, hai nước và nhân dân hai nước, có lợi cho hòa bình và phát triển trong khu vực và trên thế giới.

Hai bên thỏa thuận sẽ tăng cường các cuộc chuyến thăm cấp cao, đi sâu trao đổi kinh nghiệm về lý luận và thực tiễn trong sự nghiệp xây dựng Đảng, quản lý Nhà nước cũng như xây dựng chủ nghĩa xã hội, phát huy đầy đủ vai trò của cơ chế hợp tác giữa các ngành ngoại giao, quốc phòng, công an, an ninh..., mở rộng hợp tác thiết thực trong các lĩnh vực kinh tế thương mại, khoa học kỹ thuật, văn hóa giáo dục..., triển khai mạnh mẽ giao lưu hữu nghị giữa thanh thiếu niên hai nước, làm cho tình hữu nghị Việt Nam-Trung Quốc được lưu truyền từ thế hệ này sang thế hệ khác. Hai bên cùng nhau nỗ lực phát triển quan hệ Việt Nam-Trung Quốc "láng giềng hữu nghị, hợp tác toàn diện, ổn định lâu dài, hướng tới tương lai" và mãi mãi là "láng giềng tốt, bạn bè tốt, đồng chí tốt, đối tác tốt".

4. Hai bên đánh giá tích cực việc hai nước đã chính thức thành lập và tiến hành phiên họp đầu tiên của Ủy ban chỉ đạo hợp tác song phương Việt-Trung. Hai bên nhất trí cho rằng, sự kiện này có lợi cho việc tăng cường chỉ đạo vĩ mô, quy hoạch tổng thể và thúc đẩy toàn diện sự hợp tác trong tất cả các lĩnh vực giữa Việt Nam và Trung Quốc, điều phối giải quyết các vấn đề có thể nảy sinh trong quá trình hợp tác. Ủy ban này sẽ phát huy tác dụng quan trọng góp phần bảo đảm quan hệ láng giềng hữu nghị và hợp tác toàn diện giữa hai nước phát triển lâu dài, ổn định, lành mạnh và bền vững.

5. Hai bên hài lòng về tiến triển đã đạt được trong lĩnh vực hợp tác kinh tế-

thương mại giữa hai nước. Hai bên đồng ý trên tinh thần "bổ sung ưu thế cho nhau, cùng có lợi và cùng thắng", mở rộng hơn nữa quy mô, nâng cao chất lượng và trình độ hợp tác kinh tế thương mại. Tích cực phát triển điểm tăng trưởng mới về thương mại, duy trì đà tăng trưởng nhanh chóng kim ngạch mậu dịch song phương, thực hiện mục tiêu mới là nâng kim ngạch thương mại hai chiều lên 15 tỷ USD vào năm 2010. Từng bước cải thiện cơ cấu mậu dịch, cố gắng thực hiện phát triển cân bằng và tăng trưởng bền vững thương mại hai chiều. Tích cực ủng hộ và thúc đẩy doanh nghiệp hai nước hợp tác lâu dài và cùng có lợi trong các lĩnh vực xây dựng cơ sở hạ tầng, công nghiệp chế tạo, khai thác nguồn nhân lực, năng lượng, chế biến khoáng sản và các lĩnh vực quan trọng khác. Khẩn trương bàn bạc và thực hiện các dự án lớn như bô-xít Đác Nông... Đẩy nhanh tiến trình xây dựng "Hai hành lang, một vành đai kinh tế", thúc đẩy vững chắc, hiệu quả các dự án hợp tác cụ thể. Tăng cường hợp tác trong các thể chế kinh tế khu vực, liên khu vực và quốc tế, thúc đẩy quan hệ hợp tác kinh tế toàn diện giữa ASEAN và Trung Quốc.

Trung Quốc chúc mừng Việt Nam đã gia nhập WTO và tin tưởng rằng Việt Nam sẽ tích cực đóng góp phần mình vào các hoạt động của tổ chức này sau khi trở thành thành viên chính thức.

Hai bên đã ký và nhất trí sẽ nhanh chóng triển khai thực hiện "Hiệp định về mở rộng và đi sâu hợp tác kinh tế thương mại song phương", đề ra phương hướng tổng thể về hợp tác kinh tế thương mại giữa hai nước trong 5-10 năm tới, xác định các lĩnh vực hợp tác trọng điểm, phát huy tác dụng tích cực thúc đẩy hợp tác kinh tế thương mại giữa hai nước.

Hai bên còn ký kết Bản ghi nhớ về việc triển khai Hợp tác "hai hành lang, một vành đai kinh tế" và một số văn kiện hợp tác kinh tế khác.

6. Hai bên đánh giá tích cực những tiến triển mà hai nước đã đạt được trong việc giải quyết các vấn đề biên giới lãnh thổ. Hai bên đồng ý phối hợp chặt chẽ hơn nữa, áp dụng các biện pháp thiết thực và hiệu quả hơn, đẩy nhanh tiến độ phân giới cắm mốc biên giới trên đất liền, bảo đảm hoàn thành công tác phân giới cắm mốc trên toàn tuyến biên giới trên đất liền và ký văn bản mới về quy chế quản lý biên giới chậm nhất vào năm 2008. Tiếp tục thực hiện tốt "Hiệp định phân định Vịnh Bắc Bộ" và "Hiệp định hợp tác nghề cá Vịnh Bắc Bộ",

triển khai tốt tuần tra chung giữa hải quân hai nước, công tác điều tra liên hợp nguồn lợi cũng như kiểm tra liên hợp trong Vùng đánh cá chung, tích cực hợp tác đẩy nhanh việc thực hiện Thỏa thuận khung về hợp tác dầu khí trong Vịnh Bắc Bộ, tiến hành công tác thăm dò chung các cấu tạo dầu khí vắt ngang đường phân định, giữ gìn trật tự sản xuất nghề cá bình thường, tích cực triển khai hợp tác trong các lĩnh vực khác như nghề cá, bảo vệ môi trường, tìm kiếm cứu nạn trên biển... Hai bên tiếp tục thúc đẩy một cách vững chắc đàm phán về phân định vùng biển ngoài cửa Vịnh Bắc Bộ và tích cực trao đổi ý kiến về vấn đề hợp tác cùng phát triển ở khu vực này. Hai bên đồng ý nghiêm chỉnh tuân thủ nhận thức chung liên quan của lãnh đạo cấp cao hai nước, tiếp tục duy trì cơ chế đàm phán về vấn đề trên biển, kiên trì thông qua đàm phán hòa bình tìm kiếm giải pháp cơ bản và lâu dài mà hai bên đều chấp nhận được. Hai bên cùng nhau cố gắng giữ gìn ổn định tình hình Biển Đông, đồng thời tích cực nghiên cứu và bàn bạc vấn đề hợp tác cùng phát triển để tìm ra mô hình và khu vực phù hợp.

7. Việt Nam khẳng định kiên trì thực hiện chính sách một nước Trung Quốc, ủng hộ sự nghiệp lớn thống nhất Trung Quốc, ủng hộ "Luật Chống chia cắt đất nước", kiên quyết phản đối hành động chia rẽ "Đài Loan độc lập" dưới mọi hình thức. Mong muốn Trung Quốc sớm thực hiện thống nhất đất nước. Việt Nam không phát triển bất kỳ quan hệ chính thức nào với Đài Loan. Phía Trung Quốc bày tỏ hoan nghênh lập trường trên của phía Việt Nam.

8. Hai bên hài lòng về hợp tác giữa hai nước trong công việc quốc tế và khu vực. Hai bên khẳng định sẽ tiếp tục tăng cường phối hợp và hợp tác trong khuôn khổ đa phương như Liên hợp quốc, APEC, ASEM, ASEAN+3 (Trung Quốc, Nhật Bản, Hàn Quốc), EAS, ARF, Tiểu vùng sông Mê Công mở rộng..., cùng nhau làm hết sức mình vì hòa bình, ổn định và phát triển trong khu vực và trên thế giới.

Hai bên nhất trí cho rằng Liên hợp quốc cần góp phần nâng cao vai trò, hiệu quả trong việc đối phó với những thách thức và các mối đe dọa mới, duy trì hòa bình và an ninh quốc tế, thúc đẩy sự phát triển chung của các thành viên, phục vụ cho việc thực hiện các mục tiêu phát triển thiên niên kỷ.

Trung Quốc bày tỏ ủng hộ Việt Nam trở thành Ủy viên không thường trực Hội đồng Bảo an Liên hợp quốc nhiệm kỳ 2008-2009.

9. Tổng Bí thư, Chủ tịch nước Hồ Cẩm Đào cảm ơn Tổng Bí thư Nông Đức Mạnh, Chủ tịch nước Nguyễn Minh Triết và Đảng Cộng sản, Chính phủ và nhân dân Việt Nam đã dành cho đoàn sự đón tiếp trọng thị, nhiệt tình và hữu nghị, và trân trọng mời Tổng Bí thư Nông Đức Mạnh, Chủ tịch nước Nguyễn Minh Triết sang thăm Trung Quốc vào thời gian thuận tiện. Tổng Bí thư Nông Đức Mạnh, Chủ tịch nước Nguyễn Minh Triết bày tỏ cảm ơn và vui vẻ nhận lời.

中越联合新闻公报

（2007年5月18日）

一、应中华人民共和国主席胡锦涛邀请，越南社会主义共和国主席阮明哲于2007年5月15日至18日对中国进行国事访问。访问期间，胡锦涛主席与阮明哲主席举行会谈，全国人民代表大会常务委员会委员长吴邦国、国务院总理温家宝、中国人民政治协商会议全国委员会主席贾庆林分别会见了阮明哲主席。双方就双边关系及共同关心的国际和地区问题深入交换意见，达成广泛共识。双方一致认为，访问取得了圆满成功，有力地推动了中越睦邻友好与全面合作关系向前发展。

二、双方对中越关系不断巩固和发展表示满意，一致认为，中越友好是两国和两国人民的宝贵财富，双方应共同维护并不断发扬光大。双方同意，继续遵照长期稳定、面向未来、睦邻友好、全面合作的方针，加强高层往来，深化治党理政和社会主义理论与实践的交流，充分发挥中越双边合作指导委员会的作用，统筹规划和全面推进两国各领域合作，推动外交、国防、公安、安全等各部门合作机制有效运转，扩大经贸、科技、文化、教育、促进跨界河流水资源可持续利用等领域的务实合作，加强中越传统友好的教育，大力开展青少年友好交往，努力使两国和两国人民永做好邻居、好朋友、好同志、好伙伴，使中越友谊世代相传。

三、双方对两国经贸合作取得的长足进展表示满意，同意落实好《关于扩大和深化双边经贸合作的协定》，制订双边经贸合作发展规划，确定重点合作领域和项目，进一步提升经贸合作的规模和水平。双方同意本着优势互补、互利共赢的精神，积极开拓新的贸易增长点，保持双边贸易额快速增长，实现到2010年双边年贸易额150亿美元的目标，同时逐步改善贸易结构，努力实现双边贸易的平衡发展。双方将积极支持和推动双方企业在基础设施、制造业、人力资源开发、能源、矿产加工及其他重要领域开展长期互利合作。积极落实多农铝矿等大型项目。做好对具体合作项目的联合考察研究，以落实“两廊一圈”建设事宜。双方承诺加强在世界贸易组织等地区、跨地区及国际经济机制中的合作。中方重申承认越南市场经济地位。

四、双方认为，两国陆地边界勘界立碑工作取得明显进展。双方将进一步密切配合，确保2007年内完成实地勘界立碑工作，2008年完成全线勘界立碑任务并签署新的边界管理制度文件。继续落实好《北部湾划界协定》和《北部湾渔业合作协定》，做好两国海军联合巡逻及共同渔区资源联合调查和联合检查工作，加快落实《北部湾协议区油气合作框架协议》，力争油气勘采合作早出成果，维护正常的渔业生产秩序，积极开展北部湾渔业、环保、海上搜救、海洋科研等其他领域的合作。稳步推进北部湾湾口外海域的划界谈判并积极商谈该海域的共同开发问题。

双方同意，恪守双方已达成的有关共识，继续保持海上问题谈判机制，坚持通过和平谈判寻求双方均能接受的基本和长久的解决办法。双方愿共同努力保持南海局势稳定，均不采取使争端复杂化、扩大化的行动。积极研究和商谈共同开发问题，以便找到适合的模式和区域。

五、越方重申坚定奉行一个中国政策，支持中国统一大业，支持《反分裂国家法》，坚决反对任何形式的“台独”分裂活动。希望中国早日实现国家统一。越南不同台湾发展任何官方关系。中方对越方的上述立场表示赞赏。

六、双方对两国在国际和地区事务中的合作表示满意。重申将继续加强在联合国、亚太经合组织、亚欧会议、中国—东盟、东盟—中日韩、东亚峰会、东盟地区论坛、大湄公河次区域等多边框架下的协调与配合，共同致力于维护和促进本地区和世界的和平、稳定与发展。

双方一致认为，联合国应加强在应对新挑战和威胁，维护国际和平与安全，推动各会员国共同发展，实现千年发展目标等方面的作用及效果。中国重申支持越南成为2008—2009年度联合国安理会非常任理事国。

七、阮明哲主席对胡锦涛主席和中国人民所给予的隆重、热情、友好的接待表示衷心感谢，郑重邀请胡锦涛主席方便时访越，胡锦涛主席对此表示感谢并愉快地接受了邀请。

Thông cáo báo chí chung Trung Quốc-Việt Nam

(2007/5/18)

Nhân chuyến thăm chính thức nước Cộng hòa Nhân dân Trung Hoa của Chủ tịch nước Nguyễn Minh Triết theo lời mời của Chủ tịch nước Cộng hòa Nhân dân Trung Hoa Hồ Cẩm Đào, hai nước Việt Nam-Trung Quốc đã ra Thông cáo báo chí chung. Dưới đây là toàn văn Thông cáo này:

1. Nhận lời mời của Chủ tịch nước Cộng hòa Nhân dân Trung Hoa Hồ Cẩm Đào, Chủ tịch nước Cộng hòa Xã hội Chủ nghĩa Việt Nam Nguyễn Minh Triết đã thăm chính thức nước Cộng hòa Nhân dân Trung Hoa từ ngày 15 đến 18 tháng 5 năm 2007.

Trong thời gian chuyến thăm, Chủ tịch nước Nguyễn Minh Triết đã hội đàm với Chủ tịch nước Hồ Cẩm Đào; hội kiến với Ủy viên trưởng Ủy ban thường vụ Đại hội đại biểu nhân dân toàn quốc Ngô Bang Quốc; Thủ tướng Quốc vụ viện Ôn Gia Bảo, Chủ tịch Hội nghị hiệp thương chính trị nhân dân toàn quốc Giả Khánh Lâm. Hai bên đã đi sâu trao đổi ý kiến và đạt nhận thức chung rộng rãi về quan hệ song phương cũng như các vấn đề quốc tế và khu vực mà hai bên cùng quan tâm.

Hai bên nhất trí cho rằng chuyến thăm đã thành công tốt đẹp, thúc đẩy mạnh mẽ quan hệ láng giềng hữu nghị và hợp tác toàn diện Việt Nam-Trung Quốc tiếp tục phát triển.

2. Hai bên hài lòng nhận thấy, quan hệ giữa hai nước Việt-Trung không ngừng được củng cố và phát triển; nhất trí cho rằng tình hữu nghị Việt Nam-Trung Quốc là tài sản quý báu của hai nước và nhân dân hai nước, hai bên cần cùng nhau giữ gìn và không ngừng vun đắp.

Hai bên thỏa thuận tiếp tục tuân theo phương châm "Láng giềng hữu nghị, hợp tác toàn diện, ổn định lâu dài, hướng tới tương lai", tăng cường các chuyến thăm cấp cao, đi sâu trao đổi lý luận và thực tiễn trong xây dựng Đảng và quản lý đất nước cũng như xây dựng chủ nghĩa xã hội, phát huy đầy đủ vai trò của Ủy ban chỉ đạo hợp tác song phương Việt Nam-Trung Quốc, quy hoạch tổng thể và thúc đẩy toàn diện sự hợp tác giữa hai nước trên các lĩnh vực, thúc đẩy các cơ chế hợp tác của các ngành như ngoại giao, quốc phòng, công an, an ninh hoạt động có hiệu quả, mở rộng sự hợp tác thiết thực trong các lĩnh vực kinh tế thương mại, khoa học kỹ thuật, văn hoá giáo dục, thúc đẩy việc sử dụng bền vững tài nguyên nước các con sông chảy qua hai nước..., tăng cường giáo dục truyền thống hữu nghị Việt Nam-Trung Quốc, triển khai mạnh mẽ giao lưu hữu nghị giữa thanh thiếu niên, nỗ lực làm cho hai nước và nhân dân hai nước mãi mãi là "láng giềng tốt, bạn bè tốt, đồng chí tốt, đối tác tốt", làm cho tình hữu nghị Việt Nam-Trung Quốc được lưu truyền từ thế hệ này sang thế hệ khác.

3. Hai bên hài lòng trước những tiến triển mạnh mẽ trong quan hệ kinh tế thương mại hai nước, đồng ý thực hiện tốt "Hiệp định về mở rộng và đi sâu hợp tác kinh tế thương mại song phương", đề ra quy hoạch phát triển hợp tác kinh tế thương mại song phương, xác định những lĩnh vực và hạng mục hợp tác trọng điểm, tiếp tục nâng cao quy mô và trình độ hợp tác kinh tế, thương mại. Trên tinh thần bổ sung ưu thế cho nhau, cùng có lợi và cùng thắng, hai bên tích cực tìm kiếm những lĩnh vực tăng trưởng mậu dịch mới, duy trì đà tăng trưởng nhanh chóng kim ngạch mậu dịch song phương, thực hiện mục tiêu nâng kim ngạch mậu dịch thương mại hai chiều lên 15 tỉ USD vào năm 2010; đồng thời từng bước cải thiện cơ cấu mậu dịch, nỗ lực thực hiện sự phát triển cân bằng thương mại hai chiều. Hai bên sẽ tích cực ủng hộ và thúc đẩy các doanh nghiệp hai nước hợp tác lâu dài và cùng có lợi trong các lĩnh vực xây dựng hạ tầng cơ sở, công nghiệp chế tạo, phát triển nguồn nhân lực, năng lượng, chế biến khoáng sản và các lĩnh vực quan trọng khác. Tích cực thực hiện các hạng mục hợp tác lớn như Bô-xít Đắc Nông. Làm tốt công tác nghiên cứu khảo sát liên hợp đối với những hạng mục hợp tác cụ thể để thực hiện việc xây dựng "hai hành lang, một vành đai kinh tế". Hai bên cam kết tăng cường hợp tác trong các cơ chế kinh tế khu vực, liên khu vực và quốc tế, trong đó có WTO. Trung Quốc tái khẳng định sự

công nhận của Trung Quốc đối với quy chế kinh tế thị trường của Việt Nam.

4. Hai bên cho rằng, công tác phân giới cắm mốc biên giới trên đất liền giữa hai nước đã đạt được tiến triển rõ rệt. Hai bên sẽ phối hợp chặt chẽ hơn nữa, đảm bảo hoàn thành công tác phân giới cắm mốc trên thực địa trong năm 2007, hoàn thành nhiệm vụ phân giới cắm mốc và ký văn kiện mới về quy chế quản lý biên giới trong năm 2008.

Tiếp tục thực hiện tốt "Hiệp định phân định Vịnh Bắc bộ" và "Hiệp định hợp tác nghề cá Vịnh Bắc bộ", thực hiện tốt việc tuần tra chung giữa hải quân hai nước, công tác điều tra liên hợp nguồn lợi thủy sản cũng như kiểm tra liên hợp trong Vùng đánh cá chung, đẩy nhanh việc thực hiện Thỏa thuận khung về hợp tác dầu khí trong Vịnh Bắc bộ, cố gắng sớm có kết quả hợp tác thăm dò dầu khí, giữ gìn trật tự sản xuất nghề cá bình thường, tích cực triển khai hợp tác trong các lĩnh vực khác như nghề cá, bảo vệ môi trường, tìm kiếm cứu nạn trên biển, nghiên cứu khoa học biển…

Hai bên thúc đẩy một cách vững chắc đàm phán về phân định vùng biển ngoài cửa Vịnh Bắc bộ và tích cực trao đổi ý kiến về hợp tác cùng phát triển tại vùng biển này.

Hai bên đồng ý tuân thủ nghiêm chỉnh những nhận thức chung liên quan đã đạt được, tiếp tục duy trì cơ chế đàm phán về vấn đề trên biển, kiên trì thông qua đàm phán hòa bình tìm kiếm giải pháp cơ bản và lâu dài mà hai bên đều chấp nhận được. Hai bên cùng nhau cố gắng giữ gìn ổn định tình hình Biển Đông, không có những hành động làm phức tạp, mở rộng tranh chấp. Tích cực nghiên cứu và bàn bạc vấn đề hợp tác cùng phát triển để tìm ra mô hình và khu vực thích hợp.

5. Việt Nam khẳng định kiên trì thực hiện chính sách một nước Trung Quốc, ủng hộ sự nghiệp lớn thống nhất Trung Quốc, ủng hộ "Luật chống chia cắt đất nước", kiên quyết phản đối hành động chia rẽ "Đài Loan độc lập" dưới mọi hình thức, mong muốn Trung Quốc sớm thực hiện thống nhất đất nước. Việt Nam không phát triển bất cứ quan hệ chính thức nào với Đài Loan. Phía Trung Quốc bày tỏ hoan nghênh lập trường trên của phía Việt Nam.

6. Hai bên hài lòng về hợp tác giữa hai nước trong công việc quốc tế và khu vực. Hai bên khẳng định sẽ tiếp tục tăng cường phối hợp và hợp tác trong khuôn

khổ đa phương như Liên Hiệp Quốc, APEC, ASEM, Trung Quốc-ASEAN, ASEAN+3 (Trung Quốc, Nhật Bản, Hàn Quốc), cấp cao Đông Á, ARF, Tiểu vùng sông Mê Công mở rộng…, cùng nhau làm hết sức mình duy trì và thúc đẩy hòa bình, ổn định và phát triển trong khu vực và trên thế giới.

Hai bên nhất trí cho rằng Liên Hiệp Quốc cần tăng cường vai trò và hiệu quả trong việc đối phó với những thách thức và các mối đe dọa mới, duy trì hoà bình và an ninh quốc tế, thúc đẩy sự phát triển chung của các thành viên, thực hiện các mục tiêu phát triển thiên niên kỷ. Trung Quốc tái khẳng định ủng hộ Việt Nam trở thành Ủy viên không thường trực Hội đồng Bảo an Liên Hiệp Quốc nhiệm kỳ 2008–2009.

7. Chủ tịch nước Nguyễn Minh Triết chân thành cảm ơn Chủ tịch nước Hồ Cẩm Đào và nhân dân Trung Quốc về sự đón tiếp trọng thị, nhiệt tình và hữu nghị; trân trọng mời Chủ tịch nước Hồ Cẩm Đào sang thăm Việt Nam vào thời gian thuận tiện. Chủ tịch Hồ Cẩm Đào bày tỏ cảm ơn và đã vui vẻ nhận lời.

中越联合声明

（2008年6月1日）

一、应中国共产党中央委员会总书记、中华人民共和国主席胡锦涛的邀请，越南共产党中央委员会总书记农德孟于2008年5月30日至6月2日对中华人民共和国进行正式友好访问。访问期间，中共中央总书记、国家主席胡锦涛与农德孟总书记举行会谈，全国人大常委会委员长吴邦国、国务院总理温家宝、全国政协主席贾庆林分别会见了农德孟总书记。国家副主席习近平出席了有关活动。农德孟总书记还参观了北京奥运设施，并赴江苏省访问。

双方在坦诚友好的气氛中相互通报了各自党和国家的情况，并就两党两国关系及共同关心的国际和地区问题深入交换了意见，达成了广泛共识。双方一致认为，访问取得了圆满成功，必将对新时期中越关系的全面深入发展，对本地区和世界的和平与发展产生积极深远的影响。

二、双方强调，两国各自具有本国特色的社会主义发展道路，是符合两国人民根本利益的正确选择。越方高度评价中国改革开放30年来取得的辉煌成就，坚信中国人民一定能在建设中国特色社会主义事业中取得新的更大成就，胜利实现全面建设小康社会的奋斗目标。中方高度评价越南革新事业取得的具有历史意义的重大成就，坚信越南人民一定能够在社会主义建设事业中取得新的更大成就，胜利实现民富国强、社会公平、民主文明的目标。

越方对中国四川省遭受严重地震灾害并造成重大人员伤亡和财产损失表示深切同情和诚挚慰问，相信兄弟的中国人民一定能够早日战胜灾害，重建家园。对中国政府和人民为举办北京奥运会所做的出色筹备工作表示赞赏，并将继续全力支持中方的努力。中方对越方的上述友好情谊和支持表示衷心感谢。

三、双方对两党两国睦邻友好与全面合作关系近年来取得的丰硕成果表示满意。重申中越传统友谊是两党两国和两国人民的宝贵财富，应精心维护并不断发扬光大。双方一致同意在“长期稳定、面向未来、睦邻友好、全面合作”方针和“好邻居、好朋友、好同志、好伙伴”精神指导下，发展中越全面战略合作伙伴关系，始终牢牢把握两国关系发展的正确方向，确保两国关系长期、稳定、健康地向前发展。双方表示将在各领域继续相互支持、相互帮助，增进全面互信，深化互利合作，促进共同发展，胜利推进各自国家的社会主义建设事业；将本着“大局为重、友好协商、公平合理、互利共赢”的精神，认真落实两国领导人达成的共识，积极合作，妥善处理和解决两国关系中存在的问题；加强在国际和地区事务中的协调与配合，推动建设持久和平、共同繁荣的亚洲与世界。

四、双方强调将继续保持两党两国高层密切接触的优良传统，宣布建立领导人热线电话。双方一致同意充分发挥中越双边合作指导委员会的作用，统筹规划和全面推进两国各领域合作。建立两党中央相关部门的交流合作机制，深化治党治国和社会主义理论与实践经验的交流，继续办好两党理论研讨会，推进党政干部培训合作；推动外交、国防、公安、安全等各部门合作机制有效运转，扩大经贸、科技、文化、教育等领域的务实合作，大力开展青少年及群众团体和民间组织的友好交往，相互配合做好两国人民友好传统的宣传教育活动。

五、双方对近年来两国经贸合作展现出的良好发展势头表示满意，一致同意继续落实好《关于扩大和深化双边经贸合作的协定》，抓紧商签并实施《中越经贸合作五年发展规划》，确定重点合作领域和项目，进一步提升经贸合作的规模和水平。双方同意本着优势互补、互利双赢的精神，积极开拓新的贸易增长点，保持双边贸易额快速增长，同时采取切实有效措施改善贸易结构，实现双边贸易的平衡发展。双方将积极支持和推动双方企业在基础设施、制造业、人力资源开发、能源、矿产加工及其他重要领域开展长期互利合作。加强在多农铝矿、“两廊一圈”框架内项目和其他重大项目上的合作。双方重申加强在世界贸易组织等地区、跨地区及国际经济机制中的合作。

双方签署了《中华人民共和国政府与越南社会主义共和国政府关于植物保护和植物检疫合作的协定》、《中华人民共和国政府与越南社会主义共和国政府关于加强动物检疫和动物卫生合作的协定》及中国向越南提供优惠贷款和出口买方信贷等有关经贸合作协议。

六、双方对陆地边界勘界工作基本完成表示满意，同意进一步密切配合，积极解决剩余问题，切实加快工作进度，确保如期实现今年内完成陆地边界全线勘界立碑工作的目标，并早日签署新的边界管理制度文件，把两国陆地边界建成和平、友好、合作的纽带。继续落实好《北部湾划界协定》和《北部湾渔业合作协定》，做好共同渔区联合检查和渔业资源联合调查及海军联合巡逻工作；加快落实《北部湾协议区油气合作框架协议》，力争跨界油气勘采合作早出实质成果；维护正常的渔业生产秩序，积极开展北部湾渔业、环保、海上搜救等方面的合作。稳步推进北部湾湾口外海域划界谈判并积极商谈该海域的共同开发问题，早日启动该海域共同考察。双方同意恪守两国高层有关共识，共同维护南海局势稳定，保持海上问题谈判机制，坚持通过和平谈判寻求双方均能接受的基本和长久的解决办法，同时积极研究和商谈共同开发问题，以便找到适合的模式和区域。

七、越方重申坚定奉行一个中国政策，支持中国统一大业，坚决反对任何形式的“台独”分裂活动。越南绝不同台湾发展任何官方关系。中方对越方的上述立场表示赞赏。

八、双方对两国在国际和地区事务中的合作表示满意。双方重申将继续加强在联合国、亚太经合组织、中国—东盟等多边框架下的协调与配合，共同维护和促进世界的和平、繁荣与发展。

九、农德孟总书记对胡锦涛总书记、国家主席以及中国共产党、中国政府和中国人民所给予的隆重、热情、友好的接待表示衷心感谢，邀请胡锦涛总书记、国家主席早日再次访越。胡锦涛对此表示感谢并愉快地接受了邀请。

Tuyên bố chung Trung Quốc-Việt Nam

(2008/6/1)

1. Nhận lời mời của Tổng Bí thư Ban Chấp hành Trung ương Đảng Cộng sản Trung Quốc, Chủ tịch nước Cộng hoà Nhân dân Trung Hoa Hồ Cẩm Đào, Tổng Bí thư Ban Chấp hành Trung ương Đảng Cộng sản Việt Nam Nông Đức Mạnh đã thăm hữu nghị chính thức nước Cộng hoà Nhân dân Trung Hoa từ ngày 30/5-2/6/2008. Trong thời gian chuyến thăm, Tổng Bí thư Nông Đức Mạnh đã hội đàm với Tổng Bí thư, Chủ tịch nước Hồ Cẩm Đào; lần lượt hội kiến với Ủy viên Trưởng Ủy ban Thường vụ Đại hội đại biểu nhân dân toàn quốc Ngô Bang Quốc, Thủ tướng Quốc vụ viện Ôn Gia Bảo, Chủ tịch Ủy ban Toàn quốc Hội nghị Hiệp thương chính trị nhân dân Trung Quốc Giả Khánh Lâm. Phó Chủ tịch nước Cộng hoà Nhân dân Trung Hoa Tập Cận Bình đã tham dự các hoạt động liên quan. Tổng Bí thư Nông Đức Mạnh đã thăm Tổ hợp Olympic Bắc Kinh và thăm tỉnh Giang Tô.

Trong bầu không khí chân thành, hữu nghị và tin cậy lẫn nhau, hai bên đã thông báo cho nhau về tình hình mỗi Đảng, mỗi nước; đi sâu trao đổi ý kiến và đạt được nhận thức chung rộng rãi về quan hệ giữa hai Đảng, hai nước, cũng như về các vấn đề quốc tế và khu vực mà hai bên cùng quan tâm. Hai bên nhất trí cho rằng, chuyến thăm đã thành công tốt đẹp, chắc chắn sẽ có ảnh hưởng sâu rộng và tích cực đối với việc đi sâu phát triển toàn diện quan hệ Việt Nam-Trung Quốc trong thời kỳ mới, đối với hoà bình và phát triển của khu vực và thế giới.

2. Hai bên nhấn mạnh, con đường phát triển xã hội chủ nghĩa phù hợp với đặc điểm của mỗi nước là sự lựa chọn đúng đắn, đáp ứng lợi ích căn bản của nhân dân hai nước. Phía Việt Nam đánh giá cao những thành tựu rực rỡ mà

Trung Quốc giành được trong 30 năm cải cách mở cửa, tin tưởng vững chắc rằng, nhân dân Trung Quốc nhất định sẽ giành được những thành tựu mới to lớn hơn nữa trong sự nghiệp xây dựng chủ nghĩa xã hội đặc sắc Trung Quốc, thực hiện thắng lợi mục tiêu xây dựng toàn diện xã hội khá giả. Phía Trung Quốc đánh giá cao những thành tựu to lớn, có ý nghĩa lịch sử mà Việt Nam giành được trong sự nghiệp đổi mới, tin tưởng vững chắc rằng, nhân dân Việt Nam nhất định sẽ giành được những thành tựu mới to lớn hơn nữa trong sự nghiệp xây dựng chủ nghĩa xã hội, thực hiện thắng lợi mục tiêu dân giàu, nước mạnh, xã hội công bằng, dân chủ, văn minh.

Phía Việt Nam bày tỏ sự cảm thông sâu sắc và lời thăm hỏi chân thành đối với những mất mát to lớn về người và của do trận động đất nghiêm trọng ở tỉnh Tứ Xuyên, Trung Quốc gây ra và tin tưởng nhân dân Trung Quốc anh em nhất định sẽ sớm khắc phục được hậu quả thiên tai, ổn định cuộc sống; bày tỏ hoan nghênh đối với công tác chuẩn bị chu đáo của Chính phủ và nhân dân Trung Quốc cho Thế vận hội Olympic Bắc Kinh 2008 và sẽ tiếp tục ủng hộ mạnh mẽ những nỗ lực của phía Trung Quốc để tổ chức thành công Đại hội thể thao này. Phía Trung Quốc bày tỏ sự cảm ơn chân thành đối với tình cảm hữu nghị và sự ủng hộ nói trên của phía Việt Nam.

3. Hai bên bày tỏ hài lòng trước những thành quả to lớn đã đạt được trong quan hệ láng giềng hữu nghị, hợp tác toàn diện giữa hai Đảng, hai nước trong những năm qua; khẳng định tình hữu nghị truyền thống Việt-Trung là tài sản quý báu của hai Đảng, hai Nhà nước và nhân dân hai nước, cần hết sức gìn giữ và không ngừng phát huy mạnh mẽ. Hai bên nhất trí phát triển quan hệ đối tác hợp tác chiến lược toàn diện Việt Nam-Trung Quốc theo phương châm "láng giềng hữu nghị, hợp tác toàn diện, ổn định lâu dài, hướng tới tương lai" và tinh thần "láng giềng tốt, bạn bè tốt, đồng chí tốt, đối tác tốt"; luôn luôn nắm vững phương hướng phát triển đúng đắn của quan hệ hai nước, đảm bảo chắc chắn cho quan hệ hai nước phát triển lâu dài, ổn định và lành mạnh. Hai bên bày tỏ sẽ tiếp tục ủng hộ và giúp đỡ lẫn nhau trên các lĩnh vực, tăng cường tin cậy toàn diện lẫn nhau, đi sâu hợp tác cùng có lợi, thúc đẩy cùng nhau phát triển, thúc đẩy thắng lợi sự nghiệp xây dựng chủ nghĩa xã hội ở mỗi nước. Trên tinh thần coi trọng đại cục, hiệp thương hữu nghị, công bằng, hợp lý, cùng có lợi, cùng thắng, hai bên sẽ

nghiêm chỉnh thực hiện các nhận thức chung mà lãnh đạo hai nước đã đạt được, tích cực hợp tác để xử lý và giải quyết thoả đáng các vấn đề tồn tại trong quan hệ hai nước. Hai bên tăng cường phối hợp trong các công việc quốc tế và khu vực, cùng nhau thúc đẩy xây dựng hoà bình lâu dài, cùng phồn vinh ở châu Á và trên thế giới.

4. Hai bên nhấn mạnh sẽ tiếp tục duy trì truyền thống tốt đẹp tiếp xúc mật thiết giữa lãnh đạo cấp cao hai Đảng, hai nước; tuyên bố thiết lập đường dây nóng giữa các nhà lãnh đạo Việt Nam-Trung Quốc. Hai bên nhất trí phát huy đầy đủ vai trò của Uỷ ban chỉ đạo hợp tác song phương Việt Nam-Trung Quốc, quy hoạch tổng thể và thúc đẩy toàn diện sự hợp tác giữa hai nước trên các lĩnh vực; xây dựng cơ chế giao lưu và hợp tác giữa các cơ quan Trung ương hữu quan của hai Đảng; đi sâu trao đổi về lý luận và kinh nghiệm thực tiễn về chủ nghĩa xã hội và về xây dựng Đảng, quản lý đất nước; tiếp tục tổ chức tốt các cuộc hội thảo lý luận giữa hai Đảng; thúc đẩy hợp tác về đào tạo và bồi dưỡng cán bộ lãnh đạo, quản lý; thúc đẩy cơ chế hợp tác có hiệu quả giữa các bộ, ngành ngoại giao, quốc phòng, công an, an ninh; mở rộng hợp tác thiết thực trên các lĩnh vực kinh tế, thương mại, khoa học, kỹ thuật, văn hoá, giáo dục...; triển khai mạnh mẽ giao lưu hữu nghị giữa thanh thiếu niên, các đoàn thể quần chúng và các tổ chức nhân dân; phối hợp tổ chức các hoạt động tuyên truyền, giáo dục truyền thống hữu nghị giữa nhân dân hai nước.

5. Hai bên hài lòng trước đà phát triển tốt đẹp của mối quan hệ hợp tác kinh tế thương mại giữa hai nước trong những năm gần đây; nhất trí tiếp tục thực hiện tốt Hiệp định về mở rộng và đi sâu hợp tác kinh tế thương mại song phương; khẩn trương bàn bạc, ký kết và thực hiện tốt “Quy hoạch phát triển 5 năm về hợp tác kinh tế thương mại giữa Việt Nam và Trung Quốc”, xác định các lĩnh vực và dự án hợp tác trọng điểm; nâng cao hơn nữa quy mô và mức độ hợp tác kinh tế thương mại. Hai bên đồng ý trên tinh thần bổ sung ưu thế cho nhau, cùng có lợi, cùng thắng, tích cực tìm kiếm những lĩnh vực tăng trưởng mậu dịch mới, duy trì kim ngạch mậu dịch song phương tăng trưởng nhanh; đồng thời áp dụng những biện pháp thiết thực và có hiệu quả để cải thiện cơ cấu mậu dịch, thực hiện phát triển cân bằng mậu dịch song phương. Hai bên tích cực ủng hộ và thúc đẩy các doanh nghiệp của hai nước hợp tác lâu dài cùng có lợi trong các lĩnh vực cơ sở

hạ tầng, công nghiệp chế tạo, phát triển nguồn nhân lực, năng lượng, chế biến khoáng sản và các lĩnh vực quan trọng khác. Hai bên tăng cường hợp tác trong các dự án như: Bôxit Đắc Nông, các dự án trong khuôn khổ "Hai hành lang, một vành đai kinh tế" và các dự án lớn khác. Hai bên khẳng định tăng cường hợp tác trong các cơ chế kinh tế khu vực, liên khu vực và quốc tế như Tổ chức Thương mại thế giới...

Nhân dịp này, hai bên đã ký Hiệp định giữa Chính phủ nước Cộng hoà Xã hội chủ nghĩa Việt Nam và Chính phủ nước Cộng hoà Nhân dân Trung Hoa về hợp tác trong lĩnh vực bảo vệ và kiểm dịch thực vật, Hiệp định giữa Chính phủ nước Cộng hoà Xã hội chủ nghĩa Việt Nam và Chính phủ nước Cộng hoà Nhân dân Trung Hoa về hợp tác trong lĩnh vực thú y và kiểm dịch động vật, và một số thoả thuận kinh tế thương mại khác về việc Trung Quốc cung cấp cho Việt Nam tín dụng ưu đãi và cho vay ưu đãi bên mua.

6. Hai bên hài lòng đối với việc cơ bản hoàn thành công tác phân giới biên giới trên đất liền; đồng ý phối hợp chặt chẽ hơn nữa, tích cực giải quyết các vấn đề còn lại và đẩy nhanh tiến độ công tác, đảm bảo thực hiện đúng thời hạn mục tiêu hoàn thành toàn bộ công tác phân giới cắm mốc trên toàn tuyến biên giới trên đất liền trong năm 2008 và sớm ký văn bản mới về quy chế quản lý biên giới nhằm xây dựng đường biên giới trên đất liền giữa hai nước thành đường biên giới hoà bình, hữu nghị, hợp tác. Hai bên tiếp tục thực hiện tốt Hiệp định phân định Vịnh Bắc Bộ và Hiệp định hợp tác nghề cá Vịnh Bắc Bộ; thực hiện tốt công tác kiểm tra liên hợp cũng như điều tra liên hợp nguồn thuỷ sản trong Vùng đánh cá chung và việc tuần tra chung giữa hải quân hai nước ở Vịnh Bắc Bộ; đẩy nhanh việc thực hiện "Thỏa thuận khung về hợp tác dầu khí trong vùng thoả thuận tại Vịnh Bắc Bộ", phấn đấu sớm đạt kết quả thực chất trong hợp tác thăm dò, khai thác chung các cấu tạo dầu khí vắt ngang đường phân định Vịnh Bắc Bộ; giữ gìn trật tự sản xuất nghề cá bình thường, tích cực triển khai hợp tác nghề cá, bảo vệ môi trường, tìm kiếm cứu nạn trên biển ở Vịnh Bắc Bộ... Hai bên tiếp tục thúc đẩy một cách vững chắc đàm phán về phân định vùng biển ngoài cửa Vịnh Bắc Bộ và tích cực trao đổi ý kiến về vấn đề hợp tác cùng phát triển, sớm khởi động cùng khảo sát ở khu vực này. Hai bên đồng ý nghiêm chỉnh tuân thủ nhận thức chung liên quan của lãnh đạo cấp cao hai nước, cùng nhau giữ gìn ổn

định tình hình Biển Đông; tiếp tục duy trì cơ chế đàm phán về vấn đề trên biển, kiên trì thông qua đàm phán hòa bình tìm kiếm giải pháp cơ bản và lâu dài mà hai bên đều chấp nhận được; đồng thời tích cực nghiên cứu và bàn bạc vấn đề hợp tác cùng phát triển để tìm ra mô hình và khu vực phù hợp.

7. Phía Việt Nam khẳng định thực hiện nhất quán chính sách một nước Trung Quốc, ủng hộ sự nghiệp lớn thống nhất Trung Quốc, kiên quyết phản đối hành động chia rẽ "Đài Loan độc lập" dưới mọi hình thức; Việt Nam không phát triển bất cứ quan hệ chính thức nào với Đài Loan. Phía Trung Quốc bày tỏ hoan nghênh lập trường trên của phía Việt Nam.

8. Hai bên hài lòng về sự hợp tác giữa hai nước trong các công việc quốc tế và khu vực. Hai bên khẳng định sẽ tiếp tục tăng cường sự hợp tác và phối hợp tại các diễn đàn đa phương như Liên hợp quốc, APEC, Trung Quốc-ASEAN..., cùng nhau giữ gìn và thúc đẩy hoà bình, phồn vinh và phát triển của thế giới.

9. Tổng Bí thư Nông Đức Mạnh chân thành cảm ơn Tổng Bí thư, Chủ tịch nước Hồ Cẩm Đào và Đảng, Chính phủ và nhân dân Trung Quốc về sự đón tiếp trọng thị, nhiệt tình và hữu nghị. Tổng Bí thư Nông Đức Mạnh trân trọng mời Tổng Bí thư, Chủ tịch nước Hồ Cẩm Đào sớm sang thăm lại Việt Nam. Tổng Bí thư, Chủ tịch nước Hồ Cẩm Đào đã cảm ơn và vui vẻ nhận lời.

中越联合声明

（2008年10月25日）

一、应中华人民共和国国务院总理温家宝邀请，越南社会主义共和国政府总理阮晋勇于2008年10月20日至25日对中国进行正式访问并出席第七届亚欧首脑会议。访问期间，温家宝总理与阮晋勇总理举行会谈，中共中央总书记、国家主席胡锦涛，全国人民代表大会常务委员会委员长吴邦国分别会见了阮晋勇总理。除北京外，阮晋勇总理还赴海南省访问。

两国领导人在坦诚友好和相互理解的气氛中，就双边关系及共同关心的国际和地区问题深入交换了意见，就丰富中越全面战略合作伙伴关系的内涵达成重要共识。双方一致认为，访问取得了圆满成功，为推动中越睦邻友好与全面合作关系不断发展到新高度作出了贡献，这符合两国人民的根本利益，也有利于本地区和世界的和平、稳定与发展。

二、越方高度评价兄弟的中国人民改革开放30年来取得的辉煌成就，认为中国成功举办北京奥运会和残奥会、圆满完成神舟七号载人航天飞行和成功主办第七届亚欧首脑会议，使中国的国际地位和威望进一步提高，表示坚信中国人民一定能在建设中国特色社会主义事业中取得新的更大成就，胜利实现全面建设小康社会的奋斗目标。

中方高度评价越南人民在革新开放、实现国家工业化和现代化、改善人民生活水平的事业中取得的巨大成就，祝贺越南成功融入国际社会并担任联合国安理会非常任理事国，表示相信越南人民将胜利实现建设民富国强、社会公平、民主、文明的社会主义国家的目标。

三、双方满意地看到，中越睦邻友好合作关系取得了重要进展，双方政治互信不断增强，经贸合作成果丰硕，各部门和各地方的交流与合作日益扩大，存在问题逐步得到妥善解决。双方一致认为，在当前国际政治经济形势复杂多变的背景下，拓展和深化中越全面战略合作伙伴关系，符合两党两国和两国人民的根本利益，有利于本地区和世界的和平、稳定与发展。

四、双方就落实中越全面战略合作伙伴关系的措施达成重要共识。双方同意，保持两党两国高层密切接触，通过双边互访、热线通话、多边场合会晤等灵活多样的形式，及时就两国关系的重大问题交换意见；进一步发挥中越双边合作指导委员会的作用，统筹规划和全面推进两国各领域合作；完善各部门合作机制，落实好外交、国防、公安、安全等部门的合作协议；扩大科技、文化、教育、卫生、旅游等领域的务实合作，加强两国青少年、群众团体和民间组织的友好交往，做好对中越全面战略合作伙伴关系重要意义和具体内涵的宣传教育，使两国人民的友谊世代相传。双方同意举办形式多样的活动，隆重庆祝两国建交60周年。

五、双方同意进一步深化经贸合作，争取2010年双边贸易额达到250亿美元。双方责成中越经贸合作委员会：（一）推动落实双方正在商签的《中越经贸合作五年发展规划》；（二）为两国企业在对方国家投资创造便利；（三）尽快成立经贸合作工作组，就两国经贸合作有关具体事项相互通报情况、交换意见并就存在问题探讨解决措施；（四）在打击走私、假冒商品和商业欺诈等方面加强信息沟通、协调管理，保障边境贸易活动健康发展。

两国政府将加强指导并提供政策扶持，推动两国企业按照市场规则落实和执行业已签订的合作项目协议和经济合同，以增强双方合作信心；继续商定大型合作项目，鼓励两国大型企业在基础设施建设、交通、电力、住宅建设、设计咨询、化工、配套工业、造船等领域扩大长期互利合作。双方同意，继续落实关于开展“两廊一圈”合作的谅解备忘录，认真研究跨境经贸旅游区的有关设想，密切两国边境省份之间的关系。

双方同意加强两国经济专家之间的经验交流，为应对国际经济形势变化提出政策建议。

六、双方对陆地边界勘界工作基本完成表示满意，同意进一步密切配合，积极解决剩余问题，确保如期实现今年内完成陆地边界全线勘界立碑工作的目标，早日签署勘界议定书和新的边界管理制度协定，把两国陆地边界建成长期友好、和平稳定、互利合作的边界。双方同意在双方商定的一对口岸举行结束全线勘界立碑工作的庆祝仪式。

双方重申继续密切配合，落实好《北部湾划界协定》和《北部湾渔业合作协定》，做好北部湾共同渔区联合检查和渔业资源联合调查及海军联合巡逻工作，推动北部湾跨界油气构造勘采合作取得实质进展。稳步推进北部湾湾口外海域划界谈判并积极商谈该海域的共同开发问题，早日启动该海域共同考察。

双方就维护南海和平稳定坦诚友好地交换了意见，重申恪守两国高层共识及《南海各方行为宣言》精神，保持海上问题谈判机制，按照包括1982年《联合国海洋法公约》在内的国际法所确认的法律制度和原则，寻求双方均能接受的基本和长久的解决办法，同时积极研究和商谈共同开发问题，以便找到适合的模式和区域。在此过程中，双方将共同努力维护南海局势稳定，均不采取使争端复杂化或扩大化的行动。双方同意，本着先易后难的原则，加强在海洋科研、环境保护、气象水文预报、油气勘采、海上搜救、军舰互访、建立两国军队直接信息交流机制等领域的合作。

七、越方重申坚定奉行一个中国政策，支持中国统一大业，坚决反对任何形式的“台独”分裂活动。越南不同台湾发展任何官方关系。中方对越方上述立场表示赞赏。

八、双方就共同关心的国际和地区问题交换了意见并达成共识，对两国在联合国、世界贸易组织、亚太经合组织、亚欧会议、中国—东盟、东盟—中日韩等国际和地区事务中的密切协调与配合表示满意，同意加强在多边领域的合作，为推动建设持久和平、共同繁荣的世界作出积极贡献。

九、访问期间，双方签署了两国政府关于建立领导人热线的协定和边境卫生检疫协议以及中国向越南提供出口买方信贷的贷款总协议、关于在海防建立中国越南经济贸易合作区的合作协议、中国海洋石油总公司与越南国家油气集团战略合作协议等8份合作文件。

十、阮晋勇总理对温家宝总理以及中国共产党、中国政府和人民所给予的隆重、热情、友好的接待表示衷心感谢，邀请温家宝总理再次访问越南。温家宝总理对此表示感谢。

Tuyên bố chung Trung Quốc-Việt Nam

(2008/10/25)

Chuyến thăm hữu nghị chính thức Trung Quốc và dự Hội nghị cấp cao ASEM 7 của Thủ tướng Chính phủ Nguyễn Tấn Dũng đã thành công tốt đẹp, góp phần thúc đẩy quan hệ láng giềng hữu nghị, đẩy mạnh quan hệ đối tác hợp tác toàn diện Việt-Trung không ngừng phát triển lên một tầm cao mới vì lợi ích căn bản của nhân dân hai nước, vì hòa bình, ổn định và phát triển ở khu vực và trên thế giới. Ngày 25-10-2008, hai bên đã ra Tuyên bố chung. Báo Hànộimới xin trân trọng giới thiệu toàn văn bản Tuyên bố chung này.

1. Nhận lời mời của Thủ tướng Quốc vụ viện nước Cộng hòa nhân dân Trung Hoa Ôn Gia Bảo, Thủ tướng Chính phủ nước Cộng hòa xã hội chủ nghĩa Việt Nam Nguyễn Tấn Dũng đã thăm hữu nghị chính thức Trung Quốc và dự Hội nghị cấp cao ASEM 7 từ ngày 20 đến ngày 25-10-2008. Trong thời gian thăm, Thủ tướng Nguyễn Tấn Dũng đã hội đàm với Thủ tướng Ôn Gia Bảo và lần lượt hội kiến với các đồng chí Tổng Bí thư, Chủ tịch nước Hồ Cẩm Đào, Ủy viên trưởng Ủy ban Thường vụ đại hội đại biểu nhân dân toàn quốc Ngô Bang Quốc. Ngoài Bắc Kinh, Thủ tướng Nguyễn Tấn Dũng đã thăm tỉnh Hải Nam.

Trong không khí chân thành, hữu nghị và hiểu biết lẫn nhau, lãnh đạo hai nước đã trao đổi ý kiến về quan hệ song phương, các vấn đề quốc tế và khu vực mà hai bên cùng quan tâm, đạt được nhận thức chung quan trọng về việc làm phong phú nội hàm mối quan hệ đối tác hợp tác chiến lược toàn diện Việt Nam-Trung Quốc. Hai bên nhất trí cho rằng, chuyến thăm đã thành công tốt đẹp, góp phần thúc đẩy quan hệ láng giềng hữu nghị, hợp tác toàn diện Việt-Trung không ngừng phát triển lên một tầm cao mới vì lợi ích căn bản của nhân dân hai nước, vì hòa bình, ổn định và phát triển ở khu vực và trên thế giới.

2. Phía Việt Nam đánh giá cao thành tựu rực rỡ mà nhân dân Trung Quốc anh em đạt được sau 30 năm cải cách mở cửa; nhấn mạnh những thành công của Trung Quốc trong việc tổ chức Olympic và Paralympic Bắc Kinh, phóng tàu vũ trụ có người lái "Thần Châu 7" và tổ chức Hội nghị cấp cao ASEM 7 góp phần nâng cao thêm một bước vị thế và uy tín quốc tế của Trung Quốc; bày tỏ tin tưởng chắc chắn nhân dân Trung Quốc sẽ đạt được thành tựu mới to lớn hơn nữa trong công cuộc xây dựng CNXH đặc sắc Trung Quốc, thực hiện thắng lợi mục tiêu xây dựng xã hội khá giả toàn diện.

Phía Trung Quốc đánh giá cao thành tựu to lớn mà nhân dân Việt Nam giành được trong công cuộc đổi mới mở cửa, thực hiện công nghiệp hóa, hiện đại hóa đất nước, cải thiện đời sống nhân dân; chúc mừng những thành công của Việt Nam trong hội nhập quốc tế và đảm nhiệm vai trò Ủy viên không thường trực Hội đồng Bảo an Liên hợp quốc; bày tỏ tin tưởng nhân dân Việt Nam sẽ thực hiện thắng lợi mục tiêu xây dựng một nước xã hội chủ nghĩa, dân giàu nước mạnh, xã hội công bằng, dân chủ, văn minh.

3. Hai bên hài lòng nhận thấy, quan hệ láng giềng hữu nghị và hợp tác Việt-Trung có bước phát triển quan trọng, sự tin cậy lẫn nhau về chính trị giữa hai bên không ngừng được tăng cường, hợp tác kinh tế thương mại đạt thành quả to lớn, hợp tác giao lưu giữa các bộ ngành và các địa phương ngày một mở rộng, các vấn đề tồn tại từng bước được giải quyết ổn thỏa. Hai bên nhất trí cho rằng, trong bối cảnh tình hình kinh tế, chính trị quốc tế đang diễn biến phức tạp hiện nay, việc tiếp tục mở rộng và làm sâu sắc thêm mối quan hệ đối tác hợp tác chiến lược toàn diện Việt-Trung phù hợp lợi ích căn bản của hai Đảng, hai nước và nhân dân hai nước, có lợi cho hòa bình, ổn định và phát triển của khu vực cũng như thế giới.

4. Hai bên đạt được nhận thức chung quan trọng về những biện pháp triển khai quan hệ đối tác hợp tác chiến lược toàn diện Việt Nam-Trung Quốc. Hai bên nhất trí duy trì tiếp xúc mật thiết giữa lãnh đạo cấp cao hai Đảng, hai nước dưới các hình thức linh hoạt và đa dạng như các chuyến thăm song phương, trao đổi qua đường dây nóng, gặp gỡ tại các diễn đàn đa phương, kịp thời trao đổi ý kiến về những vấn đề quan trọng trong quan hệ hai nước; phát huy hơn nữa vai trò

của Ủy ban Chỉ đạo hợp tác song phương Việt-Trung trong việc quy hoạch tổng thể và đẩy mạnh toàn diện hợp tác giữa hai nước trên các lĩnh vực; hoàn thiện cơ chế hợp tác giữa các bộ, ngành, thực hiện tốt các thỏa thuận hợp tác giữa các ngành Ngoại giao, Quốc phòng, Công an, An ninh…; mở rộng hợp tác thiết thực trên các lĩnh vực khoa học công nghệ, văn hóa, giáo dục, y tế, du lịch…; tăng cường giao lưu hữu nghị giữa thanh thiếu niên, đoàn thể quần chúng, các tổ chức dân gian hai nước; làm tốt công tác tuyên truyền giáo dục về ý nghĩa quan trọng và nội hàm cụ thể của quan hệ đối tác hợp tác chiến lược toàn diện Việt-Trung, để tình hữu nghị của nhân dân hai nước mãi mãi lưu truyền từ thế hệ này sang thế hệ khác. Hai bên thỏa thuận sẽ cùng nhau phối hợp tổ chức các hoạt động với hình thức đa dạng, long trọng kỷ niệm 60 năm thiết lập quan hệ ngoại giao hai nước.

5. Hai bên nhất trí làm sâu sắc hơn nữa hợp tác kinh tế mậu dịch, phấn đấu nâng kim ngạch mậu dịch hai bên đạt 25 tỷ USD vào năm 2010. Hai bên giao Ủy ban Hợp tác kinh tế thương mại Việt-Trung: Đẩy mạnh thực hiện "Quy hoạch 5 năm phát triển hợp tác kinh tế mậu dịch Việt-Trung" mà hai bên đang thảo luận để ký kết; Tạo điều kiện thuận lợi để doanh nghiệp hai nước đầu tư tại nước kia; Sớm thành lập tổ công tác hợp tác kinh tế thương mại để thông báo tình hình cho nhau và trao đổi ý kiến về các công việc cụ thể trong hợp tác kinh tế thương mại, tìm các biện pháp giải quyết những vấn đề tồn tại; Tăng cường trao đổi thông tin, phối hợp quản lý chống buôn lậu, hàng giả và gian lận thương mại…, bảo đảm các hoạt động mậu dịch biên giới phát triển lành mạnh.

Chính phủ hai nước tăng cường chỉ đạo và hỗ trợ về chính sách, thúc đẩy các doanh nghiệp hai nước thực hiện và chấp hành những thỏa thuận hợp tác và hợp đồng kinh tế đã ký kết theo quy tắc thị trường để tăng cường lòng tin trong hợp tác song phương; tiếp tục trao đổi thỏa thuận về các dự án hợp tác lớn, khuyến khích các doanh nghiệp lớn của hai nước mở rộng hợp tác lâu dài, cùng có lợi trong các lĩnh vực xây dựng cơ sở hạ tầng, giao thông, điện lực, xây dựng nhà ở, tư vấn thiết kế, công nghiệp hóa chất, công nghiệp phụ trợ, đóng tàu… Hai bên nhất trí, tiếp tục thực hiện Bản ghi nhớ về triển khai hợp tác "Hai hành lang một vành đai", nghiên cứu nghiêm túc ý tưởng về khu kinh tế, thương mại, du lịch xuyên biên giới, thắt chặt mối quan hệ giữa các tỉnh biên giới hai nước.

Hai bên nhất trí tăng cường trao đổi kinh nghiệm giữa chuyên gia kinh tế hai nước, đề xuất các kiến nghị về chính sách ứng phó với những biến động của tình hình kinh tế quốc tế.

6. Hai bên bày tỏ hài lòng đối với việc cơ bản hoàn thành công tác phân giới trên bộ, đồng ý tiếp tục cùng phối hợp chặt chẽ, tích cực giải quyết vấn đề còn lại, bảo đảm thực hiện mục tiêu kết thúc công việc phân giới cắm mốc toàn tuyến biên giới trên bộ đúng thời hạn trong năm nay; sớm ký kết Nghị định thư phân giới cắm mốc và Hiệp định quy chế quản lý biên giới mới nhằm xây dựng đường biên giới hòa bình, ổn định, hợp tác, hữu nghị lâu dài giữa hai nước. Hai bên đồng ý tổ chức lễ mừng công hoàn thành toàn bộ công tác phân giới cắm mốc tại cặp cửa khẩu mà hai bên nhất trí. Hai bên khẳng định tiếp tục phối hợp chặt chẽ, thực hiện tốt "Hiệp định phân định vịnh Bắc bộ" và "Hiệp định hợp tác nghề cá vịnh Bắc bộ", làm tốt công tác kiểm tra liên hợp và điều tra liên hợp nguồn lợi thủy sản trong vùng đánh cá chung và việc tuần tra chung giữa hải quân hai nước ở vịnh Bắc bộ; thúc đẩy hợp tác thăm dò, khai thác cấu tạo dầu khí vắt ngang đường phân định vịnh Bắc bộ đạt được những tiến triển thực chất. Hai bên tiếp tục thúc đẩy một cách vững chắc đàm phán phân định khu vực ngoài cửa vịnh Bắc bộ và tích cực trao đổi về vấn đề hợp tác cùng phát triển, sớm khởi động khảo sát chung ở khu vực này.

Hai bên đã trao đổi ý kiến một cách thẳng thắn và hữu nghị về việc gìn giữ hòa bình ổn định ở biển Đông; khẳng định tuân thủ nghiêm túc nhận thức chung giữa lãnh đạo cấp cao hai nước và tinh thần "Tuyên bố về cách ứng xử của các bên ở biển Đông", duy trì cơ chế đàm phán vấn đề trên biển, căn cứ nguyên tắc và chế độ pháp lý được xác định bởi luật pháp quốc tế, bao gồm Công ước Luật Biển của Liên hợp quốc năm 1982 tìm kiếm giải pháp cơ bản và lâu dài mà hai bên có thể chấp nhận được, tích cực nghiên cứu và bàn bạc về hợp tác cùng phát triển để tìm ra mô hình và khu vực thích hợp.

Trong quá trình đó, hai bên cùng nỗ lực gìn giữ tình hình ổn định ở biển Đông, không áp dụng hành động làm phức tạp hóa hoặc mở rộng thêm tranh chấp. Hai bên đồng ý, với nguyên tắc dễ trước khó sau, tăng cường hợp tác trên các lĩnh vực như nghiên cứu khoa học hải dương, bảo vệ môi trường, dự báo khí tượng thủy văn, thăm dò khai thác dầu khí, tìm kiếm cứu hộ trên biển, tàu hải quân đi thăm lẫn nhau, xây dựng cơ chế trao đổi thông tin trực tiếp giữa quân đội hai nước.

7. Phía Việt Nam một lần nữa khẳng định việc kiên định thực hiện chính sách một Trung Quốc, ủng hộ sự nghiệp thống nhất của Trung Quốc, kiên quyết phản đối hoạt động "Đài Loan độc lập" dưới bất kỳ hình thức nào. Việt Nam không phát triển bất cứ quan hệ chính thức nào với Đài Loan. Phía Trung Quốc bày tỏ hoan nghênh lập trường trên của Việt Nam.

8. Hai bên trao đổi và đạt nhận thức chung về các vấn đề quốc tế, khu vực cùng quan tâm, bày tỏ hài lòng về sự phối hợp chặt chẽ trong các công việc quốc tế và khu vực như LHQ, WTO, APEC, ASEM, ASEAN+1, ASEAN+3, đồng ý tăng cường hợp tác trong lĩnh vực đa phương, góp phần thúc đẩy xây dựng một thế giới hòa bình lâu dài và cùng phát triển phồn vinh.

9. Trong thời gian thăm, hai bên đã ký 8 hiệp định và thỏa thuận, trong đó có Hiệp định về thiết lập đường dây nóng; Hiệp định về kiểm dịch y tế biên giới; Hiệp định khung về việc Trung Quốc cung cấp cho Việt Nam khoản tín dụng; Thỏa thuận về xây dựng khu kinh tế-thương mại Trung Quốc tại thành phố Hải Phòng; Thỏa thuận về hợp tác chiến lược giữa Tập đoàn Dầu khí Việt Nam và Công ty Dầu khí hải dương quốc gia Trung Quốc và một số thỏa thuận hợp đồng kinh tế khác.

10. Thủ tướng Nguyễn Tấn Dũng bày tỏ cảm ơn chân thành Thủ tướng Ôn Gia Bảo, Đảng Cộng sản Trung Quốc, Chính phủ và nhân dân Trung Quốc về sự đón tiếp trọng thị, nhiệt tình và hữu nghị, mời Thủ tướng Ôn Gia Bảo thăm lại Việt Nam, Thủ tướng Ôn Gia Bảo bày tỏ sự cảm ơn.

关于指导解决
中华人民共和国和越南社会主义共和国
海上问题基本原则协议

（2011年10月11日）

中华人民共和国政府代表团和越南社会主义共和国政府代表团一致认为，妥善解决中越海上问题符合两国人民的根本利益和共同愿望，有利于本地区的和平、稳定、合作与发展。双方同意根据中越领导人就海上问题达成的各项共识，在1993年《关于解决中华人民共和国和越南社会主义共和国边界领土问题的基本原则协议》基础上，遵循以下原则处理和解决海上问题：

一、以两国关系大局为重，从战略和全局高度出发，在“长期稳定、面向未来、睦邻友好、全面合作”方针和“好邻居、好朋友、好同志、好伙伴”精神指引下，坚持通过友好协商，妥善处理和解决海上问题，使南海成为和平、友好、合作之海，为发展中越全面战略合作伙伴关系、维护地区和平与稳定作出贡献。

二、本着充分尊重法理依据，同时考虑历史等其他相关因素，照顾彼此合理关切的精神，以建设性的态度，努力扩大共识，缩小分歧，不断推进谈判进程。按照包括1982年《联合国海洋法公约》在内的国际法所确认的法律制度和原则，努力寻求双方都能接受的基本和长久的解决海上争议问题的办法。

三、在海上问题谈判进程中，双方应严格遵守两国高层领导达成的协议和共识，认真落实《南海各方行为宣言》(DOC)的原则和精神。

对中越海上争议，双方将通过谈判和友好协商加以解决。如争议涉及其他国家，将与其他争议方进行协商。

四、在寻求基本和长久的解决海上问题的办法进程中，本着相互尊重、平等相待、互利共赢的精神，按照本协议第二条所述原则，积极探讨不影响双方立场和主张的过渡性、临时性解决办法，包括积极研究和商谈共同开发问题。

五、本着循序渐进、先易后难的精神解决海上问题。稳步推进北部湾湾口外海域划界谈判，同时积极商谈该海域的共同开发问题。积极推进海上低敏感领域合作，包括海洋环保、海洋科研、海上搜救、减灾防灾领域的合作。努力增进互信，为解决更困难的问题创造条件。

六、双方每年举行两次政府边界谈判代表团团长定期会晤，轮流主办，必要时可举行特别会晤。双方同意在政府代表团框架下设立热线联系机制，以便就海上问题及时沟通，妥善处理。

本协议于二〇一一年十月十一日在北京签订，一式两份，每份均用中文和越文写成，两种文本同等作准。

Thỏa thuận về những Nguyên tắc cơ bản chỉ đạo giải quyết vấn đề trên biển giữa nước Cộng hòa Nhân dân Trung Hoa và nước Cộng hòa Xã hội chủ nghĩa Việt Nam

(2011/10/11)

Hai bên nhất trí căn cứ vào những nhận thức chung mà lãnh đạo Việt Nam và Trung Quốc đã đạt được trong vấn đề trên biển, trên cơ sở "Thỏa thuận nguyên tắc cơ bản giải quyết vấn đề biên giới lãnh thổ giữa nước Cộng hòa xã hội chủ nghĩa Việt Nam và nước Cộng hòa Nhân dân Trung Hoa" năm 1993, xử lý và giải quyết vấn đề trên biển tuân theo những nguyên tắc dưới đây:

1. Lấy đại cục quan hệ hai nước làm trọng, xuất phát từ tầm cao chiến lược và toàn cục, dưới sự chỉ đạo của phương châm "láng giềng hữu nghị, hợp tác toàn diện, ổn định lâu dài, hướng tới tương lai" và tinh thần "láng giềng tốt, bạn bè tốt, đồng chí tốt, đối tác tốt", kiên trì thông qua hiệp thương hữu nghị, xử lý và giải quyết thỏa đáng vấn đề trên biển, làm cho Biển Đông trở thành vùng biển hòa bình, hữu nghị, hợp tác, đóng góp vào việc phát triển quan hệ đối tác hợp tác chiến lược toàn diện Việt Nam-Trung Quốc, góp phần duy trì hòa bình và ổn định trong khu vực.

2. Trên tinh thần tôn trọng đầy đủ chứng cứ pháp lý và xem xét các yếu tố liên quan khác như lịch sử..., đồng thời chiếu cố đến quan ngại hợp lý của nhau, với thái độ xây dựng, cố gắng mở rộng nhận thức chung, thu hẹp bất đồng, không ngừng thúc đẩy tiến trình đàm phán. Căn cứ chế độ pháp lý và nguyên tắc được xác định bởi luật pháp quốc tế trong đó có Công ước Liên hợp quốc về Luật Biển năm 1982, nỗ lực tìm kiếm giải pháp cơ bản và lâu dài mà hai bên đều

có thể chấp nhận được cho các vấn đề tranh chấp trên biển.

3. Trong tiến trình đàm phán vấn đề trên biển, hai bên nghiêm chỉnh tuân thủ thỏa thuận và nhận thức chung mà lãnh đạo cấp cao hai nước đã đạt được, thực hiện nghiêm túc nguyên tắc và tinh thần của "Tuyên bố ứng xử của các bên ở Biển Đông" (DOC).

Đối với tranh chấp trên biển giữa Việt Nam-Trung Quốc, hai bên giải quyết thông qua đàm phán và hiệp thương hữu nghị. Nếu tranh chấp liên quan đến các nước khác, thì sẽ hiệp thương với các bên tranh chấp khác.

4. Trong tiến trình tìm kiếm giải pháp cơ bản và lâu dài cho vấn đề trên biển, trên tinh thần tôn trọng lẫn nhau, đối xử bình đẳng, cùng có lợi, tích cực bàn bạc thảo luận về những giải pháp mang tính quá độ, tạm thời mà không ảnh hưởng đến lập trường và chủ trương của hai bên, bao gồm việc tích cực nghiên cứu và bàn bạc về vấn đề hợp tác cùng phát triển theo những nguyên tắc đã nêu tại Điều 2 của Thỏa thuận này.

5. Giải quyết các vấn đề trên biển theo tinh thần tuần tự tiệm tiến, dễ trước khó sau. Vững bước thúc đẩy đàm phán phân định vùng biển ngoài cửa Vịnh Bắc Bộ, đồng thời tích cực bàn bạc về vấn đề hợp tác cùng phát triển tại vùng biển này. Tích cực thúc đẩy hợp tác trên các lĩnh vực ít nhạy cảm như bảo vệ môi trường biển, nghiên cứu khoa học biển, tìm kiếm, cứu hộ cứu nạn trên biển, phòng chống, giảm thiểu thiệt hại do thiên tai. Nỗ lực tăng cường tin cậy lẫn nhau để tạo điều kiện cho việc giải quyết các vấn đề khó khăn hơn.

6. Hai bên tiến hành cuộc gặp định kỳ Trưởng đoàn đàm phán biên giới cấp Chính phủ một năm hai lần, luân phiên tổ chức, khi cần thiết có thể tiến hành các cuộc gặp bất thường. Hai bên nhất trí thiết lập cơ chế đường dây nóng trong khuôn khổ đoàn đại biểu cấp Chính phủ để kịp thời trao đổi và xử lý thỏa đáng vấn đề trên biển.

Thỏa thuận này ký tại Bắc Kinh, ngày 11 tháng 10 năm 2011, thành hai bản, mỗi bản bằng tiếng Việt và tiếng Trung, cả hai bản đều có giá trị như nhau.

中越联合声明

（2013年6月21日）

一、应中华人民共和国主席习近平邀请，越南社会主义共和国主席张晋创于2013年6月19日至21日对中华人民共和国进行国事访问。

访问期间，国家主席习近平同张晋创主席举行了会谈。国务院总理李克强、全国人民代表大会常务委员会委员长张德江分别会见了张晋创主席。两国领导人在友好坦诚的气氛中，就新形势下进一步深化中越全面战略合作和共同关心的国际地区问题深入交换意见，达成广泛共识。

除北京外，张晋创主席还前往广东省访问。

二、双方回顾了中越关系发展历程，一致认为中越友好是两国人民共同的宝贵财富，重申将遵循两国领导人多年来就发展中越友好达成的重要共识，继续坚持“长期稳定、面向未来、睦邻友好、全面合作”的方针和“好邻居、好朋友、好同志、好伙伴”的精神，不断增进战略互信，深化各领域互利合作，妥善处理存在的问题，加强在国际地区事务中的协调配合，推动中越关系长期健康稳定发展。

三、中越均处在经济社会发展的关键时期，双方视对方的发展为自身发展的机遇，同意重点在以下领域深化全面战略合作：

（一）通过双边互访、热线电话、多边场合会晤等灵活多样的形式，保持高层接触，加强战略沟通，牢牢把握两国关系发展的正确方向。中方欢迎越南领导人来华访问和参会，越方欢迎中国领导人尽早访越。

（二）双方积极评价中越双边合作指导委员会第六次会议成果，同意继续用好这一重要机制，统筹推进各领域互利合作，更好地造福两国人民。双方同意共同落实好此访期间签署的《落实中越全面战略合作伙伴关系行动计划》，推动两国务实合作取得新进展。

（三）双方对近年两党关系发展表示满意，同意深化两党合作，推进两党中央对外部门和宣传部门交流合作机制顺利运转，加强党政干部培训合作。双方同意密切配合，共同办好第九次两党理论研讨会，进一步加强治党治国经验交流，促进各自党和国家的建设。

（四）双方同意加强两国外交部合作，落实好两国外交部合作议定书，保持两部领导经常交往，举办年度外交磋商，加强两部对口司局交流。

（五）双方积极评价第七次两国防务安全磋商成果，同意保持两军高层交往，发挥好防务安全磋商机制和国防部直通电话的作用，增进双方互信。深入开展军队党务和政治工作经验交流，加强人员培训和青年军官交往。落实好此访期间签署的《中越国防部边防合作协议（修订版）》，继续开展陆地边界联合巡逻。深化边海防合作，年内开展两次两国海军北部湾联合巡逻。加强在地区多边安全事务中的沟通与协调。探讨开展防务合作的新形式、新内容，进一步深化两军合作。

（六）双方同意深化执法安全合作，充分发挥两国公安部合作打击犯罪会议机制作用，密切执法高层和业务部门互访，推进在打击跨国犯罪、维护社会治安以及执法能力建设等领域的务实合作，尽快开展各领域执法联合行动，维护两国边境地区的安全稳定。双方同意推动两国海警部门开展交流合作。双方同意下半年尽快启动《中越引渡条约》谈判。

（七）双方同意加强经济发展战略协调，落实好《中越2012—2016年经贸合作五年发展规划》及重点合作项目清单，进一步推进农业和渔业、交通运输、能源、矿业、制造业和配套工业、服务业合作以及“两廊一圈”区域合作。双方将用好双边经贸合委会机制，落实好《中国商务部和越南工贸部农产品贸易领域合作谅解备忘录》，双方同意在保持双边贸易稳定增长的基础上，积极采取有效、有力措施，促进双边贸易平衡增长，争取提前实现2015年双边贸易额600亿美元的目标。继续推进中越能源、工业园区、陆地互联互通等重大经贸合作项目建设，重点推动建设凭祥—河内高速公路等连接两国陆地边境地区的公路和铁路项目。双方同意加强双边金融合作，积极创造条件并鼓励双方金融机构向双边合作项目提供金融服务支持。继续推动双边贸易和投资便利化，包括鼓励在边境贸易中使用本币支付结算。鼓励各自企业到对方国家投资，为投资企业创造安全便利条件。

（八）双方同意继续深化农业合作，完善农业双边合作机制，加强农业科技交流与农业领域能力建设，推广包括杂交水稻在内的优质高产农作物品种，促进农产品加工与贸易发展，重点推进跨境动植物疫病防控、进出口食品安全体系建设，提高预警能力和信息共享水平。

（九）加强文化交流与合作，落实好《2011—2015年教育交流协议》、《中越文化协定2013—2015年执行计划》，在对方国家早日建成文化中心，加强在文化产业、人力资源等领域合作。双方同意下半年在华举办第二届中越青年大联欢，同时继续办好中越青年友好会见、中越人民论坛会议等活动，加大中越友好宣传，增进两国人民之间的友好感情。

（十）双方同意深化科技交流与合作，进一步发挥两国政府间科技合作联委会作用，鼓励和支持两国科技和产业界在农业、信息通讯、新能源、环保、水资源管理利用和保护等共同感兴趣的领域开展联合研究与开发、共建联合实验室和技术转移等多种形式的合作。

（十一）双方同意进一步加强两国边境省区特别是中国广东、广西、海南、云南四省（区）同越南奠边、莱州、老街、河江、高平、谅山、广宁七省之间的合作，发挥两国地方有关合作机制作用，重点推进经贸、交通基础设施、科教文卫等领域合作，促进两国边境省区的共同发展。

（十二）双方同意认真落实两国陆地边界联委会2013年工作计划，积极评价此访期间建立两国边境口岸管理合作委员会，同意推动两国边境口岸开放和升格，加强边境口岸基础设施建设和管理，改善口岸通行条件，提高口岸通行效率，服务两国经贸发展和人员往来。尽快启动中越北仑河二桥建设。双方同意下半年举行《北仑河口地区自由航行协定》和《德天瀑布地区旅游资源共同开发和保护协定》新一轮谈判，争取尽快取得实质进展。双方将加强在界河整治、跨界河流防洪减灾、水资源利用和保护领域的技术交流与合作。

（十三）双方将继续落实好《北部湾渔业合作协定》，积极探索北部湾共同渔区联合检查新方式。双方高度评价此访期间签署的《中国农业部与越南农业与农村发展部关于建立海上渔业活动突发事件联系热线的协议》，妥善处理两国海上渔业活动突发事件，使之符合两国友好关系。

四、双方就海上问题坦诚交换了意见，同意两党两国领导人就中越海上问题保持经常性的沟通和对话，从战略高度和两国关系大局出发，指导和推进海上问题的妥善解决。双方将认真落实《关于指导解决中越海上问题基本原则协议》，用好中越政府边界谈判等机制，坚持通过友好协商和谈判，寻求双方均能接受的基本和长久的解决办法，积极探讨不影响各自立场和主张的过渡性解决办法，包括积极研究和商谈共同开发问题。

双方同意本着先易后难、循序渐进的原则，加大北部湾湾口外海域工作组谈判力度，稳步推进湾口外海域划界谈判并积极推进该海域的共同开发，年内在北部湾湾口外海域启动共同考察，尽早确定合作区域和领域，落实北部湾湾口外海域工作组谈判任务。双方欢迎两国有关企业签署的中越北部湾协议区联合勘探协议修改协议，同意扩大协议区面积，延长协议期限，共同推动北部湾内跨界油气构造联合勘探尽快取得积极进展。

双方同意加大中越海上低敏感领域合作专家工作组谈判密度，年内实施中越海上联合搜救、北部湾海洋和岛屿环境管理合作研究、红河三角洲与长江三角洲海域全新世沉积演化对比研究等3个海上低敏感领域合作项目中的1至2个项目，继续推进在海洋环保、海洋科研、海上搜救、防灾减灾、海上互联互通等领域合作。

双方同意在海上争议最终解决前，保持冷静和克制，不采取使争端复杂化、扩大化的行动。同时用好两国外交部海上危机管控热线，本着建设性的态度妥善处理出现的问题，不使其影响中越关系大局以及南海和平稳定。双方同意全面有效落实《南海各方行为宣言》(DOC)，共同维护南海和平与稳定。

五、越方重申坚定奉行一个中国政策，支持两岸关系和平发展与中国统一大业，坚决反对任何形式的“台独”分裂活动。越南不同台湾发展任何官方关系。中方对此表示赞赏。

六、双方认为，中越同为发展中国家，在许多共同关心的国际地区问题上具有相似和相近的立场。双方同意加强在联合国、世贸组织、亚太经合组织、亚欧会议、东盟地区论坛、中国—东盟、东盟—中日韩、东亚峰会等多边场合的协调与配合，共同维护世界的和平、稳定与繁荣。

双方同意，以今年中国—东盟建立战略伙伴关系10周年为契机，全面落实中国同东盟国家领导人达成的各项共识，办好10周年系列纪念活动，不断拓展和深化中国同东盟在经贸、互联互通、海洋、社会人文等领域合作，为地区和平、稳定与繁荣作出更大贡献。

七、访问期间，双方签署了《中越两国政府落实中越全面战略合作伙伴关系行动计划》、《中越国防部边防合作协议(修订版)》、《中国农业部与越南农业与农村发展部关于建立海上渔业活动突发事件联系热线的协议》、《中国质量监督检验检疫总局与越南农业与农村发展部关于动植物检验检疫合作协议》、《中越陆地边境口岸管理合作委员会工作条例》、《中越两国政府关于互设文化中心的谅解备忘录》、《中国人民对外友好协会和越南友好组织联合会2013年—2017年合作备忘录》、《中国海洋石油总公司和越南油气总公司关于北部湾协议区联合勘探协议第四次修改协议》及多项经济合作文件。

八、双方对越南国家主席张晋创访华成果表示满意，一致认为此访对推动两国关系发展具有重要意义。张晋创主席对访华期间受到中方热情友好接待表示感谢，邀请国家主席习近平访问越南。国家主席习近平对此表示感谢。

Tuyên bố chung Trung Quốc-Việt Nam

(2013/6/21)

1. Nhận lời mời của Chủ tịch nước Cộng hòa Nhân dân Trung Hoa Tập Cận Bình, Chủ tịch nước Cộng hòa xã hội chủ nghĩa Việt Nam Trương Tấn Sang đã thăm cấp Nhà nước nước Cộng hòa Nhân dân Trung Hoa từ ngày 19 đến ngày 21 tháng 6 năm 2013.

Trong thời gian chuyến thăm, Chủ tịch nước Trương Tấn Sang đã hội đàm với Chủ tịch nước Tập Cận Bình; lần lượt hội kiến Thủ tướng Quốc vụ viện Lý Khắc Cường, Ủy viên trưởng Ủy ban thường vụ Đại hội đại biểu nhân dân toàn quốc Trương Đức Giang. Trong không khí thẳng thắn, hữu nghị, Lãnh đạo hai nước đã đi sâu trao đổi ý kiến và đạt nhận thức chung rộng rãi về việc làm sâu sắc thêm hợp tác chiến lược toàn diện Việt-Trung trong tình hình mới, cũng như về các vấn đề quốc tế và khu vực cùng quan tâm.

Ngoài Bắc Kinh, Chủ tịch nước Trương Tấn Sang đã thăm tỉnh Quảng Đông.

2. Hai bên đã nhìn lại quá trình phát triển quan hệ Việt-Trung, nhất trí cho rằng tình hữu nghị Việt-Trung là tài sản chung quý báu của nhân dân hai nước, khẳng định sẽ tuân theo các nhận thức chung quan trọng mà Lãnh đạo hai nước đã đạt được trong những năm qua về phát triển quan hệ hữu nghị Việt-Trung, tiếp tục kiên trì phương châm “láng giềng hữu nghị, hợp tác toàn diện, ổn định lâu dài, hướng tới tương lai” và tinh thần “láng giềng tốt, bạn bè tốt, đồng chí tốt, đối tác tốt”, không ngừng tăng cường tin cậy chiến lược, làm sâu sắc thêm hợp tác cùng có lợi trên các lĩnh vực, xử lý thỏa đáng các vấn đề còn tồn tại, tăng cường điều phối và phối hợp trong các vấn đề quốc tế và khu vực, thúc đẩy quan

hệ Việt-Trung phát triển lành mạnh, ổn định lâu dài.

3. Việt Nam và Trung Quốc đều đang ở trong thời kỳ then chốt của công cuộc phát triển kinh tế-xã hội. Hai bên coi sự phát triển của nước kia là cơ hội phát triển của nước mình, nhất trí làm sâu sắc thêm hợp tác chiến lược toàn diện với trọng tâm là các lĩnh vực dưới đây:

(i) Duy trì tiếp xúc cấp cao thông qua các hình thức linh hoạt, đa dạng như thăm song phương, điện đàm qua đường dây nóng, gặp gỡ bên lề các diễn đàn đa phương... để tăng cường trao đổi chiến lược, nắm vững phương hướng đúng đắn phát triển quan hệ hai nước. Phía Việt Nam hoan nghênh lãnh đạo Trung Quốc sớm sang thăm Việt Nam, phía Trung Quốc hoan nghênh Lãnh đạo Việt Nam sang thăm và tham dự các Hội nghị tại Trung Quốc.

(ii) Hai bên đánh giá tích cực kết quả Phiên họp lần 6 Ủy ban Chỉ đạo hợp tác song phương Việt Nam-Trung Quốc, nhất trí tiếp tục sử dụng tốt cơ chế quan trọng này, thúc đẩy tổng thể hợp tác cùng có lợi trên các lĩnh vực, mang lại nhiều lợi ích hơn cho nhân dân hai nước. Hai bên nhất trí cùng nhau thực hiện tốt "Chương trình hành động triển khai Quan hệ đối tác hợp tác chiến lược toàn diện Việt Nam-Trung Quốc" được ký kết trong chuyến thăm này, thúc đẩy hợp tác thực chất giữa hai nước đạt được tiến triển mới.

(iii) Hai bên hài lòng trước sự phát triển của quan hệ hai Đảng trong những năm qua, nhất trí làm sâu sắc thêm hợp tác giữa hai Đảng, thúc đẩy cơ chế giao lưu hợp tác giữa hai Ban Đối ngoại và Ban Tuyên giáo, Tuyên truyền của hai Đảng vận hành thuận lợi, tăng cường hợp tác trong lĩnh vực đào tạo cán bộ Đảng và Nhà nước. Hai bên nhất trí phối hợp chặt chẽ, cùng nhau tổ chức tốt Hội thảo lý luận hai Đảng lần thứ 9, tăng cường hơn nữa trao đổi kinh nghiệm về xây dựng Đảng và quản lý đất nước, thúc đẩy xây dựng Đảng và đất nước ở mỗi nước.

(iv) Hai bên nhất trí tăng cường hợp tác giữa Bộ Ngoại giao hai nước, thực hiện tốt Nghị định thư hợp tác giữa hai Bộ Ngoại giao, duy trì trao đổi thường xuyên giữa lãnh đạo hai Bộ Ngoại giao, tổ chức Tham vấn Ngoại giao thường niên và tăng cường giao lưu cấp Cục, Vụ giữa hai Bộ Ngoại giao.

(v) Hai bên đánh giá tích cực kết quả Đối thoại chiến lược quốc phòng cấp Thứ trưởng Bộ Quốc phòng lần thứ 4, nhất trí duy trì tiếp xúc cấp cao giữa quân đội hai nước, phát huy tốt vai trò của cơ chế Đối thoại chiến lược quốc phòng và đường dây điện thoại trực tiếp giữa hai Bộ Quốc phòng để tăng cường tin cậy lẫn nhau. Đi sâu trao đổi kinh nghiệm công tác Đảng và chính trị trong quân đội, tăng cường đào tạo cán bộ và giao lưu sĩ quan trẻ. Thực hiện tốt "Thỏa thuận hợp tác biên phòng giữa Bộ Quốc phòng hai nước Việt Nam-Trung Quốc" (sửa đổi) ký kết trong chuyến thăm này, tiếp tục triển khai tuần tra chung biên giới trên đất liền. Làm sâu sắc thêm hợp tác biên phòng trên đất liền và trên biển, trong năm nay triển khai hai đợt tuần tra chung giữa hải quân hai nước trong Vịnh Bắc Bộ. Tăng cường trao đổi và điều phối trong các vấn đề an ninh đa phương khu vực. Trao đổi nghiên cứu hình thức mới, nội dung mới trong triển khai hợp tác quốc phòng, làm sâu sắc thêm hợp tác giữa quân đội hai nước.

(vi) Hai bên nhất trí làm sâu sắc thêm hợp tác trong lĩnh vực thực thi pháp luật và an ninh, phát huy đầy đủ vai trò của cơ chế Hội nghị hợp tác phòng chống tội phạm giữa Bộ Công an hai nước, tăng cường các chuyến thăm cấp cao và đơn vị nghiệp vụ của cơ quan thực thi pháp luật hai bên, thúc đẩy hợp tác thực chất trong các lĩnh vực như phòng chống tội phạm xuyên biên giới, giữ gìn trật tự trị an xã hội cũng như xây dựng năng lực thực thi pháp luật, sớm triển khai các hoạt động thực thi pháp luật chung trên các lĩnh vực, duy trì an ninh và ổn định khu vực biên giới hai nước. Hai bên nhất trí thúc đẩy triển khai giao lưu hợp tác giữa cơ quan cảnh sát biển hai nước. Hai bên nhất trí sớm khởi động đàm phán về "Hiệp định dẫn độ Việt-Trung" trong nửa cuối năm nay.

(vii) Hai bên nhất trí tăng cường điều phối chiến lược về phát triển kinh tế, thực hiện tốt "Quy hoạch phát triển 5 năm hợp tác kinh tế thương mại Việt-Trung giai đoạn 2012–2016" và Danh mục các dự án hợp tác trọng điểm, thúc đẩy hơn nữa hợp tác trong các lĩnh vực như nông nghiệp, ngư nghiệp, giao thông vận tải, năng lượng, khoáng sản, công nghiệp chế tạo và phụ trợ, dịch vụ cũng như hợp tác khu vực "Hai hành lang, một vành đai."

Hai bên sẽ sử dụng tốt cơ chế Ủy ban Hợp tác kinh tế-thương mại song phương, thực hiện tốt "Bản ghi nhớ hợp tác song phương trong lĩnh vực thương mại hàng nông sản giữa Bộ Công Thương Việt Nam với Bộ Thương mại Trung Quốc"; hai bên nhất trí tích cực áp dụng các biện pháp hữu hiệu, quyết liệt để thúc đẩy cân bằng thương mại song phương trên cơ sở đảm bảo thương mại song phương tăng trưởng ổn định, cố gắng hoàn thành trước thời hạn mục tiêu đến năm 2015 kim ngạch thương mại hai chiều đạt 60 tỷ USD. Tiếp tục thúc đẩy xây dựng các dự án hợp tác kinh tế–thương mại quan trọng trong các lĩnh vực năng lượng, khu công nghiệp, kết nối giao thông trên bộ, trong đó ưu tiên thúc đẩy xây dựng các dự án đường bộ và đường sắt kết nối khu vực biên giới trên bộ hai nước như tuyến đường bộ cao tốc Lạng Sơn-Hà Nội...

Hai bên nhất trí tăng cường hợp tác trong lĩnh vực tài chính, tích cực tạo điều kiện và khuyến khích các tổ chức tài chính hai bên hỗ trợ dịch vụ tài chính cho các dự án hợp tác song phương. Tiếp tục thúc đẩy tiện lợi hóa thương mại và đầu tư song phương, bao gồm khuyến khích thanh quyết toán bằng đồng bản tệ trong trao đổi mậu dịch tại khu vực biên giới. Khuyến khích doanh nghiệp nước mình sang nước kia đầu tư, tạo điều kiện an toàn và thuận lợi cho các doanh nghiệp đầu tư.

(viii) Hai bên nhất trí tiếp tục làm sâu sắc thêm hợp tác trong lĩnh vực nông nghiệp, hoàn thiện cơ chế hợp tác song phương về nông nghiệp, tăng cường giao lưu khoa học kỹ thuật nông nghiệp và nâng cao năng lực trong lĩnh vực nông nghiệp, nhân rộng các loại giống cây trồng nông nghiệp sản lượng cao và chất lượng tốt, bao gồm các loại giống lúa lai, thúc đẩy ngành chế biến và thương mại hàng nông sản phát triển, tập trung thúc đẩy xây dựng hệ thống phòng chống dịch bệnh động thực vật xuyên biên giới và an toàn thực phẩm xuất nhập khẩu, nâng cao khả năng dự báo và mức độ chia sẻ thông tin.

(ix) Tăng cường giao lưu và hợp tác trong lĩnh vực văn hóa, thực hiện tốt "Thỏa thuận hợp tác giáo dục giai đoạn 2011–2015", "Kế hoạch hành động thực hiện Hiệp định Văn hóa Việt-Trung giai đoạn 2013–2015", sớm hoàn thành việc xây dựng Trung tâm văn hóa của nước này ở nước kia, tăng cường hợp tác trong các lĩnh vực sản nghiệp văn hóa, nguồn nhân lực. Hai bên nhất trí tổ chức Liên hoan Thanh niên Việt-Trung lần thứ 2 vào nửa cuối năm nay tại Trung Quốc, đồng thời tiếp tục tổ chức tốt các hoạt động như Gặp gỡ hữu nghị thanh niên Việt-Trung, Diễn đàn nhân dân Việt-Trung…, tăng cường tuyên truyền về tình hữu nghị Việt-Trung để gia tăng tình hữu nghị giữa nhân dân hai nước.

(x) Hai bên nhất trí làm sâu sắc thêm giao lưu hợp tác trong lĩnh vực khoa học công nghệ, phát huy hơn nữa vai trò của Ủy ban hợp tác về khoa học công nghệ giữa Chính phủ hai nước, khuyến khích và ủng hộ giới nghiên cứu và ứng dụng khoa học công nghệ hai nước triển khai hợp tác với nhiều hình thức như cùng nghiên cứu và phát triển, cùng xây dựng phòng thí nghiệm chung, chuyển giao công nghệ… trong các lĩnh vực hai bên quan tâm như nông nghiệp, công nghệ thông tin, năng lượng mới, bảo vệ môi trường, quản lý, sử dụng và bảo vệ tài nguyên nước…

(xi) Hai bên nhất trí tăng cường hơn nữa hợp tác giữa các tỉnh, khu tự trị biên giới hai nước, nhất là giữa 7 tỉnh của Việt Nam gồm Điện Biên, Lai Châu, Lào Cai, Hà Giang, Cao Bằng, Lạng Sơn, Quảng Ninh với 4 tỉnh (khu tự trị) của Trung Quốc gồm Quảng Đông, Quảng Tây, Hải Nam, Vân Nam; phát huy vai trò của cơ chế hợp tác liên quan giữa địa phương hai nước; tập trung thúc đẩy hợp tác trong các lĩnh vực kinh tế–thương mại, cơ sở hạ tầng giao thông, khoa học, giáo dục, văn hóa, y tế…; thúc đẩy các tỉnh, khu tự trị biên giới hai nước cùng phát triển.

(xii) Hai bên nhất trí thực hiện nghiêm túc Kế hoạch công tác năm 2013 của Ủy ban Liên hợp biên giới trên đất liền hai nước; đánh giá tích cực việc hai nước thành lập Ủy ban hợp tác quản lý cửa khẩu biên giới trong chuyến thăm lần này; đồng ý thúc đẩy việc mở và nâng cấp các cửa khẩu biên giới giữa hai nước; tăng cường xây dựng và quản lý cơ sở hạ tầng của các cửa khẩu biên giới, cải thiện điều kiện và nâng cao hiệu quả thông hành cho người, hàng hóa, phương tiện qua cửa khẩu nhằm phục vụ việc qua lại và phát triển kinh tế–thương mại giữa hai nước. Sớm khởi động việc xây dựng cầu Bắc Luân II Việt-Trung. Hai bên nhất trí tổ chức vòng đàm phán mới "Hiệp định về quy chế tàu thuyền đi lại tự do tại khu vực cửa sông Bắc Luân" và "Hiệp định về hợp tác và khai thác phát triển du lịch khu vực thác Bản Giốc" vào nửa cuối năm nay, cố gắng sớm đạt được tiến triển thực chất. Hai bên sẽ tăng cường trao đổi và hợp tác kỹ thuật trong các lĩnh vực quản lý sông suối biên giới, phòng chống thiên tai lũ lụt, sử dụng và bảo vệ tài nguyên nước trên sông suối xuyên biên giới.

(xiii) Hai bên sẽ tiếp tục thực hiện tốt "Hiệp định hợp tác nghề cá trong Vịnh Bắc Bộ"; tích cực nghiên cứu phương thức kiểm tra liên hợp mới tại khu vực đánh cá chung ở Vịnh Bắc Bộ. Hai bên đánh giá cao "Thỏa thuận giữa Bộ Nông nghiệp và Phát triển nông thôn Việt Nam và Bộ Nông nghiệp Trung Quốc về việc thiết lập đường dây nóng về các vụ việc phát sinh đột xuất của hoạt động nghề cá trên biển" được ký kết trong chuyến thăm lần này, xử lý thỏa đáng các vụ việc phát sinh đột xuất của hoạt động nghề cá trên biển giữa hai nước phù hợp với quan hệ hai nước.

4. Hai bên trao đổi ý kiến chân thành, thẳng thắn về vấn đề trên biển, nhất trí việc Lãnh đạo hai Đảng, hai nước duy trì trao đổi và đối thoại thường xuyên về vấn đề trên biển Việt Nam-Trung Quốc, chỉ đạo và thúc đẩy giải quyết ổn thỏa vấn đề trên biển xuất phát từ tầm cao chiến lược và đại cục quan hệ hai nước. Hai bên sẽ nghiêm túc thực hiện "Thỏa thuận về những nguyên tắc cơ bản chỉ đạo giải quyết vấn đề trên biển Việt Nam-Trung Quốc", sử dụng tốt các cơ chế như đàm phán biên giới lãnh thổ cấp Chính phủ..., kiên trì thông qua hiệp thương và đàm phán hữu nghị, tìm kiếm giải pháp cơ bản và lâu dài mà hai bên đều có thể chấp nhận được, tích cực nghiên cứu giải pháp mang tính quá độ không ảnh hưởng đến lập trường và chủ trương của mỗi bên, bao gồm tích cực nghiên cứu và bàn bạc vấn đề hợp tác cùng phát triển.

Hai bên nhất trí dựa trên nguyên tắc dễ trước khó sau, tuần tự tiệm tiến, gia tăng cường độ đàm phán của Nhóm công tác về vùng biển ngoài cửa Vịnh Bắc Bộ, vững bước thúc đẩy đàm phán phân định vùng biển ngoài cửa Vịnh Bắc Bộ và tích cực thúc đẩy hợp tác cùng phát triển tại vùng biển này, trong năm nay khởi động khảo sát chung tại vùng biển ngoài cửa Vịnh Bắc Bộ, sớm xác định khu vực và lĩnh vực hợp tác để thực hiện nhiệm vụ đàm phán của Nhóm công tác về vùng biển ngoài cửa Vịnh Bắc Bộ. Hai bên hoan nghênh Thỏa thuận sửa đổi liên quan tới Thỏa thuận thăm dò chung trong khu vực thỏa thuận ngoài khơi trong Vịnh Bắc Bộ được ký kết giữa doanh nghiệp hữu quan hai nước, nhất trí mở rộng diện tích khu vực thỏa thuận, kéo dài thời hạn thỏa thuận, cùng nhau thúc đẩy hoạt động thăm dò chung đối với cấu tạo dầu khí vắt ngang đường phân định trong Vịnh Bắc Bộ sớm đạt được tiến triển tích cực.

Hai bên nhất trí gia tăng mật độ đàm phán của Nhóm công tác chuyên viên về hợp tác trong các lĩnh vực ít nhạy cảm trên biển Việt-Trung, trong năm nay thực hiện một đến hai dự án hợp tác trong số ba dự án đã thỏa thuận, bao gồm Dự án về phối hợp tìm kiếm cứu nạn trên biển giữa Việt Nam và Trung Quốc, Dự án hợp tác nghiên cứu quản lý môi trường biển và hải đảo vùng Vịnh Bắc Bộ và Dự án nghiên cứu so sánh trầm tích thời kỳ Holocenne khu vực châu thổ sông Hồng và châu thổ sông Trường Giang; tiếp tục thúc đẩy hợp tác trong các lĩnh vực bảo vệ môi trường biển, nghiên cứu khoa học biển, tìm kiếm cứu nạn trên biển, phòng chống thiên tai và kết nối giao thông trên biển.

Trước khi tranh chấp trên biển được giải quyết dứt điểm, hai bên nhất trí giữ bình tĩnh và kiềm chế, không có hành động làm phức tạp, mở rộng tranh chấp, đồng thời sử dụng tốt đường dây nóng quản lý, kiểm soát khủng hoảng trên biển giữa Bộ Ngoại giao hai nước, xử lý thỏa đáng các vấn đề nảy sinh với thái độ xây dựng, không để các vấn đề này ảnh hưởng đến đại cục quan hệ Việt-Trung cũng như hòa bình, ổn định tại Biển Đông. Hai bên nhất trí thực hiện toàn diện, có hiệu quả "Tuyên bố về cách ứng xử của các bên ở Biển Đông" (DOC), cùng nhau duy trì hòa bình và ổn định ở Biển Đông.

5. Phía Việt Nam khẳng định kiên trì thực hiện chính sách một nước Trung Quốc, ủng hộ quan hệ hai bờ eo biển Đài Loan phát triển hòa bình và sự nghiệp lớn thống nhất Trung Quốc, kiên quyết phản đối hành động chia rẽ "Đài Loan độc lập" dưới mọi hình thức. Việt Nam không phát triển bất cứ quan hệ chính thức nào với Đài Loan. Phía Trung Quốc hoan nghênh lập trường trên của Việt Nam.

6. Hai bên cho rằng, Việt Nam và Trung Quốc cùng là hai nước đang phát triển, có lập trường tương tự và gần nhau trong nhiều vấn đề quốc tế và khu vực cùng quan tâm. Hai bên nhất trí tăng cường điều phối và phối hợp tại các diễn đàn đa phương như Liên Hợp Quốc, Tổ chức Thương mại Thế giới, Diễn đàn hợp tác kinh tế châu Á-Thái Bình Dương, Diễn đàn hợp tác Á-Âu, Diễn đàn khu vực ASEAN, Hội nghị cấp cao ASEAN và Trung Quốc, Hội nghị cấp cao ASEAN và Trung-Nhật-Hàn, Hội nghị cấp cao Đông Á..., cùng nhau duy trì hòa bình, ổn định và thịnh vượng của thế giới.

Hai bên nhất trí lấy năm nay-năm kỷ niệm 10 năm ASEAN và Trung Quốc thiết lập quan hệ đối tác chiến lược, làm cơ hội để thực hiện toàn diện nhận thức chung mà Lãnh đạo các nước ASEAN và Lãnh đạo Trung Quốc đã đạt được, tổ chức tốt các hoạt động kỷ niệm 10 năm, không ngừng mở rộng và làm sâu sắc thêm hợp tác giữa ASEAN và Trung Quốc trong các lĩnh vực kinh tế-thương mại, kết nối giao thông, hải dương, xã hội nhân văn..., đóng góp nhiều hơn nữa cho hòa bình, ổn định và thịnh vượng của khu vực.

7. Trong thời gian chuyến thăm, hai bên đã ký "Chương trình hành động giữa Chính phủ Việt Nam và Chính phủ Trung Quốc về việc triển khai quan hệ Đối tác hợp tác chiến lược toàn diện Việt Nam-Trung Quốc", "Thỏa thuận hợp tác biên phòng giữa Bộ Quốc phòng hai nước Việt Nam-Trung Quốc" (sửa đổi), "Thỏa thuận giữa Bộ Nông nghiệp và Phát triển nông thông Việt Nam và Bộ Nông nghiệp Trung Quốc về việc thiết lập đường dây nóng về các vụ việc phát sinh đột xuất của hoạt động nghề cá trên biển", "Thỏa thuận giữa Bộ Nông nghiệp và Phát triển nông thôn Việt Nam và Tổng cục giám sát chất lượng, kiểm nghiệm, kiểm dịch Trung Quốc về hợp tác trong lĩnh vực kiểm nghiệm, kiểm dịch động thực vật xuất nhập khẩu", "Điều lệ công tác của Ủy ban hợp tác quản lý cửa khẩu biên giới đất liền Việt Nam-Trung Quốc", "Bản ghi nhớ giữa Chính phủ Việt Nam và Chính phủ Trung Quốc về việc thành lập Trung tâm văn hóa tại hai nước", "Bản ghi nhớ về kế hoạch hợp tác giai đoạn 2013−2017 giữa Liên hiệp các tổ chức hữu nghị Việt Nam và Hội hữu nghị đối ngoại nhân dân Trung Quốc", "Thỏa thuận sửa đổi lần thứ 4 giữa Tập đoàn dầu khí Việt Nam và Tổng công ty dầu khí ngoài khơi quốc gia Trung Quốc liên quan tới Thỏa thuận thăm dò chung trong khu vực thỏa thuận ngoài khơi trong Vịnh Bắc Bộ" và nhiều văn kiện hợp tác kinh tế khác.

8. Hai bên hài lòng trước những kết quả đạt được trong chuyến thăm Trung Quốc của Chủ tịch nước Trương Tấn Sang, nhất trí cho rằng chuyến thăm có ý nghĩa quan trọng trong việc thúc đẩy quan hệ hai nước phát triển. Chủ tịch nước Trương Tấn Sang cảm ơn sự đón tiếp nhiệt tình, hữu nghị của phía Trung Quốc và mời Chủ tịch nước Tập Cận Bình thăm Việt Nam. Chủ tịch nước Tập Cận Bình bày tỏ cảm ơn.

新时期深化中越全面战略合作的联合声明

（2013年10月15日）

一、应越南社会主义共和国政府总理阮晋勇邀请，中华人民共和国国务院总理李克强于2013年10月13日至15日对越南社会主义共和国进行正式访问。

访问期间，李克强总理同阮晋勇总理举行会谈，同越共中央总书记阮富仲、国家主席张晋创、国会主席阮生雄举行会见。在真诚友好、相互理解的气氛中，双方就新形势下进一步深化中越全面战略合作、当前国际地区形势及共同关心的问题深入交换意见，达成广泛共识。

二、双方回顾并高度评价中越关系的发展，重申将遵循两国领导人达成的重要共识，在"长期稳定、面向未来、睦邻友好、全面合作"的方针和"好邻居、好朋友、好同志、好伙伴"的精神指引下，发展中越全面战略合作伙伴关系。双方一致认为，在当前国际政治经济形势复杂演变的背景下，加强战略沟通，进一步深化务实合作，妥善处理存在的问题，加强在国际地区事务中的协调配合，推动两国关系长期稳定健康发展，符合两党两国和两国人民的根本利益，有利于地区及世界的和平、稳定与发展。

三、双方高度评价两国高层接触具有不可替代的重要作用，同意继续保持高层接触和互访，从战略高度牢牢把握新时期两国关系发展方向。同时，通过多边场合会晤等多种形式推动高层交往，用好领导人热线电话，就双边关系及共同关心的重大问题深入沟通。

四、双方同意继续用好中越双边合作指导委员会机制，统筹推进各领域互利合作，实施好《落实中越全面战略合作伙伴关系行动计划》，使用好两国外交、国防、经贸、公安、安全、新闻和两党中央对外部门和宣传部门交流合作机制，开好双边合作指导委员会会议、合作打击犯罪会议、经贸合委会会议、两党理论研讨会，做好年度外交磋商、防务安全磋商、党政干部扩大培训等工作，有效使用国防部直通电话，加强对舆论和媒体的正确引导，为增进双方互信，维护两国关系稳定发展作出重要贡献。

五、双方一致认为，中越互为近邻和重要伙伴，均处在经济社会发展的关键阶段，从两国共同需要和利益出发，双方同意在平等互利的基础上，以下述领域为重点进一步深化全面战略合作：

（一）关于陆上合作

双方同意抓紧落实《中越2012—2016年经贸合作五年发展规划》及重点合作项目清单。建立两国基础设施合作工作组，规划并指导具体项目实施。尽快就凭祥—河内高速公路项目实施和融资方案达成一致，争取早日动工建设。双方将积极推进东兴—下龙高速公路项目，中方支持有实力的中国企业按市场原则参与该项目，并愿在力所能及的范围内提供融资支持。双方有关部门将加紧工作，适时启动老街—河内—海防铁路项目可行性研究。双方同意落实好《关于建设跨境经济合作区的备忘录》，积极研究商签《中越边境贸易协定》（修订版），为促进两国边境地区合作与繁荣发挥积极作用。

双方同意加强经贸政策协调，落实好《农产品贸易领域合作谅解备忘录》、《关于互设贸易促进机构的协定》，在保持贸易稳定增长的基础上，促进双边贸易平衡增长，争取提前实现2015年双边贸易额600亿美元目标。中方将鼓励中国企业扩大进口越南有竞争力的商品。中方将支持中国企业赴越投资兴业，也愿为更多越南企业来华开拓市场创造更便利条件。越方将为早日建成龙江和海防两个经贸合作区提供便利和协助。双方将加紧施工，推动越中友谊宫项目早日建成。

双方同意进一步深化在农业、科技、教育、文化、体育、旅游、卫生等领域的交流合作。

双方同意继续发挥两国陆地边界联委会作用，认真落实年度工作计划。召开两国口岸合作委员会首次会议，推进陆地边境口岸开放工作，尽快正式开放峒中—横模国家级口岸。推动《德天瀑布地区旅游资源共同开发和保护协定》谈判尽快取得实质进展，尽快启动《北仑河口地区自由航行协定》新一轮谈判并达成一致，早日建成北仑河公路二桥、水口至驮隆中越界河公路二桥等跨境桥梁，为两国边境地区稳定和发展奠定基础。

双方同意进一步加强两国地方特别是边境省（区）的合作，发挥两国地方有关合作机制的作用。

(二)关于金融合作

双方同意加强在金融领域的合作，积极创造条件并鼓励双方金融机构为双边贸易和投资合作项目提供金融服务。在2003年两国央行签署边境贸易双边本币结算协定基础上，继续探讨扩大本币结算范围，促进双边贸易和投资。双方决定建立两国金融合作工作组，提高双方抵御金融风险的能力，维护两国及本地区经济稳定与发展。加强多边协调与配合，共同推进东亚地区财金合作。

(三)关于海上合作

双方同意恪守两党两国领导人共识，认真落实《关于指导解决中越海上问题基本原则协议》，用好中越政府边界谈判机制，坚持通过友好协商和谈判，寻求双方均能接受的基本和长久的解决办法，积极探讨不影响各自立场和主张的过渡性解决办法，包括积极研究和商谈共同开发问题。本着上述精神，双方同意在政府边界谈判代表团框架下成立中越海上共同开发磋商工作组。

双方同意加强对现有谈判磋商机制的指导，加大中越北部湾湾口外海域工作组和海上低敏感领域合作专家工作组工作力度。本着先易后难、循序渐进的原则，稳步推进湾口外海域划界谈判并积极推进该海域的共同开发，年内启动该海域共同考察，落实北部湾湾口外海域工作组谈判任务。尽快实施北部湾海洋和岛屿环境管理合作研究、红河三角洲与长江三角洲全新世沉积演化对比研究等海上低敏感领域合作项目，继续推进在海洋环保、海洋科研、海上搜救、防灾减灾、海上互联互通等领域合作。

双方同意切实管控好海上分歧，不采取使争端复杂化、扩大化的行动，用好两国外交部海上危机管控热线，两国农业部门海上渔业活动突发事件联系热线，及时、妥善处理出现的问题，同时继续积极探讨管控危机的有效措施，维护中越关系大局以及南海和平稳定。

六、双方同意办好第二届中越青年大联欢、中越青年友好会见、中越人民大联欢等活动，为中越友好事业培养更多接班人。双方同意在越建立孔子学院，并加快推动互设文化中心、切实加强中越友好宣传，深化两国民众之间的了解与友谊。

七、越方重申坚定奉行一个中国政策，支持两岸关系和平发展与中国统一大业，坚决反对任何形式的“台独”分裂活动。越南不同台湾发展任何官方关系。中方对此表示赞赏。

八、双方同意加强在联合国、世贸组织、亚太经合组织、亚欧会议、东盟地区论坛、中国—东盟、东盟—中日韩、东亚峰会等多边场合的协调与配合，为维护世界的和平、稳定与繁荣共同努力。

双方高度评价中国—东盟关系发展取得的巨大成就，一致同意以中国—东盟建立战略伙伴关系10周年为契机，进一步增进战略信任，赞赏和欢迎中方关于缔结中国—东盟国家睦邻友好合作条约，升级中国—东盟自贸区，建立亚洲基础设施投资银行的倡议。中国与东盟开展广泛合作，促进东南亚地区和平、稳定、相互尊重和信任非常重要。

双方一致同意，全面有效落实《南海各方行为宣言》，增进互信，推动合作，共同维护南海和平与稳定，按照《南海各方行为宣言》的原则和精神，在协商一致的基础上朝着制定“南海行为准则”而努力。

九、访问期间，双方签署了《关于互设贸易促进机构的协定》、《关于建设跨境经济合作区的备忘录》、《关于成立协助中方在越实施项目联合工作组的备忘录》、《关于共同建设水口—驮隆中越界河公路二桥的协定》及其实施议定书、《关于开展北部湾海洋和岛屿环境管理合作研究的协议》、《关于长江三角洲与红河三角洲全新世沉积演化对比研究项目的协议》、《关于合作设立河内大学孔子学院的协议》及一些经济合作文件。

十、双方对中国国务院总理李克强访越成果表示满意，一致认为此访对推动两国关系发展及各领域务实合作具有重要意义。

Tuyên bố chung Trung Quốc-Việt Nam

(2013/10/15)

1. Nhận lời mời của Thủ tướng Chính phủ nước Cộng hòa xã hội chủ nghĩa Việt Nam Nguyễn Tấn Dũng, Thủ tướng Quốc vụ viện nước Cộng hòa nhân dân Trung Hoa Lý Khắc Cường đã thăm chính thức nước Cộng hòa xã hội chủ nghĩa Việt Nam từ ngày 13 đến ngày 15 tháng 10 năm 2013.

Trong thời gian chuyến thăm, Thủ tướng Lý Khắc Cường đã hội đàm với Thủ tướng Nguyễn Tấn Dũng; hội kiến với Tổng Bí thư Nguyễn Phú Trọng, Chủ tịch nước Trương Tấn Sang, Chủ tịch Quốc hội Nguyễn Sinh Hùng.

Trong không khí chân thành, hữu nghị và hiểu biết lẫn nhau, hai bên đã đi sâu trao đổi ý kiến và đạt nhận thức chung rộng rãi về việc làm sâu sắc thêm hợp tác chiến lược toàn diện Việt-Trung trong tình hình mới, cũng như tình hình quốc tế, khu vực hiện nay và các vấn đề cùng quan tâm.

2. Hai bên đã nhìn lại và đánh giá cao sự phát triển quan hệ Việt Nam-Trung Quốc, khẳng định sẽ tuân theo những nhận thức chung quan trọng mà Lãnh đạo cấp cao hai nước đã đạt được, phát triển quan hệ đối tác hợp tác chiến lược toàn diện Việt Nam-Trung Quốc theo phương châm "Láng giềng hữu nghị, hợp tác toàn diện, ổn định lâu dài, hướng tới tương lai" và tinh thần "Láng giềng tốt, bạn bè tốt, đồng chí tốt, đối tác tốt".

Hai bên nhất trí cho rằng, trong tình hình kinh tế, chính trị quốc tế diễn biến phức tạp hiện nay, việc hai bên tăng cường trao đổi chiến lược, làm sâu sắc thêm hợp tác thực chất, xử lý thỏa đáng các vấn đề còn tồn tại, tăng cường điều phối và phối hợp trong các vấn đề quốc tế và khu vực, thúc đẩy quan hệ hai nước phát triển lành mạnh, ổn định lâu dài phù hợp lợi ích căn bản của hai Đảng, hai nước và nhân dân hai nước, có lợi cho hòa bình, ổn định và phát triển của khu vực cũng như thế giới.

3. Hai bên đánh giá cao vai trò quan trọng không thể thay thế của tiếp xúc cấp cao giữa hai nước, nhất trí tiếp tục duy trì tiếp xúc và thăm viếng cấp cao, xuất phát từ tầm cao chiến lược nắm vững phương hướng phát triển quan hệ hai nước trong thời kỳ mới.

Đồng thời, thúc đẩy trao đổi cấp cao qua nhiều hình thức như gặp gỡ bên lề các diễn đàn đa phương, sử dụng tốt đường dây nóng giữa Lãnh đạo cấp cao để đi sâu trao đổi các vấn đề trọng đại trong quan hệ song phương cũng như các vấn đề cùng quan tâm.

4. Hai bên nhất trí tiếp tục sử dụng tốt cơ chế của Ủy ban Chỉ đạo hợp tác song phương Việt Nam-Trung Quốc, thúc đẩy tổng thể hợp tác cùng có lợi trên các lĩnh vực; thực hiện tốt "Chương trình hành động triển khai Quan hệ đối tác hợp tác chiến lược toàn diện Việt Nam-Trung Quốc"; sử dụng tốt các cơ chế giao lưu, hợp tác giữa các ngành Ngoại giao, Quốc phòng, Kinh tế, Thương mại, Công an, An ninh, Báo chí hai nước và giữa Ban Đối ngoại Trung ương, Ban Tuyên giáo của hai Đảng; tổ chức tốt Phiên họp Ủy ban chỉ đạo hợp tác song phương Việt Nam-Trung Quốc, Hội nghị hợp tác phòng chống tội phạm, Phiên họp Ủy ban hợp tác kinh tế thương mại, Hội thảo lý luận giữa hai Đảng; làm tốt các công tác như Tham vấn Ngoại giao thường niên, Tham vấn An ninh-Quốc phòng, đào tạo mở rộng cho cán bộ Đảng và Nhà nước; sử dụng hiệu quả đường dây điện thoại trực tiếp giữa Bộ Quốc phòng, tăng cường định hướng đúng đắn báo chí và dư luận… góp phần quan trọng cho việc tăng cường sự tin cậy giữa hai bên, duy trì phát triển ổn định quan hệ hai nước.

5. Hai bên cho rằng, Việt Nam và Trung Quốc là láng giềng và đối tác quan trọng của nhau, đều đang ở trong thời kỳ then chốt của công cuộc phát triển kinh tế-xã hội, xuất phát từ nhu cầu và lợi ích chung của hai nước, trên cơ sở bình đẳng, cùng có lợi, hai bên nhất trí làm sâu sắc thêm hợp tác chiến lược toàn diện với trọng tâm là các lĩnh vực dưới đây:

a. Về hợp tác trên bộ:

(i) Hai bên nhất trí nhanh chóng thực hiện "Quy hoạch phát triển 5 năm hợp tác kinh tế thương mại Việt-Trung giai đoạn 2012–2016" và Danh mục các dự án hợp tác trọng điểm; thành lập Nhóm công tác hợp tác về cơ sở hạ tầng giữa hai nước để quy hoạch và chỉ đạo thực hiện các dự án cụ thể; sớm đạt nhất trí về phương án thực hiện và huy động vốn đối với dự án đường bộ cao tốc Lạng Sơn-Hà Nội nhằm sớm khởi công xây dựng.

Hai bên sẽ tích cực thúc đẩy dự án đường bộ cao tốc Móng Cái-Hạ Long, phía Trung Quốc ủng hộ các doanh nghiệp có thực lực của Trung Quốc tham gia dự án này theo nguyên tắc thị trường, đồng thời sẵn sàng hỗ trợ về huy động vốn trong khả năng. Các bộ, ngành hữu quan hai nước đẩy nhanh công tác, sớm khởi động nghiên cứu khả thi dự án đường sắt Lào Cai-Hà Nội-Hải Phòng.

Hai bên nhất trí thực hiện tốt "Bản ghi nhớ về việc xây dựng các khu hợp tác kinh tế qua biên giới", tích cực nghiên cứu đàm phán ký kết "Hiệp định thương mại biên giới Việt-Trung" (sửa đổi) nhằm phát huy vai trò tích cực thúc đẩy hợp tác và phồn vinh ở khu vực biên giới hai nước.

(ii) Hai bên đồng ý tăng cường điều phối chính sách kinh tế thương mại, thực hiện tốt "Bản ghi nhớ hợp tác song phương trong lĩnh vực thương mại hàng nông sản" và "Hiệp định về việc mở Cơ quan xúc tiến Thương mại nước này tại nước kia", để thúc đẩy cân bằng thương mại song phương trên cơ sở bảo đảm thương mại tăng trưởng ổn định, phấn đấu hoàn thành trước thời hạn mục tiêu đến năm 2015 kim ngạch thương mại hai chiều đạt 60 tỷ USD.

Phía Trung Quốc khuyến khích doanh nghiệp Trung Quốc mở rộng nhập khẩu hàng hóa có tính cạnh tranh của Việt Nam, ủng hộ doanh nghiệp Trung Quốc vào Việt Nam đầu tư kinh doanh, đồng thời sẵn sàng tạo điều kiện thuận lợi hơn nữa cho doanh nghiệp Việt Nam sang Trung Quốc mở rộng thị trường.

Phía Việt Nam sẽ tạo thuận lợi, hỗ trợ sớm hoàn thành Khu công nghiệp Long Giang và Khu công nghiệp An Dương. Hai bên sẽ đẩy nhanh thi công, thúc đẩy sớm hoàn thành dự án Cung Hữu nghị Việt-Trung.

(iii) Hai bên nhất trí làm sâu sắc thêm giao lưu hợp tác trong lĩnh vực nông nghiệp, khoa học công nghệ, giáo dục, văn hóa, thể thao, du lịch, y tế…

(iv) Hai bên nhất trí tiếp tục phát huy vai trò của Ủy ban liên hợp biên giới trên đất liền giữa hai nước, thực hiện nghiêm túc Kế hoạch công tác hằng năm; tiến hành Hội nghị lần thứ nhất Ủy ban hợp tác quản lý cửa khẩu giữa hai nước, thúc đẩy công tác mở cửa, nâng cấp một số cặp cửa khẩu biên giới trên bộ, sớm chính thức mở cặp cửa khẩu quốc gia Hoành Mô-Động Trung; thúc đẩy đàm phán về "Hiệp định hợp tác bảo vệ và khai thác nguồn tài nguyên du lịch khu vực thác Bản Giốc" sớm đạt được tiến triển thực chất, sớm khởi động vòng đàm phán mới và đạt nhất trí về "Hiệp định tàu thuyền tự do đi lại tại khu vực cửa sông Bắc Luân", sớm hoàn thành xây dựng các cầu qua biên giới như cầu đường bộ Bắc Luân 2, cầu đường bộ 2 Tà Lùng-Thủy Khẩu, tạo nền tảng cho sự ổn định và phát triển của khu vực biên giới hai nước.

Hai bên nhất trí tăng cường hơn nữa hợp tác giữa các địa phương, nhất là giữa các tỉnh, khu tự trị biên giới hai nước; phát huy vai trò của cơ chế hợp tác liên quan giữa địa phương hai nước.

b. Về hợp tác tiền tệ:

Hai bên nhất trí tăng cường hợp tác trong lĩnh vực tài chính, tích cực tạo điều kiện và khuyến khích các tổ chức tài chính hai bên hỗ trợ dịch vụ tài chính cho các dự án hợp tác song phương về thương mại và đầu tư. Trên cơ sở Hiệp định thanh toán bằng đồng bản tệ song phương trong thương mại biên giới ký giữa ngân hàng Trung ương hai nước năm 2003, tiếp tục nghiên cứu việc mở rộng phạm vi thanh toán bằng đồng bản tệ, thúc đẩy trao đổi thương mại và đầu tư hai bên.

Hai bên quyết định thành lập Nhóm công tác về hợp tác tiền tệ giữa hai nước, để nâng cao khả năng phòng ngừa rủi ro tài chính tiền tệ của hai bên, duy trì ổn định và phát triển kinh tế hai nước và khu vực. Tăng cường điều phối và phối hợp đa phương, cùng nhau thúc đẩy hợp tác tài chính tiền tệ khu vực Đông Á.

c. Về hợp tác trên biển:

Hai bên nhất trí tuân thủ nhận thức chung của Lãnh đạo cấp cao hai Đảng, hai nước, nghiêm túc thực hiện "Thỏa thuận về những nguyên tắc cơ bản chỉ đạo giải quyết vấn đề trên biển Việt Nam-Trung Quốc", sử dụng tốt cơ chế đàm phán cấp Chính phủ về biên giới lãnh thổ Việt Nam-Trung Quốc, kiên trì thông qua hiệp thương và đàm phán hữu nghị, tìm kiếm giải pháp cơ bản và lâu dài mà hai bên đều có thể chấp nhận được, tích cực nghiên cứu giải pháp mang tính quá độ không ảnh hưởng đến lập trường và chủ trương của mỗi bên bao gồm tích cực nghiên cứu và bàn bạc về vấn đề hợp tác cùng phát triển. Theo tinh thần đó, hai bên đồng ý thành lập Nhóm công tác bàn bạc về hợp tác cùng phát triển trên biển trong khuôn khổ Đoàn đàm phán cấp Chính phủ về biên giới lãnh thổ Việt Nam-

Trung Quốc.

Hai bên nhất trí tăng cường chỉ đạo đối với các cơ chế đàm phán và tham vấn hiện có, gia tăng cường độ làm việc của Nhóm công tác vùng biển ngoài cửa vịnh Bắc Bộ và Nhóm công tác cấp chuyên viên về hợp tác trong các lĩnh vực ít nhạy cảm trên biển. Trên nguyên tắc dễ trước khó sau, tuần tự tiệm tiến, vững bước thúc đẩy đàm phán phân định vùng biển ngoài cửa vịnh Bắc Bộ, đồng thời tích cực thúc đẩy hợp tác cùng phát triển tại vùng biển này và trong năm nay khởi động khảo sát chung ở khu vực ngoài cửa vịnh Bắc Bộ để thực hiện nhiệm vụ đàm phán của Nhóm công tác về vùng biển ngoài cửa vịnh Bắc Bộ. Nhanh chóng thực hiện các Dự án hợp tác trong các lĩnh vực ít nhạy cảm trên biển như hợp tác nghiên cứu quản lý môi trường biển và hải đảo vùng vịnh Bắc Bộ; nghiên cứu so sánh trầm tích thời kỳ Holocenne khu vực châu thổ sông Hồng và châu thổ sông Trường Giang..., tiếp tục thúc đẩy hợp tác trên các lĩnh vực bảo vệ môi trường biển, nghiên cứu khoa học biển, tìm kiếm cứu nạn trên biển, phòng chống thiên tai và kết nối giao thông trên biển.

Hai bên nhất trí kiểm soát tốt những bất đồng trên biển, không có hành động làm phức tạp, mở rộng tranh chấp, sử dụng tốt đường dây nóng quản lý, kiểm soát tranh chấp trên biển giữa Bộ Ngoại giao hai nước, đường dây nóng về các vụ việc phát sinh đột xuất của hoạt động nghề cá trên biển giữa Bộ Nông nghiệp hai nước, xử lý kịp thời, thỏa đáng các vấn đề nảy sinh, đồng thời tiếp tục tích cực trao đổi và tìm kiếm các biện pháp có hiệu quả để kiểm soát tranh chấp, duy trì đại cục quan hệ Việt-Trung và hòa bình, ổn định trên Biển Đông.

6. Hai bên nhất trí tổ chức tốt các hoạt động như Liên hoan Thanh niên Việt-Trung lần thứ hai; Gặp gỡ hữu nghị thanh niên Việt-Trung; Liên hoan nhân dân Việt-Trung... nhằm bồi dưỡng ngày càng nhiều thế hệ tiếp nối sự nghiệp hữu nghị Việt Nam-Trung Quốc. Hai bên nhất trí thành lập Viện Khổng Tử tại Việt Nam và đẩy nhanh việc thành lập Trung tâm văn hóa của nước này ở nước kia, thiết thực tăng cường tuyên truyền về quan hệ hữu nghị Việt-Trung, làm sâu sắc sự hiểu biết và hữu nghị giữa người dân hai nước.

7. Phía Việt Nam khẳng định kiên trì thực hiện chính sách một nước Trung Quốc, ủng hộ quan hệ hai bờ eo biển Đài Loan phát triển hòa bình và sự nghiệp lớn thống nhất Trung Quốc, kiên quyết phản đối hành động chia rẽ "Đài Loan

độc lập" dưới mọi hình thức. Việt Nam không phát triển bất cứ quan hệ chính thức nào với Đài Loan. Phía Trung Quốc hoan nghênh lập trường trên của Việt Nam.

8. Hai bên nhất trí tăng cường điều phối và phối hợp tại các diễn đàn đa phương như Liên Hợp Quốc, Tổ chức Thương mại thế giới, Diễn đàn Hợp tác kinh tế châu Á-Thái Bình Dương, Diễn đàn Hợp tác Á-Âu, Diễn đàn khu vực ASEAN, Hội nghị Cấp cao ASEAN-Trung Quốc, Hội nghị Cấp cao ASEAN+3 với Trung-Nhật-Hàn, Hội nghị Cấp cao Đông Á… cùng nhau nỗ lực duy trì hòa bình, ổn định và thịnh vượng của thế giới.

Hai bên đánh giá cao những thành tựu to lớn đạt được trong phát triển quan hệ ASEAN-Trung Quốc, nhất trí lấy dịp kỷ niệm 10 năm thiết lập quan hệ đối tác chiến lược ASEAN-Trung Quốc làm cơ hội tăng cường hơn nữa tin cậy chiến lược. Phía Việt Nam hoan nghênh đề xuất của Trung Quốc về việc ký kết "Điều ước hợp tác láng giềng hữu nghị giữa các nước ASEAN và Trung Quốc", nâng cấp Khu mậu dịch tự do ASEAN-Trung Quốc, thành lập Ngân hàng Đầu tư cơ sở hạ tầng châu Á. Việc ASEAN và Trung Quốc triển khai hợp tác rộng rãi có vai trò hết sức quan trọng đối với thúc đẩy hòa bình, ổn định, tôn trọng và tin cậy lẫn nhau tại khu vực Đông Nam Á.

Hai bên nhất trí thực hiện đầy đủ, hiệu quả "Tuyên bố về cách ứng xử của các bên ở Biển Đông" (DOC), tăng cường tin cậy, thúc đẩy hợp tác, cùng nhau duy trì hòa bình, ổn định ở Biển Đông, theo tinh thần và nguyên tắc của "Tuyên bố về cách ứng xử của các bên ở Biển Đông" (DOC), trên cơ sở đồng thuận, nỗ lực hướng tới thông qua "Bộ Quy tắc ứng xử ở Biển Đông" (COC).

9. Trong thời gian chuyến thăm, hai bên đã ký "Hiệp định về việc mở Cơ quan Xúc tiến thương mại nước này tại nước kia", "Bản ghi nhớ về xây dựng khu hợp tác kinh tế qua biên giới", "Bản ghi nhớ về việc thành lập Nhóm công tác hỗn hợp hỗ trợ các dự án do doanh nghiệp Trung Quốc thực hiện tại Việt Nam", "Hiệp định về việc xây dựng cầu đường bộ 2 Tà Lùng-Thủy Khẩu" và Nghị định thư kèm theo, "Dự án hợp tác nghiên cứu quản lý môi trường biển và hải đảo vùng vịnh Bắc Bộ", "Dự án nghiên cứu so sánh trầm tích thời kỳ Holocenne khu vực châu thổ sông Hồng và châu thổ sông Trường Giang", "Thỏa thuận về việc thành lập Viện Khổng Tử tại Trường Đại học Hà Nội" và một số

văn kiện hợp tác kinh tế.

10. Hai bên bày tỏ hài lòng về kết quả chuyến thăm Việt Nam của Thủ tướng Trung Quốc Lý Khắc Cường, nhất trí cho rằng chuyến thăm lần này có ý nghĩa quan trọng đối với việc thúc đẩy quan hệ hai nước phát triển và hợp tác thiết thực trên các lĩnh vực.

中越联合声明

（2015年11月6日）

一、应越南共产党中央委员会总书记阮富仲、越南社会主义共和国主席张晋创邀请，中国共产党中央委员会总书记、中华人民共和国主席习近平于2015年11月5日至6日对越南进行国事访问。

访问期间，习近平总书记、国家主席分别同阮富仲总书记、张晋创国家主席举行了会谈，并会见了越南政府总理阮晋勇、国会主席阮生雄。两党两国领导人在友好坦诚的气氛中，就进一步深化两党两国关系及共同关心的国际和地区问题深入交换意见，达成了重要共识。

双方一致认为，访问取得了圆满成功，为巩固中越传统友谊、深化全面战略合作、促进本地区乃至世界的和平、稳定与发展作出了重要贡献。

二、双方对两国在符合本国国情的社会主义建设事业中取得的历史性伟大成就感到高兴，同意加强相互交流和借鉴，推动中国改革开放和越南革新事业向前发展，为各自社会主义建设事业注入新活力。

中方衷心祝愿越南共产党2016年初成功召开第十二次全国代表大会，相信在越南共产党领导下，越南人民将胜利实现既定目标，把越南建设成为民富、国强、民主、公平、文明的社会主义国家。

越方衷心祝愿并相信中国人民在中国共产党领导下，一定能协调推进全面建成小康社会、全面深化改革、全面依法治国、全面从严治党，胜利实现建成富强民主文明和谐的社会主义现代化国家目标。

三、双方回顾了中越建交65年来两党两国关系发展历程，一致认为由毛泽东主席和胡志明主席等老一辈领导人亲手缔造和精心培育的中越友谊是两国人民共同的宝贵财富，双方应共同继承、维护和发扬，落实好“长期稳定、面向未来、睦邻友好、全面合作”方针和“好邻居、好朋友、好同志、好伙伴”精神，牢牢把握中越友好的正确方向，加强战略沟通，增进政治互信，在相互尊重、平等互利基础上推进各领域合作，管控好和妥善处理分歧，推动中越全面战略合作伙伴关系健康稳定发展。

四、双方认为，两党两国高层保持经常接触，对增进政治互信、推动双边关系发展具有重要作用，同意通过双边互访、互派特使、热线电话、年度会晤、多边场合会晤等灵活多样的方式保持高层交往，及时就两党两国关系中的重大问题交换意见。

五、双方认为，中越均处在经济社会发展的重要时期，双方视对方的发展为自身发展的机遇，同意发挥好中越双边合作指导委员会的统筹协调作用，重点推动以下领域合作：

（一）执行好两党合作计划，深化两党中央各部门和地方特别是接壤各省（区）党组织间交流合作，继续办好理论研讨会，实施好此访期间签署的两党干部培训合作计划（2016—2020年）。积极推进中国全国人大与越南国会、中国全国政协与越南祖国阵线之间的友好交流合作，促进两国民间友好交流。

（二）落实好两国外交部合作议定书，保持两部领导经常交往，继续举办年度外交磋商，加强两部对口司局交流，实施好两部干部培训工作。越方愿为中国在越南岘港设立总领馆提供便利。

（三）保持两军高层交往，用好两军防务安全磋商、边境高层会晤机制和国防部直通电话，加强两军在边防友好交流、人员培训、军事学术研究、海军北部湾联合巡逻和军舰互访等领域交流合作，深化联合国维和及军队党务政治工作方面经验交流。加强两国海警的海上执法合作，共同维护北部湾海域和平稳定，推动中国海警局与越南海警司令部签署合作备忘录。深化执法安全合作，继续办好两国公安部合作打击犯罪会议和中国国家安全部与越南公安部副部级安全战略对话，加强在反恐、禁毒、打击电信诈骗、出入境管理、边境管控、网络安全等领域合作，开展国内安全保卫、联合追逃、非法就业管理方面的经验交流。

（四）加强两国间发展战略对接，推动“一带一路”倡议和“两廊一圈”构想对接，加强在建材、辅助工业、装备制造、电力、可再生能源等领域产能合作。加紧成立工作组，积极商签跨境经济合作区建设共同总体方案，推进中国在越前江省龙江、海防市安阳两个工业园区的建设并积极吸引投资，督促和指导两国企业实施好中资企业在越承包建设的钢铁、化肥等合作项目。

用好中越经贸合委会机制，积极研究续签《中越经贸合作五年发展规划》，加紧修订《中越边贸协定》，推动双边贸易平衡、稳定、可持续发展，努力实现2017年双边贸易额1000亿美元目标。加强在《农产品贸易领域合作谅解备忘录》框架下的合作，鼓励双方企业扩大农产品贸易合作，欢迎两国有关部门和地方探讨设立贸易促进机构。

用好基础设施合作工作组和金融与货币合作工作组，推动有关领域合作不断取得积极进展。实施好河内轻轨二号线（吉灵—河东）项目，加紧制定老街—河内—海防标准轨铁路线路规划，推进云屯—芒街高速公路等基础设施互联互通合作。

深化海关合作，共同打击跨境走私行为，继续探索促进边境口岸通关便利化的合作措施，加强两国边境口岸基础设施建设和管理，提升两国边境口岸开放合作水平。

（五）扩大科技、教育、文化、旅游、新闻等领域合作。用好两国科技合作联委会机制，积极推进技术转移、科学家交流等合作，探讨建立联合实验室。争取于2017年建成越中友谊宫并投入使用，早日在对方国家设立文化中心，办好河内大学孔子学院。加强两国媒体交流，加大对中越友好的宣传力度。继续办好中越青年友好会见、人民论坛等活动，2016年在越举办第三届中越青年大联欢。

六、继续发挥好中越陆地边界联合委员会作用，落实好此访期间签署的《北仑河口自由航行区航行协定》和《合作保护和开发德天瀑布旅游资源协定》，总结两国陆地边界三个管理文件实施五年来的情况。加强两国边境省区合作，促进边境地区发展。

七、双方就海上问题坦诚交换意见，强调恪守两党两国领导人达成的重要共识，认真落实《关于指导解决中越海上问题基本原则协议》，用好中越政府边界谈判机制，坚持通过友好协商和谈判，寻求双方均能接受的基本和长久解决办法，积极探讨不影响各自立场和主张的过渡性解决办法，包括积极研究和商谈共同开发问题。

双方宣布于2015年12月中旬启动北部湾湾口外海域共同考察海上实地作业，认为这是双方开展海上合作的重要开端。双方将稳步推进北部湾湾口外海域划界谈判并积极推进该海域的共同开发，同意加大湾口外海域工作组谈判力度，继续推进海上共同开发磋商工作组工作，加强低敏感领域合作，宣布启动中越长江三角洲与红河三角洲全新世沉积演化对比合作研究项目。

双方同意共同管控好海上分歧，全面有效落实《南海各方行为宣言》（DOC），推动在协商一致的基础上早日达成“南海行为准则”（COC），不采取使争议复杂化、扩大化的行动，及时妥善处理出现的问题，维护中越关系大局以及南海和平稳定。

八、越方重申坚定奉行一个中国政策，支持两岸关系和平发展与中国统一大业，坚决反对任何形式的“台独”分裂活动。越南不同台湾发展任何官方关系。中方对此表示赞赏。

九、双方同意继续加强在联合国、亚太经合组织、中国—东盟等多边框架内的配合，共同维护与促进世界的和平、繁荣与发展。中方支持越方成功主办2017年亚太经合组织领导人非正式会议。

十、访问期间，双方签署了《中国共产党与越南共产党干部培训合作计划（2016—2020年）》、《中华人民共和国政府与越南社会主义共和国政府关于北仑河口自由航行区航行的协定》、《中华人民共和国政府与越南社会主义共和国政府关于合作保护和开发德天瀑布旅游资源的协定》、《中华人民共和国政府与越南社会主义共和国政府关于互设文化中心的协定》、《中华人民共和国政府与越南社会主义共和国政府关于越南老街—河内—海防标准轨铁路线路规划项目可行性研究换文》、《中华人民共和国国家发展和改革委员会与越南社会主义共和国工业贸易部关于促进产能合作的谅解备忘录》、《中华人民共和国商务部与越南社会主义共和国计划投资部关于越中友谊宫项目优化设计谅解备忘录》、《中国共产党广西壮族自治区委员会与越南共产党广宁省委员会关于建立友好地方组织的交流协议》、《中国共产党云南省委员会与越南共产党老街省委员会关于开展地方党委友好交往协议》等合作文件。

十一、习近平总书记、国家主席对阮富仲总书记、张晋创国家主席以及越南共产党、政府和人民所给予的隆重、热情和友好接待表示衷心感谢。

Tuyên bố chung Trung Quốc-Việt Nam

(2015/11/6)

1. Nhận lời mời của Tổng Bí thư Ban Chấp hành Trung ương Đảng Cộng sản Việt Nam Nguyễn Phú Trọng, Chủ tịch nước Cộng hòa xã hội chủ nghĩa Việt Nam Trương Tấn Sang, Tổng Bí thư Ban Chấp hành Trung ương Đảng Cộng sản Trung Quốc, Chủ tịch nước Cộng hòa nhân dân Trung Hoa Tập Cận Bình tiến hành chuyến thăm cấp Nhà nước tới Việt Nam từ ngày 5 đến ngày 6/11/2015.

Trong thời gian chuyến thăm, Tổng Bí thư, Chủ tịch Trung Quốc Tập Cận Bình đã có các cuộc hội đàm với Tổng Bí thư Nguyễn Phú Trọng và Chủ tịch nước Trương Tấn Sang, hội kiến với Thủ tướng Nguyễn Tấn Dũng, Chủ tịch Quốc hội Nguyễn Sinh Hùng. Trong không khí hữu nghị, chân thành, thẳng thắn, lãnh đạo cấp cao hai Đảng, hai nước đã đi sâu trao đổi ý kiến và đạt được nhận thức chung quan trọng về việc làm sâu sắc hơn nữa quan hệ hợp tác giữa hai Đảng, hai nước, về các vấn đề quốc tế và khu vực cùng quan tâm.

Hai bên nhất trí cho rằng chuyến thăm đã thành công tốt đẹp, góp phần quan trọng vào việc củng cố tình hữu nghị truyền thống, làm sâu sắc quan hệ đối tác hợp tác chiến lược toàn diện Việt–Trung, thúc đẩy hòa bình, ổn định và phát triển của khu vực và thế giới.

2. Hai bên vui mừng trước những thành tựu to lớn, có ý nghĩa lịch sử của mỗi nước trong công cuộc xây dựng chủ nghĩa xã hội phù hợp với tình hình mỗi nước; nhất trí tăng cường giao lưu và tham khảo kinh nghiệm của nhau, thúc đẩy sự nghiệp đổi mới của Việt Nam và sự nghiệp cải cách, mở cửa của Trung Quốc không ngừng phát triển, tạo sức sống mới cho sự nghiệp xây dựng chủ nghĩa xã hội của mỗi nước.

Phía Việt Nam chân thành chúc và tin tưởng rằng dưới sự lãnh đạo của Đảng Cộng sản Trung Quốc, nhân dân Trung Quốc nhất định sẽ thúc đẩy hài hòa xây dựng toàn diện xã hội khá giả, đi sâu cải cách toàn diện, quản lý đất nước theo pháp luật toàn diện, quản lý đảng nghiêm minh toàn diện, thực hiện thắng lợi mục tiêu xây dựng thành công nhà nước hiện đại xã hội chủ nghĩa giàu mạnh, dân chủ, văn minh, hài hòa.

Phía Trung Quốc chân thành chúc Đảng Cộng sản Việt Nam tổ chức thành công Đại hội Đảng toàn quốc lần thứ XII vào đầu năm 2016; tin tưởng rằng dưới sự lãnh đạo của Đảng Cộng sản Việt Nam, nhân dân Việt Nam sẽ thực hiện thắng lợi các mục tiêu đề ra, xây dựng Việt Nam trở thành nước xã hội chủ nghĩa, dân giàu, nước mạnh, dân chủ, công bằng, văn minh.

3. Hai bên nhìn lại chặng đường phát triển quan hệ hai Đảng, hai nước trong 65 năm qua kể từ khi Việt Nam - Trung Quốc thiết lập quan hệ ngoại giao, nhất trí cho rằng tình hữu nghị Việt–Trung do Chủ tịch Hồ Chí Minh, Chủ tịch Mao Trạch Đông cùng các nhà lãnh đạo tiền bối đích thân xây dựng và dày công vun đắp là tài sản chung quý báu của nhân dân hai nước cần được gìn giữ, kế thừa và phát huy; thực hiện tốt phương châm "láng giềng hữu nghị, hợp tác toàn diện, ổn định lâu dài, hướng tới tương lai" và tinh thần "láng giềng tốt, bạn bè tốt, đồng chí tốt, đối tác tốt"; nắm vững phương hướng đúng đắn của tình hữu nghị Việt–Trung, tăng cường trao đổi chiến lược, củng cố tin cậy chính trị, thúc đẩy hợp tác các lĩnh vực trên cơ sở tôn trọng lẫn nhau, bình đẳng, cùng có lợi, kiểm soát tốt và giải quyết thỏa đáng bất đồng, thúc đẩy quan hệ đối tác hợp tác chiến lược toàn diện Việt–Trung phát triển lành mạnh, ổn định.

4. Hai bên cho rằng, việc duy trì tiếp xúc cấp cao thường xuyên giữa hai Đảng, hai nước có vai trò quan trọng trong việc tăng cường tin cậy chính trị, thúc đẩy phát triển quan hệ song phương; nhất trí duy trì trao đổi cấp cao thông qua các hình thức linh hoạt, đa dạng như thăm lẫn nhau, cử Đặc phái viên, điện thoại qua đường dây nóng, gặp gỡ thường niên và gặp gỡ bên lề các diễn đàn đa phương để kịp thời trao đổi ý kiến về các vấn đề quan trọng trong quan hệ hai Đảng, hai nước.

5. Hai bên cho rằng, Việt Nam và Trung Quốc đều đang trong thời kỳ phát triển kinh tế–xã hội quan trọng, hai bên coi sự phát triển của nước này là cơ hội

phát triển cho nước kia, nhất trí phát huy tốt vai trò điều phối tổng thể của Ủy ban chỉ đạo hợp tác song phương Việt - Trung, tập trung thúc đẩy hợp tác trên các lĩnh vực dưới đây:

(i) Thực hiện tốt Kế hoạch hợp tác giữa hai Đảng và làm sâu sắc các hoạt động giao lưu hợp tác giữa các tổ chức Đảng ở Trung ương và địa phương, nhất là các địa phương có chung đường biên giới; tiếp tục tổ chức tốt Hội thảo lý luận, thực hiện tốt Kế hoạch hợp tác đào tạo cán bộ hai Đảng giai đoạn 2016-2020 được ký trong chuyến thăm này. Tích cực thúc đẩy giao lưu hợp tác hữu nghị giữa Quốc hội Việt Nam với Đại hội Đại biểu Nhân dân toàn quốc Trung Quốc, giữa Mặt trận Tổ quốc Việt Nam với Hội nghị Hiệp thương Chính trị Nhân dân toàn quốc Trung Quốc; thúc đẩy giao lưu hữu nghị giữa nhân dân hai nước.

(ii) Thực hiện tốt Nghị định thư hợp tác giữa Bộ Ngoại giao hai nước, duy trì trao đổi thường xuyên giữa lãnh đạo hai Bộ, tiếp tục tổ chức Tham vấn Ngoại giao thường niên, tăng cường giao lưu giữa các Vụ/Cục tương ứng, thực hiện tốt công tác bồi dưỡng cán bộ giữa hai Bộ. Phía Việt Nam sẵn sàng tạo thuận lợi để Trung Quốc thành lập Tổng Lãnh sự quán tại Đà Nẵng, Việt Nam.

(iii) Duy trì trao đổi cấp cao giữa hai quân đội, sử dụng tốt cơ chế Đối thoại chiến lược Quốc phòng, Giao lưu hữu nghị quốc phòng biên giới Việt - Trung và đường dây thông tin điện thoại trực tiếp giữa hai Bộ Quốc phòng; tăng cường giao lưu hợp tác giữa quân đội hai nước trên các lĩnh vực như giao lưu hữu nghị biên phòng, đào tạo cán bộ, nghiên cứu học thuật quân sự, tuần tra chung trên Vịnh Bắc Bộ và tàu hải quân thăm lẫn nhau; đi sâu trao đổi kinh nghiệm về hoạt động gìn giữ hòa bình Liên hợp quốc và công tác đảng, công tác chính trị trong quân đội; tăng cường hợp tác thực thi pháp luật trên biển giữa Cảnh sát biển hai nước, cùng nhau duy trì hòa bình, ổn định trong vùng biển Vịnh Bắc Bộ, thúc đẩy ký kết Bản ghi nhớ hợp tác giữa Bộ Tư lệnh Cảnh sát biển Việt Nam với Cục Cảnh sát biển Trung Quốc. Đi sâu hợp tác trong lĩnh vực an ninh và thực thi pháp luật, tiếp tục tổ chức tốt Hội nghị hợp tác phòng, chống tội phạm giữa hai Bộ Công an và Đối thoại an ninh chiến lược cấp Thứ trưởng giữa Bộ Công an Việt Nam và Bộ An ninh Quốc gia Trung Quốc; tăng cường hợp tác trên các lĩnh vực như chống khủng bố, chống tội phạm ma túy, tội phạm lừa đảo qua mạng viễn thông, quản lý xuất nhập cảnh, quản lý biên giới, an ninh mạng, trao đổi kinh nghiệm về bảo đảm an ninh tại mỗi nước, phối hợp điều tra và truy bắt tội phạm bỏ trốn, ngăn chặn lao động bất hợp pháp v.v.

(iv) Tăng cường kết nối chiến lược phát triển giữa hai nước; thúc đẩy kết nối giữa khuôn khổ "hai hành lang, một vành đai" với sáng kiến "một vành đai, một con đường"; tăng cường hợp tác về năng lực sản xuất trên các lĩnh vực như vật liệu xây dựng, công nghiệp phụ trợ, máy móc thiết bị, điện lực, năng lượng tái tạo v.v. Khẩn trương thành lập Nhóm công tác, tích cực bàn bạc, ký kết Phương án tổng thể chung xây dựng Khu hợp tác kinh tế qua biên giới, thúc đẩy việc xây dựng và tích cực thu hút đầu tư đối với hai Khu Công nghiệp Long Giang (Tiền Giang) và An Dương (Hải Phòng) ở Việt Nam, đôn đốc và chỉ đạo doanh nghiệp hai nước thực hiện tốt các dự án hợp tác như gang thép và phân đạm do doanh nghiệp Trung Quốc nhận thầu xây dựng tại Việt Nam.

Sử dụng hiệu quả cơ chế Ủy ban hợp tác kinh tế - thương mại Việt - Trung, tích cực nghiên cứu ký tiếp "Quy hoạch phát triển 5 năm hợp tác kinh tế - thương mại Việt-Trung", khẩn trương sửa đổi "Hiệp định thương mại biên giới Việt-Trung", thực hiện thương mại song phương phát triển cân bằng, vững chắc và bền vững, phấn đấu thực hiện mục tiêu kim ngạch thương mại song phương đạt 100 tỷ USD vào năm 2017. Tăng cường hợp tác trong khuôn khổ "Bản ghi nhớ hợp tác trong lĩnh vực thương mại hàng nông sản"; khuyến khích các doanh nghiệp hai bên mở rộng hợp tác thương mại đối với các mặt hàng nông sản, hoan nghênh các cơ quan chức năng và địa phương liên quan của hai nước trao đổi thành lập Cơ quan xúc tiến thương mại.

Tăng cường vai trò Nhóm công tác hợp tác về cơ sở hạ tầng và Nhóm công tác về hợp tác tiền tệ, thúc đẩy hợp tác trên các lĩnh vực liên quan không ngừng có tiến triển tích cực. Thực hiện tốt dự án Đường sắt đô thị Cát Linh - Hà Đông; khẩn trương lập quy hoạch tuyến đường sắt tốc độ cao Lào Cai - Hà Nội-Hải Phòng, thúc đẩy hợp tác kết nối cơ sở hạ tầng như tuyến đường bộ cao tốc Móng Cái-Vân Đồn.

Đi sâu hợp tác hải quan, cùng chống các hành vi buôn lậu qua biên giới, tiếp tục tìm kiếm các biện pháp hợp tác thúc đẩy tiện lợi hóa thông quan, tăng cường xây dựng và quản lý cơ sở hạ tầng, nâng cao mức độ hợp tác mở cửa khu vực cửa khẩu biên giới giữa hai nước.

(v) Mở rộng hợp tác trên các lĩnh vực khoa học công nghệ, giáo dục, văn hóa, du lịch và báo chí v.v. Sử dụng tốt cơ chế Ủy ban liên hợp về hợp tác khoa học công nghệ giữa hai nước, tích cực thúc đẩy hợp tác về chuyển giao công nghệ, giao lưu giữa các nhà khoa học, trao đổi về việc xây dựng Phòng thí nghiệm chung. Phấn đấu hoàn thành việc xây dựng và đưa vào sử dụng Cung Hữu nghị Việt-Trung vào năm 2017, sớm thành lập Trung tâm Văn hóa nước này tại nước kia, vận hành có hiệu quả Học viện Khổng Tử tại Đại học Hà Nội. Tăng cường giao lưu báo chí hai nước, gia tăng mức độ tuyên truyền về tình hữu nghị Việt-Trung. Tiếp tục tổ chức tốt các hoạt động như Gặp gỡ hữu nghị thanh niên Việt - Trung, Diễn đàn Nhân dân, tổ chức Liên hoan thanh niên Việt-Trung lần thứ 3 tại Việt Nam vào năm 2016.

6. Tiếp tục phát huy tốt vai trò của Ủy ban liên hợp về biên giới trên đất liền Việt-Trung, thực hiện tốt "Hiệp định về tàu thuyền đi lại tại khu vực tàu thuyền đi lại tự do ở cửa sông Bắc Luân" và "Hiệp định hợp tác bảo vệ và khai thác tài nguyên du lịch thác Bản Giốc" được ký kết trong chuyến thăm này; tiến hành tổng kết tình hình 05 năm thực hiện 03 văn kiện về quản lý biên giới trên đất liền giữa hai nước. Tăng cường hợp tác giữa các tỉnh/khu biên giới, thúc đẩy sự phát triển của khu vực biên giới hai nước.

7. Hai bên đã trao đổi chân thành, thẳng thắn về vấn đề trên biển, nhấn mạnh nghiêm túc tuân thủ những nhận thức chung quan trọng đạt được giữa lãnh đạo cấp cao hai Đảng, hai nước; nghiêm túc thực hiện "Thỏa thuận về những nguyên tắc cơ bản chỉ đạo giải quyết vấn đề trên biển Việt Nam-Trung Quốc", sử dụng tốt cơ chế đàm phán cấp Chính phủ về biên giới lãnh thổ Việt-Trung, kiên trì thông qua hiệp thương và đàm phán hữu nghị, tìm kiếm giải pháp cơ bản và lâu dài mà hai bên đều có thể chấp nhận được, tích cực bàn bạc các giải pháp mang tính quá độ không ảnh hưởng đến lập trường và chủ trương của mỗi bên, bao gồm tích cực nghiên cứu và bàn bạc về vấn đề hợp tác cùng phát triển.

Hai bên tuyên bố khởi động hoạt động khảo sát chung trên thực địa tại khu vực ngoài cửa Vịnh Bắc Bộ vào trung tuần tháng 12 năm 2015, cho rằng đây là bước khởi đầu quan trọng cho việc hai bên triển khai hợp tác trên biển; thúc đẩy vững chắc đàm phán phân định vùng biển ngoài cửa Vịnh Bắc Bộ và tích cực thúc đẩy hợp tác cùng phát triển tại vùng biển này; nhất trí gia tăng cường độ đàm phán Nhóm công tác cấp chuyên viên về vùng biển ngoài cửa Vịnh Bắc Bộ, tiếp tục thúc đẩy công việc của Nhóm công tác bàn bạc về hợp tác cùng phát triển trên biển, tăng cường hợp tác trong các lĩnh vực ít nhạy cảm, tuyên bố khởi động dự án hợp tác nghiên cứu so sánh trầm tích thời kỳ Holocenne khu vực châu thổ sông Hồng và châu thổ sông Trường Giang.

Hai bên nhất trí cùng nhau kiểm soát tốt bất đồng trên biển, thực hiện đầy đủ và có hiệu quả "Tuyên bố về ứng xử của các bên ở Biển Đông" (DOC), thúc đẩy sớm đạt được "Bộ Quy tắc ứng xử ở Biển Đông" (COC) trên cơ sở hiệp thương thống nhất, không có hành động làm phức tạp, mở rộng tranh chấp; xử lý kịp thời, thỏa đáng vấn đề nảy sinh, duy trì hòa bình, ổn định ở Biển Đông và quan hệ Việt - Trung.

8. Phía Việt Nam khẳng định kiên trì chính sách một Trung Quốc, ủng hộ quan hệ hai bờ phát triển hòa bình và sự nghiệp lớn thống nhất Trung Quốc, kiên quyết phản đối hoạt động chia rẽ "Đài Loan độc lập" dưới mọi hình thức. Việt Nam không phát triển bất cứ quan hệ chính thức nào với Đài Loan. Phía Trung Quốc bày tỏ hoan nghênh lập trường trên của Việt Nam.

9. Hai bên nhất trí tiếp tục tăng cường phối hợp trong khuôn khổ đa phương như Liên hợp quốc, Diễn đàn hợp tác kinh tế châu Á - Thái Bình Dương (APEC), Hiệp hội các quốc gia Đông Nam Á (ASEAN)-Trung Quốc; cùng duy trì, bảo vệ và thúc đẩy hòa bình, phồn vinh và phát triển của thế giới. Phía Trung Quốc ủng hộ Việt Nam tổ chức thành công Hội nghị Cấp cao APEC 2017.

10. Trong thời gian chuyến thăm, hai bên đã ký các văn kiện hợp tác: "Kế hoạch hợp tác đào tạo cán bộ giữa Đảng Cộng sản Việt Nam và Đảng Cộng sản Trung Quốc giai đoạn 2016–2020", "Hiệp định về tàu thuyền đi lại tại khu vực tàu thuyền đi lại tự do ở cửa sông Bắc Luân giữa Chính phủ nước Cộng hòa xã hội chủ nghĩa Việt Nam và Chính phủ nước Cộng hòa nhân dân Trung Hoa", "Hiệp định hợp tác bảo vệ và khai thác tài nguyên du lịch thác Bản Giốc giữa Chính phủ nước Cộng hòa xã hội chủ nghĩa Việt Nam và Chính phủ nước Cộng hòa nhân dân Trung Hoa", "Hiệp định giữa Chính phủ nước Cộng hòa xã hội chủ nghĩa Việt Nam và Chính phủ nước Cộng hòa nhân dân Trung Hoa về việc thành lập Trung tâm Văn hóa nước này tại nước kia", "Công hàm trao đổi giữa Chính phủ nước Cộng hòa xã hội chủ nghĩa Việt Nam và Chính phủ nước Cộng

hòa nhân dân Trung Hoa về việc khả thi tuyến đường sắt Lào Cai - Hà Nội - Hải Phòng", "Bản ghi nhớ về việc thúc đẩy hợp tác năng lực sản xuất giữa Bộ Công Thương nước Cộng hòa xã hội chủ nghĩa Việt Nam và Ủy ban Phát triển và Cải cách Quốc gia nước Cộng hòa nhân dân Trung Hoa", "Bản ghi nhớ về việc ưu hóa thiết kế dự án Cung Hữu nghị Việt - Trung giữa Bộ Kế hoạch và Đầu tư nước Cộng hòa xã hội chủ nghĩa Việt Nam và Bộ Thương mại nước Cộng hòa nhân dân Trung Hoa", "Bản thỏa thuận giữa Tỉnh ủy Quảng Ninh, Đảng Cộng sản Việt Nam với Khu ủy Khu tự trị dân tộc Choang Quảng Tây, Đảng Cộng sản Trung Quốc về thiết lập giao lưu hữu nghị giữa các tổ chức cơ sở Đảng địa phương", "Thỏa thuận triển khai giao lưu hữu nghị Đảng bộ địa phương giữa Tỉnh ủy Lào Cai, Đảng Cộng sản Việt Nam và Tỉnh ủy Vân Nam, Đảng Cộng sản Trung Quốc"...

11. Tổng Bí thư, Chủ tịch nước Trung Quốc Tập Cận Bình chân thành cảm ơn sự đón tiếp trọng thị, thân tình và hữu nghị của Tổng Bí thư Nguyễn Phú Trọng, Chủ tịch nước Trương Tấn Sang và Đảng Cộng sản, Nhà nước và nhân dân Việt Nam.

中华人民共和国和马来西亚双边文件

Bilateral Documents between the People's Republic of China and Malaysia

中华人民共和国政府和马来西亚政府关于未来双边合作框架的联合声明

（1999年5月31日）

中华人民共和国和马来西亚(以下简称“双方”)，自1974年5月31日正式建交以来，在平等、互信、互利的基础上，在政治、经济、文化、教育、防务及其它领域建立了友好和实质性的关系。双方之间的密切交往使这种关系在友好和谐的气氛中得到进一步加强。双方保持友好合作关系不仅符合两国人民的根本利益，也有利于亚洲和世界的和平、稳定以及社会和经济发展。

在21世纪即将来临之际，双方同意共同制订一个未来双边合作的框架，从而在相互信任、相互支持的基础上建立全方位的睦邻友好合作关系。为此，本着共同的意愿和目的，双方同意优先考虑以下几个方面：

一、为进一步发展双边关系、促进本地区和世界的持久和平、稳定与繁荣而共同努力。

二、保持包括双方高层领导、政府官员的各个层次的经常性接触和互访，增进双方企业及人民之间的交流，以促进中马双边关系全面、持续地发展。

三、加强两国外交部年度高官磋商机制，就共同关心的双边、地区和国际问题交换意见。磋商将由双方轮流主办。

四、在平等互利原则的基础上扩大贸易、投资、银行、金融、国防、安全、教育、科技、信息、卫生、交通、环境、农业、林业、矿业、文化、旅游、青年和体育等领域的友好互利合作，并承诺：

（一）通过下列措施进一步促进双边贸易与投资往来并加强工业合作：

1. 同意消除贸易和投资障碍以提供良好的市场环境；

2. 提高有关贸易法规的透明度；

3. 通过更频繁的信息交流来鼓励和支持双向投资的增长；

4. 促进投资以及合作到第三国共同投资；

5. 鼓励双方工商部门发挥更积极的作用。

（二）加强在金融领域的交流与合作。根据对等原则，为相互在对方国家开设银行和开展银行业务提供必要的便利。共同致力于改革和改进国际金融管理制度，建立一个有利于各方的国际金融新秩序。

（三）为进一步发展防务合作关系，除加强两军高层交往外，应促进各个层次的互访，包括考察、军舰互访、培训、信息/情报交流、组织研讨会和开展互利研究与开发。在国防工业领域，双方将鼓励国防工业公司官员互访，举办展览、研讨会及讲习班以探讨联合或合作生产项目的可能性。

（四）促进双方执法机关之间的合作和相互协助，在交换刑事信息和预防、打击有组织跨国犯罪、经济犯罪、走私毒品和精神药物、走私武器和炸药、贩卖人口以及其它犯罪活动方面建立更密切的联系。

（五）根据一九九七年六月二十日签订的谅解备忘录，加强教育领域尤其是科技教学方面的合作与交流，以增进双方的学术和技术交流。

（六）根据一九九二年七月十三日签订的《科学技术合作协定》，加强科技领域的合作，特别是在双方共同感兴趣的领域进行合作研究和技术交流，并在地区和国际论坛就共同关心的问题加强磋商。

（七）加强信息和通讯领域的合作。

（八）促进在医学研究、药品生产、传统医学、消费者保护和传染病防控方面的合作。加强双方政府及官员在联合国教科文组织、联合国儿童基金会、世界卫生组织和其它国际卫生合作机构内的协调与合作。

（九）增进空中、陆地和海上交通领域的合作。双方将共同努力推动湄公河流域开发计划项下的新加坡—昆明铁路项目。这符合中马两国及本地区其它国家的长远和共同利益。

（十）促进环境管理和可持续发展领域的合作，加强就包括落实多边环境协议在内的全球环境问题的磋商，进一步推动清洁技术、环境教育、环境意识和环境保护等方面的信息交流合作。

（十一）在农业、林业、矿业和木材业产品领域扩大工艺和技术交流，提高产品质量，改进生产，增加附加值。

（十二）有计划、有组织地推动文化交流，考虑签订双边文化合作协定。

（十三）鼓励双方旅游部门采取措施加强合作，增加游客人数，拓展旅游市场，提高旅游促销技巧。

（十四）鼓励和促进体育运动领域的合作，包括体育运动管理、训练及运动医学方面的合作。在青年培养及交流计划方面开展更密切的合作。

五、确认相互尊重独立、主权和领土完整。马方按照其一个中国的政策，重申承认中华人民共和国政府是中国的唯一合法政府，台湾是中华人民共和国领土不可分割的一部分。

六、重申《联合国宪章》、和平共处五项原则、《东南亚友好合作条约》所确立的原则以及包括互不干涉内政在内的其它公认的原则，应作为指导双方关系的基本准则。

七、继续在东盟、东盟地区论坛、亚太经济合作组织、亚欧会议、世贸组织和联合国等多边场合就共同关心的地区和国际问题加强磋商与合作，促进地区及国际和平与发展。

八、加强中华人民共和国和东盟之间友好关系的发展。双方认识到中马之间的密切合作及双方作出的重要贡献促进了中华人民共和国和东盟及东盟与中日韩关系的发展。

九、维护南中国海的和平与稳定，根据公认的国际法原则，包括1982年《联合国海洋法公约》，通过双边友好协商和谈判促进争议的解决。

十、促进多极世界和公正、合理的国际政治经济新秩序的建立。

十一、重申各国有权选择自己的社会、政治和经济制度，任何国家都不应以任何借口干涉他国内政。

十二、促进发展中国家团结，支持发展中国家平等参与国际事务并在新的世界秩序中占有自己应有的位置。

如一方要求，双方外交部长将共同对本框架文件进行复审。任何可能出现的问题、争议或分歧均应由双方通过友好协商加以解决。

本声明于1999年5月31日在北京签署。

Joint Statement between the Government of the People's Republic of China and the Government of Malaysia on Framework for Future Bilateral Cooperation

(31 May 1999)

The People's Republic of China (PRC) and Malaysia (hereinafter referred to as "the two sides") have enjoyed substantive and friendly relations, based on equality, mutual trust and benefit, in the political, economic, cultural, educational, defense and other fields since the formal establishment of bilateral diplomatic relations on 31 May, 1974. These relations have been strengthened by close contacts which have brought about an environment of harmony and amity. The friendly relations and cooperation between the two sides not only accord with the fundamental interests of the two people, but also contribute to the peace, stability and social and economic development in Asia and the world at large.

As the 21st century approaches, both sides agree to work together on a Framework of Future Bilateral Cooperation so as to bring about an all-directional relationship and good neighborliness, friendship and cooperation based on mutual trust and support. In this regard, the two sides, sharing similar aspirations and objectives, hereby agree that priority be given to the following:

1. TO UNDERTAKE concerted efforts to further develop the bilateral relations and to promote lasting peace, stability and prosperity in the region and in the world at large.

2. TO MAINTAIN close and frequent contacts and exchanges of visits at all levels, including government leaders and officials, the private sector, and their peoples in order to contribute to a comprehensive and sustained development of

PRC-Malaysia bilateral relations.

3. TO STRENGTEN the mechanism of annual meetings between senior officials of their respective Foreign Ministries for consultations on bilateral, regional and international issues of mutual concern. The consultations will be hosted by the two sides alternately.

4. TO EXPAND friendly and mutually beneficial cooperation in the fields of trade, investment, banking and finance, defense, security, education, science and technology, information, health, transport, environment, agriculture, forestry, mining, culture, tourism, youth, and sports based on the principles of equality and mutual benefit, by undertaking the following:

a) To promote better bilateral trade and investment flows, and improve industrial cooperation by:

i) agreeing to provide a conducive market environment, through identification and removal of trade and investment impediments,

ii) improving transparency of trade related regulations,

iii) encouraging and supporting increased mutual investment, through more frequent exchanges of information,

iv) undertaking investment promotion, and joint investment in third countries, and

v) encouraging a pro-active role for the business sectors of both sides.

b) To intensify exchanges and cooperation in the field of finance. Each side will provide necessary facilities for the establishment and operation of the other's banks in its territory based on reciprocity. The two sides will work together to reform and improve the international financial regulatory system and to establish a new international finance order to the benefit of all sides.

c) To promote defense cooperation by facilitating the exchange of visits at various levels, including study visits, ship visits, training, exchange of information/intelligence, organizing of seminars, and undertaking mutual beneficial research and development besides exchange of high ranking military officers. In the area of defense industry, both sides will encourage reciprocal visits by officials of the defense industry companies and organize exhibitions, seminars and workshops to explore the possibility of identifying joint or coproduction projects.

d) To promote cooperation and mutual assistance between their respective law enforcement agencies to develop closer contacts in the exchange of information on criminal matters and in preventing and combating organized cross-border crimes, economic crimes, trafficking of narcotic drugs and psychotropic substance, trafficking of firearms and explosives, trafficking of humans, and other criminal activities.

e) To enhance cooperation and exchanges in the field of education, in line with the Memorandum of Understanding of 20th June 1997, with special focus to be placed in the area of science and technology so as to enable the two sides to promote the academic and technological exchanges.

f) To enhance cooperation in the fields of science and technology between the two sides, in accordance with the Agreement of Cooperation in Science and Technology of 13th July, 1992, with special emphasis being given to joint research and technological exchanges in areas of mutual interests and to forge greater consultation on issues of common concern at regional and international fora.

g) To enhance cooperation in the field of information and communication.

h) To promote cooperation in medical research, pharmaceutical production, traditional medicine, consumer protection, and epidemic prevention and control and to strengthen the coordination and cooperation between their governments and officials within the framework of UNESCO, UNICEF, WHO and other such international organizations that cooperate in the area of public health.

i) To enhance cooperation in the area of air, land and maritime transport. The two sides will jointly work to promote the Singapore-Kunming Rail Project of the Mekong Valley Development Program, which will serve the long term and common interest of not only the PRC and Malaysia, but also other countries in the region.

j) To promote cooperation in the areas of environmental management and sustainable development, to forge greater consultation on global environmental concerns including the implementation of Multilateral Environment Agreements, promote stronger cooperation in information exchange such as on cleaner technology, environmental education and awareness and conservation.

k) To promote and expand technical and technological exchanges and to improve quality, production and added value of agriculture, forestry, mining and timber products.

l) To promote cultural exchanges in a structured and organized manner, and to consider the signing of a bilateral agreements on cultural corporation.

m) To encourage the tourism sector of the two sides, to take steps to intensify bilateral cooperation, increase tourist arrivals, expand their tourism markets and improve marketing techniques.

n) To encourage and promote cooperation in the field of sports including in sports administration, training and sports medicine, and to establish closer cooperation in youth development and youth exchange programs.

5. TO AFFIRM the respect for the independence, sovereignty and territorial integrity of each other. The Malaysian side, in line with its "One China" policy, reaffirms its recognition that the government of the People's Republic of China is the sole legal government of China, and that Taiwan is an inalienable part of the territory of the People's Republic of China.

6. TO REAFFIRM that the United Nations Charter, the Five Principles of Peaceful Coexistence, the principles established in the Treaty of Amity and Cooperation (TAC) in Southeast Asia and other universally recognized principles, including the principle of non-interference in each other's internal affairs, should be the basic norms governing the relations between the two sides.

7. TO CONTINUE to strengthen consultations and cooperation on regional and international issues of common concerns at ASEAN, ARF, APEC, WTO, UN and other multilateral fora, so as to enhance regional and international peace and development.

8. TO ENHANCE the development of friendly relations between ASEAN and the PRC, recognizing that close PRC-Malaysia cooperation and the vital contributions made by the both sides have helped promote ASEAN-PRC and ASEAN+3 (the PRC, Republic of Korea and Japan) relations.

9. TO MAINTAIN peace and stability in the South China Sea, and to promote the settlement of disputes through bilateral friendly consultations and negotiations in accordance with universally recognized principles of international law, including the 1982 United Nations Convention on the Law of the Sea.

10. TO PROMOTE the establishment of the multipolar world and a new equitable and rational international political and economic order.

11. TO REAFFIRM the right of each country to choose its own social, political and economic system and that no country shall interfere in other countries' internal affairs on whatever pretext.

12. TO PROMOTE the unity amongst developing countries and support developing countries to participate in international affairs on an equal footing and to take their rightful place in the new world order.

This Framework for Future Bilateral Cooperation will be jointly reviewed by the Ministers of Foreign Affairs of the two sides at the request of either side. Any problem, dispute or difference which may arise shall be settled by mutual and friendly consultations between the two sides.

Done at Beijing this 31 day of May one thousand nine hundred and ninety nine.

中华人民共和国与马来西亚联合公报

（2004年5月31日）

应中华人民共和国国务院总理温家宝的邀请，马来西亚总理阿卜杜拉·艾哈迈德·巴达维于2004年5月27至31日对中国进行了正式访问。此次访问也是为了纪念中国与马来西亚建交三十周年。访问期间，巴达维总理会见了中国国家主席胡锦涛，与中国国务院总理温家宝举行了会谈，并与中国国务院副总理黄菊共同出席了庆祝中马建交三十周年招待会。两国领导人在诚挚友好的气氛中就双边关系及共同关心的国际和地区问题深入交换意见，达成了广泛共识。

两国领导人对中马建交三十年来在政治、经贸、文化、教育、军事等各领域合作取得的进展表示满意，强调相互信任及开展对话是增进双方友好关系的重要基础。两国领导人一致认为，进一步发展中马关系，积极推进两国战略合作符合双方的根本利益。

两国领导人回顾了1974年中马《建交公报》有关原则，重申将继续坚持两国1999年5月31日签署的关于未来双边合作《联合声明》的精神，并认为上述两份文件对中马关系的未来发展具有重要指导意义。两国领导人强调将继续推进文件中确定的有关合作，并达成如下共识：

——继续保持两国领导人之间的经常交往，推动两国执政党、议会、中央政府各部门、地方政府以及民间社团之间的交流与合作，不断丰富中马关系的内涵。双方将继续进行两国外交部之间的年度磋商，讨论双边关系及共同关心的国际和地区问题。

——充分利用两国经济的比较优势，巩固和深化中马经贸合作。

——争取2010年中马贸易额取得显著增长。双方欢迎两国有关部门签署《加强WTO/TBT合作的谅解备忘录》和《加强WTO/SPS合作的谅解备忘录》。

双方同意本着互谅互让的精神、根据世界贸易组织的有关原则，妥善处理可能出现的贸易纠纷，推动两国贸易平衡发展。

——马方表示承认中国的完全市场经济地位。

——欢迎双方企业参与对方国家的基础设施建设，中方愿对中国企业赴马投资兴业提供融资便利。双方还将继续鼓励两国企业在第三国进行联合投资。

——双方将积极推进两国农业合作，抓紧落实两国政府2003年签署的《农业合作协定》，加强在水稻种植、水产养殖及其他相关领域的农业技术研发合作。

——继续加强两国在交通、能源和金融等领域的合作。双方同意在2003年《中华人民共和国政府与马来西亚政府关于双边劳务合作谅解备忘录》的基础上，继续加强对两国劳务合作的管理。

——双方认为科学技术对于两国的发展具有重要意义，将继续强化两国《科技合作协定》确定的有关合作，同时积极开拓新的合作领域。中方愿与马方共同开展在生物科技和中药等领域的研发与培训合作。中方将鼓励中国科研机构和高科技企业参与马来西亚“生物谷”计划。双方将继续落实《中华人民共和国政府和马来西亚政府关于空间合作及和平利用外层空间的协定》，并愿与有关国家共同推动成立亚太空间合作组织。

——双方将进一步拓展文化、教育、卫生等领域的交流与合作，同意续签《中华人民共和国政府与马来西亚政府教育合作谅解备忘录》，并表示愿意加强对两国留学人员的规范管理。双方强调签署《中华人民共和国政府与马来西亚政府卫生合作谅解备忘录》的重要性，决定建立疫情通报机制，加强传染病防治合作。

——相互尊重国家独立、主权和领土完整。马方重申坚持一个中国政策，认为台湾是中华人民共和国不可分割的一部分。

——双方高度评价中国与东盟关系近年来取得的巨大发展。两国领导人表示愿继续加强在10+3框架下的合作，并推动中国—东盟自由贸易区的建设。马方赞赏中方对东盟一体化进程、特别是在东盟湄公河流域开发和东盟东部增长区方面所作的积极贡献。

——为促进地区和世界的和平与发展，双方同意进一步加强在联合国、东盟地区论坛、亚太经合组织、亚欧会议、世界贸易组织及其他多边组织中的协调与配合。双方同意将继续致力于维护南海地区的和平与稳定，并根据包括1982年《联合国海洋法公约》在内的公认的国际法准则，积极寻求以双边友好协商和谈判的方式解决有关争议。双方表示愿对落实《南海各方行为宣言》的后续行动进行积极研究。

——双方认为和平、安全与发展是当今世界的主题与关切。国际社会应尊重世界多样性，提倡国际关系民主化，促进多边主义，主张通过协商与谈判和平解决国际争端，共同推动建立公正合理的国际政治经济新秩序。双方强调国际社会应切实维护联合国的权威，支持联合国在重大国际事务中发挥主导作用。双方认为经济全球化既是机遇也是挑战，发展中国家应加强南南合作，推动南北对话，积极参与国际经济合作，促进经济全球化朝着有利于共同繁荣的方向发展。

——双方重申反对一切形式的恐怖主义，强调国际社会应加强反恐合作，标本兼治，反对将恐怖主义与特定的宗教和民族相联系。双方主张国际社会应共同防范恐怖主义威胁。

——双方对中东和伊拉克局势表示严重关切，呼吁国际社会应为和平解决上述问题作出更大努力。双方对朝核问题六方会谈取得的积极进展表示欢迎，马方高度赞赏中方为和平解决半岛核问题所作的不懈努力。中方高度赞赏马来西亚作为不结盟运动主席国和伊斯兰会议组织主席国在国际和地区事务中所发挥的重要作用。

马方对巴达维总理及代表团访华期间受到的热情友好接待表示感谢。巴达维总理邀请中国领导人在方便的时候访问马来西亚，中国领导人愉快地接受了邀请。

二〇〇四年五月三十一日于北京

Joint Communiqué between the People's Republic of China and Malaysia

(31 May 2004)

At the invitation of H.E. Wen Jiabao, Premier of the State Council of the People's Republic of China, H.E. Dato'Sri Abdullah Ahmad Badawi, Prime Minister of Malaysia paid an official visit to China from 27 to 31 May 2004. The visit was also to mark the 30th anniversary of the establishment of diplomatic relations between the People's Republic of China and Malaysia. During the visit, Prime Minister Abdullah met with H.E. Hu Jintao, President of the People's Republic of China, held official talks with Premier Wen Jiabao, and together with Vice Premier Huang Ju, attended the commemorative reception of the 30th anniversary of China-Malaysia diplomatic relations. The two sides had an in-depth exchange of views on bilateral, regional and international issues of mutual interest in a friendly and cordial atmosphere, the leaders of both countries reached broad consensus on the issues discussed.

The leaders of the two countries noted with satisfaction the significant progress in cooperation in the political, economic, trade, culture, education, defense and other fields made by the two countries since the establishment of diplomatic relations 30 years ago. They underlined the importance of mutual trust and understanding and a spirit of dialogue as the basis for enhancing constructive and friendly relations. They expressed their shared commitment to consolidate the existing bilateral relations and work for greater cooperation between China and Malaysia in strategic areas to serve the fundamental interests of both countries.

The leaders recalled the principles enshrined in the Communique on the Establishment of Diplomatic Relations signed in 1974 and further reiterated their full endorsement and support for the Joint Statement on Framework for the Future Bilateral Cooperation between China and Malaysia signed in Beijing on 31 May 1999. They reaffirmed the significance and relevance of the two Documents in guiding the future development of China-Malaysia relations. Both leaders stressed that they would intensify efforts to implement the various cooperation programmes outlined in the Documents and have agreed on the following:

—**TO MAINTAIN** regular communications between the leaders of the two countries and at all levels including ruling parties, legislative bodies, government agencies, non-governmental organization, the private sector and their peoples to sustain a comprehensive development of China-Malaysia bilateral relations. The two sides would continue with the annual consultations between their respective Ministries of Foreign Affairs, through which matters of bilateral, regional and international issues of common concern could be discussed.

—**TO EXPLOIT** the comparative economic advantages of their respective economies in order to strengthen and deepen economic cooperation.

—**TO INCREASE** two-way trade to a significant level by 2010. The two sides welcomed the signing of the Memorandum of Understanding on Strengthening the Cooperation of WTO/TBT and the Memorandum of Understanding on the Strengthening the Cooperation of WTO/SPS by the two countries. The two sides also agreed to resolve any arising trade disputes in the spirit of mutual understanding and cooperation in accordance with the relevant principles of the World Trade Organization. The two sides also agreed to strive for a balance of trade.

—**TO RECOGNIZE** China's full market economy status by the Malaysian side.

—**TO WELCOME** the participation of enterprises from both countries in the development of infrastructure in each other's countries. The Chinese side expressed its readiness to provide financing facilities for Chinese enterprises investing in Malaysia. The two sides will continue to encourage their enterprises to make joint investment in a third country.

—**TO STRENGTHEN** cooperation in the field of agriculture and agreed to step up the implementation of the Agreement on Agricultural Cooperation signed by the two governments in 2003. Cooperation in agricultural R&D in rice planting, aquaculture and other related fields would also be pursued.

—**TO IMPROVE** cooperation between the two countries in the field of transportation, energy and finance. The two sides undertook to enhance the management of labor cooperation following the signing of the MOU on labor in 2003.

—**TO RECOGNIZE** the significance in the application of science and technology in the development of both countries. In this connection both sides would pursue new areas of cooperation in this sector while strengthening the existing areas of cooperation under the Agreement of Science and Technology Cooperation. The Chinese side welcomes Malaysia's interest to collaborate in R&D projects and training, particularly in the fields of biotechnology and Chinese traditional medicine. The Chinese side would encourage Chinese scientific and research institutions and high-tech enterprises to take part in the Bio-Valley project of Malaysia. The two sides also expressed their readiness to continue to implement the Agreement on Space Cooperation and the Peaceful Use of Outer Space signed by the two countries. The two sides are willing to work together with other relevant countries towards the establishment of the Asia-Pacific Space Cooperation Organization.

—**TO EXPAND** exchanges and cooperation in the fields of culture, education and public health. The two sides agreed for both countries to renew the Memorandum of Understanding between the Government of the People's Republic of China and the Government of Malaysia on Cooperation in the Field of Education and expressed the willingness to enhance the regulation on the intake of students studying in each other's country. The two sides underlined the importance of the signing of the Memorandum of Understanding between the Government of the People's Republic of China and the Government of Malaysia on Cooperation in the Field of Public Health, and decided to establish an epidemic reporting mechanism to enhance cooperation in prevention and control of infectious diseases.

—**TO AFFIRM** the respect for the independence, sovereignty and territorial integrity of each other. The Malaysian side emphasizes its adherence to the One-China policy and recognizes that Taiwan is an inalienable part of the territory of the People's Republic of China.

—**TO ACKNOWLEDGE** the tremendous progress in China-ASEAN relations in recent years, the two leaders expressed their readiness to continue to strengthen cooperation in the ASEAN+3 process and the development of the ASEAN-China Free Trade Area. The Malaysian side also expressed appreciation for China's active contribution to ASEAN's efforts towards closer integration especially in the development of ASEAN-Mekong Basin and the Brunei, Indonesia, Malaysia and the Philippines East ASEAN Growth Area (BIMP-EAGA).

—**TO ENHANCE** regional and international peace and development, the two sides agreed to further strengthen consultations and coordination at the UN, ARF, APEC, ASEM, WTO and other multilateral fora. Both sides also agreed to maintain peace and stability in the South China Sea and to promote the settlement of disputes through friendly bilateral consultations and negotiations in accordance with universally recognized principles of international law, including the 1982 United Nations Convention on the Law of the Sea. The two sides expressed their readiness to study the follow-up actions on the implementation of the Declaration on the Conduct of Parties in the South China Sea.

—**TO ACKNOWLEDGE** that peace, security and development are currently the main themes and concerns to the world. The international community should respect world diversity, advocate democracy in international relations, promote multilateralism, advocate settlement of international disputes through peaceful consultation and negotiation, and work together for the establishment of a fair and just international political and economic order. The two sides emphasized that the international community should undertake effective measures to safeguard the authority of the UN and support its leading and central role in major international affairs. Both sides also believed that the economic globalization presents both opportunities and challenges. Developing countries should enhance the South-South cooperation, promote North-South dialogue, and take proactive approach in international economic cooperation so as to ensure that economic globalization develops in a way that is conducive to common prosperity.

—**TO REAFFIRM** their commitment in the fight against terrorism in all its forms and manifestations and stressed that the international community should enhance cooperation and address both the symptoms and root causes of terrorism. They also reiterate their opposition to linking terrorism with any specific religion or ethnic group. The two sides maintain that the international community should strengthen cooperation in addressing this menace.

—**TO EXPRESS** their deep concern over the situation in the Middle East and Iraq. They called on the international community to make greater efforts for the peaceful settlement of the issues in the region. The two sides also welcomed the positive progress made in the Six-Party Talks on the nuclear issue of the Korean Peninsula. The Malaysian side expressed its appreciation to China for its sustained efforts to seek a solution to resolve the issue. The Chinese side expressed its appreciation of Malaysia's role as the current Chairman of the Non-Aligned Movement and the Organization of the Islamic Conference.

The Malaysian side expressed its appreciation for the warm hospitality extended to H.E. Prime Minister Dato'Seri Abdullah Ahmad Badawi and his delegation during his visit to China. Prime Minister Abdullah extended an invitation to the Chinese leaders to visit Malaysia at their convenience. The Chinese leaders accepted his invitation with pleasure.

Beijing, 31 May 2004

中华人民共和国和马来西亚联合公报

（2005年12月15日）

应马来西亚总理达图·斯里·阿卜杜拉·艾哈迈德·巴达维的邀请，中华人民共和国国务院总理温家宝于2005年12月15日对马来西亚进行正式访问。

温家宝总理会见了马来西亚最高元首端古·赛义德·西拉杰丁，与巴达维总理举行了会谈。双方在诚挚友好的气氛中就中马关系及共同关心的国际和地区问题坦诚地交换了意见，达成了广泛共识。

两国领导人对1974年建交以来中马关系取得的显著进展表示满意，认为中马关系的发展给两国和两国人民带来了实实在在的利益，为促进本地区的和平、稳定与繁荣作出了积极贡献。

两国领导人回顾了1974年中马《建交公报》有关原则，重申将继续坚持两国1999年5月31日签署的《关于未来双边合作联合声明》及2004年5月29日发表的《中马联合公报》的精神，一致认为上述三份文件对中马关系未来发展具有重要的指导意义。

两国领导人认为，巴达维总理2004年5月访华期间，双方一致同意将积极推进中马战略性合作，为两国关系的长远发展指明了方向。为进一步拓展和深化中马战略性合作，双方达成如下共识：

——保持两国高层互访，加强两国政府、议会、政党及各界人士之间的交往。中方欢迎马领导人明年出席在南宁举行的中国—东盟博览会并顺访中国，马方对此表示感谢。

——为促进双边合作，双方将加强外交、经贸、科技领域的磋商与合作机制。

——两国外交部将制定中马战略性合作行动计划，对两国各领域合作进行全面规划。双方一致认为上述行动计划应同两国各自发展战略和区域合作进程紧密结合起来。

——继续扩大双边贸易和双向投资，积极推进贸易、投资自由化和便利化进程，努力实现2010年两国贸易额达到500亿美元的目标，加强双方在农业、高新科技、信息通讯技术、资源开发、基础设施建设和旅游等重点领域的合作，积极鼓励两国企业联合到第三国投资，继续支持两国商务理事会等机构在促进两国工商界合作方面发挥积极作用。

——为推动中马经贸合作的长远发展，双方同意就商签中马紧密经济伙伴关系协议进行可行性研究。

——双方注意到两国企业正在进行的能源合作，承诺努力推进该领域的合作。双方同意支持两国有关企业探讨在油气领域设立合资公司。

——双方欢迎于2005年12月15日签署《中华人民共和国政府和马来西亚政府卫生合作谅解备忘录》和《中华人民共和国政府和马来西亚政府教育合作谅解备忘录》。卫生合作包括人力资源开发、初级卫生保健、药品、传染病控制、医学卫生研究与开发、食品安全和传统医学。教育合作涵盖各个层次。

——双方期望在水利、海洋科技和生物科技领域开展合作。

——双方期望在央行货币互换及其他金融领域加强合作。

——双方积极评价两国合作举办郑和下西洋600周年的纪念活动，同意进一步加强文化交流。双方将继续支持中马友好协会和马中友好协会在促进两国民间友好交往中更好地发挥积极作用，大力推动青年交流，使中马友好世代相传。双方同意组织两国青年开展互访活动。

——双方认为加强旅游合作对增进两国人民的相互了解与友谊具有重要意义，同意在扩大航权、出入境便利等方面加强磋商与合作。

——拓展人力资源开发合作。中方感谢马方在马来西亚技术合作计划框架下向中方人员提供的培训机会。双方将继续鼓励两国各部门开展灵活多样的培训合作。

——积极开展两国在打击跨国犯罪等非传统安全领域的信息交流与合作，共同维护本地区的安宁。

——推进两国国防安全领域的磋商与合作，扩大两军交流。双方积极评价两国国防部今年 9 月签署的《防务合作谅解备忘录》，同意在此谅解备忘录框架下尽早启动中马防务安全磋商机制。双方还表示愿积极探讨军工军贸合作。

——马方欢迎中方愿参与马六甲海峡安全合作，同意讨论合作形式，如情报信息的交换与分享。中方承认包括马来西亚在内的海峡沿岸国依照《联合国宪章》和其他公认的国际法维护海峡主权和安全。马方欢迎中方作为海峡主要使用国为海峡的安全作出积极贡献。

——马方重申坚持一个中国政策，认为中国的发展有利于促进本地区的和平、稳定和繁荣。中方感谢马方在中国和平统一问题上给予的理解和支持。

——中方对马方成功主办第九次中国—东盟(10+1)和东盟与中日韩(10+3)领导人会议及首届东亚峰会表示诚挚的祝贺。双方表示将加强合作，共同致力于推进东亚区域合作进程。

——双方高度评价中国与东盟关系取得的长足进展，中方高度赞赏马方在推进中国与东盟合作中所发挥的重要作用。双方同意继续致力于落实中国与东盟战略伙伴关系的行动计划，推进中国—东盟自由贸易区建设，共同举办好明年中国与东盟对话合作15周年的庆祝活动。马方欢迎中方积极参与东盟东部增长区建设，支持中方继续主办好中国—东盟博览会。双方表示将进一步拓展中国与东盟湄公河流域开发合作。

——双方重申将继续致力于维护南海地区的和平与稳定，同意与其他东盟国家一道落实《南海各方行为宣言》后续行动。双方欢迎并支持有关国家本着“搁置争议、共同开发”的精神探讨在南海争议海域开展务实合作。双方愿意把南海看作联系中国与东盟的友谊之海、合作之海。

——双方积极评价东盟与中日韩(10+3)合作取得的成果，支持以10+3为主渠道推进东亚共同体的建设进程。双方认为，东亚峰会为东亚合作搭建了新的平台，有利于调动各种积极因素促进东亚的发展。中方重申将继续支持东盟在东亚合作进程中发挥主导作用，马方对此表示赞赏。

——双方对中东局势表示关切，呼吁国际社会应为和平解决有关问题作出更大努力。双方对朝鲜半岛核问题六方会谈取得的积极进展表示欢迎。中方高度赞赏马来西亚作为不结盟运动主席国和伊斯兰会议组织主席国在国际和地区事务中所发挥的重要作用。

——双方欢迎2005年9月联合国成立60周年首脑会议通过的《成果文件》，认为当务之急是要落实千年发展目标，切实帮助发展中国家解决发展问题。

——双方同意加强在联合国改革进程中的协调与配合，认为联合国改革应有助于提高联合国的作用、权威和效率，维护世界和平与安全以及应对新挑战和新威胁的能力。双方认为安理会改革应从联合国长远利益出发，根据国际关系民主化原则，在广泛协商的基础上优先增加发展中国家的代表性，寻求兼顾各方利益的解决办法。

——双方同意在亚洲合作对话、东盟地区论坛、亚太经济合作组织、亚欧会议、亚拉论坛、世界贸易组织等多边机制中继续保持良好的协调与配合。

双方对温家宝总理访马取得的积极成果表示满意，一致认为此访将进一步加强两国关系。

温家宝总理对马来西亚政府和人民给予的热情友好接待向巴达维总理表示感谢，并邀请巴达维总理在方便的时候再次访华。巴达维总理愉快地接受了邀请。

二〇〇五年十二月十五日于吉隆坡

Joint Communiqué between the People's Republic of China and Malaysia

(15 December 2005)

1. At the invitation of the Honourable Dato' Seri Abdullah bin Haji Ahmad Badawi, Prime Minister of Malaysia, H.E. Wen Jiabao, Premier of the State Council of the People's Republic of China, paid an official visit to Malaysia on 15 December 2005.

2. Premier Wen had an audience with His Majesty Tuanku Syed Sirajuddin Putra Jamalullail, Yang di-Pertuan Agong of Malaysia and held talks with Premier Minister Abdullah Badawi. The two sides had candid exchanges of views on China-Malaysia relations and regional and international issues of common interest in a cordial and friendly atmosphere, and reached broad consensus.

3. The leaders of the two countries expressed satisfaction with the remarkable progress in China-Malaysia relations since the establishment of diplomatic ties in 1974. They believed that the growth of bilateral relations has brought about tangible benefits to the two countries and peoples, and has made important contribution to peace, stability and prosperity in the region.

4. The leaders of the two countries reviewed the relevant principles set forth in the China-Malaysia Joint Communique on the Establishment of Diplomatic Relations of 1974, and reaffirmed their commitment to the spirit enshrined in the Joint Statement on the Framework for Future Bilateral Cooperation signed on 31 May 1999 and the Joint Communique between China and Malaysia issued on 31 May 2004. They agreed that these three documents are of great importance in

guiding the future development of China–Malaysia relations.

5. The leaders of the two countries expressed the view that the common understanding to vigorously promote China–Malaysia strategic cooperation, which the two sides reached during Prime Minister Abdullah Badawi's visit to China in May 2004, has provided direction for the long-term development of bilateral relations. In order to further expand and deepen China–Malaysia strategic cooperation, the two sides have agreed on the following:

i) The two sides will keep up high-level exchanges of visits, and strengthen exchanges between the Governments, parliaments, political parties and people of all walks of life of the two countries. The Chinese side welcomed Malaysia leaders to visit China and attend China–ASEAN Expo to be held in Nanning next year. The Malaysian side expressed its thanks for the invitation.

ii) In order to strengthen bilateral cooperation, the two sides will enhance the mechanism of consultation and cooperation in the diplomatic, economic, trade, scientific and technological fields.

iii) The Foreign Ministries of the two countries will draw up a plan of action for China–Malaysia strategic cooperation to map out a comprehensive plan for bilateral cooperation in various fields. The two sides agreed that this plan of action shall be fully compatible with their respective development strategies and the process of regional cooperation.

iv) The two sides will continue to expand bilateral trade and mutual investment, vigorously push forward trade and investment liberalization and facilitation, and strive to increase bilateral trade to US$ 50 billion a year by 2010. They will enhance cooperation in key areas, such as agriculture, hitech, ICT, development of resources, infrastructure and tourism. They will actively encourage businesses of the two countries to make joint investment in third countries, and continue to support the positive role of business councils and other institutions of the two countries in promoting cooperation between the two business communities.

v) In order to promote the long-term development of China–Malaysia trade and economic cooperation, the two sides agreed to conduct feasibility studies on a China–Malaysia Economic Partnership Agreement (EPA).

vi) The two sides took note of the ongoing corporate sector cooperation in the energy sector and undertook to work hard to push forward cooperation in this area. The two sides agreed to support their relevant companies in pursuing joint ventures in oil and gas.

vii) The two sides welcomed the signing of the Memorandum of Understanding between the Government of the People's Republic of China and the Government of Malaysia on Cooperation on Health and the Memorandum of Understanding between the Government of Malaysia and the Government of the People's Republic of China on Cooperation in the Field of Education on 15 December, 2005. The cooperation in health includes human resource development, primary health care, pharmaceuticals, control of infectious diseases, medical and health research development, food safety and traditional and complementary medicine. Cooperation in education will involve education at all levels.

viii) The two sides looked forward to collaborating in the areas of water services and conservancy, marine science and technology, and biotechnology.

ix) The two sides also looked forward to further collaboration in central bank currency swap and in other areas in the financial sector.

x) Both sides spoke highly of the collaboration of the two countries in holding commemorative activities for the 600th anniversary of Zheng He's voyage and agreed to further strengthen cultural exchanges between the two countries. The two sides will continue to support the positive role of the China-Malaysia Friendship Association and the Malaysia-China Friendship Association in promoting friendly people-to-people exchanges between the two countries and will strongly promote contacts among the youth, so as to pass on China-Malaysia friendship from generation to generation. The two sides agreed to jointly organize an exchange of visits for the youth of the two countries.

xi) The two sides believed that promoting tourism cooperation is of great significance to enhancing mutual understanding and friendship between the two peoples and agreed to further consultations and cooperation in areas such as expansion of air traffic rights and facilitation of entry and exit.

xii) The two sides would expand cooperation in human resource development. The Chinese side thanked the Malaysian side for providing training opportunities for Chinese personnel under the framework of Malaysian Technical Cooperation Programme. The two sides would continue to encourage their departments to carry out training cooperation of diversified forms.

xiii) The two sides will actively conduct information exchange and cooperation in non-traditional security areas such as combating cross-border crimes and will work together for peace in the region.

xiv) The two sides will promote consultation and cooperation in defense and security areas and expand military to military exchanges between the two countries. The two sides spoke highly of the Memorandum of Understanding between the Ministry of National Defense of the People's Republic of China and the Ministry of National Defense of Malaysia on Bilateral Defense Cooperation signed last September and agreed to launch under the framework of this Memorandum the "China Malaysia Defense and Security Talks" mechanism as soon as possible. The two sides also expressed their readiness to look into cooperation in defense industry and trade.

xv) The Malaysia side welcomed China's willingness to cooperate on security of the Straits of Malacca and agreed to discuss the modalities of such cooperation including exchanging and sharing of intelligence and information. The Chinese side recognized the sovereignty of the Straits in accordance with the Charter of the United Nations and international law. The Malaysian side welcomed the interest of the Chinese side, as one of the major user states, in contributing to the security of the Straits of Malacca.

xvi) The Malaysian side reaffirmed its One China policy and maintained that China's development would be in the interest of regional peace, stability and prosperity. The Chinese side thanked the Malaysian side for its understanding and support on the question of the peaceful reunification of the country.

xvii) The Chinese side expressed its sincere congratulations to the Malaysian side on its successful hosting of the 9th ASEAN Plus Three and ASEAN-China Summit and the First East Asia Summit. The two sides expressed their readiness to strengthen cooperation and jointly promote East Asia regional cooperation.

xviii) The two sides spoke highly of the considerable progress achieved in

China–ASEAN relations. The Chinese side highly appreciated the important role of Malaysia in promoting China–ASEAN cooperation. The two sides agreed to continue to carry out the Plan of Action to Implement the Joint Declaration on China–ASEAN Strategic Partnership for Peace and Prosperity, promote the building of China–ASEAN Free Trade Area and jointly ensure the success of the commemorative activities for the 15th anniversary of China–ASEAN dialogue relations. The Malaysian side welcomed China's participation in the development of the Brunei Darussalam–Indonesia–Malaysia–the Philippines East ASEAN Growth Area (BIMP–EAGA) and supported the Chinese side to continue to host the China–ASEAN Expo. The two sides expressed their readiness to further expand China–ASEAN cooperation in Mekong Basin development.

xix) The two sides reaffirmed their commitment to maintaining peace and stability in the South China Sea and agreed to work with other ASEAN countries to implement the follow-up to the Declaration on Conduct of Parties in the South China Sea. The two sides welcomed and supported discussions among countries concerned on practical cooperation in the disputed areas in the South China Sea in the spirit of "shelving disputes and going in for common development". The two sides would like to see the South China Sea as a sea of friendship and cooperation linking China and ASEAN.

xx) The two sides spoke positively of the achievement in the 10+3 cooperation and supported the building of an East Asia Community through the main channel of 10+3. The two sides agreed that the East Asia Summit offers a new platform for East Asia cooperation, which will help mobilize various positive factors for the development in East Asia. The Chinese side reaffirmed its support for ASEAN's leading role in the East Asia cooperation process, which the Malaysia side appreciated.

xxi) The two sides expressed concerns over the Middle East situation and called on the international community to make greater efforts for peaceful settlement of the relevant issues. The two sides welcomed the positive progress in the Six-Party Talks on the nuclear issue on the Korean Peninsula. The Chinese side highly appreciated the important role of Malaysia in international and regional affairs in its capacity as Chairmen of the Non-Aligned Movement and the Organization of the Islamic Conference.

xxii) The two sides welcomed the 2005 World Summit Outcome Document adopted at the Summit on the 60th anniversary of the UN in September 2005 and believed that the pressing task is to implement the MDGs and help, in real earnest, address the development issue in developing countries.

xxiii) The two sides agreed to strengthen coordination and cooperation in the process of UN reform and held that reform should help improve the role, authority and efficiency of the UN and its capacity to maintain world peace and security and deal with new challenges and threats. The two sides maintained that the reform of the Security Council must take into account the long-term interest of the UN, give priority to a broader representation of developing countries and seek a solution accommodating the interests of all parties on the basis of extensive consultations in accordance with the principle of democratization of international relations.

xxiv) The two sides agreed to maintain good coordination and cooperation in multilateral mechanisms including the ACD, ARF, APEC, ASEM, FEALAC and WTO.

6. The two sides expressed satisfaction with the positive outcome of Premier Wen Jiabao's visit to Malaysia and agreed that the visit would further enhance relations between the two countries.

7. Premier Wen Jiabao expressed appreciation to Prime Minister Abdullah Badawi for the warm and gracious hospitality accorded to him by the Government and people of Malaysia and invite Prime Minister Abdullah Badawi to visit China again at a convenient time. Prime Minister Abdullah Badaw accepted the invitation with pleasure.

Kuala Lumpur

December 15, 2005

中华人民共和国和马来西亚联合新闻稿

（2013年10月5日）

一、应马来西亚最高元首阿卜杜勒·哈利姆陛下邀请，中华人民共和国主席习近平阁下于2013年10月3日至5日对马来西亚进行国事访问。访问期间，习近平会见了哈利姆最高元首，与纳吉布总理举行会谈，并会见了前总理马哈蒂尔。

二、双方高度评价中马关系发展，一致同意将中马战略性合作关系提升为全面战略伙伴关系。这标志着双方在贸易、投资、旅游、教育、金融服务业、基础设施建设和防务等各领域合作迈上新台阶。这一新的伙伴关系要求双方加强接触，增进两国各领域合作。双方重申愿保持密切高层接触，深化各领域友好交流与合作，推动中马关系取得新发展。

三、此访期间签署的《中华人民共和国政府与马来西亚政府经贸合作五年规划》（2013—2017年）明确了双边贸易发展路线图，确定了2017年达到1600亿美元的贸易新目标。中马经济合作富有活力，其中最突出的是2012年4月启动的中马钦州产业园区和2013年2月启动的马中关丹产业园区，上述规划将给双方经济合作注入新的动力。

四、双方原则欢迎中国在马来西亚哥打基纳巴卢和槟城，马来西亚在中国南宁设立总领事馆。双方同意继续加强两国民间往来和地方合作。

五、双方欢迎将2014年确定为“中马友好交流年”。2014年中国和马来西亚将庆祝两国建交40周年，届时中国大熊猫赴马将标志两国伙伴关系迈上新台阶。两国将举行青年交流、文艺团体互访等一系列庆祝活动，进一步促进两国教育、文化、旅游等领域交流与合作。

六、双方高度评价中国—东盟关系发展取得的巨大成就，一致同意以中国—

东盟建立战略伙伴关系10周年为契机，进一步增进战略信任，推动缔结中国—东盟国家睦邻友好合作条约，提升中国—东盟自贸区合作水平。中国与东盟开展广泛合作，促进东南亚地区和平、稳定、相互尊重和信任非常重要。

七、双方同意继续致力于维护地区和平与稳定，主张通过和平、友好对话与磋商解决争议。

二〇一三年十月五日于吉隆坡

Joint Press Release between the People's Republic of China and Malaysia

(5 October 2013)

1. At the invitation of His Majesty Seri Paduka Baginda Yang Di-Pertuan Agong XIV Almu'tasimu Billahi Muhibbuddin Tuanku AlHaj Abdul Halim Mu'adzam Shah ibni Al-Marhum Sultan Badlishah of Malaysia, His Excellency Xi Jinping, the President of the People's Republic of China undertook a State Visit to Malaysia from 3–5 October 2013. During the visit, President Xi Jinping met His Majesty Seri Paduka Baginda Yang Di-Pertuan Agong XIV and held talks with the Honourable Dato' Sri Mohd Najib Tun Abdul Razak, Prime Minister of Malaysia. President Xi Jinping also met the Honourable Tun Dr. Mahathir Mohamad, former Prime Minister of Malaysia.

2. The two sides spoke highly of the progress of Malaysia–China relationship and agreed to elevate the Malaysia–China Strategic Cooperation to "Comprehensive Strategic Partnership". It marked a new level of the bilateral cooperation of the two countries in various fields, namely trade, investment, tourism, education, financial services, infrastructure development and defence. This new level of partnership entails engagement in enhancing cooperation between the two countries. Both sides also reaffirmed their shared desire to maintain close high-level contacts, deepen friendly exchanges and cooperation in all fields as well as to promote new development of Malaysia–China relationship.

3. The Five Year Programme for Economic and Trade Cooperation Between the Government of Malaysia and the Government of the People's Republic of China (2013–2017) which was signed during the visit outlined a clear roadmap

of a new bilateral trade goal of USD160 billion by 2017. The Programme will add impetus to the already vibrant economic cooperation with the most visible being the China-Malaysia Qinzhou Industrial Park which was launched in April 2012 and Malaysia-China Kuantan Industrial Park in February 2013.

4. In principle, both Malaysia and China welcomed the establishment of the Chinese Consulate-General offices in Kota Kinabalu and Penang of Malaysia as well as a Malaysian Consulate-General office in Nanning of China. The two sides agreed to continuously enhance bilateral people-to-people exchanges and local-level cooperation.

5. The two sides welcomed the designation of the year 2014 as the "Malaysia-China Year of Friendly Exchanges" and both sides agreed that the arrival of the giant pandas to Malaysia will signify a new level of partnership between the two countries especially when Malaysia and China celebrate the 40th anniversary of the establishment of diplomatic relations in the same year. The two countries would undertake a series of celebration activities including the exchanges of youth groups and art troupes, promoting exchanges and cooperation in such fields as education, culture and tourism between the two countries.

6. The two sides spoke highly of the tremendous achievement in ASEAN-China relations, agreed to take the 10th anniversary of ASEAN-China Strategic Partnership as an opportunity to further enhance strategic confidence, push forward the conclusion of a treaty of good neighborliness and friendly cooperation between ASEAN countries and China as well as to elevate cooperation level of the ASEAN-China Free Trade Area. It is indeed very important for ASEAN and China to collaborate extensively in promoting peace, stability, mutual respect and confidence building in the Southeast Asian region as a whole.

7. The two sides agreed to remain committed to maintaining peace and stability in the region, maintaining that disputes should be resolved through peaceful and friendly dialogues and consultations.

中华人民共和国和马来西亚建立外交关系40周年联合公报

（2014年5月31日）

一、值此中华人民共和国和马来西亚建立外交关系40周年之际，应中华人民共和国国务院总理李克强邀请，马来西亚总理达图·斯里·穆罕默德·纳吉布·宾·敦·阿卜杜尔·拉扎克于2014年5月27日至6月1日对中国进行正式访问。

二、访问期间，中国国家主席习近平会见了纳吉布总理，李克强总理同纳吉布总理举行会谈，中国全国人民代表大会常务委员会委员长张德江会见了纳吉布总理。双方全面回顾和总结了中马关系40年来取得的成就，对两国关系未来发展作出规划，就推进两国各领域交流与合作深入交换意见，并达成广泛共识。

三、双方一致认为，1974年建交以来，中马两国不断拓展和深化双边关系，给双方带来实实在在的利益，也为促进两国和本地区的繁荣与进步发挥了重要作用。双方重申将进一步加强在广泛领域的协调与合作，共同促进两国和本地区的和平、稳定、安全、和谐与发展。

四、双方忆及马来西亚1974年在东南亚国家联盟中率先同中国建立外交关系，并在开启中国—东盟对话进程中发挥重要作用。中方对此表示赞赏。

五、双方回顾了1974年《中华人民共和国政府和马来西亚政府联合公报》中确立的相关原则，重申这一联合公报和两国此后发表或签署的其他文件在指导中马关系长期发展中的重要性。这些文件包括1999年5月31日《中华人民共和国政府和马来西亚政府关于未来双边合作框架的联合声明》、2004年5月31日《中华人民共和国和马来西亚联合公报》、2005年12月15日《中华人民共和国和马来西亚联合公报》、2009年6月3日《中华人民共和国政府与马来西亚政府关于中马战略性合作共同行动计划》和2013年10月5日《中华人民共和国和马来西亚联合新闻稿》。

六、双方承诺相互尊重国家独立、主权和领土完整。马方重申坚定奉行一个中国政策，承认中华人民共和国政府是代表全中国的唯一合法政府，台湾是中国不可分割的一部分，支持两岸关系和平发展和中国和平统一大业。

七、双方高度评价习近平主席2013年10月3日至5日对马来西亚国事访问取得的丰硕成果，并认为这次访问将两国关系提升为全面战略伙伴关系，对未来两国关系的长远发展具有十分重要的意义。双方重申将在相互尊重、互惠互利、造福两国人民的基础上，积极致力于建设中马全面战略伙伴关系。

八、双方认为，40年来中马两国交往与合作显著加强。双方在政治、贸易、投资、旅游、教育、金融服务、基础设施建设和执法、安全、防务等众多领域的合作取得重要进展和成就。双方重申将致力于深化和拓展上述领域的互利合作。

九、双方同意，在当前复杂的国际和地区形势下，两国构建更加紧密的全面战略伙伴关系尤为重要。双方重申将从战略大局和长远出发，在相互尊重、平等互利基础上深化互信，加强合作，共同努力将双边关系提升到新的高度。

十、双方重申将保持密切的高层往来，加强双边关系战略规划，通过外交部战略磋商等双边交流机制和其他领域各层级官员的经常性接触，就涉及双方利益的双边和重大国际地区问题交换意见。

十一、双方表达了对2014年3月8日以来失踪的马来西亚航空吉隆坡至北京MH370航班乘客和机组人员家属的深切同情和慰问。纳吉布总理就中国在MH370客机前一阶段搜寻过程中给予马来西亚的支持与帮助向中国政府表达诚挚谢意。马方赞赏中国为国际搜寻行动作出的积极贡献，认为在26个国家参与的大规模国际搜寻行动中，中国派出最多数量的舰船、飞机和专家，协助马来西亚主导的国际搜寻行动。中国参与搜寻的力度是前所未有的。马方承诺将继续搜寻工作，直至找到MH370客机。中方对此表示欢迎。双方同意继续密切合作，在南印度洋澳大利亚西海岸水域开展水下搜寻。马来西亚也欢迎中国参与下一阶段搜寻工作。

十二、双方赞赏马来西亚、中国和澳大利亚于2014年5月5日至7日就MH370客机下阶段搜寻工作举行了三方会议。三国坚定承诺将继续加大搜寻力度。中国承诺在过渡阶段使用自有设备参加深海探测，这对下阶段水下搜寻行动至关重要，马来西亚对此表示欢迎。马方也欢迎中国在下阶段搜寻行动中参与部署侧扫声呐设备。

十三、双方对两国经贸合作稳步发展感到满意，同意将进一步促进双边贸易多元化增长。双方积极评价中国—马来西亚钦州产业园区和马来西亚—中国关丹产业园区取得的进展。面对当前全球金融和经济挑战，双方重申将共同努力保持经济增长。为强化双边贸易纽带，双方将进一步深化在清真产业领域的合作，加强马来西亚输华燕窝检验检疫交流与合作，在马来西亚棕榈油对华出口、绿色橡胶材料在华推广和质量检测以及品牌建设、促进贸易便利化等方面加强合作。

十四、双方同意根据2013年10月签署的《中华人民共和国政府与马来西亚政府经贸合作五年规划》（2013年—2017年），积极鼓励和支持双向投资，努力实现2017年双边贸易额1600亿美元的目标。双方同意扩大并推进在特许经营、建造、建筑和设计服务、电讯、垃圾和水处理、港口开发与物流、铁路、银行与金融服务、医疗卫生、教育、康体养生、在华清真产品与服务等领域的合作。

十五、双方重申将加强在医疗领域，特别是中医药领域的合作。双方认识到中医药的潜力，认为两国开展合作和专家交流将使双方共同受益。双方同意加强合作，发掘马来西亚草药作为传统医疗手段的效用。

十六、双方表达了在中马全面战略伙伴关系框架下，就宏观经济政策加强对话，并逐步扩大至双方共同关心的国际、地区及国内财经议题的意愿。双方将进一步促进双边金融合作，加强两国央行在货币政策、金融发展、金融稳定以及国际金融体系改革方面的交流与对话。两国央行将进一步加快本币用于两国贸易结算和投资，并推动必要配套基础设施的建设。

十七、双方重申愿扩大教育、文化、青年、出入境管理、防务、安全、农业、媒体、旅游、体育等领域合作。

十八、双方确认，为纪念中马建交40周年，并加强双方在有关领域的科研合作，中国一对大熊猫于2014年5月21日抵达马来西亚。这体现了中国人民对马来西亚人民的友好情谊。这对在马来西亚生活的大熊猫代表中马之间长期存在的友谊和密切关系。马方将确保这对大熊猫在马来西亚受到良好的照顾，并期待双方在大熊猫合作研究领域取得进展。

十九、双方对两国政府《高等教育学位学历互认协议》的全面落实表示欢迎，呼吁加强专家交流与学生往来，以实现2020年中国—东盟“双十万”学生流动计划，以及马来西亚在马培养20万名国际留学生的目标，确保更多人从高等教育中受益。

二十、双方同意加强科学、技术和创新领域的合作，推动在共同感兴趣的领域共建联合实验室，推动共建中马技术转移中心，促进两国青年科学家交流。双方同意于2014年10月在中国北京举行的首届中马科学、技术和创新联委会会议期间讨论有关合作细节。

二十一、双方同意进一步提升两国农业合作水平，重点开展在作物种植、畜牧及水产养殖、动植物疫病防控、能力建设及农业投资等领域的交流与合作。双方愿加强检验检疫领域合作，愿就达成进出口水生动物检验检疫协议共同作出努力。中方同意进一步研究马来西亚提出的扩大对华出口菠萝蜜、菠萝及其他热带水果等农产品的市场准入问题。中方还考虑在符合新检验检疫准入要求的前提下允许现有马来西亚生产商继续向中国出口牛奶及奶制品。

二十二、双方同意加强防务合作，增进两国防务部门间的友好、理解与协调。有关合作包括高层交往与会议、联合训练、人员培训、建立两军联络热线、海军舰船互访等。两国还签署国防科技工业领域合作谅解备忘录，同意本着平等互利的原则推进在国防科技工业领域的合作。

二十三、双方同意进一步加强学术、文化、媒体、体育等领域的交流，增进两国民众间的相互理解，巩固中马传统友谊。双方同意鼓励更多本国民众赴对方国家访问，进一步扩大游客互访规模。

二十四、双方欢迎两国就马来西亚在南宁及中国在槟城、哥打基纳巴卢设立新的总领事馆达成协议。双方一致认为，马来西亚驻南宁总领事馆和中国驻槟城及驻哥打基纳巴卢总领事馆的设立，将进一步便利两国人民往来，促进双边交流与合作。

二十五、双方一致认为，多边事务合作是两国全面战略伙伴关系的重要组成部分。双方同意加强与其他发展中国家的沟通与协调，促进本地区和地区间合作，推动发展中国家更多地参与重大国际事务。

二十六、双方同意将共同努力，深化中国与东盟合作，欢迎中国和东盟领导人提出的包括“2+7合作框架”、共同建设21世纪海上丝绸之路在内的重要倡议。马来西亚欢迎中国提出的建设中国—东盟命运共同体的建议，也欢迎建立亚洲基础设施投资银行，并愿参与该进程。双方一致同意推进区域全面伙伴关系谈判进程。双方还将在东盟与中日韩、东亚峰会及其他有关会议框架下保持密切沟通。中国支持马来西亚2015年担任东盟轮值主席国。双方同意于2015年2月1日至6日在马来西亚联合主办2015年东盟地区论坛救灾演习。

二十七、马方确认将出席中国在北京主办的2014年亚太经合组织领导人非正式会议。

二十八、双方一致认为，在应对国际金融危机过程中，中马两国为保持各自国内经济增长采取重要举措，为全球经济复苏作出了积极贡献。双方一致认为，国际货币基金组织和世界银行正在进行的改革应进一步深化，赋予发展中国家更多代表性和话语权。国际金融机构应向受危机影响的发展中国家提供更多实质性帮助。发展中国家在国际和地区组织中的代表性应得到进一步加强。双方呼吁发达国家采取积极举措应对危机，并希望有关举措不损害发展中国家利益。

二十九、双方反对采用贸易保护主义措施应对国际金融危机。两国将继续在世界贸易组织框架下开展工作，愿合作推动多哈回合谈判尽早达成均衡成果。谈判成果应符合多哈授权，特别是与中马在内的发展中国家的发展目标保持一致。

三十、双方强调维护南海和平、安全与稳定及航行自由安全的重要性。双方强调，各直接有关的主权国家应保持克制并根据包括1982年《联合国海洋法公约》在内公认的国际法原则，通过友好磋商和谈判以和平方式解决分歧。双方一致认为，不直接相关方干涉和介入有关争议无助于解决问题，反而会使上述分歧进一步复杂化。

三十一、双方将同其他东盟国家一道努力，全面有效落实《南海各方行为宣言》，在协商一致的基础上积极、稳步推动磋商进程，朝着制定“南海行为准则”而努力。

三十二、纳吉布总理对他本人及马来西亚代表团受到中国政府和人民热情友好接待表示感谢，并邀请李克强总理在双方方便时访问马来西亚。李克强总理愉快地接受了邀请。

二〇一四年五月三十一日于北京

Joint Communiqué between the People's Republic of China and Malaysia in Conjunction with the 40th Anniversary of the Establishment of Diplomatic Relations

(31 May 2014)

1. At the invitation of His Excellency Premier Li Keqiang of the State Council of the People's Republic of China, His Excellency Dato' Sri Mohd Najib bin Tun Abdul Razak, Prime Minister of Malaysia, paid an official visit to the People's Republic of China from 27 May to 1 June 2014, in conjunction with the 40th anniversary of the establishment of diplomatic relations between China and Malaysia.

2. During the visit, His Excellency President Xi Jinping of the People's Republic of China met with Prime Minister Dato' Sri Mohd Najib, His Excellency Premier Li Keqiang held talks with Prime Minister Dato' Sri Mohd Najib, and His Excellency Chairman Zhang Dejiang of the Standing Committee of China's National People's Congress met with Prime Minister Dato' Sri Mohd Najib. Both sides took full stock of the progress made over the last 40 years in China-Malaysia relations, set up plans for the future development of their bilateral relations, exchanged views on exchanges and cooperation in various fields and reached extensive consensus.

3. Both sides agreed that, since the establishment of diplomatic relations in 1974, the two countries have continuously strengthened the breadth and depth of bilateral relations. This has brought many mutual benefits and contributed significantly to enhancing prosperity and progress for both countries and the region as a whole. Both sides reaffirmed their commitment to strengthening

coordination and cooperation in various fields to promote peace, stability, security, harmony and growth in both countries and the region.

4. Both sides recalled that Malaysia was the first country of the Association of Southeast Asia Nations (ASEAN) to establish diplomatic relations with China in 1974 and played an instrumental role in bringing China into the ASEAN fold as a Dialogue Partner, for which the Chinese side expressed its appreciation to the Malaysian side.

5. Both sides reviewed the relevant principles set forth in the China-Malaysia Joint Communiqué on the Establishment of Diplomatic Relations of 1974 and reaffirmed the importance of the 1974 Joint Communique and subsequent other documents jointly issued by both countries, namely, Joint Statement on the Framework for Future Bilateral Cooperation of 31 May 1999, Joint Communiqué Between the People's Republic of China and Malaysia of 31 May 2004, Joint Communiqué between the People's Republic of China and Malaysia of 15 December 2005, Joint Action Plan on China-Malaysia Strategic Cooperation between the Government of the People's Republic of China and the Government of Malaysia of 3 June 2009 and the Joint Press Release between the People's Republic of China and Malaysia of 5 October 2013, in guiding the long-term development of China-Malaysia relations.

6. Both sides reiterated their respect for each other's independence, sovereignty and territorial integrity. The Malaysian side reiterated its firm adherence to the one China policy, recognized that the government of the People's Republic of China is the sole lawful government representing the whole of China, and Taiwan is an inalienable part of the Chinese territory, and supported peaceful development of cross-Straits relations and China's peaceful reunification.

7. Both sides applauded the fruitful outcome of the State Visit of President Xi Jinping to Malaysia from 3-5 October 2013 and agreed that the visit was of great importance to the long-term development of their bilateral relations as underscored by the elevation of China-Malaysia relations to Comprehensive Strategic Partnership. The two sides reaffirmed their commitment to working together in building a positive, comprehensive strategic China-Malaysia partnership based on mutual respect and mutual benefits which serve the interests

of the Chinese and Malaysian peoples.

8. Both sides recognized that engagements and collaborations between the two countries had significantly intensified over the last 40 years. Substantive progress and achievements had been made through cooperation in various fields namely political, trade, investment, tourism, education, financial services, infrastructure development, law enforcement, security and defence. Both sides reaffirmed their commitment to working further to broaden and deepen the cooperation and collaboration in those areas of mutual benefits.

9. Both sides agreed that, in the current complex international situation, it was all the more important for both countries to build a stronger strategic and comprehensive partnership. Both sides reaffirmed their commitment to handling bilateral relations with a strategic, comprehensive and long-term perspective, deepening mutual trust and enhancing cooperation on the basis of mutual respect, equality and mutual benefits and working to elevate bilateral cooperation to new heights.

10. Both sides reaffirmed their commitment to maintain close high-level exchanges, improve strategic planning of bilateral relations and exchange views on bilateral and major international and regional issues of mutual interest through bilateral exchange mechanisms such as the strategic consultation between the Ministries of Foreign Affairs of both countries, and regular engagements between officials at all levels in various fields.

11. Both sides expressed deep empathy and sympathy to the relatives of all passengers and crew aboard Malaysian Airlines flight MH370 which has gone missing since 8 March 2014 while en route from Kuala Lumpur to Beijing. Prime Minister Dato' Sri Mohd Najib expressed to the Chinese government Malaysia's sincere gratitude for the support and assistance rendered by China in helping Malaysia to search for MH370. The Malaysian side appreciated the positive contribution made by China to the international search operation and believe that, in the massive international search operation which have witnessed the participation of 26 countries, China alone had deployed the most number of vessels, aircraft and experts to assist the Malaysia-led international search operations to locate the missing aircraft of MH370, the scale of China's

participation in the search operation was unprecedented in its history. The Chinese side welcomed the assurance by the Malaysian side of Malaysia's commitment to continue the search for MH370 until it is found. Both sides agreed to continue to work closely together in the sub-surface search operation for MH 370 in the southern Indian Ocean off the west coast of Australia. Malaysia also welcomed China's participation in the next phase of search.

12. Both sides appreciated Malaysia, China and Australia's holding of a Tripartite Meeting on 5 and 7 May 2014 to discuss the way forward for the new phase of the search for MH370. All countries have made a firm commitment for the search to be a continuous and intensified efforts. Malaysia welcomed China's commitment in participating in the bathymetric survey using its assets in the transitional phase which is essential to the subsequent sub-surface search operations. Malaysia also welcomed China's participation in deploying assets for side scan sonar in the subsequent search operations.

13. Both sides noted with satisfaction the steady development of bilateral economic and trade cooperation and undertook to make further efforts to diversify and promote growth of bilateral trade. Both sides applauded the progress of the China-Malaysia Qinzhou Industrial Park and Malaysia-China Kuantan Industrial Park. In the face of the on-going global financial and economic challenges, both sides reaffirmed that China and Malaysia would work to maintain economic growth. Towards enhancing bilateral trade ties, both sides stood ready to deepen cooperation in the Halal industries, strengthen communication and cooperation on inspection and quarantine of bird's nest and strengthen palm oil exports from Malaysia to China, collaborate in promoting green rubber materials in China and its quality testing, collaborate in brand building activities and generally, facilitating trade.

14. Both sides agreed to actively encourage and support two-way investment as stipulated in the Five Year Programme for Economic and Trade Cooperation between China and Malaysia (2013-2017) signed in October 2013, and work towards the realisation of bilateral trade target of USD 160 billion by 2017. In this regard, both sides agreed to further expand and boost their trade relations in the franchising, construction, architectural & design services, ICT, waste and

water treatment, port development and logistics, railway, banking and financial services, healthcare and medical supplies, education, spa and wellness, halal products and services in China.

15. Both sides reaffirmed the commitment to enhancing closer cooperation in healthcare, notably in the field of Traditional Chinese Medicine (TCM). The two sides recognised the potential of TCM and the mutual benefits that could be reaped via joint collaborations and exchanges of expertise between both our countries. Both sides also agreed to enhance cooperation towards recognising Malaysian herbals for traditional healthcare treatment.

16. Both sides expressed readiness to strengthen dialogue on macro-economic policies within the framework of China–Malaysia Comprehensive Strategic Partnership and step up cooperation on international, regional or domestic fiscal and financial issues of mutual interest. Both sides will further promote bilateral financial cooperation and intensify exchanges and dialogue on monetary policy, financial development and stability, and reform of the international financial system between their central banks. The two central banks will work to further accelerate the use of local currencies settlement for trade and investment between the two countries and promote the development of the necessary supporting infrastructure.

17. Both sides reiterated readiness to broaden cooperation in such areas as education, culture, youth, immigration, defence, security, agriculture, media, tourism and sports.

18. Both sides recognized that, in the purpose of commemorating the 40th anniversary of establishment of diplomatic relations between China and Malaysia and strengthening the bilateral cooperation on scientific research in the related areas, China sent a pair of giant pandas to Malaysia on 21 May 2014. This embodied the friendly sentiments of the Chinese people to the Malaysian people. The pair of giant pandas in Malaysia represent to the long-standing friendship and close relationship between China and Malaysia. The Malaysian side would ensure that the pair of pandas be well taken care of and look forward to the progress in the field of giant pandas scientific research cooperation.

19. The two sides welcomed the full implementation of the Framework

Agreement to Facilitate Mutual Recognition in Academic Higher Education Qualifications between the two Governments and called for enhanced flow of experts and students in both directions to achieve the China-ASEAN Double 100,000 Student Mobility Goals and Malaysia's aspiration for educating 200,000 international students in Malaysia by year 2020 to help ensure that more people would enjoy the benefits of higher education.

20. The two sides agreed to strengthen cooperation on science, technology and innovation, promote the establishment of joint laboratories in the areas of common interests and China-Malaysia Center for Technology Transfer, and enhance exchange of young scientists between the two countries. Both sides agreed to discuss the related cooperation in details during the 1st China-Malaysia Joint Committee Meeting on Science, Technology and Innovation to be held in Beijing, China in October 2014.

21. The two sides agreed to further intensify cooperation in the field of agriculture, mainly focusing on crops plantation, livestock, fisheries and aquaculture, animal and plant diseases prevention and control, capacity building, as well as agricultural investment. Both sides expressed readiness to strengthen cooperation in the field of inspection and quarantine and would make joint efforts to enter into Protocol on Inspection and Quarantine of Imported and Exported Live Aquatic Animals. The Chinese sides agreed to further study the request by Malaysia to gain market access into China for an expanded export of its agriculture products including jackfruit, pineapple and other tropical fruits, as well as to expedite the inspection and registration of Malaysian dairy producers. Chinese side will also consider allowing continued importation of milk and dairy products from existing Malaysian producers pending approvals for new inspection and quarantine access requirements.

22. Both sides agreed to strengthen defence cooperation to enhance rapport, understanding and coordination between the defence agencies of China and Malaysia. The aforesaid cooperation may include exchange of high-level visits and meetings, joint exercises, personnel training, setting up a hotline for communication between the two Armed Forces, and exchange of port-call visits by both navies. Both countries also agreed to promote cooperation in defence

science, technology and industry based on the principles of equality and mutual benefit with the signing of the Memorandum of Understanding on Cooperation in the field of Science, Technology and Industry for National Defence.

23. The two sides agreed to promote mutual understanding between the two peoples and consolidate the China-Malaysia traditional friendship through exchanges between the academic, cultural, media and sports communities. The two sides agreed to encourage more of their nationals to visit each other countries and enlarge the number of tourists.

24. The two sides welcomed the exchange of documents pertaining to the establishment of Malaysia's new Consulate General in Nanning and China's two new Consulates General in Penang and Kota Kinabalu. Both sides agreed that the establishment of Malaysia's Consulate General in Nanning and China's Consulates General in Penang and Kota Kinabalu would further facilitate the people-to-people ties between the two countries and promote bilateral exchanges and cooperation.

25. The two sides agreed that their cooperation in multilateral affairs is an important component of China-Malaysia comprehensive strategic partnership. The two sides agreed to improve communication and coordination with other developing countries to promote regional and inter-regional cooperation and increase the participation of developing countries in major international affairs.

26. The two sides agreed to work together to deepen ASEAN-China cooperation, and welcomed the initiatives proposed by both ASEAN and Chinese leaders including the "2+7 cooperation framework" and the establishment of the 21st century Maritime Silk Road. Malaysia welcomes the Chinese proposal of an ASEAN-China community of common destiny. Malaysia also welcomes the establishment of Asian Infrastructure Investment Bank and expressed readiness to participate in the process. Both sides agreed to advance with the negotiations on Regional Comprehensive Economic Partnership (RCEP). Both sides would maintain close communication within the framework of ASEAN plus Three and the East Asia Summit and other related Meetings. China supports Malaysia's chairmanship of ASEAN in 2015. Both sides have agreed to jointly hold the ASEAN Regional Forum Disaster Relief Exercise 2015 (ARF DiREx 2015) in

Malaysia from 1-6 February 2015.

27. The Malaysian side affirmed participation in the 2014 APEC Economic Leaders' Meeting to be hosted by China in Beijing.

28. Both sides shared the view that in tackling the international financial crisis, China and Malaysia had both taken important measures to maintain economic growth at home and have made positive contribution to international economic recovery. Both sides are also of the view that the on-going reform of the International Monetary Fund (IMF) and the World Bank should be further deepened so as to give more representation and say to developing countries. The two sides shared the view that international financial institutions should provide more substantial assistance to the developing countries affected by the crisis. Both sides were also of the view that the representation of developing countries should be enhanced in various regional and international organizations. Both sides urged the developed countries to take active measures to address the crisis and expressed the hope that the measures would not undermine the interests of developing countries.

29. Both sides were against the practice of addressing the international financial crisis with trade protectionist measures. Both countries would continue to work within the framework of the World Trade Organization (WTO) and stood ready to work together to achieve an early conclusion and balanced outcome of the Doha Development Agenda (DDA) negotiations. Outcomes achieved thus far must be preserved in accordance with its mandate, particularly development objectives for such developing countries as China and Malaysia.

30. Both sides underscored the importance of maintaining peace, security and stability as well as upholding freedom and safety of navigation in the South China Sea. Both sides emphasized that all sovereign states directly concerned shall exercise self-restraint and settle their differences by peaceful means, through friendly consultations and negotiations, and in accordance with universally recognised principles of international law, including the United Nations Convention on the Law of the Sea 1982. Both sides recognised the fact that intervention or involvement of parties not directly concerned could be counter-productive and further complicate the aforementioned differences.

31. Both sides, together with the other ASEAN Member States, would work hard to achieve a full and effective implementation of the Declaration on the Conduct of Parties in the South China Sea (DOC), and to make efforts to ensure positive and steady progress of consultations for the conclusion of the Code of Conduct in the South China Sea (COC) on the basis of consensus.

32. Prime Minister Dato' Sri Mohd Najib expressed his appreciation for the warm welcome and gracious hospitality accorded to him and the Malaysian delegation during the visit by the Chinese Government and people and invited Premier Li Keqiang to visit Malaysia at a convenient time to both sides. Premier Li accepted the invitation with pleasure.

Beijing, 31 May 2014

中华人民共和国和马来西亚联合声明

（2015年11月23日）

一、应马来西亚总理达图·斯里·穆罕默德·纳吉布·宾·敦·阿卜杜尔·拉扎克邀请，中华人民共和国国务院总理李克强于2015年11月20日至23日赴马来西亚出席东亚合作领导人系列会议并对马来西亚进行正式访问。

二、访问期间，李克强总理同纳吉布总理举行会谈。双方回顾了近年来中马关系发展成就，特别是对2014年5月两国领导人在北京签署联合公报后中马全面战略伙伴关系发展取得的成果表示欢迎。

三、双方重申致力于在相互尊重的基础上发展积极、全方位的中马伙伴关系，推进两国政治、经济、人文、安全等领域合作，进一步提升中马全面战略伙伴关系水平，服务于两国人民的利益和福祉。

四、双方强调，相互信任和理解作为提升建设性紧密关系的基石十分重要。加强两国领导人以及各个层级包括执政党、立法机构、政府部门、非政府组织、私营部门间密切交往将推动两国关系向全方位和战略方向发展。双方将继续发挥好两国外交部战略磋商等双边交流机制作用，就共同关心的问题交换意见，推动两国关系持续发展。

五、马方欢迎中方提出的共建丝绸之路经济带和21世纪海上丝绸之路（“一带一路”）合作倡议，双方同意在该框架下加强发展战略对接，推进务实合作。

六、中方认为，在过去五年，马来西亚政府和经济实现良好转型，全球竞争指数排名持续上升。马方新经济模式和国家转型计划中的项目管理和金融监管原则将促进符合双方利益的项目快速落实。

七、双方认为两国加强产能和装备制造合作潜力巨大，对于推动双边贸易增长、促进共同发展具有重要意义，同意进一步发挥各自优势，加强产能领域的合作。双方欢迎两国签署《关于加强产能与投资合作的协定》。

八、双方同意继续推动“两国双园”协调发展，共同探讨推进钢铁、船舶、通讯、电力、轨道交通等重点领域合作。

九、为促进两国经贸合作，双方同意根据两国经贸合作五年规划，进一步扩大双边贸易规模，积极鼓励和支持双向投资，促进民营企业的参与，支持两国中小企业和服务机构之间合作。

十、基于深化合作的良好意愿，双方欢迎中国商务部和马来西亚贸易与工业部签署《关于进一步推进中马经贸投资发展的合作计划》，相信该计划将进一步提升两国经济合作水平。

十一、双方欢迎在日益增长的跨境贸易、投资和资金流动中扩大两国本币使用，密切金融合作，包括货币互换和跨境抵押安排、人民币和马币间直接交易、在吉隆坡指定人民币清算行以及向马方提供500亿元人民币合格境外机构投资者（RQFII）额度等，以促进两国间日益紧密的经济联系。

十二、双方同意促进市场主体准入和知识产权尤其是商标领域合作，共同支持知识产权权利相关的市场活动，促进双方信息和理念交流，便利知识产权权利人和潜在合作伙伴开展知识产权活动。双方欢迎两国签署《关于政府市场主体准入和商标领域合作谅解备忘录》。

十三、双方同意进一步提升两国农业合作水平，召开第五次农业联合工作组会议，加强两国棕榈油贸易合作，欢迎签署《马来西亚输华棕榈油质量安全的谅解备忘录》。

十四、双方同意根据两国海洋科技合作协议，召开中马海洋科技合作联委会第三次会议。双方欢迎建立中马联合海洋科研中心，推动海洋科技合作。

十五、双方同意加强包括航天领域在内的科技合作，欢迎两国政府尽快签署空间合作及和平利用外层空间的协定，推动双方开展遥感、全球导航及其他卫星技术应用合作。

十六、双方领导人积极评价两国防务和军队建设领域的良好合作，包括成功举行2014年12月两军首次联合桌面推演和2015年9月两军首次联合实兵演练，相信未来两国防务合作将取得更加丰硕的成果。

十七、双方同意进一步加强执法安全合作，增进两国执法安全部门间的友好交往，开展执法安全磋商，实施好刑事司法协助条约。

十八、双方重申将全面落实两国政府高等教育学位学历互认协议。鉴于基础教育合作十分重要，两国将继续推动在该领域开展合作。双方同意进一步加强人文和媒体等领域合作，开展青年代表团互访，欢迎中方在马来西亚设立文化中心。双方愿鼓励更多本国民众赴对方国家参观旅游，进一步增进人员往来。

十九、双方领导人高度评价马方主办2015年东亚合作领导人系列会议取得的成果。中方对马方成功主办东亚合作领导人系列会议和东盟共同体宣布建成表示祝贺，积极评价马担任东盟轮值主席国期间为中国—东盟关系发展所做的贡献。双方支持发展中国—东盟战略伙伴关系，进一步增进战略互信，提升中国—东盟自贸区水平。

二十、双方重申根据国际法公认原则维护南海和平、安全与稳定及航行自由的重要性。

二十一、双方强调，各直接有关的主权国家应根据包括1982年《联合国海洋法公约》在内公认的国际法原则，通过友好磋商和谈判以和平方式解决分歧和争议，各国应保持克制，避免采取使问题复杂化或导致局势升级的行动。

二十二、双方重申致力于全面有效落实《南海各方行为宣言》，并同其他东盟国家一道，争取在协商一致的基础上早日达成“南海行为准则”。

二十三、中方对马方在李克强总理和代表团访问期间给予的热情友好接待表示感谢。

二〇一五年十一月二十三日于吉隆坡

Joint Statement between the People's Republic of China and Malaysia

(23 November 2015)

1. At the invitation of the Honourable Dato' Sri Mohd Najib bin Tun Abdul Razak, Prime Minister of Malaysia, His Excellency Li Keqiang, Premier of the State Council of the People's Republic of China, paid an official visit to Malaysia and attended the 10th East Asia Summit and Related Summits in Kuala Lumpur from 20 to 23 November 2015.

2. During the official visit, the Honourable Dato' Sri Mohd Najib Tun Abdul Razak, had a bilateral meeting with Premier Li Keqiang. Both sides took stock of the progress and achievements made over the years and welcomed the developments under the Malaysia-China Comprehensive Strategic Partnership, especially after the signing of the Joint Communique between both leaders in May 2014 in Beijing, China.

3. Both sides reaffirmed their commitment to working together in building a positive, wide-ranging Malaysia-China partnership based on mutual respect and mutual benefits and continue to further strengthen the cooperation in the political, economic, cultural and security areas and further strengthening the Comprehensive Strategic Partnership, which serve the interests and well-being of the peoples of the two countries.

4. Both sides underlined the importance of trust and understanding as the basis for enhancing constructive and cordial relations. Regular communications between the leaders of the two countries and at all levels including ruling parties, legislative bodies, government agencies, non-governmental organizations, the

private sector and their peoples to sustain a comprehensive strategic development of Malaysia–China bilateral relations. Both sides will continue to make full use of the bilateral exchange mechanisms such as the strategic consultation meeting between the Ministries of Foreign Affairs of both countries to exchange views on the issues of common interests so as to promote the sustained development of Malaysia–China relations.

5. Malaysia welcomed China's initiative of jointly establishing the Silk Road Economic Belt and the 21st Century Maritime Silk Road (One Belt and One Road). Both sides agreed to develop synergy and appropriate strategies to enhance cooperation under the above framework guided at all times by each other's prevailing program management and financial governance guidelines.

6. China recognised the dramatic transformations in Malaysia's government and economy in these past 5 years as shown by the sustained upswing of the country's position in the global competitiveness indices. China views that the principles of program management and financial governance as outlined in Malaysia's New Economic Model (NEM) and national transformation programs should be emulated and used to enable fast delivery of programs of mutual interest.

7. Both sides realized the huge potential that could be derived from the cooperation in production capacity and high-end equipment manufacturing between both countries, which would be significant to the further growth in bilateral trade and promoting common development. In this regard, both sides agreed to collaborate and to further leverage on each other's strengths in production capacity. Both sides welcomed the signing of the "Agreement between the two Governments on Cooperation in Enhancing Production Capacity and Investment".

8. Both sides agreed to continue to facilitate the coordinated development of the two countries' industrial twin parks project and jointly explore the opportunities of promoting cooperation in the priority areas such as iron and steel manufacturing, ship building, ICT, power generation and rail transportation.

9. To facilitate the already vibrant economic and trade cooperation, both sides will further enhance bilateral trade, actively encourage and support two-

way investment, promote the involvement of the private sector and support cooperation between the small-medium enterprises and service institutions of the two countries as stipulated in the "Five Year Programme for Economic and Trade Cooperation".

10. Both sides appreciated the goodwill between the two countries. In this regard, both sides welcomed the signing of the Cooperation Programme to Enhance Malaysia-China Trade, Economic and Investment Cooperation between the Ministry of International Trade and Industry of Malaysia and the Ministry of Commerce of the People's Republic of China. Both sides expressed confidence that this Cooperation Programme would further strengthen and consolidate existing economic cooperation and collaboration between the two countries.

11. Both sides welcomed the extensive financial cooperation between the two countries through facilitating the use of local currencies to support the growing cross-border trade, investment and financial flows between the two countries over the years. These initiatives include the currency swap and cross-border collateral arrangements, the direct currency trading between renminbi and ringgit, the designation of a renminbi clearing bank in Kuala Lumpur and the granting of 50 billion Renminbi Qualified Foreign Institutional Investor (RQFII) quota to Malaysia. These tangible outcomes highlight the growing economic and financial linkages between China and Malaysia.

12. Both sides agreed to enhance cooperation in the field of registration of market entities and intellectual property especially in trademarks and to work together to promote cooperation in support of IP rights-related marketplace activities; to promote the exchange of information and cross-fertilization of ideas as well as to facilitate IP rights transactions between IP owners and potential partners. Both sides welcomed the signing of the "Memorandum of Understanding between the Government of Malaysia and the Government of People's Republic of China in the Fields of Registration of Market Entities and Trademark".

13. Both sides agreed to further intensify cooperation in the field of agriculture and will hold the 5th Agriculture Joint Working Group Meeting. Both sides will also strengthen cooperation in palm oil trade and welcomed the

signing of the "Memorandum of Understanding between the two Governments on Quality and Safety of Malaysian Palm Oil Exports to China".

14. Both sides agreed to hold the 3rd Malaysia-China Joint Committee Meeting on Marine Science and Technology as outlined under the Agreement on Cooperation in the Field of Marine Science and Technology between the two Governments. Both sides welcomed the establishment of China-Malaysia Joint Centre for Marine Scientific & Technology Co-research, in promoting cooperation in marine science and technology.

15. Both sides agreed to enhance cooperation in science and technology, including that in space and welcomed the early signing of the Memorandum of Understanding between the two Governments on Space Cooperation and the Peaceful Use of Outer Space so as to promote the cooperation in the fields of application of remote sensing, global navigation and other satellite technologies.

16. Both leaders commended the excellent cooperation between the defence and military establishments, particularly with the successful conclusion of the first Table Top Exercise (TTX) and the first Field Training Exercise (FTX) Peace and Friendship, which were held in December 2014 and September 2015, respectively. The leaders also expressed their confidence for more substantive defence engagements in the near future.

17. Both sides agreed to further strengthen cooperation in the area of law enforcement and security. Malaysia and China will continue to enhance the exchange of friendly visits between the law enforcement and security agencies of Malaysia and China, continue to hold the law enforcement and security consultations and effectively implement the Treaty on Mutual Legal Assistance in Criminal Matters.

18. Both sides reiterated that they would fully implement the Framework Agreement to Facilitate Mutual Recognition in Higher Education Qualifications between the two Governments, acknowledged the importance of the cooperation in the field of basic education and reassured continuous commitments in promoting more collaboration between both countries, agreed to further strengthen cooperation in the fields of culture and media, enhance exchange of visits between the youths of the two countries and welcomed the establishment of China's

Cultural Centre in Malaysia. Both counties would also encourage their nationals to visit each other's country to further enhance people-to-people contacts.

19. The two leaders spoke highly of the achievements attained during in the 27th ASEAN Summit and Related Summits chaired by Malaysia in 2015. The Chinese side congratulated Malaysia on successfully hosting the 27th ASEAN Summit and Related Summits as well as the establishment of the ASEAN Community and appreciated the contributions of Malaysia as the Chair of ASEAN to the development of ASEAN-China relations. Both sides agreed ASEAN-China Strategic Partnership as an opportunity to further enhance strategic confidence to elevate cooperation level of the ASEAN-China Free Trade Area.

20. Both sides reiterated the importance of ensuring the maintenance of peace, security and stability, as well as upholding freedom of navigation in and over-flight above the South China Sea in accordance with universally recognised principles of international law.

21. Both sides emphasised the need for all sovereign states directly concerned to resolve their differences and disputes by peaceful means, through friendly negotiations and consultations, in accordance with universally recognised principles of international law, including the 1982 United Nation Convention on the Law of the Sea (1982 UNCLOS). Both sides further emphasised the need for all states to exercise self-restraint in the conduct of activities, and to avoid actions that would complicate or escalate tensions in the South China Sea.

22. Both sides reaffirmed their commitment to the full and effective implementation of the Declaration on the Conduct of Parties in the South China (DOC) in its entirety, and to work, together with the other ASEAN Member States, towards the early establishment of the Code of Conduct in the South China Sea (COC) on basis of consensus.

23. The Chinese side expressed its appreciation for the warm welcome and gracious hospitality accorded to Premier Li Keqiang and his delegation during the visit.

PUTRAJAYA, 23 November 2015

中华人民共和国和马来西亚
联合新闻声明

（2016年11月3日）

一、应中华人民共和国国务院总理李克强邀请，马来西亚总理纳吉布于2016年10月31日至11月5日对中华人民共和国进行正式访问。

二、访问期间，中华人民共和国主席习近平会见了纳吉布总理，国务院总理李克强同纳吉布总理举行会谈，全国人大常委会委员长张德江同纳吉布总理举行会见。双方就推进中马全面战略伙伴关系以及共同关心的地区和国际问题深入交换意见。

三、双方认为，自1974年中马建交以来，两国保持经常性互访，将中马关系提升至新高度。过去42年来，两国在许多领域开展了重大合作。双方回顾了近期的高层互访，包括2013年习近平主席对马进行国事访问、2014年纳吉布总理正式访华和2015年11月李克强总理正式访马，认为上述访问进一步深化了两国真诚、友好的双边关系。

四、双方一致认为，中马关系正处于历史最高水平，将继续通过领导人、政府、政党和企业间经常性交流和互访予以加强。双方回顾并欢迎两国关系取得的成果，决心从政治、经济、社会发展及地区安全合作等各领域进一步提升和强化中马全面战略伙伴关系。

五、双方同意确保中马关系面向未来、富有活力、繁荣发展，以造福两国民众。

六、双方强调，相互信任和相互尊重是双边关系与合作的坚实基础，再次强调应坚持两国主权和领土完整原则。马方重申坚定奉行一个中国政策，支持两岸关系和平发展和中国和平统一。

七、双方欢迎2015年马来西亚驻南宁总领事馆、中国驻槟城总领事馆和中国驻哥打基纳巴卢总领事馆分别开馆，2016年马来西亚在西安设立总领事馆。两国互设领馆表明双方友好关系进一步发展。

八、马来西亚高度重视其作为中国政府2013年提出的丝绸之路经济带和21世纪海上丝绸之路（“一带一路”）倡议沿线重要国家的地位。

九、根据中方数据，2015年中马贸易总额为972.9亿美元，2016年1－8月双方贸易额为542.8亿美元。自2009年以来中国是马来西亚最大贸易伙伴，2015年中马贸易额占马外贸总额的15.8%。2008年以来马来西亚是中国在东盟最大的贸易伙伴。

十、双方通过联合进展报告确认了《经贸合作五年规划（2013—2017）》取得的成果。两国领导人坚信在频密的高层互访和重大倡议推动下，中马经贸合作未来将更加强劲。

十一、双方高度重视在马来西亚南部铁路项目上的合作，欢迎拟议中的马来西亚东海岸铁路项目，有意发掘潜力，就基础设施建设项目开展合作，从战略层面促进相关地区的互联互通，带来潜在经济发展机遇，推动经济社会发展。这将包括技术转移、人力资源开发、当地采购以及基建行业其他长期合作。

十二、双方期待进一步加强双边贸易、投资和经济交流，倡议之一是就两国政府《关于避免双重征税和防止偷税漏税协定》换函，确认两国国有企业的资质。

十三、双方认为，海港在地区基础设施发展中具有关键作用。双方将继续推动两国海港合作，支持中马港口联盟发展，实现21世纪海上丝绸之路的愿景。

十四、双方积极评价两国在打击电信犯罪、境外追逃、反恐等领域的合作成果，同意进一步加强执法安全和反恐合作，增进两国执法安全部门间的友好交往，为维护地区安全稳定作出积极贡献。

十五、双方乐见两国重签《防务合作谅解备忘录》，相信两国国防机构间持续逐步扩大交往、密切友好合作将进一步强化双边关系。双方认识到增进两国防务领域合作的重要性，欢迎中国国防科工局与马来西亚国防部签署《关于共同开发建造马海军滨海任务舰合作框架协议》。

十六、双方一致认为，旅游业为推动中马人员往来发挥着重要作用。自2016年3月马方实施电子签证和免签计划以来，赴马中国游客人数大幅增长。双方同意加强与航空公司和旅行机构联合营销，通过消费者展和网站做好推广，推动更多两国游客赴对方国家旅游，在民间层面增进中马传统友谊和理解。双方认识到，电子商务和网络营销在促进旅游业发展方面发挥着日益重要的作用。

十七、双方重申将加强并致力于实现两国更全面和互利的空中运输合作。

十八、双方欢迎两国续签《教育合作谅解备忘录》，此举将进一步加强并推动中马教育交流取得进展。厦门大学马来西亚分校是两国高等教育合作新的里程碑，将为当地社会培养亟需的优秀人才，深化中马两国友谊。

十九、双方将共同努力落实两国政府间《文化合作协定》和《2014年至2019年执行计划》，鼓励和支持双方文化机构和文化团组互访交流，共同支持在马设立中国文化中心。

二十、双方讨论了中国扩大进口马来西亚产品的前景。马来西亚希望扩大对华出口棕榈油，扩大马棕榈油在华市场份额。

二十一、双方愿通过签署《农业合作谅解备忘录》，提升包括农产品贸易在内的农业合作，促进农业投资，加强能力建设和农业科技交流。

二十二、双方相信，签署《马来西亚输华毛燕的检验检疫和兽医卫生条件议定书》将增强中国消费者对马来西亚农产品的信心，促进两国农业贸易。双方希望未来在符合检验检疫准入要求的前提下给予马来西亚农产品更多市场准入。

二十三、两国领导人赞赏中方支持东盟共同体建设，努力实现《东盟共同体愿景2025》，欢迎中国—东盟合作取得积极进展，欢迎中国和东盟庆祝建立对话关系25周年。双方还讨论了《落实中国—东盟面向和平与繁荣的战略伙伴关系联合宣言的行动计划（2016—2020）》的执行进展。

二十四、双方同意继续加强在东盟与中日韩（10+3）、东亚峰会（EAS）、东盟地区论坛（ARF）等区域合作机制中的协调与配合。

二十五、双方就南海局势发展交换了意见，强调维护南海和平、安全和稳定及各国根据国际法享有的航行与飞越自由的重要性。

二十六、双方强调各直接有关主权国家应根据包括1982年《联合国海洋法公约》在内的国际法原则，通过友好磋商和谈判以和平方式解决分歧。双方进一步强调各方应保持克制，避免采取使南海局势复杂化或紧张升级的行动。双方认为，不直接相关方介入有关争议无助于问题的解决。

二十七、双方将同其他东盟国家一道，努力确保《南海各方行为宣言》全面有效落实，推进“南海行为准则”磋商，争取早日在协商一致的基础上达成“准则”。

二十八、马来西亚担任联合国安理会非常任理事国期间，中方同马方开展了良好的建设性合作，共同履行了联合国安理会的职责。马方对此表示赞赏。

二十九、马方对此次正式访问期间中方给予纳吉布总理及马来西亚代表团的热情欢迎和友好接待表示诚挚感谢。

二〇一六年十一月三日于北京

Joint Press Statement of the People's Republic of China and Malaysia

(3 November 2016)

1. At the invitation of His Excellency Li Keqiang, Premier of the State Council of the People's Republic of China, the Honourable Dato' Sri Mohd Najib Tun Abdul Razak, Prime Minister of Malaysia, undertook an official visit to the People's Republic of China from 31 October to 5 November 2016.

2. During the visit, the Honourable Dato' Sri Mohd Najib Tun Abdul Razak called on H.E. Mr. Xi Jinping, President of the People's Republic of China, and held talks with H.E. Mr. Li Keqiang, Premier of the State Council. He also met with H.E. Mr. Zhang Dejiang, Chairman of the Standing Committee of the National People's Congress of China. Both sides had in-depth exchange of views on enhancing China-Malaysia Comprehensive Strategic Partnership, regional and international issues of common interest.

3. Both sides shared the similar views that the regular exchange of visits between Malaysia and China had elevated Malaysia-China relations to greater heights, ever since diplomatic ties were established in 1974. Over the course of 42 years, numerous significant cooperation in many areas were achieved. Both leaders recalled the recent high level visits undertaken by both sides including the State Visit by President Xi Jinping to Malaysia in 2013, the Official Visit by the Honorable Dato' Sri Mohd Najib Tun Abdul Razak to China in 2014 and the Official Visit by Premier Li Keqiang to Malaysia in November 2015. The leaders agreed that these visits have enabled both countries to further deepen their current cordial and friendly ties.

4. Both sides agreed that Malaysia-China bilateral relations is currently at its highest level and will continue to be strengthened through regular communications and exchange of visits between the leaders, government and party officials and business enterprises from both sides. Both sides reviewed and welcomed the bilateral achievements and were determined to further enhance and strengthen the existing Malaysia-China Comprehensive Strategic Partnership in various areas including political, economic and social development, as well as regional security cooperation.

5. Both sides agreed to ensure that Malaysia–China relationship continues to remain forward-looking, dynamic and prosperous for the benefit of the people of both friendly countries.

6. Both sides underscored the importance of maintaining mutual trust and respect as the foundation for the solid bilateral relations and cooperation between Malaysia and China. Both leaders also reemphasised the need to uphold the principles of sovereignty and territorial integrity of the two countries. Malaysia reiterated its firm adherence to the One-China policy and supported peaceful development of cross-Straits relations and China's peaceful reunification.

7. Both sides welcomed the opening of the Consulate General of Malaysia in Nanning and the Consulate General of China in Penang and Kota Kinabalu respectively in 2015, as well as the new Consulate General of Malaysia in Xi'an in 2016. The establishment of the Consulate Offices by Malaysia and China respectively is a testament of the ever-growing bilateral relations between the two friendly countries.

8. Malaysia highly valued its place as one of the important countries under the Silk Road Economic Belt and 21st Century Maritime Silk Road (Belt and Road) Initiative proposed by the Chinese government in 2013.

9. Based on China's statistics, the total volume of bilateral trade was registered at USD97.29 billion in 2015 and USD54.28 billion for the period of January–August 2016. Since 2009, China is Malaysia's largest trading partner and the trade volume with China in 2015 accounted for 15.8 percent of Malaysia's external trade. Among ASEAN countries, Malaysia has been China's largest trading partner since 2008.

10. The endorsement of the Joint Progress Report is a recognition of the achievements made under the 'Five Year Program for Economic and Trade Cooperation' (2013-2017). Both leaders believed that economic and trade cooperation between Malaysia and China will grow even stronger in the years ahead leveraging on major initiatives and frequent high level visits involving the two nations.

11. Both sides attached great importance to the ongoing cooperation on Malaysia's South Double Track Railway, welcomed the proposed East Coast Rail Line project in Malaysia, and expressed their intention to explore potentials for future cooperation on infrastructure projects, which will strategically improve the connectivity of the regions involved, and eventually enhance the socio-economic development from the potential economic opportunities. This will include among others, transfer of technology, strengthening human capital development, consumption of local content and other long-term cooperation in the infrastructure industry.

12. Both sides looked forward to further enhancing bilateral trade and investment as well as economic exchanges. The initiative, among others, is through the Exchange of Notes to confirm the status of state-owned Institutions from each country under the Agreement between the Government of Malaysia and the Government of the People's Republic of China for the Avoidance of Double Taxation and the Prevention of Fiscal Evasion with Respect to Taxes on Income.

13. Both sides agreed that seaports play a vital role in regional infrastructure development. They will continue to promote cooperation between seaports in Malaysia and China and support the development of China-Malaysia Port Alliance to realize the vision of the 21st Century Maritime Silk Road.

14. Both sides spoke positively of fruitful cooperation in areas of combating telecommunication crime, overseas pursuit, counter-terrorism and agreed to further strengthen law enforcement and counter-terrorism cooperation, enhance friendly exchanges among law enforcement and security agencies in order to make contributions to safeguarding regional security and stability.

15. Both sides are pleased with the renewal of the "Memorandum of

Understanding on Bilateral Defence Cooperation." Malaysia and China believed that the continuous and incremental engagements and close rapport between the defence establishments will further strengthen the existing relations. Realising the importance of expanding defence ties between Malaysia and China, both sides welcomed the signing of the "Framework of Cooperation on Joint Development and Construction of the Littoral Mission Ship for the Royal Malaysian Navy (RMN)" between the State Administration for Science, Technology and Industry for National Defense of China (SASTIND) and Ministry of Defence of Malaysia (MINDEF).

16. Both sides agreed that the tourism industry has always been an important element of Malaysia–China people-to-people exchanges. Following the introduction of eVISA and eNTRI programmes in March 2016, Malaysia is seeing a growing number of inbound tourists from China to Malaysia. Both sides agreed to strengthen the joint marketing with airlines and travel agencies and promotion efforts such as consumer fairs and websites to further increase the number of tourist arrivals in both countries, which will consolidate Malaysia-China traditional friendship and understanding at the grassroots level. Both sides recognized the growing importance of e-commerce and online marketing for tourism promotions.

17. Malaysia and China reaffirmed their commitment to strengthen and work towards a more comprehensive and mutually beneficial air transport cooperation between the two countries.

18. Both sides welcomed the renewal of the Memorandum of Understanding on Cooperation in the Field of Education which will strengthen and make progress in educational exchanges between Malaysia and China. The establishment of Xiamen University Malaysia Campus marked a new milestone of tertiary education cooperation between the two countries. The University will provide talents for local community to strengthen the friendly ties between two countries.

19. Both sides shall endeavor to jointly implement the Agreement on Cultural Cooperation and the Cultural Executive Programme for 2014-2019, encourage the exchange of visits between the cultural institutions and groups,

and jointly support the establishment of the China Cultural Center in Malaysia.

20. Both sides discussed the prospect of strengthening imports of commodity products by China. Malaysia is ready to increase the exports of Malaysian palm oil to China and increase the market share for Malaysian palm oil in China.

21. Both sides expressed their intention to enhance cooperation in agriculture including trade of agricultural products, promote the investment in agriculture, and strengthen capacity building and communication in the field of agricultural science and technology through the signing of Memorandum of Understanding on Agricultural Cooperation.

22. Both sides also believed that the signing of Protocol on Inspection, Quarantine and Veterinary Hygiene Requirements for the Exportation of Raw-unclean Edible-Birdnest from Malaysia to China will increase Chinese consumers' confidence in Malaysian agricultural products and further promote trade in agriculture between both countries. Both sides hoped that more market access will be given to other Malaysia agricultural products pending approvals for inspection and quarantine access requirements in the future.

23. Both leaders appreciated China's commitment to support ASEAN Community-building towards the realization of ASEAN Community Vision 2025. The leaders welcomed the good progress in ASEAN-China cooperation and welcomed the celebration of the 25th Anniversary of ASEAN-China Dialogue Relations. Both sides also discussed the progress made in the implementation of the Plan of Action to implement the Joint Declaration on ASEAN-China Strategic Partnership for Peace and Prosperity for the period 2016-2020.

24. Both sides agreed to continue coordination and collaboration in regional mechanisms including ASEAN Plus Three (APT), East Asia Summit (EAS) and ASEAN Regional Forum (ARF).

25. Both sides exchanged views on the developments in the South China Sea and underscored the importance of maintaining peace, security and stability, as well as upholding freedom of navigation in and over-flight in the South China Sea, in accordance with international laws.

26. Both sides emphasised the need for all sovereign states concerned to

to resolve their differences by peaceful means through friendly consultations and negotiations, in accordance with universally recognised principles of international law, including the 1982 United Nations Convention on the Law of the Sea. Both sides further emphasised the need for all parties to exercise self-restraint in the conduct of activities, and to avoid actions that would complicate or escalate tensions in the South China Sea. Both sides recognised that the involvement of parties not directly concerned could be counter-productive.

27. Both sides, together with the ASEAN Member States, would work hard to ensure the full and effective implementation of the Declaration on the Conduct of Parties in the South China Sea (DOC) in its entirety, as well as pushing forward consultations to ensure the early establishment of a "Code of Conduct" in the South China Sea (COC) on basis of consensus.

28. Malaysia expressed appreciation for the excellent and constructive cooperation between Malaysia and China towards fulfilling the mandate of the United Nations Security Council during Malaysia's non-permanent membership of the Security Council.

29. Malaysia expressed its sincere appreciation for China's warm welcome and hospitality accorded to the Honourable Dato' Sri Mohd Najib Tun Abdul Razak and the Malaysian delegation during the Official Visit.

中华人民共和国和文莱达鲁萨兰国双边文件

Bilateral Documents between the People's Republic of China and the Brunei Darussalam

中华人民共和国与文莱达鲁萨兰国联合公报

（2004年9月22日）

一、应中华人民共和国主席胡锦涛邀请，文莱达鲁萨兰国苏丹和国家元首苏丹·哈吉·哈桑纳尔·博尔基亚·穆伊扎丁·瓦达乌拉陛下于2004年9月20至22日对中国进行工作访问。

二、访问期间，胡锦涛主席与苏丹陛下举行了会谈。两国领导人在诚挚友好的气氛中就加强双边关系及共同关心的地区和国际问题交换了意见。全国人大常委会委员长吴邦国会见了苏丹陛下。

三、双方对中、文建交13年来在政治、经贸、文化、教育、卫生、司法、防务等领域合作取得的进展表示满意。双方一致认为发展中、文友好合作符合两国和两国人民的根本利益，表示愿共同推动双边关系迈上一个新台阶。

四、双方强调1991年《建交公报》和1999年《联合公报》所确定的原则，包括相互尊重主权和领土完整以及互不干涉内政等原则，对两国友好关系发展具有重要指导意义。文方重申将继续坚定坚持一个中国政策，认为台湾是中华人民共和国不可分割的一部分。中方对此表示赞赏。

五、双方同意继续保持两国领导人经常交往，推动两国各层次官员交流。双方还一致同意拓展全方位合作，以增进相互了解与信任。为鼓励两国民间交往，双方对“中国与文莱友好协会”的成立表示欢迎。

六、双方注意到两国签署《高等教育合作谅解备忘录》和《最高法院合作谅解备忘录》，表明双方有关部门希望建立更加密切联系的意愿正不断加强。

七、双方同意加强经贸联系，扩大贸易和双向投资，争取2010年双边贸易额达到10亿美元。文莱承认中国的完全市场经济地位。

八、双方还一致认为两国有关部门签署《促进贸易、投资和经济合作谅解备忘录》将有利于两国政府加强和扩大农业、能源、旅游、交通、通讯和基础设施建设等领域的双边合作。双方对两国有关部门签署《避免双重征税和防止偷漏税的协定》表示欢迎。

九、鉴于工商界对经济发展的重要贡献，双方鼓励两国企业在已经确定的合作领域进行投资。双方欢迎中国企业参与文莱油气资源的勘探开发。

十、关于地区合作，双方赞赏中国与东盟关系近年来取得的显著进展，一致同意密切合作，共同推动中国东盟战略伙伴关系的发展。双方重申致力于中国—东盟自贸区的建设。双方同意通过现有的东盟与中、日、韩（10+3）合作机制进一步推动东亚合作。中方重申将支持东盟在东亚合作进程中继续发挥主导作用。在次区域合作方面，文方欢迎中方支持并参与地跨文莱、印度尼西亚、马来西亚和菲律宾的东盟东部增长区建设。

十一、双方表示将继续致力于维护南海地区的和平与稳定，与东盟其他国家一道落实《南海各方行为宣言》后续行动。双方还表示愿探讨在南海开展合作的途径。关于东北亚局势，文方赞赏中方在六方会谈中发挥的重要作用，认为会谈有助于维护地区和平、安全与稳定。

十二、双方同意加强两国在联合国、东盟地区论坛、亚太经合组织、亚欧会议、世界贸易组织以及其他国际和地区组织中的协调与配合，以进一步促进和平、稳定与发展。

十三、双方重申致力于打击一切形式的恐怖主义，主张反恐应采取综合措施，包括应设法解决产生恐怖主义的根源问题。双方还表示反对将恐怖主义与特定的民族或宗教相联系，并呼吁加强国际反恐合作。

十四、苏丹陛下对在华访问期间受到的热情友好接待表示感谢，并邀请中国领导人在方便的时候访问文莱。中国领导人接受了邀请，并期待着有机会访问文莱。

Joint Communiqué between The People's Republic of China and Brunei Darussalam

(22 September 2004)

I. At the invitation of President Hu Jintao of the People's Republic of China, Head of State of Brunei Darussalam H.M. Sultan Haji Hassanal Bolkiah Mu'izzaddin Waddaulah paid a working visit to China from September 20 to 22, 2004.

II. During the visit, President Hu Jintao had a meeting with H.M. Sultan. The leaders of the two countries exchanged views on strengthening the bilateral relations and on regional and international affairs in a sincere and friendly atmosphere. Chairman of the Standing Committee of the National People's Congress Wu Bangguo met with H.M. Sultan.

III. Both sides are satisfied with the progress in their cooperation on political affairs, trade, culture, education, health, justice and defense over the past 13 years since they established diplomatic relations. Both sides agreed that friendly cooperation between China and Brunei is in the interest of the two countries and their people. They said that they are ready to push bilateral relations up to a new stage.

IV. Both sides emphasized that the principles defined in the "Communiqué on the Establishment of Diplomatic Relations" of 1991 and the "Joint Communiqué" of 1999, including the principles of mutual respect of sovereignty and territorial integrity and non-interference of the other's internal affairs, are of guiding significance to the development of the friendly relations between the two countries. Brunei reiterated that it will continue to firmly uphold the one-

China policy and consider Taiwan an inseparable part of the People's Republic of China. China appreciates this.

V. Both sides agree to maintain frequent exchanges between leaders of the two countries and to promote exchanges between officials at various levels. Both sides agree to explore all-around cooperation to enhance mutual understanding and confidence. To encourage non-governmental exchanges between the two countries, both sides welcome the establishment of the "Association on the Friendship between China and Brunei".

VI. Both sides noticed that the two countries have signed the "Memorandum of Understanding on Higher Education Cooperation"and the "Memorandum of Understanding on Supreme Court", which demonstrates that the willingness of relevant agencies of the two countries to develop closer relations is being strengthened.

VII. Both sides agree to strengthen economic relations, expand trade and two-way investments, so that the bilateral trade volume can reach US$ 1 billion. Brunei acknowledges China's complete market economy status.

VIII. Both sides agree that the "Memorandum of Understanding on Enhancing Trade, Investment and Economic Cooperation" signed by related agencies of the two countries will help governments of the two countries to strengthen and expand the bilateral relations in areas such as agriculture, energy, tourism, transportation, communications and infrastructure construction. Both sides welcome the signing of the "Agreement for the Avoidance of Double Taxation and the Prevention of Fiscal Tax Evasion" between related agencies of the two countries.

IX. In view of the significant contributions made by the industrial and commercial communities to economic development, both sides encourage enterprises of the two countries to invest in identified cooperation areas. Both sides welcome Chinese businesses to participate in the exploitation of oil and gas resources in Brunei.

X. With regard to regional cooperation, both sides appreciate remarkable improvement in the relationship between China and ASEAN and agree on close cooperation in a bid to jointly promote the development of the China-ASEAN strategic partnership. Both sides reiterate being committed to the development of China–ASEAN free trade area. Both sides agree to further facilitate cooperation among East Asian countries through the current 10+3 cooperative mechanism between ASEAN, China, Japan and South Korea. In sub-regional cooperation, Brunei applauds that China supports and participates the development of Brunei–Indonesia–Malaysia – the Philippine East ASEAN Growth Area.

XI. Both sides express continued commitment to safeguarding the peace and stability in the South China Sea and to following up, with other ASEAN countries, the "Declaration on the Conduct of Parties in The South China Sea." Both sides express the willingness to discussing ways of cooperation in the South China Sea. With respect to the situation in northeast Asia, Brunei appreciates China's important role in the Six-Party Talks and is of the opinion that the talks will be helpful to maintaining regional peace, safety and stability.

XII. Both sides agree to strengthen coordination and cooperation between the two countries in the United Nations, ASEAN Regional Forum, APEC, ASEM, World Trade Organization and other international and regional organizations, so as to further promote peace, stability and development.

XIII. Both sides reiterate their commitment to fighting all forms of terrorism and propose that comprehensive measures be adopted in the fight again terrorism, for example, measures should be taken to tackle the root causes of terrorism. Both sides also express the objection to associating anti-terrorism with certain ethnic groups or religions, and appeal for strengthened international cooperation on anti-terrorism.

XIV. H.M. Sultan expressed his gratitude to China's warm and friendly hospitality during his visit, and invited China's leaders to visit Brunei at their convenience. The Chinese leaders accepted the invitation and look forward to the opportunity to visit Brunei.

中华人民共和国和文莱达鲁萨兰国联合新闻公报

（2005年4月21日）

应文莱达鲁萨兰国苏丹和国家元首苏丹·哈吉·哈桑纳尔·博尔基亚·穆伊扎丁·瓦达乌拉陛下邀请，中华人民共和国主席胡锦涛阁下于2005年4月20至21日对文莱达鲁萨兰国进行国事访问。

访问期间，胡锦涛主席与苏丹陛下举行了会谈。双方在亲切友好的气氛中就中文关系及共同关心的国际地区问题交换了意见，并达成广泛共识。

两国领导人对自1991年建交以来，中文关系取得的显著进展表示满意，认为双方在政治、经济、文化、教育、卫生、司法、军事等领域均进行了友好和富有成效的合作。双方重申将坚持互相尊重主权和领土完整、互不干涉内政的原则，共同推动中文睦邻友好合作关系取得更大发展。

双方一致认为保持高层交往和促进各层次的人员交流对两国关系发展具有重要意义。两国领导人对文莱—中国友好协会的成立表示欢迎，认为这将成为增进了解、扩大交流的新渠道。

双方同意加强经贸合作，进一步扩大贸易和相互投资，重申将致力于实现2010年双边年贸易额达到10亿美元的目标。两国领导人对双方企业为中文经贸合作作出的贡献表示赞赏。双方表示愿在能源领域保持长期合作，并进一步加强在交通、通讯和基础设施建设等领域的合作。

双方一致认为旅游业对促进国家经济发展、增加就业具有重要作用。双方同意在现有合作谅解备忘录的框架下加强合作，相互提供更多便利，促进两国往来游客数量的增长。

两国领导人对双方就互免持外交、公务护照人员签证进行换文表示欢迎，认为这将为两国官员的工作提供便利，并有利于双方开展更紧密的合作。

双方同意加强在卫生领域的合作，对两国卫生部门签署2005至2007年度卫生合作执行计划表示欢迎。

文方重申坚持一个中国政策，赞赏和支持中方为实现国家和平统一、维护台海和亚太地区和平稳定所作的努力。

双方高度评价中国与东盟友好关系近年来取得的积极进展，重申愿进一步加强合作，在中国与东盟战略伙伴关系框架下推动中国—东盟自由贸易区建设。中方重申支持东盟在东亚合作进程中发挥主导作用，文方对此表示欢迎，并感谢中方长期以来对东盟东部增长区建设的支持。

双方重申将继续致力于维护南海地区的和平与稳定，积极探讨在南海开展合作。双方同意与其他东盟国家共同落实《南海各方行为宣言》后续行动，并实施本地区的建立信任措施。

双方一致认为保持亚太地区和平与稳定对地区繁荣和发展至关重要，文方赞赏中方在维护朝鲜半岛和平稳定方面发挥的建设性作用。

双方同意继续加强在东盟地区论坛、亚太经济合作组织、亚欧会议、联合国、世界贸易组织及其他地区和国际组织中的协调与配合。

苏丹陛下感谢胡锦涛主席应邀访文。胡锦涛主席对访问期间文方给予的热情友好接待表示感谢，并邀请苏丹陛下和其他王室成员再次访华。

Joint Press Communiqué between the People's Republic of China and Brunei Darussalam

(21 April 2005)

At the invitation of His Majesty Sultan Haji Hassanal Bolkiah Mu'izzaddin Waddaulah, Sultan and Yang Di-Pertuan of Brunei Darussalam, His Excellency Hu Jintao, President of the People's Republic of China, paid a State Visit to Brunei Darussalam from 20 to 21 April 2005.

During the visit, President Hu Jintao held bilateral talks with His Majesty the Sultan.The two sides had an exchange of views and reached broad common understanding on bilateral relations and international and regional issues of common interest in an atmosphere of goodwill and friendliness.

Both sides expressed satisfaction with the remarkable progress of bilateral relation since the establishment of diplomatic relations in 1991, and recognized the friendly and effective cooperation between two countries in the political, economic, cultural, educational, health, legal, defense and other fields. Both sides reiterated their adherence to the principles of mutual respect for sovereignty and territorial integrity and non-interference in each other's internal affairs and their desire to push forward the development of China-Brunei good-neighborly, friendly relations of cooperation.

Both sides recognized the importance of maintaining high-level contacts and promoting exchanges between officials at all levels to the development of bilateral relations. The two leaders welcomed the establishment of the Brunei-China Friendship Association as another channel for deepening understanding and expanding linkages.

Both sides agreed to enhance economic cooperation and further expand trade and two-way investment, and recalled a commitment to reach a bilateral trade target of US$ 1 billion by 2010. The two leaders commended the contributions of the private sector to the bilateral economic cooperation. Both sides expressed their willingness to maintain long-term cooperation. Both sides expressed their willingness to maintain long-term cooperation in the energy sector and further strengthen cooperation in transportation, telecommunications and infrastructure.

Both sides recognized the significance of the tourism sector in generating economic and employment opportunities.

The two leaders welcomed the *Exchange of Notes on Mutual Visa Exemption for Diplomatic, Official and Service Passport Holders* and agreed that this will facilitate the work of officials from both sides and enable them to work more closely together.

Both sides agreed to intensify bilateral cooperation in the field of health, and welcomed the *Plan of Action on Health Cooperation* signed by health departments of the two countries for the period from 2005 to 2007.

The Brunei side reiterated its adherence to the One China policy, and expressed its appreciation of and support to China's effort for peaceful national reunification, peace and stability in the Taiwan Straits and in Asia-Pacific.

Both sides highly evaluated the positive development of friendly relations between China and ASEAN in recent years, and reaffirmed their commitment to strengthen cooperation and to work closer to promote a China-ASEAN Free Trade Area within the framework of the China-ASEAN strategic partnership. The Chinese side also reiterated its view that ASEAN should continue to play the primary role in conducting East Asian cooperation. The Brunei side welcomed this view and expressed appreciation for China's continued support in the development of the Brunei-Indonesia-Malaysia-Philippines—East ASEAN Growth Area(BIMP-EAGA).

Both sides reaffirmed their commitment to maintain peace and stability in the South China Sea and actively explore ways of cooperation in this region. They agreed to carry out the follow-up activities of the *Declaration on the Conduct of Parties in the South China Sea* together with the other ASEAN countries and expressed willingness to participate in confidence-building measures in the region.

Both sides recognized the importance of maintaining peace and stability in the Asia-Pacific to prosperity and development of the region. The Brunei side expressed its appreciation of the constructive role that China is playing in maintaining peace and stability in the Korean Peninsula.

Both sides agreed to further enhance the coordination and cooperation at the *ARF, APEC, ASEM, UN, WTO* and other regional and international organizations.

His Majesty expressed his appreciation to President Hu Jintao for accepting the invitation to visit Brunei Darussalam. President Hu Jintao expressed his appreciation for the warm hospitality accorded to him during the visit and extend invitations to His Majesty and other members of the Royal Family to visit China again.

中华人民共和国和文莱达鲁萨兰国联合声明

（2013年4月5日）

一、应中华人民共和国主席习近平阁下的邀请，文莱达鲁萨兰国苏丹和国家元首苏丹·哈吉·哈桑纳尔·博尔基亚·穆伊扎丁·瓦达乌拉陛下于2013年4月4日至7日对中国进行国事访问。访问期间，习近平主席同哈桑纳尔苏丹举行了双边会谈，国务院总理李克强、全国人大常委会委员长张德江分别会见了哈桑纳尔苏丹一行。哈桑纳尔苏丹还将赴海南省出席4月7日举行的博鳌亚洲论坛2013年年会开幕式并致辞。

二、在会谈会见中，中国领导人高度评价哈桑纳尔苏丹为中文关系发展所作重要贡献，特别提及2011年双方为庆祝两国建交20周年开展的重要活动。双方强调，应进一步加强中文传统友谊，传承两国间密切的历史文化联系。

三、两国元首重申了以1991年《中华人民共和国政府和文莱达鲁萨兰国苏丹陛下政府关于两国建立外交关系的谅解备忘录》、1999年和2004年《中华人民共和国与文莱达鲁萨兰国联合公报》和2005年《中华人民共和国和文莱达鲁萨兰国联合新闻公报》确立的原则和精神为基础，通过各领域合作深化双边关系的政治意愿。

四、两国元首重申，将相互尊重主权和领土完整，互不干涉内政。文方重申将继续坚持一个中国政策，支持两岸关系和平发展与中国和平统一大业，中方对此表示赞赏。

五、两国元首认为，中国和文莱互为重要合作伙伴，双方为实现共同繁荣与发展密切合作，为地区和平与稳定作出了贡献。在这一伙伴关系基础上，两国元首同意秉持友好和善意的精神，以和平共处五项原则、《东南亚友好合作条约》以及其他公认的国际法准则为指导，建立中文战略合作关系，以增进两国和本地区的和平、稳定与繁荣。

六、两国元首一致认为，应保持经常性双边交往，加强两国外交磋商、经贸磋商等各层次机制合作。两国元首指出，增进相互理解和政治信任，加强双边合作在两国关系发展中发挥着重要作用。

七、考虑到中文各自国内发展战略，两国元首同意进一步提升两国经贸合作水平，在交通、通讯、基础设施建设、金融等领域开展密切合作。两国元首鼓励双方企业探讨在基础设施建设等领域建立合资企业的机会。

八、两国元首对双方2011年11月签署的《中华人民共和国政府和文莱达鲁萨兰国政府关于能源领域合作谅解备忘录》表示欢迎，对双方此后在商业、炼油、石化及公私领域合作所取得的进展感到高兴。

九、两国元首特别提及2011年11月签署的《中国海洋石油总公司与文莱国家石油公司油气领域商业性合作谅解备忘录》，并对2013年4月2日在北京签署的中国海油与文莱国油合作协议表示欢迎，此举将继续深化双方在能源领域的合作。

十、两国元首同意支持两国有关企业本着相互尊重、平等互利的原则共同勘探和开采海上油气资源。有关合作不影响两国各自关于海洋权益的立场。

十一、两国元首同意，在2009年5月签署的《中华人民共和国农业部与文莱达鲁萨兰国工业及初级资源部农业合作谅解备忘录》和2012年4月签署的《中华人民共和国商务部与文莱达鲁萨兰国工业及初级资源部关于农业领域经贸合作的谅解备忘录》基础上，进一步加强在农业、清真食品、农业食品、水产养殖等领域的交流与合作。双方鼓励和支持本国企业按照市场化原则，在平等互利基础上扩大农产品进出口贸易。中方欢迎文方继续参与中国举办的各种博览会、交易会，包括每年在南宁举办的中国—东盟博览会。两国元首鼓励双方企业就在清真食品和渔业产业建立合资企业进行合作，共同拓展国际市场。

十二、两国元首回顾了2003年9月签署的《中华人民共和国国防部与文莱达鲁萨兰国国防部关于军事交流的谅解备忘录》，对双方现有防务安全合作表示满意。两国元首同意进一步深化防务安全合作，保持两军经常性互访，加强在人员培训、非传统安全领域及地区安全机制中的合作，进一步促进地区和平与稳定。哈桑纳尔苏丹赞赏中方一直以来对文莱国际防务展的支持，欢迎中方参与2013年6月在文莱举行的东盟防长扩大会框架下的人道主义救援和军事医学联合演习。

十三、两国元首支持双方加强人员往来，深化在打击跨国犯罪、执法能力建设、情报信息交流等领域的合作。

十四、两国元首提及2011年11月签署的《中华人民共和国卫生部和文莱达鲁萨兰国卫生部卫生合作2012年至2015年度执行计划》有关落实情况。两国元首强调，双方应重视加强在卫生普及、传染病预控、传统中医药、非传染性疾病防控、母婴健康、康复医疗、实验室服务和护理服务等领域的培训与研究合作。

十五、两国元首对两国在文化和体育领域的交流感到满意，同意进一步加强在相关领域的合作。

十六、两国元首强调，应根据2004年签署的《中华人民共和国教育部与文莱达鲁萨兰国教育部关于高等教育合作谅解备忘录》，继续保持教育领域交流与合作。两国元首鼓励进一步加强两国在教育领域的联系。

十七、两国元首同意根据2006年9月签署的《中华人民共和国政府和文莱达鲁萨兰国苏丹陛下政府旅游合作谅解备忘录》，加强双方旅游合作，为两国旅游业协会和旅游企业创造交流机会，学习借鉴对方管理经验，促进两国旅游产业发展。

十八、两国元首同意深化宗教领域的合作，继续开展两国政府宗教部门之间的互访交流。两国元首同意继续加强两国特别是伊斯兰教界在学术研究、朝觐、公益慈善等方面合作。

十九、两国元首认为，青年是两国经济社会发展的重要人力资源。鉴此，两国元首同意继续鼓励两国青年组织加强在包括中国—东盟合作框架等机制内的合作。哈桑纳尔苏丹欢迎赴文莱工作的中国青年志愿者为文莱汉语学习和医疗科学所作的贡献。

二十、中方赞赏东盟为维护地区和平、稳定与繁荣作出的努力，包括在推进东亚合作中发挥的重要作用。中方表示将继续为东盟共同体建设提供力所能及的支持和帮助，愿加强同东盟在10+3、东亚峰会等更广泛机制内的合作，共同维护东亚的和平、发展与繁荣。哈桑纳尔苏丹感谢中方长期以来为东盟发展和共同体建设所作的积极贡献。

二十一、中方祝贺文莱担任2013年东盟轮值主席国，将全力支持文莱办好包括东亚峰会在内的一系列重要会议。两国积极评价中国—东盟建立对话关系以来，特别是2003年建立中国—东盟面向和平与繁荣的战略伙伴关系后，中国—东盟合作所取得的显著成就，一致认为应继续拓展和深化中国与东盟在政治安全、经贸、互联互通、海洋、社会人文以及国际地区事务中的合作。

二十二、两国元首同意进一步加强在贸易、投资和经济合作等领域合作，包括开展项目合作或成立合资企业，共同为消除本地区贫困、推进东盟一体化作出积极贡献。哈桑纳尔苏丹对中方作为发展伙伴长期支持东盟东部增长区(文莱、印尼、马来西亚、菲律宾)发展表示赞赏。

二十三、两国元首认为，区域全面经济伙伴关系协定谈判的启动，充分展现了东亚各国加强经济合作、实现区域经济一体化的决心。两国元首强调，希望相关谈判本着开放、平等、互利的原则，尽早取得进展。中方表示，对所有有利于亚太地区经济融合和共同繁荣的合作倡议持开放态度。哈桑纳尔苏丹对此表示赞赏。

二十四、两国元首同意在联合国、世界贸易组织等国际场合继续加强在共同关心领域的磋商。哈桑纳尔苏丹赞赏中方为应对国际金融危机所作持续努力，希望中方继续支持东盟参与二十国集团事务。

二十五、两国元首重申，将继续致力于维护南海地区的和平与稳定，敦促有关各方继续保持克制，增进互信，加强合作。两国元首强调应由直接有关的主权国家根据包括1982年《联合国海洋法公约》在内的公认的国际法原则，通过和平对话和协商解决领土和管辖权争议。两国元首希望有关国家进一步落实《南海各方行为宣言》，朝最终制定“南海行为准则”而努力。

二十六、文莱达鲁萨兰国苏丹和国家元首感谢中方在访问期间给予他本人和代表团的热情友好接待，期待着习近平主席和其他中国领导人早日访问文莱。

Joint Statement between the People's Republic of China and Brunei Darussalam

(5 April 2013)

1. At the invitation of His Excellency Xi Jinping, President of the People's Republic of China, His Majesty Sultan Haji Hassanal Bolkiah Mu'izzaddin Waddaulah, Sultan and Yang Di-Pertuan of Brunei Darussalam, made a State Visit to the People's Republic of China from 4 to 7 April 2013. During the visit, His Majesty held bilateral talks with His Excellency Xi Jinping, and met with His Excellency Li Keqiang, Premier of China's State Council as well as His Excellency Zhang Dejiang, Chairman of the Standing Committee of China's National People's Congress. His Majesty will also attend and address the opening ceremony of the 2013 Annual Conference of the Boao Forum for Asia to be held on 7 April 2013 in Hainan Province.

2. At the bilateral meetings, the Chinese Leaders highly commended the significant contribution made by His Majesty on the development of China-Brunei Darussalam relations and noted the important initiatives that were undertaken by China and Brunei Darussalam to celebrate the 20th anniversary of the official establishment of China-Brunei Darussalam diplomatic relations in 2011. Both sides underlined the importance of further strengthening the long-standing friendship, reflecting the close historical and cultural ties between the two countries.

3. The Leaders reiterated their political will to deepen bilateral relations through cooperation in various fields, on the basis of the principles and spirit enshrined in the Memorandum of Understanding between the People's Republic

of China and Brunei Darussalam issued in 1991, the Joint Communiques issued in 1999 and 2004 respectively, as well as the Joint Press Statement issued in 2005.

4. The Leaders reiterated their mutual respect for sovereignty, territorial integrity and non-interference in each other's internal affairs. Brunei Darussalam reiterated that it will continue to adhere to the one China policy, and support the peaceful development of cross-Straits relations and the peaceful reunification of China. China appreciated the above-mentioned position.

5. The Leaders recognised that China and Brunei Darussalam are important partners working closely for common prosperity and development, contributing to regional peace and stability. On the basis of this partnership, the Leaders agreed to establish China-Brunei Strategic Cooperative Relationship aimed at enhancing peace, stability and prosperity of the two countries and the region, in the spirit of friendship and goodwill, as well as on the basis of the Five Principles of Peaceful Coexistence, the Treaty of Amity and Cooperation in Southeast Asia and other universally recognised norms of international law.

6. The Leaders agreed to maintain frequent exchanges and strengthen bilateral mechanisms including diplomatic, economic and trade consultations, at all levels. The Leaders noted that enhanced mutual understanding and political trust and bilateral cooperation have played an important part in developing the close relations shared by both countries.

7. In recognition of the two countries' domestic development strategies, the Leaders agreed to further promote the level of bilateral economic and trade cooperation and work closely together in transportation, communications, infrastructure and finance. The Leaders encouraged their respective enterprises to explore joint venture opportunities, particularly in infrastructure development.

8. The Leaders welcomed the signing of the Memorandum of Understanding between the Government of the People's Republic of China and the Government of His Majesty the Sultan and Yang Di-Pertuan of Brunei Darussalam on the cooperation in the Energy Sector in November 2011, and were pleased to note the increased cooperation between the two countries as a result of this, particularly in the areas of commercial cooperation, refining, petrochemicals and

public-private sector cooperation.

9. In this regard, the Leaders further noted the signing of the Memorandum of Understanding between China National Offshore Oil Corporation (CNOOC) and Brunei National Petroleum Company Sendirian Berhad (PetroleumBRUNEI) on Commercial Cooperation in the Oil and Gas Sector which was also signed in November 2011, and welcomed the signing of the Cooperation Agreement between CNOOC and PetroleumBRUNEI on 2 April 2013, in Beijing, which will continue to deepen cooperation in the energy sector between the two sides.

10. The Leaders agreed to support relevant enterprises of the two countries to carry out joint exploration and exploitation of maritime oil and gas resources following the principle of mutual respect, equality and mutual benefit. Such cooperation shall not be interpreted as to prejudice the position of the respective countries in relation to maritime rights and interests.

11. The Leaders noted the Memorandum of Understanding between the Ministry of Agriculture of the People's Republic of China and the Ministry of Industry and Primary Resources of the Government of His Majesty the Sultan and Yang Di-Pertuan of Brunei Darussalam on Agricultural Cooperation signed in May 2009 and the Memorandum of Understanding between the Ministry of Commerce of the People's Republic of China and the Ministry of Industry and Primary Resources of the Government of His Majesty the Sultan and Yang Di-Pertuan of Brunei Darussalam on Economic and Trade Cooperation in the Agriculture Sector signed in April 2012. In this regard, they agreed to further strengthen exchanges and cooperation in agriculture, halal food products, agrifoods and aquaculture. Both sides encouraged and supported their enterprises to increase the trade of agricultural products on the basis of market rules and equality and mutual benefit, and the Chinese side welcomed Brunei Darussalam's continued participation in various expositions and trade fairs held by China, including the annual China-ASEAN Expo held in Nanning. The Leaders encouraged enterprises of both countries to cooperate in developing ventures in the halal food industry and fisheries industry and the international market.

12. The Leaders recalled the Memorandum of Understanding on Military

Exchanges between the Ministry of Defence of Brunei Darussalam and the Ministry of National Defence of the People's Republic of China signed in September 2003 and expressed satisfaction with the existing cooperation in defence and security. The Leaders agreed to further deepen such cooperation through regular exchanges of visits, personnel training, cooperation in non-traditional security fields and in regional security mechanisms, in further promoting regional peace and stability. His Majesty extended his appreciation to China for its continued support of the Brunei International Defence Exhibition (BRIDEX) and welcomed its participation in the ADMM-Plus Humanitarian Assistance and Disaster Relief and Military Medicine Exercise (ADMM-Plus HADR and MM Ex) to be held in Brunei Darussalam in June 2013.

13. The Leaders also supported efforts to enhance bilateral personnel exchanges and deepen cooperation activities in fields such as combating transnational crimes, capacity building, and information exchange.

14. The Leaders noted with pleasure the implementation of the Plan of Action on Health Cooperation between the Ministry of Health of the People's Republic of China and the Ministry of Health of the Government of His Majesty the Sultan and Yang Di-Pertuan of Brunei Darussalam for 2012-2015 signed in November 2011. In this regard, the Leaders underlined the importance of continuing to cooperate in training and research in the fields of Health Promotion; Communicable Diseases Control and Surveillance; Traditional Chinese Medicine; Noncommunicable Diseases Prevention and Control; Maternal and Child Health; Rehabilitation Medicine; Laboratory Services; and Nursing Services.

15. The Leaders noted with satisfaction that cultural and sports exchanges between the two countries have been developing well and agreed to further strengthen cooperation in these areas.

16. The Leaders emphasised the importance of continuing exchanges and cooperation in education as highlighted in the Memorandum of Understanding between the Ministry of Education of the People's Republic of China and the Ministry of Education of Brunei Darussalam on Cooperation in the Field of Higher Education signed in 2004. Both Leaders encouraged further efforts in

promoting educational linkages between both countries.

17. The Leaders recalled the Memorandum of Understanding between the Government of the People's Republic of China and the Government of His Majesty the Sultan and Yang Di-Pertuan of Brunei Darussalam on Tourism Cooperation signed in September 2006. The Leaders expressed the need to continue to strengthen tourism cooperation to provide both countries with opportunities for exchanges between tourism organisations, travel agencies, and tour operators; learn from each other's management experiences, and enhance the development of their respective tourism industries.

18. The Leaders also agreed to deepen cooperation in the field of religion and maintain exchanges of visits between their respective religious affairs departments. The Leaders agreed to continue to strengthen such cooperation, especially among the Islamic communities, and for academic research, pilgrimage, public welfare and charity .

19. The Leaders regarded the youth as an important human resource for both nations' economic and social development. In this regard, the Leaders agreed to continue encouraging youth organizations of the two countries to foster closer cooperation including under the China-ASEAN framework. His Majesty welcomed the contributions of the young Chinese volunteers in the areas of Chinese language studies and health sciences in Brunei Darussalam's institutions.

20. The Chinese side appreciated ASEAN's efforts on maintaining regional peace, stability and prosperity, including ASEAN's major role in promoting East Asia Cooperation. The Chinese side expressed its continued support and assistance within its capacity to ASEAN's community building efforts, and strengthen its cooperation with ASEAN through wider regional mechanisms such as ASEAN Plus Three and the East Asia Summit (EAS), to jointly safeguard peace, development and prosperity in East Asia. His Majesty thanked China for its long-term positive contribution to ASEAN's development and community building process.

21. The Chinese side congratulated Brunei Darussalam for assuming the chairmanship of ASEAN of 2013, and pledged their full support to Brunei

Darussalam in the latter's efforts for several important occasions including the EAS. Both sides also spoke highly of the remarkable progress of China-ASEAN dialogue relations especially after the establishment of China-ASEAN Strategic Partnership for Peace and Prosperity in 2003. Both sides agreed to continuously expand and deepen the cooperation between China and ASEAN in political security, economic and trade, connectivity, maritime, social-cultural, and regional and international affairs.

22. The Leaders agreed to further strengthen cooperation in such fields as trade, investment and economic cooperation, including joint projects/ventures, and to make positive contributions to poverty eradication in the region and promotion of ASEAN integration. His Majesty expressed appreciation for China's continued support as a development partner in BIMP-EAGA (Brunei Darussalam, Indonesia, Malaysia, Philippines—East Asia Growth Area).

23. The Leaders believed that the launching of negotiations on the Regional Comprehensive Economic Partnership Agreement (RCEP) fully demonstrated the resolve of East Asian countries in strengthening economic cooperation and realizing regional economic integration. The Leaders stressed the need to make progress on the negotiations at an early date, in the principle of openness, equality and mutual benefit. His Majesty also expressed appreciation for China's open attitude towards all cooperative initiatives conducive to economic integration and common prosperity in the Asia-Pacific region.

24. The Leaders also agreed to continue enhancing consultations on areas of common interests in international fora, such as the United Nations and the World Trade Organization. His Majesty expressed appreciation towards China's continued international efforts in addressing the global financial crisis and expressed hope that China will continue to support ASEAN's participation in the G20.

25. The Leaders reaffirmed their commitment to maintaining peace and stability, the continued exercise of self-restraint by all parties concerned, and the promotion of mutual trust, confidence and cooperation in the South China Sea. They underscored the importance of resolving territorial and jurisdictional disputes through peaceful dialogue and consultations by sovereign states

directly concerned, and in accordance with universally recognised principles of international law, including the 1982 United Nations Convention on the Law of the Sea (UNCLOS). The Leaders looked forward to the further implementation of the Declaration on the Conduct of the Parties in the South China Sea (DOC), making efforts towards eventually formulating a code of conduct in the South China Sea .

26. His Majesty Sultan and Yang Di-Pertuan of Brunei Darussalam expressed his appreciation for the warm welcome and kind hospitality extended to him and his delegation during his visit to China, and looked forward to receiving His Excellency Xi Jinping and other Chinese leaders to Brunei Darussalam.

中华人民共和国和文莱达鲁萨兰国联合声明

（2013年10月11日）

一、应文莱达鲁萨兰国苏丹和国家元首苏丹·哈吉·哈桑纳尔·博尔基亚·穆伊扎丁·瓦达乌拉陛下邀请，中华人民共和国国务院总理李克强阁下于2013年10月9日至11日对文莱进行正式访问。李克强总理还出席了2013年10月9日至10日在文莱举行的东亚领导人系列会议。

二、访问期间，李克强总理与苏丹陛下举行了会谈，双方在和谐友好的气氛中就双边关系以及共同关心的地区和国际问题深入交换了意见。

三、双方对1991年两国建交以来双边关系取得的显著成就表示高兴。两国领导人回顾了中文之间密切的历史和文化联系，对两国长期以来的关系表示肯定。双方重申以1991年《中华人民共和国政府和文莱达鲁萨兰国苏丹陛下政府关于两国建立外交关系的谅解备忘录》、1999年和2004年《中华人民共和国与文莱达鲁萨兰国联合公报》、2005年《中华人民共和国和文莱达鲁萨兰国联合新闻公报》和2013年《中华人民共和国和文莱达鲁萨兰国联合声明》中确立的原则和精神为基础，通过各领域合作深化双边关系的政治意愿。

四、双方重申相互尊重主权和领土完整，互不干涉内政。李克强总理赞赏文莱继续坚持一个中国政策，支持两岸关系和平发展与中国和平统一大业。

五、双方认为，中国和文莱互为紧密的合作伙伴，双方为实现共同繁荣与发展密切合作，为地区和平与进步作出贡献。双方鼓励各自官员开拓思路，进一步加强2013年4月习近平主席和苏丹陛下一致同意建立的中文战略合作关系。

六、双方同意保持双边交往的频度，加强两国外交、政治、经贸等各层级的磋商机制。双方同意进一步加强在经贸、能源、基础设施、农渔业、防务、教育和人文交流等领域的合作。

七、双方对中文在能源领域，特别是中国海洋石油总公司(中国海油)与文莱国家石油公司（文莱国油）之间的现有合作表示满意，对中国海油与文莱国油近期签署关于成立油田服务领域合资公司的协议表示欢迎。双方鼓励各自官员根据2013年4月5日中文联合声明第十条所表述的原则为基础，探讨两国相关企业在其他方面共同勘探和开采海上油气资源。

八、双方注意到2003年9月两国签署《中华人民共和国国防部与文莱达鲁萨兰国国防部关于军事交流的谅解备忘录》后防务领域取得的积极进展，愿不断加强两军在高层互访、团组往来、人员培训等领域的交流与合作。苏丹陛下欢迎更多的中方防务人员赴文莱皇家国防学院进修。苏丹陛下感谢中方对2013年6月在文莱举行的第一届东盟防长扩大会议框架下人道主义救援、减灾和军事医学联合演习所作的贡献，以及出席2013年8月在文莱举行的第二届东盟防长扩大会议。苏丹陛下期待中方出席2013年12月在文莱举办的文莱国际防务展。

九、双方认为，人员交流以及教育、旅游、文化和体育领域的合作在增进两国人民友谊方面发挥着重要作用。

十、双方欢迎中方志愿者继续在文莱相关机构为文莱汉语教学、体育和医疗科学事业发展作出贡献。

十一、苏丹陛下赞赏中方对文莱担任2013年东盟轮值主席国工作的支持，以及为促进本地区和平、稳定、发展与繁荣所作贡献，赞赏中方支持东盟通过自身引领的东盟与中日韩（10+3）、东亚峰会（EAS）和东盟地区论坛（ARF）等机制，在不断演变的区域架构中发挥主导作用。

十二、李克强总理祝贺文莱成功举办第16次中国—东盟领导人会议，赞赏中国—东盟对话伙伴关系，特别是2003年中国与东盟建立战略伙伴关系以来取得的进展。双方积极评价中国和东盟战略伙伴关系10周年系列庆祝活动。苏丹陛下赞赏李克强总理在此次中国—东盟领导人会议上重申中国长期坚持与东盟致力于友谊和伙伴关系的睦邻友好政策。

十三、苏丹陛下赞赏中方提出的打造中国—东盟自贸区“升级版”、设立亚洲基础设施投资银行、启动中国—东盟海上合作基金支持项目等倡议，以加强中国与东盟的经贸、投资、互联互通、海上等领域合作。苏丹陛下同时高度评价中方作为“东盟东部增长区”发展伙伴，加大参与并支持次区域层面经济发展。

十四、双方重申，将继续在亚太经合组织、亚欧会议、联合国和世界贸易组织等其他地区国际场合就共同关心的问题加强磋商。苏丹陛下期待中方明年担任亚太经合组织东道主，赞赏中方为增强世界经济所作出的努力，希望两国继续密切合作，共同促进强劲、可持续和平衡发展。苏丹陛下还对中方支持东盟继续参加二十国集团峰会表示赞赏。

十五、双方强调应由直接有关的主权国家根据包括1982年《联合国海洋法公约》在内的公认的国际法原则，通过和平对话和协商解决领土和管辖权争议。双方重申将致力于全面有效落实《南海各方行为宣言》，维护地区和平、稳定和安全，增进互信，加强合作。双方欢迎2013年9月15日在中国苏州举行的落实《南海各方行为宣言》第六次高官会，及在落实《南海各方行为宣言》框架下就“南海行为准则”进行的磋商取得的积极进展，认为应以循序渐进和协商一致的方式稳步推进“南海行为准则”进程。

十六、李克强总理感谢文方在访问期间给予的热情友好接待，期待着苏丹陛下和文莱其他王室成员在不久的将来访问中国。

Joint Statement between Brunei Darussalam and the People's Republic of China

(11 October 2013)

1. At the invitation of His Majesty the Sultan Haji Hassanal Bolkiah Mu'izzaddin Waddaulah, Sultan and Yang Di-Pertuan of Brunei Darussalam, His Excellency Li Keqiang, Premier of the State Council of the People's Republic of China, made an official visit to Brunei Darussalam on 9–11 October 2013. His Excellency was also in Brunei Darussalam to attend the ASEAN Related Summits on 9–10 October 2013.

2. During the visit, His Excellency held talks with His Majesty and had an in-depth exchange of views on bilateral relations as well as on regional and international issues of common concern in a warm and cordial atmosphere.

3. The two sides expressed pleasure over the excellent progress in bilateral relations since the establishment of diplomatic relations in 1991. They reaffirmed the long-standing relations between Brunei Darussalam and China, reflecting the close historical and cultural ties between the two countries. They reiterated their political will to deepen bilateral relations through cooperation in various fields, on the basis of the principles and spirit enshrined in the Memorandum of Understanding between the People's Republic of China and Brunei Darussalam issued in 1991, the Joint Communiques issued in 1999 and 2004 respectively, the Joint Press Statement issued in 2005 and the Joint Statement issued in 2013.

4.The two sides reaffirmed their mutual respect for sovereignty, territorial integrity and non-interference in each other's internal affairs. His Excellency expressed appreciation for Brunei Darussalam's continued commitment to the One

China policy, as well as its support for the peaceful development of cross-straits relations and the peaceful reunification of China.

5.The two sides recognised that Brunei Darussalam and China are close partners working for common prosperity and development, contributing to regional peace and progress. In this regard, they encouraged their respective officials to look into ways to further strengthen the Brunei–China Strategic Cooperative Relationship, as agreed between His Majesty and President Xi Jinping in April 2013.

6. The two sides agreed to maintain frequent exchanges and strengthen bilateral consultative mechanisms at all levels, including diplomatic, political and economic consultations. They also agreed to further enhance bilateral cooperation in economics, energy, infrastructure, agriculture and fisheries, defence, education and people-to-people exchanges.

7. The two sides expressed satisfaction with the ongoing energy cooperation between Brunei Darussalam and China, in particular, between Brunei National Petroleum Company Sendirian Berhad (Petroleum BRUNEI) and China National Offshore Oil Corporation (CNOOC). They welcomed the recent signing of an agreement between PB and CNOOC, on a joint venture on oil field services. They also encouraged their respective officials to study other aspects of joint exploration and exploitation of maritime oil and gas resources by the relevant enterprises of the two countries on the basis of the principles set out in paragraph 10 of the Brunei Darussalam–China Joint Statement of 5 April 2013.

8. The two sides noted the positive progress made in defence cooperation facilitated by the *Memorandum of Understanding on Military Exchanges between the Ministry of Defence of Brunei Darussalam and the Ministry of National Defence of the People's Republic of China* signed in September 2003 and expressed their willingness to continuously strengthen exchanges and cooperation in such areas as high-level visits, delegation exchanges and personnel training between the two armed forces. In this regard, His Majesty welcomed more Chinese defence officials to study at the Royal Brunei Armed Forces Defence Academy. His Majesty appreciated China's contribution to the 1st ASEAN Defence Ministers' Meeting-Plus Humanitarian Assistance and

Disaster Relief and Military Medicine Exercise (ADMM-Plus HADR & MM Ex) held in June 2013 and participation in the 2nd ADMM-Plus in August 2013 in Brunei Darussalam. His Majesty also looked forward to China's participation in the Brunei International Defence Exhibition (BRIDEX) to be held in Brunei Darussalam in December 2013.

9. The two sides recognised the important role of people-to-people exchanges, cooperation in education, tourism, culture and sports in further strengthening relations between the peoples of Brunei and China.

10. The two sides welcomed the continued contribution of Chinese Volunteers in the areas of Chinese language, sports and health sciences in Brunei Darussalam institutions.

11. His Majesty expressed appreciation for China's support of Brunei Darussalam's ASEAN Chairmanship in 2013; contribution to the development and the promotion of peace, stability and prosperity in the region; and continued support for ASEAN's centrality in the evolving regional architecture through the various ASEAN-led processes, including the ASEAN Plus Three (APT), the East Asia Summit (EAS) and the ASEAN Regional Forum (ARF).

12. His Excellency congratulated Brunei Darussalam on the successful convening of the 16th ASEAN-China Summit and noted with appreciation the progress of ASEAN-China Dialogue Relations, particularly since the establishment of the ASEAN-China Strategic Partnership in 2003. The two sides lauded the various Commemorative Activities undertaken by ASEAN and China to celebrate the 10th Anniversary of the Strategic Partnership. In this respect, His Majesty commended His Excellency's renewed call for China's long-term good-neighbourly policy of friendship and partnership with ASEAN at the recent ASEAN-China Summit.

13. His Majesty expressed appreciation for China's initiative to upgrade the ASEAN-China Free Trade Area (ACFTA), set up an Asian infrastructure investment bank and launch a host of projects with support from the ASEAN-China Maritime Cooperation Fund, in an effort to boost trade and investment, connectivity and maritime cooperation between ASEAN and China. At the same time, His Majesty also valued China's growing involvement, as a development

partner of BIMP-EAGA, in supporting economic development at the sub-regional level.

14. The two sides reiterated their commitment to continue enhancing consultations on areas of common interest in other regional and international fora such as APEC, ASEM, the UN and WTO. His Majesty looked forward to China's Chairmanship of APEC next year. His Majesty expressed appreciation towards China's efforts to strengthen the global economy and hoped for Brunei Darussalam and China to continue working closely together towards promoting strong, sustainable and balanced growth. His Majesty also expressed appreciation for China's support for ASEAN's continued participation in the G-20 Summits.

15. The two sides underscored the importance of resolving territorial and jurisdictional disputes through peaceful dialogue and consultations by sovereign states directly concerned, and in accordance with universally recognised principles of international law, including the 1982 United Nations Convention on the Law of the Sea (UNCLOS). They reiterated their commitment to the full and effective implementation of the Declaration on the Conduct of the Parties in the South China Sea (DOC) in maintaining peace, stability and security, and promoting mutual trust, confidence and cooperation in the region. In this regard, they welcomed the positive outcomes of the 6th Senior Officials'Meeting on the Implementation of the DOC in Suzhou, China on 15 September 2013, including the official consultations on the Code of Conduct in the South China Sea (COC) within the framework of implementing the DOC. They noted that consultations on the COC should be pushed forward in a gradual and step-by-step manner, and on the basis of consensus.

16.His Excellency expressed his appreciation for the warm welcome and kind hospitality accorded to him and his delegation during the visit and looked forward to welcoming His Majesty and other members of the royal family to visit China in the near future.

中华人民共和国和印度尼西亚共和国双边文件

Bilateral Documents between the People's Republic of China and the Republic of Indonesia

中华人民共和国和印度尼西亚共和国联合新闻公报

（1999年12月3日）

应中华人民共和国主席江泽民阁下的邀请，印度尼西亚共和国总统瓦希德阁下于1999年12月1日至3日对中华人民共和国进行国事访问。

访问期间，江泽民主席同瓦希德总统举行了会谈，就双边关系以及一些共同关心的重大地区和国际问题进行了有益的探讨，并取得了广泛共识和谅解。双方一致认为，瓦希德总统对中国的访问取得了圆满成功，对未来两国关系的深入发展具有重要意义。

双方回顾了1990年复交以来两国关系的发展情况，对各领域合作取得的进展表示满意。双方认为，发展平等、互利、相互理解和相互尊重的中、印尼友好合作关系符合两国的根本利益。双方认为，加强两国友好合作关系有利于促进本地区和世界的和平、稳定与繁荣。

双方认识到，世纪之交，中、印尼两国关系正面临进一步改善和发展的重要契机。双方重申将以和平共处五项原则和万隆会议十项原则为基础，进一步巩固业已存在的传统友谊，共同致力于建立和发展长期稳定的睦邻互信全面合作关系。为此，两国外交部将尽快制订关于面向21世纪合作的框架文件。

双方认为，两国高层保持经常互访和接触有利于两国友好关系的健康稳定发展。双方同意充分利用业已存在的磋商机制，加强两国政府部门、议会、政党、军队及民间团体之间的友好交往，积极开展文化、教育、卫生、住房、体育和旅游等领域的合作，推动两国友好合作关系全面深入发展。

双方充分肯定两国在经贸合作方面所取得的成绩，同意进一步扩大在贸易、投资、科技、工业、农业、林业及种植业、渔业、能源、矿产、通信和金融等方面的互利合作。双方将共同致力于促进建立一个更加良好的经贸合作环境；增加贸易法规的透明度和非歧视性；鼓励双方企业界开展密切交往和多种形式的互利合作，并定期举行投资促进会。为落实两国领导人达成的合作意向，双方商定，明年上半年召开两国经贸联委会第五次会议，中方将尽早派企业家代表团访问印尼。

双方重申坚持相互尊重独立、主权和领土完整的原则。中方表示支持印尼政府在维护国家统一和领土完整方面的努力，认为印尼的稳定和繁荣有利于本地区的和平与发展。印尼方重申继续坚持一个中国的政策，并承认中华人民共和国政府是代表全中国人民的唯一合法政府，台湾是中国不可分割的一部分。

双方就当前地区经济形势交换了看法。中方高兴地看到，包括印尼在内的本地区有关国家经济复苏正取得积极进展。印尼方对中国自亚洲经济和金融危机发生以来所给予的不断支持表示赞赏。双方认为，亚洲国家应坚持自己的价值观，走符合本国实际的发展道路，并建立起更加广泛的合作，共同应对经济全球化带来的机遇和挑战。

双方对近年来中国和东盟友好关系不断发展并取得积极成果表示满意。中方赞赏印尼方为推动中国—东盟关系的发展所发挥的作用，支持印尼为进一步加强东盟的团结合作以及推动东盟在国际和地区事务中发挥更大作用所作的努力。双方重申将继续致力于中国—东盟睦邻互信友好合作关系的发展。双方对最近在马尼拉举行的东盟和中、日、韩领导人非正式会晤所取得的进展和重要意义给予高度评价，愿继续为推进对地区和平、稳定和繁荣至关重要的东亚对话与合作进程作出贡献。

双方认为，当前国际局势正在发生深刻的变化，多极化已成为国际关系发展的总趋势。双方强调，联合国宪章、和平共处五项原则、万隆会议十项原则和公认的国际关系基本准则应继续成为更加公正和平衡的国际政治、经济和安全新秩序的基础，必须得到所有国家的尊重。任何国家都无权以任何借口干涉其他主权国家的内部事务。 双方重申了人权普遍性原则应与各国国情、包括文化背景相结合的立场。双方认为，应基于合作、对话、非对抗精神和尊重国家主权和不干涉内政原则，在国际范围内就促进人权交换看法。

双方认为，人权问题不能通过牺牲国家主权和国家间主权平等的原则来解决，不能违背或破坏联合国本身赖以成立的原则。 双方支持制定普遍有效的准则，通过实施双边和多边协议来裁减武器，尤其是大规模杀伤性武器。如不履行此类条约，地区和世界和平与稳定将受到威胁。双方认为，反弹道导弹条约

（ABM）对于维护国际和平、安全与战略稳定具有重要意义。双方认为，东南亚无核武器区条约对促进地区与国际和平与稳定作出了重要贡献。中方重申愿签署该条约议定书。

双方重申将进一步加强在联合国、世贸组织、亚太经合组织、亚欧会议等多边场合磋商与合作。双方重申将继续支持发展中国家的团结合作和不结盟运动，为建立公正、合理的国际政治经济新秩序以及维护世界和平与稳定作出共同努力。

瓦希德总统对中华人民共和国政府和人民所给予的热情友好款待表示感谢，并邀请江泽民主席阁下早日访问印度尼西亚共和国，江泽民主席愉快地接受了邀请。

一九九九年十二月三日于北京

Joint Press Communiqué of the People's Republic of China and the Republic of Indonesia

(3 December 1999)

At the invitation of His Excellency Jiang Zemin, President of the People's Republic of China, His Excellency KH Abdurrahman Wahid, President of the Republic of Indonesia paid a state visit to the People's Republic of China from December 1 to 3, 1999.

During the visit, President Jiang Zemin and President Wahid held talks in which they conducted useful discussions on bilateral relations and major international and regional issues of common interest, and reached broad agreement. Both sides believe that President Wahid's visit to China is a complete success and is of important significance to deepened development of China-Indonesia relations in the future.

The two sides reviewed the progress of the bilateral relations following the resumption of diplomatic ties in 1990 and expressed their satisfaction with the progress made in all areas of cooperation. The two sides maintain that the friendly relations and cooperation on a basis of equality, mutual benefit, mutual understanding and respect conform to the fundamental interests of the two peoples and contribute to the peace, stability and prosperity both in the region and the world.

The two sides have come to the view that at the turn of the century, China-Indonesia relations are faced with important opportunities for further improvement and growth. The two sides reaffirmed their willingness to consolidate the existing traditional friendship on the basis of the Five Principles of Peaceful Coexistence and the Ten Principles of Bundung Conference, and reiterated their joint commitment to the establishment and development of a long-term and stable relationship of good-neighborliness, mutual trust and all-round cooperation. To this end, foreign ministries of the two countries will work out and sign a framework document on the 21st century-oriented cooperation at an early date.

The two sides believe that frequent exchange of high-level visits and contacts conduces to the sound and steady development of the bilateral friendly relations. The two sides agree to make full use of the existing forums of bilateral consultations, strengthen the friendly exchanges between government departments, parliaments, political parties, military circles and non-governmental organizations of the two countries, and intensify cooperation in such areas as culture, education, health, sports and tourism, so as to promote the all-round and indepth development of the bilateral friendly relations and cooperation.

The two sides fully endorse the achievements the two countries have made in trade and economic cooperation, and are willing to further expand their mutually beneficial cooperation in areas such as trade, investment, science and technology, industry, agriculture, fishery, energy, mining, telecommunication and finance. The two sides will make concerted efforts to promote a more conducive environment for better trade and economic cooperation, increase transparency and impartiality of trade related regulations, impel closer contacts and mutually beneficially cooperation of various forms between business communities of the two sides, and hold regular joint investment promotion. In order to materialize the intended cooperation agreed upon by leaders of the two countries, the two sides have decided through consultation that the fifth Sino-Indonesian joint economic and trade commission will meet in the first half of next year and that the Chinese side will send an entrepreneurs' delegation to Indonesia at the earliest possible date.

The two sides emphasize that they will adhere to the principle of mutual respect for independence, sovereignty and territorial integrity. The Chinese side supports the Indonesian Government in its efforts to maintain national unity and territorial integrity. The Chinese side holds that stability and prosperity in Indonesia is conducive to the regional peace and development. The Indonesian side reiterates that the Government of the People's Republic of China is the sole legal government representing the entire Chinese people, Taiwan is an inalienable part of the Chinese territory and that Indonesia will continue to pursue the one China policy.

The two sides exchanged views on the current regional economic situation. The Chinese side notes with pleasure that thanks to their efforts, Indonesia and other countries concerned in the region are making positive progress in their economic recovery. The Indonesian side appreciates the continuing support of China to Indonesia since the outbreak of the Asian financial crisis. The two sides believe that the Asian countries should uphold their own values, choose their development path in line with their actual national conditions, and conduct more extensive cooperation so as to jointly confront challenges brought by the economic globalization.

The two sides expressed satisfaction over the continuous development and positive results of China-ASEAN friendly relations in recent years. The Chinese side appreciates Indonesia's positive role in promoting the development of China-ASEAN relations and supports Indonesia in its efforts to enhance ASEAN solidarity and cooperation and push for a bigger ASEAN role in international and regional affairs. The Indonesian side reaffirms its continued commitment to a China-ASEAN friendly and cooperative relationship of good-neighborliness and mutual trust. The two sides highly evaluate the progress in the informal leadership meeting between ASEAN, China, Japan and ROK, and stand ready to contribute to the further progress of the East Asian cooperation process.

The two sides are of the view that profound changes are taking place in the international situation and that multipolarization is a general trend in establishing a more just and balanced world order. The two sides emphasize that the United Nations Charter, the Five Principles of Peaceful Coexistence and the universally-recognized basic norms governing international relations are the basis for a new international political, economic and security order, and should therefore be observed by all. No country has the right to interfere in other sovereign states' internal affairs under whatever pretext.

The two sides reaffirm their position that both the universality of human rights and the domestic conditions of each country should be respected. The two sides consider it essential to exchange views on the issue of human rights at the international level based on the spirit of cooperation, dialogue and non-confrontation as well as respect for state sovereignty. The two sides maintain that the human rights issues can not be solved by sacrificing the principle of state sovereignty and sovereign equality among nations as there must be a solution that does not demolish a principle on which the United Nations itself was founded.

The two sides support the endeavors of forging a universal and effective compliance with the implementation of the provisions of bilateral as well as multilateral agreements on the limitation and disarmament of weapons, in particular weapons of mass destruction. Failure to comply with these treaties will only threaten regional and global stability. The two sides agree that the Anti-Ballistic Missile (ABM) Treaty remains the cornerstone for the maintenance of international peace, security and strategic stability. The development of any Theater Missile Defense (TMD) system in the Asia-Pacific region is not conducive to strengthening the regional security. On the contrary, it will only impel arms race and result in increased tension, which is disadvantageous to regional peace, stability and development.

The two sides reiterate that they will strengthen their consultation and cooperation at UN, WTO, APEC, ASEM and other multilateral organizations, continue to support the solidarity and cooperation among the Third World countries, and the Non-Aligned Movement, and that they are willing to work together for the establishment of a fair and equitable new international political and economic order and for the maintenance of world peace and stability.

President Wahid thanked the Government and people of the People's Republic of China for the gracious hospitality, and invited President Jiang Zemin to visit the Republic of Indonesia at an early date. President Jiang Zemin accepted the invitation with pleasure.

中华人民共和国和印度尼西亚共和国关于未来双边合作方向的联合声明

（2000年5月8日）

中华人民共和国和印度尼西亚共和国（以下简称“双方”）自1990年8月8日恢复外交关系以来，两国间双边关系迅速发展，在各个领域的互利合作不断扩大。两国最高领导人、政府和人民为推动双方友好合作关系持续发展一直进行着不懈的努力。双方认为，在平等、互利、相互理解和相互尊重的基础上，巩固和加强中、印尼友好合作关系，符合两国的根本利益，有利于促进本地区和世界的和平、稳定与繁荣。

双方一致认为，世纪之交，中、印尼两国关系正面临进一步改善和发展的重要契机。为巩固业已存在的传统友谊，加强双方21世纪在各领域的合作，双方同意建立和发展长期稳定的睦邻互信全面合作关系。为此，双方同意共同制订一个未来双边合作方向的框架，并达成以下共识：

一、双方重申将以《联合国宪章》、和平共处五项原则、万隆会议十项原则、《东南亚友好合作条约》所确定的原则以及公认的国际法原则为基础，进一步加强双边关系，促进本地区和世界的持久和平、稳定与繁荣。

二、双方认为，两国高层保持经常互访和接触有利于两国友好关系的健康稳定发展。双方将加强两国政府机构、议会、政党、军队及民间团体之间的友好交往，鼓励两国政府各层次官员保持经常性的互访与交流。两国外交机构将定期举行外交磋商，并充分利用各种场合保持经常性的会晤。

三、双方同意充分利用业已存在的磋商机制，就双边和多边范围各领域的合作进行探讨。双方将继续保持并加强经贸技术合作联委会、科技合作联委会、双边领事磋商以及双边地区安全对话等机制。由双方外交部长牵头的中、印尼政府间双边合作联合委员会将作为两国政府间保持沟通和磋商的高层机制，从宏观上为两国各领域合作提供政策指导和导向。双方还认为，上述磋商论坛对双方在共同关心的双边、地区和国际问题上的相互理解和支持是必要的，并具有重要意义。

四、双方将在平等互利、公正合理、相互尊重、相互理解的基础上加强贸易、投资、科技、农业、畜牧业、渔业、医药卫生、工业、林业、能源、交通、矿产、电信及信息、金融、民间交往、青年及体育、旅游业、教育、司法协助、防务、政治和地区安全等领域的友好合作，以促进地区和世界的持久和平、稳定和繁荣。为此，双方将共同致力于：

（一）促进建立一个更具吸引力的、更有利以及更好的经贸合作环境。通过交换信息和加强协调，增加贸易法规的透明度和非歧视性。

（二）简化投资程序，定期举行投资促进会，推动双向投资不断发展，并提供切实保障。鼓励双方企业界开展密切交往和多种形式的互利合作，包括双方在第三国进行的经贸合作。

（三）采取建设性的政策，开拓有潜力并有利于双方的新的合作领域，发挥双方私营部门在开展各领域合作方面的积极、主动的作用。

（四）积极促进学术和技术交流，鼓励在包括信息技术在内的高新技术领域以及科技成果商品化方面的联合研究和开发。

（五）加强在农业、畜牧业、农业机械以及农产品加工等方面的互利合作，商谈签署《农业合作谅解备忘录》。根据两国《林业合作备忘录》，加强林业的交流与合作。

（六）为加强渔业合作，双方主管部门可直接对话，并就渔业合作达成一项互利协议或安排的可能性进行探讨。

（七）根据双方现有有关协定，进一步加强在工业和矿产开发方面的互利合作。

（八）加强金融领域的交流与合作，共同致力于改革和改进国际金融管理制度，为建立一个有利于各方的国际金融新秩序而继续努力。

五、双方愿共同努力并采取切实有效的措施，加强在两国同意的领域内的友好交流与合作。

（一）进一步促进在医学、医药特别是传统医药的研究和生产、消费者保护以及传染病预防与控制方面的合作。

（二）加强两国文化艺术交流与合作并尽早签署文化协定，双方分别建立友好协会，积极鼓励民间团体开展交往，并提供必要的便利。

（三）在平等互利的基础上积极促进旅游业合作，为两国人民保持经常交往提供便利，包括通过深入交换信息加强在旅游合作方面的联系，简化双方的签证手续，为吸引更多旅客首先讨论扩大两国间空中航线的可能性。

（四）充分利用双方各自优势，加强在城市规划、住房和公共设施建设以及环境保护方面的交流与互利合作。

（五）促进两国教育和学术界的交流与合作，通过双方的奖学金计划项目交换留学生，鼓励专家和学者之间保持经常交往，组织两国的研究人员、专家和学者开展共同研究。

（六）密切在青年、体育方面的交流与合作。

六、双方愿相互尊重对方的法律制度，密切司法交流，加强在打击跨国有组织犯罪、贩毒、走私、计算机犯罪、经济犯罪及其他犯罪活动中的执法合作。

七、双方将在联合国、世界贸易组织、亚太经合组织、亚欧会议、东盟、东盟地区论坛、东盟和中华人民共和国、日本、韩国领导人非正式会晤等多边场合，就共同关心的地区和国际政治、经济、安全等问题加强磋商与合作，促进地区和国际的和平与发展。

八、双方重申坚持相互尊重独立、主权和领土完整的原则。中方认为印尼的稳定、完整和繁荣有利于本地区的和平与发展，支持印尼政府在维护国家统一和领土完整、促进国内各民族和解以及平等基础上的和睦方面的努力。印尼方重申继续坚持一个中国的政策，承认中华人民共和国政府是代表全中国人民的唯一合法政府，台湾是中国不可分割的一部分并支持中国的和平统一进程。

九、双方对近年来中国和东盟友好关系不断发展并取得积极成果表示满意。中方赞赏印尼方为推动中国—东盟关系的发展所发挥的作用，支持印尼为进一步加强东盟的团结合作以及推动东盟在国际和地区事务中发挥更大作用所作的努力。双方重申将继续致力于中国—东盟睦邻互信伙伴关系的发展。

十、双方认为，在有关国家政府和人民的不懈努力下，本地区经济已逐步摆脱金融危机带来的负面影响，正在走向复苏。亚洲特别是东亚国家在经过必要的调整后，将继续成为世界经济最有活力、最有希望的地区之一。双方强调，亚洲国家应坚持自己的价值观，走符合本国实际的发展道路，并建立起更加广泛的合作，共同应对经济全球化带来的机遇和挑战。

十一、双方相信，尽管存在着风险与挑战，谋求和平、安全、稳定、繁荣与合作仍是本地区和世界形势的主流，多极化已成为国际关系发展的总趋势。双方强调，《联合国宪章》、和平共处五项原则、万隆会议十项原则和公认的国际关系基本准则应继续成为更加公正和平衡的国际政治、经济和安全新秩序的基础，必须得到所有国家的尊重。任何国家都无权以任何借口干涉其他主权国家的内部事务。

十二、双方重申了人权普遍性原则应与各国国情、包括文化背景相结合的立场。双方认为，应基于合作、对话、非对抗精神和尊重国家主权和不干涉内政原则，在国际范围内就促进人权交换看法。双方认为，人权问题不能通过牺牲国家主权和国家间主权平等的原则来解决，不能违背或破坏联合国本身赖以成立的原则。

十三、双方重申通过和平方式解决国际争端的重要性，呼吁亚太地区和全世界就促进信心和信任采取合作措施。双方认为，反弹道导弹条约（ABM）和东南亚无核武器区条约对于维护国际和平、安全与战略稳定具有重要意义。双方支持制定普遍有效的准则，通过实施双边和多边协议来裁减武器，尤其是大规模杀伤性武器。如不履行此类条约，地区和世界和平与稳定将受到威胁。

十四、双方重申将继续支持发展中国家的团结合作和不结盟运动，鼓励发展中国家平等参与国际事务并在新的世界秩序中占有自己应有的位置。

十五、双方承诺为促进双边关系的不断发展，为建立公正、合理的国际政治经济新秩序以及维护世界稳定与繁荣作出共同努力。如双方认为有必要，并应任何一方要求，两国外长将共同对此份关于未来双边合作方向的联合声明进行审查。该联合声明的解释和适用中如出现困难、分歧或争议，双方将在协商一致的基础上，通过友好磋商加以解决。

本声明于二〇〇〇年五月八日在北京签署。

Sino-Indonesia Joint Statement on Bilateral Cooperation

(8 May 2000)

Since the restoration of diplomatic relations between the People's Republic of China and the Republic of Indonesia (hereinafter referred to as "the two sides") on 8 August 1990, the bilateral relationship between the two countries has developed rapidly and their mutually beneficial cooperation has continued to expand in all areas. The top leaders, governments and people of the two countries have been working tirelessly for the continued development of the friendly relations and cooperation between the two sides. The two sides maintain that to consolidate and strengthen the friendly relations and cooperation on the basis of equality, mutual benefit, mutual understanding and respect between the two countries conforms to the fundamental interests of the two nations and contributes to peace, stability and prosperity in the region and the world.

The two sides are of the view that at the turn of the century China-Indonesia relations are faced with important opportunities for further improvement and growth. In order to consolidate the existing traditional friendship, strengthen bilateral cooperation in all areas in the 21st century, the two sides agree to establish and develop a long-term and stable relationship of good-neighborliness, mutual trust and all-round cooperation. To this end, the two sides have agreed to jointly work out a framework on future directions of bilateral cooperation and reached agreement on the following:

1. The two sides reaffirm their willingness to further strengthen the bilateral ties and promote lasting peace, stability, and prosperity in the region and the world on the basis of the United Nations Charter, the Five Principles of Peaceful

Coexistence, the Ten Principles of the Bandung Conference, the Principles enshrined in the Treaty of Amity and Cooperation in Southeast Asia, as well the universally-acknowledged principles of international law.

2. The two sides believe that frequent exchanges of high-level visits and contacts are conducive to the sound and steady development of the bilateral friendly relations. They will promote the friendly exchange of visits between government agencies, parliaments, political parties, the military and non-governmental organizations and encourage regular exchange of visits between government officials of the two countries at various levels. Their diplomatic institutions will conduct regular diplomatic consultations and make full use of various functions to hold meetings.

3. The two sides agree to take full advantage of the existing forums of consultations to explore ways of bilateral and multilateral cooperation in all areas. The two sides will continue to maintain and strengthen such mechanisms as the Joint Commission on Economic, Trade and Technical Cooperation; the Joint Commission on Science and Technology Cooperation; Bilateral Consultation on Consular Affairs and Bilateral Dialogue on Regional Security. The Joint Commission between the Governments of China and Indonesia headed by the two Foreign Ministers of the two sides will serve as a high-level mechanism for communication and consultations between the two Governments and provide policy guidance and directions at macro level to bilateral cooperation in various fields. Both sides also consider it important and relevant to have these forums for consultation as a venue to gain mutual understanding and support on bilateral, regional and international issues of mutual interest to the two sides.

4. The two sides will increase their friendly cooperation in such areas as trade, investment, science and technology, agriculture, animal husbandry, fishery, health and medicine, industry, forestry, energy, transportation, mining, telecommunications and information, finance, people-to-people contacts, youth and sports, tourism, education, legal assistance, defense, and political and regional security on the basis of equality and mutual benefit, fairness and justice, and mutual respect and mutual under-standing, with a view to promoting lasting peace, stability and prosperity of the region and the world.

To this end, the two sides will be jointly committed to:

A. Promote a more attractive, more favorable and better environment for economic cooperation and trade; increase transparency and impartiality of trade-related regulations through the exchange of information and the increased coordination;

B. Simplify investment procedures, hold regular investment promotion activities, and facilitate the continued growth of two- way investment with practical safeguards; encourage closer contacts and mutually beneficial cooperation of various forms between business communities of the two sides, including bilateral economic cooperation and trade in a third country;

C. Adopt a constructive policy, open up and expand new areas with potentials for mutually beneficial cooperation, and allow their private sectors to play an active and positive role in cooperation in all areas;

D. Actively facilitate academic and technological exchanges and encourage joint research and development projects in high-and new-tech areas, including information technology, as well as the commercialization of scientific and technological achievements;

E. Strengthen the mutually beneficial cooperation in such areas as agriculture, animal husbandry, agricultural machinery and the processing of agricultural produce, sign a memorandum of understanding (MOU) on agricultural cooperation through consultation; enhance exchanges and cooperation in forestry in accordance with the MOU on Forestry Cooperation between the two countries;

F. Strengthen fishery cooperation and explore the possibility of concluding a mutually beneficial agreement or arrangement on fishery cooperation through the direct dialogue between the competent authorities of the two sides;

G. Further enhance the mutually beneficial cooperation in industry and the development of mineral resources in accordance with the relevant existing agreements concluded by the two sides;

H. Strengthen the exchanges and cooperation in the financial area, jointly commit themselves to reforming and improving the international financial regulatory regime; make continued efforts to establish a new international financial order favorable to all sides.

5. The two sides are ready to work together and take practical and effective measures to enhance their friendly exchanges and cooperation in the areas agreed upon by the two countries.

A. Further promote cooperation in medical science and medicine, especially in the research and production of traditional medicine, protection of consumers as well as the prevention and control of infectious diseases;

B. Enhance exchanges and cooperation between the two countries in culture and arts, conclude a cultural agreement at an early date, reciprocally establish friendship associations between the two sides, actively encourage exchanges between non-governmental organizations, and provide necessary facilities to this end;

C. Actively promote cooperation in tourism on the basis of equality and mutual benefit and provide facilities for regular exchanges between the two peoples, including developing closer links for tourism cooperation through an in-depth exchange of information, simplifying visa procedures between the two sides and initially discussing the possibility of new flight routes across the two countries in an effort to attract more tourists;

D. Make full use of their respective advantages and step up their exchanges and mutually beneficial cooperation in city planning, housing, construction of public facilities and environmental protection;

E. Facilitate exchanges and cooperation between their educational and academic communities, exchange students through scholarship programs provided by the two sides, encourage regular exchanges between experts and scholars; and organize joint research between the academicians, experts or scholars of the two sides;

F. Work for increased exchanges and cooperation in youth activities and sports.

6. The two sides will respect each other's legal systems, enhance their judicial exchanges and strengthen their law enforcement cooperation in combating organized cross-border crimes, drug-trafficking, smuggling, cyber-crimes, economic crimes, and other criminal activities.

7. The two sides will strengthen their consultation and cooperation at UN,

WTO, APEC, ASEM, ASEAN, ARF, the Informal Leadership Meeting between ASEAN and the People's Republic of China, Japan, the Republic of Korea and other multilateral organizations on regional and international political, economic, security and other issues of common interest, thus promoting peace and development in the region and the world.

8. The two sides reiterate their commitment to the principles of mutual respect for independence, sovereignty and territorial integrity. The Chinese side holds that Indonesia's stability, integrity and prosperity are conducive to peace and development in the region, and supports the Indonesian Government in its efforts to maintain national unity and territorial integrity and to facilitate ethnic reconciliation and promote harmony in the country on the basis of equality. The Indonesian side reiterates its continuing adherence to the One China policy and its recognition that the Government of the People's Republic of China is the sole legal government representing the entire Chinese people and that Taiwan is an inalienable part of China and supports the process of peaceful reunification of China.

9. The two sides are satisfied with the continuous development of China-ASEAN friendly relations and the positive results achieved in recent years. The Chinese side appreciates the role Indonesia plays in promoting the development of China-ASEAN relations and supports its efforts in enhancing ASEAN solidarity and cooperation and pushing for a bigger ASEAN role in international and regional affairs. The two sides reaffirm their continued commitment to a China-ASEAN partnership of good-neigh-borliness and mutual trust.

10. The two sides are of the view that thanks to the unremitting efforts of the governments and peoples of the relevant countries, the economies in the region have gradually freed themselves from the harmful effect of the financial crisis and are now on their way to recovery. Asia, East Asian countries in particular, after necessary economic restructuring, will continue to be one of the most dynamic and promising regions in the world economy. The two sides stress that Asian countries should uphold their own values, choose their development path suited to their actual national conditions, and conduct more extensive cooperation so as to jointly respond to opportunities and challenges brought by

the economic globalization.

11. The two sides believe that in face of the risks and challenges, to seek peace, security, stability, prosperity and cooperation remains the main trend in the region and the world at large, and multi-polarization has become a general trend in international relations. The two sides emphasize that the United Nations Charter, the Five Principles of Peaceful Coexistence, the Ten Principles of the Bandung Conference and the universally recognized basic norms governing international relations should continue to be the basis of a just and more balanced new international political, economic and security order, and should therefore be observed by all nations. No country has the right to interfere in the internal affairs of other sovereign states under any pretext.

12. The two sides reaffirm their position that both the principle of universality of human rights and the national particularities of each country, including its cultural background, should be respected. They consider it essential to exchange views on the promotion of human rights at the international level in the spirit of cooperation, dialogue and non-confrontation as well as respect for the principles of state sovereignty and non-interference in each other's internal affairs. They maintain that human rights issues must not be solved at the expense of the principles of state sovereignty and sovereign equality among nations or in contravention or violation of the principles on which the United Nations itself was founded.

13. The two sides reaffirm the importance of resolving international disputes by peaceful means and call on the Asian-Pacific countries and the rest of the world to take cooperative measures to build up confidence and trust. The two sides agree that the Anti-Ballistic Missiles (ABM) Treaty and the Treaty on the Southeast Asia Nuclear-Weapon-Free Zone play an important role in maintaining international peace, security and strategic stability. The two sides support the endeavors of forging a universal and effective compliance with the implementation of the provisions of bilateral as well as multilateral agreements on disarmament, disarmament of weapons of mass destruction in particular. Failure to comply with these treaties will only threaten regional and global peace and stability.

14. The two sides reaffirm that they will continue to support the solidarity and cooperation among developing countries, and the Non-Aligned Movement, and encourage developing countries to participate in international affairs on an equal footing and to seek an appropriate place in the new international order.

15. The two sides undertake to work together for the continued development of the bilateral relationship, the establishment of a fair and equitable new international political and economic order and the maintenance of world stability and prosperity. The Ministers of Foreign Affairs of the two countries will jointly review this Joint Statement on the Future Directions of Bilateral Cooperation if the two sides deem it necessary and at the request of either side. Any difficulty, differences and disputes regarding the interpretation and application of this Joint Statement which may arise, shall be resolved by the two sides on the basis of consensus through friendly consultation.

Done in Beijing, this 8th day of May, Two Thousand.

中华人民共和国与印度尼西亚共和国关于建立战略伙伴关系的联合宣言

（2005年4月25日）

为纪念中华人民共和国和印度尼西亚共和国建交五十五周年、万隆会议召开五十周年、联合国成立六十周年，我们作为中国和印度尼西亚共和国国家元首，共同回顾了双边关系发展历程。

我们一致认为，中国和印尼已成为重要的合作伙伴。作为两个发展中大国，我们应从战略高度处理长远利益，把两国关系推上一个新高度，造福两国和两国人民，并为发展中国家的团结合作和人类的和平发展事业作出新的贡献。

为此，我们同意建立中华人民共和国与印度尼西亚共和国战略伙伴关系。

这一战略伙伴关系应是不结盟、非排他的关系，旨在促进两国和两国人民的和平、稳定与繁荣。这一战略伙伴关系应以《联合国宪章》、和平共处五项原则、万隆会议十项原则、《东南亚友好合作条约》以及其他公认的国际法为准则。

这一战略伙伴关系应是加强中国—东盟战略伙伴关系的重要支柱，也是发展中国家南南合作的重要组成部分。这一战略伙伴关系应成为区域、跨区域及国际论坛和组织开展密切协调与合作的一个基础，旨在致力于建立全面、互利的纽带，迎接新千年的挑战，并促进地区和世界的和平、稳定与繁荣。

这一战略伙伴关系应以加强政治与安全合作、深化经济与发展合作、促进社会文化合作、扩大民间交往为主要内涵。

为此，我们达成以下共识：

一、政治与安全合作

（一）加强高层经常性互访与沟通，促进相互接触与联系，推动双方就共同关心和关注的双边、地区和国际问题开展对话：

1. 建立国务委员和统筹部长级别的对话机制，加强中印尼关系与双方合作；

2. 巩固由两国外长牵头的中印尼政府间双边合作联委会在协调与审议现有对话机制方面的作用；

3. 加强中印尼高官级磋商在落实双边各级对话机制所作决定方面的作用，并探讨需要时在双方达成一致的基础上在各个合作领域增设适当级别的机制；

4. 鼓励中印尼立法机关直接交往，并在东盟议会组织、亚洲议会和平协会、各国议会联盟等国际议会组织中保持协调与合作。

（二）继续促进两国在相互尊重独立、主权和领土完整原则上的相互理解、相互支持。中国支持印度尼西亚共和国政府为维护国家统一和领土完整所作的努力。印尼重申继续奉行一个中国政策，承认中华人民共和国政府是代表全中国的唯一合法政府，台湾是中国不可分割的一部分。印尼支持中国的和平统一进程。

（三）继续致力于联合国系统的有效改革与民主化进程，推动多边主义，增强联合国在维护和促进国际和平、安全及可持续发展方面的作用，并保障发展中国家在联合国决策过程中拥有更大的参与权和共享权。

（四）通过亚非新型战略伙伴关系加强与亚非国家的合作，加强与不结盟运动国家和77国集团的合作，共同应对全球化和不断变化的世界环境所带来的挑战，确保发展中国家在全球化进程中充分受益。

（五）再次肯定东盟通过建设东盟共同体在促进地区合作方面发挥的作用，再次肯定中国通过参与东盟东部增长区等项目在支持东盟工作方面发挥的作用。

（六）共同鼓励所有核武器国家签署《东南亚无核武器区条约》议定书。一俟有关各方就议定书遗留问题达成各方均能接受的解决方案，中国将尽快签署《东南亚无核武器区条约》议定书。

（七）推动落实《南海各方行为宣言》，使南中国海成为合作平台和友谊桥梁。

（八）促进双方在防务和军事领域的互信，推动各自国防工业发展，积极探讨建立防务安全磋商机制。

（九）鼓励双方执法和情报部门间开展合作，通过落实现有合作协议，共同应对恐怖主义、走私、贩毒、贩卖人口、洗钱、网络犯罪及其他跨国有组织犯罪活动等非传统安全问题，并积极探讨建立磋商机制，根据各自国家法律促进其他适宜领域的合作。

（十）密切开展海上合作，提升能力建设，建立海上问题磋商与合作机制。

（十一）加强在打击各种形式的恐怖主义方面的合作。两国反对将恐怖主义与特定的宗教和民族相联系，主张反恐行动应完全遵循《联合国宪章》的宗旨和原则以及其他公认的国际法准则。

二、经济和发展合作

（十二）进一步推动双边、地区和国际合作，本着平等互利、优势互补、形式多样的原则保持经济持续增长，促进双方经济伙伴关系和经济独立。

（十三）加强与国际组织的合作，确保发展中国家在公正、平衡的情况下从多边贸易体系和贸易自由化进程中充分受益。双方强调在实现联合国千年发展目标和其他国际上达成一致的发展目标上进行合作的重要性。

（十四）加快落实《中国—东盟全面经济合作框架协议》，开放并推动货物和服务贸易，创建透明、自由、便利的投资制度。

（十五）巩固双方经贸科技联委会机制，探讨各领域合作的新思路、新途径、新方式。

（十六）促进投资合作，加强双方投资部门及私营企业间的相互了解和联系，创造更有利的经济、社会、政治和法律环境，保证投资流动。

（十七）发展各自中小企业，开展资助、人力资源开发、扩大市场准入的合作，并拓展其他可能开展合作的领域。

（十八）促进金融稳定，加强在培育资本市场，完善资金流动预警机制方面的技术互助。

（十九）加快落实现有机制，加强农业、林业和渔业领域合作，提高上述领域人力资源开发、科技开发、技术援助、生产率和多样化、可持续管理和能力建设的水平。加强双方在打击非法伐木、非法捕鱼方面的合作。

（二十）加强能源政策的对话与磋商，进一步发挥中印尼能源论坛的作用，开展政策交流，加强油气和矿产领域的交流与合作，鼓励更多企业参与联合能源资源勘探开发，建立商业上可行的本地区能源运输网络，推动能源的可持续发展，包括开发可再生能源、提高能源利用率、节约能源以及和平利用核能。

（二十一）加强道路、桥梁、港口、电力、通讯等基础设施建设的合作。印尼欢迎中国参与这一领域合作。两国也强调有必要充分利用现有机制，并探讨在陆、海、空交通运输领域扩大合作。

（二十二）加强科技合作，在食品、以生物技术为重点的医药、能源、交通、信息、通讯和国防领域开展人力资源开发和联合研究。

（二十三）推动两国政府、民间组织和公众在环境保护领域的交流与合作。

三、社会文化合作

（二十四）在平等、公正的基础上重视人权和基本自由，遵循《联合国宪章》和其他国际人权文件的原则，致力于在社会各层面和国际社会中保护上述人权和自由。

（二十五）促进文化相互尊重，开展双方旅游、艺术、新闻、体育、青年团体和民间组织的合作，确保中印尼友谊世代相传。

（二十六）加强教育合作，积极开展培训交流，鼓励相互教学对方语言。

（二十七）加强流行性和非流行性疾病防治的合作和能力建设。

（二十八）加强在预防和处理自然灾害方面的区域和跨区域合作，建立先进的预警、紧急救助和灾后重建机制。

本宣言于二〇〇五年四月二十五日在雅加达签订，一式两份，每份均以中文、印尼文和英文写成，三种文本同等作准。

Joint Declaration between the People's Republic of China and the Republic of Indonesia on Strategic Partnership

(25 April 2005)

In commemoration of the 55th anniversary of the establishment of diplomatic relations between the Republic of Indonesia and the People's Republic of China, the 50th anniversary of the Asian–African Conference, and the 60th anniversary of the United Nations, we, the Heads of State of the Republic of Indonesia and the People's Republic of China, have reviewed the development of bilateral relations between our two countries.

We agree that Indonesia and China have become important partners for cooperation and that, as two major developing countries, we should develop a strategic perspective in addressing our long-term interests and take our relations to a new level to the benefit of our two countries and peoples as well as to make new contributions to solidarity and cooperation among the developing countries and to peace and development of mankind.

In view of this, we hereby agree to the establishment of the Strategic Partnership between the Republic of Indonesia and the People's Republic of China.

The Strategic Partnership shall be a non-aligned and non-exclusive relationship aimed at promoting peace, stability and prosperity of the two countries and its peoples.

The Strategic Partnership shall conform to principles set out in the UN Charter, the Five Principles of Peaceful Coexistence, the Ten Principles of the Asian–African Conference, the Treaty of Amity and Cooperation in Southeast Asia, and other universally recognized norms of international law.

The Strategic Partnership shall be an important pillar in strengthening

ASEAN–China strategic partnership as well as a critical component of South-South cooperation among developing countries.

The Strategic Partnership shall provide a basis for close coordination and cooperation in regional, inter regional, and international fora and organizations with a view to building comprehensive and mutually beneficial ties in meeting the challenges of the new millennium and strengthening regional and international peace, stability and prosperity.

The Strategic Partnership shall focus on strengthening political and security cooperation, deepening economic and development cooperation, enhancing socio-cultural cooperation, and expanding non-governmental exchanges.

To these ends, we have agreed as follows:

A. Political and Security Cooperation

1.To increase regular high-level bilateral exchanges and interactions as a means to improve contacts and communications as well as promote dialogue on bilateral, regional and international topics of common interests and concerns, through;

a. Establishing a dialogue mechanism at the State Councillor/Coordinating Minister level for greater relations and cooperation between Indonesia and China;

b. Consolidating the Indonesia–China Joint Commission for Bilateral Cooperation (JCBC), headed by the Foreign Ministers of both countries, in coordinating and reviewing activities within existing Indonesia–China dialogue mechanisms;

c. Strengthening the role of Indonesia–China consultations at the Senior Officials level in implementing decisions made at each levels of bilateral dialogue mechanism as well as in exploring, if and when necessary and based on mutual consensus, the need for additional mechanisms at appropriate levels in various areas of cooperation; and

d. Encouraging exchanges and direct contacts between the legislative bodies of Indonesia and China and their coordination and cooperation within international parliamentary organizations such as the ASEAN Inter-Parliamentary

Organization (AIPO), the Association of Asian Parliaments for Peace (AAPP), and the Inter-Parliamentary Union (IPU).

2.To continuously promote mutual understanding and support in our commitment to the principles of mutual respect for independence, sovereignty and territorial integrity of both countries. China supports the Government of the Republic of Indonesia in its efforts to maintain national unity and territorial integrity. Indonesia reiterates its continuing adherence to the one China policy and its recognition that the Government of the People's Republic of China is the sole legal government representing all of China and that Taiwan is an inalienable part of China and supports the process of peaceful reunification of China.

3.To sustain efforts towards the effective reform and greater democratization of the UN system, with a view to promote multilateralism, reinforce the role of the UN in maintaining and promoting international peace and security and sustainable development, as well as ensure greater participation for and share among developing countries in its decision-making processes.

4.To strengthen cooperation with Asian and African countries through the New Asian–African Strategic Partnership (NAASP) as well as with countries of the Non-Aligned Movement (NAM) and the Group of 77 in facing the challenges of globalization and the changing world environment and in ensuring that developing countries fully share the benefits of globalization.

5.To reaffirm the role of ASEAN in developing regional cooperation through the pursuit of the ASEAN Community as well as the role of China in sustaining the efforts of ASEAN through programs such as BIMP–EAGA.

6.To cooperate in encouraging all Nuclear Weapon states to sign the Protocol to the Treaty on the Southeast Asia Nuclear Weapons-Free Zone. China will sign the Protocol as soon as possible once a solution to the unresolved question on the Protocol is reached and accepted by all parties concerned.

7. To enhance the implementation of the Declaration on the Conduct of Parties in the South China Sea as a means to make the South China Sea a platform for cooperation and a bridge of friendship.

8. To promote mutual confidence and trust in defense and military fields with a view to developing each other's defense industries and actively exploring

the possibility of setting up defense and security consultation mechanism.

9.To encourage cooperation among law enforcement and intelligence agencies in addressing non-traditional security issues such as terrorism, smuggling, drug-trafficking, trafficking of persons, money laundering, cyber crime, and other transnational organized crimes through implementing existing cooperation agreements; actively exploring the possibility of setting up a consultation mechanism; and promoting other areas of cooperation where appropriate and in accordance with the national laws of the respective countries.

10. To work closely in maritime issues through enhancing capacity-building and setting up a mechanism for maritime consultation and cooperation.

11. To strengthen cooperation in the fight against terrorism in all its forms and manifestations. Both countries are against linking terrorism with a particular religion and ethnic group and maintain that the campaign against terrorism should be conducted in full conformity with the purposes and principles of the Charter of the United Nations and in accordance with universally recognized norms of international law.

B. Economic and Development Cooperation

12.To promote greater cooperation at the bilateral, regional and international levels in sustaining economic growth under the principles of equality, mutual benefit, complementarities and diversity in order to both enhance economic partnership and establish economic independence.

13.To strengthen cooperation within international organizations to ensure that developing countries fully reap the benefits of the multilateral trading system and process of trade liberalization in a fair and balanced manner. The two countries stress the importance of strengthening cooperation in realizing the UN Millennium Goals and other internationally agreed development goals and targets.

14.To expedite the implementation of the ASEAN-China Framework Agreement on Comprehensive Economic Cooperation as a means to liberalize and promote trade in goods and services as well as create a transparent, liberal and facilitating investment regime.

15.To consolidate the Joint Commission on Economic, Trade and Technical

Cooperation with a view to exploring new concepts, approaches and modalities of various areas of cooperation.

16.To enhance investment cooperation by increasing mutual understanding and networking among investment authorities, including the private sectors, and by creating more conducive eco-socio-political and legal climates for the flow of investments.

17.To jointly develop each other's small and medium local enterprises and industries through financing, human resource development, expanding market access, and identifying possible areas of cooperation.

18.To promote greater financial stability through enhancing mutual technical assistance in developing capital markets and an early warning system to monitor capital flows.

19.To expedite the implementation of existing mechanisms in furthering cooperation in the fields of agriculture, forestry, and fishery, with a view to enhancing human resources development, technology, technical assistance, productivity and diversification, sustainable management and capacity building in these fields, and strengthen cooperation against illegal logging and illegal fishing.

20.To step up dialogue and consultation on energy policy and give further scope to the China-Indonesia Energy Forum to allow for policy exchanges, strengthen exchanges and cooperation in the fields of oil, gas and mining, encourage greater participation by enterprises in joint energy resource exploration and development, and establish a commercially viable regional energy transportation network, with a view to promoting sustainable energy development, including the development of renewable energy, energy efficiency, energy conservation, and nuclear energy for peaceful purposes.

21.To strengthen cooperation in the development of infrastructures such as roads, bridges, ports, as well as power and telecommunications facilities. Indonesia welcomes China's participation in this field. The two countries also stress the importance of maximizing on existing mechanisms and exploring potential areas for further cooperation in the fields of land, air and maritime transportation.

22.To strengthen scientific and technological cooperation in implementing human resource development and joint research in the fields of food, medicine with emphasis on biotechnology, energy, transportation, information and communication, and defense.

23.To promote environmental protection through exchanges and cooperation among the governments, non-governmental organizations and the general public.

C. Socio-Cultural and Other Cooperation

24.To value human rights and fundamental freedoms on the basis of equality and equity, and strive to protect such rights and freedoms in all levels of society and within the international community in accordance to the principles of the UN Charter and other international human rights instruments.

25.To enhance cultural mutual respect through conducting cooperation in tourism, arts, media, sports and among youth groups and non-governmental organizations in order to ensure that the China–Indonesia friendship is carried forward from generation to generation.

26.To promote education cooperation through active training exchanges as well as the teaching of each other's languages.

27.To strengthen cooperation and capacity-building in efforts to prevent and control communicable and non-communicable diseases.

28.To work closely in enhancing regional and inter-regional cooperation in the field of natural disaster prevention and management through developing advanced early warning, emergency relief and post-disaster reconstruction mechanisms.

Done in Jakarta on 25 April 2005, in duplicates in the Indonesian, Chinese, and English languages, all texts being equally authentic.

中华人民共和国政府和印度尼西亚共和国政府关于进一步加强战略伙伴关系的联合公报

（2011年4月29日）

一、应印度尼西亚共和国总统苏西洛·班邦·尤多约诺邀请，中华人民共和国国务院总理温家宝于2011年4月28日至30日对印度尼西亚共和国进行正式访问。

二、访问期间，温家宝总理和苏西洛总统在亲切友好的气氛中举行会谈，就双边关系及共同关心的国际和地区问题深入交换了意见，达成重要共识。双方对访问成果感到满意，认为访问将成为中印尼战略伙伴关系发展的重要里程碑。

三、双方回顾了两国友好互利合作关系取得的新进展，一致认为，中印尼关系已进入全面发展的新阶段，具有地区和全球战略意义。双方同意在中印尼战略伙伴关系框架下，进一步增进在政治领域业已存在的紧密关系，深化和扩大经贸往来，促进文化交流和民间交往，扩大国际合作。

政治

四、双方重申将继续奉行相互尊重独立、主权和领土完整的原则。苏西洛总统重申印尼坚持一个中国政策的一贯立场，支持中国和平统一进程。温家宝总理对印尼方这一立场表示赞赏，并重申中国坚定支持和尊重印尼的国家统一、领土完整和主权。

五、双方对2010年1月21日签订的《中华人民共和国政府与印度尼西亚共和国政府关于落实战略伙伴关系联合宣言的行动计划》感到满意，一致同意采取具体措施落实好行动计划，推进两国各领域务实合作。

六、双方认识到加强两国领导人互访和完善高级别战略对话机制的重要性。双方同意进一步加强印尼政治、法律、安全统筹部长和中国国务院国务委员之间的双边磋商，责成两国外长联委会每年召开一次会议，履行监督、评估各领域现有双边合作，并寻找新的合作机遇的机制职能以加强两国战略伙伴关系。同时，双方同意保持在两国防务与安全磋商、经贸和技术合作联委会等机制下的对话与合作。

七、双方欢迎签署《中华人民共和国外交部和印度尼西亚共和国外交部关于共同行动的谅解备忘录》，以加强两国外交部合作，包括开展相互交流、外交官培训、政策规划研究以及建立两国外交部各级别官员间热线电话等。

八、中方欢迎印尼即将在上海开设总领馆。双方认为，这将有利于进一步深化两国关系。

九、双方重申海上合作对发展两国战略伙伴关系的重要意义，承诺继续加强在航行安全、海上安全、海军合作、渔业开发活动、打击非法、不报告及不受管制的渔业捕捞活动、海洋科研环保等领域的交流与合作。双方欢迎签署《关于修订〈中华人民共和国国家海洋局和印度尼西亚共和国海洋渔业部关于海洋领域合作谅解备忘录〉的议定书》。

经济、贸易和投资

十、双方对双边经济关系的积极发展表示满意。双方相信，两国贸易额达到500亿美元的目标有望提前实现，同意努力实现2015年两国贸易额达到800亿美元的新目标。双方强调和重申以平衡和可持续发展的方式实现上述目标。

十一、为此，温家宝总理重申中方坚定致力于扩大从印尼进口并为此提供便利，通过增加中国在印尼工业领域的投资等措施提高印尼工业能力。

十二、双方欢迎两国政府签署《中华人民共和国政府和印度尼西亚共和国政府关于扩大和深化双边经济贸易合作的协定》，并决心通过互利互惠的方式落实好上述协定。

十三、双方同意积极鼓励和支持两国企业增加和扩大双向投资，包括推动双方相关协会间建立直接对话。印尼欢迎中国增加对印尼制造业、高新技术、农业、林业、渔业、清洁能源和旅游业等领域的投资。

十四、印尼欢迎中国企业在平等互利基础上，特别是在公私伙伴合作框架下，参与印尼公路、桥梁、港口、电站和水资源开发等基础设施发展。双方同意就印尼经济走廊的发展加强合作。中方也希望就经济合作区的发展同印尼方加强合作。

十五、双方再次承诺将推进两国农业领域合作，特别是在技术转让、能力建设、粮食储备管理、杂交水稻、共同研发以及应对粮食安全相关问题方面的合作。

十六、双方强调，将巩固扩大两国在油气、煤炭、电力领域的合作，并积极探索新能源和可再生能源领域的合作机会。为此，双方强调，充分利用中国—印尼能源论坛，加快实现两国在能源领域的合作目标。

防务和安全

十七、双方一致认为，为应对二十一世纪传统和非传统安全挑战，两国应进一步加强战略防务合作。为此，双方承诺，进一步加强包括联合演习、海上安全、国防工业在内的防务及其能力建设领域的合作，并加强在非传统安全领域的交流与合作。

社会和文化

十八、双方一致认为，建立双边合作机制，加强防灾、减灾领域协商与协调非常重要，其中包括信息、经验共享及相关人员培训。

十九、双方强调相互尊重对方的传统文化，同意进一步加强艺术、电影、媒体、展览以及双方达成一致的其他领域的交流与合作。

二十、双方同意进一步推动两国教育领域合作，在教育及相关机构鼓励语言教学，促进学生交流和学者交流，扩大奖学金规模，推进互相承认学历学位工作。

二十一、双方同意加强两国青年和青年组织间互访，加强体育合作。

二十二、双方同意推动旅游合作，鼓励联合宣传推广，鼓励两国游客互访。

二十三、双方同意促进两国学术界交流，加深两国国民间业已存在的友好关系，增进双方相互理解与信任。双方进一步鼓励双方智库加强交流。

地区和国际问题

二十四、双方强调中国和印尼在促进亚太地区和平与稳定方面拥有广泛共同利益，为此，双方支持构建和完善开放、包容、互利的合作框架。双方重申，将坚定致力于在中国—东盟、东盟与中日韩、东亚峰会(EAS)、东盟地区论坛(ARF)、亚太经合组织、亚欧会议等多边框架下加强协调与合作，共同应对国际和地区问题。双方致力于促进区域贸易和投资自由化与便利化、区域经济一体化和经济技术合作以及为本地区的稳定和发展作出贡献。

二十五、双方高度评价中国与东盟二十年来始终保持密切合作关系。温家宝总理表示相信，在印尼担任东盟主席国期间，中国—东盟关系将得到进一步提升。

二十六、双方承诺将继续支持东盟在东亚峰会中的主导作用。双方相信，2011年11月在巴厘举行的东亚峰会将进一步推动各成员国密切合作，以进一步实现本地区的共同稳定、共同安全和共同繁荣。

二十七、双方一致认为，中印尼在多边领域中的合作是两国战略伙伴关系的重要组成部分。作为主要发展中国家，中印尼加强对话与合作将为国际社会应对重大挑战作出贡献。中国和印尼愿在联合国、二十国集团和世界贸易组织框架下保持密切磋商。同时，双方将加强与其他发展中国家的协调，在重大国际问题上维护发展中国家的主张和利益，推动建立持久和平、共同繁荣的和谐世界。

二十八、双方强调，应对气候变化应在可持续发展框架下进行，应基于《联合国气候变化框架公约》及其《京都议定书》的原则和规定，应在坎昆会议成果的基础上继续落实"巴厘路线图"授权，推动南非德班气候变化会议取得积极成果。

二十九、双方满意地看到，中国和印尼在应对国际金融危机带来的挑战中采取了积极有效措施，保持了各自经济增长，并为全球经济复苏作出了重要贡献。双方支持加快落实和深化国际货币基金组织和世界银行的改革，实现二十国集团匹兹堡峰会确定的量化改革目标，将就此保持密切磋商与协调。

三十、温家宝总理对苏西洛总统以及印尼政府和人民在此次正式访问期间给予他本人和代表团的热情款待表示衷心感谢，这充分体现了两国和两国人民间长久的友谊和互利合作关系。

Joint Communiqué between the Government of the Republic of Indonesia and the Government of the People's Republic of China on Further Strenthening China–Indonesia Strategic Partnership

(29 April 2011)

1. At the invitation of President Susilo Bambang Yudhoyono of the Republic of Indonesia, Premier Wen Jiabao of the State Council of the People's Republic of China paid an official visit to the Republic of Indonesia on 28–30 April 2011.

2. During the visit, Premier Wen Jiabao and President Yudhoyono held talks in a cordial and friendly atmosphere. They had an in-depth exchange of views on bilateral relations and regional and international issues of shared interest, and reached important agreements. Both sides felt satisfied with the results of the visit and believed that the visit would serve as an important milestone in the development of China–Indonesia strategic partnership.

3. The two sides reviewed the friendly and mutually beneficial cooperation between the two countries and recent progress made in their bilateral relations, and shared the view that China–Indonesia relations had entered a new stage of comprehensive development and acquired regional and global strategic significance. The two sides agreed to take further steps to enhance the existing close relations in the political field, deepen and widen economic and trade ties, promote cultural exchanges and people-to-people interaction and expand international cooperation under the framework of China–Indonesia strategic partnership.

Political

4. The two sides reiterated their commitment to the continued adherence to the principles of mutual respect for the independence, sovereignty and territorial integrity of both countries. President Yudhoyono reaffirmed Indonesia's long standing position of the one China policy and supported the process of peaceful reunification of China. Premier Wen Jiabao appreciated Indonesia's position and reaffirmed China's firm support, and respect for Indonesia's national unity, territorial integrity and sovereignty.

5. The two sides expressed satisfaction over the *Plan of Action for the Implementation of the Joint Declaration on Strategic Partnership between the Government of the People's Republic of China and the Government of the Republic of Indonesia* signed on 21 January 2010, and agreed to take concrete measures to implement the Plan of Action and promote pragmatic cooperation in various fields between the two countries.

6. The two sides recognized the importance of intensifying mutual visits among leaders of the two countries and enhancing high level strategic dialogue mechanism. Both sides agreed to further strengthen bilateral consultation between the Coordinating Minister for political, Legal and Security Affairs of Indonesia and the State Councilor of the State Council of China and tasked the Joint Commission for Bilateral Cooperation (JCBC) co-chaired by Minister for Foreign Affairs of the two countries to convene annually and to function as the mechanism to monitor and review the existing bilateral cooperation in various fields and identify new cooperative opportunities so as to enhance the strategic partnership while maintaining the dialogue and cooperation under the mechanisms such as the Defense and Security Consultation and the Joint Commission on Economic, Trade and Technical Cooperation.

7. Both sides welcomed and supported the signing of the *Memorandum of Understanding between the Ministry of Foreign Affairs of the People's Republic of China and the Ministry of Foreign Affairs of the Republic of Indonesia on Joint Activities* aimed at intensifying cooperation between both Foreign Ministries, namely on mutual exchanges, training for diplomats, policy planning and research as well as the establishment of hotlines between officials of the

Foreign Ministries at various levels.

8. The Chinese side welcomed the forthcoming opening of the Consulate General of the Republic of Indonesia in Shanghai. Both sides believed that this will further deepen the relations between the two countries.

9. The two sides stressed the importance of maritime cooperation in developing China-Indonesia strategic partnership and would be committed to further strengthening exchanges and cooperation in the fields of safety of navigation maritime security, navy-to-navy cooperation, fisheries development activities, combating IUU (Illegal, Unreported and Unregulated) fishing, marine scientific research and environmental protection. Both sides welcomed the signing of the Protocol Amending the Memorandum of Understanding on Marine Cooperation between the State Oceanic Administration of the People's Republic of China and the Ministry of Marine Affairs and Fisheries of the Republic of Indonesia.

Economic, Trade and Investment

10. The two sides expressed satisfaction at the positive development in bilateral economic relations. Both sides believed that the initial target of US$50 billion in trade volume could be achieved ahead of schedule and therefore agreed to strive toward a new target of US$80 billion in trade volume by 2015. The two sides emphasized and reaffirmed that this trade target will be achieved in a balanced and sustainable manner.

11. In this respect, Premier Wen Jiabao reiterated China's firm commitment to facilitate and promote more imports from Indonesia, and enhance Indonesia's industrial capacity through, among others,increasing China's investment in the industrial sectors in Indonesia.

12. Both sides welcomed the signing of the *Agreement on Expanding and Deepening Bilateral Economic and Trade Cooperation between the Government of the Republic of Indonesia and the Government of the People's Republic of China* and are determined to implement the said agreement in a mutually beneficial way.

13. The two sides agreed to actively encourage and support their enterprises to increase and expand two-way investment flows, including promoting direct

dialogue between relevant associations from both sides. The Indonesian side welcomed the increased Chinese investment in the fields of manufacturing industries, high and new technologies, agriculture and forestry, fishery, clean energy, and tourism.

14. The Indonesian side welcomed the participation of Chinese enterprises in infrastructure development, including roads, bridges, ports, power plants and water resources development particularly under the cooperative framework of public-private-partnership(PPP) based on partnership, equality and mutual benefit. Both sides agreed to strengthen the cooperation on the development of Indonesian economic corridors. The Chinese side also hopes to strengthen the cooperation with the Indonesian side on the development of the Economic and Trade Cooperation Zone.

15. The two sides reaffirmed their commitment to the furtherance of the bilateral cooperation in the field of agriculture, particularly with respect to technology transfer, capacity building, food stock management, hybrid rice, joint research and development, including effort to address food security related issues.

16. The two sides underlined their readiness to solidify and expand cooperation in oil and gas, coal and electricity, and actively explore cooperation opportunities in new and renewable energies. In this respect, both sides emphasized the importance of optimizing the China–Indonesia Energy Forum (ICEF) as a forum to accelerate the achievement of the common goals of the two countries in energy cooperation. The two sides agreed to establish a cooperative mechanism on clean energy.

Defense and Security

17. The two sides shared the view on the importance of further strengthening strategic defense cooperation to address traditional and non-traditional security challenges of the 21st century. In this regard, both sides were committed to further enhancing the implementation of defense and capacity-building cooperation, including joint exercises, maritime security, national defense industry and exchanges and cooperation in non-traditional security fields.

Social and Cultural

18. The two sides shared the view on the importance of establishing a bilateral cooperative mechanism to enhance consultation and coordination in disaster preparedness and mitigation, including among others, sharing of information and best practices as well as training for relevant personnel.

19. The two sides reiterated their respect for each other's traditional culture and agreed to further enhance exchanges and cooperation in art, film, media, exhibition and cooperation in other fields as agreed upon by both sides.

20. The two sides agreed to further promote bilateral cooperation in the field of education by means of promoting language teaching in various educational and other relevant institutions, facilitating student and lecturer exchanges, increasing the scale of scholarships, and promoting mutual recognition of academic degrees.

21. Both sides agreed to intensify exchanges of visits between young people and youth organizations as well as to strengthen cooperation on sports.

22. The two sides agreed to further promote cooperation in tourism, including encouraging joint promotion and mutual visits of tourists between the two countries.

23. The two sides agreed to promote stronger academic exchanges with a view to deepening the existing friendly relations and increasing mutual understanding and trust between the peoples of the two countries. The two sides further encouraged more intensive interactions between their think tanks.

Regional and International

24. The two sides emphasized that China and Indonesia share broad common interests in promoting peace and stability in the Asia-Pacific region and therefore support the establishment and improvement of an open, inclusive and mutually beneficial cooperation framework. The two sides reaffirmed their firm commitment to enhance coordination and cooperation in multilateral frameworks such as ASEAN+1, ASEAN+3, East Asia Summit (EAS), ASEAN Regional Forum (ARF), APEC and ASEM and to undertake joint efforts in addressing international and regional issues. The two sides were committed to advancing

regional trade and investment liberalization and facilitation, regional economic integration, economic and technological cooperation, and to contributing to regional peace, stability and development.

25. On ASEAN, both sides highly valued ASEAN and China relations which have reached 20 years of close cooperation. In this respect, Premier Wen Jiabao expressed his confidence that under the chairmanship of Indonesia, China-ASEAN relations would be further enhanced.

26. The two sides were committed to continuously supporting the role of ASEAN as the main driving force of the East Asia Summit. Both sides were confident that the upcoming East Asia Summit in Bali in November 2011 would further promote closer cooperation between members on common stability, common security and common prosperity in the region.

27. The two sides shared the view that cooperation in multilateral fora is an important part of China-Indonesia strategic partnership. Enhanced dialogue and cooperation between China and Indonesia, as two major developing countries, will contribute to the international effort in addressing major challenges. The two sides therefore expressed their readiness to maintain close consultation under the framework of the United Nations, the G20 and the WTO. The two sides would also enhance coordination with other developing countries to uphold the positions and interests of developing countries on major international issues and promote the building of a harmonious world of lasting peace and common prosperity.

28. The two sides emphasized that climate change should be tackled under the framework of sustainable development in keeping with the principles and provisions of the United Nations Framework Convention on Climate Change and the Kyoto Protocol, and that efforts should be made to continue implementing the mandate of the Bali Roadmap on the basis of the outcomes of the Cancun Conference and push for positive outcomes at the Durban Climate Change Conference.

29. The two sides noted with satisfaction that China and Indonesia have actively and effectively taken measures to address the challenges brought by the international financial crisis and maintained growth of their respective

economies, thus contributing to global economic recovery. The two sides expressed their support to expedite and deepen the reform of the International Monetary Fund and the World Bank towards achieving the quantified reform goals as set out at the G20 Summits, and agreed to maintain close consultation and coordination in this field.

30. Premier Wen Jiabao expressed his sincere gratitude to President Susilo Bambang Yudhoyono and the Government and people of Indonesia for the warm welcome and hospitality accorded to him and the Chinese Delegation during this official visit, which reflected the bonds of long standing friendship and mutually beneficial cooperation between the two countries and their peoples.

中华人民共和国和印度尼西亚共和国联合声明

（2012年3月24日）

一、应中华人民共和国主席胡锦涛阁下的邀请，印度尼西亚共和国总统苏西洛·班邦·尤多约诺阁下于2012年3月22日至24日对中国进行国事访问。

二、中国政府和人民给予苏西洛总统及印尼代表团热情友好接待，高度评价苏西洛总统此访对深化中印尼战略伙伴关系的重要意义。

三、苏西洛总统对胡锦涛主席和中国政府与人民在其访问期间给予他和印尼代表团热情款待表示衷心感谢，这彰显了两国和两国人民间的持久友谊和全面合作。

四、访华期间，胡锦涛主席在北京同苏西洛总统举行了会谈，全国人大常委会委员长吴邦国和国务院总理温家宝分别会见了苏西洛总统，中共中央政治局常委李长春与苏西洛总统共同会见了两国青年代表，苏西洛总统还同中国知名企业家代表见面。中国清华大学向苏西洛总统授予荣誉博士学位，表彰他领导印尼为促进本国经济发展和本地区和平、稳定与发展所发挥的作用。

五、在会谈会见中，两国领导人对中印尼自2005年4月25日建立战略伙伴关系以来各领域合作取得的进展表示满意。双方承诺将中印尼战略伙伴关系提升到更高水平。

政治、防务和安全领域

六、双方重申将继续奉行相互尊重主权、独立和领土完整的原则。苏西洛总统重申印尼坚持一个中国政策，支持两岸关系和平发展和中国和平统一大业。

胡锦涛主席赞赏印尼方立场，重申中国尊重和支持印尼为维护国家统一和领土主权完整所作的努力。

七、双方一致认为，应保持两国高层密切协调和磋商，继续完善现有各层级对话机制。2012年2月28日，中国国务院国务委员戴秉国与印尼政治法律安全统筹部长苏扬托在北京一致同意将双边副总理级对话机制会议由两年一次增加为一年一次，两国领导人对此表示赞赏。双方还表示，将根据两国关系发展需要，积极探讨进一步充实该机制对话的内容。双方欢迎两国外交部长尽早共同主持召开双边合作联委会第二次会议。

八、在防务安全领域，双方欢迎并支持两国安全防务部门加强沟通与合作，同意推动落实联演联训、国防工业以及非传统安全领域的合作。中方欢迎印尼成立和平安全中心，表示愿积极支持在该中心设立汉语中心。

九、双方高兴地看到，两国在司法、执法领域合作取得进展，一致认为双方应积极推动《中国和印尼引渡条约》尽早生效，两国执法部门应进一步密切高层互访和业务团组交流，深化在打击跨国犯罪和恐怖主义、禁毒、执法能力建设领域以及在情报信息交流、案件协查、缉捕和遣返犯罪嫌疑人等方面的高效、务实合作，共同维护两国国内安全和社会稳定。

经济发展领域

十、双方对两国经济合作稳步推进表示满意，同意继续致力于扩大和深化双边经贸合作。双方还同意进一步发挥好现有中印尼经贸联委会机制作用，积极推进两国各类经济合作机制建设，并在必要时就经济事务举行更高级别的双边磋商，共同推动中印尼经贸合作长期健康顺利发展。

十一、在贸易领域，两国领导人高兴地看到，近年来双边贸易额稳步上升，对双方在2015年前实现800亿美元贸易目标表示乐观。双方重申愿继续加快实现双边贸易顺利、平衡、可持续发展进程。

十二、在投资领域，双方将继续鼓励两国企业增加和拓展双向投资。苏西洛总统欢迎中国企业在印尼增加投资，参与印尼产业能力建设。

十三、在基础设施领域，中方重申将继续参与印尼基础设施发展项目，特别是印尼2011—2025年经济发展总体规划包括的项目。

十四、在经贸规划合作方面，双方同意结合中国“十二五”规划和印尼2011—2025年经济发展总体规划共同编制《中印尼经贸合作五年规划》。两国经贸部门于2012年3月15日至16日召开中印尼经济合作工作组第一次会议，正式启动规划编制工作。

十五、在工业领域，双方同意全面积极落实两国在2006—2011年签署的各项产业合作协议。

海上合作领域

十六、双方积极评价两国在海洋领域进行富有成效的合作，欢迎两国签署海上合作谅解备忘录，同意成立海上合作委员会并启动两国海上合作基金。

十七、双方承诺继续加强在航行安全、海上安全、海军合作、海洋科研环保、海上搜救、船舶建造、海上能力建设和渔业等领域的合作，继续加强在国际海事组织等国际场合的协调与配合。双方同意共同推进“蓝色经济”，继续支持中印尼海洋与气候中心开展互利合作项目。

科技领域

十八、双方同意进一步发挥好两国科技联委会作用，不断深化在信息通信、农业、海洋渔业、生物科技和生物医药技术等领域的合作。

十九、中方感谢印尼长期支持中国远望号航天测量船赴印尼相关海域实施北斗导航卫星发射海上测控任务，重申将进一步加强两国航天合作，支持印尼航天技术发展。

粮食、水和能源安全

二十、双方对自然灾害和部分地区不断加剧的政治经济动荡给全球粮食、水和能源安全带来的影响深表关注。双方重申将继续加强双边合作与协调，共同应对粮食、水和能源安全问题。

二十一、在农业领域，双方同意加强在粮食生产及农产品质量安全领域的合作，并积极探讨在两国农业部2001年签署的农业合作谅解备忘录框架下开展务实合作。

二十二、在能源领域，鉴于平价的能源供应是两国实现可持续发展的必要条件，双方认为有必要保证能源安全。因此，双方同意进一步发挥好两国能源论坛作用，巩固和拓展在油气、矿产和电力等领域的合作，积极探讨开发新能源和可再生能源的合作机会。印尼方向中方介绍了印尼为完善矿产资源管理所作的努力，期待中国企业增加对印尼矿业的投资，并承诺将继续为包括中国投资者在内的外国投资者营造更加有利的投资环境。

二十三、在水安全领域，双方同意加强在水资源可持续管理、综合性水利枢纽开发、涉水灾害防御以及水处理方面的合作。

社会和文化领域

二十四、双方高兴地看到，两国在文化、教育、科技、旅游、档案和青年交流领域的合作取得进展，一致认为加强上述领域的合作将进一步深化相互了解与信任。

二十五、在文化领域，双方认为应进一步加强合作，促进两国文化产业方面的交流。双方同意建立两国部长牵头的人文交流合作机制。

二十六、在教育领域，双方积极评价孔子学院和印尼研究中心为促进中印尼文化交流和加强两国语言培训发挥的作用，表示将进一步加强两国教育机构间的合作，继续加强两国学生和教师交流。

二十七、在青年交流领域，双方欢迎2012年开展100名青年交流互访项目，并支持继续开展这一项目。

二十八、在旅游领域，双方认为两国在旅游领域合作潜力巨大，鼓励两国相关机构包括私营部门加强合作，增加互访游客人数，扩大对旅游业的投资，为两国游客提供便利。

二十九、在档案领域，双方同意进一步加强在文化遗产、历史文献和文献保护领域的合作。

国际和地区事务

三十、两国领导人还就共同关心的国际和地区问题交换意见，强调两国更紧密的伙伴关系对加强多边主义、促进地区和国际和平、稳定与经济发展具有重要意义。双方赞赏并相互支持彼此在全球和本地区发挥更大作用，重申加强伙伴关系，在双方共同关心的国际和地区问题上保持协调与配合，共同致力于本地区乃至世界的和平、稳定与繁荣。

三十一、两国领导人强调，中国和印尼有必要在以东盟为主导的地区合作框架下加强配合与协调。2011年中国和东盟共同庆祝建立对话关系20周年，双方高度评价中国—东盟战略伙伴关系取得的成就，承诺将推动中国—东盟自贸区建设、互联互通取得积极成果，不断拓展和深化中国同东盟在政治、安全、经济和社会文化等领域的合作。中方重申将坚定支持东盟一体化和共同体建设，支持东盟在区域合作中发挥主导作用，尊重各方在10+3、东亚峰会上达成的共识，包括《东亚峰会互利关系原则宣言》。

三十二、双方强调，各方已就《南海各方行为宣言》后续指针达成一致，这有利于继续维护南海地区和平、安全和稳定。各方应继续确保全面有效地落实《南海各方行为宣言》，用好中国—东盟海上合作基金，加强务实合作，并朝着在协商一致基础上最终制定“南海行为准则”而努力。

三十三、双方一致认为，建立东南亚无核武器区对维护本地区的和平和稳定具有重要意义。双方愿共同努力，推动《东南亚无核武器区条约》议定书早日签署。

三十四、双方支持有关各方推进六方会谈进程，全面均衡落实9·19共同声明所确定的各项目标。

三十五、双方欢迎缅甸取得的积极进展，强调保持这一势头具有重要意义，呼吁西方国家解除对缅甸的经济制裁，相信这将有助于缅甸促进社会和经济发展。

三十六、关于地区经济一体化，双方强调，本地区国家间加强互联互通和开展密切、互利、可持续的贸易与投资合作具有重要意义，双方将为此加强协调与合作。

三十七、双方对近期中东和北非局势表示关注，呼吁冲突各方立即停止一切暴力行动，通过包容性和平对话和政治协商寻求各方均可接受、反映各派意愿的解决办法。双方强调应根据《联合国宪章》的宗旨和原则以及相关国际法和国际准则实现上述目标。

三十八、双方对霍尔木兹海峡持续的紧张局势造成的影响深表关注，认为油价上涨将导致通胀压力上升，进而加剧发展中国家贫困问题，还将进一步恶化许多国家业已存在的高通胀问题。双方呼吁国际社会敦促有关各方保持最大限度的克制，采取措施缓解该地区紧张局势。

三十九、双方讨论了欧元区主权债务问题及其对全球经济的负面影响，承诺在这一问题上加强双边和包括国际货币基金组织、二十国集团、亚欧会议在内多边合作框架下的协调与合作。双方还将继续呼吁维护发展中国家的发展权。

四十、中方表示将全力支持印尼担任2013年亚太经合组织东道主。双方承诺将加强协调与配合，致力于实现茂物目标，并继续维护开放性地区主义，在发展中经济体和发达经济体制定的不同时间表内，继续保持本地区开放、自由的贸易和投资势头。考虑到各经济体发展程度不同，双方重申将加强合作，进一步加强经济技术合作，全面实现茂物目标。

四十一、会谈结束后，胡锦涛主席和苏西洛总统出席了下列合作文件的签字仪式：

（一）《中华人民共和国政府和印度尼西亚共和国政府海上合作谅解备忘录》

（二）《中华人民共和国政府和印度尼西亚共和国政府关于加强禁毒合作的谅解备忘录》

（三）《中华人民共和国国家档案局和印度尼西亚共和国国家档案馆档案合作

谅解备忘录》

（四）《中华人民共和国海关总署和印度尼西亚中央统计局关于对外货物贸易统计数据交换的谅解备忘录》

（五）《中华人民共和国国家旅游局和印度尼西亚共和国旅游与创意经济部关于中国公民赴印度尼西亚旅游实施方案的谅解备忘录修订案》

（六）《中华人民共和国国家海洋局和印度尼西亚共和国海洋与渔业部关于发展中国—印尼海洋和气候中心的安排》

四十二、双方对苏西洛总统此次国事访问的成果表示满意，相信此访将为进一步增进双边关系、加强两国合作和提升中印尼战略伙伴关系奠定坚实基础。

Joint Statement between the People's Republic of China and the Republic of Indonesia

(24 March 2012)

1. At the invitation of the President of the People's Republic of China, H.E. Mr. Hu Jintao, President of the Republic of Indonesia, H.E. Dr. Susilo Bambang Yudhoyono paid a state visit to China on 22–24 March 2012.

2. The government and people of China accorded President Yudhoyono and the Indonesian Delegation warm and cordial reception and highly commended the importance of the visit in enhancing China–Indonesia Strategic Partnership.

3. President Yudhoyono expressed sincere gratitude to President Hu and the Government and people of China for the warm welcome and hospitality accorded to him and the Indonesian Delegation during this state visit, which reflect the bonds of the longstanding friendship and multi-faceted cooperation between the two countries and their peoples.

4. During his State Visit to China, President Yudhoyono held talks with President Hu Jintao and met with the Chairman of the Standing Committee of the National People's Congress Wu Bangguo and Premier Wen Jiabao of the State Council, and the representatives of youths from both countries together with Li Changchun, Member of the Standing Committee of the Political Bureau of the CPC Central Committee. President Yudhoyono also met with prominent Chinese business leaders in Beijing. President Yudhoyono received a honoris causa doctorate degree from Tsinghua University for his leadership and accomplishment in advancing Indonesia's economic progress and its role in promoting peace, stability and development in the region.

5. In the bilateral discussions leaders of both countries expressed satisfaction with the enhancement of bilateral relations in all areas, notably since the establishment of strategic partnership between the People's Republic of China and the Republic of Indonesia on 25 April 2005. The leaders were also committed to elevating the China-Indonesia strategic partnership to a higher ground.

Political, Defense and Security Areas

6. The two sides reiterated their commitment to the continued adherence to the principles of mutual respect for the independence, sovereignty and territorial integrity of both countries. President Yudhoyono reaffirmed Indonesia's long standing position of the one China policy and supported the process of peaceful reunification of China. President Hu appreciated Indonesia's position and reaffirmed China's firm support, and respect for Indonesia's efforts to maintain national unity, territorial integrity and sovereignty.

7. The two leaders underlined the importance of maintaining close coordination and consultation between the two countries at the highest level and optimizing their existing bilateral dialog mechanisms at all levels. Both leaders therefore commended the decision of Mr. Djoko Suyanto, Coordinating Minister for Political, Legal and Security Affairs of Indonesia and Mr. Dai Bingguo, State Councilor of the State Council of China in Beijing on 28 February 2012 to intensify their bilateral consultation mechanism from biennial to annual basis. Both sides agreed to further substantiate the mechanism in accordance with the need of the development of bilateral relations. The two leaders also welcomed the forthcoming Second Joint Commission for Bilateral Cooperation (JCBC) co-chaired by the Ministers for Foreign Affairs of the two countries, which would be convened in the second semester of 2012.

8. On defense and security, both sides welcomed and supported the intensifying interactions and cooperation between security and defense institutions of the two countries and agreed to push forward the implementation of various cooperation including joint exercises and trainings, exchanges and cooperation in national defense industry and non-traditional security fields.

The Chinese side welcomed the establishment of Indonesia Peace and Security Center (IPSC) and expressed willingness to assist the development of Chinese Language department within the language center in the IPSC.

9. Both sides noted with pleasure the enhancement in the judicial and the law enforcement cooperation. They agreed for the early entry into force of the Treaty between the People's Republic of China and the Republic of Indonesia on Extradition, and the law enforcement agencies of the two countries should strengthen the exchanges of high level and operational visits, deepen efficient and pragmatic cooperation in the fields of combating transnational crimes, countering terrorism, narcotics control, capacity building as well as information and intelligence exchange, assistance in investigation of cases, apprehension and repatriation of criminal fugitive suspects, for maintaining national security and social stability in both countries.

Economic and Development Areas

10. Both sides noted with satisfaction the solid and progressive economic cooperation and reaffirmed their commitment to stepping up efforts to broaden and deepen the increasingly intertwined economic ties with a view to realizing a more sustained, balanced and healthy bilateral economic partnership based on mutual respect, mutual benefit and equal treatment. Both sides therefore agreed to optimize and actively advance various types of bilateral economic cooperation mechanisms, including the China–Indonesia Joint Commission on Economic, Trade, and Technical Cooperation and the convening of a higher-level bilateral consultation on economic issues when necessary.

11. On trade, both sides were delighted to note that the volume of trade between Indonesia and China has increased steadily in the past few years and were optimistic that the target of US$ 80 billion bilateral trade value by 2015 could be accomplished. Both sides reiterated their firm commitment to stepping up efforts to realize smooth, balanced and sustainable two-way trade relations.

12. On investment, both sides were determined to continue encouraging enterprises of the two countries to increase and expand two-way investment flows. President Yudhoyono invited Chinese enterprises to increase their

investment and participate in augmenting the industrial capacity in Indonesia.

13. On infrastructure, the Chinese side reaffirmed China's commitment to participating in Indonesia's infrastructure development projects, particularly those covered in the Master Plan on Acceleration and Expansion of Indonesia's Economic Development 2011–2025 (MP3EI).

14. On economic and trade planning cooperation, both sides agreed to draw up an Indonesia-China Five-year Development Program for Trade and Economic Cooperation in the light of the MP3EI and China's "Twelfth Five-Year" Plan. The 1st working group meeting on bilateral economic cooperation between the two countries' trade Ministries in Beijing on 15–16 March 2012 officially started the process.

15. On industry, both sides agreed to push forward the full and effective implementation of various industrial cooperation agreements signed between the two countries during 2006–2011.

Maritime

16. Both sides shared a positive assessment of the effective cooperation in the maritime field, welcomed the signing of the Memorandum of Understanding on Maritime Cooperation, agreed to establish a Maritime Cooperation Committee and launch the Maritime Cooperation Fund.

17. Both sides were committed to strengthening cooperation on safety of navigation, marine environment, maritime security, navy-to-navy cooperation, ship building, maritime capacity building and fishery, and further enhancing coordination and cooperation in international arena including the International Maritime Organization. Both sides agreed to jointly promote the "Blue Economy" and continue to support the Indonesia-China Center for Ocean and Climate (ICCOC) in further developing mutually beneficial concrete projects.

Science and Technology

18. Both sides agreed to optimize the Joint Commission on Science and Technology of the two countries to further deepen bilateral cooperation in this field, particularly ICT, agriculture, marine and fishery, bio technology and bio

medical sciences.

19. The Chinese side appreciated Indonesia's continued support towards China's Yuanwang scientific instrumentation ship sailing into designated Indonesian sea areas to carry out TTC support for COMPASS navigation satellite launch missions. The Chinese side reiterated its commitment to further strengthening space cooperation between the two countries and assisting the development of Indonesia's space technology.

Food, Water and Energy Security Areas

20. Both sides expressed deep concern over the natural disasters and the increasing political and economic instability in some parts of the world that negatively affected the world's food, water and energy security. Both sides therefore reiterated their readiness to strengthen bilateral cooperation and coordination in addressing food, water and energy security issues.

21. On agriculture, both sides agreed to intensify cooperation on food production and safety of agricultural products, and to explore practical cooperation under the framework of the Memorandum of Understanding between the Ministry of Agriculture of the People's Republic of China and the Ministry of Agriculture of the Republic of Indonesia on Agricultural Cooperation signed in 2001.

22. On energy, both sides recognized the need to ensure energy security in the light of growing demand for affordable energy supplies as a necessary condition to ensure their sustainable national development. Both sides therefore agreed to continue to promote the role of the bilateral Energy Forum, gear up efforts to further solidify and expand cooperation in oil and gas, mining and electricity, and actively explore cooperation opportunities in new and renewable energy. The Indonesian side briefed the Chinese side on Indonesia's efforts to improve the management of its mining resources. The Indonesian side expected that Chinese enterprises invest more in Indonesia's mining industry, and reiterated its commitment to continue creating conducive investment atmosphere for foreign investors, including those of China.

23. On water security, both sides agreed to strengthen bilateral cooperation

in the fields of sustainable water resources management, multipurpose water projects, water related disaster mitigation and water treatment.

Social and Culture Areas

24. Both sides noted with pleasure the enhancement of bilateral cooperation in the fields of culture, education, science and technology, tourism, archives and youth exchange. They concurred that strengthening cooperation in these areas would further deepen mutual understanding and trust.

25. On culture, both sides concurred that it is necessary to enhance bilateral cooperation, and to promote cultural exchange in the field of cultural industry. They agreed to establish a cultural and people-to-people exchange mechanism headed by relevant ministers of the two countries.

26. On education, both sides underlined the role played by the Confucius institutes in Indonesia and the Indonesia Study Centers in China to promote better understanding of Indonesian and Chinese cultures and to provide language proficiency training programs. Both sides called for increasing partnership between educational institutions of the two countries and were determined to continue intensifying student and lecturer exchanges.

27. On youth exchange, both sides welcomed the program of mutual visit involving one hundred youths in 2012 and supported the continuation of such program.

28. On tourism, both sides recognized that there are still so much untapped potentials that both countries could jointly develop in the tourism sector. Both sides therefore encouraged the relevant institutions of the two countries, including private sector, to strengthen cooperation to increase two-way flow of tourists and to promote greater investment in tourism-related fields with a view to better serving tourist of both countries.

29. On archives, both sides agreed to further cooperate in the areas of heritage, historical documentation and conservation.

Regional and International Issues

30. Both sides also exchanged views on regional and international affairs

of common concern and stressed the importance of closer Indonesia-China partnership in strengthening multilateralism and in promoting regional and international peace, stability and economic development. They appreciated and supported each other in playing a greater role both regionally and globally. They reiterated that they would strengthen partnership, maintain cooperation and coordination on international and regional issues of common concern, and remain committed to peace, stability and prosperity in the region and beyond.

31. Within the regional framework, both sides emphasized the need for China and Indonesia to strengthen their collaboration and coordination and ensure ASEAN's centrality within the ASEAN cooperative framework. Both sides applauded the achievements of ASEAN-China partnership which in 2011 celebrated its 20th anniversary. They were committed to obtaining fruitful gains from the China-ASEAN Free Trade Area and the connectivity between China and ASEAN, and expressed their commitment to further broadening and deepening political, security, economic, social and cultural cooperation between China and ASEAN. The Chinese side reaffirmed China's support for the ASEAN integration, the building of ASEAN Community and ASEAN's centrality in regional cooperation and respected the consensus reached in ASEAN+3 and EAS, including on the Declaration of the East Asia Summit on the Principles for Mutually Beneficial Relations.

32. Both sides stressed the need to intensify efforts to ensure the effective and full implementation of the Declaration on the Conduct of Parties in the South China Sea (DOC), especially after the adoption of the Guidelines of the DOC in order to continue the maintenance of peace, security and stability in the South China Sea, and underlined the need to make good use of the China-ASEAN Maritime Cooperation Fund and strengthen practical cooperation. Both sides were committed to working on the basis of consensus towards the eventual adoption of a code of conduct in the South China Sea.

33. Both sides shared the view on the significance of the establishment of the Southeast Asia Nuclear-Weapon-Free Zone for the maintenance of peace and stability in the region and therefore were ready to stepping up efforts to the early signing of the Protocol to the SEANWFZ Treaty.

34. Both sides supported all parties concerned in promoting the Six-party Talks process and implementing the goals set out in the September 19th Joint Statement in a comprehensive and balanced way.

35. Both sides welcomed the significant positive developments in Myanmar and underscored the importance of maintaining a strong momentum in this regard. Both sides reiterated their call for the lifting of economic sanctions on Myanmar which would significantly contribute to the socio-economic development of Myanmar.

36. On regional economic integration, both sides emphasized the importance of realizing greater connectivity and strong, mutually beneficial and sustainable trade and investment cooperation among nations in the region and were determined to strengthen coordination and cooperation toward these goals.

37. Both sides shared concern of the recent developments in the Middle East and North Africa and urged all parties concerned to immediately end all acts of violence and called for inclusive peaceful dialogue and political settlement in finding mutually acceptable solutions reflecting the will and aspirations of their peoples. They stressed the need to attain that goal in accordance with the purposes and principles of the Charter of the United Nations and relevant international laws, norms and principles.

38. Both sides expressed profound concern of the impacts of the continued tension in the Strait of Hormuz, especially the rise in oil prices that creates inflationary pressure, which in turn, both directly and indirectly, raises poverty level in developing countries. Such development would also worsen the already high inflation level faced by many countries. Both sides urged the international community to call on all parties concerned to exercise maximum restraint and to initiate concrete steps to reduce tension in the region.

39. Both sides discussed the sovereign debt problems in the Eurozone and its negative impact to the global economy. Both sides were committed to intensifying coordination and cooperation on addressing this issue, both within the bilateral and multilateral cooperative frameworks, such as the International Monetary Fund, G20 and the Asia-Europe Meeting. Both sides were also determined to continue voicing and advancing the development rights of

developing countries.

40. The Chinese side expressed full support on Indonesia's chairmanship in APEC in 2013. Both sides were committed to strengthening cooperation and coordination towards the achievements of the Bogor Goals, while maintaining open regionalism and momentum in realizing open and free trade and investment in the region, within the differentiated time frame for developed and developing economies. Cognizant of the various level of development across APEC economies, both sides reaffirmed commitments to cooperate and push for effective economic and technical cooperation in the common aspiration for the realization of the Bogor Goals.

41. At the conclusion of their bilateral discussion, President Yudhoyono and President Hu attended the signing ceremony of the following documents:

a. Memorandum of Understanding between the Government of the People's Republic of China and the Government of the Republic of Indonesia on Maritime Cooperation;

b. Memorandum of Understanding between the Government of the People's Republic of China and the Government of the Republic of Indonesia on Cooperation in Narcotic Drugs, Psychotropic Substances and Precursor Chemicals Control;

c. Memorandum of Understanding between the State Archives Administration of the People's Republic of China and the National Archives of the Republic of Indonesia Concerning Archives Cooperation;

d. Memorandum of Understanding between the General Administration of Customs of the People's Republic of China and the BPS Statistical Indonesia on Exchange of External Merchandise Trade Statistical Data;

e. Arrangement between the National Tourism Administration of the People's Republic of China and the Ministry of Tourism and Creative Economy of the Republic of Indonesia on the Implementation Plan of Outbond Travel by Chinese Citizens to the Republic of Indonesia;

f. Arrangement between the State Oceanic Administration of the People's Republic of China and the Ministry of Marine Affairs and Fisheries of the Republic of Indonesia on the Development of the China–Indonesia Center for

Ocean and Climate.

42. Both sides expressed satisfaction with the results of the state visit of President Yudhoyono to China and were confident that they would lay down a stronger foundation for promoting closer bilateral ties and cooperation as well as for taking the China-Indonesia strategic partnership to a higher level.

中华人民共和国政府与印度尼西亚共和国政府海上合作谅解备忘录

（2012年3月24日）

中华人民共和国政府和印度尼西亚共和国政府（以下简称“双方”），

为进一步推动双边关系发展；

注意到两国在航行安全、海上安全、海军对话与合作、海洋科研与环境保护等领域业已开展的富有成效的合作；

认识到扩大和深化双方海上合作对丰富两国战略伙伴关系内涵、造福两国人民具有重要意义；

认识到加强两国海上合作有利于增进双方相互理解与信任，推动睦邻友好关系发展；

忆及一九八二年十二月十日通过的《联合国海洋法公约》中有关条款；

也忆及二〇〇五年四月二十五日发表的《中华人民共和国与印度尼西亚共和国关于建立战略伙伴关系的联合宣言》、二〇一〇年一月二十一日签订的《中华人民共和国政府和印度尼西亚共和国政府关于落实战略伙伴关系联合宣言的行动计划》以及二〇一一年四月二十九日发表的《中华人民共和国政府和印度尼西亚共和国政府关于进一步加强战略伙伴关系的联合公报》中的有关内容；

遵照双方各自国内法律和法规；

达成协议如下：

第一条 目标

双方将建立一个合作机制，进一步加强在航行安全、海洋环境和海上安全等海上领域的双边合作。

第二条 合作领域

双方将推动以下领域的海上合作：

(一)航行安全:

交流航行安全信息;

提供海上安全航行助航设备及相关设施;

开展马六甲海峡和新加坡海峡沿岸国与使用国间的对话合作;

(二)海洋环境和渔业:

1. 交流海洋环境信息;

2. 保护海洋环境和生态环境;开展海上溢油、防污染技术合作交流;

3. 开展打击、预防、制止和消除非法、不报告、不管制捕捞活动技术合作交流;

4. 开展海洋科研、观测和培训项目;

(三)海上安全:

1. 交流海上安全信息;

2. 提供海上监控管理协助;

3. 合作打击走私、贩毒、人口贩卖、跨国有组织犯罪、针对海上船舶犯罪、海盗以及其他海上非法行为;

4. 开展两国海军互访等交流活动,增强两军关系与其他相关合作;

(四)其他领域:

1. 海上搜救合作;

2. 船舶建造和供应,包括维护和修理;

3. 海上能力建设项目;

4. 在国际海事组织、国际水文组织、政府间海洋学委员会和国际航标协会等国际场合的合作;

5. 双方认为必要的其他合作领域。

第三条 海上合作委员会

一、双方同意成立海上合作委员会(以下简称“委员会”),由两国外交部副部长共同担任主席,双方政府相关部门代表作为成员。

二、委员会是双方海上合作指导机构,主要职责如下:

(一)为双方海上合作提供政策指导;

(二)从战略高度和长远角度规划双方海上合作重点领域和项目;

(三)对重大问题作出决策;

(四)指导和监督中印尼海上合作基金使用情况;

三、委员会每年举行一次会议,在两国轮流举行,如有需要,经双方同意可以召开委员会特别会议。

四、委员会向两国外长联委会及两国副总理级对话机制报告。

第四条 海上合作技术委员会

一、双方同意成立海上合作技术委员会（以下简称“技术委员会”），由两国外交部高级别官员共同担任主席，两国相关政府部门代表作为成员。

二、技术委员会是双方海上合作的执行机构，主要职责如下：

（一）规划、审批、推进、监督合作项目；

（二）就项目执行情况和未来合作向委员会作出报告并提出建议；

三、经双方同意，技术委员会每年举行一次会议和/或特别会议，在两国轮流举行。

第五条 海上合作基金

一、基金主要职责是为双方开展海上合作提供资金支持，用于选定的项目。

二、中方提供十亿元人民币作为启动资金。今后可根据实际需要，经协商一致，由双方筹集后续资金。

第六条 知识产权

在本谅解备忘录框架下取得的成果，如无一般性国际协议规定，应在各自领土内遵守所在国有关保护知识产权及相关权利的法律和规定。

第七条 修改

只有双方通过磋商达成共识并以书面形式确认，才可修改本谅解备忘录。

第八条 分歧解决

双方在本谅解备忘录执行过程中出现的任何分歧将通过友好协商解决。

第九条 生效、期限和终止

一、本谅解备忘录自双方签字之日起生效。有效期为五年，除一方提前六个月以书面形式通知另一方终止本谅解备忘录外，本谅解备忘录将在期满后自动延期五年，并按此法顺延。

二、自本谅解备忘录生效之日起，二〇〇五年四月二十五日签订的《中华人民共和国政府与印度尼西亚共和国政府海上合作谅解备忘录》即行终止。

三、如终止本谅解备忘录，双方将明确相关条件，以决定本谅解备忘录框架内所有进行中活动的进一步发展。

本谅解备忘录由以下经各自政府授权代表签署，以昭信守。

本谅解备忘录于二〇一二年三月二十四日在北京签订，一式两份，每份均用中文、印尼文和英文写成，三种文本同等作准。如对文本的解释发生分歧，以英文本为准。

Memorandum of Understanding on Maritime Cooperation between the Government of the People's Republic of China and the Government of the Republic of Indonesia

(March 2012)

The Government of the People's Republic of China and the Government of the Republic of Indonesia (hereinafter referred to as "the Parties");

DESIRING to further promote the existing bilateral relations between the two countries;

NOTING the fruitful and effective cooperation between the two countries in the fields of, among others, safety of navigation, maritime security, dialogue and cooperation between the two navies, marine scientific research and environmental protection;

RECOGNIZING the importance of expanding and deepening maritime cooperation between the Parties for enriching the bilateral strategic partnership to the benefit of the two peoples;

REALIZING that closer maritime cooperation between the two countries enhances their mutual trust and understanding and promotes the development of their good-neighborly and friendly relationship;

RECALLING the relevant provisions of the United Nations Convention on the Law of the Sea of 10 December 1982;

RECALLING ALSO the relevant contents in Joint Declaration between the People's Republic of China and the Republic of Indonesia on Strategic Partnership issued on 25 April 2005, the Plan of Action for the Implementation of the Joint Declaration on Strategic Partnership between the Government of the People's

Republic of China and the Government of the Republic of Indonesia signed on 21 January 2010 and the Joint Communique between the Government of the People's Republic of China and the Government of the Republic of Indonesia on Further Strengthening the China-Indonesia Strategic Partnership issued on 20 April 2011;

PURSUANT TO the respective national laws and regulations of the Parties;

Have agreed as follows:

Article 1 Objectives

The Parties shall establish a framework for further strengthening the bilateral maritime cooperation mechanism in the maritime fields, such as safety of navigation, marine environment, and maritime security.

Article 2 Areas of Cooperation

The Parties shall promote the development of the maritime cooperation through the following areas:

1. Safety of Navigation:

(1) Exchange of information on safety of navigation;

(2) Provision of aids-to-navigation for safety of navigation and its related facilities;

(3) Cooperation in dialogues between the Littoral States and User States of the Straits of Malacca and Singapore;

2. Marine Environment and Fisheries:

(1) Exchange of information on marine environment;

(2) Maritime environmental and ecological protection; Technical exchanges and cooperation on oil spill at sea and pollution prevention;

(3) Technical exchanges and cooperation to combat, prevent, deter and eliminate illegal, unregulated and unreported (IUU) fishing;

(4)Marine scientific research, observation and training program;

3. Maritime Security:

(1) Exchange of information on maritime security;

(2) Provisions of aids for maritime surveillance, monitoring and management;

(3) Cooperation in such areas as combating smuggling, drug-trafficking,

trafficking in person, transnational organized crimes, crimes against ships at sea, piracy, and any other unlawful acts at sea;

(4) Exchanges among the armed forces in such areas as navy mutual visits, to enhance military to military relations and other relevant cooperation;

4. Other Areas:

(1) Maritime search and rescue (SAR) cooperation;

(2)Construction and provision of ships, including maintenance and repair;

(3) Capacity building programs on maritime issues;

(4)Cooperation in various international forum such as International Maritime Organization (IMO), International Hydrographic Organization (IHO), Intergovernmental Oceanographic Commission (IOC) and International Association of Lighthouse Authorities (IALA);

(5) Other areas of cooperation deemed necessary by the Parties.

Article 3 Maritime Cooperation Committee

1. The Parties agree to establish Maritime Cooperation Committee (hereinafter referred to as the "MCC") which shall be Co-Chaired by the Vice Minister for Foreign Ministry from the respective countries, with its members consisting of representatives from relevant government agencies from each Party.

2. The MCC is a steering organ for the maritime cooperation between the Parties with the following mandates:

(1) Providing policy guidance on maritime cooperation mechanism between the Parties;

(2) Planning the key areas and projects of maritime cooperation between the Parties from a strategic height and a long-term perspective;

(3) Making decision on important issues;

(4) Guiding and supervising the use of China-Indonesia Maritime Cooperation Fund;

3. The MCC shall meet annually in China or Indonesia alternately, and may convene special meetings whenever deemed necessary upon mutual consent of the Parties.

4. The MCC shall report to the bilateral dialogues between the Ministers

for Foreign Affairs of the two countries and between the State Councilor of the People's Republic of China and the Coordinating Minister for Political, Legal and Security Affairs of the Republic of Indonesia.

Article 4 Technical Committee on Maritime Cooperation

1. The Parties agree to establish Technical Committee on Maritime Cooperation (hereinafter referred to as the "TCM") which shall be Co-Chaired by the respective high ranking officials from the Ministry of Foreign Affairs with its members consisting of representatives from the relevant government agencies.

2. The TCM is the executive organ for the maritime cooperation between the Parties and is responsible for the following tasks:

(1) Planning, approving, promoting and supervising the cooperation projects;

(2) Reporting to the MCC on the implementation of the projects and for future cooperation and making recommendations to the MCC.

3. The TCM shall convene annual meeting and/or special meetings in China or Indonesia alternately, based upon mutual consent of the Parties.

Article 5 Maritime Cooperation Fund

1. The main task of the Maritime Cooperation Fund is to provide financial support for the maritime cooperation between the Parties by funding the approved projects.

2. The Chinese side shall provide 1 billion RMB as the starting fund. The Parties may seek for follow-up funds in the future based on practical needs and under mutual consent.

Article 6 Intellectual Property Rights

Any result of activities performed under this Memorandum of Understanding shall be subject to the laws and regulations concerning the protection of intellectual property rights and related rights in the respective territories of the Parties insofar as these are not covered by a general agreement of an international character.

Article 7 Amendment

Any amendment to this Memorandum of Understanding shall only be made after mutual consent achieved by consultation, and written confirmation be made by both Parties.

Article 8 Settlement of Disputes

Any dispute that may occur between the Parties in implementing this Memorandum of Understanding will be settled amicably through Consultations.

Article 9 Entry into Force, Duration and Termination

The Memorandum of Understanding will come into force upon signature by both Parties. It will remain in force for five years and will be automatically renewed for another period of five years and thereafter accordingly, unless terminated at any time by either Party by giving prior notification to the other Party, at least 6 (six) months in advance.

Upon the entry into force of this Memorandum of Understanding, the Memorandum of Understanding between the Government of the People's Republic of China and the Government of the Republic of Indonesia on Maritime Cooperation signed by the Parties on 25 April 2005 shall terminate.

Upon the termination of this Memorandum of Understanding, the Parties will determine the further course of all ongoing activities concluded in the framework of this Memorandum of Understanding in clearly defined terms and conditions.

IN WITNESS THEREOF, being duly authorized by their respective Governments concerned, the undersigned signed this Memorandum of Understanding.

Done at Beijing on March 24, 2012, in duplicate in the Chinese, Indonesian, and English languages, all texts being equally authentic. In case of divergence in interpretations, the English text will prevail.

中印尼全面战略伙伴关系未来规划

（2013年10月3日）

一、应印度尼西亚共和国总统苏西洛·班邦·尤多约诺邀请，中华人民共和国主席习近平于2013年10月2日至3日对印度尼西亚共和国进行国事访问。习近平主席还将于10月5日至8日赴巴厘岛出席亚太经合组织第二十一次领导人非正式会议。

二、访问期间，习近平主席同苏西洛总统在亲切友好的气氛中举行了会谈，就双边关系及共同关心的国际地区问题广泛深入交换意见，达成重要共识。习主席还会见了副总统布迪奥诺、人协主席西达尔托和国会议长马祖基。双方对访问成果感到满意，认为此次访问具有历史性意义，将开辟两国关系新纪元。

三、习近平主席同苏西洛总统高度评价中印尼战略伙伴关系取得的积极进展，一致认为，两国关系呈现出全方位、多层次、高水平的良好发展势头，为两国人民带来了福祉。

四、两国元首认为，中国和印尼在全球经济和国际事务中的作用持续上升，为两国加快经济社会发展，抵御当前这些需要合作应对的复杂艰难挑战带来了机遇。中国和印尼继续为促进亚洲的和平、稳定和繁荣而共同努力，符合两国的共同利益。

五、鉴此，双方一致同意，在2005年4月25日签署的《中华人民共和国和印度尼西亚共和国关于建立战略伙伴关系的联合宣言》和2010年1月21日签署的《中华人民共和国政府和印度尼西亚共和国政府关于落实战略伙伴关系联合宣言的行动计划》基础上，将双边关系提升为全面战略伙伴关系。为此，两国将重点加强以下领域合作：

政治、防务和安全

六、两国元首强调将在涉及彼此核心利益与重大关切问题上继续相互支持。苏西洛总统重申印尼坚持一个中国政策，支持两岸关系和平发展和中国和平统一大业。习近平主席赞赏印尼方立场，重申中国尊重和支持印尼为维护国家统一和领土完整所作的努力。

七、两国元首同意两国领导人保持定期互访，并进一步发挥副总理级对话、双边合作联委会以及其他双边机制作用，促进双方合作。

八、两国元首积极评价两国防务合作取得的成果，承诺将通过防务安全磋商等机制进一步增进互信，推动联演联训、海上安全、国防工业以及非传统安全领域的合作。

九、两国元首同意进一步加强司法、执法领域合作，深化打击跨国犯罪、非法移民、恐怖主义、人口贩卖、网络犯罪、经济犯罪以及禁毒、执法能力建设领域务实合作，承诺在情报信息交流、案件协查、缉捕和遣返犯罪嫌疑人、追缴犯罪资产等方面相互支持。双方同意进一步加强双边反恐磋商机制，推动中国公安部和印尼警察总部、中国最高人民检察院和印尼最高检察院、中国司法部和印尼司法人权部在法律事务和打击跨国犯罪等领域加强合作。

经济和发展合作

十、两国元首同意充分利用现有各层级对话机制，加强统筹规划与协调，加强两国副总理级官员在经济领域的磋商，共同寻求更多合作机遇，应对经济和发展领域的挑战。

十一、两国元首欢迎签署中印尼经贸合作五年发展规划，同意积极落实好该规划，共同推动两国经济和发展合作健康稳定发展。两国元首认为，加强两国金融合作具有重要意义。

十二、两国元首指示两国官员继续积极努力，以实现两国贸易额在2015年达到800亿美元的目标，并更加重视实现强劲、平衡、可持续、稳步增长的贸易。两国元首认为双方投资具有巨大发展潜力。中方将继续鼓励中国企业增加对印尼直接投资。

十三、两国元首认同加强工业合作的重要性和互利性。双方欢迎和支持中国企业在印尼建立印尼—中国综合产业园区。中方注意到印尼方希望中国企业在爪哇和巴厘以外的地区投资建设综合产业园区。两国元首认为有关合作将为双边贸易和投资合作注入新的活力。

十四、习近平主席重申中方将继续鼓励和支持中国企业积极参与印尼基础设施建设项目，特别是印尼2011—2025年经济发展总体规划包含的项目。两国元首同意双方将探讨在印尼六大经济走廊框架下开展经济合作，即苏门答腊走廊（自然资源和能源）；爪哇走廊（服务和工业）；加里曼丹走廊（矿业和能源）；巴厘—努沙登加拉走廊（旅游、食品和农业）；苏拉威西走廊（农业、种植业、渔业和矿业）；巴布亚—马鲁古走廊（食品、能源和矿业）。

十五、苏西洛总统欢迎和鼓励中国对印尼互联互通基础设施建设加大投资和贡献，如铁路、桥梁、高速公路、港口和机场。两国元首也认识到加强造船和飞机工业等合作以促进空中和海上运输合作的重要性。

十六、两国元首一致认为有必要加强两国之间的互联互通，包括建立海上、航空和信息通讯直接联系。双方同意探讨两国产业园区、港口和机场之间开展合作的可能性。

十七、两国元首同意重启两国农业合作谅解备忘录，加强双边农业合作磋商以及在粮食生产与加工、食品安全、化肥和农产品互惠贸易等领域开展务实、全面的合作，保障粮食安全。

十八、两国元首认为，能源安全对两国实现可持续发展至关重要。为此，两国元首同意进一步发挥好两国能源论坛作用，扩大在油气、矿业和电力等领域的合作，积极探讨新能源和可再生能源合作机会。

海上、航天和科技

十九、两国元首高度评价两国海上合作取得的积极进展，充分肯定海上合作委员会发挥的重要作用，同意推动尽快全面落实双方业已达成一致的、由中印尼海上合作基金支持的项目。两国元首也鼓励双方进一步加强在航行安全、海上安全、海军合作、海洋科研与环保、海上搜救、渔业、蓝色经济等领域的务实合作，加快推进中印尼海洋与气候中心发展等项目建设。

二十、两国元首欢迎签署《中华人民共和国农业部与印度尼西亚共和国海洋渔业部渔业合作谅解备忘录》，鼓励双方继续加强在捕捞、养殖、人员培训和打击非法、未报告、无管制捕鱼等方面的合作。两国元首还欢迎双方在印尼设立两国渔业合作基地，增强粮食安全，提高印尼渔业水平。

二十一、两国元首同意充分发挥两国科技联委会作用，促进两国研究人员交流，深化各领域科技与创新合作。两国元首一致认为，共建联合实验室是双方保持长期、持续合作的重要方式，将积极支持建设中印尼生物技术联合实验室。两国元首决心大力推动技术转移合作，促进科技企业发展。习近平主席重申中方在未来3年资助不少于15名印尼青年科学家到中国与中方科研人员共同开展科研活动。

二十二、两国元首欢迎签署政府间航天合作协议，同意成立两国航天合作联合委员会，加强在航天测控、卫星研制、卫星发射、卫星应用、共建遥感卫星数据共享与应用平台等领域的合作。双方还同意在气象和气候领域密切合作，并开展联合研发。

社会、文化合作

二十三、两国元首同意进一步深化人文交流，扩大民间往来，增进两国人民之间的了解和友谊。

二十四、两国元首同意推动两国高校和学术机构通过教师和学生交流以及结好等方式加强合作，为促进两国语言培训和文化交流发挥更大作用。两国元首鼓励双方学生到对方国家留学。习近平主席重申中国将继续通过多种渠道向印尼学生提供奖学金。

二十五、两国元首欢迎继续开展青年交流项目，将在未来5年每年向对方国家派遣100名青年进行访问，以传承和弘扬两国传统友谊。

二十六、两国元首同意推动大熊猫在印尼合作研究和科莫多巨蜥在华合作研究野生动物保护项目。

二十七、两国元首认为，人文交流对加强和扩展双边关系至关重要。中国和印尼互为重要的入境旅游客源国和出境旅游目的地国家。双方同意共同努力，推动两国人员往来到2015年实现200万人次的目标。为此，双方欢迎两国续签旅游合作谅解备忘录，同意联合开展旅游推介活动，促进旅游便利化，提高能力建设，鼓励扩大对旅游产业的投资。

二十八、两国元首同意加强媒体交流与合作，以增加相互报道的全面性、客观性和准确性。双方同意加强公共外交方面的合作，鼓励进一步扩大两国智库、高校、研究所等学术机构的交流与合作，继续办好“中印尼关系研讨会”等交流活动。

国际和地区合作

二十九、两国元首强调各国人民自主选择社会制度和发展道路的重要性，主张在国际关系中弘扬平等互信、包容互鉴、合作共赢的精神，共同维护国际公平正义。双方主张加强联合国在促进国际和平、安全和发展上的核心作用，增强其应对新威胁与新挑战的能力。双方支持对联合国安理会进行改革，以更好地履行《联合国宪章》赋予的维护国际和平与安全的职责。安理会改革应通过民主、耐心协商，寻求“一揽子”解决改革所涉及各类问题的方案，推动改革朝有利于维护联合国整体利益和会员国团结的方向发展。

三十、两国元首欢迎和支持中国和印尼在全球和本地区发挥更大作用，重申愿在国际和地区问题上加强协调与配合，共同致力于本地区乃至世界的和平、稳定与繁荣。为此，双方同意开展两国外交部多边事务磋商。

三十一、两国元首高度评价中国—东盟战略伙伴关系发展取得的显著成就，一致认为应继续拓展和深化中国与东盟在政治、安全、经济、贸易、中国—东盟自贸区、互联互通、海洋、社会、文化等重点领域的合作，本着开放、平等、互利以及公平发展和共同繁荣的原则，落实双方重大合作倡议。习近平主席重申，中国支持东盟发展，支持东盟共同体建设，支持东盟在区域合作中发挥主导作用。

三十二、两国元首同意，中国和东盟应共同推动区域合作，加强在国际地区事务中的协调与合作，维护共同安全、共同稳定和共同繁荣的地区利益。两国元首深信，区域全面经济伙伴关系协定是东盟主导的区域一体化的重要平台，双方将本着开放、平等、互利以及公平发展和共同繁荣的原则推动谈判进程。

三十三、两国元首一致认为，维护南海和平稳定是本地区国家的共同责任。中国、印尼及其他东盟国家愿共同努力，全面有效落实《南海各方行为宣言》，增进互信，推动合作，共同维护南海和平稳定，按照《南海各方行为宣言》的原则和精神，在协商一致的基础上朝着制定“南海行为准则”而努力。双方欢迎中国—东盟特别外长会，也欢迎最近举行落实《南海各方行为宣言》第六次高官会并在落实《宣言》框架下就“南海行为准则”举行磋商。

三十四、习近平主席重申支持印尼作为东道主举办2013年亚太经合组织第二十一次领导人非正式会议。双方承诺将加强协调与配合，推动会议在支持多边贸易体制、促进区域经济一体化以及加强地区互联互通、促进基础设施建设发展与投资等方面取得务实成果。印尼重申支持中国2014年在北京举办亚太经合组织领导人非正式会议。

三十五、两国元首重申双方将进一步加强在二十国集团框架内的协调与合作，推动二十国集团峰会在实现世界经济强劲、可持续和平衡增长，扩大就业，改革国际货币金融体系方面作出切实贡献，并在二十国集团框架下就全球性发展问题开展合作。

三十六、两国元首认为，中国和印尼在气候变化、多哈回合谈判、能源和粮食安全、国际金融机构改革和全球经济治理等重大全球性问题上拥有共同利益。双方同意就上述问题以及在联合国可持续发展大会后续进程和2015年后国际发展议程相关讨论中加强协调。

三十七、会谈结束后，习近平主席和苏西洛总统出席了下列合作文件的签字仪式。

《中华人民共和国政府和印度尼西亚共和国政府经贸合作五年发展规划》

《中华人民共和国政府和印度尼西亚共和国政府关于印度尼西亚—中国综合产业园区的协定》

《中华人民共和国政府和印度尼西亚共和国政府关于探索与和平利用外层空间的合作协议》

《中华人民共和国农业部与印度尼西亚共和国海洋渔业部渔业合作谅解备忘录》

《中国气象局与印度尼西亚共和国气象、气候和地球物理局气象和气候领域合作谅解备忘录》

《中华人民共和国国家旅游局和印度尼西亚共和国旅游与创意经济部旅游合作谅解备忘录》

三十八、2013年10月3日举行的中印尼商务午餐会期间，两国企业签署了总额超过200亿美元的商业协议。

三十九、习近平主席和夫人彭丽媛对苏西洛总统及夫人阿妮给予的热情款待表示感谢。

四十、两国元首对习近平主席对印尼进行国事访问所取得的成果表示满意，深信这将为加强中印尼全面战略伙伴关系注入新的动力。

Future Direction of Indonesia-China Comprehensive Strategic Partnership

(3 October 2013)

1. At the invitation of H.E. Dr. H. Susilo Bambang Yudhoyono, the President of the Republic of Indonesia, H.E. Xi Jinping, the President of the People's Republic of China, paid a state visit to Indonesia on 2-3 October 2013. President Xi Jinping will also attend the 21st APEC Economic Leaders' Meeting to be held in Bali on 6-8 October 2013.

2. During the visit, President Yudhoyono and President Xi Jinping held extensive and in-depth talks in an amicable and friendly atmosphere and reached important consensus on bilateral relations as well as international and regional issues of common concern. President Xi Jinping also met with H.E. Vice President Boediono, H.E. Sidarto Danusubroto, Chairman of the People's Consultative Assembly, and H.E. Marzuki Ali, Speaker of the People's Representative Assembly. The two sides were satisfied with the outcome of the visit, and believed that the historic visit would usher in a new era for the bilateral relationship.

3. President Yudhoyono and President Xi Jinping commended the progress made in the Indonesia-China Strategic Partnership. The two sides believed that the relationship had presented a good momentum of all-round, multi-dimensional and high-level development, and had brought benefits to the two peoples.

4. The two Leaders also recognized that Indonesia's and China's increasing role in the global economy and international affairs has generated significant opportunities for accelerated economic and social development of the two

countries to weather the existing intricate and difficult challenges which required a collaborative response. It is also in the common interest of Indonesia and China to continue working together to enhance the prospects for peace, stability and prosperity in Asia.

5. Therefore, the two Leaders agreed to elevate the bilateral relationship to the level of **Comprehensive Strategic Partnership** building on the Joint Declaration on Strategic Partnership between Republic of Indonesia and the People's Republic of China signed on 25 April 2005 and the 2010–2015 Plan of Action for the Strategic Partnership between the Government of the Republic of Indonesia and the Government of the People's Republic of China signed on 22 January 2010. To this end, the two countries will strengthen cooperation in the following key areas, among others:

POLITICAL, DEFENCE AND SECURITY

6. The two Leaders emphasized that they would continue to enhance mutual support on issues involving the two countries' core interests and major concern. President Yudhoyono reiterated Indonesia's adherence to the One-China policy, and its support for peaceful development of the relationship across the Taiwan Straits as well as the peaceful reunification of China. President Xi Jinping appreciated Indonesia's position and reiterated China's respect and support for Indonesia's national unity and territorial integrity.

7. The two Leaders agreed to maintain regular exchange of visits between leaders of the two countries and further optimize the various bilateral consultation mechanisms, including the Coordinating Minister/Vice-Premier level consultation and the Joint Commission for Bilateral Cooperation, so as to promote cooperation between the two sides.

8. President Yudhoyono and President Xi Jinping commended the achievement in bilateral defense cooperation, and undertook to further enhance mutual trust through such mechanisms as defense and security consultations, and to push forward cooperation in joint military exercises and training, maritime security, defense industry, as well as non-traditional security areas.

9. The two Leaders agreed to further enhance judicial and law enforcement

cooperation, deepen practical cooperation in combating transnational crimes, illegal migrants, terrorism, trafficking in persons, cyber-crimes, economic crimes as well as in capacity building for narcotics control and law enforcement. The two sides undertook to support each other in areas such as information and intelligence sharing, case investigation, as well as searching, arresting and repatriation of criminal suspects, recovering criminal assets. The two sides agreed to intensify the bilateral counter-terrorism consultation mechanism. The two sides agreed to continue promoting cooperation between the National Police of Indonesia and the Ministry of Public Security of China; Office of the Attorney General of Indonesia and the Supreme People's Procuratorate of China; as well as between the Ministry of Law, and Human Rights of Indonesia and the Ministry of Justice of China to advance cooperation, including in legal affairs and in combating trans-national crimes.

ECONOMIC AND DEVELOPMENT COOPERATION

10. Both Leaders agreed to make the most of the existing dialog mechanisms at all levels, enhance overall planning and coordination, and promote Coordinating Minister/Vice-Premier level consultation in economic fields in effort to explore greater cooperation opportunities and address economic and development challenges.

11. The two Leaders welcomed the signing of the China-Indonesia Five year Development Program for Trade and Economic Cooperation, and agreed to actively implement the program, with a view to jointly pushing forward the sound and solid expansion of bilateral economic and development cooperation. Both Leaders also recognized the importance of strengthening financial cooperation between the two countries.

12. The two Leaders tasked relevant officials of both countries to continue working vigorously to achieve the US$ 80 billion by 2015 by putting more emphasis on realizing strong, balanced, sustainable and steady growing two-way trade. The two Leaders were also of the view that the two-way investment cooperation had great potentials to grow and expand. The Chinese side will continue encouraging Chinese enterprises to increase direct investment in

Indonesia.

13. The two Leaders shared their view on the importance and mutual benefit of intensifying industrial cooperation. Both sides therefore supported and welcomed the establishment of Indonesia-China Integrated Industrial Parks by Chinese enterprises in Indonesia. The Chinese side recognized the Indonesian side's wish that Chinese enterprises could expand their investment in integrated industrial parks outside Java and Bali. Both Leaders believed that such cooperation would inject new vitality into bilateral trade and investment cooperation.

14. President Xi Jinping reaffirmed China's readiness to continue encouraging and supporting the active participation of Chinese enterprises in the infrastructure development of Indonesia, particularly those covered in the Master Plan for Acceleration and Expansion of Indonesia's Economic Development 2011-2015. The two Leaders therefore agreed that both countries should explore further bilateral economic cooperation between Indonesia and China in accordance to the MP3EI's corridors, namely: Sumatera Corridor (natural resources and energy); Java Corridor (services and industry); Kalimantan Corridor (mining and energy); Bali-Nusa Tenggara Corridor (tourism, food, and agriculture); Sulawesi Corridor (agriculture, plantation, fishery, and mining); and, Papua-Maluku Corridor (food, energy, and mining).

15. President Yudhoyono welcomed and encouraged China's greater investment in and contribution to the infrastructural connectivity in Indonesia, such as railways, bridges, highways, seaports and airports. Both Leaders also recognized the importance of strengthening cooperation in the field of air and sea transport by, among others, intensifying cooperation in ship and airplane industries.

16. The two Leaders shared the view on the need to enhance connectivity between the two countries through establishing direct links by sea, air and digital communication. Both sides agreed to explore possible cooperation between industrial zones, seaports and airports of the two countries.

17. The two Leaders agreed to enhance bilateral cooperation in ensuring food security and to strengthen practical and integrated cooperation in various

fields supportive of food security by, among others, promptly revitalizing the Memorandum of Understanding on Agricultural Cooperation and the bilateral consultation on agricultural cooperation and intensifying collaboration in food production and processing, food safety, fertilizers and mutually beneficial trade in agricultural products.

18. The two Leaders shared the view that energy security is crucial to the sustainable development of both countries. Therefore, they agreed to optimize the bilateral energy forum, expand cooperation in oil, gas, mining and electricity sectors, and actively explore opportunities for new and renewable energy cooperation.

MARITIME, AEROSPACE, SCIENCE AND TECHNOLOGY

19. The two Leaders commended the positive progress in maritime cooperation between the two countries. They fully acknowledged the important role of Indonesia-China Maritime Cooperation Committee and agreed to push forward the prompt and full implementation of the mutually agreed joint projects financed by the China-Indonesia Maritime Cooperation Fund. Both Leaders also encouraged both countries to further strengthen practical cooperation in areas such as navigation safety, maritime security, navy cooperation, marine scientific research and environmental protection, maritime search and rescue, fishery as well as blue economy, and speed up such projects as the Indonesia-China Center for Ocean and Climate (ICCOC).

20. The two Leaders welcomed the signing of the Memorandum of Understanding on Fishery Cooperation between the Ministry of Agriculture of the People's Republic of China and the Ministry of Marine Affairs and Fisheries of the Republic of Indonesia, and encouraged the two countries to strengthen cooperation in areas such as fishing, aquaculture, personnel training and combating illegal, unreported and unregulated (IUU) fishing. The two Leaders also welcomed the idea of establishing bilateral fishery cooperation bases in Indonesia in effort to enhance food security and advance the capacity of Indonesia's fishery industry.

21. The two Leaders agreed to give full play to the role of the joint

committee of science and technology in promoting bilateral exchanges of researchers and deepening scientific and innovation cooperation in various fields. Both Leaders also acknowledged the importance of establishing a joint laboratory, a mechanism to maintain long-term and sustained cooperation, and agreed to actively support the development of a joint biotechnology laboratory. Both Leaders were determined to push forward cooperation in technology transfer and to facilitate development of technology enterprises. President Xi Jinping affirmed China's readiness to provide grants to at least fifteen Indonesian young scientists to carry out research in China with Chinese researchers in the next three years.

22. Both Leaders welcomed the signing of the agreement on inter-governmental aerospace cooperation, and agreed to establish a joint aerospace cooperation committee to strengthen cooperation in aerospace surveying and tracking, and satellite development, launch and application; and joint development of remote sensing satellite data application and sharing platform. They also agreed to promote close cooperation on meteorology and climatology as well as joint research and development in these fields.

SOCIAL AND CULTURAL COOPERATION

23. The two Leaders agreed to deepen cultural contacts, expand non-governmental exchanges and enhance the understanding and friendship between peoples of the two countries.

24. The two Leaders agreed to promote a more active role of universities and academic institutions of the two countries in strengthening bilateral language and cultural exchanges, including by intensifying exchange of lecturers and students, and twinning programs. The two Leaders also encouraged Indonesian students to study in China and Chinese students to study in Indonesia. President Xi Jinping reaffirmed China's offer for more scholarships to Indonesian students through various channels.

25. The two Leaders welcomed the continuation of youth exchange program between the two countries where in the next five years, each side will send one hundred youths each year to visit the other's country, to carry forward the

traditional friendship of the two countries.

26. The two Leaders agreed to push forward wildlife conservation projects, namely the collaborative research of giant panda in Indonesia and komodo dragon in China.

27. The two Leaders shared the view on the importance of people-to-people connection in strengthening and broadening the bilateral relationship. They recognized that Indonesia and China are each other's important inbound tourism market and outbound tourism destinations and therefore agreed to step up effort to increase two-way tourists flows aiming at 2 million by 2015. To this end, both sides welcomed the renewal of the MoU on Tourism Cooperation and agreed to, among others, intensify joint promotion activities, travel facilitation, capacity building, and encourage more investment in tourism industries.

28. The two Leaders agreed to strengthen media exchanges and cooperation to increase the comprehensiveness, objectivity and accuracy of each country's news coverage on the other. Both Leaders also agreed to enhance cooperation on public diplomacy. They further encouraged the expansion of exchanges and cooperation between think tanks, universities, research institutions and other academic organizations, and continue to hold the Indonesia-China Relations Seminar and other exchange activities.

INTERNATIONAL AND REGIONAL COOPERATION

29. The two Leaders underscored the importance for people of all countries to decide independently their own social systems and development paths, and maintained that the equality, mutual trust, inclusiveness, mutual learning and win-win cooperation should be upheld in international relations and concerted efforts should be made to safeguard international equity and justice. Both Leaders supported the strengthening central role of the United Nations in promoting international peace, security and development, and enhancing its ability to address new threats and challenges. The two Leaders supported the reform of the UN Security Council to enable it to better fulfill its responsibility of maintaining international peace and security enshrined in the Charter of the United Nations. Both Leaders also underlined that Security Council reform should be pursued

through democratic and patient consultations to seek a package solution that addresses all of the issues involved, and ensure that the reform is promoted in a way that is conducive to safeguarding the overall interests of the United Nations and the unity of its Member States.

30. The two Leaders welcomed and supported a greater role played by Indonesia and China in both global and regional affairs. They reiterated their readiness to strengthen cooperation and coordination on international and regional issues, and reaffirmed their commitment to peace, stability and prosperity in the region and beyond. In this regard, the two Leaders agreed to hold consultations on multilateral affairs between the Ministries of Foreign Affairs of the two countries.

31. Both Leaders highly commended the outstanding achievements of China-ASEAN strategic partnership, and shared the view that China and ASEAN should continue to expand and enhance cooperation in the political, security, economic, trade including through the ASEAN-China Free Trade Agreement, connectivity, marine, social, cultural and other key fields, as well as in implementing major cooperation proposals under the principles of openness, equality, mutual benefit, equitable development and common prosperity. President Xi Jinping reiterated that China supported the development and community building of ASEAN and its leading role in regional cooperation.

32. The two Leaders agreed that ASEAN and China should work together to promote regional cooperation, strengthen cooperation in international and regional affairs, and safeguard the common regional interest of common security, stability and prosperity. Both Leaders were confident that the agreement on the Regional Comprehensive Economic Partnership (RCEP) would serve as an important platform for ASEAN-led regional integration. They would also push forward RCEP negotiations under the principles of openness, equality and mutual benefit, equitable development and common prosperity.

33. The two Leaders agreed that it is the common responsibility of the countries in the region to maintain peace and stability in the South China Sea. China, Indonesia and other ASEAN countries shall work together to fully and effectively implement the Declaration on the Conduct of Parties in the South

China Sea (DOC), enhance mutual trust, promote cooperation, and maintain peace and stability in the South China Sea. They agreed to work towards the eventual adoption of a code of conduct (COC) in the South China Sea following the principles and spirit of the DOC. They welcomed the Special ASEAN-China Foreign Ministers' Meeting. They also welcomed the subsequent 6th Senior Officials Meeting held recently on the implementation of the DOC and the consultations on the COC in the South China Sea under the framework of implementing the DOC.

34. President Xi Jinping reaffirmed China's support for Indonesia's hosting and chairing of the 21st APEC Economic Leaders' Meeting in Bali in October 2013. Both Leaders undertook to further strengthen cooperation and coordination, so to ensure that the meeting produces tangible results for the region, such as support of multilateral trading system, promotion of regional economic integration, enhanced regional connectivity and stronger infrastructure development and investment. President Yudhoyono reiterated Indonesia's supports for China's hosting of the 2014 APEC Economic Leaders' Meeting in Beijing.

35. Both Leaders reaffirmed Indonesia's and China's commitment to strengthening coordination and cooperation within the G20 framework so that it can make concrete contributions to the realization of strong, sustainable and balanced growth, enhancing job creation, reforming the international monetary and financial architecture and collaborating on global development issues in the G20. The Indonesian side appreciated China's proposal to host the G20 Summit in 2016.

36. Both Leaders acknowledged that China and Indonesia share common interests in major global issues such as climate change, the Doha Round negotiations, energy and food security, reform of international financial institutions and global economic governance. Both Leaders agreed to strengthen coordination in the above-mentioned issues and in discussions concerning the follow-up to the United Nations Conference on Sustainable Development and the post-2015 international development agenda.

37. Upon conclusion of their talks, President Xi Jinping and President

Yudhoyono witnessed the signing ceremony of the following cooperation documents:

• Indonesia–China Five Years Economic Development Programs;

• Agreement between the Government of the People's Republic of China and the Government of the Republic of Indonesia on Indonesia–China Integrated Industrial Park;

• Agreement between the Government of the Republic of Indonesia and the Government of the People's Republic of China on cooperation in the Exploration and Peaceful Use of Outer Space;

• Memorandum of Understanding between the Ministry of Agriculture of the People's Republic of China and the Ministry of Marine Affairs and Fisheries of the Republic of Indonesia on Fisheries Cooperation;

• Memorandum of Understanding between the Indonesia Meteorology, Climatology and Geophysics Agency (BMKG) and the China Meteorological Administration on Meteorology and Climatology Cooperation;

• Memorandum of Understanding Between the State Ministry of Tourism and Creative Economy of the Republic of Indonesia and the National Tourism Administration of the People's Republic of China on Tourism Cooperation

38. During the Indonesia–China Business Meeting held on 3 October 2013, business communities of the two countries signed commercial agreements valued to more than US$ 20 billion.

39. President Xi Jinping and Madame Peng Liyuan expressed their gratitude for the warm hospitality extended by President Susilo Bambang Yudhoyono and Madame Ani Bambang Yudhoyono.

40. The two Leaders expressed satisfaction with the results of the state visit of President Xi Jinping to Indonesia and were confident that they would inject further momentum for the enhancement of Indonesia–China Comprehensive Strategic Partnership.

中华人民共和国和印度尼西亚共和国关于加强两国全面战略伙伴关系的联合声明

（2015年3月27日）

一、应中华人民共和国主席习近平邀请，印度尼西亚共和国总统佐科·维多多于2015年3月25日至28日对中国进行国事访问并出席博鳌亚洲论坛2015年年会。

二、访问期间，习近平主席同佐科总统在亲切友好气氛中举行会谈，就双边关系及共同关心的国际地区问题广泛深入交换意见，达成重要共识。国务院总理李克强、全国人大常委会委员长张德江也分别会见佐科一行。

三、两国元首对两国关系发展表示满意并强调，中印尼建立全面战略伙伴关系以来，政治互信不断加深，务实合作成果丰硕，人文交流日益密切。两国关系持续深入发展符合两国人民共同利益，也为地区和平稳定和世界发展繁荣作出重要贡献。双方应共同努力，使两国全面战略伙伴关系在新形势下更加体现主权平等、相互尊重、相互信任、互利互惠、团结协作的特性。

四、两国元首一致认为，中国和印尼在地区和多边层面拥有广泛共同利益，在维护地区和平稳定、促进世界繁荣发展、全面推动南南合作、应对全球性议题方面是重要合作伙伴，应加强战略沟通与协作。

两国元首一致同意未来双方将重点加强以下领域合作：

政治、防务和安全领域

五、双方同意继续保持高层交往势头，加强两国领导人间互动沟通，做好两国关系顶层设计，及时就双边关系和共同关心的问题交换意见，增进互信，扩大共识。两国元首一致同意将尽快商签《中印尼全面战略伙伴关系未来五年行动计划》。两国元首一致同意，作为中印尼全面战略伙伴关系重要组成部分，双方应积极推动各领域可行、互利的具体合作项目。

六、双方强调将充分发挥由中国国务院国务委员分别与印尼政治、法律和安全统筹部长、经济统筹部长牵头的中印尼副总理级对话和高层经济对话、两国外交部长牵头的政府间双边合作联委会等各领域、各层级交流合作机制作用，统筹协调两国各领域合作，为中印尼全面战略伙伴关系向纵深发展做好科学设计和总体规划。两国元首支持建立由中国负责人文交流事务的副总理和印尼人类发展与文化统筹部长牵头的中印尼副总理级人文交流机制。

七、双方同意进一步加强司法、执法领域合作，加强在打击跨国犯罪、禁毒、反贪、追逃追赃、网络安全、出入境管理以及执法能力建设领域务实合作，承诺在情报信息交流、案件协查、缉捕和遣返犯罪嫌疑人等方面相互支持。双方将尽快签署中国公安部和印尼警察总部关于打击跨国犯罪的有关合作文本。双方愿在力所能及范围内继续在执法培训和技术装备等方面相互支持。

八、双方认为，恐怖主义是人类公敌。双方将在情报交流、联合侦讯、网络反恐、去极端化等领域加强合作，共同应对恐怖主义威胁。双方将积极在提高各自反恐能力建设方面相互支持。

九、双方积极评价两国防务合作成果，承诺将进一步加强军事高层交往，用好防务安全磋商、国防科技工业合作联委会、海军对话等机制，提升联演联训、军工军贸、军舰互访、人员培训、多边安全等领域合作水平。双方一致鼓励建立两国其他军种间的对话平台。

十、两国元首表示，双方将在涉及彼此核心利益的重大问题上继续给予对方坚定支持，继续奉行和平共处五项原则，相互尊重主权、独立和领土完整。习近平主席表示，中国支持印尼政府为维护国家统一和领土完整所作努力。佐科总统重申，印尼坚定奉行一个中国政策，支持中国和平统一事业。

贸易、投资和经济发展领域

十一、双方认为，习近平主席提出的建设“21世纪海上丝绸之路”重大倡议和佐科总统倡导的“全球海洋支点”战略构想高度契合。双方同意发挥各自优势，加强战略交流和政策沟通，推动海上基础设施互联互通，深化产业投资、重大工程建设等领域合作，推进海洋经济、海洋文化、海洋旅游等领域务实合作，携手打造“海洋发展伙伴”。

十二、双方欢迎中印尼高层经济对话首次会议于2015年1月26日在北京举行，承诺积极落实中印尼经贸合作五年发展规划，尽快签署《中华人民共和国和印度尼西亚共和国经贸合作五年发展规划优先项目清单》，共同推动两国经贸和投资合作长期、健康、平衡、可持续发展。双方同意落实中国—东盟自由贸易区有关协议，以改善全面市场准入条件。双方欢迎中国国家发展和改革委员会与印尼经济统筹部签署《中印尼经济合作谅解备忘录》。

十三、中方将鼓励企业扩大进口印尼产品，为印尼企业来华举办贸促活动提供便利。双方同意扩大双向投资规模，鼓励各自企业到对方国家投资，支持探讨重签中印尼投资保护协定，并按照双方法律规定保护投资者合法利益。双方欢迎中国国家开发银行与印尼国有企业部签署共同支持中国优质企业与印尼国有企业的合作谅解备忘录。

十四、双方同意深化基础设施与产能合作，鼓励两国企业在铁路、公路、港口、码头、机场等基础设施领域，在电力、光伏、钢铁、有色金属、造船、建材等产能领域开展交流与合作。双方同意就比通经济特区等项目保持密切沟通，深入探讨具体合作设想和方式。双方欢迎中国国家发展和改革委员会与印尼国有企业部签署《中印尼基础设施与产能合作谅解备忘录》和《中印尼雅加达—万隆高铁合作谅解备忘录》。

十五、双方支持两国企业就印尼第一期1000万千瓦燃煤电站租赁运营开展合作。中方欢迎印尼未来五年电站发展规划，同意鼓励中国企业寻找互利投资机遇。印尼方欢迎中方参与印尼下一阶段3500万千瓦电站建设，并愿与中方积极探讨在电网规划、建设、运营和维护方面合作。双方同意使用环保、可持续技术开展电站建设互利合作。

十六、双方承诺将加快推进中印尼综合产业园区建设，并尽快成立两国政府间协调委员会。印尼方表示将尽快出台园区配套优惠政策，为更多中国企业根据印尼法律法规入园提供保障和便利，加快推进园区建设。

十七、双方同意发挥两国能源论坛作用，尽早召开第五次中印尼能源论坛，加强中印尼海陆油气资源开发、炼化、储存以及煤炭、电力等领域合作，探讨水电、太阳能、风能等清洁能源领域合作，尽早签署《中华人民共和国政府和印度尼西亚共和国政府关于和平利用核能协议》，推动中印尼能源合作向更多层次、更宽领域发展。

十八、双方同意用好中印尼农业联委会机制作用，加强在杂交水稻种植、经济作物开发、农业技术交流、动物疫病防控、食品安全等领域合作，探讨建立农业合作产业园区和水稻合作生产园区。加强两国检验检疫合作，促进两国农产品贸易顺利发展。

十九、中方将继续通过双多边金融渠道为印尼基础设施和大项目建设提供融资支持。双方同意在两国双边本币互换协议执行层面加强合作，并探讨进一步扩大本币结算规模。双方积极评价亚洲基础设施投资银行对于促进区域互联互通和经济发展的重要意义，表示将与有关各方共同努力将亚投行打造成专业高效的基础设施投融资平台。

二十、双方同意将积极开展税务合作，共同为加强全球税收合作，打击国际逃避税，帮助发展中国家和低收入国家提高税收征管能力而努力，为两国投资和经贸往来提供有利的税收环境。双方欢迎签署中印尼避免双重征税协定议定书及谅解备忘录。

二十一、双方同意加强两国航空运输合作，以促进中印尼经贸、旅游合作及人文交流。

海上、航天、科技领域

二十二、双方积极评价两国海上合作取得的长足进展，认为应继续用好两国海上合作委员会机制和中印尼海上合作基金，加快推进“海事卫星地面站建设”、“中印尼国家联合海上搜救沙盘推演”和“中印尼海洋与气候中心建设”等项目，并继续加强在航行安全、海上安全、海上搜救、海洋科研环保等领域务实合作。欢迎中国交通运输部和印尼国家搜救局签署《中印尼海上搜救合作谅解备忘录》。

二十三、双方充分肯定中印尼航天合作联委会机制在推动两国航天合作中的重要作用，欢迎中国国家航天局和印尼航空航天研究院签署《2015—2020中印尼航天合作大纲》，进一步明确两国未来航天合作领域和重点方向。双方同意将继续加强在卫星遥感、卫星通信、卫星导航、卫星发射服务、航天测控、探空火箭、航天基础设施、卫星分系统及零部件、空间科学、人员交流培训、航空技术等领域的合作，全面提高两国航天合作水平。印尼方愿继续根据印尼国家法律和双边协议为中方测控船只赴印尼海域执行测控任务提供便利。中方愿在探空火箭能力建设方面与印尼方进行合作。

二十四、双方同意在两国政府间科技联委会框架下，积极推进共建中印尼技术转移中心、生物技术联合实验室、遥感卫星数据共享与服务平台、青年科学家交流等合作，并探讨核电技术交流、科技创新政策等领域合作。

文化、社会领域

二十五、2015年是中印尼建交65周年。双方同意将“和平繁荣伙伴”作为纪念两国建交65周年的主题。两国元首一致同意共同规划并举办庆祝活动，总结有益经验，深化双方相互了解与信任，传承并发扬两国传统友谊。

二十六、双方认识到文化中心对传播本国文化，加深相互了解具有积极作用，愿尽早商签互设文化中心谅解备忘录，并于时机成熟时启动相关文化中心建设。双方还将探讨新签两国政府文化合作协定和文化交流执行计划，不断密切两国文化交流。

二十七、双方一致认为青年是两国关系的未来，加强青少年交流有利于传承两国传统友谊和中印尼全面战略伙伴关系的长远可持续发展。双方同意继续开展每年向对方国家派遣100名青年访问交流项目，中方将继续邀请印尼优秀青年代表来华参加东盟青年干部培训班。

二十八、双方同意在有关双边教育合作协议框架下，加强在学生交流、语言教学、高等教育和职业培训等领域务实合作，加快商签互认高等教育学位学历协议。印尼方积极评价孔子学院在汉语传播方面的重要作用。中方欢迎在北京和广州建立印尼研究中心。印尼方邀请中方派员赴印尼参加印尼艺术和文化奖学金项目和高级别外交官培训。中方将继续通过多种渠道向印尼提供奖学金，欢迎更多印尼学生来华求学深造。

二十九、中方欢迎印尼政府近期宣布给予中国公民免旅游签证待遇。两国同意进一步开展旅游合作，力争两国公民年度往来早日突破200万人次。双方同意推进文化遗产旅游合作。为此，印尼邀请中国游客赴印尼体验“重走郑和路”旅游新项目。双方同意致力于通过中印尼旅游合作联合工作组探讨互利项目和倡议，并在多边场合讨论旅游议题时加强磋商，协调立场。双方将积极推进中国大熊猫赴印尼合作研究项目和印尼科莫多巨蜥赴中国合作繁育项目。

三十、双方将进一步扩大两国媒体、智库、高校、研究所等机构交流合作，办好“感知中国”、“中印尼关系研讨会”等交流活动，继续邀请印尼宗教人士访华。

国际和地区事务

三十一、双方认为，中印尼在维护亚洲及世界和平、稳定与繁荣方面拥有共同利益，担负共同责任。双方支持世界多极化和国际关系民主化，主张推动国际秩序和国际体系朝着公正合理的方向发展。双方认为，国际社会应通过对话与合作，消除贫困，缩小南北差距，促进各文明、文化和宗教间和谐与合作，实现共同繁荣。

三十二、双方重申联合国在维护全球和平稳定和促进共同发展方面发挥重要作用，致力于同国际社会一道加强联合国体系，使其能在有效、合理的多边基础上解决全球问题。双方均认为联合国成立70周年意义重大，愿在联合国系列纪念活动中保持沟通协调。中国和印尼一致认为，联合国改革应该是全方位和多层面的，也应是全面、透明、包容、平衡的，需遵循《联合国宪章》有效、负责地予以推进，应充分尊重该组织的政治性及其作为政府间、全球性民主国际组织的特性。双方支持对安理会进行改革，以更好地履行《联合国宪章》赋予的维护国际和平与安全的职责。安理会改革应增加发展中国家代表性和发言权，并通过民主、耐心的政府间谈判，协商寻求兼顾各方利益和关切的全面解决方案，推动改革朝有利于维护联合国整体利益和会员国团结的方向发展。

三十三、双方认识到中国和印尼在联合国维和行动中的重要作用，欢迎各自扩大参与联合国维和行动的努力。中方欢迎印尼方提出的“维和愿景4000”。双方同意推进在维和方面的合作。

三十四、双方一致认为，万隆会议是亚非国家自主举办的历史性国际会议，树立了发展中国家联合自强、反殖反霸的伟大旗帜，在和平、独立、社会公正基础上推进世界秩序建设。会议倡导“团结、友谊、合作”的万隆精神，至今仍对国际关系具有指导意义。中国支持印尼举办万隆会议60周年相关纪念活动，愿与印尼方密切配合，推动亚非各国增进互信，深化南南合作，实现共同发展。

三十五、中方祝贺东盟将建成亚洲地区首个次区域共同体，重申支持东盟共同体建设，支持东盟在东亚合作中的主导地位，支持东盟为地区和平、稳定与繁荣作出更大贡献。中方将继续为东盟一体化建设进程提供力所能及的支持和帮助，愿同包括印尼在内的东盟国家加强在中国—东盟、东盟与中日韩（10+3）、东亚峰会、东盟地区论坛、其他由东盟主导的机制等区域合作机制内的合作，共同维护东亚和平、发展与繁荣。

三十六、关于南海问题，双方重申致力于全面有效落实《南海各方行为宣言》，并在协商一致的基础上尽早达成“南海行为准则”。双方强调通过磋商和谈判以和平方式解决南海分歧和争议的迫切必要。

三十七、双方高度评价中国—东盟战略伙伴关系发展，认为中国与东盟合作不仅促进了中国和东盟国家的经济社会发展，也为地区和平、稳定与繁荣作出积极贡献。印尼方欢迎中方在中国—东盟“2+7合作框架”内的各项提议和倡议。双方致力于加强中国和东盟间的政策协调和务实合作。

三十八、双方高度评价2013年、2014年分别在印尼巴厘岛和中国北京举办的亚太经合组织（APEC）领导人非正式会议在实现茂物目标、区域经济一体化、互联互通、经济创新发展与改革、可持续公平增长等方面取得的重大务实成果。双方一致同意在APEC内加强协作，共同推动亚太自贸区建设，落实《十年期互联互通蓝图》、《经济创新发展、改革与增长共识》等会议成果，为亚太长远发展和共同繁荣作出积极贡献。

三十九、中方欢迎印尼担任环印度洋联盟2015至2017年主席国。作为联盟对话伙伴国，中方相信印尼将引领联盟在海上安全、贸易投资便利化、渔业管理、灾害风险管理、学术科技、旅游文化交流等六大优先领域有效开展深度合作。

四十、双方一致同意在二十国集团、亚欧会议等多边组织中加强合作，积极考虑相互支持各自候选人竞选国际组织职位，就重大国际问题经常性交换意见，加强在气候变化、多哈回合谈判、能源和粮食安全、国际金融机构改革和全球经济治理等重大全球性问题上的沟通协调，共同维护发展中国家利益。为此，印尼方表示将支持中方主办2016年二十国集团峰会。中方欢迎印尼方在联合国框架内在维护国际和平与安全方面发挥更大作用。

四十一、会谈结束后，习近平主席和佐科总统共同出席了两国有关合作文件的签字仪式。

Joint Statement on Strenthening Comprehensive Strategic Partnership between the People's Republic of China and the Republic of Indonesia

(27 March 2015)

1. At the invitation of President Xi Jinping of the People's Republic of China, President Joko Widodo of the Republic of Indonesia paid a state visit to China and attended the Boao Forum for Asia (BFA) Annual Conference from 26 to 28 March 2015.

2. During the visit, President Xi Jinping and President Joko Widodo held friendly talks, had an in-depth exchange of views on bilateral relations and a wide range of international and regional issues of shared interest, and reached important consensus. Premier Li Keqiang of the State Council and Chairman Zhang Dejiang of the Standing Committee of China's National People's Congress will also meet with President Joko Widodo.

3. The two Presidents expressed their satisfaction with the development of bilateral relations, stressing that since the establishment of comprehensive strategic partnership, the two countries have deepened political mutual trust, reaped rich fruits in practical cooperation, and strengthened people-to-people and cultural exchanges. The continuous deepening of China-Indonesia relations serves the common interests of the peoples of the two countries, and greatly contributes to regional peace and stability and world development and prosperity. The two sides should make joint efforts to highlight the distinctive features of the comprehensive strategic partnership, namely sovereign equality, mutual respect,mutual trust,mutual benefit, reciprocity, unity and coordination, in the

new era.

4. The two Presidents held the view that China and Indonesia share extensive interests in regional and multilateral arenas. As important partners in maintaining regional peace and stability, promoting world prosperity and development, advancing South-South cooperation, and addressing global issues, the two countries should strengthen strategic communication and coordination.

The two Presidents agreed to enhance cooperation in the priority areas as follows:

Political, Defense and Security

5. The two sides agreed to maintain high-level exchanges, enhance interaction and communication between the Leaders of the two countries, develop a master plan for bilateral relations and conduct timely exchange of views on bilateral relations and issues of shared interest to promote mutual trust and build up consensus. The two Presidents agreed to sign the Five-Year Plan of Action for China–Indonesia Comprehensive Strategic Partnership at an early date. The two Presidents also agreed that, as an integral part of the Comprehensive Strategic Partnership between China and Indonesia, both sides should actively promote concrete, doable and mutually beneficial cooperation projects in various areas.

6. The two sides agreed to fully leverage the role of cooperation mechanism in various areas and at various levels, such as the Bilateral Dialogue between China's State Councilor and Indonesia's Coordinating Minister for Political, Legal and Security Affairs and the High-Level Economic Dialogue between China's State Councilor and Indonesia's Coordinating Minister for Economic Affairs, as well as Joint Commission for Bilateral Cooperation between the Ministers of Foreign Affairs of the two countries, so as to better coordinate bilateral cooperation in various fields, and make scientific design and overall plan for deepening China–Indonesia comprehensive strategic partnership. The two Presidents endorsed the establishment of the People-to-People Exchange Mechanism at the Coordinating Minister-Vice Prime Ministerial Level between China and Indonesia to be led by China's Vice Premier for people-to-people

exchanges and Indonesia's Coordinating Minister for Human Development and Cultural Affairs.

7. The two sides agreed to further enhance cooperation in judicial and law enforcement affairs, especially in combating transnational crimes, anti-drug trafficking, anti-corruption, extradition of corrupt officials who have fled abroad and asset recovery, cyber-security, enhancing border entry and exit management, law enforcement capacity building, and exchanging support in intelligence sharing, investigation, arrest and repatriation of suspects. The two sides would sign the Agreement/ Memorandum of Understanding on Cooperation in Preventing and Combating Transnational Crime between the Ministry of Public Security of China and the Indonesian National Police at an early date. The two sides will continue to provide support for each other in law enforcement training, technology and equipment within the realm of their respective capabilities.

8. The two sides agreed that terrorism is the common enemy of humanity. The two sides will strengthen cooperation in intelligence exchange, joint investigation, countering cyber terrorism and eradication of extremism, and jointly deal with the threat of international terrorism. The two sides will actively support each other in building their respective anti-terrorism capabilities.

9. The two sides spoke highly of the fruits of bilateral defense cooperation and were committed to further strengthening high-level military exchanges, making good use of such mechanisms as defense and security consultation, joint commission of defense technology and industry, as well as navy dialogue. The two sides agreed to raise the level of cooperation in joint exercises and training, military industry and trade, mutual visits of military vessels, personnel training and multilateral security. The two sides agreed to encourage the establishment of dialogue forums between other armed forces of the two countries.

10. The two Presidents agreed that the two sides will give each other firm support on important issues concerning their respective core interests, continue to uphold the five principles of peaceful coexistence, and respect each other's sovereignty, independence and territorial integrity. President Xi Jinping reaffirmed China's support for the efforts of the Indonesian government to maintain national unity and territorial integrity. President Joko Widodo reiterated

Indonesia's firm commitment to the One China Policy, and support for China's peaceful reunification.

Trade, Investment and Economic Development

11. The two sides held the view that the initiative of the 21st-Century Maritime Silk Road proposed by President Xi Jinping and the strategy of the Global Maritime Fulcrum initiated by President Joko Widodo are highly complementary to each other. The two sides agreed to synergize them to each other's advantages, strengthen strategy and policy communications, advance maritime infrastructure connectivity, deepen cooperation in industrial investment and major project construction, enhance practical cooperation in maritime economy, maritime culture, maritime tourism, so as to develop a Maritime Partnership together.

12. The two sides welcomed the first meeting of the High Level Economic Dialogue in Beijing on 26 January 2015. Both sides pledged to actively implement The Five-Year Development Plan of China–Indonesia Economic and Trade Cooperation and to finalize the List of Priority Projects at an early date with a view to bolstering investment and long-term, healthy, balanced and sustainable growth of bilateral trade cooperation. The two sides agreed to implement the related free trade agreements between China and ASEAN, so as to improve overall market access conditions. The two sides welcomed the signing of the Memorandum of Understanding between the National Development and Reform Commission of the People's Republic of China and the Coordinating Ministry for Economic Affairs of the Republic of Indonesia on Economic Cooperation.

13. China agreed to encourage its enterprises to increase imports of Indonesian products and support Indonesian enterprises in holding trade-promotion activities in China. The two sides agreed to expand two-way investment, encourage their enterprises to invest in the other side and support the discussion on the possibility of a new China–Indonesia agreement on investment protection to protect the lawful rights of investors taking into account certain laws and regulations of both countries. The two sides welcomed the signing of

the Memorandum of Understanding on Mutual Support of Cooperation between the Chinese Qualified Enterprises and Indonesia State-owned Enterprises.

14. Both sides agreed to deepen infrastructure and industrial cooperation, encourage the enterprises of both countries to conduct exchanges and cooperation in the above-mentioned areas such as railways, roads, ports, docks, airports, electric-power, solar-power, steel, nonferrous metal, shipbuilding and building materials. The two sides agreed to maintain close communication on the development of the Bitung Economic Special Zone and other projects, and explore specific ways and methods for carrying out cooperation. The two sides welcomed the signing of the Memorandum of Understanding on Infrastructure and Industrial Cooperation and Memorandum of Understanding on Cooperation on the Jakarta-Bandung High Speed Rail Project between the National Development and Reform Commission of the People's Republic of China and the Ministry of State-owned Enterprises of the Republic of Indonesia.

15. The two sides support the enterprises of both countries to conduct cooperation on the lease and operation of the first-phase 10,000MW coal power plants in Indonesia. The Chinese side welcomed Indonesia's new plan to develop power plants for the next five years and agreed to encourage Chinese enterprises to look for mutually beneficial investment opportunities. The Indonesia side welcomed the Chinese side to participate in the construction of the 35,000MW power plant in the next phase and stands ready to explore cooperation in the planning, construction, operation and maintenance of electrical grids with the Chinese side. The two sides agreed to conduct cooperation on the construction of power plant through environmentally sustainable technologies on a mutually beneficial basis.

16. The two sides promised to speed up the construction of China-Indonesia Integrated Industrial Parks and establish the inter-governmental coordinating committee as soon as possible. The Indonesian side will introduce preferential policies for the industrial parks to provide safeguard and facilitation for more Chinese enterprises to enter the park in accordance with the Indonesian laws and regulations, so as to accelerate the development of the Industrial Parks.

17. The two sides agreed to better leverage the role of the China-Indonesia

Energy Forum, hold the 5th China-Indonesia Energy Forum at an early date, strengthen cooperation in the development, refinery and storage of land-sea oil and gas resources as well as coal mining and power generators, explore cooperation in clean energy sectors such as water, solar and wind power, work for the early signing of the Arrangement between the Government of the People's Republic of China and the Government of the Republic of Indonesia for Cooperation in Peaceful Uses of Nuclear Energy and push for multi-level and wide-ranging energy cooperation between China and Indonesia.

18. The two sides agreed to make full use of the China-Indonesia Joint Committee on Agriculture, strengthen cooperation in the fields of hybrid rice planting, commercial crops development, agriculture technology exchange, food safety and animal disease prevention and control, and explore the feasibility of establishing the Agriculture Cooperation Industrial Park and the Rice Cooperation Production Park. The two sides will strengthen cooperation in inspection and quarantine to facilitate trade in agriculture products.

19. China will continue to provide financing support for Indonesia's infrastructure construction and large projects through bilateral and multilateral financial channels. The two sides agreed to strengthen cooperation in the implementation of bilateral local currency swap agreement and explore the possibility of further enlarging the scale of local currency settlement. The two sides applauded the significant role of Asian Infrastructure Investment Bank (AIIB) in promoting regional connectivity and economic development and were committed to making joint efforts with the related parties to build AIIB into a professional and efficient platform for infrastructure investment and financing.

20. The two sides agreed to actively conduct taxation cooperation and work to enhance global taxation cooperation, combat international tax evasion and help developing countries and low-income countries build up capabilities in terms of taxation and related administration. The two sides agreed to create favorable taxation environment for investment, economic cooperation and trade between the two countries. The two sides welcomed the signing of the Protocol to and Memorandum of Understanding on the Agreement between the Government of the People's Republic of China and the Government of the Republic of Indonesia

for the Avoidance of Double Taxation and the Prevention of Fiscal Evasion with Respect to Taxes on Income.

21. The two sides agreed to enhance air transport cooperation between the two countries so as to facilitate the growth of economic, trade and tourism relations, as well as people-to-people contact between China and Indonesia.

Maritime, Aeronautics, Science & Technology

22. The two sides applauded the progress the two countries had achieved in maritime cooperation and agreed to make full use of the China-Indonesia Maritime Cooperation Committee (MCC) and China-Indonesia Maritime Cooperation Fund (MCF) to speed up the implementation of such programs as "remote sensing satellite application ground station", "China-Indonesia joint table-top exercise of maritime search and rescue" and "the China-Indonesia center for ocean and climate", and continue to strengthen practical cooperation in navigation safety, maritime security, maritime search and rescue, maritime scientific research and environmental protection. The two sides welcomed the signing of Memorandum of Understanding on Maritime Search and Rescue Cooperation between the Ministry of Transport of the People's Republic of China and the National Search and Rescue Agency (BASARNAS) of the Republic of Indonesia.

23. The two sides fully recognized the important role of China-Indonesia Space Cooperation Committee in promoting space cooperation between the two countries, and welcomed the signing of the 2015-2020 Aerospace Cooperation Outline between National Space Administration of the People's Republic of China and National Institute of Aeronautics and Space of the Republic of Indonesia which further made clear key areas and directions of China-Indonesia space cooperation in the future. The two sides agreed to strengthen cooperation in earth observation, satellite telecommunication, satellite navigation, satellite launching service, telemetry, tracking and control, sounding rocket, space facilities, satellite subsystem/instrument/component/material, space science, personnel training and education, and aeronautics technology, so as to raise the level of China-Indonesia space cooperation. The Indonesian side is ready

to continue providing facilitation for Chinese vessels to carry out telemetry, tracking and control missions in Indonesian waters in accordance with the Indonesian national laws and bilateral agreements. Further, the Chinese side is ready to cooperate with the Indonesian side concerning with the capacity building on the sounding rocket technology.

24. The two sides advance the various cooperation initiatives under the framework of the Joint Committee on Science and Technology including the China-Indonesia Center for Technology Transfer, joint biological technology lab, remote satellite data sharing and service platform and exchange of young scientists, and explore cooperation on nuclear power technologies and science and technology innovation policies.

Cultural and Social Affairs

25. The year 2015 marks the 65th Anniversary of the establishment of China-Indonesia diplomatic relations. The two sides agreed that "partnership for peace and prosperity" will be the overarching theme of the 65th Anniversary. The two sides further agreed to jointly plan and hold celebration activities, sum up good experience, deepen mutual understanding and trust, and carry forward traditional friendship.

26. The two sides recognized the positive role of cultural centers in promoting national culture and enhancing mutual understanding, and stood ready to negotiate and sign at an early date the MOU on the establishment of cultural centers and, as soon as feasible, start the related construction. The two sides will also explore to the possibility of signing an inter-governmental cultural cooperation agreement and action plan on cultural exchanges to continuously enhance cultural exchanges between the two countries.

27. The two sides shared the view that youth is the future of bilateral relations, and enhancing youth exchanges could help carry forward the traditional friendship between the two countries into future generations and ensure the long-term sustainable development of China-Indonesia comprehensive strategic partnership. The two sides agreed to continue the annual 100 Youth Exchange Program. The Chinese side will continue to invite outstanding Indonesian youth

representatives to participate in the ASEAN youth cadre training program.

28. The two sides agreed to enhance practical cooperation in student exchange, language education, higher education and vocational training under the framework of the relevant bilateral education cooperation agreements, and speed up the negotiations for the signing of the Agreement on the Mutual Recognition of Higher Education Degrees and Diplomas. The Indonesian side commended the important role of Confucius Institutes in promoting the Chinese language. The Chinese side welcomed the establishment of Indonesian Studies Centers in Beijing and Guangzhou. The Indonesian side offered the Chinese participants to take part in the Indonesian Arts and Culture Scholarship program as well as in the Senior-Level Diplomatic Training in Indonesia. The Chinese side will continue to provide scholarships to Indonesia through various channels, and welcome more Indonesian students to study in China.

29. China welcomed the recent announcement by the government of Indonesia to waive tourist visa requirements for Chinese citizens. The two sides agreed to further promote tourism cooperation so as to reach the annual target of over 2 million exchange of visits at an early date. The two sides also agreed to promote cooperation in cultural heritage tourism. In this regard, Indonesia invited Chinese tourists to appreciate its new tourism package to trace the voyage of Admiral Zheng He in Indonesia. The two sides were committed to exploring mutually beneficial projects and initiatives through the Indonesia–China Joint Working Group on Tourism Cooperation and enhancing consultation and coordination to synergize their positions on tourism issues discussed in multilateral fora. The two sides will also work to advance a collaborative program on ex-situ conservation of Giant Panda and Komodo Dragon.

30. The two sides will further expand exchanges and cooperation between their media agencies, think-tanks, colleges and universities and research institutes, and ensure the success of the relevant exchange activities, including "Experience China" and "Seminar on China–Indonesia Relations". China will continue to invite Indonesian religious figures to visit China.

International and Regional Affairs

31. The two sides held the view that, as two big developing countries, China and Indonesia share common interests and responsibilities in maintaining peace, stability and prosperity of Asia and the world. The two sides support multi-polarity and democracy in international relations and stand for international order and system developing towards justice and equity. The two sides shared the view that the international community should eliminate poverty, narrow the North-South gap, promote harmony and cooperation among civilizations, cultures and religions, as well as achieve common prosperity through dialogue and cooperation.

32. The two sides reaffirmed the important role of the United Nations in maintaining global peace and stability and promote common development, and were committed to strengthening the UN system with other members of the international community, in order to enable the UN to resolve global issues on an effective, reasonable and multilateral basis. The two sides recognized the significance of the 70th founding anniversary of the UN and stood ready to maintain communication and coordination in the series of UN commemoration activities. The two sides shared the view that the UN reform should be an all-dimensioned and multi-layered process as well as comprehensive, transparent, inclusive, and balanced in nature, and pursued in an effective and accountable manner, fully respecting the political nature of the Organization as well as its intergovernmental, universal and democratic character, consistent with the UN Charter. The two sides supported the reform of the Security Council with the purpose of better fulfilling its obligation to maintain international peace and security as stipulated in the UN Charter. The Security Council reform should be made to increase the representation and voice of developing countries, achieved by adopting a package solution through consultation which accommodates the interests and concerns of all parties through democratic and patient inter-governmental negotiations, so as to carry forward the reform in a way serving the UN's overall interest and unity of all UN member states.

33. Both sides recognized the important role played by China and Indonesia in peace-keeping missions of the United Nations and welcomed the efforts by

both sides to expand participation in the peace-keeping missions. The Chinese side welcomed Indonesia's Vision 4,000 Peacekeepers. The two sides agreed to promote bilateral cooperation in peacekeeping.

34. The two sides shared the view that the Bandung Conference was a historical international conference held independently by Asian and African countries, and it rallied developing countries around the great banner of unity, self-reliance, the struggle against colonialism and hegemonism as well as the promotion of world order based on peace, independence, and social justice. The Bandung spirit of "unity, friendship and cooperation" advocated by the Conference remains relevant to the contemporary international relations. China supports Indonesia to hold the relevant commemorative activities of the 60th anniversary of the Bandung Conference, and will work closely with the Indonesian side to promote mutual understanding among Asian and African countries, deepen South-South cooperation and achieve common development.

35. China congratulated ASEAN on the establishment of the first sub-regional community in Asia, and reaffirmed its support for ASEAN centrality in East Asia cooperation, and its support for ASEAN efforts to make a bigger contribution to regional peace, stability and prosperity. China will continue to provide every possible support and assistance to the process of ASEAN Community building, enhance the cooperation with ASEAN countries including Indonesia in such regional cooperation mechanisms as ASEAN Plus One, ASEAN Plus Three, East Asia Summit (EAS) and ASEAN Regional Forum (ARF), as well as other ASEAN led-mechanisms, and jointly uphold peace, development and prosperity in East Asia.

36. On the South China Sea, the two sides reaffirmed their commitments to the full and effective implementation of the Declaration of the Conduct of Parties in the South China Sea and the early conclusion of Code of Conduct in the South China Sea on the basis of consensus through consultations. Both sides underlined the imperative necessity to resolve differences and disputes in the South China Sea by peaceful means, through consultations and negotiations.

37. The two sides applauded the development of China–ASEAN Strategic Partnership, and held the view that China–ASEAN cooperation not only makes

positive contribution to the economic and social development of China and ASEAN countries, but also to peace, stability and prosperity in the region. Indonesia welcomed China's proposals and various initiatives under the "2+7 Cooperation Framework" for China–ASEAN relations. The two sides are committed to enhancing policy coordination and conducting practical cooperation between China and ASEAN.

38. The two sides applauded the major concrete achievements in terms of implementing Bogor Goals, regional economic integration, connectivity, innovative development, economic reform and growth, and sustainable and fair growth at Asia–Pacific Economic Cooperation (APEC) Leaders' Informal Meetings held in Bali, Indonesia in 2013 and Beijing, China in 2014. The two sides agreed to strengthen the coordination under APEC framework, move towards the establishment of Asia–Pacific Free Trade Area, and implement APEC Connectivity Blueprint for 2015–2025, APEC Accord on Innovative Development, Economic Reform and Growth among other Meetings' results, so as to make positive contributions to long-term development and universal prosperity of Asia-Pacific region.

39. The Chinese side welcomed Indonesia's chairmanship of the Indian Ocean Rim Association (IORA) 2015–2017. As a dialogue partner of IORA, the Chinese side was confident that Indonesia would lead IORA towards deeper and more effective cooperation in six priority areas: maritime safety and security; trade and investment facilitation; fisheries management; disaster risk management; academic, science and technology; as well as tourism and cultural exchanges.

40. The two sides agreed to enhance cooperation in international multilateral organizations such as G20 and ASEM, positively consider exchange reciprocal supports to their respective candidatures in international organizations, conduct regular exchange of views on major international issues, strengthen communication and coordination on major global issues such as climate change, Doha Round negotiations, energy and food security, reform of international financial institutions and global economic governance, and jointly uphold the interests of developing countries. In this regard, the Indonesian side expressed

its willingness to support China in hosting the G20 summit in 2016. The Chinese side supported Indonesia playing a greater role in maintaining international peace and security under the framework of the United Nations.

41. After their talks, President Xi Jinping and President Joko Widodo attended the signing ceremony of the related cooperation documents between the two countries.

中华人民共和国国家海洋局与印度尼西亚共和国海洋与渔业部海洋领域合作谅解备忘录

（2015年3月26日）

中华人民共和国国家海洋局和印度尼西亚共和国海洋与渔业部（以下简称“一方”，共同称“双方”）；

认识到《联合国海洋法公约》（UNCLOS 1982）的精神以及双方对保护、管理和可持续利用海洋资源的共同关注；

根据中华人民共和国政府和印度尼西亚共和国政府于2012年3月23日在北京签署的海上合作谅解备忘录；

考虑到中华人民共和国与印度尼西亚共和国于2005年4月25日在雅加达签署的战略伙伴联合声明；

愿意更替中华人民共和国国家海洋局与印度尼西亚共和国海洋与渔业部于2007年11月10日签署的《中华人民共和国国家海洋局和印度尼西亚共和国海洋与渔业部海洋领域合作谅解备忘录》，以及2011年4月29日签署的《关于修订〈中华人民共和国国家海洋局和印度尼西亚共和国海洋与渔业部海洋领域合作谅解备忘录〉的议定书》；

考虑到中印尼海洋和气候中心建设的重要性，该中心由双方共有、管理和监督，旨在促进双方的海洋合作。

遵守两国各自现行的法律法规，

达成以下协议：

第一条 目标

本谅解备忘录的目的是为海洋合作提供框架。

第二条 合作领域

双方将在以下领域开展合作：

（一）海洋科学研究与开发，包括勘探、观测与调查；

（二）海岸带和小岛屿综合管理，包括海景、海洋空间规划、环境保护、防灾减灾；

（三）人力资源能力建设，包括正式和职业教育、联合举办座谈会、研讨班、讨论会、科学家培训和交流；

（四）防止、阻止和消除非法、无管制和未报告的捕捞，包括破坏性捕鱼行为；

（五）政府官员互访；

（六）经双方同意的数据和信息交换；

（七）发展"蓝色经济"；

（八）应对气候变化，提高海洋与海岸带地区应对极端气候事件的能力。

第三条 海洋合作联委会

（一）为执行本谅解备忘录，双方同意成立海洋合作联合委员会。

（二）为顺利实施本谅解备忘录，海洋合作联合委员会应包括双方相关的其他部委和机构。

（三）海洋合作联合委员会可以每年轮流在中华人民共和国和印度尼西亚共和国举办至少一次会议，日期由双方约定。

（四）海洋合作联合委员会的作用如下：

1.指导本谅解备忘录框架下的合作并制定实施安排；

2.推进和监督本谅解备忘录框架下的合作；

3.交流合作进展信息，并对本谅解备忘录框架下的合作在实施过程中产生的问题进行商议和提出解决建议；

4.就海洋合作方面的其他重要问题进行交流和商议。

第四条 实施安排

应按照经过双方同意的实施安排，开展本谅解备忘录第二条中确定的合作内容。

第五条 财务安排

（一）双方应认识到第二条中确定的合作是在双方各自的财务能力允许的条件下开展的。双方应根据已有资金情况，根据一事一议的原则就每一个财务安排达成一致。

（二）可用资金包括海上合作基金，该基金根据2012年3月23日在北京签署的《中华人民共和国政府与印度尼西亚共和国政府海上合作谅解备忘录》设立，并经海上合作委员会通过。海上合作基金的使用将根据双方同意的实施安排做进一步落实。

第六条 知识产权保护

（一）双方中的一方为执行该谅解备忘录框架下的活动所获得的知识产权由这一方所有；

（二）未获得另一方的书面许可之前，任何一方在任何出版物、文件和/或文章上不得使用对方的名字、标志和/或任何官方徽章。

第七条 遗传资源

双方重申根据《生物多样性公约》的条款，特别是双方事前知情同意的原则以及公平合理的利益共享原则获得遗传资源。一方有权根据本国法律获取遗传资源，并努力创造条件促进获取基因资源的透明化。

第八条 保密

双方未经事先书面同意，应确保不得将在本谅解备忘录下相互提供和共享的数据与信息，包括开展联合研究所取得的成果转让或提供给第三方。

第九条 修订

经双方协商同意并以书面确认方可对本谅解备忘录进行修订。修订内容应构成本谅解备忘录不可分割的一部分，于双方商定之日起生效。

第十条 争议解决

双方基于本谅解备忘录的相关事项产生的任何分歧和争议，将通过友好磋商和谈判解决。

第十一条 生效、有效期及终止

（一）本谅解备忘录经双方签署生效，有效期为五年。在期满六个月前经双方书面同意可续签。

（二）任何一方可随时以书面方式通知另一方终止本谅解备忘录。

（三）本谅解备忘录的终止不影响双方已同意的且在该备忘录下开展的任何合作活动的有效性和持续性。

（四）自本谅解备忘录生效之日起，双方于2007年11月10日签署的《中华人民共和国国家海洋局和印度尼西亚共和国海洋与渔业部海洋领域合作谅解备忘录》，以及2011年4月29日签署的《关于修订〈中华人民共和国国家海洋局和印度尼西亚共和国海洋与渔业部海洋领域合作谅解备忘录〉的议定书》同时终止。

下列代表，经各自政府正式授权，在本协议上签字为证。

于2015年3月26日在北京签署，一式两份，中文、印尼文和英文版本具有同等效力。若中文和印尼文翻译时产生歧义，以英语文本为准。

Memorandum of Understanding between the State Oceanic Administration of the People's Republic of China and the Ministry of Marine Affairs and Fisheries of the Republic of Indonesia on Marine Cooperation

(26 March 2015)

The State Oceanic Administration of the People's Republic of China and the Ministry of Marine Affairs and Fisheries of the Republic of Indonesia, hereinafter referred to singularly as "the Party" and collectively as "the Parties";

RECOGNIZING the United Nations Convention on The Law of The Sea (UNCLOS) 1982 and the common concern of the Parties on the conservation, management and sustainable utilization of marine resources;

REFERRING to the Memorandum of Understanding on Maritime Cooperation between the Government of the People's Republic of China and the Government of the Republic of Indonesia, signed on 23rd March 2012 in Beijing;

TAKING INTO ACCOUNT the Joint Declaration between the People's Republic of China and the Republic of Indonesia on Strategic Partnership Declaration, signed on 25th April 2005 in Jakarta;

DESIRING to supersede the Memorandum of Understanding between the State Oceanic Administration of the People's Republic of China and the Ministry of Marine Affairs and Fisheries of the Republic of Indonesia on Marine Cooperation, signed on 10th November 2007, and Protocol Amending the Memorandum of Understanding on Marine Cooperation between the State

Oceanic Administration of the People's Republic of China and the Ministry of Marine Affairs and Fisheries of the Republic of Indonesia, signed on 29th April 2011;

CONSIDERING the importance of Indonesia-China Center for Ocean and Climate (ICCOC) and its development as a center, which is affiliated, managed and supervised by the Parties, with the purpose of promoting development of marine cooperation;

PURSUANT to the prevailing laws and regulations of the respective Parties' Countries;

HAVE AGREED as follows:

ARTICLE I

OBJECTIVE

The objective of this Memorandum of Understanding is to set up framework in the field of marine cooperation.

ARTICLE II

AREAS OF COOPERATION

The Parties shall pursue the following areas of cooperation:

1. Marine scientific research and development including exploration, observation and survey;
2. Integrated coastal and small islands management including seascape, marine spatial planning, conservation, disaster preparation and mitigation;
3. Human resources capacity building including formal and vocational education, joint symposia, seminar, workshop, training and exchange of scientist;
4. Prevention, deterrence and elimination of Illegal, Unreported and Unregulated (IUU) Fishing including destructive fishing practices;
5. Exchange of government officials visit;
6. Sharing of data and information as mutually agreed upon by the Parties;
7. Development of Blue Economy;
8. Addressing climate change, and building the capacity of coping with extreme weather events in the ocean and coastal regions.

ARTICLE III

JOINT COMMITTEE ON MARINE COOPERATION

1. The Parties agreed to establish a Joint Committee on Marine Cooperation for the implementation of this Memorandum of Understanding.

2. The Joint Committee on Marine Cooperation shall include the relevant ministries or agencies concerned of the Parties for the purpose of the successful implementation of this Memorandum of Understanding.

3. The Joint Committee on Marine Cooperation may meet alternately in the People's Republic of China and the Republic of Indonesia at least once a year at dates agreed upon by the Parties.

4. The roles of the Joint Committee on Marine Cooperation are as follows:

a. To guide and develop arrangement for the implementation of the areas of cooperation under this Memorandum of Understanding;

b. To promote and monitor the implementation of the areas of cooperation of this Memorandum of Understanding;

c. To exchange information on cooperation progress, as well as to consult and formulate recommendation to solve any problems that may occur in the implementation on the areas of cooperation under this Memorandum of Understanding; and

d. To communicate and consult other important issues on marine cooperation.

ARTICLE IV

IMPLEMENTING ARRANGEMENT

The implementation of the cooperation set forth in Article II of this Memorandum of Understanding shall be carried out through Implementing Arrangements to be agreed upon by the Parties.

ARTICLE V

FINANCIAL ARRANGEMENT

1. The Parties shall realize that the cooperation set forth in the Article II is specified within their own liabilities and financial capabilities. The Parties shall

mutually agree upon any financial arrangement arising therein on a case-by-case basis subject to the availabilities of funds.

2. Such available fund may include the Maritime Cooperation Fund, as endorsed by the Maritime Cooperation Committee, established under the Memorandum of Understanding on Maritime Cooperation between the Government of the People's Republic of China and the Government of the Republic of Indonesia, signed on 23rd March 2012 in Beijing. The disbursement of the Maritime Cooperation Fund shall be further arranged in an Implementing Arrangement agreed upon by the Parties.

ARTICLE VI

INTELLECTUAL PROPERTY RIGHTS

1. Any intellectual property rights brought by one of the Parties for the implementation of activities under this Memorandum of Understanding shall remain the property of the Party.

2. Either Party prohibits the use of the name, logo and/or official emblem of any of the Parties on any publication, document and/or paper without the prior written approval.

ARTICLE VII

GENETIC RESOURCES

The Parties reaffirm that access to genetic resources shall be carried out in accordance with the provisions of the Convention on Biological Diversity (CBD), particularly the principles of prior informed consent and of fair and equitable benefit sharing. Each Party shall have the authority to determine access to genetic resources in accordance with its domestic legislation and endeavor to create conditions to facilitate transparent access to genetic resources.

ARTICLE VIII

CONFIDENTIALITY

The Parties shall ensure that the data and information mutually provided or shared including the result of joint research carried out under this Memorandum of Understanding, are not transferred or supplied to a third party without prior written consent of the Parties.

ARTICLE IX

AMENDMENT

Amendment to this Memorandum of Understanding can only be made after mutual consent achieved by the consultation and confirmation in writing by the Parties. Such amendment shall form as an integral part of this Memorandum of Understanding and shall enter into force on such date as may be determined by the Parties.

ARTICLE X

SETTLEMENT OF DISPUTES

Any differences or disputes that may arise between the Parties relating to any matters under this Memorandum of Understanding will be settled amicably through consultations and negotiations between the Parties.

ARTICLE XI

ENTRY INTO FORCE, DURATION AND TERMINATION

1. This Memorandum of Understanding shall enter into force upon the signature of the Parties and shall remain effective for 5 (five) years. It may be renewed by mutual written consent in 6 (six) months prior to the expiration date.

2. Each Party may terminate this Memorandum of Understanding at any time upon written notification.

3. The termination of this Memorandum of Understanding shall not affect the validity and duration of any activity made under this Memorandum of Understanding as mutually agreed upon by the Parties.

4. Upon the entry into force of this Memorandum of Understanding, the Memorandum of Understanding between the Ministry of Marine Affairs and Fisheries of the Republic of Indonesia and the State Oceanic Administration of the People's Republic of China on Marine Cooperation, signed on 10th November 2007 and its Protocol Amending, signed on 29th April 2011 shall be

terminated.

IN WITNESS WHEREOF, the undersigned, being duly authorized thereto by their respective Governments, has signed this Memorandum of Understanding.

DONE at Beijing on this 26th day of March in the year of 2015, in duplicate, in Indonesian, Chinese and English languages, all texts being equally authentic. In case of any divergence of interpretations of the Indonesian and Chinese texts, the English text shall prevail.

中华人民共和国和日本国双边文件

中華人民共和国と日本国両国間の文書

中华人民共和国和日本国渔业协定

（1997年11月11日）

中华人民共和国政府和日本国政府，忆及一九七二年九月二十九日发表的《中华人民共和国政府和日本国政府联合声明》，考虑到包括一九七五年八月十五日签订的《中华人民共和国和日本国渔业协定》在内的渔业领域的传统合作关系，为按照制订于一九八二年十二月十日的《联合国海洋法公约》的宗旨建立两国间新的渔业秩序，养护和合理利用共同关心的海洋生物资源，维护海上正常作业秩序，经友好协商，达成协议如下：

第一条

本协定的适用水域（以下称“协定水域”）为中华人民共和国的专属经济区和日本国的专属经济区。

第二条

一、缔约各方根据互惠原则，按照本协定及本国有关法令，准许缔约另一方的国民及渔船在本国专属经济区从事渔业活动。

二、缔约各方的授权机关，按照本协定附件一的规定，向缔约另一方的国民及渔船颁发有关入渔的许可证，并可就颁发许可证收取适当费用。

三、缔约各方的国民及渔船在缔约另一方专属经济区按照本协定及缔约另一方的有关法令从事渔业活动。

第三条

缔约各方考虑到本国专属经济区资源状况、本国捕捞能力、传统渔业活动、相互入渔状况及其他相关因素，每年决定在本国专属经济区的缔约另一方国民及渔船的可捕鱼种、渔获配额、作业区域及其他作业条件。该决定应尊重第十一条规定设置的中日渔业联合委员会的协商结果。

第四条

一、缔约各方应采取必要措施，确保本国国民及渔船在缔约另一方专属经济区从事渔业活动时，遵守本协定的规定以及缔约另一方有关法令所规定的海洋生物资源的养护措施及其他条件。

二、缔约各方应及时向缔约另一方通报本国有关法令所规定的海洋生物资源的养护措施及其他条件。

第五条

一、缔约各方为确保缔约另一方的国民及渔船遵守本国有关法令所规定的海洋生物资源的养护措施及其他条件，可根据国际法在本国专属经济区采取必要措施。

二、被逮捕或扣留的渔船及其船员，在提出适当的保证书或其他担保之后，应迅速获得释放。

三、缔约各方的授权机关，在逮捕或扣留缔约另一方的渔船及其船员时，应通过适当途径，将所采取的行动及随后所施加的处罚，迅速通知缔约另一方。

第六条

第二条至前条的规定适用于协定水域中除以下1及2所指水域以外的部分。

1. 第七条第一款规定的水域；

2. 北纬二十七度以南的东海的协定水域以及东海以南的东经一百二十五度三十分以西的协定水域（南海的中华人民共和国的专属经济区除外）。

第七条

一、下列各点顺次用直线连结而围成的水域（以下称“暂定措施水域”）适用本条第二款及第三款的规定。

1. 北纬三十度四十分、东经一百二十四度十点一分之点
2. 北纬三十度、东经一百二十三度五十六点四分之点
3. 北纬二十九度、东经一百二十三度二十五点五分之点
4. 北纬二十八度、东经一百二十二度四十七点九分之点
5. 北纬二十七度、东经一百二十一度五十七点四分之点
6. 北纬二十七度、东经一百二十五度五十八点三分之点
7. 北纬二十八度、东经一百二十七度十五点一分之点
8. 北纬二十九度、东经一百二十八度零点九分之点
9. 北纬三十度、东经一百二十八度三十二点二分之点
10. 北纬三十度四十分、东经一百二十八度二十六点一分之点
11. 北纬三十度四十分、东经一百二十四度十点一分之点

二、缔约双方根据第十一条规定设置的中日渔业联合委员会的决定，在暂定措施水域中，考虑到对缔约各方传统渔业活动的影响，为确保海洋生物资源的维持不受过度开发的危害，采取适当的养护措施及量的管理措施。

三、缔约各方应对在暂定措施水域从事渔业活动的本国国民及渔船采取管理及其他必要措施。缔约各方在该水域中，不对从事渔业活动的缔约另一方国民及渔船采取管理和其他措施。缔约一方发现缔约另一方国民及渔船违反第十一条规定设置的中日渔业联合委员会决定的作业限制时，可就事实提醒该国民及渔船注意，并将事实及有关情况通报缔约另一方。缔约另一方应在尊重该方的通报并采取必要措施后将结果通报该方。

第八条

缔约各方为确保航行和作业安全，维护海上正常作业秩序并顺利及时处理海上事故，应对本国国民及渔船采取指导及其他必要措施。

第九条

一、缔约一方的国民及渔船在缔约另一方沿岸遭遇海难或其他紧急事态时，缔约另一方应尽力予以救助和保护，同时迅速将有关情况通报对方的有关部门。

二、缔约一方的国民及渔船，由于天气恶劣或其他紧急事态需要避难时，可按本协定附件二的规定，经与缔约另一方有关部门联系后，到缔约另一方港口等避难。该国民及渔船应遵守缔约另一方的有关法令，并服从有关部门的指挥。

第十条

缔约双方为渔业科学研究和海洋生物资源的养护而进行合作。

第十一条

一、缔约双方为实现本协定的目的，设立中日渔业联合委员会（以下称“渔委会”），渔委会由缔约双方政府各自任命的两名委员组成。

二、渔委会的任务如下：

（一）协商与第三条规定有关的事项、与第六条第 2 项所指水域有关的事项，并向缔约双方政府提出建议。协商事项包括如下内容：

1. 第三条规定的缔约另一方国民及渔船的可捕鱼种、渔获配额及其他具体作业条件的事项；

2. 有关维持作业秩序的事项；

3. 有关海洋生物资源状况和养护的事项；

4. 有关两国间渔业合作的事项。

（二）协商和决定与第七条规定有关的事项；

（三）根据需要，就本协定附件的修改向缔约双方政府提出建议；

（四）研究本协定的执行情况及其他有关本协定的事项。

三、渔委会的一切建议和决定须经双方委员一致同意方能实施。

四、缔约双方政府应尊重本条第二款第（一）项的建议，并按照本条第二款第（二）项的决定采取必要措施。

五、渔委会每年召开一次会议，在中华人民共和国和日本国轮流举行。根据需要，经缔约双方同意可召开临时会议。

第十二条

本协定各项规定不得认为有损缔约双方各自关于海洋法诸问题的立场。

第十三条

一、本协定的附件（包括根据本条第二款规定修改后的附件），为本协定不可分割的组成部分。

二、缔约双方政府可以书面协议修改本协定的附件。

第十四条

一、本协定经缔约双方履行为生效所必要的各自国内法律手续后，自两国政府通过换文达成协议之日起生效。本协定有效期为五年，之后有效至根据本条第二款的规定终止为止。

二、缔约任何一方，在最初五年期满时或在其后，可提前六个月以书面形式通知缔约另一方，随时终止本协定。

三、一九七五年八月十五日签订的《中华人民共和国和日本国渔业协定》自本协定生效之日起失效。

本协定于一九九七年十一月十一日在东京签订，一式两份，每份都用中文和日文写成，两种文本同等作准。

中华人民共和国政府代表	日本国政府代表
徐敦信	小渊惠三

附件一：

缔约各方根据本协定第二条第二款的规定，采取以下许可措施：

一、缔约各方的授权机关在接到缔约另一方授权机关发来的有关本协定第三条规定决定的书面通报后，向缔约另一方的授权机关申请发给在缔约另一方专属经济区从事渔业活动的本国国民及渔船许可证。缔约另一方的授权机关按照本协定及本国的有关法令颁发许可证。

二、缔约各方的授权机关应以书面形式向缔约另一方的授权机关通报有关入渔的手续规定（包括许可证的申请和颁发、捕鱼数据的提供、渔船标识及捕捞日志的填写等手续规定）。

三、获得许可的渔船应将许可证置于驾驶舱明显之处，并明确显示缔约另一方规定的渔船标识。

附件二：

按以下规定实施本协定第九条第二款的规定：

一、中华人民共和国政府指定的联络部门为管辖有关港口的港务监督部门。日本国政府指定的联络部门为管辖避难港口等的海上保安厅的各管区海上保安本部。

二、具体联系方法在本协定第十一条规定设置的中日渔业联合委员会上相互通报。

三、缔约各方的渔船与缔约另一方指定的联络部门进行联系的内容有：船名、呼号、当时船位（纬度、经度）、船籍港、总吨位和全长、船长姓名、船员数、避难理由、请求避难的目的地、预计到达时间、通讯联络方法。

协议议事录

中华人民共和国政府代表及日本国政府代表就本日签订的《中华人民共和国和日本国渔业协定》（以下称“协定”）有关条款，同意记录下列事项：

一、两国政府表示将继续坦诚进行两国关于专属经济区和大陆架划界的磋商，并努力达成双方都能接受的协议。此外，两国政府表示协定第七条第一款规定的暂定措施水域的设定，不得认为有损两国有关专属经济区和大陆架划界的各自立场。

二、两国政府表示，鉴于两国传统和合作的渔业关系，在实施协定和与第三国建立渔业关系时，双方在协定第七条第一款规定的水域北限线以北的东海部分水域，尊重现有的渔业活动，考虑缔约另一方传统作业及该水域的资源状况，不使缔约另一方在该水域的渔业利益受到不正当的损害。

中华人民共和国政府代表　　　　　　　　日本国政府代表

徐敦信　　　　　　　　　　　　小渊惠三

一九九七年十一月十一日于东京

日本国外务大臣小渊惠三阁下：

我荣幸地提及本日签订的《中华人民共和国和日本国渔业协定》，并谨阐述中华人民共和国政府意向如下：

以中日两国为确保本协定第六条第2项所指水域的海洋生物资源的维持不受过度开发的危害而进行合作为前提，在该水域不将本国有关渔业的法令适用于日本国民。

顺致敬意。

中华人民共和国驻日本国特命全权大使

徐敦信

一九九七年十一月十一日于东京

（译文）

中华人民共和国驻日本国特命全权大使徐敦信阁下：

本大臣荣幸地提及本日签订的《日本国和中华人民共和国渔业协定》，并谨阐述日本国政府意向如下：

以日中两国为确保本协定第六条第2项所指水域的海洋生物资源的维持不受过度开发的危害而进行合作为前提，在该水域不将本国有关渔业的法令适用于中国国民。

顺致敬意。

日本国外务大臣

小渊惠三

一九九七年十一月十一日于东京

（译文）

中华人民共和国驻日本国特命全权大使徐敦信阁下：

本大臣荣幸地提及本日签订的《日本国和中华人民共和国渔业协定》，并谨阐述如下：

一、根据本协定第三条规定，中华人民共和国政府要求本协定生效后五年内，中国鱿鱼钓渔船应可在日本海及北太平洋日本国专属经济区内进行作业，免交入渔费，作业船数及渔获量不应超过一九九六年的实际数量。

二、本大臣对此意向如下：日本国政府注意到并原则接受中方的要求，将根据该水域的渔业资源状况，由本协定第十一条规定设置的日中渔业联合委员会协商确定具体实施办法。

顺致敬意。

日本国外务大臣

小渊惠三

一九九七年十一月十一日于东京

漁業に関する日本国と中華人民共和国との間の協定

（略称）中国との漁業協定

平成　九年　十一月　十一日　東京で署名
平成　十年　四月　三十日　国会承認
平成　十二年　三月　三十一日　効力発生のための公文の交換の閣議決定
平成　十二年　三月三十一日　北京で効力発生のための公文の交換
平成　十二年　四月　五日　公布及び告示
（条約第二号及び外務省告示第一五七号）
平成　十二年　六月　一日　効力発生

目次

中国との漁業協定

三四三

中国との漁業協定

三四四

漁業に関する日本と中華人民共和国との間の協定

前文

日本国政府及び中華人民共和国政府は、千九百七十二年九月二十九日に発出された日本国政府と中華人民共和国政府の共同声明を想起し、千九百七十五年八月十五日に署名された日本国と中華人民共和国政府との間の漁業に関する協定に基づく関係を含む漁業の分野における伝統的な協力関係を考慮し、千九百八十二年十二月十日に作成された海洋法に関する国際連合の条約の趣旨に沿った新しい漁業秩序を両国の間に確立し、共に関心を有する海洋生物資源を保存し及び合理的に利用し並びに海上における正常な操業の秩序を維持するため，友好的な協議を経て、次のとおり協定した。

協定の適用範囲

第一条

この協定が適用される水域（以下「協定水域」という。）は日本国の排他的経済水域及び中華人民共和国の排他的経済水域とする。

相互入会いの許可制

第二条

1 各締約国は、相互利益の原則に立って、この協定及び自国の関係法令に従い、自国の排他的経済水域において他方の締約国の国民及び漁船が漁獲を行うことを許可する。

2 各締約国の権限のある当局は、この協定の付属書Iの規定に基づき、他方の締約国の国民及び漁船に対し入漁に関する許可証を発給する。当該権限のある当局は、許可証の発給に関し妥当な料金を徴収することができる。

3 各締約国の国民及び漁船は、他方の締約国の排他的経済水域において、この協定及び当該他方の締約国の関係法令に従って漁獲を行う。

沿岸国による操業条件等の決定

第三条

各締約国は、自国の排他的経済水域における資源状況、自国の漁獲能力、伝統的な漁業活動及び相互入会いの状況その他の関連する要因を考慮し、自国の排他的水域における他方の締約国の国民及び漁船の漁獲が認められる魚種、漁獲割当量、操業区域その他の操業の条件を毎年決定する。この決定は第十一条の規定に基づいて設置される日中漁業共同委員会における協議の結果を尊重して行われる。

他国水域における操業

第四条

1 各締約国は、自国の国民及び漁船が他方の締約国の排他的経済水域において漁獲を行うときは、この協定の規定及び他方の締約国の関係法令に定める海洋生物資源の保存措置その他の条件を遵守することを確保するために必要な措置をとる。

2 各締約国は、他方の締約国に対し、自国の関係法令に定める海洋生物資源の保存措置その他の条件につき、遅滞なく通報を行う。

沿岸国の法令の遵守

第五条

1 各締約国は、自国の関係法令に定める海洋生物資源の保存措置その他の条件を他方の締約国の国民及び漁船が遵守することを確保するために、国際法に従い、自国の排他的経済水域において、必要な措置をとることができる。

2 拿捕または抑留された漁船及びその乗組員は、適当な担保またはその他の保証の提供の後に速やかに釈放される。

3 各締約の権限のある当局は、他方の締約国の漁船及びその乗組員を拿捕し又は抑留した場合には、とられた措置及びその後科された罰について、適当な経路を通して他方の締約国に速やかに通報する。

相互入会い措置をとらない水域

第六条

第二条から前条までの規定は、協定水域のうち次の（a）及び（b）の水域を除く部分について適用する。

（a）第七条Ⅰに定める水域

（b）北緯二十七度以南の東海の協定水域及び東海より南の東経百二十五度三十分以西の協定水域（南海における中華人民共和国の排他的経済水域を除く。）

中国との漁業協定

暫定措置水域の共同規制

第七条

1 次に掲げる各点を順次に直線で結ぶ線によって囲まれる水域（以下「暫定措置水域」という。）においては、2及び3の規定を適用する。

（a）北緯三十度四十分、東経百二十四度十．一分の点

（b）北緯三十度、東経百二十三度五十六．四分の点

（c）北緯二十九度、東経百二十三度二十五．五分の点

（d）北緯二十八度、東経百二十二度四十七．九分の点

(e) 北緯二十七度、東経百二十一度五十七.四分の点
(f) 北緯二十七度、東経百二十五度五十八.三分の点
(g) 北緯二十八度、東経百二十七度十五.一分の点
(h) 北緯二十九度、東百二十八度零. 九分の点
(i) 北緯三十度、東経百二十八度三十二.二分の点
(j) 北緯三十度四十分、東経百二十八度二十六.一分の点
(k) 北緯三十度四十分、東経百二十四度十.一分の点

2 両締約国は、第十一条の規定に基づいて設置される日中漁業共同委員会における決定に従い、暫定措置水域において、各締約国の伝統的な漁業活動への影響を考慮しつつ、海洋生物の維持が過度の開発によって脅かされないことを確保するために、適当な保存措置及び量的な管理措置をとる。

3 各締約国は、暫定措置水域において漁獲を行う自国の国民及び漁船に対し、取り締りその他の必要な措置をとる。各締約国は、当該水域において漁獲を行う他方の締約国の国民及び漁船に対し、取り締りその他の措置をとらない。ただし、一方の締約国は、他方の締約国の国民及び漁船が第十一条の規定に基づいて設置される日中漁業共同委員会が決定する操業についての規制に違反していることを発見した場合には、その事実につき当該国民及び漁船の注意を喚起するとともに、当該他方の締約国に対し、その事実及び関連する状況を通報することができる。当該他方の締約国は、その通報を尊重して必要な措置をとった後、その結果を当該一方の締約国に対して通報する。

航行及び操業の安全の確保

第八条

各締約国は、自国の国民及び漁船に対し、航行及び操業の安全の確保、海上における正常な操業の秩序の維持並びに海上における事故の円滑かつ迅速な処理のため、指導その他の必要な措置をとる。

海難救助及び緊急避難

第九条

1 いずれか一方の締約国の国民及び漁船が他方の締約国の沿岸において海難その他の緊急事態に遭遇した場合には、他方の締約国は、できる限りの援助及び保護を与えるとともに、当該一方の締約国の関係当局にこれらに関

する状況を速やかに通報する。

2 いずれかの一方の締約国の国民及び漁船は，荒天その他の緊急事態のため避難する必要がある場合には、この協定の付属書IIの規定に従って他方の締約国の関係当局に連絡した後、当該他方の締約国の港等に避難することができる。この場合において、当該国民及び漁船は、当該他方の締約国の関係法令及び関係当局の指示に従わなければならない。

資源の保存のための協力等

第十条

両締約国は、漁業に関する科学的研究及び海上生物資源の保存のための協力を行う。

漁業委員会の設置

第十一条

1 両締約国は、この協定の目的を達成するため、日中漁業共同委員会（以下「漁業委員会」という。）を設置する。漁業委員会は、両締約国の政府が任命するそれぞれ二人の委員で構成する。

2 漁業委員会の任務は、次のとおりとする。

(1) 第三条の規定に関する事項及び第六条（b）の水域に関する事項について協議し、各締約国の政府に勧告する。これらの協議を行う事項には、次のものが含まれる。

(a) 第三条に規定する他方の締約国の国民及び漁船の漁獲が認められる魚種、漁獲割当量その他の具体的な操業の条件に関する事項

(b) 操業の秩序の維持に関する事項

(c) 海洋生物資源の状況及び保存に関する事項

(d) 両締約国間の漁業についての協力に関する事項

(2) 第七条の規定に関する事項について協議し、決定する。

(3) 必要に応じ、この協定の付属書の修正に関し、両締約の政府に勧告する。

(4) この協定の実施状況その他のこの協定に関する事項について検討する。

3 漁業委員会のすべての勧告及び決定は、双方の委員の合意によってのみ行う。

4 両締約国の政府は、2（1）の勧告を尊重し及び2（2）の決定に従って必要な措置をとる。

5 漁業委員会は、毎年一回、日本国又は中華人民共和国で交互に会合する。漁業委員会は、必要に応じ、両締約国の間の合意により臨時に会合することができる。

海洋法に関する諸問題

第十二条

この協定のいかなる規定も、海洋法に関する諸問題についての両締約国のそれぞれの立場を害するものとみなしてはならない。

付属書の位置付け及びその修正手段

第十三条

1 この協定の付属書（2の規定に従って修正された後の付属書を含む。）は、この協定の不可分の一部を構成する。

2 両締約国の政府は、文書による合意により、この協定の付属書を修正することができる。

協定の効力発生、終了及び旧協定の失効等

第十四条

1 この協定は、その効力発生のために国内法上必要とされる手続がそれぞれの国において完了した後、両締約国の政府の間の公文の交換によって合意されるひに効力を生ずる。この協定は、五年間効力を有する。その後は、2の規定に従ってこの協定が終了するまで効力を有する。

2 いずれの一方の締約国も、他方の締約国に対し、六箇月前に文書による予告を与えることにより、最初の五年の期間の満了の際またはその後いつでもこの協定を終了させることができる。

3 千九百七十五年八月十五日に署名された日本国と中華人民共和国との間の漁業に関する協定は、この協定の効力発生の日に効力を失う。

末文

千九百九十七年十一月十一日に東京で、ひとしく正文である日本語及び中国語により本書二通を作成した。

日本国政府のために
小渕恵三

中華人民共和国政府のために
徐敦信

中国との漁業協定

付属書I

各締約国は、この協定の第二条2の規定に基づき、許可に関する次の措置をとる。

1 各締約国の権限のある当局は、他方の締約国の権限のある当局からこの協定の第三条に規定する決定ににについての書面による通報を受領した後、当該他方の締約国の権限のある当局に対し、当該他方の締約国の排他的経済水域において漁獲を行うことを希望する自国の国民及び漁船に対する許可証の発給のための申請を行う。当該他方の締約国の権限のある当局は、この協定及び自国の関係法令に従って、この許可証の発給を行う。

2 各締約国の権限のある当局は、他方の締約国の権限のある当局に対し、入漁に関する手続き規則（許可証の申請及び発給、漁獲に関する情報の提出、漁船の標識並びに操業日誌の記載に関する手続き規則を含む。）を書面により通報する。

3 許可を受けた漁船は、許可証を操舵室の見やすい場所に掲示し、他方の締約国の定めｍル漁船の標識を明確に表示しなければならない。

付属書II

この協定の第九条2の規定の実施に関しては、次に定めるところによる。

1 日本国政府が指定する連絡先は、避難する港等を管轄する海上保安庁の各管区海上保安本部とする。中華人民共和国政府が指定する連絡先は、関係港を管轄する港務監督部門とする。

2 具体的な連絡方法については、この協定の第十一条の規定に基づいて設置される日中漁業共同委員会において相互に通報する。

3 一方の締約国の漁船が他方の締約国の指定する連絡先に連絡する内容は次のとおりとする。

船名、識別信号、現在位置（緯度、経度）、船籍港、総トン数及び全長、船長の氏名、乗組員数、避難の理由、避難を求める目的地、到着予定時刻並びに通信連絡の方法

合意された議事録

日本国政府代表及び中華人民共和国政府代表は、本日署名された漁業に関する日本国と中華人民共和国政府との間の協定（以下「協定」という。）の関係条項に関連し、次の事項を記録することに合意した。

1 両政府は、両国の排他的経済水域及び大陸棚の境界画定に関する協議を誠実に継続し、双方に受け入れ可能な合意が得られるよう努めることを表明した。また、両政府は、協定第七条1に規定する暫定措置水域の設定に関し、双方の排他的経済水域及び大陸棚の境界画定に関する立場を損なうものとみなしてはならないことを表明した。

2 両政府は、両国の伝統的且つ協力的な漁業関係にかんがみ、協定の実施及び第三国との漁業関係の構築に際し、双方が協定第七条1に規定する水域の北側の境界線以北の東海の一部水域において現有の漁業活動を尊重し、他方の国の伝統的操業及び当該水域の資源状況に配慮し、当該他方の国の当該水域における漁業の利益が不当に損なわれることのないようにする意向を表明した。

千九百九十七年十一月十一日に東京で

日本政府のために	中華人民共和国政府のために
小渕恵三	徐敦信

（漁業に関する日本国と中華人民共和国との間の協定第六条（b）の水域に関する書簡）

日本側書簡

日本国駐在中華人民共和国特命全権大使　徐敦信閣下

本大臣は、本日署名された漁業に関する日本国と中華人民共和国との間の協定に言及するとともに、次の通り申し述べる光栄を有します。

日本国政府は、日中両国が同協定第六条（b）の水域における海洋生物資源の維持が過度の開発によって脅かされないことを確保するため協力関係にあることを前提として、中国国民に対して、当該水域において、漁業に関する自国の関係法令を適用しないとの意向を有している。

本大臣は、以上を申し進めるに際し、ここに閣下に向かって敬意を表します。

千九百九十七年十一月十一日に東京で

日本国外務大臣

小渕恵三

中国側書簡

（訳文）

日本国外務大臣　小渕恵三閣下

本使は、本日署名された漁業に関する日本国と中華人民共和国との間の協定に言及するとともに、次のとおり申し述べる光栄を有します。

中華人民共和国政府は、日中両国が同協定第六条（b）の水域における海洋生物資源の維持が過度の開発によって脅かされないことを確保するため協力関係にあることを前提として、日本国民に対して、当該水域において、漁業に関する自国の関係法令を適用しないとの意向を有している。

本使は、以上を申し進めるに際し、ここに閣下に向かって敬意を表します。

千九百九十七年十一月十一日に東京で

日本国駐在中華人民共和国

特命全権大使　徐敦信

（中国のいか釣りの実績に関する日本側書簡）

日本国駐在中華人民共和国特命全権大使　徐敦信閣下

本大臣は、本日署名された漁業に関する日本国と中華人民共和国との間の協定に言及するとともに、次の通り申し述べる光栄を有します。

1 同協定第三条の規定に基づき、中華人民共和国政府は、協定の発効後五年の間、中国のいか釣り漁船が日本海及び北太平洋の日本国の排他的経済水域において操業ができること、入漁費用が免除されること並びに操業隻数及び漁獲量は千九百九十六年の実際の数量を超えないものとされるべきことを要望した。

2 日本国政府は、中国側の要望に留意するとともに、これを原則的に受け入れ、当該水域における漁業資源の状況を踏まえつつ、同協定第十一条の規定に基づいて設置される日中漁業共同委員会において具体的実施方法につき協議し及び確定する意向である。

本大臣は、以上を申し進めるに際し、ここに閣下に向かって敬意を表します。

千九百九十七年十一月十一日に東京で

日本国外務大臣　小渕恵三

（参考）

この協定は、日中両国について平成八年に発行した国連海洋法条約の趣旨を踏まえ、原則として沿岸国が自国の排他的経済水域において海洋生物資源の管理を行うことを基本とする新たな漁業秩序を日中間に確立するため締結したものであり、昭和五十年八月十五日に署名された中国との漁業協定（昭和五十年二国間条約集及び条約集第二五一四号参照）に代わるものである。

中日联合新闻公报

（2006年10月8日）

一、应中华人民共和国国务院总理温家宝邀请，日本国内阁总理大臣安倍晋三于2006年10月8日至9日对中华人民共和国进行了正式访问。中华人民共和国主席胡锦涛、全国人民代表大会常务委员会委员长吴邦国和国务院总理温家宝分别与安倍晋三首相举行了会见和会谈。

二、中日双方一致认为，邦交正常化34年来，中日两国各领域的交流与合作不断拓展和深化，相互依存进一步加深，中日关系成为两国最重要的双边关系之一；推动中日关系健康稳定地持续发展，符合两国基本利益；共同为亚洲以及世界的和平、稳定与发展作出建设性贡献，是新时代赋予两国和两国关系的新的庄严责任。

三、双方同意，继续遵守《中日联合声明》、《中日和平友好条约》和《中日联合宣言》的各项原则，正视历史，面向未来，妥善处理影响两国关系发展的问题，让政治和经济两个车轮强力运转，把中日关系推向更高层次。双方同意，努力构筑基于共同战略利益的互惠关系，实现中日两国和平共处、世代友好、互利合作、共同发展的崇高目标。

四、双方认为，两国领导人之间的交往与对话对两国关系的健康发展具有重要意义。日方邀请中国领导人访问日本，中方对此表示感谢，并原则同意。双方同意通过外交渠道进行协商。双方同意两国领导人在国际会议场合经常举行会谈。

五、中方强调，中国的发展是和平的发展，中国将同包括日本在内的各国共同发展、共同繁荣。日方对中国走和平发展道路和中国改革开放以来的发展给包括日本在内的国际社会带来巨大机遇给予积极评价。日方强调，日本战后六十多年一直走作为和平国家的道路，今后将继续走作为和平国家的道路。中方对此表示积极评价。

六、双方确认，为使东海成为和平、合作、友好之海，应坚持对话协商，妥善解决有关分歧；加快东海问题磋商进程，坚持共同开发大方向，探讨双方都能接受的解决办法。

七、双方同意，在政治、经济、安全、社会、文化等领域促进各层次交流与合作。

——以能源、环保、金融、信息通信技术、知识产权保护等领域为重点，深化互利合作。

——在经济领域推进部长级对话、相关部门之间的磋商和官民对话。

——以2007年中日邦交正常化35周年为契机，通过举办中日文化、体育交流年，大力开展两国人民尤其是青少年交流，增进两国人民之间的友好感情。

——通过中日安全对话和防务交流，增进安全领域互信。

——年内启动中日学术界共同历史研究。

八、双方同意，加强在国际和地区事务中的协调与合作。

双方对包括核试验问题在内朝鲜半岛最近的形势深表忧虑。双方确认，愿与有关各方一道，根据六方会谈共同声明推进六方会谈进程，通过对话与协商，共同合作致力于实现朝鲜半岛无核化，维护东北亚地区的和平与稳定。

双方确认，就东亚区域合作、中日韩合作加强协调，共同推进东亚一体化进程。

双方赞成对联合国包括安理会进行必要、合理的改革，愿就此加强对话。

九、日方对安倍晋三首相访华期间中方给予的热情友好接待表示感谢。

2006年10月8日在北京发表。

日中共同プレス発表

平成18年10月8日

1. 安倍晋三日本国内閣総理大臣は、温家宝中華人民共和国国務院総理の招待に応じ、2006年10月8日から9日まで中華人民共和国を公式訪問した。安倍総理は、胡錦濤中華人民共和国主席、呉邦国全国人民代表大会常務委員会委員長、温家宝国務院総理とそれぞれ会見、会談を行った。

2. 日本側及び中国側双方は、国交正常化後34年間、日中両国間の各分野における交流と協力が絶え間なく拡大・深化し、相互依存が更に深まり、日中関係が両国にとり最も重要な二国間関係の一つとなったとの認識で一致した。また、双方は、日中関係の健全かつ安定的な発展の持続を推進することが、両国の基本的利益に合致し、アジア及び世界の平和、安定及び発展に対して共に建設的な貢献を行うことが、新たな時代において両国及び両国関係に与えられた厳粛な責任であるとの認識で一致した。

3. 双方は、日中共同声明、日中平和友好条約及び日中共同宣言の諸原則を引き続き遵守し、歴史を直視し、未来に向かい、両国関係の発展に影響を与える問題を適切に処理し、政治と経済という二つの車輪を力強く作動させ、日中関係を更に高度な次元に高めていくことで意見の一致をみた。双方は、共通の戦略的利益に立脚した互恵関係の構築に努力し、また、日中両国の平和共存、世代友好、互恵協力、共同発展という崇高な目標を実現することで意見の一致をみた。

4. 双方は、両国の指導者の間の交流と対話が両国関係の健全な発展に重要な意義を有すると考える。日本側より中国の指導者の日本訪問を招待したのに対し、中国側は感謝の意を表明し、原則的にこれに同意し、双方は、外交ルートを通じて協議することで意見の一致をみた。双方は、両国の指導者が国際会議の場においても頻繁に会談を行うことで意見の一致をみた。

5. 中国側は、中国の発展は平和的発展であり、中国が日本をはじめとする各国と共に発展し、共に繁栄していくことを強調した。日本側は、中国の平和的発展及び改革開放以来の発展が日本を含む国際社会に大きな好機をもたらしていることを積極的に評価した。日本側は、戦後60年余、一貫して平和国家として歩んできたこと、そして引き続き平和国家として歩み続けていくことを強調した。中国側は、これを積極的に評価した。

6. 双方は、東シナ海を平和・協力・友好の海とするため、双方が対話と協議を堅持し、意見の相違を適切に解決すべきであることを確認した。また、双方は、東シナ海問題に関する協議のプロセスを加速し、共同開発という大きな方向を堅持し、双方が受入れ可能な解決の方法を模索することを確認した。

7. 双方は、政治、経済、安全保障、社会、文化等の分野における各レベルでの交流と協力を促進することで意見の一致をみた。

エネルギー、環境保護、金融、情報通信技術、知的財産権保護等の分野を重点として、互恵協力を強化する。

経済分野において、閣僚間の対話、関係当局間の協議や官民の対話を推進する。

2007年の日中国交正常化35周年を契機として、日中文化・スポーツ交流年を通じ、両国民、特に青少年の交流を飛躍的に展開し、両国民の間の友好的な感情を増進する。

日中安全保障対話や防衛交流を通じて、安全保障分野における相互信頼を増進する。

日中有識者による歴史共同研究を年内に立ち上げる。

8. 双方は、国際問題及び地域問題における協調と協力を強化することで意見の一致をみた。

双方は、核実験の問題を含む最近の朝鮮半島情勢に深い憂慮を表明した。この関連で、双方は、関係方面と共に、六者会合の共同声明に従って六者会合プロセスを推進し、対話と協議を通じて、朝鮮半島の非核化の実現、北東アジア地域の平和と安定の維持のため、協力して共に力を尽くすことを確認した。

双方は、東アジア地域協力、日中韓協力における協調を強化し、東アジアの一体化のプロセスを共に推進することを確認した。

双方は、国連について安保理改革を含む必要かつ合理的な改革を行うことに賛成し、これにつき対話を強化する意向を表明した。

9. 日本側は、安倍晋三内閣総理大臣の中国訪問期間中における中国側の心のこもった友好的な接遇に対し、感謝の意を表明した。

2006年10月8日北京で発表した。

中日联合新闻公报

（2007年4月11日）

一、应日本国政府邀请，中华人民共和国国务院总理温家宝于2007年4月11日至13日对日本进行了正式访问。访日期间，温家宝总理与安倍晋三内阁总理大臣举行了会谈，还将会见明仁天皇，在日本国会发表演讲，并与日本各界人士进行广泛接触。

二、中日双方确认，将继续遵循《中日联合声明》、《中日和平友好条约》和《中日联合宣言》的各项原则。

三、双方决心正视历史，面向未来，共同开创两国关系的美好未来。关于台湾问题，日方表示坚持在《中日联合声明》中表明的立场。

四、双方再次确认，根据2006年10月安倍首相访华时双方发表的《中日联合新闻公报》，努力构筑“基于共同战略利益的互惠关系”（以下称战略互惠关系），实现中日两国和平共处、世代友好、互利合作、共同发展的崇高目标，并就构筑战略互惠关系达成以下共识：

（一）战略互惠关系的基本精神是：

中日两国共同为亚洲以及世界的和平、稳定与发展作出建设性贡献，是新时代赋予两国的庄严责任。基于这一认识，今后中日两国将全面发展在双边、地区及国际等各层次的互利合作，共同为两国、亚洲以及世界作出贡献，在此过程中相互获得利益并扩大共同利益，藉此推动两国关系发展到新的高度。

（二）战略互惠关系的基本内涵是：

1. 相互支持和平发展，增进政治互信。保持并加强两国高层往来。努力提高各自政策的透明度。扩大和深化两国政府、议会、政党的交流与对话。

2. 深化互利合作，实现共同发展。加强在能源、环保、金融、信息通信技术、知识产权保护等领域的合作，充实和完善合作机制。

3. 加强防务对话与交流，共同致力于维护地区稳定。

4. 加强人文交流，增进两国人民相互理解和友好感情。广泛开展两国青少年、媒体、友城、民间团体之间的交流。开展丰富多彩的文化交流。

5. 加强协调与合作，共同应对地区及全球性课题。共同致力于维护东北亚和平与稳定，坚持通过对话和平解决朝鲜半岛核问题，实现朝鲜半岛无核化目标。双方赞成联合国包括安理会进行必要、合理的改革。支持东盟在东亚区域合作中发挥重要作用，共同在开放、透明、包容等三项原则基础上促进东亚区域合作。

五、双方决定为构筑战略互惠关系开展具体合作，达成以下成果：

（一）加强对话交流，增进相互理解

1. 高层交往安排

两国领导人保持经常性往来，在国际会议场合继续举行经常性会晤。

2. 中日经济高层对话机制

两国总理共同出席机制启动会议，启动了这一机制，分别提名曾培炎副总理和麻生太郎外相为机制共同主席，明确了机制构成和任务，确认了两国经济及经济合作对世界经济的重要性，并就今年年内在北京举行第一次会议达成一致。

3. 外交当局对话

双方确认，两国外长就双边及共同关心的地区和国际问题保持密切合作，加强中日战略对话、中日安全对话、中日经济伙伴关系磋商、中日联合国改革问题磋商、中日非洲问题磋商、中日外交部发言人磋商等涉及广泛领域的各层次对话。

4. 防务交流

中国国防部长应邀于今年秋季访日。双方就尽早实现中国海军军舰访日，其后日本海上自卫队军舰访华达成一致。加强两国防务当局联络机制，防止发生海上不测事态。

5. 人员往来和青少年交流

中方同意开通虹桥机场与羽田机场之间的定期国际客运包机航班。

双方结合纪念中日邦交正常化35周年，共同实施日本向中国19个直航城市派遣总计两万人规模访问团计划。

日方宣布将根据“21世纪东亚青少年大交流计划”，今后5年大规模邀请中国高中生访日，中方对此表示欢迎。双方就双向实施两国青少年大规模交流计划达成一致。

6. 文化交流

双方密切配合，确保中日文化体育交流年取得积极成果。双方就在对方首都互设文化中心达成一致。

（二）加强互利合作

1. 能源、环保合作

双方对发表《关于进一步加强环境保护合作的联合声明》表示欢迎。双方确认在认真致力于解决全球性环境问题的同时，就重点开展渤黄海区域和长江流域等重要水域水污染防治、建设循环型社会、防止大气污染、应对气候变化、防止海洋漂浮垃圾、防治酸雨及沙尘暴等合作达成一致。

双方对举行第一次部长能源政策对话和发表关于加强两国在能源领域合作的联合声明表示欢迎，同意重点推进节能环保商务示范项目，加强两国在节能、煤炭、核能等能源领域以及亚洲地区节能多边框架内的合作。

双方确认，支持中日民间绿化合作委员会的工作，进一步推进日本民间团体等在华植树造林合作事业，并在可持续森林经营方面开展合作。

2. 农业合作

双方就积极开展农业领域合作达成一致。中方表示同意进口符合中国检疫标准的日本大米，日方对此表示欢迎。双方将继续积极协商相互进出口农产品问题。

3. 朱鹮

中方同意向日本提供两只朱鹮，日方对此表示感谢。双方同意开展朱鹮保护合作。

4. 医药领域合作

双方同意推进以应对新型流感和癌症为重点的中日医学合作构想。关于癌症防治合作，日方表示将尽早派遣由官方和民间有关人员组成的代表团到中国交流，中方对此表示欢迎。

5. 知识产权

双方同意，在相互尊重、互利共赢的基础上，加强知识产权领域的对话与合作，共同促进知识产权运用与保护水平的不断提高，以推动两国经济关系顺利发展。

6. 中小企业博览会

日方同意应邀作为主宾国与中方共同主办将于9月在广州举办的中小企业博览会。

7. 信息通信技术领域合作

双方同意，进一步加强和推动双方在下一代移动通信和下一代网络等信息通信领域的合作。

8. 金融领域合作

双方同意，进一步加强在金融和金融监管领域的合作关系。

9. 刑事司法领域合作

双方同意，作为加强中日在刑事司法领域合作关系的重要一环，将努力争取年内关于缔结中日刑事司法协助条约的谈判达成实质性共识。双方同意继续推进关于缔结中日引渡条约和被判刑人移管条约事项的磋商。

（三）地区和国际事务合作

1. 联合国改革

双方同意就联合国改革问题加强对话与沟通，努力增加共识。中方愿意看到日本在国际事务中发挥更大的建设性作用。

2. 六方会谈合作

双方再次确认，根据2005年9月19日六方会谈共同声明推进六方会谈进程，通过对话与协商，共同合作致力于实现朝鲜半岛无核化，维护东北亚地区的和平与稳定。双方一致认为，六方应共同努力，全面落实2007年2月13日六方会谈关于起步阶段行动的共同文件。日方就解决包括绑架问题在内的日朝间悬案、推进日朝邦交正常化谈判的方针作了说明。中方对日本国民有关人道主义关切表示理解和同情，希望这一问题早日得到解决，期待日朝关系取得进展，愿为此提供必要协助。

3. 投资交流

双方同意，为尽早达成一个务实共赢的中日韩投资协议和制定中日韩改善商务环境行动计划作出努力。

4. 经济合作

双方一致认为，将于2008年结束的日本对华日元贷款为中国经济建设和中日经济合作发挥了积极作用，中方对此表示感谢。双方同意就合作向第三国提供援助问题进行对话。

六、为妥善处理东海问题，双方达成以下共识：

（一）坚持使东海成为和平、合作、友好之海。

（二）作为最终划界前的临时性安排，在不损害双方关于海洋法诸问题立场的前提下，根据互惠原则进行共同开发。

（三）根据需要举行更高级别的磋商。

（四）在双方都能接受的较大海域进行共同开发。

（五）加快磋商进程，争取在今年秋天就共同开发具体方案向领导人报告。

七、双方对设立“处理日本遗弃在华化学武器日中联合机构”表示欢迎。为加快销毁进程，日方表示将根据中方提议引进移动式处理设备进行作业，中方对此表示欢迎。

八、中方对日方在温家宝总理访日期间所给予的热情友好接待表示感谢。

日中共同プレス発表

温家宝中華人民共和国国務院総理は、日本国政府の招待に応じ、2007年4月11日から13日まで公賓として日本を公式訪問した。温家宝総理は、日本滞在中、安倍晋三内閣総理大臣と会談を行った。また、天皇陛下に謁見し、国会において演説を行い、日本の各界の人々と幅広く接触を行う。

日中双方は、日中共同声明、日中平和友好条約及び日中共同宣言の諸原則を引き続き遵守することを確認した。

双方は、歴史を直視し、未来に向かい、両国関係の美しい未来を共に切り開くことを決意した。

台湾問題に関し、日本側は、日中共同声明において表明した立場を堅持する旨表明した。

双方は、2006年10月の安倍総理訪中の際に双方が発表した「日中共同プレス発表」に基づき、「共通の戦略的利益に立脚した互恵関係」(以下「戦略的互恵関係」という。)の構築に努力し、また、日中両国の平和共存、世代友好、互恵協力、共同発展という崇高な目標を実現することを再確認するとともに、「戦略的互恵関係」の構築に関し、以下の共通認識に達した。

(1)「戦略的互恵関係」の基本精神は、以下のとおりである。

日中両国が、アジア及び世界の平和、安定及び発展に対して共に建設的な貢献を行うことが、新たな時代において両国に与えられた厳粛な責任である。このような認識の下、日中両国は、将来にわたり、二国間、地域、国際社会等様々なレベルにおける互恵協力を全面的に発展させ、両国、アジア及び世界のために共に貢献し、その中で互いに利益を得て共通利益を拡大する。そのことにより、両国関係を新たな高みへと発展させていく。

(2)「戦略的互恵関係」の基本的な内容は、以下のとおりである。

(イ) 平和的発展を相互に支持し、政治面の相互信頼を増進する。両国のハイレベルの往来を維持し強化する。それぞれの政策の透明性の向上に努める。両国の政府、議会、政党間の交流と対話を拡大し深化させる。

(ロ) 互恵協力を深化させ、共同発展を実現する。エネルギー、環境保護、金融、情報通信技術、知的財産権保護等の分野における協力を強化し、協力のメカニズムを充実させ整備する。

(ハ) 防衛分野における対話及び交流を強化し、共に地域の安定に向け力を尽くす。

(ニ) 人及び文化の交流を強化し、両国民の相互理解及び友好的感情を増進する。両国の青少年、メディア、友好都市、民間団体の間の交流を幅広く展開し、多種多様な文化交流を展開する。

(ホ) 協調と協力を強化し、地域及び地球規模の課題に共に対応する。北東アジアの平和と安定の維持に共に力を尽くし、朝鮮半島の核問題を対話を通じて平和的に解決することを堅持し、朝鮮半島の非核化という目標を実現する。国際連合が安保理改革を含め必要で合理的な改革を行うことに賛成する。ASEANが東アジアの地域協力において重要な役割を果たすことを支持し、共に開放性、透明性、包含性の三つの原則の基礎の上に東アジアにおける地域協力を促進する。

双方は、「戦略的互恵関係」の構築のため具体的な協力を行うことを決定し、以下の成果を得た。

(1) 対話と交流の強化・相互理解の増進

(イ) 首脳レベルの交流

両国の指導者は、頻繁な往来を維持するとともに、国際会議の場において引き続き頻繁に会談を行う。

(ロ) 日中ハイレベル経済対話

両総理は、立上げ会合に共に出席し、同対話を立ち上げることとし、それぞれ麻生太郎外務大臣及び曾培炎副総理を同対話の共同議長に指名し、対話の構成及び任務を明確にし、両国の経済及び経済面における両国の協力の世界経済に対する重要性を確認し、年内に北京において第一回会合を行うことで一致した。

（ハ）外交当局間の対話

双方は、両外相が二国間問題及び共に関心を有する地域・国際問題について緊密な協力を維持することを確認し、日中戦略対話、日中安全保障対話、日中経済パートナーシップ協議、国連改革に関する日中協議、アフリカに関する日中協議、日中外務報道官協議等、幅広い分野に及ぶ様々なレベルの対話を強化していくことを確認した。

（ニ）防衛交流

中国国防部長は招待に応じ本年秋に訪日する。双方は、中国海軍艦艇の訪日、その後の日本国海上自衛隊艦艇の訪中を早期に実現することで一致した。また、両国の防衛当局間の連絡メカニズムを整備し、海上における不測の事態の発生を防止する。

（ホ）人的往来及び青少年交流

中国側は、虹橋空港と羽田空港との間の定期的な国際旅客チャーター便の開設に同意した。

双方は、日中国交正常化35周年に合わせ、日本からの直行便を有する中国の19の都市に、総計2万人規模の訪問団を派遣するなどの計画を共に実施する。

また、日本側より、「21世紀東アジア青少年大交流計画」に基づき、今後5年間、中国の高校生を日本に大きな規模で招きたい旨表明し、中国側はこれを歓迎した。双方は、両国の青少年の大規模交流計画を双方向で実施することで一致した。

（ヘ）文化交流

双方は緊密に協力し、日中文化スポーツ交流年が積極的な成果を得ることを確保する。双方は、互いに相手国の首都に文化センターを開設することにつき一致した。

(2) 互恵協力の強化

（イ）エネルギー・環境協力

双方は、「環境保護協力の一層の強化に関する共同声明」の発表を歓迎し、日中双方の地球規模環境問題に対する真摯な取組を確認するとともに、渤海、黄海区域及び長江流域等重要な水域における水質汚濁防止、循環型社会の構築、大気汚染防止、気候変動対策、海洋漂流ゴミ防止、酸性雨及び黄砂対策等の協力を重点的に展開していくことで一致した。

双方は、第一回エネルギー閣僚政策対話 他のサイトへの開催及び日中間のエネルギー分野における協力強化に関する共同声明の発表を歓迎し、省エネルギー・環境ビジネス推進モデルプロジェクトを始め、省エネ、石炭、原子力等のエネルギー分野や、アジア地域における省エネルギーの推進など多国間の枠組みにおける両国の協力を重点的に強化していくことで一致した。

双方は、日中民間緑化協力委員会の活動を支持し、日本の民間団体などによる中国での植林協力事業を一層促進すること、また、持続可能な森林経営にも両国が協力して取り組んでいくことを確認した。

(ロ) 農業協力

双方は、農業分野での協力を積極的に展開していくことで一致した。中国側は、中国の検疫基準に合致する日本産米の輸入に同意し、日本側はこれを歓迎した。双方は、双方の農産物の輸出問題について、引き続き積極的に協議を行っていくこととした。

(ハ) トキ

中国側は、日本に二羽のトキを提供することに同意し、日本側は謝意を表明した。双方は、トキ保護に関する協力を展開することで一致した。

(ニ) 医薬品分野における協力

双方は、新型インフルエンザ対策及びがん対策を重点とする日中医学協力構想を推進していくことで一致した。日本側は、がん対策の協力について、官民の関係者からなるミッションを早期に中国に派遣して交流を行う旨伝達し、中国側はこれを歓迎した。

(ホ) 知的財産権

双方は、相互尊重、互恵で双方が利益を得るとの基礎の上に、知的財産権分野における対話と協力を強化し、知的財産権の運用及び保護の水準を不断に高め、もって日中間の経済面での協力を円滑に発展させていくことで一致した。

(ヘ) 中小企業博覧会

日本側は、要請に応じ、9月に広州にて開催される中小企業博覧会について主賓国として中国側と共同で同博覧会を主催することに同意した。

(ト) 情報通信技術分野における協力

双方は、次世代移動通信及び次世代ネットワーク等の情報通信分野における協力を一層強化し推進していくことで一致した。

(チ) 金融分野における協力

双方は、金融及び金融監督の分野における協力関係を一層強化していくことで一致した。

（リ）刑事司法分野における協力

双方は、日中間の刑事司法分野における協力関係を強化していく重要な一環として、日中刑事共助条約締結交渉の年内実質合意に向け努力していくことで一致した。双方は、また、日中犯罪人引渡条約及び受刑者移送条約の締結に関する事項についての協議を引き続き推進することで一致した。

(3) 地域・国際社会における協力

（イ）国連改革

双方は、国連改革問題について対話と意思疎通を強化し、共通認識を増やすべく努力することで一致した。中国側は、日本が国際社会で一層大きな建設的役割を果たすことを望んでいる。

（ロ）六者会合における協力

双方は、六者会合の2005年9月19日の共同声明に従って六者会合プロセスを推進し、対話と協議を通じて、朝鮮半島の非核化を実現し、北東アジア地域の平和と安定を維持するため、共に協力して力を尽くすことを再確認した。また、双方は、2007年2月13日に六者会合が達成した「初期段階の措置」に関する共同文書を六者が共に努力して全面的に実施すべきであるとの認識で一致した。日本側は、拉致問題を含む日朝間の懸案事項を解決し、日朝国交正常化交渉を進める方針を説明した。中国側は、日本国民の人道主義的関心に対して理解と同情を示し、この問題の早期解決を希望するとともに、日朝関係が進展することへの期待を表明し、このため必要な協力を提供したい旨表明した。

（ハ）投資交流

双方は、実務的で共に利益を得る日中韓投資協定の早期合意及び日中韓ビジネス環境改善行動アジェンダの策定のため然るべく努力していくことで一致した。

（ニ）経済協力

双方は、2008年に終了する日本の対中円借款が、中国の経済建設及び経済面での日中協力に積極的役割を果たしたとの認識で一致し、中国側はこのことに対して感謝の意を表明した。双方は、協力して第三国に援助を提供する問題について対話を行うことで一致した。

双方は、東シナ海問題を適切に処理するため、以下の共通認識に達した。

(1) 東シナ海を平和・協力・友好の海とすることを堅持する。

(2) 最終的な境界画定までの間の暫定的な枠組みとして、双方の海洋法に関する諸問題についての立場を損なわないことを前提として、互恵の原則に基づき共同開発を行う。

(3) 必要に応じ、従来よりハイレベルの協議を行う。

(4) 双方が受入れ可能な比較的広い海域で共同開発を行う。

(5) 協議のプロセスを加速させ、本年秋に共同開発の具体的方策につき首脳に報告することを目指す。

双方は、「中国における日本の遺棄化学兵器の処理に関する日中連合機構」の設立に対して歓迎の意を表明した。また、日本側は、中国側の提案を踏まえ、廃棄のプロセスを加速するため、移動式処理設備を導入して作業を進めていくことを表明し、中国側はこれを歓迎した。

中国側は、温家宝総理の日本訪問期間中における日本側の心のこもった友好的な接遇に対し、感謝の意を表明した。

2007年4月11日　東京にて発表した。

中华人民共和国政府和日本国政府关于加强交流与合作的联合新闻公报

（2008年5月7日）

应日本国政府邀请，中华人民共和国主席胡锦涛于2008年5月6日至10日对日本进行国事访问，与福田康夫内阁总理大臣举行了富有成果的会谈，双方发表了《中日关于全面推进战略互惠关系的联合声明》。为落实上述联合声明，双方达成如下共识：

一、日方邀请胡锦涛主席出席今年7月在北海道洞爷湖举行的八国集团同有关国家领导人对话会议，中方表示将认真积极研究。

二、中方邀请福田康夫首相出席今年10月在北京举行的第七届亚欧首脑会议，日方表示将认真积极研究。

三、日方提议今年秋天在日本举行中日韩领导人会议，中方表示将认真积极研究。

四、双方积极评价中日战略对话为推动中日关系改善与发展所发挥的重要作用，将继续重视这一对话。

五、在今年4月东京召开的中日外交部发言人磋商中，双方一致认为，为进一步增进两国人民相互了解，双方应在报道和宣传方面进行合作，加强两国宣传报道部门的直接联络机制，共同努力向两国媒体提供客观、准确的信息。双方对此表示欢迎，将在双方方便的时候在北京举行下次磋商。

六、为增进两国防务部门之间的相互信任，日本防卫大臣将于年内访华。

七、双方对今年3月举行的中日防务安全磋商表示欢迎。为加深两国防务部门之间的相互理解，将继续举行高级别防务安全磋商。

八、继今年2月日本联合参谋长访华后，中国人民解放军空军司令员将于今年6月访日，海军司令员、副总参谋长将于今年下半年分别访日。

九、继中国人民解放军海军舰艇去年11月访日后，日本海上自卫队舰艇将于今年6月访华。

十、为防止海上发生不测事态，建立中日防务部门海上联络机制首轮专家组磋商于4月下旬在北京举行，双方对此表示欢迎，将继续为早日建立该机制作出努力。

十一、双方将就扩大军兵种、防务相关教育机构、研究机构间的交流进行探讨。

十二、双方将探讨在联合国维和行动（PKO）、灾害救援等领域合作的可能性。

十三、为加深两国防务部门之间的相互理解和对对方国家的了解，双方同意加强中国人民解放军青年军官和日本自卫队年轻干部互访，年内将相互邀请约15名尉官级干部访问对方国家一周左右。

十四、新一届中日友好21世纪委员会在两国领导人的关心下，为推动中日关系改善和发展提出了有益建议，双方对此表示积极评价，期待该委员会今年底提交最终报告。

十五、双方积极评价中日共同历史研究发挥的作用，同意继续开展这一研究。

十六、双方对去年两国人员往来达到500万人次表示欢迎，今后将继续扩大人员交往，为增进相互理解进行密切合作。

十七、双方对“中日青少年友好交流年”顺利启动表示满意。双方确认，今后4年每年开展4000人规模的青少年交流，并将为最大限度有效开展青少年交流作出努力。

十八、双方一致同意持之以恒地开展青少年友好交流，呼吁两国各界为促进青少年交流加强合作。

十九、双方一致认为，进一步加强两国中青年干部交流具有积极意义，今后将继续支持开展这一领域的交流与合作。

二十、双方一致希望北京奥运会取得成功，希望以北京奥运会为契机，进一步促进两国人民交流，增进相互理解和友谊。

二十一、双方对签署两国关于互设文化中心的协定表示欢迎，期待该中心为促进两国人民的相互理解发挥积极作用。

二十二、双方积极致力于人文领域的交流与合作，鼓励相关部门和社会团体在文化遗产保护等领域开展共同研究。

二十三、去年12月福田首相访华时，日方提出加强北京大学对日交流的计划，双方对有关准备工作取得进展表示欢迎，将继续为进一步加强知识界交流进行合作。

二十四、中日经济高层对话首次会议去年12月在北京召开，两国有关部长们会聚一堂，就各自宏观经济政策、包括气候变化问题在内的节能环保、贸易投资、检验检疫、地区及国际经济问题等开展跨部门直接对话，增进了相互理解，并为今后解决问题和推进合作指明了方向。双方对此表示高度评价。下次对话拟于今年秋天在东京举行。

二十五、两国相关部门签署了《关于互利共赢推动可持续经济发展一揽子合作的框架协议》、《关于继续加强节能环保领域合作的备忘录》和《关于推进中小企业领域合作备忘录》三个协议。双方对此表示欢迎，并一致同意继续推动上述合作。

二十六、双方对当前的原油价格表示忧虑。双方一致同意继续开展中日部长级能源政策对话，探讨能源领域互惠合作。

二十七、双方表示，在煤炭领域技术合作方面，推动中方煤炭火力发电厂的设备诊断、设备改造、人才培训。双方将继续开展通过捕集和封存煤炭火力发电厂产生的二氧化碳（CCS）提高石油采收率（EOR）方面的实证研究。双方对继续开展钢铁、水泥领域的节能环境诊断表示欢迎。

二十八、双方认为，“中日节能环保商务示范项目”进展顺利，将与中国地方政府共同努力，进一步推进该项目，加强项目挖掘和成果普及。

二十九、双方高度评价通过日方培训节能人才在中国的节能法及节能政策方面取得的进展和成果。双方同意，今后在开展政策研修的同时，日方向中国派遣节能监测领域的有关专家，并对中方进一步加强节能体制建设和企业的能源管理提供支持。

三十、双方将推动建设与环境相关的研究生院网络，促进环境人才培养。

三十一、双方对福田康夫首相访华时确定的“中日节能环保合作咨询窗口”今年4月正式启动表示欢迎，并将努力通过这一窗口促进两国节能环保产业的发展。

三十二、双方同意，鉴于核能发电对保障能源安全及防止地球变暖的重要性，将加强在该领域的合作。

三十三、双方认为，包括双方在内的主要能源消费国，有必要就节能方面的政策措施等广泛交换意见，共享信息。

三十四、双方对天津市和北九州市、神户市在循环经济、节能环保方面开展合作表示欢迎，并将继续给予支持。

三十五、双方对两国环保部门签署合作实施小城镇分散型污水处理示范项目备忘录表示欢迎。

三十六、双方对两国合作推动沙尘暴共同研究取得进展表示评价，将继续促进亚洲国家在包括二氧化硫等大气环境领域的交流与合作。

三十七、双方将促进关于兼顾防治公害和减缓气候变化协同效应的具体合作。

三十八、双方对两国主管部门起草关于促进中国农村地区饮水安全供给及介绍并推广日本在普及简易自来水管道方面的成功经验等的备忘录表示欢迎，并将为实施备忘录进行合作。

三十九、关于有效管理水资源、预防水污染、治理水灾等水资源领域合作，双方认为，水是最易受地球变暖影响的资源，将从应对气候变化角度出发，进一步加强上述领域合作。

四十、双方积极评价两国政府间林业合作及中日民间绿化合作委员会的扎实工作。同时，将针对全球森林减少及退化问题，加强植树造林、打击非法采伐，促进亚洲地区森林恢复与可持续经营。

四十一、双方在坚持“不与人争粮、不与粮争地”的原则下，就发展生物燃料开展信息交换与技术交流。

四十二、双方高兴地看到，中方向日方提供的朱鹮正在顺利繁殖，今后将继续加强在朱鹮保护和野外放飞方面的合作。

四十三、为增进中日两国人民的友好感情，中方同意向日方提供一对大熊猫，共同开展合作研究，日方对此表示感谢。

四十四、双方愿继续进行矿物资源领域的对话，开展建设性讨论。双方达成共识，年内在双方认为方便的时间举行中日稀土交流会议，以便进一步深化该领域的交流与合作。

四十五、双方将继续加强知识产权领域的合作，利用两国知识产权交流的现有工作机制，交换知识产权立法、执法及行政审批的信息；增强双方企业间知识产权保护和利用的经验交流；共同开展各类人才的知识产权培训，扩大知识产权制度的影响力。

四十六、双方对中日韩改善商务环境行动计划达成一致表示欢迎。同时，双方对签署《关于就贸易投资相关法律制度开展研究交流的备忘录》表示欢迎，将加强贸易投资法律的交流与合作。

四十七、双方对两国有关部门签署《关于促进技术贸易顺利发展的合作备忘录》表示欢迎。

四十八、双方对两国有关部门签署《关于促进中小企业顺利开展海外业务的合作备忘录》表示欢迎，今后将创造更为宽松的商务环境，进一步推动中小企业合作。

四十九、双方将为保护两国人民生命和健康进一步加强合作。对于此次出现的冷冻加工食品中毒案件，双方将为尽早查明真相进一步加强调查与合作。

五十、双方对迄今为止在动植物检疫领域内的合作予以积极评价，并愿意进一步加强双方的合作和交流。妥善解决存在的技术问题，促进贸易的顺利发展。中方允许日本精米正式对华出口，日方对此表示欢迎。日方允许中国新鲜南瓜对日出口，中方对此表示欢迎。

五十一、双方积极评价信息通信领域开展的政策磋商，并将致力于共同促进信息通信领域的合作。

五十二、双方积极评价近期中日在加强金融及金融监管领域合作方面取得的成果，包括东京证券交易所开设北京代表处等，并表示今后将继续加强在该领域的合作。

五十三、双方对中日迄今为止的农业合作予以积极评价，愿进一步在现有机制下加强合作。

五十四、双方将进一步扩大旅游交流，积极推进在铁道、物流、海运、航空等领域的合作。

五十五、双方在去年年底官民访华团取得的成果的基础上继续开展癌症防治合作，促进中日医学交流，继续派遣官民使节团进行交流。双方将加强医药领域的信息交换。

五十六、双方将加快关于地球观测和预测的工作进度，共享数据和成果，努力构筑全球地球观测系统（GEOSS）。双方将推进气候变化领域的科学技术研究交流。

五十七、双方对草签中日领事协定表示欢迎，将争取尽快正式签署并完成生效手续。

五十八、双方将为《中日刑事司法协助条约》早日生效而加倍努力。

五十九、双方将开始关于缔结中日罪犯引渡条约的谈判，同时酌情尽早开始关于缔结中日被判刑人移管条约的谈判，争取同时签署两个条约。

六十、双方将根据《禁止化学武器公约》的规定，进一步加强合作，尽早销毁中国境内日本遗弃化学武器。

六十一、为实现亚洲经济持续稳定增长，双方认为开展清迈倡议多边化、亚洲债券市场倡议等区域财金合作十分重要，将共同推动这一合作取得更大进展。

六十二、日方表示，将按照日朝平壤宣言，解决包括核问题和人道问题在内的有关悬而未决问题，清算不幸的历史，实现日朝邦交正常化。双方确认日朝关系取得进展的重要性，中方表示，愿提供必要协助。

六十三、双方今年4月在北京举行了联合国改革问题司长级磋商，就联合国包括安理会改革问题等交换了意见，并一致同意今后继续进行磋商。

六十四、双方对签署中日关于应对气候变化合作的联合声明表示欢迎。

六十五、双方去年11月在北京举行了向第三国援助问题司局级对话，探讨了分享援外经验及在援外领域开展合作的可能性，并将继续开展工作层面的对话。

六十六、双方去年9月在东京举行了非洲政策司局级磋商，就各自对非政策及非洲形势等坦率交换了意见，并同意继续就开展可能的合作加强磋商。中方期待今年5月在日本召开的第4次非洲发展东京国际会议（TICAD）为促进非洲发展取得更大成果。

六十七、双方于今年4月在北京举行了湄公河政策对话，并就湄公河次区域现状、各自对湄公河次区域政策和促进湄公河次区域开发、贸易投资等问题展开了广泛讨论，双方对此表示欢迎。

六十八、双方去年5月在东京举行了中日军控与防扩散磋商，就当前国际军控和防扩散领域的主要问题广泛交换了意见，并将继续进行磋商。

六十九、双方同意在平等和相互尊重的基础上就人权问题进行对话，推动国际人权领域的对话与合作。

七十、双方认为，目前全球经济面临许多新的课题和困难，年内成功结束多哈回合谈判符合各方的共同利益，有助于加强多边贸易体制，维护世界经济的稳定和增长。双方将继续合作，推动多哈谈判达成广泛和平衡的协议，实现发展目标。

二〇〇八年五月七日东京

日中両政府の交流と協力の強化に関する共同プレス発表

胡錦濤中華人民共和国主席は、日本国政府の招待に応じ、2008年5月6日から10日まで国賓として日本国を公式訪問し、福田康夫日本国内閣総理大臣と実りある会談を行った。双方は、「戦略的互恵関係」の包括的推進に関する日中共同声明を発表し、同共同声明を着実に実施するため、以下の共通認識に達した。

1. 日本側は、胡錦濤主席を本年7月に北海道洞爺湖において開催されるG8首脳会議アウトリーチ・セッションに招待し、中国側はこれを真剣かつ積極的に検討する旨表明した。

2. 中国側は、福田総理を本年10月に北京において開催されるアジア欧州会合（ASEM）第7回首脳会合に招待し、日本側はこれを真剣かつ積極的に検討する旨表明した。

3. 日本側は、本年秋に日本国において日中韓首脳会議を開催することを提案し、中国側はこれを真剣かつ積極的に検討する旨表明した。

4. 双方は、日中戦略対話が日中関係の改善及び発展に果たしている重要な役割を積極的に評価し、同対話を引き続き重視していく。

5. 双方は、本年4月に東京において開催された日中外務報道官協議において、両国国民間の相互理解を更に深めるため、報道及び広報の面で協力し、両国報道担当部局間の直接の連絡体制を強化すること、両国メディアに対し客観的かつ正確な情報を提供するよう共に努力することで一致したことを歓迎し、次回協議を双方の都合の良い時期に北京において開催する。

6. 両国防衛当局間の相互信頼を増進するため、本年中に日本国の防衛大臣が訪中する。

7. 双方は、本年3月に開催された日中防衛当局間協議を歓迎した。両国防衛当局間の相互理解を深めるため、引き続きハイレベルでの防衛当局間協議を継続する。

8. 本年2月の統合幕僚長の訪中に続き、本年6月に中国人民解放軍空軍司令員が、本年後半に海軍司令員及び副総参謀長がそれぞれ訪日する。

9. 昨年11月の中国人民解放軍海軍艦艇の訪日に続き、本年6月に日本国海上自衛隊艦艇が訪中する。

10. 双方は、海上における不測の事態の発生を防止するため、4月下旬に北京において日中防衛当局間の海上連絡メカニズム設立のための第1回共同作業グループ協議が開催されたことを歓迎するとともに、早期に当該メカニズムが設立されるよう引き続き努力する。

11. 双方は、軍種間、防衛関係の教育機関・研究機関間の交流の拡大を検討していく。

12. 双方は、国際連合平和維持活動（PKO)、災害救援等の分野での協力の可能性を検討していく。

13. 双方は、両国防衛当局間の相互理解及び相手国への理解を深めるため、中国の人民解放軍青年将校と日本の自衛隊若手幹部との相互訪問を強化することで一致し、年度内にそれぞれ15名程度の尉官級幹部を相手国へ1週間程度相互招聘することで一致した。

14. 双方は、新日中友好21世紀委員会が、両首脳の関心の下、日中関係の改善及び発展のために有益な提言を行ってきたことを積極的に評価し、同委員会が本年末に最終報告書を提出することを期待する。

15. 双方は、日中歴史共同研究の果たす役割を高く評価し、今後も継続していく。

16. 双方は、昨年の両国間の人的往来が延べ500万人規模に達していることを歓迎し、今後も引き続き、人的交流を拡大し、相互理解を深めるため緊密に協力する。

17. 双方は、「日中青少年友好交流年」の順調な立ち上げに満足の意を表明する。双方は、今後4年間、毎年4000名規模の青少年交流を実施することを確認し、最大限有効な青少年交流が行われるよう努力する。

18. 双方は、日中青少年友好交流を長期にわたり継続的に行っていくことで一致し、両国の各界に青少年交流促進の協力を強化するよう呼びかける。

19. 双方は、両国中堅幹部の交流を一層強化することが積極的な意義を

有し、今後この分野における交流及び協力に取り組むことを引き続き支持することで一致した。

20. 双方は、北京オリンピックを成功させ、北京オリンピックを契機に、両国国民の交流が一層促進され、相互理解と友情が増進されることを希望する。

21. 双方は、文化センターの相互設置に関する協定が署名されたことを歓迎し、同センターが、両国国民の相互理解の促進に積極的役割を果たすことへの期待を表明した。

22. 双方は、人文分野における交流及び協力に積極的に取り組み、関係部門及び社会団体が文化遺産の保護等の分野で共同研究を行うことを奨励する。

23. 昨年12月の福田総理訪中時に、日本側は北京大学の対日交流強化のためのプランを提案した。双方は、関連の準備が進められていることを歓迎し、知的交流の更なる強化のため協力を継続する。

24. 双方は、昨年12月に北京で行われた第1回日中ハイレベル経済対話において、両国の関係閣僚が一堂に会して、それぞれのマクロ経済政策、気候変動を含む省エネ・環境、貿易・投資、検査・検疫及び地域・国際的な経済問題について、部門を越えた直接対話を行ったことにより、相互理解が促進され、今後の問題解決や協力推進への指針が示されたことを高く評価した。次回対話は、本年秋を目途に東京で開催する方向で検討する。

25. 双方は、両国関係部門が、「持続可能な経済発展に資する互恵関係構築を推進していくための包括協力文書」、「省エネルギー・環境分野における協力の継続強化に関する覚書」及び「中小企業分野の協力推進に関する覚書」の3つの文書に署名したことを歓迎し、引き続き協力を推進していくことで一致した。

26. 双方は、現在の石油価格に対する懸念を表明した。また、双方は、継続的に日中エネルギー閣僚政策対話を行い、エネルギー分野における互恵的協力について検討していくことで一致した。

27. 双方は、石炭分野における技術協力として、中国の石炭火力発電所における設備診断・設備改造・人材育成を推進する。双方は、石炭火力発電所からの二酸化炭素の隔離・貯蔵（CCS）を通じて、石油回収率の向上（EOR）の実証研究を継続的に展開する。また、双方は、鉄鋼及びセメント分野の省エネルギー環境診断を引き続き推進することを歓迎する。

28. 双方は、「日中省エネルギー・環境ビジネス推進モデルプロジェクト」が順調に進行していることを確認し、中国の地方政府と共に努力して同プロジェクトを一層推進させ、プロジェクトの発掘とその成果の普及を強化する。

29. 双方は、省エネルギー政策に係る受入研修を通じて中国の省エネルギー法及び中国の省エネルギー政策が進展したことを高く評価する。双方は、今後、政策研修を実施すると同時に、日本側が中国側に対し省エネルギー計測の分野の省エネ関連に係る専門家を派遣し、中国側が省エネ制度の確立と企業のエネルギー管理を更に強化するよう支援することに同意する。

30. 双方は、環境関連の大学院ネットワークの構築を推進し、環境人材の養成を進める。

31. 双方は、福田総理が訪中した際に確認した「日中省エネ環境協力相談窓口」が本年4月から業務を開始したことを歓迎するとともに、本窓口により両国の省エネ環境保護ビジネスの発展を促進するよう努力する。

32. 双方は、原子力発電のエネルギー安全保障と地球温暖化防止に対する重要性に照らし、この分野における協力を強化することに同意する。

33. 双方は、双方を含む主要なエネルギー消費国が、省エネルギーに関する政策手法等につき、幅広く情報を共有し、意見交換を行う必要性を共有する。

34. 双方は、天津市と北九州市・神戸市との循環経済、省エネ・環境保護分野における協力を歓迎するとともに、引き続き支持していく。

35. 双方は、両国の環境保護部門が農村地域等における分散型排水処理モデル事業協力実施に関する覚書に署名したことを歓迎する。

36. 双方は、両国の協力により黄砂の共同研究が進展していることを評価し、引き続きアジア諸国の二酸化硫黄等を含む大気環境分野における交流と協力を促進する。

37. 双方は、公害対策等と気候変動の緩和を両立させるコベネフィットアプローチに関する具体的な協力を促進する。

38. 双方は、両国主管部門が中国の農村地域における水安全供給及び日本における簡易水道普及に係る成功経験の紹介等に関する覚書を起草したことを歓迎し、覚書の実施のために協力を行っていく。

39. 双方は、水資源の効率的管理、水質汚濁の予防、治水災害対策等の水資源分野における協力について、水が地球温暖化の影響を最も受けやすい資源であると認識し、気候変動への適応の観点からも、この分野の協力を一層強化していく。

40. 双方は、両政府間の森林・林業協力及び日中民間緑化協力委員会の着実な活動を積極的に評価するとともに、世界的な森林減少及び劣化の抑制の問題に対して、植林・違法伐採取り締まりを強化し、アジア地域における森林回復及び持続可能な経営を促進する。

41. 双方は、食料と競合しないとの原則を堅持しつつ、バイオマス燃料の発展について、情報交換及び技術交流を行う。

42. 双方は、中国から日本に提供されたトキが順調に繁殖していることを喜ばしく思うとともに、今後もトキ保護及び野生復帰に関する協力を引き続き強化する。

43. 日中両国国民の友好的感情を増進するため、中国側は、日本側に一対のパンダを提供し、共同で協力研究を行うことに同意し、日本側はこれに謝意を表明した。

44. 双方は、鉱物資源分野に係る対話を継続し、建設的議論を行っていくことを希望するとともに、当該分野における交流と協力をより一層深めるため、年内の双方にとり都合の良い時期に、レアアース交流会議を開催することで共通認識に達した。

45. 双方は、知的財産権分野における協力を引き続き強化し、両国の知的財産権交流の既存のワーキング・メカニズムを利用して、知的財産権の立法、執行及び行政審査実務に関する情報交換を行う。双方の企業間で知的財産権の保護及び利用の経験交流を強化する。知的財産人材育成を共同して行い、知的財産権制度の影響力を拡大する。

46. 双方は、日中韓ビジネス環境改善アクション・アジェンダについて、日中間で意見の一致を見たことを歓迎する。また、「貿易・投資関連法律制度の研究交流に関する覚書」が署名されたことを歓迎し、貿易投資法律の交流・協力を強化する。

47. 双方は、両国関係部門が「技術貿易の発展と円滑化に関する協力覚書」に署名したことを歓迎する。

48. 双方は、両国の関係部門が「中小企業海外事業展開円滑化協力のための覚書」に署名したことを歓迎するとともに、今後、中小企業のビジネス・投資の円滑化を更に推進していく。

49. 双方は、両国国民の生命・健康を守るために、協力を一層強化していく。双方は、このたび発生した冷凍加工食品の中毒事案につき、一刻も早い真相究明のため、日中双方で捜査及び協力を一層強化していく。

50. 双方は、これまでの動植物検疫分野における協力を積極的に評価し、双方の協力・交流を一層強化し、存在する技術的問題を適切に解決し、貿易の順調な発展を促進することを希望することで一致した。中国側は、日本産精米の正式な対中輸出を許可し、日本側は、これを歓迎した。日本側は、中国産生鮮かぼちゃの対日輸出を許可し、中国側は、これを歓迎した。

51. 双方は、情報通信分野における政策協議を積極的に評価し、情報通信分野における協力を共に促進していくよう努力する。

52. 双方は、東京証券取引所の北京事務所の開設等を含め、最近の日中の金融及び金融監督管理分野における協力の強化で得られた成果を積極的に評価し、今後も引き続き当該分野における協力を強化することを表明した。

53. 双方は、日中の農林水産分野におけるこれまでの協力を高く評価し、既存のメカニズムを活用してこれを更に推進していく。

54. 双方は、観光交流を更に拡大させ、鉄道、物流、海運、航空等の分野における協力を積極的に推進する。

55. 双方は、昨年末の官民共同ミッションで得られた成果の基礎に立ち、引き続きがん予防協力に取り組み、日中医学交流を促進し、官民ミッションを派遣して交流を行う。また、双方は、医薬品分野における情報交換の強化等を図っていく。

56. 双方は、地球観測・予測の取り組みを加速するとともに、得られたデータや成果の共有を行い全球地球観測システム（GEOSS）の構築に取り組む。また、双方は、気候変動分野における科学技術研究交流を推進していく。

57. 双方は、日中領事協定締結交渉が実質合意に至ったことを歓迎するとともに、早期に署名し、発効のための手続を了するよう努める。

58. 双方は、日中刑事共助条約の早期発効のため努力を加速する。

59. 双方は、日中犯罪人引渡条約の締結交渉を開始するとともに、その時の状況を踏まえて日中受刑者移送条約の締結交渉についても速やかに開始する。両条約は同時期の署名を目指す。

60. 双方は、「化学兵器禁止条約」の規定に基づき、協力を一層強化し、中国における日本の遺棄化学兵器の廃棄をできるだけ早く進める。

61. 双方は、アジア経済の持続的かつ安定した成長を実現するために、チェンマイ・イニシアチブのマルチ化やアジア債券市場育成イニシアチブ等、地域財政金融協力に取り組むことが非常に重要であると認識し、この協

力を共に推進し、更に大きな進展を得る。

62. 日本側は、日朝平壌宣言に従い、核問題、人道問題等の懸案事項を解決し、不幸な過去を清算し、日朝国交正常化を図るとの方針を表明した。双方は、日朝関係が前進することの重要性を確認し、中国側は、必要な協力を行う旨述べた。

63. 双方は、本年4月に北京で行われた国連改革に関する局長級協議において、安保理改革を含む国連の問題等につき意見交換を行い、今後とも協議を継続していくことで一致した。

64. 双方は、「日本国政府と中華人民共和国との気候変動に関する共同声明」の発表を歓迎した。

65. 双方は、昨年11月に北京で行われた第三国援助問題に関する局長級対話において、対外援助に関する経験の共有及び対外援助の分野における協力の可能性を検討した。双方は、引き続き、実務レベルで対話を継続していく。

66. 双方は、昨年9月に東京で行われたアフリカ局長級協議において、各々の対アフリカ政策及びアフリカ情勢等について率直な意見交換を行い、可能な協力のため引き続き協議を強化していくことで一致した。また、中国は、日本で本年5月に開催される第4回アフリカ開発会議（TICAD IV）がアフリカの発展の促進に向けてより大きな成果を収めることへの期待を表明した。

67. 双方は、本年4月に北京で行われた日中メコン政策対話において、メコン地域の現状、各々の対メコン地域政策、メコン地域の開発、貿易投資の促進等の問題について幅広い議論を行ったことを歓迎した。

68. 双方は、昨年5月に東京で行われた日中軍縮・不拡散協議において、最近の国際軍縮、不拡散の分野における主要な問題について幅広い意見交換を行った。双方は、引き続き協議を行っていく。

69. 双方は、平等と相互尊重の基礎の上に、人権問題について対話を行い、国際人権分野における対話と協力を進めることで一致した。

70. 双方は、現在、世界経済が多くの新たな課題と困難に直面しており、ドーハ・ラウンドを年内に成功裡に妥結させることが各国の共通利益に合致し、多角的貿易体制の強化及び世界経済の安定と成長の維持に資すると認識した。双方は、ドーハ・ラウンドが広範かつバランスのとれた合意に達するよう推進し、その目標を実現するために引き続き協力していく。

2008年5月7日　東京

中日关于全面推进战略互惠关系的联合声明

（2008年5月7日）

应日本国政府邀请，中华人民共和国主席胡锦涛于2008年5月6日至10日对日本国进行国事访问。访问期间，胡锦涛主席会见了明仁天皇，并同福田康夫内阁总理大臣举行会谈，就全面推进战略互惠关系达成广泛共识。双方发表联合声明如下：

一、双方一致认为，中日关系对两国都是最重要的双边关系之一。两国对亚太地区和世界的和平、稳定与发展有着重要影响，肩负着庄严责任。长期和平友好合作是双方唯一选择。双方决心全面推进中日战略互惠关系，实现中日两国和平共处、世代友好、互利合作、共同发展的崇高目标。

二、双方重申，1972年9月29日发表的《中日联合声明》、1978年8月12日签署的《中日和平友好条约》及1998年11月26日发表的《中日联合宣言》构成中日关系稳定发展和开创未来的政治基础，确认继续恪守三个文件的各项原则。双方确认，继续坚持和全面落实2006年10月8日及2007年4月11日发表的《中日联合新闻公报》的各项共识。

三、双方决心正视历史、面向未来，不断开创中日战略互惠关系新局面。双方将不断增进相互理解和相互信任，扩大互利合作，使中日关系的发展方向与世界发展潮流相一致，共同开创亚太地区和世界的美好未来。

四、双方确认，两国互为合作伙伴，互不构成威胁。双方重申，相互支持对方的和平发展。双方确信，坚持和平发展的中国和日本将给亚洲和世界带来巨大机遇和利益。

中国自改革开放以来取得的发展给包括日本在内的国际社会带来了巨大机遇，日方对此表示积极评价。中国愿为构建持久和平、共同繁荣的世界作出贡献，日方对此表示支持。

日本在战后60多年来，坚持走作为和平国家的道路，通过和平手段为世界和平与稳定作出贡献，中方对此表示积极评价。双方同意就联合国改革问题加强对话与沟通，努力增加共识。中方表示重视日本在联合国的地位和作用，愿意看到日本在国际事务中发挥更大的建设性作用。

双方坚持通过协商和谈判解决两国间的问题。

五、日方重申，继续坚持在《日中联合声明》中就台湾问题表明的立场。

六、双方决定在以下五大领域构筑对话与合作框架，开展合作。

（一）增进政治互信

双方确认，增进政治安全互信对构筑中日战略互惠关系具有重要意义。双方决定：

——建立两国领导人定期互访机制，原则上隔年互访，在多边场合频繁举行会晤。加强政府、议会、政党间的交流和战略对话机制，就双边关系和各自内外政策及国际形势加强沟通，努力提高政策透明度。

——加强安全保障领域的高层互访，促进多层次对话与交流，进一步加深相互理解和信任。

——为进一步理解和追求国际社会公认的基本和普遍价值进行紧密合作，不断加深对在长期交流中共同培育、共同拥有的文化的理解。

（二）促进人文交流，增进国民友好感情

双方确认，不断增进两国人民特别是青少年之间的相互了解和友好感情，有利于巩固中日世代友好与合作的基础。为此，双方决定：

——广泛开展两国媒体、友城、体育、民间团体之间的交流，开展丰富多采的文化交流及知识界交流。

——持之以恒地开展青少年交流。

（三）加强互利合作

双方确认，中日两国作为对世界经济有重要影响的国家，将为世界经济的可持续增长作出贡献，决定重点开展以下合作：

——在能源和环境领域开展合作是我们对子孙后代和国际社会的义务，基于这一认识，要特别加强在这一领域的合作。

——在贸易、投资、信息通讯技术、金融、食品及产品安全、知识产权保护、商务环境、农林水产业、交通运输及旅游、水、医疗等广泛领域开展互利合作，扩大共同利益。

——从战略高度有效运用中日经济高层对话。

——共同努力，使东海成为和平、合作、友好之海。

（四）共同致力于亚太地区的发展

双方确认，中日两国作为亚太地区重要国家，将就本地区事务保持密切沟通，加强协调与合作。双方决定重点开展以下合作：

——共同致力于维护东北亚地区和平与稳定。共同推动六方会谈进程。双方一致认为，日朝关系正常化对东北亚地区的和平与稳定具有重要意义。中方对日朝解决有关问题，实现关系正常化表示欢迎和支持。

——本着开放、透明和包容的原则，促进东亚区域合作，共同推动建设和平、繁荣、稳定和开放的亚洲。

（五）共同应对全球性课题

双方确认，中日两国在21世纪对世界的和平与发展肩负更大责任，愿就重大国际问题加强协调，共同推动建设持久和平、共同繁荣的世界。双方决定开展以下合作：

——双方将在《联合国气候变化框架公约》框架下，根据“共同但有区别的责任及各自能力”的原则，按照巴厘路线图积极参与构建2012年之后有实效的应对气候变化国际框架。

——双方确认能源安全、环境保护、贫困、传染病等全球性问题是双方面临的共同挑战，双方将从战略高度开展有效合作，共同为推动解决上述问题作出应有贡献。

二〇〇八年五月七日于东京

「戦略的互恵関係」の包括的推進に関する日中共同声明

胡錦濤中華人民共和国主席は、日本国政府の招待に応じ、2008年5月6日から10日まで国賓として日本国を公式訪問した。胡錦濤主席は、日本国滞在中、天皇陛下と会見した。また、福田康夫内閣総理大臣と会談を行い、「戦略的互恵関係」の包括的推進に関し、多くの共通認識に達し、以下のとおり共同声明を発出した。

双方は、日中関係が両国のいずれにとっても最も重要な二国間関係の一つであり、今や日中両国が、アジア太平洋地域及び世界の平和、安定、発展に対し大きな影響力を有し、厳粛な責任を負っているとの認識で一致した。また、双方は、長期にわたる平和及び友好のための協力が日中両国にとって唯一の選択であるとの認識で一致した。双方は、「戦略的互恵関係」を包括的に推進し、また、日中両国の平和共存、世代友好、互恵協力、共同発展という崇高な目標を実現していくことを決意した。

双方は、1972年9月29日に発表された日中共同声明、1978年8月12日に署名された日中平和友好条約及び1998年11月26日に発表された日中共同宣言が、日中関係を安定的に発展させ、未来を切り開く政治的基礎であることを改めて表明し、三つの文書の諸原則を引き続き遵守することを確認した。また、双方は、2006年10月8日及び2007年4月11日の日中共同プレス発表にある共通認識を引き続き堅持し、全面的に実施することを確認した。

双方は、歴史を直視し、未来に向かい、日中「戦略的互恵関係」の新たな局面を絶えず切り開くことを決意し、将来にわたり、絶えず相互理解を深め、相互信頼を築き、互恵協力を拡大しつつ、日中関係を世界の潮流に沿って方向付け、アジア太平洋及び世界の良き未来を共に創り上げていくことを宣言した。

双方は、互いに協力のパートナーであり、互いに脅威とならないことを確認した。双方は、互いの平和的な発展を支持することを改めて表明し、平和的な発展を堅持する日本と中国が、アジアや世界に大きなチャンスと利益をもたらすとの確信を共有した。

(1) 日本側は、中国の改革開放以来の発展が日本を含む国際社会に大きな好機をもたらしていることを積極的に評価し、恒久の平和と共同の繁栄をもたらす世界の構築に貢献していくとの中国の決意に対する支持を表明した。

(2) 中国側は、日本が、戦後60年余り、平和国家としての歩みを堅持し、平和的手段により世界の平和と安定に貢献してきていることを積極的に評価した。双方は、国際連合改革問題について対話と意思疎通を強化し、共通認識を増やすべく努力することで一致した。中国側は、日本の国際連合における地位と役割を重視し、日本が国際社会で一層大きな建設的役割を果たすことを望んでいる。

(3) 双方は、協議及び交渉を通じて、両国間の問題を解決していくことを表明した。

台湾問題に関し、日本側は、日中共同声明において表明した立場を引き続き堅持する旨改めて表明した。

双方は、以下の五つの柱に沿って、対話と協力の枠組みを構築しつつ、協力していくことを決意した。

(1) 政治的相互信頼の増進

双方は、政治及び安全保障分野における相互信頼を増進することが日中「戦略的互恵関係」構築に対し重要な意義を有することを確認するとともに、以下を決定した。

両国首脳の定期的相互訪問のメカニズムを構築し、原則として、毎年どちらか一方の首脳が他方の国を訪問することとし、国際会議の場も含め首脳会談を頻繁に行い、政府、議会及び政党間の交流並びに戦略的な対話のメカニズムを強化し、二国間関係、それぞれの国の国内外の政策及び国際情勢についての意思疎通を強化し、その政策の透明性の向上に努める。

安全保障分野におけるハイレベル相互訪問を強化し、様々な対話及び交流を促進し、相互理解と信頼関係を一層強化していく。

国際社会が共に認める基本的かつ普遍的価値の一層の理解と追求のために緊密に協力するとともに、長い交流の中で互いに培い、共有してきた文化について改めて理解を深める。

(2) 人的、文化的交流の促進及び国民の友好感情の増進

双方は、両国民、特に青少年の間の相互理解及び友好感情を絶えず増進することが、日中両国の世々代々にわたる友好と協力の基礎の強化に資することを確認するとともに、以下を決定した。

両国のメディア、友好都市、スポーツ、民間団体の間の交流を幅広く展開し、多種多様な文化交流及び知的交流を実施していく。

青少年交流を継続的に実施する。

(3) 互恵協力の強化

双方は、世界経済に重要な影響力を有する日中両国が、世界経済の持続的成長に貢献していくため、以下のような協力に特に取り組んでいくことを決定した。

エネルギー、環境分野における協力が、我々の子孫と国際社会に対する責務であるとの認識に基づき、この分野で特に重点的に協力を行っていく。

貿易、投資、情報通信技術、金融、食品・製品の安全、知的財産権保護、ビジネス環境、農林水産業、交通運輸・観光、水、医療等の幅広い分野での互恵協力を進め、共通利益を拡大していく。

日中ハイレベル経済対話を戦略的かつ実効的に活用していく。

共に努力して、東シナ海を平和・協力・友好の海とする。

(4) アジア太平洋への貢献

双方は、日中両国がアジア太平洋の重要な国として、この地域の諸問題において、緊密な意思疎通を維持し、協調と協力を強化していくことで一致するとともに、以下のような協力を重点的に展開することを決定した。

北東アジア地域の平和と安定の維持のために共に力を尽くし、六者会合のプロセスを共に推進する。また、双方は、日朝国交正常化が北東アジア地域の平和と安定にとって重要な意義を有しているとの認識を共有した。中国側は、日朝が諸懸案を解決し国交正常化を実現することを歓迎し、支持する。

開放性、透明性、包含性の三つの原則に基づき東アジアの地域協力を推進し、アジアの平和、繁栄、安定、開放の実現を共に推進する。

(5) グローバルな課題への貢献

双方は、日中両国が、21世紀の世界の平和と発展に対し、より大きな責任を担っており、重要な国際問題において協調を強化し、恒久の平和と共同の繁栄をもたらす世界の構築を共に推進していくことで一致するとともに、

以下のような協力に取り組んでいくことを決定した。

「気候変動に関する国際連合枠組条約」の枠組みの下で、「共通に有しているが差異のある責任及び各国の能力」原則に基づき、バリ行動計画に基づき2013年以降の実効的な気候変動の国際枠組みの構築に積極的に参加する。

エネルギー安全保障、環境保護、貧困や感染症等のグローバルな問題は、双方が直面する共通の挑戦であり、双方は、戦略的に有効な協力を展開し、上述の問題の解決を推進するために然るべき貢献を共に行う。

2008年5月7日、東京

中日东海问题原则共识

（2008年6月）

一、关于中日在东海的合作

为使中日之间尚未划界的东海成为和平、合作、友好之海，中日双方根据2007年4月中日两国领导人达成的共识以及2007年12月中日两国领导人达成的新共识，经过认真磋商，一致同意在实现划界前的过渡期间，在不损害双方法律立场的情况下进行合作。为此，双方迈出了第一步，今后将继续进行磋商。

二、中日关于东海共同开发的谅解

作为中日在东海共同开发的第一步，双方将推进以下步骤：

（一）由以下各坐标点顺序连线围成的区域为双方共同开发区块：

1. 北纬29°31′，东经125°53′30″
2. 北纬29°49′，东经125°53′30″
3. 北纬30°04′，东经126°03′45″
4. 北纬30°00′，东经126°10′23″
5. 北纬30°00′，东经126°20′00″
6. 北纬29°55′，东经126°26′00″
7. 北纬29°31′，东经126°26′00″

（二）双方经过联合勘探，本着互惠原则，在上述区块中选择双方一致同意的地点进行共同开发。具体事宜双方通过协商确定。

（三）双方将努力为实施上述开发履行各自的国内手续，尽快达成必要的双边协议。

（四）双方同意，为尽早实现在东海其它海域的共同开发继续磋商。

三、关于日本法人依照中国法律参加春晓油气田开发的谅解

中国企业欢迎日本法人按照中国对外合作开采海洋石油资源的有关法律，参加对春晓现有油气田的开发。

中日两国政府对此予以确认，并努力就进行必要的换文达成一致，尽早缔结。双方为此履行必要的国内手续。

東シナ海における日中間の協力について（日中共同プレス発表）

（2008年ろく月）

日中双方は、日中間で境界がいまだ画定されていない東シナ海を平和・協力・友好の海とするため、2007年4月に達成された日中両国首脳の共通認識及び2007年12月に達成された日中両国首脳の新たな共通認識を踏まえた真剣な協議を経て、境界画定が実現するまでの過渡的期間において双方の法的立場を損なうことなく協力することにつき一致し、そして、その第一歩を踏み出した。今後も引き続き協議を継続していく。

日中間の東シナ海における共同開発についての了解

2008年6月18日

双方は、日中間の東シナ海における共同開発の第一歩として以下を進めることとする。

1. 以下の座標の各点を順次に結ぶ直線によって囲まれる区域を双方の共同開発区域とする。

（1）北緯29度31分東経125度53分30秒

（2）北緯29度49分東経125度53分30秒

（3）北緯30度04分東経126度03分45秒

（4）北緯30度00分東経126度10分23秒

（5）北緯30度00分東経126度20分00秒

（6）北緯29度55分東経126度26分00秒

(7) 北緯29度31分東経126度26分00秒

2. 双方は、共同探査を経て、互恵の原則に従って、上述の区域の中から双方が一致して同意する地点を選択し、共同開発を行う。具体的な事項については双方が協議を通じ確定する。

3. 双方は、上述の開発の実施に必要な二国間合意をそれぞれの国内手続を経て早期に締結すべく努力する。

4. 双方は、東シナ海のその他の海域における共同開発をできるだけ早く実現するため、継続して協議を行う。

白樺（中国名:「春暁」）油ガス田開発についての了解

2008年6月18日

中国企業は、日本法人が、中国の海洋石油資源の対外協力開発に関する法律に従って、白樺（中国名:「春暁」）の現有の油ガス田における開発に参加することを歓迎する。

日中両政府はこれを確認し、必要な交換公文に合意し、早期に締結すべく努力する。双方はその締結のために必要な国内手続をとる。

中日就处理和改善中日关系达成四点原则共识

（2014年11月7日）

一、双方确认将遵守中日四个政治文件的各项原则和精神，继续发展中日战略互惠关系。

二、双方本着“正视历史、面向未来”的精神，就克服影响两国关系政治障碍达成一些共识。

三、双方认识到围绕钓鱼岛等东海海域近年来出现的紧张局势存在不同主张，同意通过对话磋商防止局势恶化，建立危机管控机制，避免发生不测事态。

四、双方同意利用各种多双边渠道逐步重启政治、外交和安全对话，努力构建政治互信。

日中関係の改善に向け，これまで両国政府間で静かな話し合いを続けてきたが，今般，以下の諸点につき意見の一致をみた。

平成26年11月7日

1. 双方は，日中間の四つの基本文書の諸原則と精神を遵守し，日中の戦略的互恵関係を引き続き発展させていくことを確認した。

2. 双方は，歴史を直視し，未来に向かうという精神に従い，両国関係に影響する政治的困難を克服することで若干の認識の一致をみた。

3. 双方は，尖閣諸島等東シナ海の海域において近年緊張状態が生じていることについて異なる見解を有していると認識し，対話と協議を通じて，情勢の悪化を防ぐとともに，危機管理メカニズムを構築し，不測の事態の発生を回避することで意見の一致をみた。

4. 双方は，様々な多国間・二国間のチャンネルを活用して，政治・外交・安保対話を徐々に再開し，政治的相互信頼関係の構築に努めることにつき意見の一致をみた。

中华人民共和国和大韩民国双边文件

중화인민공화국 과 대한민국 양자 문건

中华人民共和国政府和大韩民国政府渔业协定

中华人民共和国政府和大韩民国政府，根据一九八二年十二月十日《联合国海洋法公约》的有关规定，为养护和合理利用共同关心的海洋生物资源，维护海上正常作业秩序，加强和发展渔业领域的相互合作，经友好协商，达成协议如下：

第一条

本协定的适用水域（以下称“协定水域”）为中华人民共和国的专属经济区和大韩民国的专属经济区。

第二条

一、缔约各方按照本协定和本国有关法律、法规的规定，准许缔约另一方的国民及渔船在本国专属经济区从事渔业活动。

二、缔约各方授权机关根据本协定附件一及本国有关法律、法规的规定向缔约另一方国民及渔船发放入渔许可证。

第三条

一、缔约各方每年决定缔约另一方国民及渔船在本国专属经济区的可捕鱼种、渔获配额、作业时间、作业区域及其他作业条件，并通报缔约另一方。

二、缔约各方决定第一款所规定事项时应考虑到本国专属经济区的海洋生物资源状况、本国捕捞能力、传统渔业活动、相互入渔状况及其他相关因素，并应尊重根据第十三条的规定设立的中韩渔业联合委员会的协商结果。

第四条

一、缔约一方的国民及渔船进入缔约另一方专属经济区从事渔业活动，应遵守本协定及缔约另一方有关法律、法规的规定。

二、缔约各方应采取必要措施，确保本国国民及渔船在缔约另一方专属经济区从事渔业活动时，遵守缔约另一方有关法律、法规所规定的海洋生物资源的养护措施及其他条件和本协定的规定。

三、缔约各方应及时向缔约另一方通报本国有关法律、法规所规定的海洋生物资源的养护措施及其他条件。

第五条

一、缔约各方为确保缔约另一方的国民及渔船遵守本国有关法律、法规所规定的海洋生物资源的养护措施及其他条件，可根据国际法在本国专属经济区采取必要措施。

二、被扣留或逮捕的渔船或船员，在提出适当的保证书或其他担保之后，应迅速获得释放。

三、缔约一方在扣留或逮捕缔约另一方的渔船或船员时，应通过适当途径，将所采取的行动及随后所施加的处罚，迅速通知缔约另一方。

第六条

第二条至第五条的规定适用于协定水域中除第七条、第八条和第九条所指水域以外的部分。

第七条

一、下列各点顺次用直线连接而围成的水域（以下称“暂定措施水域”）适用第二款及第三款的规定。

1.北纬37度00分，东经123度40分之点（A 1）

2.北纬36度22分23秒，东经123度10分52秒之点（A 2）

3.北纬35度30分，东经122度11分54秒之点（A 3）

4.北纬35度30分，东经122度01分54秒之点（A 4）

5.北纬34度00分，东经122度01分54秒之点（A 5）

6.北纬34度00分，东经122度11分54秒之点（A 6）

7.北纬33度20分，东经122度41分之点（A 7）

8.北纬32度20分，东经123度45分之点（A 8）

9.北纬32度11分，东经123度49分30秒之点（A 9）

10.北纬32度11分，东经125度25分之点（A 10）

11.北纬33度20分，东经124度08分之点（A 11）

12.北纬34度00分，东经124度00分30秒之点（A 12）

13.北纬35度00分，东经124度07分30秒之点（A 13）

14.北纬35度30分，东经124度30分之点（A 14）

15.北纬36度45分，东经124度30分之点（A 15）

16.北纬37度00分，东经124度20分之点（A 16）

17.北纬37度00分，东经123度40分之点（A 17）

二、缔约双方为养护和合理利用海洋生物资源，应按照根据第十三条的规定设立的中韩渔业联合委员会的决定，在暂定措施水域采取共同的养护措施和量的管理措施。

三、缔约各方在暂定措施水域对从事渔业活动的本国国民及渔船采取管理和其他必要措施，不对缔约另一方国民及渔船采取管理和其他措施。缔约一方发现缔约另一方国民及渔船违反中韩渔业联合委员会的决定时，可就事实提醒该国民及渔船注意，并将事实及有关情况通报缔约另一方。缔约另一方应尊重对方的通报，并在采取必要措施后，将结果通报对方。

第八条

一、自本协定生效之日起四年内，下列（一）及（二）各点顺次用直线连接而围成的水域（以下称“过渡水域”）适用第二款至第四款的规定。

（一）中方一侧过渡水域坐标

1.北纬35度30分，东经121度55分之点（C 1）

2.北纬35度00分，东经121度30分之点（C 2）

3.北纬34度00分，东经121度30分之点（C 3）

4.北纬33度20分，东经122度00分之点（C 4）

5.北纬31度50分，东经123度00分之点（C 5）

6.北纬31度50分，东经124度00分之点（C 6）

7.北纬32度20分，东经123度45分之点（C 7）

8.北纬33度20分，东经122度41分之点（C 8）

9.北纬34度00分，东经122度11分54秒之点（C 9）

10.北纬34度00分，东经122度01分54秒之点（C 10）

11.北纬35度30分，东经122度01分54秒之点（C 11）

12.北纬35度30分，东经121度55分之点（C 12）

（二）韩方一侧过渡水域坐标

1.北纬35度30分，东经124度30分之点（K 1）

2.北纬35度00分，东经124度07分30秒之点（K 2）

3.北纬34度00分，东经124度00分30秒之点（K 3）

4.北纬33度20分，东经124度08分之点（K 4）

5.北纬32度11分，东经125度25分之点（K 5）

6.北纬32度11分，东经126度45分之点（K 6）

7.北纬32度40分，东经127度00分之点（K 7）

8.北纬32度24分30秒，东经126度17分之点（K 8）
9.北纬32度29分，东经125度5 7分30秒之点（K 9）
10.北纬33度20分，东经125度28分之点（K 10）
11.北纬34度00分，东经124度35分之点（K 11）
12.北纬34度25分，东经124度33分之点（K 12）
13.北纬35度30分，东经124度48分之点（K 13）
14.北纬35度30分，东经124度30分之点（K 14）

二、为在过渡水域逐步实施专属经济区制度，缔约各方应采取适当措施，逐步调整并减少在缔约另一方一侧过渡水域作业的本国国民及渔船的渔业活动，以努力实现平衡。

三、缔约双方在过渡水域应采取与第七条第二款和第三款相同的养护和管理措施，还可采取联合监督检查措施，包括联合乘船、勒令停船、登临检查等。

四、缔约双方各自对在缔约另一方一侧过渡水域作业的本国渔船发放许可证，并相互交换渔船名册。

五、本协定生效之日起四年后，过渡水域适用第二条至第五条的规定。

第九条

缔约双方在第七条第一款规定的暂定措施水域北限线所处纬度以北的部分水域及第七条第一款规定的暂定措施水域和第八条第一款规定的过渡水域以南的部分水域，维持现有渔业活动，不将本国有关渔业的法律、法规适用于缔约另一方的国民及渔船，除非缔约双方另有协议。

第十条

缔约各方为确保航行和作业安全，维护海上正常作业秩序并顺利及时处理海上事故，应对本国国民及渔船采取指导及其他必要措施。

第十一条

一、缔约一方的国民及渔船在缔约另一方沿岸遭遇海难或其他紧急事态时，缔约另一方应尽力予以救助和保护，同时迅速将有关情况通报对方的有关部门。

二、缔约一方的国民及渔船，由于天气恶劣或其他紧急事态需要避难时，可按本协定附件二的规定，与缔约另一方有关部门联系，到缔约另一方港口等处避难。该国民及渔船应遵守缔约另一方的有关法律、法规，并服从有关部门的指挥。

第十二条

缔约双方为开展养护和合理利用海洋生物资源的科学研究（包括交换必要资料），应加强合作。

第十三条

一、缔约双方为便于实施本协定，设立中韩渔业联合委员会（以下称“渔委会”）。渔委会由缔约双方各自任命的一名代表和若干名委员组成，必要时可设立专家组。

二、渔委会的任务如下：

（一）协商如下事项，并向缔约双方政府提出建议：

1.第三条规定的缔约另一方国民及渔船的可捕鱼种、渔获配额及其他具体作业条件的事项；

2.有关维持作业秩序的事项；

3.有关海洋生物资源状况和养护的事项；

4.有关两国间渔业合作的事项。

（二）根据需要，可就本协定附件的修改向缔约双方政府提出建议。

（三）协商和决定与第七条、第八条规定有关的事项。

（四）研究本协定的执行情况及其他有关本协定的事项。

三、渔委会的一切建议和决定须经双方代表一致同意。

四、缔约双方政府应尊重第二款第（一）项的建议，并按照第二款第（三）项的决定采取必要措施。

五、渔委会每年召开一次会议，在中华人民共和国和大韩民国轮流举行。根据需要，经缔约双方同意可召开临时会议。

第十四条　本协定各项规定不得认为有损缔约双方各自关于海洋法诸问题的立场。

第十五条　本协定的附件为本协定不可分割的组成部分。

第十六条

一、本协定经缔约双方履行各自国内法律程序后，自换文通知之日起生效。

二、本协定有效期为五年，之后有效至根据第三款的规定终止为止。

三、缔约任何一方在最初五年期满时或在其后，可提前一年以书面形式通知缔约另一方，随时终止本协定。

以下经各自政府授权的代表在本协定上签字，以昭信守。

本协定于二〇〇〇年八月三日在北京签订，一式两份，每份都用中文和韩文写成，两种文本同等作准。

中华人民共和国政府代表　　大朝民国政府代表

唐家璇　　权丙铉

（签字）　　（签字）

附件一：

缔约各方根据本协定第二款第二款的规定，采取以下入渔许可措施：

一、缔约各方授权机关在接到缔约另一方授权机关发来的本协定第三条规定的决定的书面通报后，向缔约另一方授权机关申请发给希望在缔约另一方专属经济区从事渔业活动的本国国民及渔船入渔许可证。缔约另一方授权机关按照本协定及本国有关法律、法规的规定颁发许可证。缔约各方授权机关发放许可证时可收取适当费用。

二、缔约各方授权机关应以书面形式向缔约另一方授权机关通报有关入渔的手续规定（包括许可证的申请和颁发、渔获量统计资料的提供、渔船标识及捕捞日志的填写等）。

三、获得许可的渔船应将许可证置于驾驶舱明显之处，并明确显示缔约另一方规定的渔船标识。

附件二：

本协定第十一条第二款的规定按以下规定实施：

一、中华人民共和国政府指定的联络部门为管辖有关港口的港务监督部门。大韩民国政府指定的联络部门为海洋警察部门。

二、具体联系方法在根据本协定第十三条的规定设立的中韩渔业联合委员会上相互通报。

三、缔约各方的渔船与缔约另一方指定的联络部门进行联系的内容有：船名、呼号、当时船位（纬度、经度）、船籍港、总吨位、全长、船长姓名、船员数、避难理由、请求避难的目的地、预计到达时间和通讯联络方法。

谅解备忘录

中华人民共和国政府代表和大韩民国政府代表就二〇〇〇年八月三日签署的《中华人民共和国政府和大韩民国政府渔业协定》（以下称“协定”）的有关规定，达成如下谅解：

一、双方在协定第七条第一款规定的暂定措施水域北限线所处纬度线以北的韩方一侧部分水域及第七条第一款规定的暂定措施水域和第八条第一款规定的过渡水域以南的中方一侧部分水域，尊重沿岸国有关渔业的现行法律、法规，并采取必要措施，使本国国民及渔船遵守这些法律、法 规。

二、双方相互通报第一款提及的有关法律、法规，并为圆满实施这些法律、法规，通过根据协定第十三条的规定设立的中韩渔业联合委员会就具体方案进行协商。

本备忘录于二〇〇〇年十一月二十日在北京签署，自协定生效之日起有效。

中华人民共和国农业部部长	大韩民国驻中华人民共和国特命全权大使
陈耀邦	洪淳瑛

중화인민공화국 정부와 대한민국 정부간의 어업에 관한 협정

중화인민공화국 정부와 대한민국 정부는,

1982년 12월 10일자 "해양법에 관한 국제연합협약" 의 관련규정에 따라, 공동관심사항인 해양생물자원의 보존과 합리적 이용을 도모하고, 해상에서의 정상적인 조업질서를 유지하며, 어업분야에서의 상호협력을 강화•증진하기 위하여, 우호적인 협상을 통하여,

다음과 같이 합의하였다.

제 1 조

이 협정이 적용되는 수역(이하 "협정수역"이라 한다)은 중화인민공화국의 배타적경제수역과 대한민국의 배타적경제수역으로 한다.

제 2 조

1. 각 체약당사자는 이 협정과 자국의 관계법령의 규정에 따라, 자국의 배타적경제수역에서 타방체약당사자의 국민 및 어선이 어업활동을 하는 것을 허가한다.

2. 각 체약당사자의 권한있는 당국은 이 협정의 부속서 I 및 자국의 관계법령의 규정에 따라 타방체약당사자의 국민 및 어선에 대하여 입어허가증을 발급한다.

제 3 조

1. 각 체약당사자는 자국의 배타적경제수역에서 타방체약당사자의 국민 및 어선에게 허용하는 어획가능어종•어획할당량•조업기간•조업구역 및 기타 조업조건을 매년 결정하고, 이를 타방체약당사자에게 통보한다.

2. 각 체약당사자는 제1항에 정한 사항을 결정함에 있어서 자국의 배타적경제수역내 해양생물자원의 상태, 자국의 어획능력, 전통적 어업활동, 상호입어의 상황 및 기타 관련요소를 고려하여야 하며, 제13조의 규정에 의하여 설치되는 중•한 어업공동위원회의 협의결과를 존중하여야 한다.

제 4 조

1. 일방체약당사자의 국민 및 어선은 타방체약당사자의

배타적경제수역에서 어업활동을 함에 있어서 이 협정과 타방체약당사자의 관계법령의 규정을 준수하여야 한다.

2. 각 체약당사자는 자국의 국민 및 어선이 타방체약당사자의 배타적경제수역에서 어업활동을 함에 있어서 타방체약당사자의 관계법령에 규정된 해양생물자원의 보존조치 및 기타 조건과 이 협정의 규정을 준수하도록 필요한 조치를 취하여야 한다.

3. 각 체약당사자는 자국의 관계법령에 규정된 해양생물자원의 보존조치와 기타 조건을 타방체약당사자에게 지체없이 통보하여야 한다.

제 5 조

1. 각 체약당사자는 자국의 관계법령에 규정된 해양생물자원의 보존조치와 기타 조건을 타방체약당사자의 국민 및 어선이 준수하도록 국제법에 따라 자국의 배타적경제수역에서 필요한 조치를 취할 수 있다.

2. 나포되거나 억류된 어선 또는 승무원은 적절한 보증금이나 기타 담보를 제공한 후에는 즉시 석방되어야 한다.

3. 일방체약당사자는 타방체약당사자의 어선 또는 승무원을 나포하거나 억류한 경우에는 취하여진 조치와 그 후에 부과된 처벌에 관하여 타방체약당사자에게 적절한 경로를 통하여 신속하게 통보하여야 한다.

제 6 조

제2조 내지 제5조의 규정은 협정수역중 제7조·제8조 및 제9조에서 지정한 수역을 제외한 부분에 대하여 적용한다.

제 7 조

1. 다음 각목의 점을 순차적으로 직선으로 연결하는 선에 의하여 둘러싸이는 수역(이하 "잠정조치수역"이라 한다)에 대하여는 제2항 및 제3항의 규정을 적용한다.

가. 북위 37도 00분, 동경 123도 40분의 점 (A1)
나. 북위 36도 22분 23초, 동경 123도 10분 52초의 점 (A2)
다. 북위 35도 30분, 동경 122도 11분 54초의 점 (A3)
라. 북위 35도 30분, 동경 122도 01분 54초의 점 (A4)
마. 북위 34도 00분, 동경 122도 01분 54초의 점 (A5)
바. 북위 34도 00분, 동경 122도 11분 54초의 점 (A6)
사. 북위 33도 20분, 동경 122도 41분의 점 (A7)
아. 북위 32도 20분, 동경 123도 45분의 점 (A8)
자. 북위 32도 11분, 동경 123도 49분 30초의 점 (A9)
차. 북위 32도 11분, 동경 125도 25분의 점 (A10)

카. 북위 33도 20분, 동경 124도 08분의 점 (A11)
타. 북위 34도 00분, 동경 124도 00분 30초의 점 (A12)
파. 북위 35도 00분, 동경 124도 07분 30초의 점 (A13)
하. 북위 35도 30분, 동경 124도 30분의 점 (A14)
거. 북위 36도 45분, 동경 124도 30분의 점 (A15)
너. 북위 37도 00분, 동경 124도 20분의 점 (A16)
더. 북위 37도 00분, 동경 123도 40분의 점 (A17)

2. 양 체약당사자는 해양생물자원의 보존과 합리적 이용을 위하여, 제13조의 규정에 의하여 설치되는 중•한 어업공동위원회의 결정에 따라 잠정조치수역에서 공동의 보존조치 및 양적인 관리조치를 취하여야 한다.

3. 각 체약당사자는 잠정조치수역에서 어업활동을 하는 자국의 국민 및 어선에 대하여 관리 및 기타 필요한 조치를 취하고, 타방체약당사자의 국민 및 어선에 대하여는 관리 및 기타 조치를 취하지 아니한다. 일방체약당사자가 타방체약당사자의 국민 및 어선이 중•한 어업공동위원회의 결정을 위반하는 것을 발견한 경우, 그 사실에 대하여 해당 국민 및 어선의 주의를 환기시킬 수 있으며, 그 사실 및 관련 정황을 타방체약당사자에게 통보할 수 있다. 타방체약당사자는 그 통보를 존중하여야 하며, 필요한 조치를 취한 후 그 결과를 상대방에게 통보한다.

제 8 조

1. 이 협정이 발효한 날부터 4년까지 다음 (1) 및 (2)의 각 점을 순차적으로 직선으로 연결하는 선에 의하여 둘러싸이는 수역(이하 "과도수역"이라 한다)에 대하여는 제2항 내지 제4항의 규정을 적용한다.

(1) 중국측 과도수역 좌표

가. 북위 35도 30분, 동경 121도 55분의 점 (C1)
나. 북위 35도 00분, 동경 121도 30분의 점 (C2)
다. 북위 34도 00분, 동경 121도 30분의 점 (C3)
라. 북위 33도 20분, 동경 122도 00분의 점 (C4)
마. 북위 31도 50분, 동경 123도 00분의 점 (C5)
바. 북위 31도 50분, 동경 124도 00분의 점 (C6)
사. 북위 32도 20분, 동경 123도 45분의 점 (C7)
아. 북위 33도 20분, 동경 122도 41분의 점 (C8)
자. 북위 34도 00분, 동경 122도 11분 54초의 점 (C9)
차. 북위 34도 00분, 동경 122도 01분 54초의 점 (C10)

카. 북위 35도 30분, 동경 122도 01분 54초의 점 (C11)
타. 북위 35도 30분, 동경 121도 55분의 점 (C12)
(2) 한국측 과도수역 좌표
가. 북위 35도 30분, 동경 124도 30분의 점 (K1)
나. 북위 35도 00분, 동경 124도 07분 30초의 점 (K2)
다. 북위 34도 00분, 동경 124도 00분 30초의 점 (K3)
라. 북위 33도 20분, 동경 124도 08분의 점 (K4)
마. 북위 32도 11분, 동경 125도 25분의 점 (K5)
바. 북위 32도 11분, 동경 126도 45분의 점 (K6)
사. 북위 32도 40분, 동경 127도 00분의 점 (K7)
아. 북위 32도 24분 30초, 동경 126도 17분의 점 (K8)
자. 북위 32도 29분, 동경 125도 57분 30초의 점 (K9)
차. 북위 33도 20분, 동경 125도 28분의 점 (K10)
카. 북위 34도 00분, 동경 124도 35분의 점 (K11)
타. 북위 34도 25분, 동경 124도 33분의 점 (K12)
파. 북위 35도 30분, 동경 124도 48분의 점 (K13)
하. 북위 35도 30분, 동경 124도 30분의 점 (K14)

2. 각 체약당사자는 과도수역에서 점진적으로 배타적경제수역 제도를 실시하기 위하여 적절한 조치를 취하여야 하며, 타방체약당사자측 과도수역에서 조업을 하는 자국의 국민 및 어선의 어업활동을 점진적으로 조정•감축하여 균형을 이루도록 노력한다.

3. 양 체약당사자는 과도수역에서 제7조제2항 및 제3항과 동일한 보존 및 관리조치를 취하여야 하고, 또한 공동승선•정선•승선검색 등을 포함한 공동감독검사 조치를 취할 수 있다.

4. 양 체약당사자는 각각 타방체약당사자측 과도수역에서 조업하는 자국 어선에게 허가증을 발급하고, 또한 그 어선의 명부를 상호 교환한다.

5. 이 협정이 발효한 날부터 4년이 경과한 후에는 과도수역에 대하여 제2조 내지 제5조의 규정이 적용된다.

제 9 조

양 체약당사자는 제7조제1항에 지정된 잠정조치수역의 북단이 위치한 위도선 이북의 일부수역과 제7조제1항에 지정된 잠정조치수역 및 제8조제1항에 지정된 과도수역 이남의 일부수역에서는 양 체약당사자간에 별도의 합의가 없는 한 현행 어업활동을 유지하며 어업에 관한 자국의 법령을 타방체약당사자의 국민과 어선에 대하여 적용하지 아니한다.

제 10 조

각 체약당사자는 항행 및 조업의 안전을 확보하고, 해상에서의 정상적인 조업질서를 유지하며, 해상사고를 원활하고 신속하게 처리하기 위하여 자국의 국민 및 어선에 대하여 지도 기타 필요한 조치를 취하여야 한다.

제 11 조

1. 일방체약당사자의 국민 및 어선이 타방체약당사자의 연안에서 해난이나 기타 긴급사태를 당한 경우, 타방체약당사자는 가능한 한 구조 및 보호를 제공함과 동시에 이에 관한 상황을 일방체약당사자의 관계당국에게 신속히 통보하여야 한다.

2. 일방체약당사자의 국민 및 어선은 악천후나 기타 긴급한 사태로 피난할 필요가 있을 때에는 이 협정의 부속서 II의 규정에 따라 타방체약당사자의 관계당국에 연락을 취하고 타방체약당사자의 항구 등에 피난할 수 있다. 해당 국민 및 어선은 타방체약당사자의 관계법령을 준수하고 관계당국의 지시를 따라야 한다.

제 12 조

양 체약당사자는 해양생물자원의 보존과 합리적 이용에 관한 과학적 연구(필요한 자료교환을 포함한다)를 위하여 협력을 강화하여야 한다.

제 13 조

1. 양 체약당사자는 이 협정의 실시를 더욱 용이하게 하기 위하여 중•한 어업공동위원회(이하 "위원회"라 한다)를 설치한다. 위원회는 양 체약당사자가 각각 임명하는 1인의 대표 및 약간명의 위원으로 구성되며, 필요한 경우 전문분과위원회를 설치할 수 있다.

2. 위원회의 임무는 다음과 같다.

(1) 아래 사항을 협의하고 양 체약당사자의 정부에게 권고한다.

가. 제3조의 규정에 의하여 타방체약당사자의 국민 및 어선에게 허용하는 어획가능어종•어획할당량 기타 구체적 조업조건에 관한 사항

나. 조업질서의 유지에 관한 사항

다. 해양생물자원의 상태와 보존에 관한 사항

라. 양국간 어업협력에 관한 사항

(2) 필요한 경우, 이 협정의 부속서의 개정과 관련하여 양 체약당사자의 정부에게 권고할 수 있다.

(3) 제7조 및 제8조의 규정에 관한 사항을 협의하고 결정한다.

(4) 이 협정의 집행현황과 기타 이 협정과 관련된 사항을 연구한다.

3. 위원회의 모든 권고와 결정은 양 체약당사자 대표간의 합의에 의하여서만 이를 한다.

4. 양 체약당사자의 정부는 제2항(1)의 권고를 존중하고, 제2항(3)의 결정에 따라 필요한 조치를 취하여야 한다.

5. 위원회는 중화인민공화국과 대한민국에서 교대로 매년 한차례씩 회의를 개최한다. 필요한 경우 양 체약당사자의 합의를 거쳐 임시회의를 개최할 수 있다.

제 14 조

이 협정의 어떠한 규정도 해양법상의 제반 사안에 관한 각 체약당사자의 입장을 저해하는 것으로 해석되어서는 아니된다.

제 15 조

이 협정의 부속서는 이 협정의 불가분의 일부를 구성한다.

제 16 조

1. 이 협정은 양 체약당사자가 각자 국내법상의 절차를 완료한 후, 이를 통보하는 공한을 서로 교환하는 날부터 그 효력이 발생한다.

2. 이 협정은 5년간 유효하며, 그 후에는 제3항의 규정에 따라 종료될 때까지 계속하여 유효하다.

3. 일방체약당사자는 타방체약당사자에게 1년전에 서면으로 통보하여 최초 5년 기한의 만료시 또는 그 후 언제라도 이 협정을 종료시킬 수 있다.

이상의 증거로서 아래 대표는 각자의 정부로부터 정당하게 권한을 위임받아 이 협정에 서명하였다.

2000년 8월 3일 북경에서 서명하였으며, 동등하게 정본인 중국어 및 한국어로 각 2부 작성하였다.

중화인민공화국 정부를 위하여 　　　　　　　　　　대한민국 정부를 위하여

부속서 Ⅰ

각 체약당사자는 이 협정 제2조제2항의 규정에 의하여 입어허가에 관한 아래 조치를 취한다.

1. 각 체약당사자의 권한있는 당국은 타방체약당사자의 권한있는 당국으로부터 이 협정 제3조에 정한 결정을 서면으로 통보받은 후 타방체약당사자의 권한있는 당국에게 타방체약당사자의 배타적경제수역에서 어업활동을 하고자 하는 자국의 국민과 어선에 대한 입어허가증의 발급을 신청한다. 타방체약당사자의 권한있는 당국은

이 협정 및 자국의 관계법령의 규정에 따라 허가증을 발급한다. 각 체약당사자의 권한있는 당국은 허가증의 발급에 있어 적절한 요금을 징수할 수 있다.

2. 각 체약당사자의 권한있는 당국은 입어에 관한 절차규정(허가증의 신청과 발급, 어획량에 관한 통계자료제출, 어선의 표지 및 조업일지의 기재 등)을 타방체약당사자의 권한있는 당국에게 서면으로 통보하여야 한다.

3. 허가를 받은 어선은 허가증을 조타실의 보이기 쉬운 장소에 부착하고, 타방체약당사자가 규정한 어선 표지를 명확히 표시하여야 한다.

부속서 II

이 협정 제11조제2항의 규정은 아래 규정에 따라 실시한다.

1. 중화인민공화국 정부가 지정하는 연락처는 관련 항구를 관할하는 항구감독기관으로 한다. 대한민국 정부가 지정하는 연락처는 해양경찰관서로 한다.

2. 구체적인 연락방법에 대하여는 이 협정 제13조의 규정에 의하여 설치되는 중•한 어업공동위원회에서 상호 통보한다.

3. 각 체약당사자의 어선이 타방체약당사자가 지정하는 연락처에 연락하는 내용은 다음과 같다.

선박명•호출신호•현재위치(위도•경도)•선적항•총톤수•전장•선장의 성명•선원수•피난이유•피난요청목적지•도착예정시각 및 통신연락방법